Creative Economy

Series editors

Stephen Hill, Professor Emeritus, University of Wollongong, Australia
Kazuo Nishimura, Professor, Research Institute for Economics and Business Administration (RIEB) and Interfaculty Initiative in the Social Sciences (IISS), Kobe University, Japan; Fellow, The Japan Academy, Japan
Tadashi Yagi, Professor, Doshisha University, Japan

Editorial Board

Nobuko Kawashima, Professor, Doshisha University, Japan
Sebastine Lechevalier, Professor, École des Hautes Études en Sciences Sociales (EHESS), France
Yoshifumi Nakata, Professor, Doshisha University, Japan
Andy Pratt, Professor, University of City London, UK
Masayuki Sasaki, Professor, Doshisha University, Japan
Toshiaki Tachibanaki, Professor, Kyoto Women's University, Japan
Makoto Yano, Professor, Kyoto University, Japan
Roberto Zanola, Professor, University of Eastern Piedmont, Italy

As the global economy has developed, we have seen severe competition and polarisation in income distribution. With this drastic change in the economic system, creativity with a high market value has come to be considered the main source of competiveness. In addition to the improvement of competitiveness, however, we are required to work toward fairness in society.

This series covers research on creative economies that are based on humanity and spirituality to enhance the competitiveness, sustainability, peace, and fairness of international society. We define a creative economy as a socio-economic system that promotes those creative activities with a high market value and leads to the improvement of society's overall well-being.

Through this series, we intend to propose various policy recommendations that contribute to the prosperity of international society and improve the well-being of mankind by clarifying the concrete actions that are needed.

More information about this series at http://www.springer.com/series/13627

Stomu Yamash'ta · Tadashi Yagi
Stephen Hill
Editors

The Kyoto Manifesto for Global Economics

The Platform of Community, Humanity, and Spirituality

 Springer

Editors
Stomu Yamash'ta
Doshisha University
Kyoto
Japan

and

Sound Core Co., Ltd.
Kyoto
Japan

Tadashi Yagi
Faculty of Economics
Doshisha University
Kyoto
Japan

Stephen Hill
Faculty of Law, Humanities and the Arts
University of Wollongong
Wollongong, NSW
Australia

ISSN 2364-9186   ISSN 2364-9445 (electronic)
Creative Economy
ISBN 978-981-10-6477-7   ISBN 978-981-10-6478-4 (eBook)
https://doi.org/10.1007/978-981-10-6478-4

Library of Congress Control Number: 2017954268

© The Editor(s) 2018
This work is subject to copyright. All rights are reserved by the Publisher, whether the whole or part of the material is concerned, specifically the rights of translation, reprinting, reuse of illustrations, recitation, broadcasting, reproduction on microfilms or in any other physical way, and transmission or information storage and retrieval, electronic adaptation, computer software, or by similar or dissimilar methodology now known or hereafter developed.
The use of general descriptive names, registered names, trademarks, service marks, etc. in this publication does not imply, even in the absence of a specific statement, that such names are exempt from the relevant protective laws and regulations and therefore free for general use.
The publisher, the authors and the editors are safe to assume that the advice and information in this book are believed to be true and accurate at the date of publication. Neither the publisher nor the authors or the editors give a warranty, express or implied, with respect to the material contained herein or for any errors or omissions that may have been made. The publisher remains neutral with regard to jurisdictional claims in published maps and institutional affiliations.

Printed on acid-free paper

This Springer imprint is published by Springer Nature
The registered company is Springer Nature Singapore Pte Ltd.
The registered company address is: 152 Beach Road, #21-01/04 Gateway East, Singapore 189721, Singapore

Preface

This book, *The Kyoto Manifesto for Global Economics*, had a quite extraordinary birth.

Master Stomu Yamash'ta was the midwife.

Music, and concern for the suffering of others within our current world from conflict, inequality, and unfairness, provided the stimulus for conception. Humanity, our spirituality, and power of human community provided nurture. The newborn child of the ideas is destined to be a leader of humanity's future.

Two stars came into alignment as prequel to the delivery.

The first star was rising over Japan.

> In April 2013, the Center for the Study of Creative Economy was founded within Doshisha University, Kyoto, under the overall supervision of Prof. Nobuko Kawashima, and with Prof. Tadashi Yagi as Director. The mandate of the Center was to research, understand, and stimulate creative activity in the economy as well as to identify ways for creativity to provide a resource for the community as a whole.

Master Stomu Yamash'ta came by.

His commitment, for a long time, has been to explore the spiritual base for creativity, in particular, through the harmony of sacred music, as a way of building peace and harmony for humanity as a whole. Tadashi Yagi and the Center team immediately realized that our spirituality and humanity must be fostered if creative action is to develop and stay alive in the longer term and remain substantial in depth. For humanity's deeper spirituality is its ultimate source.

In consequent partnership, Stomu founded and supported the St. Core Research Group in cooperation with the Center. The primary purpose of the St. Core program is to explore the depth of humanity and spirituality as the underlying platform for creativity, and thus, understand and promote creative solutions to the problems such as conflict and inequality which have been staked into the heart of our global humanity by economic "progress" and self-interest.

Stomu's vision was to bring together science, art, and religion in this quest for resolution and consequent peace. He invited many professors and artists into the St. Core program, thus substantially enriching its quality as a research project anchored in superior real-world practice.

The second star aligned, hovering, as it was, over Indonesia.

In parallel with the Kyoto initiatives, Stomu met with Rano Sianturi, Director of the Indonesian NGO, "Sacred Bridge," and Stephen Hill, previously a UNESCO Regional Director and Representative (Ambassador), based in Jakarta from 1995 to 2006. The meeting was in 2013 and in Bali. Its intention was to explore an initial plan to develop a Culture Center in Bali—with a particular focus on the sacred, and art/music.

Stephen and Rano had been working closely together since 1996, using music and performance in the promotion of peace and the healing of children such as those caught up in Muslim-Christian conflicts, street gangs, and those orphaned and traumatized by the Aceh Tsunami of December 2004.

Rano was both inspiration and committed supporter of these programs. Stephen brought in support, UN endorsement, and shared in helping to develop Rano's vision—with strong assistance and visionary ideas from his UNESCO Culture Specialist, Philippe Delanghe, and a quite extraordinarily committed team of local UNESCO support staff.

As an associated venture, they organized an International Sacred Music Concert to celebrate the oncoming Millennium at Midnight on December 31, 1999. Stephen was the fund-raiser, supporter, and close collaborator from the United Nations—along with Philippe Delanghe. Rano was the main organizer and inspiration. Stomu was the star performer.

Collaboratively, they wanted to show to the world—on behalf of the United Nations—that if we are to reflect on the next one thousand years, this must be in spiritual and human terms, not commercial. "Sacred Music" performers were brought in from all over the world—Africa, Europe, the USA, Asia, and Indonesia—and, in particular, Japan, with Stomu as leader.

The UNESCO Office had previously supported a number of (large scale, i.e, audiences of 5,000 plus) Sacred Bridge-organized concerts for local Indonesian youth prior to this, all with local professional rock musician stars who donated their time, all focused on providing images of emancipating ideas, even working around serious censorship by the "New Order" Government regime prior to the downfall of President Soeharto in May 1998.

These emancipatory music programs were very effective, in particular, in healing where there was conflict and trauma for children, and in developing awareness of wider humanitarian concerns among the young.

Stomu generously accepted to perform at the Bali Millenium Concert, so a very close relationship between Rano and himself was forged, along with Philippe, and subsequently, with Stephen Hill.

From 2006, Stephen, retired from the United Nations, returned to his previous University at Wollongong, Australia, and was awarded his lifelong Emeritus Professor status by the University Council. He subsequently has worked particularly on the development of community empowerment along with support of the repressed indigenous people of West Papua and maintained his friendship with Rano who invited Stephen to Bali to meet with Stomu. Among many other commitments and abilities, Rano taught a Cultural Economics Program at MIT in the USA each year so was a wise and informed "bridge" between the sacred, creativity and music, and economics.

Alignment of the two stars in 2013—over Japan and Indonesia, led to discussions then the Kyoto International Symposium Series, initiated in June 2014. Professor Tadashi Yagi took on the role of visionary champion and organizer.

Rano Sianturi was directly involved and spoke at the 2014 Kyoto 1 Symposium. He subsequently became very ill and has not been able to be directly engaged since. We all, however, owe Rano an enormous debt of gratitude for his humanity, vision, commitment, generosity, and inspiration. He is both our own very dear friend and a friend to humanity as a whole.

Colleagues from the Center for the Study of Creative Economy have been outstanding in their commitment, expertise, and support of what is now a four-year program.

In particular, we express our appreciation for the continuous support of overall Director, Prof. Nobuko Kawashima, and for the implementation management by Madoka Watanabe and her team. We are honored by the continuing generous financial support of the Japan Ministry of Education, Culture, Sports, Science and

Technology, and indebted to Doshisha University for the vision and support in developing and conducting the Kyoto Symposium Series. Additionally, we are grateful for the immediate interest then commitment of Springer Books to publish and promote "The Kyoto Manifesto for Global Economics."

Finally, we offer our heartfelt appreciation to all the contributors to the Kyoto Symposium Series, and in particular, to the authors now collected into the current book, for their generous gift of time, commitment, and inspiration.

Kyoto, Japan
                                                         Stomu Yamash'ta
A Creator for Modern Percussion's Music and On Zen Ceremony for Sacred Music

Kyoto, Japan   Tadashi Yagi

Wollongong, Australia   Stephen Hill
AM, FWIF, FTSE, FRSN, Ph.D.

May 2017

Contents

Overture: The Sacred Symphony

1 The Path: From the Sacred Harmony of Humanity
   to a New Economics 3
   Stomu Yamash'ta, Tadashi Yagi and Stephen Hill

First Movement: 'Recognizing the Need for Change'

2 The Survivability of Humanity Within the Current Global
   Economic Paradigm 13
   Stephen Hill

3 Human and Nature Revisited: The Industrial Revolution,
   Modern Economics and the Anthropocene 35
   Ryuichi Fukuhara

4 Dimensions of Change Within the Economics Mainstream 63
   Tadashi Yagi

5 Ethics of Economics in Late Stage Capitalism:
   Postmodern Chords 89
   C. Edward Arrington and Grace Gonzalez Basurto

Second Movement: 'Foundation Stones of Spirituality'

6 The Three Foundations of Kyoto's Traditional Culture 107
   Manami Oka

7 Supplement for Chapter 6: The Wisdom
   of Traditional Kyoto Culture 129
   Tadashi Yagi

8 Listen to the Stone—Searching for Spiritual Harmony
   in Polyphonic Coexistence 131
   Stomu Yamash'ta

9 Zero and Emptiness (Vacuum/Void) in Physics
   and Chemistry 141
   Kazuyoshi Yoshimura

10 Supplement for Chapter 9: Impression and Comment
   on "Zero and Emptiness (Vacuum Void) in Physics
   and Chemistry" by Kazuyoshi Yoshimura 157
   Stomu Yamash'ta

11 Next Civilization and Spirituality 163
   Tadao Takemoto

12 Spirituality as the Source of Human Creativity:
   Insights from India 179
   Akio Tanabe

Third Movement: 'The Dynamic of Creativity'

13 The Essence of Creativity 197
   Stomu Yamash'ta and Tadashi Yagi

14 Trust, Not Competition, as a Source of the Creative Economy 223
   Stomu Yamash'ta and Tadashi Yagi

15 Creative Organizations 237
   Tadashi Yagi

Fourth Movement: 'Building the Kyoto Platform for Change'

16 A Self-similar Dynamic Systems Perspective of "Living" Nature:
   The Self-nonself Circulation Principle Beyond Complexity 257
   Masatoshi Murase

17 'Sacred Silence'—The Stillness of Listening to Humanity 285
   Stephen Hill

18 'Community': Platform for Sustainable Change 309
   Stephen Hill

19 Evolution of Community and Humanity from Primatological
   Viewpoints 329
   Juichi Yamagiwa

20 Eminent Otherness: Toward an Economy of Hospitality 359
   C. Edward Arrington

21 Building the Harmony of Humanity 375
   Stephen Hill

22 The Future of Capitalism and the Islamic Economy 395
   Shinsuke Nagaoka

23 **Buddhist Economics: A Cultural Alternative** 417
Juewei Shi

24 **Informal Economy and Diversity: The Role
of Micro-producers** 437
Tadashi Yagi

25 **"The Future's Not What It Used to Be"—Ogden Nash** 449
Stephen Hill

**The Conclusions Suite Finale: 'The Kyoto Manifesto—From
Exploration of the Sacred Essence of Humanity to Daily Life and
Economics'**

26 **"The Sacred Symphony" (Overture)** 479
Stephen Hill, Stomu Yamash'ta and Tadashi Yagi

27 **Recognizing the Need for Change (First Movement)** 485
Stephen Hill, Stomu Yamash'ta and Tadashi Yagi

28 **"Foundation Stones of Spirituality" (Second Movement)** 493
Stephen Hill, Stomu Yamash'ta and Tadashi Yagi

29 **"The Dynamic of Creativity" (Third Movement)** 501
Stephen Hill, Stomu Yamash'ta and Tadashi Yagi

30 **"Building the Kyoto Platform for Change" (Fourth Movement)**... 509
Stephen Hill, Stomu Yamash'ta and Tadashi Yagi

31 **The Way Forward** 521
Stephen Hill, Stomu Yamash'ta and Tadashi Yagi

Encore

32 **"The Kyoto Manifesto for Global Economics". "The Platform
of Community, Humanity and Spirituality"** 527
Stephen Hill, Stomu Yamash'ta and Tadashi Yagi

Index 535

About the Editors

Stomu Yamash'ta is Creator for Modern Percussion's Music. He was born in Kyoto, studied music at Kyoto Horikawa Senior High School of Music, Interlochen Arts Academy, and Berklee College of Music, and took percussion lesson under Prof. S. Goodman at Julliard School in USA. His innovation and acrobatic drumming style earned him many accolades. In the 1960s, he performed with Seiji Ozawa music by Toru Takemitsu and Hans Werner Henze among others and became a great master of percussion at a young age. At the turn of the 1970s, he formed the rock supergroup "GO," which made an incredible impact in the world by taking its lead in fusion/music going beyond the different genres of music. In the 1980s, he began pursuing Buddhism music at Toji Temple in Kyoto and established a new style of music. From his encounter with a stone instrument "sanukite" which has a wide range far more than any other instruments, he is currently the art director of "On Zen Ceremony" which is a ceremony incorporating Shinto, Zen, and world of spiritual music.

Tadashi Yagi is a Professor of the Faculty of Economics at Doshisha University. He holds a Ph.D. in Economics, awarded by Nagoya University in 1996. His research areas are wide-ranging, including public economics, human resources management, income distribution, welfare economics, and cultural economics. He has written many papers in refereed academic journals and chapters in edited volumes. The important papers are "Economic Growth and the Riskiness of Investment in Firm-Specific Skills" (with Taichi Maki and Koichi Yotsuya), European Economic Review (2005), "Income Redistribution through the Tax System: A Simulation Analysis of Tax Reform," (with Toshiaki Tachibanaki), Review of Income and Wealth (1998), "Public Investment and Interregional Output —Income Inequalities," (with Nobuhiro Okuno), Regional Science and Urban Economics (1990). Recent works include "Moral, Trust and Happiness-Why does trust improves happiness?", Journal of Organizational Psychology (2017), "How Parenting Affects Children's Futures: Empirical Study in Japan,"(with Kazuo Nishimura), Journalism and Mass Communication, January 2017, Vol. 7, No. 1,

35–45, "Knowledge Creation by Consumers and Optimal Strategies of Firms," Journal of Knowledge Economy (2014).

Stephen Hill is Emeritus Professor, University of Wollongong, Australia and a prominent Australian scientist and diplomat. He has degrees and has written extensively in multiple disciplines. Originally, a research chemist (Sydney University and Unilever), he also was awarded Australia's first Business Administration Ph.D. (Melbourne University) and after academic positions in Chicago, Sussex, and Sydney was appointed as Foundation Professor of Sociology at the University of Wollongong at age 30. He has lived and worked in the USA, Europe, and Asia, been policy consultant to most Asian countries, and founded three research centers including a Center of Excellence of the Australian Research Council. From 1995 to 2006, he was Asia-Pacific Regional Director for Science for the UN Agency UNESCO, and Representative (Ambassador), based in Indonesia. He was responsible for major UN science, education, media freedom, culture, world heritage and peace initiatives, and reforms in the region, as well as being commissioned by the director-general to reform and decentralize the UN Agency globally. Now retired, an Emeritus Professor of the University of Wollongong, he has been awarded several State Awards including Member, Order of Australia, and continues to write and be involved in community empowerment and human rights initiatives.

Overture: The Sacred Symphony

Chapter 1
The Path: From the Sacred Harmony of Humanity to a New Economics

Stomu Yamash'ta, Tadashi Yagi and Stephen Hill

1 Building Our Critique: Asserting Our Humanity

The following book, "The Kyoto Manifesto for Global Economics" is a product of three Annual International Symposia, hosted in early June each year in Kyoto by Doshisha University from 2014 to 2016. These Symposia are now identified as Kyoto 1 (2014), Kyoto 2 (2015) and Kyoto 3 (2016).

The objective of this sequence has been to build progressively a series of society-centered platforms on which we can erect a new approach to economics, one that emphasizes people and their spirituality as the end, and economic activity as the means.

In *Kyoto 1*, we explored the dimensions of communication, in particular across cultures, the significance of common values, in particular, humane and spiritual values, and 'listening' across the multicultural world to promote global cooperation. In *Kyoto 2*, we took the next step to explore the power of 'community', the expression of our humanity, and the power of engaged communities as a transformative force.

S. Yamash'ta (✉)
Center for the Study of the Creative Economy, Doshisha University, Kyoto, Japan

Sound Core Co., Ltd., Kyoto, Japan
e-mail: info@sound-core.jp

T. Yagi
Faculty of Economics, Doshisha University, Kyoto, Japan
e-mail: tyagi@mail.doshisha.ac.jp

S. Hill
University of Wollongong, Wollongong, Australia
e-mail: sthill@uow.edu.au

© The Editor(s) 2018
S. Yamash'ta et al. (eds.), *The Kyoto Manifesto for Global Economics*,
Creative Economy, https://doi.org/10.1007/978-981-10-6478-4_1

In *Kyoto 3*, we moved further onto the global stage to explore 'harmony'—both within and across societies today. Here, we also focused participation in the Symposium down from the two hundred or so participants earlier to just the authors finally involved in the book, along with a small group of directly relevant commentators.

Finally, in 2017, we presented our overall conclusions from the first three Kyoto symposia at *Kyoto 4* for international review prior to final publication.

A brief quote from Australian social survey expert, Hugh Mackay (2007), reflects what we wish to understand and change:

We used to live in a society. Now we live in an economy.

2 Dimensions of Our Critique

The book will present the dimensions of a *new* paradigm for economic-oriented action which seeks to reverse this progressive capture of our humanity into subservience to the demands of an enormously powerful global economics regime.

The demand for change is urgent and critical. At stake is the very survival of humanity beyond the 21st century.

Mainstream neo-classical economists, in general, and unquestioning participants in the economic system, do not seem to realize how close they are to the abyss—partying on in the excitement of stock market gambling, powering global influence for separate economic advantage, living the profits-supported 'good life' … whilst the luxury bus in which they travel together is carrying them, and us, towards an un-crossable precipice—absolute limits to growth-based economic enterprise.

The solution lies, not in theory but in return to the strength that resides in our *humanity* and its universal quest beyond the everyday world—though expressed in many forms and doctrines—to our ultimate source of meaning, commitment and strength—our collective spirituality … reversing the valence of the earlier observation from Hugh Mackey—recapturing 'society' from its command by global economic assumptions and practice.

We are, however, unlikely to change economics and its 'frame' for society overnight. Certainly not at a theoretical level where the forces of academic, government and commercial interest, power and practice, are very strongly embedded and those who might seek to invade firmly rejected. All, of course based on the assumptions authoritatively protected at the center of the 'economic frame' that rejects the legitimacy of an alternative perspective and marginalizes the critical lessons that can be drawn from 'political economy' and the more creative insights that lie at the margins of mainstream national economic interest.

At the core of these mainstream assumptions is the principle of *self-interest-based global competitiveness*—rather than 'social harmony', and price-based exchange rather than gift, values which are inscribed in *stone* in the platform of global economics—and increasingly within contemporary society, in *silicon*-based systems of (instant) internet commerce, managed by automatic algorithm rather than human choice.

Behind the scenes are the puppet masters—a very small highly concentrated set of interlocked "super-entity" *financial institutions*, which control the majority of the monetary value of all transnational corporations. At the core of world production and trade is thus a single interest … making financial profit—to the severe cost of human equity and life—where 2.2 billion people must survive on less than two dollars per day.

All world society is now deeply embedded within this global economy. We can no longer hope to overwhelm its dynamic by direct confrontation, but must work from within. Realistically, we may be able to moderate the more negative dynamics of global economic competition, but not destroy it.

Equally, we cannot expect to radically transform the basic economic theory that underscores global economic competition. This task is one that would require substantial and dedicated expert thinking *within* mainstream economic practice and theory, and could lead either to premature dismissal by those whose expertise, lives and worldviews are totally committed, for example, to a 'monetarist' or 'new classical macroeconomics' paradigm, or to lack of traction with a more general audience.

Instead, our entry point for change is to expose and attack weaknesses of the economic system and its underlying assumptions which deny the priority of a sustainable, empowered and harmonious humanity.

We need to start with demonstration of the negative impact on the daily lives, social cohesion and meaning of life for the people; expand consciousness of what is otherwise hidden; and then identify immediate practical actions that make a difference, along with ways to expand this influence from there based on the power of our shared humanity.

Our objective, we suggest, is to present a persuasive argument that the current system will doom us to serious failure as a world society, in terms ultimately of ecological sustainability and social/human sustainability in a world otherwise wracked by conflict and threat of annihilation.

But then to offer a realistic alternative.

Ultimately, this will need to start from the 'humanity' of individuals—across all spheres of the economy and its governance, the power of 'community' that captures the power of people confirming each other and acting together, and ultimately, our spirituality, the ultimate essence of what humanity is and can aspire to.

Back to the essence of our humanity, a quest and need for 'harmony'.

The only way transformation will then follow is if *the people* assert their power.

3 Drawing from Wider Knowledge

The intentional (and unique) approach we have taken is to draw from the full spectrum of human and academic knowledge in developing our critique of current global economic thought and practice from a 'humanistic' perspective. We draw from philosophy—including across Eastern versus Western thought, and critique of 'liberalism'; sociology; cultural anthropology; primatology—as it relates to early humanity; political economics; mainstream post 1972 economics; politics; and … more, including from direct experience working to empower disadvantaged communities through the United Nations.

Furthermore, our analysis is informed deeply from the practice of searching for what is 'sacred', the ultimate essence of our humanity, what we *can* be as a human race—empowered, fulfilled individuals, deeply sharing and caring for each other across our separate cultural and life worlds. Stomu Yamash'ta's 'On Zen' performances which bring different religions and cultures together across their dividing boundaries into a single search through sacred music, translate quite directly into inspiration and understanding. Explorations in quantum theory complement by exploring harmonic interconnectedness through lessons from natural science.

The book therefore refers into contemporary scientific knowledge, but is not limited to it—for as the quite extraordinary chapter by philosopher, Tadeo Takemoto, demonstrates, we need to move beyond the logic of natural science as unique arbiter of truth to the existential state of 'Being Now' to truly explore and assert out humanity and spirituality in a future civilization.

4 Principles Behind the Structure of the Book

The ultimate goal of this book is to build a future based on the "harmony of humanity". We draw our source from humanity's exploration of its deepest essence, its spirituality.

In keeping with the creation of our "Manifesto" in Kyoto, woven into the structure of the book are *lessons from Shinto*, the millenia-old ethnic religion and way of life of Japan, historically formed as a *connectedness* of contemporary Japanese life with its ancient past—with lessons drawn from long human history and experience.

The word "Shinto" or "way of the gods" is derived from "shin" meaning "spirit" or "kami", and "tō" meaning philosophic "path" or study. "Kami" refers to the "essences" of our world—across all forms in nature, and their *collective* energy, a singular divinity which manifests in many forms—rocks, trees, rivers, animals, places—and people. Shinto therefore brings together past and the present, nature, deities (or spiritual ideals) and human beings … and purification, or, in the language of the book, the re-establishment of the order between nature, humans and their spiritual ideals.

Each of the International Symposia was preceded by a performance by Stomu Yamash'ta of 'On-Zen' in the awe-inspiring Daitokuji Buddhist Temple of Kyoto, a ceremony which brought Buddhist and Shinto religion and ritual together in a celebration of peace. Stomu's instrument is made of a very special stone, Sanukite —with the extraordinary tonal qualities described in Chap. 8 by Stomu, and Chap. 11 by Tadeo Takemoto.

This instrument presents the very essence of Shinto, with designs drawn from ancient China prior to the Bronze Age, producing harmonies that relate humanity and spirituality to the entire natural world from which the stone is drawn, and from which Stomu derives his sacred music inspiration.

In contemporary society, we are losing this connection. In Chap. 8, Stomu contrasts natural sound, as produced from Sanukite stone, to the increasing use of digitized and systemized technologies in contemporary society to achieve higher efficiency in the commercialization of music. But, particularly through 'sampling' technology in music, wave motions and wave lengths of digital sounds are no longer those of nature. As a key example, "psychoacoustic" or "perceptual coding" is used, for the sake of *compressing* recordings by eliminating auditory resolution beyond the ability of most people to hear. With Sanukite stone, on the other hand, frequencies can exceed 500,000 Hz, way beyond the human hearing range. But this is the range where stimulation of brain activity, concentration and even healing can occur.

As Stomu Yamash'ta concludes, the digitized sound source both *unifies* human thought orientation and creativity at the same time as it *weakens* them—leading to a decline in multidimensional thinking and originality, to an increasingly non-diversified world where cultural variation disappears. Even more important, humanity and nature are intertwined in a cosmos of energy derived from both 'existence' and 'non-existence'—material vs non-material—as explained in Yoshimuru's Chap. 8 on quantum physics and Yamash'ta's Supplementary Chap. 9. It is intrinsically not possible to digitize this ever-changing world. Yamash'ta therefore leaves us with the critical question,

> "While living with continuously changing phenomena and existences, how can we human beings harmonize (*through increasingly digitized representation*) with nature and establish an interacting relationships with it."

On the other hand, the music of Sanukite deeply conveys the relation of humanity and spirituality to the timeless harmonics of the entire natural world from which the stone is drawn, and the harmony of humanity. This is the music of a "polyphony"—a musical structure which brings two or more simultaneous lines of independent melody together as with the parallel elements of Shinto.

We have therefore adopted a *musical* structure for our presentation of the book to mirror this deeper connectedness of humanity. Inspired by the Shinto "*polyphony*" we have translated its essence into the more contemporary form—that of the "*symphony*". The book is therefore presented as a series of inter-connected Symphonic Movements, each related to what went before, but also moving on into new harmonies until resolution in the final crescendos that echo from our conclusions through the theatre of our future.

Even so, many diverse voices can be heard within every 'Movement'—and, as the reader will see, they fundamentally connect the human with nature, indeed with the cosmos, in what can only be described as a polyphony dressed up in the formal robes of a symphonic performance.

Our end-goal however is to *draw* from both the experience and philosophy of this spiritual depth to build a new *economics*, to construct a deeply *human* platform on which we can stand to see more clearly and comprehensively, providing us with the light to re-assess the economically driven structures and values which in the 21st Century essentially control modern globalised life.

In keeping with a Shinto perspective, our book is centred in and draws inspiration from the 'place' and 'spiritual history' of Kyoto, where we held our three International Symposia exploring humanistic alternatives to current global economics. This 'place' context is presented in Chap. 6 on "Kyoto" by Manami Oka, and Tadashi Yagi's Supplement, Chap. 7.

Again, with the inspiration of Stomu Yamash'ta, *the four voices*, or expressions of 'spirit' are dealt with through the text, ie:

"*Sound Spirit Voice*"—understanding of consciousness which is constituted from language referring to the surrounding world of experience, as in Stephen Hill's Chap. 17, "Sacred Silence—The Stillness of Listening to Humanity", and Tadao Takemoto's Chap. 11, "Next Civilization and Spirituality".

"*Material Spirit Voice*"—understanding of "place" and environmental concerns (largely measured by natural science investigation), as well as of economics the objectives of which are to accumulate *material* benefits—even, as E.F. Schumacher observes, where a modern economy is "propelled by a frenzy of greed and indulges in an orgy of envy" … "not accidental features but the very causes of its expansionist success." (Schumacher 1973, p. 18)

On 'place' and environmental concerns, we have, in the 'First Movement' of our 'Symphony', Chap. 3 by Ryuichi Fukuhara, "Human Nature Revisited" and Chap. 2 by Stephen Hill, "The Survivability of Humanity within the Current Global Economic Paradigm". Oka's Chap. 6 and Yagi's Chap. 7 supplement relate the materiality of place with its deeper spirit.

On economics, chapters of particular relevance are Chap. 4 by Tadashi Yagi, "Dimensions of Change within the Economics Mainstream", Chap. 5 by Grace Gonzalez and Ed Arrington, "Ethics of Economics in Late Stage Capitalism: Postmodern Chords", Chap. 14 by Stomu Yamash'ta and Tadashi Yagi, "Trust Not Competition as Source of the Creative Economy", and a series of Chapters in the Fourth Movement' of the book prior to the Conclusions Suite, all of which move forward from alternative economics frameworks – Chap. 22 on "Islamic Economy" (Shinsuke Nagaoka), Chap. 23 on "Buddhist Economics" (Juewei Shi), Chap. 24, "Informal Economy and Diversity" (Tadashi Yagi), and Chap. 20, "Eminent Otherness – Towards an Economy of Hospitality" (Ed Arrington).

On natural science, Kazuyoshi Yoshimuru's quantum physics support for the nature of harmony developed by Stomu Yamash'ta refers the impact of spiritual music to basic principles of physics (Chap. 9) and Yamash'ta's supplement (Chap. 10), and Stephen Hill's Chap. 2 on the "Survivability of Humanity" refer evidence of environmental danger directly to support from natural science investigation, as does Ryuichi Fukuhara's Chap. 3 on "Human and Nature Revisited".

"Voice of Spirit": The 'voice' of understanding which moves beyond 'Sound Voice', the language of consciousness. It is the voice of humanity when the separative 'noise' of language is suspended, for example with the power of music to communicate and transform – beyond words, as demonstrated in Stephen Hill's Chap. 17, "Sacred Silence" depicting when children caught in trauma and violent conflict were 'healed' through music, in Stomu Yamash'ta's Chap. 8, "Listening to the Stone", Tadao Takemoto's Chap. 11, "Next Civilization and Spirituality", and Juewei Shi's Chap. 23 on "Buddhist Economics".

"Voice of Mathematical Spirit": The voice of natural science, logic and calculation. This 'voice' is essential in understanding what we are dealing with in environmental destruction, in the logic of action in the physical world which will work, and in calculation of consequences and future trends of which we must be aware and with which we must deal.

Chapters already introduced under the 'natural science' dimension of "material voice" align with "the voice of mathematical spirit". However, other chapters warn of being trapped into believing that natural science and mathematics are the ultimate arbiters of the truth of *humanity*. In particular, Tadeo Takemoto's Chap. 11 "Next Civilization and Spirituality' observes how we must suspend scientific logic to progress".

Being Now, the state of consciousness he argues is basic to dealing with the development of a fully humanistic next civilization. Stephen Hill's argument in his Chap. 21. "Building the Harmony of Humanity" also warns of the potential distortion or trivialization of the whole created by depending too much on mathematized exploration of the holistic quality of humanity and society.

The 'Voice of Mathematical Spirit' is therefore a divided voice. A voice of investigative strength in knowing what is happening in our physical world. But it is also a voice of distortion if applied too comprehensively to the whole human being and the peoples' spirituality.

The connecting tissue which holds these voices together in the structure of our argument is the human quality of *creativity*, the particular focus of our 'Third Movement' in the book, "The Dynamic of Creativity"—including seven chapters stretching from the essence of what creativity is, its underlying values, and its application in policy and organization for a positive future. In particular, see Chaps. 6 and 7, Manami Oka and Tadashi Yagi's Chapters on "Kyoto"; Chap. 13: Stomu Yamash'ta and Tadashi Yagi's "The Essence of Creativity'; Chap. 14, Stomu Yamash'ta and Tadashi Yagi's "Trust Not Competition as Source of the Creative Economy"; and, Chap. 15, Tadashi Yagi's "Creative Organization".

With these four voices of spirit and the connecting tissue of creativity woven throughout the text, our overall "Symphony" is a "*Sacred Symphony*"—progressively discovering and asserting the "energy generative of a thing"—the "natural order"—the "divine", the "human", "how people should live"

Movements of the Symphony follow:

Overture: 'The Sacred Symphony'
First Movement: 'Recognizing the Need for Change'
Second Movement: 'Foundation Stones of Spirituality'
Third Movement: 'The Dynamic of Creativity'
Fourth Movement: 'Building the Kyoto Platform for Change'
The Conclusions Suite Finale: 'The Kyoto Manifesto—From Exploration of the Sacred Essence of Humanity to Daily Life and Economics'
Encore

5 The Kyoto Manifesto for Global Economics

Thus the book stretches to the ultimate frame and expression of our humanity and drive—the sacred.

This is not your more 'normal' academic text. Instead, it is an inspired search for humanity-lost within the noise of globalization and its supportive economics.

It has been the intention therefore of the Kyoto Series of Symposia, and the book that now follows, to provide some guidance based on ….

"Listening to the Harmony of Humanity"

There is no time however for procrastination. As we said earlier, "the demand for change is urgent and critical. At stake is the very survival of humanity beyond the 21st century."

Our Conclusions are therefore derived and presented as a definitive call for action drawn from our three Annual International Kyoto Symposia which prepared the way. Inspired by the 'place', the 'spirituality of Kyoto, and by a search across a very broad range of disciplines and experience, and by connection with the sacred music and performances of 'On Zen' which have brought Zen and Shinto ritual together for harmony and peace as background to our understanding and discussions.

The product of 'listening to the harmony of humanity' is therefore ….

"*THE KYOTO MANIFESTO FOR GLOBAL ECONOMICS*"

References

Mackay, H. (2007). Advance Australia … Where?' Hachett, Australia. (Used in radio interviews when promoting the Advance Australia book: Personal communication).
Schumacher, E. F. (1973). *Small is beautiful—Economics as if people mattered*. New York: Harper and Row.

First Movement: 'Recognizing the Need for Change'

Chapter 2
The Survivability of Humanity Within the Current Global Economic Paradigm

Stephen Hill

1 Introduction: Reaching Beyond the 'Tipping Point'

In many ways the 21st Century is pushing world society to its 'tipping point'. And, if we continue to allow our society to be ruled by current economic assumptions we are in very severe danger of falling down the precipice of annihilation that irrevocably confronts us on the other side.

I do not believe this is an extremist view. I always have avoided such a position. *But*, every indicator of progressive change, e.g.: in population, impact on our limited environment, loss of community and resilience, and bellicose defence of established economic advantage in an unequal world … are heading in this one direction.

We would be foolish to close our eyes. We are writing and discussing in a context of urgency.

It is the intention of Chap. 2 to expose the urgency for change in the current global economics paradigm which is pushing us irrevocably towards the precipice.

Later chapters will propose ways forward to make change happen—but based on rediscovering and asserting the essential power of our humanity as the platform for future global economics.

2 The "Faustian Bargain" of Our Globalized World

So, how did the contemporary shadow of economics start to enshroud the essence of human community and lead us to this tipping point?

S. Hill (✉)
University of Wollongong, Wollongong, Australia
e-mail: sthill@uow.edu.au

The answer is its apparent attractiveness which kept society quiescent during the progressive handover of power to a limited globally controlling economic elite who now call the shots but for self-interested advantage rather than humanity's benefit as a whole.

Additionally, from the other side of 'attractiveness', the answer includes the fact that those who needed to survive *had* to participate within the rigors of the new 'factory' based employment from the late 18th Century onwards that powered the world's take-off into a globalized industry based economy. And then adjust as the 'external' *systems* that progressively fed capitalist expansion through technological innovation and progress—Transport (at first, railways) …. Power (electricity) … Urbanization and Consumerism … and now … Internet Connectedness, progressively commanding available employment choices and peoples' lives (Hill 1988).

2.1 A 'Faustian' Bargain

Our world's progress over the last two to three centuries towards an increasingly 'globalized economy' has been a *Faustian Bargain.*'

"Faust", in a classic German legend, is an ambitious scholar who is highly successful yet dissatisfied with his life. This leads him to make a pact with the Devil, representative of evil, via the Devil's agent, Mephistopheles, exchanging his soul for unlimited knowledge and worldly pleasures. "Faust" and the expression "to strike a Faustian Bargain" means to be willing to sacrifice anything to satisfy a limitless desire for knowledge or power (Wikipedia 2016).

2.2 The Devil's Blessing

The 'Devil' has delivered.

Indeed, with the advent of industrialization from the late 18th Century onwards, and the obeisance of people to increasingly technologically complex systems of production and supply to consumers, world society as a whole has been rewarded with exponentially increasing knowledge and power (Hill 1988).

There is no question that world society as a whole has benefitted.

Commitment to economic growth has expanded access to wealth for many.

As striking examples:

> India's economy, previously one of the poorest in the world with a very small elite and a very large poverty stricken population, now has a strong developing middle class in between so is divided into thirds, i.e.: the rich, an emerging broad middle class and a very poor underclass.

> The middle class and their consumer lifestyle is an increasingly powerful force within the Indian economy. The number of households with a disposable income of more than $10,000 has leapt from around 2.5 million in 1990 to nearly 50 million in 2015, according to Euromonitor International (Breene 2016).
>
> The 'underclass', inhabitants of the traditional 'caste' system which previously riveted the poor into an inescapable place of disadvantage, is starting to see light of opportunity. 'Caste' was officially outlawed over sixty years ago. But, socially the constraint remained—in spite of government action to assist people from 'scheduled castes'. Today, 'caste' still remains as a shadow on opportunity, but this social remnant is steadily dissolving and often expressed more in socio-economic status terms than caste per se (Sankaran 2013; Agrawal 2015, 2016).

China, a poor peasant society in the 1960s is now a leading world industrial economic power.

The Republic of Korea, an economy equivalent in wealth to Bangladesh in the late 1950s is now also a major economic power, a consumer based modern society.

All over the last half century.

The dynamic of change behind each of these examples, is the capture of (technological) *knowledge,* and the economic *power* to use it (Hill 1986).

> I have been in the fortunate position of being involved, researching and consulting since 1965 in Asia's scientific and technological development and policies for most of this time, living and working directly in three of the countries and consulting with many others as well as the relevant international agencies. I was additionally the United Nations Regional Asia Pacific Director for Science (within UNESCO) for the 44 countries of the region for the mid-1995 to mid-2000s decade and a UN Ambassador responsible for UNESCO's whole mandate for five, that is, with responsibility for supporting national development, equity, and peace through science, education, culture, world heritage, communication and freedom of expression and peace initiatives on behalf of the UN as a whole. So, I have been privileged to see and be involved in the history first hand for over 50 years, almost since the start. My conclusions are therefore based on personal experience as well as academic review.

Scientific and technological innovation has massively enhanced economic growth, and as a side-product, generally increased the life chances and comfort of the general population and even of the very poor, though broad ranging access to wealth remains a problem—particularly for those apart from the elite in poorer and less democratically ruled societies.

Based on the relative freedoms of increasing and more broadly distributed wealth, an expanding number of people have the freedom to move beyond simply surviving or looking after just their own benefit to pay attention to *altruism* for others. The collective commitment of most governments to the post-1945 United Nations and its altruistic and peace objectives, the development of care-centered NGOs serving the poor and disadvantaged, are demonstration. World society as a whole, now *cares*.

Such global concern would have been unthinkable in early 19th Century European society when slavery was a common path to wealth for their masters, colonial control of 'primitives' was the basis of central empire wealth, and poor children simply died if they got sick or had no food—*in the back streets of the wealth capitals of the time,* just around the corner from where the elite were partying.

Further, whilst there persist many regimes today which control openness of communication of their people, the international 'norm' now *is* freedom of expression—thus, the possibility of transformation where the public is openly informed and public pressure can apply force to redress inequity or repression. Freedom of expression, not only exposes excesses and corruption in the systems of economy and governance. It also offers alternatives, even radical ideas to which the broader society can become committed.

No contemporary society is healthy, resilient, free, or able to cope with radical change without freedom of expression. And I say this from the real-life perspective of having this as a central element of my practical responsibilities within UNESCO for over a decade (mid 1990s to mid 2000s) in Asia and the Pacific—the United Nations organization responsible, amongst other things, for globally promoting and ensuring freedom of expression and media (Hill 2005; UNESCO 2005).

Again, a very positive product of globalized economic development and the freedoms it has provided, ultimately for the individual freedom and human rights of all … or, perhaps more accurately, *many*.

2.3 Payback to the Devil

The 'other' side of the Faustian Bargain however is what we have sacrificed and how we are equipped to handle the future *now*. According to the Legend of Faust, the 'Devil' claims the benefits *back* after a limited period of time.

We have reached this time limit.

As Kenneth Boulding observed in 1973,

> Anyone who believes that exponential growth can go on forever within a finite world is either a madman or an economist. (Boulding 1973)

Boulding continues. Any positive rate of growth whatever eventually carries a human population to an unacceptable magnitude, no matter how small the rate of growth may be unless the rate of population growth can be reduced to zero before the population reaches an unacceptable size.

Consequently, based on the sheer arithmetic of growth, Boulding derives what he terms his "dismal theorem",

> If the only thing which can check the growth of population is starvation and misery, then the population will grow until it is sufficiently miserable and starving to check its growth,

And, the second even worse theorem, "the utterly dismal theorem",

> If the only thing which can check the growth of population is starvation and misery, the ultimate result of any technological improvement is to enable a larger number of people to live in misery than before and hence to increase the total sum of human misery (Boulding 1988; McCloskey 2013)

The immediacy of this finite end point in a closed system was seen by Boulding, hence his metaphor of a *"Spaceman Economy"* in the mid 1960s, that is, "one where earth has become a single spaceship without unlimited reservoirs of anything". Boulding contrasts this with the economy of the past, a *"Cowboy Economy"*—symbolic of America's limitless plains, associated with "reckless, exploitative, romantic, and violent behavior", an 'open' economy where increasing consumption and production are regarded as good things (Boulding 1966).

Shortly thereafter, in the early 1970s, the world started to wake up to the immediacy and significance of this 'closed sphere' concept of our future - to the absolute limitation on the physical resources needed to sustain humanity, including in the very air we breathe and the temperature of the earth that fundamentally supports our food and welfare. As declared by the influential Club of Rome in 1972 and based on detailed computer modeled projections, there *are* limits to growth! (Meadows et al. 1972).

It seems however that we have taken a half century of new evidence, calls for action, and slowly evolving public consciousness, before we took Boulding seriously, or, for that matter, seriously paid attention to the well-based predictions of the Club of Rome.

Evidence for the significance of Boulding's observation now surrounds us—concerning *impact* on our physical environment, accelerating population growth, and massive and increasing concentration of ownership and control that globally even affects access to humanity's stocks of food. Indeed, the projected consequences of the 'Business As Usual' scenario of the 1972 Club of Rome Report, have been compared very recently to actual data over the time period, and show remarkable alignment. *The modeled consequence is imminent collapse of the global economy and environment*, "where standards of living fall at rates faster than they have historically risen due to disruption of normal economic functions" (Turner 2014).

3 Dimensions of Threat to Humanity

3.1 The Danger of Ecological Disaster

Potential ecological disaster is already rising as an all-encompassing hurricane of transformation over the horizon of current contemporary life.

The link to the rapacious energy-intensive expansion of human productive enterprise across our whole world is undeniable within the mainstream of scientific evaluation.

For its Fifth Report, launched on 18th March 2015, the United Nations Intergovernmental Panel on Climate Change drew together 744 scientists from 70 countries to review 12,000 of the latest relevant scientific studies. Every conclusion was accompanied by the results of a 'level of probability' survey of all scientists involved. Amongst many observations of imminent environmental threat, the UN Panel conclude,

> Warming of the atmosphere and ocean system is *unequivocal*.
> (United Nations 2015)

Meanwhile, the World Meteorological Organization (WMO) concluded in its *Greenhouse Gas Bulletin* in September 2014:

> "Increase in atmospheric CO_2 from 2012 to 2013 was 2.9 parts per million (ppm), the largest year-to-year increase in 30 years. ... just 9 ppm away from an average level some scientists believe could cause enough sea level rise, drought and severe weather to significantly harm human populations across the globe." WMO Secretary General, Michael Jarraud concluded, "we are running out of time." (WMO 2013; Atkin 2014)

> As this book is published, in 2018, we have already breached this tipping point.

At the center of continuing exploitation of this planet is population growth. To take but one evocative example,

> 'If the population of China walked past you, eight abreast, the line would never end because of the rate of reproduction.'

China is just one model of a previously universally poor country with new development initiatives integrated into the global economy, although it is the most dramatic. Chinese citizens now have increasingly high consumption aspirations that can only be fed by high economic growth rates in China and a global expanding industrialized economic system. Increasing demand on our fragile and limited environment.

At stake: extinction of animal and plant species essential for our survival, and explosion of population needing to be fed, sheltered and ... sustained in a world that is intrinsically limited but within which all those touched by globalization's aspirations, seek to consume *more*.

Even if one takes an extraordinarily optimistic view of the future of our current global economic design and casts forward one or two centuries, the trend curve of impact on our limited global resources simply *has* to stop sometime. We are presently living by an economic paradigm that intrinsically *has* to self-destruct.

The only question is *when?*

3.2 Wealth and Inequality

As Thomas Piketty authoritatively demonstrates from detailed studies of 20 countries over 250 years in his recent widely read and applauded book, '*Capitalism in the 21st Century*', increasing globalization and economic competition in the 21st Century is directly associated with *increasing* inequality, not less. Rate of capital return in developed countries is persistently greater than rate of economic growth and as a result, already acquired wealth grows, whilst structural equality in access to wealth, erodes (Piketty 2014).

At the center of Piketty's conclusions is that the core of expanding inequality is inherited assets. International NGO, Oxfam, estimates that over the next 20 years, just 500 people will hand on $(US)2.1 *trillion* to their heirs, a sum larger than the annual GDP of India, a country of 1.3 billion people (Eliott 2017).

The result is that today, the top 0.01% of the world's people (one hundred thousandths of total) control 30% of the world's wealth ($(US)16.7 trillion) whilst the lowest 99.1% of the world's population control just 19% ($(US)10.3 trillion) (James 2012). The OECD has recently released a report demonstrating that the richest 10% earn over ten times that of the poorest 10%. The poorest are losing ground and the wealth gap is widening (Babones 2014).

These comparisons are dramatic. Perhaps most dramatic of all however is the conclusion of the Report released by Oxfam on January 16th 2017 to mark the annual meeting of political and business leaders in Davos, Switzerland for The World Economic Forum.

> Eight men own the same wealth as the 3.6 billion people who make up the poorest half of humanity. (Oxfam 2017; Eliott 2017)!
>
> *Eight men!*
>
> And the Oxfam Report then outlines how the super-rich employ networks of tax havens to avoid fair taxation, wealth managers to ensure secure investment returns not available to ordinary savers, and use their money and connections to ensure government policy that supports them. *Over half* of the world's billionaires either inherited their wealth or accumulated it from industries connected with corruption and cronyism. (Oxfam 2017).

At the lower end of this economic inequity it remains obscene that *2.2 billion people* or *over 34% of the entire current world population of seven billion people*, live below a mere two dollars per day poverty line (World Bank 2015a). They are likely to not even have access to safe water, decent food, any welfare or health support, or education, so live in the pit of desperation to survive and for their children to grow up to maturity. For them, an enriching and empowered life is likely to be ground down into little more than a fantasy.

3.3 Inequality and Division

It is not just *level* of wealth that is the problem.

Economic growth has produced *greater* not less equity along with consequent *consciousness* of division, and it is this consciousness of difference rather than absolute level of income that most impacts on a sense of inequity (Alisina et al. 2004; Oishi et al. 2011; Ferrer-i-Carbonell 2014).

Awareness of division is deeply erosive of *community* and its power as the social and cultural context for living and meaning for *all* of its participants. When the *community* is *divided*—in particular when some are denied access even to decent food, health, security and shelter, our shared humanity is impoverished whilst a minority bask in increased wealth and personal opportunity.

The lesson applies as much to contemporary 'modern' societies and their cities as it does to traditional people within remote regions of the developing world. Internal community tension *will* follow.

3.4 Concentration of Global Economic Control—Impact on Survivability and Community

Meanwhile, the power to continue this unequal access to new wealth lies in the hands of a very small number of company board room directors.

In 2007, Based on a database of 37 million companies and investors worldwide, the Swiss Federal Institute of Technology in Zurich analyzed all 43,000 transnational corporations, the share ownerships linking them, and concluded that *a mere 147 inter-locking companies controlled nearly 40% of the monetary value of all transnational corporations.*

> The majority of these economic "super-entity" companies are *financial institutions*—not directly responsible for producing anything - just financial puppeteers pulling the strings of the world.
>
> With a single CEO in overall charge of each, it is hardly worth calculating how small this percentage of the world's population is - of those who have major control over the economic and lifestyle inequity of all, i.e.: 0.00021%! This is the central interconnected controlling force in the world economy. Around them, there are another 590 major global corporations, that is, a total of 737 business entities which, together, control 80% of the world economy, but led by the core 'super-entities' (Upbin 2011; Peralta 2013; Vitali et al. 2011).

It is important therefore to realise that it is not just the small *numbers* of controlling corporations which matter, but their networking and collusion. We are therefore not dealing with a full global *free-market* economy as conservative economic theorists might hope for, but one controlled by inter-connected monopolies, with a central more powerful group, the so-called "super-entities", setting the pace - and market influences - which are followed by the rest.

If, as observed from the Swiss data noted above, the majority of controlling entities are indeed *financial institutions*, the consequence is that world trade and economy is even more firmly set into the *single* criterion of *profit* ... rather than wider interest and responsibility.

If, at the centre, only profit matters, then whatever social or ecological responsibility issues confronted by the companies which are collected under the central financial corporation's umbrella, have to be dealt with lower down in the hierarchy. The lower level production company must produce PROFIT and in the course of doing this, handle the 'obstructions to profit' required by responsiveness to either their local governmental restrictions or share-holder concern about responsible use of labour in developing countries or environmental impact. But, as far as the over-riding financial institution is concerned, all of this is irrelevant. What matters is the lower level company's final PROFIT as it is up to the lower level companies to handle whatever constraints there might have been on final profitability.

In other words, the core global controlling financial institutions have no care for human values, ecology or shareholder constraints. Their business is the end-product, just, PROFIT!

And ... meanwhile, just *eight men* own the resulting assets equivalent to *half* of the rest of the world's people! With a bit of a squeeze you could fit them all into one of Donald Trump's golf carts. And 68% of this poor half of the world's people are struggling to earn just a two dollar coin every single day!

Whilst this minuscule percentage of the world's population has enormous control over the world's people, they too are embedded within the 'grammar' of global economic capitalism. The CEOs will not earn their multi-million dollar bonuses or ensure their companies thrive unless they abide by global capital's rules. The danger is that this tiny group has enormous power to call the shots, and are *most* able to exploit the rules for greatest profit—what happens to the other 99.99979% of the *people* is a secondary consideration.

3.5 Food Insecurity

One direct and critical consequence is that control and limitation of the biodiversity of humanity's main staple crops now lies firmly in the hands of a very limited number of the executives of transnational corporations.

In the last few decades, the U.S. has led a radical shift to commercialization, consolidation, and control of seed ownership. The top ten seed firms, with a majority stake owned by U.S. corporations, account for 73%. Three agrichemical firms—Monsanto, DuPont, and Syngenta—now control 53% of the global commercial seed market. These *three* corporations make more than *$11.8 billion* annually (Action Group 2008). This is equivalent to the entire 2013 national GDP for the nations of Mauritius or Mongolia and three times the GDP of Fiji (World Bank 2015b).

Based on industry statistics, The Action Group on Erosion, Technology and Concentration (the ETC Group) estimates that Monsanto's biotech seeds (including those licensed to other companies) accounted for 87% of the total world area devoted in 2007 to farming from genetically engineered seeds.

Genetically manipulated seeds, designed to resist *present* insects and the application of herbicides (even sold from the companies controlling the new seeds), are increasingly spreading across all world agriculture (Action Group 2008).

Leading the way is the United States. The vast majority of the four major commodity crops in the U.S. are genetically engineered varieties: soybean (93% transgenic in 2010), cotton (88%), corn (86%), and canola (64%). Seeds containing genes patented by Monsanto account for more than 90% of soybeans grown in the U.S. and 80% of U.S.-grown corn (Center for Food Safety 2013).

Control cuts deeply into human survivability as seeds are increasingly engineered *genetically to not reproduce*, so farmers must purchase seeds from Monsanto every year—even in the most desperately poor countries of the world, whilst biodiversity is limited to what exists in Monsanto's laboratories, not the outside world (Sarich 2013).

Although the normal long-term practice of farmers to save costs, Monsanto has declared it a *crime* for the farmers to keep the seeds (which are not yet genetically sterile in Monsanto's production program) for the next season from the crops grown from Monsanto's original genetically modified seeds. Monsanto prosecutes accordingly. In 2003, farmer, Ken Ralph from Covington, Tennessee, was ordered to serve prison time and to repay Monsanto $165,649 for about 41 tons of genetically engineered cotton and soybean seed he was found to have saved from the production of his own crops in violation of the agreement. Monsanto meanwhile claimed it had filed 73 civil lawsuits against farmers over the previous five years for a similar offence (Shinkle 2003).

As "The Action Group on Erosion, Technology and Concentration" (the ETC Group), also highlights about the "privatization of a commons" in its report, 'Who Owns Nature?':

> In the first half of the 20th century, seeds were overwhelmingly in the hands of farmers and public-sector plant breeders. In the decades since, (biotechnology companies) have used intellectual property laws to commodify the world seed supply — a strategy that aims to control plant germ-plasm and maximize profits by eliminating farmers' rights. ... In less than three decades, a handful of multinational corporations have engineered a fast and furious corporate enclosure of the first link in the food chain (Action Group 2008).

The level of danger to humanity's resilience against natural mutation of pests and loss of our entire food sources is enormous. 'Local' farmers, local community food supplies and economies, are now slaves to "a handful of multinational corporations".

3.6 The Enslavement of Nation States

Moving even further down this path of concentrated control over global society is a disturbing development.

Beginning in 2015, negotiations have been progressing between the European Union and the United States towards a major new trade agreement, the 'Transatlantic Trade and Investment Partnership' (TTIP). Negotiations have been carried out mostly in secret. The objective of TTIP, as a bilateral trade agreement, is to produce a common market across the European Union and the United States. To ease the way it seeks to reduce the regulatory barriers for big business, for example in food safety law, environmental legislation, banking regulations, jobs and the sovereign powers of individual nations. A parallel multilateral trade arrangement also has been developing for the Pacific countries and the United States, the Trans Pacific Partnership (TPP). Indeed it was already signed but had yet to be ratified. (Wikipedia 2017)

That is, until Donald Trump was elected President of the United States and after coming into office on Friday 20th January 2017 and three days later signed Executive Orders withdrawing United States involvement in negotiating these multilateral trade deals. (Diamond and Bash 2017) Meanwhile the UK was in the process of withdrawing from the EU in the decision known as BREXIT further complicating the arrangement. It is possible both TTIP and TPP may be revitalized, for example, with China taking a central role in a new Trans Pacific Partnership. But, nothing is sure at the time of writing.

It is however very likely, given the pressure from corporations advantaged by the deals that, following a temporary hiatus, one form or another of the TTIP and TTP will finally be implemented.

What matters most of all is the additional power these trade deals potentially give to large international corporations. Whilst there are very disturbing consequences for the other issues in the final agreements, by far the biggest threat to global society is TTIP's assault on democracy that follows from agreed corporate power. A similar power is given to private corporations under the TPP.

Under both, 'Investor-State Dispute Settlements' (ISDS), allow companies *to sue governments* if those governments' policies cause a loss of corporate profits. In other words, unelected transnational corporations will be able to dictate the policies of democratically elected governments.

Already, ISDSs are in place in other bi-lateral trade agreements internationally. Amongst around 500 business versus nation cases are currently proceeding. A Swedish energy company, Vattenfall, is suing the German Government for billions of dollars because the Government decided to phase out nuclear power plants in the wake of the Fukushima Disaster in Japan (Independent 2015).

National public health policy is being sacrificed on the altar of the power of international corporation profit interests.

Whatever Donald Trump may do in the short term, TTIP (and perhaps, TPP) are likely to be the next staging points in the continuing march of globalization over the power of the people. And the Investor-State Dispute Settlements system, already cemented into place, will expand globally.

Global economics gone mad!

A handful of transnational corporation CEOs, under this deal, potentially control our national Sovereignty and the will of the people, including you and me.

3.7 Learned Helplessness

Against this backdrop of concentrated power elsewhere, it is no wonder then that in many cases developing country communities have *learned* helplessness, i.e.: "We can't do it and do not have the knowledge, someone elsewhere must; otherwise we follow the externally controlled economic and power rules given to us!" … (and thus, stay safe, out of gaol and alive). Power is located so far away.

The global economy not only invades but disempowers alternative action at the same time.

4 Confronting Humanity's Challenges—Targets for Social Action

The future is *now*!

What we must deal with *now*, our starting points for social action, are five *social challenges* for humanity—associated with globalization's progress across the essence of our humanity and equity, marching as it is to the rhythm of current economic assumptions … or, as is the case with current ISIS Islamic extremism, *against* the secular power of globalization.

4.1 Divisiveness

The first target to be addressed is the increasing pressure from divisiveness, conflict, and war—forged in the fire of increasing inequality.

> *Day-by-day Survival*: The danger is predicated on the need for many people across the globe to obtain, or have to fight for, their very basic water and food requirements to survive, or their need to make ultimate sense of liberation from the impoverished world of their immediate experience.
>
> > As I reported earlier, *2.2 billion people, 34% of the world population, live below a $2 per day poverty line.* If I may suggest, in Australia, or Japan, or any other developed country, probably most of us would hardly be bothered to find a two dollar coin lost amongst other things in the bottom of our purse or pocket when we are purchasing an ice cream for the kids.

What follows is the force of desperation. People fighting for the right to simply stay alive.

Invariably this is likely to cut a division through a previously harmonious society between "us" and "them" and to destroy the very heart of compassion that otherwise sustains 'community'.

4.2 Ideological Extremism

Additionally, the danger of divisiveness to be addressed is the consequent power of ideological extremism—to appeal to those who are desperately disadvantaged, or excited by the youthful freedom to jump—under the legitimation of a total belief system, or for the sake of being 'heroes' within it, out of all other morality … to kill, to rape, to rampage … because it is now OK. The power of an absolute belief! Globalization and its secular values are the 'legitimized' enemy.

Most significant at this point in time is the Islamic fundamentalist terrorist organization based in the Middle East, now alternately referring to itself as the "Islamic State in Iraq and Syria" (ISIS) or the "Islamic State in Iraq and the Levant" (ISIL). It rapidly became a major force of terrorism.

As the leader of ISIS, Abu Bakr Al-Baghdadi, declared in 2015, "the faith was never a "religion of peace', but rather 'a religion of war'" (Beattie 2015).

ISIS grew out of al-Qaeda, forged by Sunni militants after the 2003 US-led invasion of Iraq, becoming a major force in the country's subsequent sectarian insurgency. The United States invaded to remove a constructed fantasy of 'weapons of mass destruction' under the dictatorial rule of Saddam Hussein, but had no game plan of what to do next. Capitalizing on the subsequent withdrawal of US troops and the widespread anger amongst Sunnis about the sectarian policies of the Shia-led post-invasion government of Iraq supported by the US, the group overran large swathes of northern and western Iraq, and became "Islamic State". By joining the rebellion against Syria's authoritarian ruler, Bashar al-Assad, in 2011, ISIS found a safe-haven and easy access to weapons.

As a consequence, ISIS was able to rapidly take over control of a territory across Syria and Iraq of around 78,000 km^2 (30,100 square miles) by 2014, proclaimed the creation of a "Caliphate", or, State under direction of a religious leader claiming succession from Muhammad … and called themselves "The Islamic State". A Caliphate does not recognize alternate territorial borders. A population of over ten million people was estimated then to be under ISIS control across their 'Caliphate' (Beattie 2015, BBC 2017).

Apart from political control, ISIS exerted authority over a range of industrial and commercial activities, natural resources and commodities, from oil to agricultural products and minerals. Based on conservative estimates, ISIS controlled revenue in excess of US$2 billion (Black et al. 2014).

However, ISIS's longer term power is that they do not just embark on the most extreme of terrorist action to frighten those who have different (even different Islamic) beliefs to their doctrine, but build their terror and control, community by community, rather than fight a battle at international level such as has been the project of Al Qaida. ISIS follows up by carefully building a new society, with rules, laws and taxes, according to their fundamentalist ideology—delivered with extreme violence to those who do not follow their command. Their power to sustain their impact ultimately is in *building an economy and community* by *their* rules.

> In its quest to establish *administrative and civil control* over its conquered territory, ISIS immediately moves in with a full administrative system to control everything from hospitals, to education, to football. It has implemented taxes on a variety of commercial activities. In Mosul alone, ISIS is believed to raise US$8 million in taxes each month. (Brisard and Martinez 2015)

This was the situation and power of ISIS at the time when we addressed its significance in the course of our three year Kyoto program to develop our Kyoto Manifesto for a New Economics, that is, in June 2014.

The main point of this analysis was to show the immense power of a terrorist group that captured into extreme terrorist violence not only the engagement of disadvantaged and repressed people under corrupt regimes serving their own private interests within an international capitalism system. ISIS worked through *building* the administrative and community support for those taken over—according to ISIS Caliphate rules and with extreme violence to ensure compliance … but still, not just leaving control to terrorist violence, but also through building community engagement … of a sort!

However, since 2014, the situation of ISIS has changed, primarily as they have met with massive military opposition on an international front.

> ISIS subsequently lost 14% of its territory in 2015 under attack from Syria, Iraq, Turkey, the United States and Russia—although battles in Syria are immensely complex in terms of who is involved, who they are fighting, and what is the consequence.
>
> In 2016, ISIS lost one quarter of the territory they previously controlled in Iraq and Syria, bringing their overall territorial control down from 78,000 to 60,400 km^2 (23,300 square miles) in December 2016. Along with the fall of Mosul in June 2017, ISIS lost another 60% of their territory whilst their revenue had dropped from US $2 billion to $875 million (BBC 2017).
>
> The impact on the people of Syria, in particular, has been totally traumatic. As at February 2016, 11.5% of Syria's population had been wounded or killed since 2011 including 470,000 deaths. The vast majority of deaths— 400,000—were caused by violence, while 70,000 came as an indirect result of the war—the collapse of the country's health-care infrastructure, lack of access to medicine, poor sanitation, the spread of communicable diseases, falling vaccination rates, food scarcity and malnutrition. Another 1.88 million Syrians have been injured (Boghani 2016).

According to the UN Refugee Agency, UNHCR, 6.5 million people, including 2.8 million children, have been displaced within Syria, the biggest internally displaced population in the World (UNHCR 2016).

Meanwhile, ISIS strategies have reacted to its defeats by moving directly into confrontation with the globalized world—in their homes

With a sophisticated strategy of radicalization, particularly of the impressionable young, ISIS is encouraging random terrorist attacks by individuals or independent groups across the world—not planned from ISIS, but 'inspired' by 'conversion', often via internet and social group influence. The purpose, as expressed by Al-Qaeda leader Ayman al-Zawahiri in a video message released on December 1st 2015: 'Because they are the leaders of the contemporary "crusader campaign"', that is, against secular, globalization values that conflict with Sunni Islam's most extremist doctrinal demands (Europol 2016.)

Although its global strategy has adjusted under pressure of defeat within the intended 'Caliphate', ISIS represents the power of religious-based *division* against the possible *harmony* of a globalized world. Our wider *humanity* is at stake when such violent division remains within.

4.3 Military Conflict

Most dangerous of all consequences of global divisiveness to be addressed is the paranoid and self-centered action of those who have enough but wish to preserve it no matter what by whatever means of economic, coercive and military power they possess.

The technological power that now is held in the paranoid control of the very few is strong enough to annihilate the human race entirely through nuclear war within, as a worst case scenario, 30 min.

This destruction of humanity could be initiated not just from the superpower United States or Russia, but even from a local border dispute between India and Pakistan, or North and South Korea, Israel and the Arab world, or terrorists who are able to access nuclear bomb capability from ineffectively guarded stockpiles of weaponary in failed states or Russia.

A so-called 'limited nuclear strike' in any of these conflicts could create a global winter with the power to destroy all food sources for our surivival— within a year.

The scariest thing of all is that our human world could well be annihilated by a simple mistake. This *has almost happened* several times over the last 34 years.

In 1983 for example, the Soviet Union was poised to launch massive nuclear attack on the United States because of an error in their 'Dead Hand' nuclear retaliation system. In case of the complete annihilation of the Soviet leadership from a US 'first strike', the system's technology would *automatically* take over, delivering a comprehensive 'second strike' on the United States by intercontinental ballistic nuclear missiles.

The system picked up what the computers interpreted as a massive missile strike from the US, and was sending urgent signals to respond before it was too late.

A single individual, Lt Colonel Stanislov Petrov, stood between peace and World War III and the total destruction of humanity. He commanded 'Serpukhov-15', a top-secret missile attack early warning system located south of Moscow.

In spite of the data and screaming alarms, he paused and refused to follow established orders because he judged that the warning of an immediate missile strike from the United States *might be* a technological error (Hoffmann 2009).

It was. The Soviet satellites had picked up the sun at dusk glinting on poised missiles in North Dakota and technologically interpreted this as the flames of rockets being launched.

We came within minutes of the destruction of our world.

Without Petrov's good judgment, most of humanity would have been annihilated over 30 years ago.

If any of us were still here today, we would probably be fighting each other with bows and arrows for whatever scarce and radiated food supplies were around, and delivering genetically crippled children. 'Humanity' would have disappeared along with all reminders of past cultures.

Petrov was dismissed and marginalized in the Soviet Union because he did not follow established orders. The international community has only very recently recognised Petrov's importance and rewarded him—now, a very old man.

The new rulers of the world, the cockroaches, would otherwise be marching.

4.4 Dealing with 'not Having an Alternative'

The fourth danger is to our ability to find the new solutions needed to address these concerns.

As global industrialized economic 'progress' continues, *'global warming' of our ecology is directly associated with 'global freezing' of humanity*—marginalizing our humanity in the interests of economic progress. Marginalizing our human power to respond. "Freezing" our human solutions to problems into what appeared to work in the past, but not solving the problems now that the global economic paradigm surrounding world society has created.

We need a new mind-set.

However, with globalization we are losing the human values lessons for survival that we can learn from traditional societies that have been sustainable for millennia, and from 'eastern' cultural and social values that both historically and in the present have a great deal to offer but fit uncomfortably into current global economic paradigms.

The remote tribal societies of West Papua, to take but one example, some of the last peoples to confront the modern world, have sustained their existence for 10,000 years by their values. (Hill 2017)

Can we?

Throw away the arrogance of our 'modernized' beliefs, and we have a great deal to learn from the integrity of west Papua values and choices. Currently their world, their culture and even their lives are being destroyed by direct repression from Indonesia's military and international profit oriented interests (Hill 2017).

On the other hand, Eastern cultures can offer us important lessons for change as well.

I need to be clear to avoid romanticized stereotypes. Cultures and societies of China, Japan, and other countries of the 'East' are themselves now well embedded in the global economic framework. The 'language' of cultural difference in economic and organizational practice is largely played out within the 'grammar' of globalization. Equally, Eastern societies historically have been no more societies of peace than those of the West.

However, there is much to be learnt from the 'spiritual'—expressed in traditional values and rituals that celebrate enriched vision, balance and our 'togetherness' as humanity.

This issue is dealt with through our Second Movement, "Foundation Stones of Spirituality".

4.5 Dealing with the Danger of the Erosion of Human Spirituality

The fifth danger within a globalized society that is stamped by its 'western' global economic benefit assumptions, is loss of our *spirituality*. Our ultimate human vision of meaning and connectedness, is increasingly being marginalized or disguised in fake clothing.

Humanity's spirituality is intrinsically inclusive, not exclusive, for as soon as we marginalize others, we separate ourselves from our own shared humanity.

However, spirituality—celebration of the sacredness, ultimate vision and connectedness of our humanity and its relationship to the cosmos and eternity—is not to be confused with institutionalized religion, although potentially, religious devotion may well offer a path.

> When enclosed in institutional boundaries that *separate*, spiritual potential may well be co-opted into serving local 'church' or religious *institutions* rather than engaging and enriching our wider community and its collective vision. The extreme case of religious commitment to ISIS's version of the Sunni interpretation of Islam is a particular case in point.

Where human *spirituality* is not at the center, one confronts *interest*.

> First, this interest may be in maintaining institution-based property or financial ownership, and the institution's wider financial base and *institutional* longevity.
>
> Second, and most important to *religious* affiliation may be the need or *interest* at a personal level for an absolute belief base to support personal identity along with its secure meaning, perhaps to offer forgiveness or release from everyday life anxiety, and even for the future security of being 'saved' in our 'afterlife'.
>
> Or, as with the case of the Sunni ISIS followers, being secure as a 'martyr' that all is OK for a totally blessed afterlife—for males, even with 72 virgins at their personal disposal, 'houris'—undefiled, pure, wives—a particular reward in the *Sunni's* faith.
>
> Women unfortunately do not get the same deal. Instead, following a devoted life on this earth, they will become beautiful, happy, and without jealousy in their afterlife—potentially with husbands who never grow bored of their wives and prefer them over all the houris on offer. One female suicide bomber projected that she would become "chief of the 72 virgins, the fairest of the fair" (Tsai 2010).

Our *humanity* may well be expressed within and by religious institutions, but it most certainly is not limited by the boundaries of any one of them that separate 'this' belief group off from communion with and care for others.

'Humanity' is intrinsically ecumenical.

Furthermore, the direct forces of globalized economics may well extract spirituality out of institutionalized religion by *co-opting or replacing* spirituality with the marketing campaigns of large commercial enterprise, e.g.: for some revivalist movements requiring a dedicated percentage of income from committed members for benefit largely of the leader or expansion of the institution; or commercial interests selling 'religious' or 'belief' products.

Finally, religious institutions may *demand* for their own institutional and economic survival their pre-eminence for salvation *above* the wider community (i.e.: separation), or intolerance of alternatives - particularly, as expressed in fundamentalist movements such as with ISIS at present or for that matter, any religion that denies that God, or ultimate connection to the universe, can be approached through a *variety* of human paths.

> It is significant, as observed earlier, that ISIS's success is based not just on terrorism but in refashioning the invaded communities' social world within an enforced economic system, anchoring longer term strength back into a refashioned community. Empathy, sharing, tolerance for all humanity, ultimately *spirituality,* are lost. But, after ISIS fighters originally swept across the Iraq city of Mosul, they took power, and to show they could bring stability to daily life, immediately reduced the price of bread (Shubert 2015).

ISIS controls the newly invaded society through determining its economy and rigid administration controlled from *outside* the local community's will or voice—a veiled mirror of the Western capitalist global economic and ideological control they despise! In spite of its protestations against the West, ISIS remains embedded in the values and dynamics of global economics and uses profits from, for example, sale of oil, in the international economy to fund its terrorist enterprise. *Spirituality* has been denied in particular through assertion of the practice of public beheading of innocents who happened to believe in an alternative path to God.

This is *not* what our global humanity and its ultimate essence, our spirituality, can be!

5 A Final Word

The world's current globalized economic systems are therefore leading humanity towards a dangerous precipice in the 21st Century: a continuing rush towards the edge of ecological disaster for the separate profit of some but not all; divisiveness that must inevitably lead to conflict and war; and, loss of shared meaning that otherwise provides the basic resilience of our world society to respond.

In the long term, we are impoverishing the very essence of what humanity *can* be, our shared spiritual core and ultimate potential, lives worth living not just for the rich, but for all. For if humanity is divided and impoverished, so too are we all within our very existential selves.

"We used to live in a society. Now, we live in an economy"

The threats to our continued survival and humanity follow from the power of this economic context, its values, and demands for selfishness.

It is time to reverse the valence of this relationship.

This is the objective of our "Kyoto Manifesto for Global Economics".

References

Action Group on Erosion, Technology and Concentration (the ETC Group). (2008). *Who owns nature? Corporate power and the final frontier in the commodification of life*. http://www.etcgroup.org.files/publications/707/01/pdf, November 12, 2008.

Agrawal, R. (2015, August 28). Why India is still fighting over caste system'. *CNN*. http://edition.cnn.com/2015/08/28/asia/india-gujarat-caste-protests/.

Agrawal, R. (2016, February 24). India's caste system: Outlawed but still omnipresent. *CNN*. http://edition.cnn.com/2016/02/23/asia/india-caste-system/.

Alisina, A., Di Tella, R., & Mac Culloch, R. (2004). Inequality and happiness: Are European and Americans different? *Journal of Public Economics, 88*(9–10), 2009–2042.

Atkin, E. (2014, September 10). UN scientists see largest CO_2 increase in 30 years: We are running out of time. *Climate Progress/News Investigation*. http://www.nationofchange.org/un-scientists-see-largest-co2-increase-30-years-we-are-running-out-time-1410361126.

Babones, S. (2014). *The great recession has widened the gap between the developed world's affluent and everyone else*. http://inequality.org/oecd-report-inequality-rising-faster/#sthash.lxeGwbiP.dpuf.

BBC. (2017. January 20). Islamic state and the crisis in Iraq and Syria in maps. *News*. http://www.bbc.com/news/world-middle-east-27838034.

Beattie, J. (2015, May 15). Islam is a religion of war, not a religion of peace. *Western Journalism*. http://www.westernjournalism.com/isis-leader-islam-is-a-religion-of-war-not-a-religion-of-peace/.

Black, I., Abouzeid, R., Tran, M., Maher, S., Tooth, R., & Chulov, M. (2014). 'The terrifying rise of ISIS: $2ba in loot, online killings and an army on the run'. *The Guardian*. https://www/theguardian.com/world/2014/jun/16/terrifying-rise/

Boghani, P. (2016, February 11). A staggering new death toll for Syria's War—470,000. *PBS Frontline*. http://www.pbs.org/wgbh/frontline/article/a-staggering-new-death-toll-for-syrias-war-470000/.

Boulding, K. E. (1966). *The economics of the coming spaceship earth*. http://www.geocities.com/RainForest/3621/Boulding.htm.

Boulding, K. E. (1973). Attributed in: United States Congress, House (1973), Energy, Reorganization Act of 1973: Hearings. Ninety-third Congress, first session on H.R. 11510, p. 248.

Boulding, K. E. (1988). Quoted in McCloskey, Deidre (2013) 'What Boulding said went wrong with economics, a quarter century on'. p. 126. Routledge Volume edited by Wilfred Dolfsma: http://www.deirdremccloskey.com/editorials/boulding.php.

Breene, K. (2016, November 7). 6 surprising facts about India's exploding middle class. *World Economic Forum*. https://www.weforum.org/agenda/2016/11/6-surprising-facts-about-india-s-exploding-middle-class/.

Brisard, J.-C., & Martinez, D. (2014). Islamic state: The economy-based terrorist funding. *Thomas Reuters Consulting* (Accelus). http://accelus.thomsonreuters.com/sites/default/files/GRC01815.pdf.

Center For Food Safety and Save Our Seeds (2013). *Seed giants vs. U.S. farmers* (p. 5). http://www.centerforfoodsafety.org/files/seed-giants_final_04424.pdf.

Diamond, J., & Bash, D. (2017, January 24). Trump signs order withdrawing from TPP, reinstate "Mexico City policy" on abortion. *CNN Politics*. http://www.cnn.com/.../trans-pacific-trade-deal-withdrawal-trumps-first-executive-order/.

Eliott, L. (2017, January 16). World's eight richest people have same wealth as poorest 50%. *The Guardian*. https://www.theguardian.com/global-development/2017/jan/16/worlds-eight-richest-people.

Europol. (2016). Changes in modus operandi of Islamic State terrorist attacks. Review held by experts from Member States and Europol on 29th November and 1st December 2015, The Hague, 18 January. https://www.europol.europa.eu/sites/default/files/documents/changes_in_modus_operandi_of_islamic_state_terrorist_attacks/.

Ferrer-i-Carbonell, A. (2014). Inequality and happiness. *Journal of Economic Surveys, 28*(5), 1016–1027.

Hill, S. (1986). eighteen cases of technology transfer to Asia/Pacific Countries. *Science and Public Policy, 13*(3), 162–169.

Hill, S. (1988). *The tragedy of technology—Freedom vs liberation in the late 20th `century*. London: Pluto Press.

Hill, S. (2005, May 3). Opening remarks. *World Press Freedom Day. Jakarta, Indonesia*. Available from UNESCO Office, Jakarta. www.unesco.or.id.

Hill, S. (2017). *Captives for Freedom – Hostages, Negotiation and the Future of West Papua*. Port Moresby. University of Papua New Guinea Press.

Hoffmann, D. E. (2009). The dead hand—The untold story of the Cold War Arms Race and its dangerous legacy. New York: Doubleday. (Pulitzer Prize Winner).

Independent. (2015). *What is TTIP? And six reasons why the answer should scare you*, October 16, 2015. 16 http://www.independent.co.uk/voices/comment/what-is-ttip-and-six-reasons-why-the-answer-should-scare-you-9779688.html.

James, H. (2012). The price of offshore revisited: New estimates for missing global private wealth, income, inequality, and lost taxes (PDF) (p. 5). *Tax Justice Network*, July 2012. Retrieved April 15, 2015.

McCloskey, D. (2013). What Boulding said went wrong with economics, a quarter century on (p. 126). Routledge Volume edited by Wilfred Dolfsma (forthcoming). http://www.deirdremccloskey.com/editorials/boulding.php.

Meadows, D. H., Meadows, D. L., Randers, J., & Behrens III, W. W. (1972). *Limits to growth—A report for the club of Rome's project on the predicament of mankind*. New York: Universe Books.

Oishi, S., Kesebir, S., & Diener, E. (2011). Income disparity makes people unhappy—Study. *Psychological Science*. http://inequality.org/happiness-and-inequality-study/.

Oxfam. (2017). An economy for the 99 percent. January 16. https://www.oxfam.org/en/research/economy-99/. See also Oxfam International Press Release, January 16, 2017, Just 8 men own same wealth as half the world. https://www.oxfamorg/en/pressroom/pressreleases/2017-01-16/just-8-men-own-same.

Peralta, N. A. (2013, May 14). Ownership control, transnational corporations and financial power. *Mappingignorance*. http://mappingignorance.org/2013/05/14/ownership-control-transnational-corporations-and-financial-power/.

Piketty, T. (2014). *Capitalism in the twenty-first century* (trans: Arthur Goldhammer). Cambridge MA & London: Belknap Press of Harvard University Press.

Sankaran, L. (2013, June 15). Caste is not past. *The New York Times: Sunday Review*. http://www.nytimes.com/2013/06/16/opinion/sunday/caste-is-not-past.html.

Sarich, C. (2013. October 21). The 10 companies controlling the world's seed supply. *Nation of change/News Analysis*. http://www.nationofchange.org/10-companies-controlling-world-s-seed-supply-1382363748.

Shinkle, P. (2003, June 19). Monsanto sends seed-saving farmer to prison. *Agribusiness Examiner*, No. 246. http://www.rense.com/general38/saver.htm.

Shubert, A. (2015, April 21). How ISIS controls life from birth to foosball. *CNN*. http://www.cnn.com/2015/04/21/middleeast/isis-documents/.

Tsai, M. (2010, March 29). Do female suicide bombers get 72 virgins too? *Slate*. http://www.slate.com/articles/news_and_politics/recycled/2010/03/honey_im_dead.html.

Turner, G. (2014). *Is global collapse imminent? An updated comparison of the limits to growth with historical data* (p. 3). Research Paper No. 4, University of Melbourne. Melbourne Sustainable Society Institute, August.

UNESCO. (2005). *Annual report, Jakarta Office* (pp. 7–8; 144–145). http://www.unesdoc.unesco.org/images/0015/001505/150521e.pdf.

United Nations. (2015). Intergovernmental panel on climate change, 'Synthesis Report', the 'Fifth Assessment Report' launched on 18th May. http://www.ipcc.ch/report/ar5/syr/.

UNHCR. (2016). *Internally displaced people*. http://www.unhcr.org/sy/29-internally-displaced-people.html.

Upbin, B. (2011, October 22). The 147 companies that control everything. *Forbes*. http://www.forbes.com/sites/bruce.

Vitali, S., Glattfelder, J. B., & Batison, S. (2011). The network of global corporate control. *PLoS ONE 6*(10). https://doi.org/10.1371/journal.pone.0025995.

Wikipedia. (2016). *Faust*, April, 25, 2016. https://en.wikipedia.org/wiki/Faust.

Wikipedia. (2017). *Trans-Pacific partnership*. https://en.wikipedia.org/wiki/Trans-Pacific-Partnership/.

World Bank. (2015a). *Poverty overview*, April, 06. www.worldbank.org/en/topic/poverty/overview.

World Bank. (2015b). *GDP (current US$), 2015 (based on World Bank National Accounts Data and OECD National Accounts Data Files)*. http://worldbank.org/indicator/NY.GDP.MKTP.CD.

World Meteorological Organization (WMO). (2013). The state of greenhouse gases in the atmosphere based on global observations through 2013. *Greenhouse Gas Bulletin*, 10, September 9. https://www.wmo.int/pages/mediacentre/pressreleases/documents/1002_GHG_Bulletin.pdf.

Chapter 3
Human and Nature Revisited: The Industrial Revolution, Modern Economics and the Anthropocene

Ryuichi Fukuhara

> What we observe is not nature itself, but nature exposed to our method of questioning
> —Werner Heisenberg

1 Tragedy of the Aral Sea—A Collapse of the Interconnection of Human and Nature

In 1998, for my research on the status of local fishery at the disappearing Aral Sea in Kazakhstan, I visited Karateren village close to the Syr Darya, one of the two major tributaries together with the Amu Darya, that had been feeding water to the Aral Sea for millennia. On the coast near the river mouth of the Syr Darya, I saw there many trucks, bulldozers and laborers working on a sand dike stretching out over shallow water towards the opposite side of the bank of the Aral Sea. They were building up the closure dike to prevent outflow from the northern part to the southern part of the Aral Sea. This last-ditch effort, initiated by the local administration, was to save only the small northern part from disappearing. As far as I heard from construction workers and local officials, the closure dike collapsed several times during construction, and it sometimes became a deadly accident due to seasonal floods, poor construction planning and absolute lack of budget. They also did lack the sophisticated hydraulic information, so the construction was undertaken in an impromptu manner without any help from the central government and the international community. Since the fall of the Soviet Union in 1991 when the Aral Sea was already in dire straits, its final fate was handed down primarily to the two new independent states, Kazakhstan and Uzbekistan. It seemed Uzbekistan almost gave up the further effort since the water of the Amu Darya had not reached the Aral even in the 1980s while Kazaks still had a

---

R. Fukuhara (✉)
The Center for the Study of the Creative Economy, Doshisha University, Kyoto, Japan
e-mail: ryuichi.fukuhara@gmail.com

© The Editor(s) 2018
S. Yamash'ta et al. (eds.), *The Kyoto Manifesto for Global Economics*, Creative Economy, https://doi.org/10.1007/978-981-10-6478-4_3

hope to protect the last piece of the sea and the flow of the Syr Darya. Attempts by locals however looked miserably incompetent at that time as the scale of construction work gave me an impression that the inability of mankind to fix nature, considering the magnitude of man-induced destruction on environment.

Until the 1970s, Karateren was a vibrant fisherman village on the shore, where warehouses, small shipyards and fish processing factories ran business as constituents of the local fishery, the one and only livelihood of the village. It was still the very fisherman village when I visited simply because villagers did have any other option, if they had to remain in the middle of the desert, but continued the fish catch after the sea coast receded away beyond the horizon. Fishermen, once sailed out from the village port next door, had to go 30 km away by truck to catch seawater flounders near the river mouth of the Syr Darya. Flounders were of course not indigenous species in the low saline water but stocked in order to sustain the local fishery since the ten-time increase of water salinity extinguished native fresh and brackish water fish species. The history of fisheries in the Aral Sea dated back to the Neolithic period as proven by archeological excavations. In the late 1950s the fisheries yielded about 46,000 tons annually, then declined to 6700 tons by the late 1970s and dropped to merely 1000 tons in the early 80s. At their best time, catches had been transported across the whole country, and fed millions of starved people during the country's famine in the early Soviet time. Nonetheless, such an old glory of the Aral Sea fishery was totally gone with the desert wind. The long-term relations between human and the Aral Sea almost came to an end.

The Aral Sea was with slightly more than 67,000 km^2 the fourth largest lake till the 1960s, following Caspian Sea, Lake Superior and Lake Victoria. The terminal lake with salinity averaging 1%, one third of the seawater, was inhabited by brackish and freshwater fish species. The extensive deltas of the Amu Darya and the Syr Darya sustained the rich diversity of fauna and flora in the sensitive brackish-freshwater ecosystem. The Aral Sea's water level was stable with the balance between annual inflow and net evaporation so it was in long-term equilibrium with a maximum lake level variation of less than one meter (Micklin 2007).

The Aral Sea had started to change dramatically since the early 1960s after the groundbreaking of the Karakum Canal in 1954, one of the largest irrigation canals in the world at that time, to divert water from the Amu Darya across the Karakum Desert in Turkmenistan. This new engineering scheme was to cultivate "cotton", one may called "White Gold". To achieve cotton self-sufficiency was the very important political and economic goal of the Soviet Union in the post war era as emphasized in Joseph Stalin's speech in 1946 (CIA 1955). Expansion of irrigated areas between 1965 and 2000 markedly reduced the inflows to the Aral Sea. The annual average of total inflow decreased to 43 km^3 and the annual average of net groundwater inflow was estimated 2.5 km^3, whereas net evaporation was 57 km^3, giving a deficit of 12 km^3. The gap between river inflow and net evaporation was particularly noticeable during the 1970s and 1980s, with water balance deficits for both periods above 30 km^3 annually. Consequently, the sea shrink exacerbated over these two decades; since 1960 up to January 2006, the Aral separated into two parts,

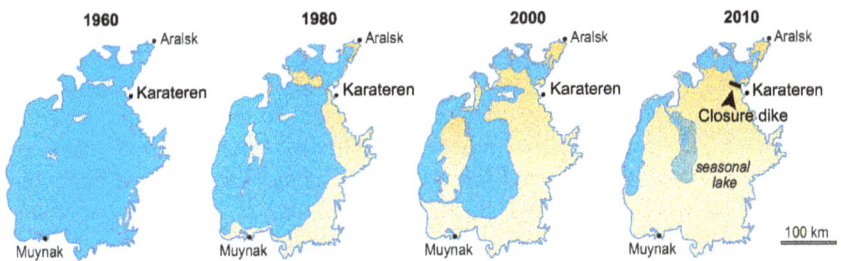

Fig. 1 Changing profile of the Aral Sea from 1960 to 2010 (cited from UNEP and ENVSEC 2011, modified by author)

and the level of the Small Aral fell by 13 m and the Large Aral fell by 23 m (Micklin 2007). A channel named the Berg Strait connected the two lakes, the channel people tried to close as I witnessed in 1998, with flow from the Small to the Large Aral. At the end, the area of both seas taken together diminished by 74% and the volume by 90% (Fig. 1).

In addition to immeasurable impacts on the aquatic ecosystem and local climate, the dried-up sea bed, so-called Aral-kum desert, produced dust storms laden with chemicals and pesticides from the intensive agriculture occurring along the two rivers. This in turn led to increased air and water pollution levels, and crop damage as much as 1000 km away. Cancers, respiratory diseases, anemia, miscarriages, and kidney and liver diseases soared in the region. Thousands of people were forced to abandon their homes as their livelihoods dried up and their health was threatened. The situation continued to worsen until the restoration program launched by the international communities came into effect. As part of such efforts, the engineering-sound Berg Strait dike was completed later in 2005 with assistances from the international community, leading to keep the water level and to drop the salinity level of the small Aral Sea to some extent. Accordingly, locals around the northern part experience fewer sand storm, more rain; improved water availability, air quality and health conditions even though it was very modest recovery.

Considered as the worst environmental disaster in the 20th century, the Aral Sea tragedy provides the most striking example of the interconnections between the health of an ecosystem and that of the economy, community, and people dependent on that ecosystem (Postel 2000), and the thirst for cotton certainly lay at the center of the Aral Sea's environmental catastrophe.

2 Cotton—A Crop of the Industrialization and the Modern Economy

In India there were trees growing wild, which produce a kind of wool better than sheep's wool in beauty and quality, which the Indians use for making their clothes.

—Herodotus, wrote in 400 BC

The story of cotton has much more to tell us however. Indeed, cotton has influenced human history for at least 5000 years, was at the heart of the Industrial Revolution around the turn of the 19th century, shaped the modern globalized economy, and still remains a powerful determinant of current economic behavior.

Cotton is known to have been cultivated in India for more than 5000 years, and it was native spices of *Gossyplum arboretum*, producing a short staple fiber. The cotton production, not only cultivation but also techniques of ginning, spinning, yarning and weaving to make textiles and fabrics, spread slowly to the east, north and west. By roughly the 13th century, it arrived from west Africa to Japan. In Africa, there was also an indigenous cotton, *G. harbaceum* similar to the Asian one. By contrast, South Americans including Mayans and Incans grew *G. barbadense*, which produced the longer staple fiber. By the mid 19th century, one variety became dominated cotton cultivation, *G. hirsutum*, also known as American Upland, a native in Central America and West Indies, and now 90% of all cotton production is cultivars deprived from this variety. American Upland was preferred in modern cotton cultivation because of its quality of skinny, straight-long and fine white fiber; more suitable than other three varieties to process by the new mechanical textile production.

As we can see the origins of domesticated cotton varieties, cotton requires warm to hot temperatures with low humidity and plenty of sunshine. Cotton needs about 180 frost-free days to mature from its emergence to fruiting so that its cultivation areas inevitably must have a dry climate with hot temperatures and low rainfall in the planting and harvesting seasons since the rainfall after the open of cotton hulls would be fatal to market values of cotton fibers. It was a reasonable option, at least economically, for the Soviet Union to irrigate water to the very dry Karakum desert to establish their own "cotton belt" just like large-scale cotton plantations were developed in American South to provide England with raw cotton in the 18th century. Since cotton was regarded as a proxy of "World Power" (Scherer 1916) at that time, when Czarist Russia gained control over Central Asia in the 19th century, Russian businessmen immediately started growing American Upland cotton there. In the late 19th and early 20th centuries, one-third of total irrigated lands were devoted to cotton production. Since then the Czarist Russia as well as the Communism Soviet stuck to the cotton self-sufficiency within their territory. It might be in an economically suitable, but not in an environmentally sustainable way.

Due to its biological root of the wet tropical origin, cotton has naturally remained a "thirsty crop" that requires plenty of water—to gulp down all water of the Aral Sea. Dutch Hydrologist Arjen Hoekstra, who developed Water Footprint concept,[1] mentioned "If there is one single crop to be elected for its most disastrous effect on natural water flows and water quality in river basins, cotton has a good chance of winning". He continues "the blame should not be placed on cotton, but on the people who

---

[1] A water footprint is the real amount of freshwater used, including pollution, by individuals, groups or companies in order to make goods or provide services used by the community, proposed as an alternative water use indicator in 2002. This concept was inspired by British geographer Tony Allen's idea of "Virtual Water" (Allen 1997).

decided to grow it at too large a scale in unsuitable regions" (Hoekstra 2013). From hydrological point of view, cotton cultivation annually consumes approximately 2.5% of the total water withdrawal globally (Chapagain et al. 2006), jeopardizing local water sustainability in many places such as Deccan Plateau in India, Pakistan, China and the United States. Cotton also requires other environmental costs, not only water but soil fertility, in places where cotton cultivation was practiced. Even before modern era in China's lower Yangtze region, huge amounts of soybean cake fertilizer had to be imported (mostly from Manchuria) to replenish the overworked soil. In Japan, plenty small fish catches were used as fertilizer for cotton-growing fields (Pomeranz and Topik 2006). Cotton also could attract many kinds of pests and be infected by a range of diseases which can affect the quality of fiber and seed, the yield and the production cost. For that reason, cotton in modern agriculture, in addition to fertilizers, demands many other inputs; it consumed 5.7% by value of all the protection chemicals and 16.5% by value of all insecticide in 2013; Biotech cotton was planted on 23 million ha or 68% of the world cotton area in 2012/13. In the same year, 72% of the cotton produced and 73% of the cotton traded internationally originated from biotech varieties. In two hundred years, cotton has become a crop of the modern economy in such a sense that it needs a combination of various fruits of modern sciences as well as is produced and traded as a global commodity.

Then, who are precisely to be blamed for the expansion of cotton cultivation resulting in the disappearance of the Aral Sea in the last century? On this point, Brad Stevens Richter denies such particularity to the Marxism or Communism with regard to environmental degradation, but rather suggests its historical relevance to Christianity and the Enlightenment. In the Soviet Union, instead of a supernatural being, a supernatural institution—Man and the (Communist) Party—became the new Gods, the mediator between environment and society, who were legitimized to view nature techno-centrically for planned economic growth. After all, it was nothing but a derivation of the Cartesian doctrine, "nature to be mastered by man" (Richter 1997). Cotton lay not only at the center of early Soviet planned economy. When the Industrial Revolution is referred, technical innovations on new machineries, new energy sources and prime movers, and more efficient production system and institutional improvements have been more focused, not on raw materials; after all, whether or not the Industrial Revolution could go on depended on the availability of raw cotton.

Before the dawn of the Industrial Revolution, India was a relatively urbanized and commercialized nation, and was the world's main producer of cotton textiles and had a substantial export trade to Britain, many European continental countries too, and other parts of the world. Indian cotton products were also used for the slavery trade in Africa since the Indian fine textiles and fabrics were considered much better in quality than any other European textile products. Moreover, woolen products, then main textile products producible in Europe, had no demand in African tropical and subtropical climate. European merchants therefore penetrated in South and Southeast Asia, and established the trading network that importing exotic goods from Asia to exchange them with slaves in Africa, and to send slaves for the plantations in the New World. Cotton product as a global commodity thus was served as a medium of exchange to sustain the slavery trade.

This trade pattern started to change in 1733 with John Kay's invention of a flying shuttle, one of the first of inventions associated with cotton industry; the most important innovation allowing cheaper, mass-scale production of cloth came in 1785 with Edmund Cartwright's power loom (initially powered by steam). These technological innovations on cotton production was literally revolutionary; the industrialized process in England became almost as 300 time efficient as the traditional textile manufacturing in India. Generally speaking, the Industrial Revolution has been widely considered by historians as a tipping point dividing human history. The process of sustained economic growth that historians believe began between 1750 and 1830 drastically altered the socio-economic system of the West. Nobel Economics laureate Douglass North summarizes socio-economic changes invoked by the Industrial Revolution as follows (North 1981).

1. Population growth occurred at an unprecedented rate. Demographers estimate that the world population was approximately eight hundred million in 1750. It was in excess of four billion by 1980, and now we are seven billion.
2. The Western world achieved a standard of living which had no counterpart in the past. The average citizen enjoyed luxuries which were not available to even the richest man of earlier societies. Moreover, the average length of life almost doubled in the developed countries.
3. In the Western world agriculture ceased to be the dominant economic activity; industry and service sectors of the economy replaced it in significance. This change was made possible by the tremendous increase in agricultural productivity.
4. In consequence, the Western world became an urban society with all that term implies concerning increasing specialization, division of labor, interdependence, and inevitable externalities.
5. Continuous technological change became the norm. New sources of energy were harnessed to do men's work and new material and substances constantly created to satisfy human wants.

While these developments are not in question, how these changes occurred and why in Europe not in Asia or other region have been at the center of debate for a long time. For example, North regards the Industrial Revolution as an acceleration in the rate of technical and scientific innovation, enabled by improvement of specified property rights. The increasing market size and better specified property rights over inventions could raise the rate of return on innovating. It was this set of developments which paved the way for the real revolution in technology, which was the wedding of science and technology.

On the other hand, since the environmental movements in the West in the 1970s, the origins of the Industrial Revolution have been revisited from an ecological perspective, paying more attentions to unaccounted social and environmental costs. American historian Ted Steinberg, one of the pioneers who discussed the Industrial Revolution in this regard, wrote "One major assumption has continuity throughout human history: Humankind can never escape from the biological need to sustain itself. All epochs share a common biological threat. From the Pleistocene Age to industrial society, humankind has engaged in a long-standing struggle with the natural world, constantly manipulating and exploiting it for the sake of human existence" (Steinberg 1986). In this long process of humankind's struggle, nature was increasingly conceived as discrete bundles of commodities,—of wood, land, water as a process of commodification, that has made nature tradable in the market system. Steinberg then concluded that the Industrial Revolution had redefined the environment as a vast "natural resource". It is very central to industrialization that has been restructuring drastically mankind's relationship with nature, so that an ecological perspective on the Industrial Revolution provides alternative route to understanding its origins and consequences (Steinberg 1986).

Both views look plausible explanations on the Industrial Revolution; in fact, the current status of our society and the environment could provide room with debates on the two separate perspectives on the nature-human relationship until quite recently. Let us first focus on its consequences, namely our modern globalized economy, at the onset of which cotton played a critical role.

3 The Modern Globalized Economy that Brought an Era of the Anthropocene

Is Earth F**ked?[2]

—Brad Werner, American geophysicist

Many scholars point out that cotton shaped the modern globalized economy, and the modern economy has changed the world, in particular, in terms of the human-nature relationship. Recent discussions on increasing impacts by socio-economic activities, represented by climate change, may provide a new watershed to revisit the relationship. A set of 12 graphs in Fig. 2 shows our socio-economic trends since the mid-18th century. It illustrates that we started to grow drastically since the Industrial Revolution, and our growth has accelerated exponentially after the World War II. This presents a triumph of humanity with modern sciences, technologies and sophisticated institutions; mankind finally could break out of the ecological constraints that hampered our further growth before the pre-modern period for a long time. The globalized economic paradigm that frames our current economic order after the end of the Cold War is indubitably a key to mankind's unprecedented prosperity.

This set of 12 graphs are firstly presented in 2004 by the International Biosphere and Geosphere Program under the International Council of Science, and then

---

[2]The title of the invited presentation in the American Geophysical Union 2012 Fall Meeting. His pessimistic answer was "In sum, the dynamics of the global coupled human-environmental system within the dominant culture precludes management for stable, sustainable pathways and promotes instability" (Werner 2012).

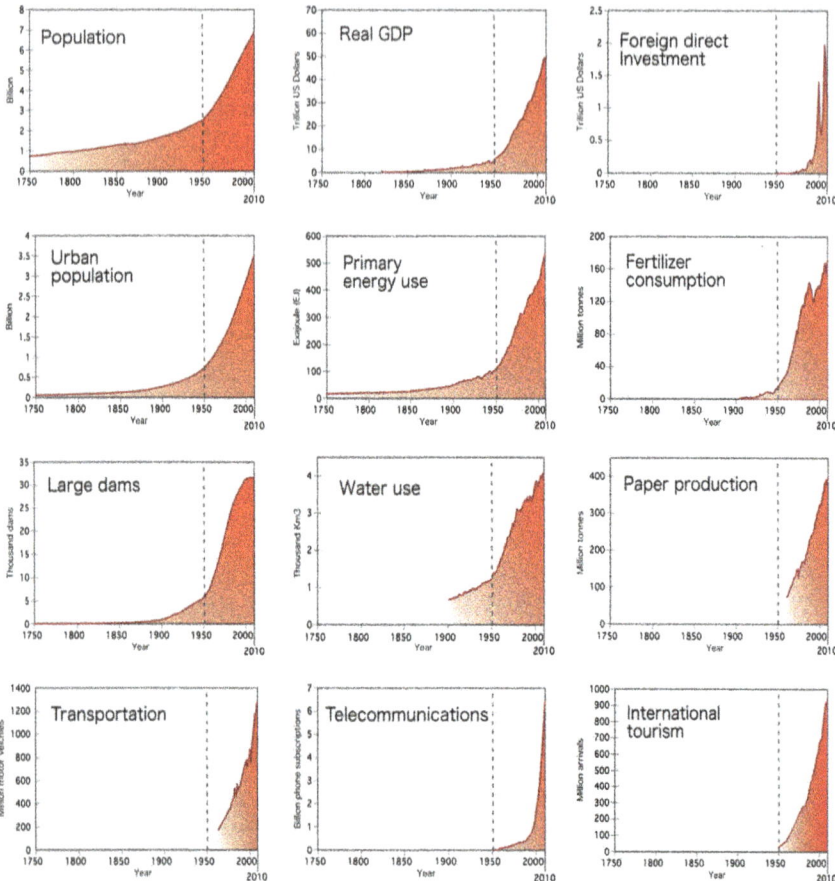

Fig. 2 Trends from 1750 to 2010 in globally aggregated indicators for socio-economic developments (data obtained from http://www.igbp.net. Original sources of each indicator are to be referred in Steffen et al. 2015)

updated in 2015 using data to 2010. There is however another set of 12 graphs shown in Fig. 3. X-axes have the same time scale with the first set, from 1750 to 2010, but this second set presents the changes of the Earth System by selected indicators (Steffen et al. 2015). A growing imprint of the human enterprise on the Earth System from the start of the Industrial Revolution onwards was expected but the dramatic change in magnitude and rate of the human imprint from about 1950 onwards was beyond presumption when the graphs was firstly developed in 2004. That phenomenon was already well known to environmental historians such as McNeill (2000) but generally not to Earth System scientists, and never to economists.

Two sets of graphs are called "Earth Dashboard" or "Great Acceleration Graph". For some economists, policy makers and entrepreneurs, the first set is something to

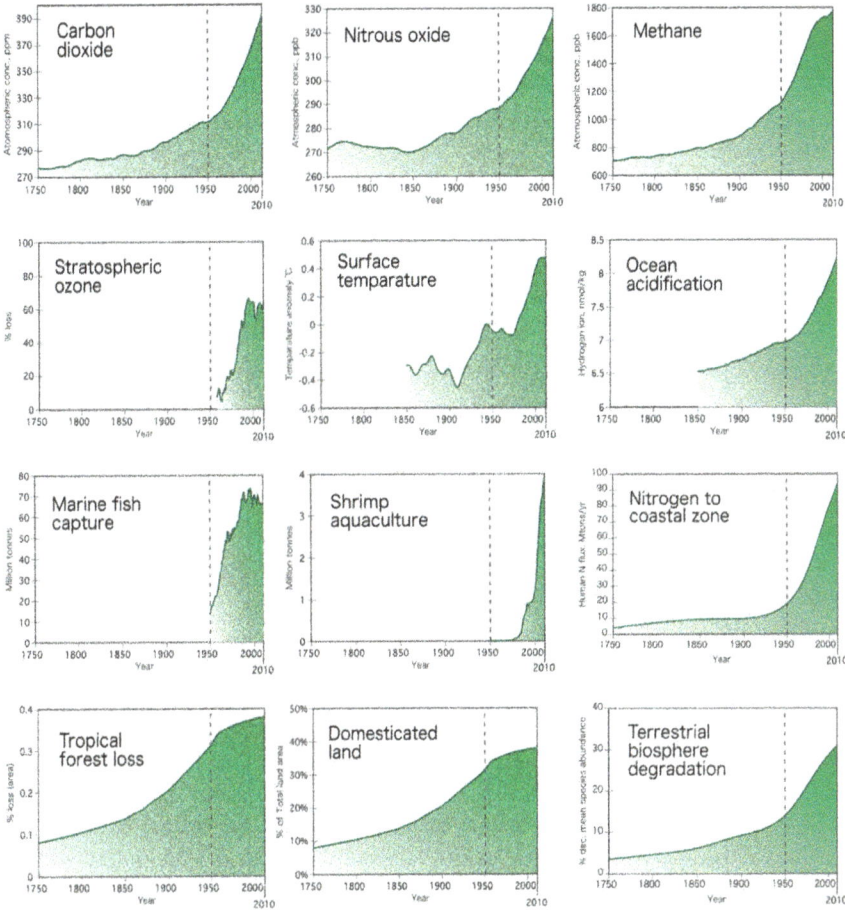

Fig. 3 Trends from 1750 to 2010 in indicators for the structure and functioning of the Earth System (data obtained from http://www.igbp.net. Original sources of each indicator are to be referred in Steffen et al. 2015)

prove the mankind's glorious trajectories of the modern economy in the last two and half centuries guided by modern economic thoughts. On the other hand, earth scientists, ecological conservationists and their allies are deeply concerned with trends shown in the second set that systemic failures of the Earth's life sustaining system seem looming in the horizon. Both sets of graphs certainly describe the current status of the Earth on which we live, but look like as if there were two different planets; one Earth with the full potential for ever-lasting human prosperity with a business-as-usual scenario, another heading to the planetary environmental catastrophe due to human's greeds. Earth Dashboard implies two divided understandings on past, present and the future of human beings' dependence on the Earth system, and this dualistic view induced by the two sets of indicators may recall Karl

Polanyi's observation on "economics", the author of *"Great Transformation"* in which he analyzed the new type of civilization emerging in the 19th century based on the self-regulating "market system". It reads;

> The substantive meaning of economic derives from man's dependence for his living upon nature and his fellows. It refers to the interchange with his natural and social environment, in so far as this results in supplying him with the means of material want satisfaction.
>
> The formal meaning of economic derives from the logical character of the means–ends relationship, as apparent in such words as 'economical' or 'economizing'. It refers to a definite situation of choice, namely, that between the different uses of means induced by an insufficiency of those means.
>
> (Polanyi 1957)

Following line of his thoughts, the modern economy has been gradually dominated by "the formal meaning of economic" substantiated in the first set of graphs while ignoring "the substantive meaning of economic" which represents mankind's primal dependence on the Earth ecosystem so as to meet all energetic and material needs as well as our social and cultural foundations. The gap in-between two meanings of economic has become much wider.

Arbitrary though it may be, I could not think it was just a coincidence that the Soviet Union made such an anthropocentric decision on the Aral Sea ecosystem in the 1950s. Indeed, the mid-20th century will be soon periodized as the opening of new geological epoch of the Earth history. Accumulative anthropogenic impacts on the Earth are now so unprecedentedly enormous even at the geological scale that the "Anthropocene", Geology of mankind, needs to be declared, according to an official expert group who presented the recommendation to the 35th International Geological Congress in South Africa in August 2016. The expert group stated that the new geological epoch should begin around 1950, and the radioactive elements dispersed across the planet by nuclear bombs and their tests would be likely to be adopted as the key evidence although an assemblage of other scientific evidences such as increasing atmospheric carbon level, nitrogen cycle disturbance, plastic pollution, soot from power stations, rapid loss of biological diversity and even bones of the domestic chicken, that has become the largest population among avian species, are now under consideration. After those geological and geophysical evidences being reviewed extensively by broader experts, it is expected that the beginning of the Anthropocene will be officially declared within two or three years to come. It is a little bit ironical that Donald Worster, American historian who pioneered the field of environmental history, called the day on 16 July 1945 the beginning of "the Age of Ecology" which inaugurated on the desert outside Alamogordo, New Mexico with a dazzling fireball of light and swelling mushroom cloud of radioactive gases (Worster 1994). That day is probably to be declared as the very opening of the Anthropocene.

The "current" epoch, the Holocene, lasts the 12,000 years of stable interglacial climate during which all our civilization, society and economy have been developed. The ecologically stable states had continued for thousands of years, which enabled human being to make shift from hunting and gathering to settled agrarian societies. The warmer climate also assisted humans to develop economically, socially, culturally and intellectually in such a way that the Holocene climate guaranteed the three fundamental requirements for the survival and development of humanity; stable climate, the proper circulation of water and nutrients, and the diversity of life forms. Stable climate was a minimum precondition for survival and urged the shift to the agrarian societies, and water and nutrients were indispensable for agriculture. The biological diversity meant that the mankind could have wider options to use for foods and clothes to utilize so as to contribute to expanding human's habitable range, departing from Africa to every small corner of continents and islands except the Antarctic. During the Holocene, our survivability in principle had to submit to the availability of these three requirements principally governed by the natural order beyond the mankind's capacity. In other words, mankind could only alter the very surface of the Earth such as deforestation for expansion of farmlands, diversion of rivers for irrigation and so forth during the Holocene when human species could never alter the earthly geophysical system.

The striking acceleration of socio-economic upward trends has started since the mid-20th century onward.

The population explosion and unprecedented economic growth have accompanied carbon dioxide emissions from internal combustion engines, sea level rise, the global mass extinction of species, and the massive transformation of land by deforestation and desertification as well as oceanic acidification.

Steffen et al. (2007) call this period "Great Acceleration", not only as an echo of the aforementioned Polanyi's book "*Great Transformation*" but also as an accelerating departure from the Holocene to the new geological epoch.

The most different and critical point to divide between the previous epoch and the new epoch is that mankind intendedly or unintendedly has acquired an ability to alter the Earth system. Now that the astronomical and geophysical forcing in the Holocene, and even though the entire Quaternary (2.588 million years to the present), which had been the drivers of the Earth system for 4.6 billion years, could be approximated to zero in comparison with the impact of current anthropogenic pressures, in particular in the last six decades of Great Acceleration in terms of the rate of change of the Earth System. Gaffney and Steffen insist that the reducing risk of leaving the glacial-interglacial limit of cycle of the late Quaternary for an unpredicted future will require the rage of change of the Earth System to become approximately zero (Gaffney and Steffen 2017). In the case of the Anthropocene, efforts to achieve the long-term survivability of a global civilization implies that *Homo sapiens* will deliberately and rapidly reduce its impacts on the Earth System so that they are more comparable in magnitude and more synergistic with astronomical forcing, geophysical forcing and particularly internal dynamics of the Earth System. Alternatively, continued increases in human activities could well lead to abrupt changes in the Earth System that could trigger societal collapse, forcibly reducing human forcing dramatically and returning control of the system to astronomical, geophysical and internal forces. The legacy of the impacts of human forcing on internal forcing through changes in the biosphere could, however, be discernible in the internal dynamics of the Earth System for millions of years (Williams et al. 2015).

Although human activities had been no more than a subset of the internal forces of the Earth system till quite recently (in geological time scale), the modern mainstream economics has not seriously considered any possible feedback loops with the outside of economic system that it has supposed, as many heretical ecological economists have criticized. Ernst "Fritz" Schumacher prophetically stated in his 1973 famous book "*Small is beautiful: a study of economics as if people mattered*" as,

> Until fairly recently the economists have felt entitled, with tolerably good reason, to treat the entire framework within which economic activity takes place as given, that is to say, as permanent and indestructible. It was no part of their job and, indeed, of their professional competence, to study the effects of economic activity upon the framework. Since there is now increasing evidence of environmental deterioration, particularly in living nature, the entire outlook and methodology of economics is being called into question (Schumacher 1973).

Then another question I wish to address in this chapter is how and when has such an idea that "the entire framework is regarded as given" been mainstreamed in modern globalized economics paradigm? In so doing, how did a fault line between the market economy and the Earth system come into being? The first clue can date back to 1865 when William Stanley Jevons pointed out the importance of fossil energy for the socio-economic systems in his "The Coal Question". His statement in its introduction reads; "coal in truth stands not beside but entirely above all other commodities. It is the material source of the energy of the country—the universal aid—the factor in everything we do. With coal, almost any feat is possible or easy; without it we are thrown back into the lubricous poverty of early times" (Jevons 1865). This perception may be the beginning of blessing the increase in per capita energy and material consumption as "economic growth" that constitutes the modern economic thoughts originating in the late 18th century.

4 Revisiting the Industrial Revolution—The Origin of the Anthropocene

> Without slavery there would be no cotton, without cotton there would be no modern industry
>
> —Karl Marx

Although the beginning of new geological epoch will be set at the mid 20th century, no one would refute that the Industrial Revolution opened up a Pandora's Box that has caused unintended and unpredictable enormous environmental changes. It was at the end of the 19th when Arnold Toynbee, who first invented the Industrial Revolution as a subject of historical investigation and discussed its origin based on the two aspects; division of labor or specialization and steam technology. Ever since, the conventional center of the Industrial Revolution narratives has rested on the techno-institutional Western superiority and the mastering of inanimate powers. In such narratives, the divide between pre-modern and modern was common, and the increasing superiority of the modernized West over the rest of the world was justified or even necessarily destined. One of the prominent works in this line was David Landes's "*Unbound Prometheus*", in which he defined the Industrial Revolution as "the final victory of humanity over the natural order (represented by Prometheus, the mythical figure who stolen fire from the gods)" by virtue of new technologies and social values (Landes 2003). Likewise, Mokyr (1990) explained "the difference between rich nations and poor nations" rooted in the Industrial Revolutions, stating rich nations that acquired the ability "to control and manipulate nature and people for productive ends is superior" (Mokyr 1990).

When it comes to the role of fossil energy in this line of argument, British historical demographer Tony Wrigley (2010) develops a flow diagram that depicts the achievements of the Industrial Revolution, in which coal rifted environmental constraints and illuminated what Jevons called by the escape which coal provided from the "laborious poverty" of the organic economy in the pre-modern period (Fig. 4). This diagram shows the structure of the organic pre-industrial economy and the escape route into the unconstrained growth. In the pre-modern organic economy, only the link between pressure on land and real income per head is negative, which represents that growth is self-constrained by ecological factors in the closed system, where all energy and materials deprives from contemporary and relatively recent primary production almost driven by the solar energy within the national boundary. What the fossil energy (as longer-term resultants of accumulated biomass by the primary production) enabled was the opening of a new route which circumvents "pressure on the land". This escape route on the rightmost of the diagram has a positive sign linking the consumption energy to real income growth, bypassing negatives imposed by ecological constraints. Elegantly the British economic take-off for the modern economy is explained, but there should be something missing from this rosy view. Otherwise, there would be no anthropogenic cause for environmental changes towards the Anthropocene.

There are some criticisms on conventional perspectives on modern economic growth and the Industrial Revolution. Stefania Barca points out that underneath this kind of the narratives lies a series of more or less implicit assumption about the distinction between society-nature as well as north-south relationship (Barca 2011). As Stephen Hill also refers to in Chap. 2 of this book, "increasing environmental degradation" and "growing inequality between rich and poor" (Barbier 2015) are two of the major challenges of the current globalized economics paradigm, and these threats have deprived from what Kenneth Pomeranz calls the "Great Divergence", which denotes the socio-economic process by which the Western world overcame premodern growth constraints and emerged during the 19th century as the most powerful and wealthy world civilization of all time, overriding the rest of other regional cores, in particular, Qing China, Mughal India, Tokugawa Japan and the Ottoman Empire (Pomeranz 2000). Pomeranz insists that trade was central to the British industrialization because the principal fiber of the textile revolution, cotton, was always an import that Britain could not grow at home due to its biological features aforementioned in Sect. 2. Cotton import to Britain in 1780

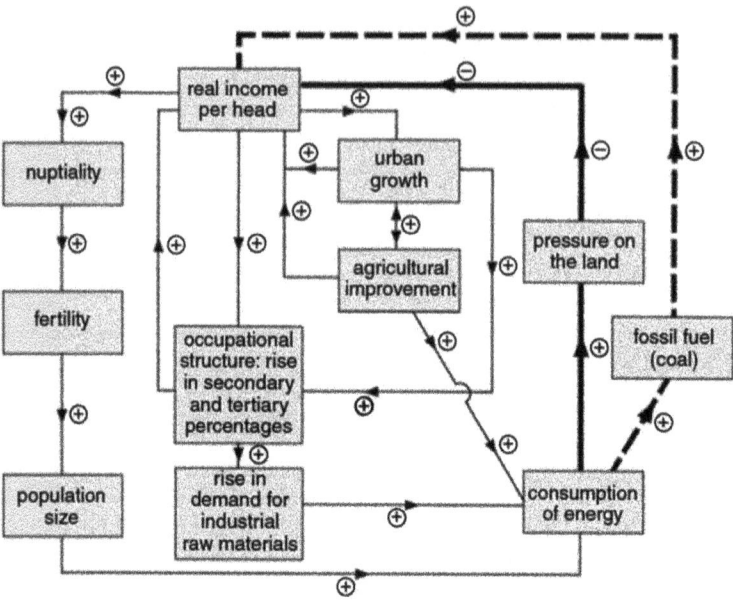

Fig. 4 Old organic economy and the escape route to further economic growth (Wrigley 2010)

was 7 million lb, and seventy years later in 1850, the cotton import accounted for 663 million lb. In the meantime, the cotton textile industry expanded 30-fold by 1830, and the workforce employed in this industry was as large as 800,000 already in 1806 (Riello 2013). Its scale doubled every ten years up to the middle of the 19th century with twice the rate of other economic sectors in Britain. As a result, the cotton industry accounted for 22% of British industrial value added (it was 2.6% in 1780), and 50% of British merchandise exports in 1831; during the years 1780–1860 it sustained an average rate of Total Factor Production growth of 2.6% per year while contributing to about a quarter of the economy's total TFP growth (Crafts 1985).

The early industrial age constituted many sectors more than textile sectors, yet cotton, not any other fiber such as wool and flax, had remained a decisive sector of industrialization process in England. Foreign trade to procure raw materials and to sell final products also remained the prime mover of economic growth although it has been an under-appreciated or disregarded in part of the Industrial Revolution victorious narratives. Not only cotton, but also foreign supplies of other primary products were crucial to other sectors to underpin the social structural changes. In an industrialization process, a shift of workforce from the agricultural sector to the industrial sector would take place as the standard economics textbook teaches, which means that unless the rapid growth of the non-farming population had to be matched by equally rapid growth in agricultural productivity, workers would not be able to eat without an increase in food imports (Pomeranz 2000). This is because agricultural productivity is more bound to environmental constraints than industrial productivity. While the mechanized textile production increased by three hundred times as much as traditional manufacturing within the early decades of mechanization, an average agricultural yield per acre in the 21st century modestly has quadrupled from that in the 19th century (Smil 2011). Thus, industrialization almost always has to go with a sharp increase in trade. In fact, it was not only import of raw cotton that increased but also other commodities. According to the Trading Consequences project,[3] ten of the top important commodities imported to Britain during the 19th century were cotton, wool, wheat, sugar, tea, butter, silk, flax, rice and guano. These imports can be divided to three groups: (a) raw material inputs for industrialized production; cotton, silk and flax, (b) raw material inputs to feed factory workers; wheat, sugar, tea and rice, and raw materials for agricultural land productivity; guano—seabird's excrement that is rich in nitrogen, phosphate and potassium to be used for fertilizers.

These raw materials were neither home-grown nor possible to be self-sufficient in Britain, so it was limitation of domestic supplies that had set an "organic" ceiling on the rate of economic growth and the size of national economy for long periods. By importing raw materials and export final products in the scope of increasing demand and supply, Britain first could exceed that ceiling, scale up their economy, accumulate their wealth and save their land and labor necessary to procure raw materials to use for other purposes, such as technological innovation. In this regard, Alf Hornborg (2006) compared necessary inputs of land and labor embedded in the textile exports from Britain with those in some commodities imported from American South and its colonial peripheries such as the West Indies based on the historical trade records. Then he concludes that unequal exchanges of environmental footprints were underlying in the Industrial Revolution and the economic success of the British textile industry in the late 18th and early 19th century (Hornborg 1998, 2006). Likewise, guano, ranked on the 10th place of the British important import list, together with nitrates, were massively transferred from Peru and Chile to enrich the soil fertility in Britain, American South and other European countries in the 19th century. British monopoly over the trade of guano and nitrate from Peru and Chile led to their substantial dependence on extraction sectors, caused a series of warfare, and eventually ended in collapse of their national economies after overexploitation of guano and substitution of nitrate. The latter was realized by the Haber-Bosch process, the artificial nitrogen fixation process invented in the beginning of the 20th century. These facts are completely out of sight from Wrigley's diagram; what the escape route by fossil energy hypostasized was to utilize land, labor and resources in distant places of others.

The idea of Great Divergence in light of the Anthropocene are fertilizing debates to reconsider how the costs and benefits of modern economic growth since the

---

[3]The Trading Consequences project is a multi-institutional, international collaboration between environmental historians in Canada and computer scientists in the UK that uses text-mining software to explore more than 250,000 historical documents related to international commodity trading in the British Empire during the 19th century, and its impact on the economy and environment. See http://tradingconsequences.blogs.edina.ac.uk/about/.

Industrial Revolution has been unequally distributed among different social groups and among different areas, and how seeds of two major threats for our society have been sown in the modern economic paradigm and grown as our current social and economic frame. It is nothing but an attempt to challenge against the prevailing logic of externalities rigidly anchored in the mainstream neoclassical economics theory, namely that tends to account only for financial and material gains within the market system, leaving social and environmental costs as "external" to be underestimated as much as possible, such external costs occurring outside the market are mostly to be imposed on distant others.

In summary of our interpretation of the Industrial Revolution in Kyoto Manifesto context, it is inspiring that American historian Frederic Jonsson's observation drawn from recent discussions on the origins of the Industrial Revolution; "the idea of the Anthropocene suggests that the Industrial Revolution constituted not a conclusive escape from material limits imposed by national boundaries, but a temporary reprieve bought with finite fossil fuel stock, which in turn may be undone by climate change and other environmental threats unleashed unwittingly by economic development" (Jonsson 2012).

5 Beyond "Mastery Over Nature" in the Globalized Economics Paradigm

> Irrational, because all human action whatever consists in altering the spontaneous course of Nature, and all useful action consists in improving it
>
> —John Stewart Mill

How this misconception of "a conclusive escape from material limits" has been embedded in the modern economic paradigm? The Industrial Revolution enormously transformed the economy by altering the biophysical and energetic orders that characterized the pre-modern economy, on which environmental constraints were robustly imposed. The idea of "mastery over nature" had been gradually theorized in the modern economic thoughts, following up with the ballooned economic growth that was actually going on. It was not vice versa; the development of modern economic theories did not precede actual economic growth. In fact, early classical economists did not fully recognize the implication of the Industrial Revolution although they were living in the middle of the process. Adam Smith wrote The Wealth of Nations in 1776 at the early stage of the Industrial Revolution, but he did not mention them. Instead, he predicted that his portion of merchants, farmer and handicraftsmen would continue to increase its wealth at a moderate pace by further specialization and trade. In his 1798 writing, Thomas Malthus dismally forecasted as "the power of population is indefinitely greater than the power in the earth to produce subsistence for man" although his dismal tone was somehow weakened in the 1803 revision; "though the future prospects respecting the mitigation of the evils arising from the principle of population may not be so bright as we could wish, yet they are far from being entirely disheartening". David Ricardo suggested in 1817 that rising rents would absorb any increase in productivity, namely diminishing returns of land, and his famous theory on comparative advantage referred to the reciprocal trade of final goods, not to the asymmetrical trade between raw materials and final goods that were made of traded raw materials. Those great figures in classical economics shared a common sense; human's socio-economy was supposed to obey the immutable natural order. What really happened on the British economy within a next hundred years however was going beyond their assumptions; the population tripled, some villages grew into big cities, the average income doubled, the agricultural output lost its share in the national income from 50% to 20%. Although Malthus and Ricardo's works slowly moved towards unlocking that natural limit, classical economic theorists were still left behind the real changes of the economy.

The decisive pivot in the evolution of economic theory took place in the mid 19th century as was necessary to have an ex post explanation for contemporary economic transformation. American Philosopher Margaret Schabas argues that economics was gradually "denaturalized" during the move from the aforementioned classical political economy to neoclassical economics in attempting to interpret ongoing transformation. That is, the economy was progressively divorced and treated as autonomous from the realm of natural and biophysical process. It came to be rooted in physically unfettered, abstract "utilities", individual psychology, introducing the methodological individualism of "Homo Economicus". She attributes this pivot to John Stuart Mill as the most important instigator, saying that "the distinction that Mill draws….between the natural and the artificial has far-reaching consequences for his broader program for social reform, hence, for his economic thought" (Schabas 2006). On the other hand, Mill was known to propose the idea of "stationary state" as he was concerned with the relationship between economic growth and human well-being, asking "Towards what ultimate point is society tending by its industrial progress? When the progress ceases, in what condition are we to expect that it will leave mankind?". Mill also stated his *"On Nature"* as,

> Any attempt to shape natural phenomena to the convenience of mankind could easily seem to be an interference with the government of those superior Beings; and though life couldn't have been maintained, much less made pleasant, without perpetual 'interferences' of this kind, each new one was presumably made in fear and trembling, until experience had shown that it could be ventured on without attracting the vengeance of the gods.

(Mill 1874)

The theme in his essay "On Nature" was not about political economy but natural theology. Conceivably however his statement on nature looks contradictory to his concerns with economic growth, so as to be hard to conclude to what extent his perspective on the relationship between mankind and nature was reflected on his economic thoughts. Nonetheless, it was Mill as Schabas pinpointed, who actually transformed much of classical economic thoughts with respect to value and distribution. In particular, his contribution to supply and demand equilibrium theory as a more general explanation of price and value was a historical turning point towards modern mainstream neoclassical economics. The reciprocal demand and supply analysis of the international values to determine terms of trade has also remained at the heart of the standard international trade theory. As we can see, however, trade of raw materials with final products fueling the Industrial Revolution was never equally reciprocal from the beginning. Both demand of raw cotton to produce cotton textile and fabrics and supply of final products to sell were imperative for Britain to sustain its unleashed economic growth, while it was not for India who did not have any reason to supply raw cotton and demand English cotton textile as then world largest cotton producer and exporter. The Industrial Revolution in Britain and other European countries was nothing but "deindustrialization" for China and India, which took two hundred years for them to overcome and catch up the predecessors (Parthasarathi 2011). In this respect, Gandhi, who had own economic ideas much farther off the mainstream economics, once made his comment on the reciprocal theory, "the law of supply and demand is a devilish law" (cited from Dasgupta 1996).

Mill had given birth to the very root of economic imbalance, contrary to what Mill manifested as "the best state for human nature is that in which, while no one is poor, no one desires to be richer, nor has any reason to fear being thrust back by the efforts of others to push themselves forward" (Mill 1848). Following Polanyi's definition, the law of supply and demand can be read as "substantive" values would set to be determined by "formal" values through the self-regulating market mechanism. This value determination process was legitimized to explain the physical phenomena of the 19th century's international trades; hereby others' nature was deprived, and others' environmental and social costs came to be discounted. Thus, the distinction between human and nature had founded in the current global economics paradigm ever since till today.

Then, what is necessary to relink "denaturalized" modern economics with the natural physical world? Leading scholars of the Anthropocene debates have listed up the broad group of research questions for sciences to work on: (1) societal goals for the future; (2) major trends and dynamics that might favor or hinder them; (3) and factors that might propel or impede transformations towards desirable futures. In order to address these questions, they emphasize the necessity of the development of novel approach integrating natural and social sciences as wells the humanities beyond what is current today (Bai et al. 2016). When it comes to economics, it in principle takes a disciplinary and reductionist approach, and presupposes a sort of certainty and calculability in order to predict or to engineer "economy" based on the Newtonian mechanical and deterministic worldview (Mirowski 1989), while such an approach, not only in economics but other modern academic disciplines, has proven to be insufficient to address complex societal issues with unclear system boundaries, multiple interactions across natural and social systems, different temporal and spatial scales, and deep influences by human values, behavior, and culture and institutions.

Besides, some scholars think modes premised on a human-nature dualism are totally unacceptable. This is not only because such dualisms helped to legitimate and facilitate the Anthropocene in ways that produced large social inequalities through the appropriation of other's nature (Schmidt et al. 2016). Rather, the Anthropocene is not merely forcible re-convergence of human and nature as we were used to in the pre-modern society, but also a new formulation of how humans are understood with regard to the Earth system (Hamilton and Grinevald 2015). A quest for a new formulation to overcome the human-nature dualism however is a venture far from the economist traditional terrain because questioning such relationship per se has never been a major topic of discussion in economics; we therefore would be better guided by anthropologists, whose academic discipline has centered deciphering perplexed relations between human being and nature, or non-human being, sometimes in an astonishing way.

The idea that there is one nature and many cultures, one way things really are and many ways of understanding them, seems central to the anthropological enterprise. Yet this premise is essentially ethnocentric since the nature that supposedly stands behind all cultures is the one defined by modern science, a truth which belongs to Western culture. This is what Bruno Latour (1993) calls the "modern constitution" drawing on the discussion by French anthropologist Philippe Descola to undermine its centralities. Descola (2013) points out that the division of between nature and culture embedded in Western thought is not old as conventionally believed, and then he analyzes the various ways in which anthropologists have understood the relation of nature and culture. He makes two related claims; that each culture has its own way of knowing the world and that knowing cannot be separated from a variety of practices that situate the know in its cultural context. Descola concludes from these premises that "nature" is not the same thing in different cultures and so the knowledge of it cannot be compared as between cultures, and calls it "relative universalism" posing as its basic condition the relation of natural phenomenon with human existence since it allows each culture to have its own truth (Descola 2013, 2014). This idea does not limit to what Feenberg points out that Descola's relative universalism has a similarity with Max Horkheimer's view on truth in history (Feenberg 2014). French geographer Augustine Berque (2005) suggests its correspondence to what Japanese philosopher Tetsuro Watsuji conceptualized in *Fûdo* (1935) as "milieu as the structural moment of human existence". Furthermore, Berque assumes that Watsuji's conception of milieu was influenced by Jacob von Uexküll's distinction between *Umgebung* (the environment as a universal set of objectives) and *Umwelt* (the milieu proper to a certain species, resulting from this species' singular interpretation of the environment) (Berque 2005). At the same time, Berque also refers to Japanese naturalist, one of the founders of Japanese primatology, Kinji Imanishi (1941), who did not refer to Watsuji, nor to the concept of milieu as differing from the environment, but expressed that same idea in his own words with the formula of "subjectivation of the environment, environmentalization of the subject" (Berque 2016). In the context of this chapter's discourse with regard to human and nature in terms of the modern globalized economy that has been shaped by appropriation of distant others' nature through the international trade, I would rather refer to what Said (1993) stated in *"Culture and Imperialism"*. It reads; "If there is anything that radically distinguishes the imagination of anti-imperialism, it is the primacy of the geographical in it. Imperialism after all is an act of geographical violence through which virtually every space in the world is explored, chartered, and finally brought under control.

For the native, the history of colonial servitude is inaugurated by the loss of locality to the outsider, its geographical identify must thereafter be searched for and somehow restored .... Because of the presence of the colonizing outsider, the land is recoverable at first only through imagination" (Said 1993). Thus, the modern globalized economy that perceives a given unitary environment has exploited others' nature, depriving others' its geographical identity, jeopardizing others' existence, and consequently threatening the sustainability of the life supporting system provided by the Earth.

In search for a new foundation of relinking nature and economy, I am of course not free at all from my own geographical identity and cultural context, namely being Japanese and Buddhism follower. Having said that, from our perspective of Kyoto Manifesto, consideration of a painting by the 18th century Japanese artist Itoh Jakuchū (1716–1800) may be suggestive as a representation of Japanese view on the natural realm to explore a possible reconciliation between human-nature relationship (Harris 1998). The painting shows a variety of vegetables arranged around a central image which happens to be a large radish laying on a mat or bed of some sort (Fig. 5). The number of vegetables and fruits appeared, representing blessings bestowed by nature, varies depending on scholars, but the largest number was suggested by Itoh (2008), who expanded its digital image and counted 88 varieties from domesticated vegetables of local products to wild mushrooms and nuts (Itoh 2008). For those who does not any information on vegetables in Japan as well as on Buddhism, this painting looks just a still-life ink painting. This painting however does not just depict vegetables and fruits, but is titled "*Kasai Neman-zu* (Vegetable Nirvana)"; the composition of this painting is a coded reference to the Buddha's death scene (Parinirvana), which has customarily centered on a reclining Shakyamuni (represented by a large radish at the center) surrounded by mourners (represented by vegetables, fruits, mushrooms and nuts). A proper interpretation of the work is only possible once we have factored in the doctrine of the Buddhahood of grasses and plants (*somoku jobutsu* in Japanese). This term means grasses and plants attain Buddhahood. Not only for plants but also for any beings, there are other similar terms such as *somoku-kokudo-shikkai-jobutsu*, *mujo-jobutsu*, which respectively means plants as well as non-sentiment beings—soil, water, stone and mountain—can attain Buddhahood. As such, Japanese conventionally did not distinguish between human and non-human beings as all are equally belonging to the Buddha's natural realm. Moreover, it was likely that the painting was donated to the Buddhist temple in 1792 in commemoration of the death of the painter's eldest brother. The painting thus served as a twin memorial to the Buddha and to Jakuchū's brother. The painter also was born as a fourth-generation member of a family of greengrocers at the corner of the biggest market street in Kyoto, so the work can also be read as a celebration of the hereditary occupation, an occupation with which Jakuchū, as the new head of the family, will have to become more fully involved. Yoshiaki Shimizu concludes that the complex metaphoric commemoration tends to be absent in other cultures and must be regarded as "indigenously Japanese" (Shimizu 1992). Yet there is more than Shimizu's conclusion in this painting. Itoh (2008) examined the contemporary botanical encyclopedia and recipe

Fig. 5 Kasai Nehan zu (Vegetable Nirvana) by Itoh Jakuchu. (This image may not be reprinted or reproduced in any form, in whole or part, without the expressed written permission by the Kyoto National Museum.)

books, and then suggested that vegetables appeared in the painting were carefully selected by prioritizing vegetables and fruits that are useful to make preserves and nonperishables in preparation of famine, which frequently occurred in the end of the 17th century in Japan. One of serial famines was caused by the huge volcanic eruption, which meant the famine was a part of the natural order beyond human agency. The painting was first contributed to the Buddhist temple, supposed to be shown in public at Buddhist holiday, so it was used to enlighten people, by indicating useful harvests in the painting, how to survive in case that nature would treat people adversely, that is to say, the way to live in harmony with the Buddha's nature at any hard time. I would reconfirm that implications of Vegetable Nirvana deeply connected to our culture and tradition, and this may work even only for Kyoto locally. Nevertheless, if our reconciliation with nature need collective and multiple wisdom in order to overcome human-nature dualism, Jakuchū's painting suggests a possible way forward; he certainly embodied personal, social, economic, ecological and religious respects in one painting, subliming it to the masterpiece, not to contribute to upper-class people, but to share among his local community.

6 Cotton Again in the Intricate Web of Our Current Globalized Economy

Things derive their being and nature by mutual dependence and are nothing in themselves

—Nagarjuna

Aleppo, known to be one of the oldest continuously inhabited cities in the world, locates at the crossroads of ancient trade routes. Cotton cultivated in the Fertile Crescent along the Tigris and Euphrates rivers was blended with wool to make fustian fabrics in Aleppo, then exported to Europe by Venetian merchants till the 17th century. Even after the maritime trade route between Asia and Europe was developed, as the recent study has revealed, Aleppo remained the important trade center on the land route more than having been conventionally considered (Faroqhi 2009). The Industrial Revolution however wiped Aleppo out of the global cotton map, a synonym of the global economic map at that time. After several hundred years, the Battle of Aleppo that began on July 2012 as part of escalation of the Syrian Civil War has reminded Europe of the name of the old trade center by shocking images of isolated people in the besieged city, devastated fights and aerial bombardments as well as by "dirty cotton".

Center for Analysis for Terrorism reported in 2015 that ISIS controls 75–80% of Syria's cotton production due to its control over the al-Raqqa and Deir ez-Zor regions along the Euphrates river. According to the report, around 12,000 tons, 100 million cotton t-shirts could be made of by that amount, were sold in 2015 via intermediaries, primarily to Turkish brokers, with Turkish spinners and clothes manufacturers being based near the Syrian border. Cotton sales brought in some $15 M for ISIS in 2015, equivalent to 1% of its total revenue (Center for Analysis of Terrorism 2016). The low prices charged by ISIS, at around 70% of the market value, makes it attractive. Cheap cotton is always preferable for fast fashion industries based on the global North, so that newspapers in European countries, the main importer of Turkish cotton and its products, reported this issue in alarm.

If the supermarket is the highest temple of the modern food system as Raj Patel described in his provocative book about the global food system, "*Stuffed and Starved*" (Patel 2008), the fast-fashion store could be the highest shrine of the global textile and apparel industries that the Industrial Revolution and the modern economy have given birth to. Retailers are constantly stocking their shelves and showcases with new designs, new colors and new materials that are priced at extremely low cost, always spurring consumers' appetite by advertisement in all kinds of media. Rich consumers are blessed with a wide variety of choices to meet their demands, often tempted to purchase more than necessary. The standard textbook of economics teaches us that more consumption of more variety of more goods enhances our utility. As a result, the volume of clothing waste has doubled in the past twenty years, from 7 to 14 million tons in the United States, with 15% of clothing waste being reused or recycled.

The rapid cycle of cloth consumption partly due to the fast fashion industry has also resulted in the increase of the global trade of second-hand clothes, the value of which has reached 4.17 billion USD in 2014, quadrupled from 1995; mostly from the rich countries in the global North to the poor in Asia, Africa and Latin America (UN Comtrade 2016). This is a part of reuse or recycle of clothing waste. Oxfam already warned in 2005 that although the second-hand clothes trade has clear consumer benefit, in particular for poorer people, it makes a cultural shift from "indigenous or traditional style fashion" to more "Western style", and more importantly, it will be likely to undermine the local textile industries and employments (Baden and Barber 2005). Andrew Brooks (2015), British geographer, takes up the case in Mozambique, the major raw cotton producer in Eastern Africa, where the local textile industries have been killed by the inundation of the second-hand clothes from the global North because the local industries could not compete with cheap imports. Shifting agriculture to light industry are taught as the first step to industrialization, which is a synonym towards "economic growth" in the standard economic theory, but imported second-hand clothes to Mozambique deprive of such opportunity to economic "take-off" and keep them as one of global raw cotton suppliers maintained by 1.2 million people to generate just 35 million USD annual revenue in the 2013/2014 season. It means the cotton cultivation and export can generate only 30 USD per capita annually. That is why Brooks calls cotton "Mother of Poverty" (Brooks 2015). Cotton was once the golden goose for Britain in the Industrial Revolution to become a forerunner of modern globalized economy while it works opposite in Mozambique two hundred and fifty years later.

In addition, regardless of either being made of cotton or synthetic fibers, the rapid cycle of cloth production, consumption and disposal require further environmental burdens that could exacerbate changes of the Earth system. Possibility that environmental degradation causes to increase instability in the modern social, political and economic system is not a new subject, though. As a very recent case, the 2007–2010 drought that hit the Fertile Crescent was the worst one in the instrumental record, causing widespread crop failure and a mass migration of famers to urban centers. For Syria, a country governed poorly by an authoritarian regime with unsustainable agricultural and environmental policies, the drought had a catalytic effect, combined with the high price of foods in the international market by late 2010 that increased by 40% over the year, thereby triggering the ongoing Syrian Civil War (Gleick 2014). This regional drought itself is considered worsened by accumulated impacts of anthropogenic activities, as indicated by the analysis of observations and climate model simulations. Century-long observed trends in precipitation, temperature, and sea-level pressure, supported by climate model results, strongly suggest that anthropogenic forcing has increased the probability of severe and persistent droughts in the Fertile Crescent region, and made the occurrence of a 3-year drought as severe as that of 2007–2010 2–3 times more likely than by natural variability alone (Kelley et al. 2015). It can be concluded, unfortunately, that human influences on the climate system are implicated in the current Syrian Civil War.

The Syrian Civil War has many other roots, including long-standing political, religious and sociological disputes within the country as well as economic dislocation from both global and regional factors and worsening environmental factors. Environmental factors can be further classified into domestic aspects such as poor water management in the agricultural sector, and into global aspects such as impacts on climate variability and regional hydrological regime. Reversely, repercussions of the Syrian Civil War are not contained at the country or regional level, rather is spreading across the Western world, shaking the stability and reliability of the socio-economic system in several ways. The influx of the refugees and the resultant rise of right-wing parties in the EU political climate are growing concerns just to name only a few. Homer-Dixon calls such cascading and escalating phenomenon the "synchronous failure" of entangled system of economics, climate and the supply-chains securing water, food and energy (Homer-Dixon et al. 2015). In fact, the comprehensive analysis on the relationship between climate and human conflict confirms that anomalies of precipitation and temperatures could increase systematically the risk of conflict (Hsiang et al. 2013). Given the potential changes in climate and degradation of ecosystem are projected, amplified rates of human conflict could represent a large and critical social impact of the Anthropocene in both global North and South, affecting each other.

This chapter takes up cotton as a way to explore causes and consequences of the current globalized economic paradigm, and how it finally takes us to the opening of a new geological era. Originally it was not, cotton has become so ubiquitous in our daily life across the globe, so it is sometimes difficult imagine why and how cotton has become so affluent and so cheap. Additionally, this chapter addresses that cotton shaped not only the modern economic paradigms, but also how cotton still plays multiple roles in our challenges, that are inextricably intertwined with many other factors.

Cotton growing is still practiced in the Aral Sea basin in Uzbekistan, the fifth largest cotton exporter, and their cultivation system is criticized by "most labor exploitative" imposed by the authoritarian regime. Although the Aral Sea disappeared, the business-as-usual practices are ongoing in a socially inadequate, economically not-so-profitable and environmentally unsustainable manner. Forced and child labors in cotton production in Uzbekistan have been often taken up in the international community, leading to ethical boycott of Uzbek cotton by the international companies in the global North while those companies want more and cheaper "clean" cotton in order to sustain their "business as usual". More and cheaper cotton to foster economic growth causes challenges of the globalized modern economics paradigm, and, as it turned out, these challenges are not detachable from possible disturbances of the Earth system. Without disenchanting such fundamental inertia underpinning our current economy and social order, we are not likely to meaningfully confront our challenges at local and global levels. As tried in this chapter by tracing cotton's trajectory as the first globalized commodity, uncovering the very roots and practices of the modern globalized economic paradigm may help reconsider the human-nature relationship in a broader perspective. This relation has been distorted by the taken-for-granted economic norm for more than two centuries, but such distortion should be addressed as it is the very fundamental of our survivability on the Earth.

References

Allan, J. A. (1997). Virtual water: A long term solution for water short Middle Eastern economies? Paper presented at the British Association Festival of Science, Water and Development Session. London: University of Leeds.

Baden, S., & Barber, C. (2005). *The impact of the second-hand clothing trade on developing countries*. OXFAM.

Bai, X., van der Leeuw, S., O'Brien, K., Berkhout, F., Biermann, F., Brondizio, E. S., et al. (2016). Plausible and desirable futures in the Anthropocene: A new research agenda. *Global Environmental Change, 39*, 351–362.

Barbier, E. (2015). Nature and wealth—Overcoming environmental scarcity and inequality. Palgrave McMillan.

Barca, S. (2011). Energy, property, and the industrial revolution narrative. *Ecological Economics, 70*(7), 1309–1315.

Berque, A. (2005). A basis for environmental ethics. *Diogenes, 207*, 3–12.

Berque, A. (2016). Nature, culture: Trajecting beyond modern dualism. *Inter Faculty, 7*(0).

Brooks, A. (2015). *Clothing poverty: The hidden world of fast fashion and second-hand clothes*. London: Zed House.

Center for Analysis of Terrorism. (2016). *ISIS financing in 2015*.

Central Intelligence Agency. (1955). *Soviet cotton production in the post war period*. CIA/SC/RR 94.

Chapagain, A. K., Hoekstra, A. Y., Savenije, H. H. G., & Gautam, R. (2006). The water footprint of cotton consumption: An assessment of the impact of worldwide consumption of cotton products on the water resources in the cotton producing countries. *Ecological Economics, 60*(1), 186–203.

Crafts, N. F. R. (1985). *British economic growth during the industrial revolution*. Clarendon Press.

Dasgupta, A.K. (1996). *Gandhi's economic thought*. Routledge.

Descola, P. (2013). *The ecology of others*. Prickly Paradigm Press.

Descola, P. (2014). *Beyond nature and culture (Paperback version)*. The University of Chicago Press.
Faroqhi, S. (2009). Ottoman cotton textiles* The story of a success that did not last, 1500–1800. In G. Riello & P. Parthasarathi (Eds.), *The spinning world a global history of cotton textiles, 1200–1850*. Oxford University Press.
Feenberg, A. (2014). The many natures of Philippe Descola, reflections on the ecology of others. *Science as Culture, 23*(2), 277–282.
Gaffney, O., & Steffen, W. (2017). The Anthropocene equation. *The Anthropocene Review, 54*(1), 1–9.
Gleick, P. H. (2014). Water, drought, climate change, and conflict in Syria. *Weather, 6*(3), 331–340.
Hamilton, C., & Grinevald, J. (2015). Was the Anthropocene anticipated? *The Anthropocene Review, 2*(1), 59–72.
Harris, I. (1998). Buddhism and the discourse of environmental concern: Some methodological problems considered. In M. E. Turcker & D. R. Williams (Eds.), *Buddhism and ecology—The interconnection of dharma and deems*. Harvard University Press.
Hoekstra, A. Y. (2013). *Water footprint of modern consumer society*. Routledge.
Homer-Dixon, T., Walker, B., Biggs, R., Crépin, A.-S., Folke, C., Lambin, E. F., et al. (2015). Synchronous failure: The emerging causal architecture of global crisis. *Ecology and Society, 20*(3), Art 6–16.
Hornborg, A. (1998). Towards an ecological theory of unequal exchange: Articulating world system theory and ecological economics. *Ecological Economics, 25*(1), 127–136.
Hornborg, A. (2006). Footprints in the cotton fields: The Industrial Revolution as time–space appropriation and environmental load displacement. *Ecological Economics, 59*(1), 74–81.
Hsiang, S. M., Burke, M., & Miguel, E. (2013). Quantifying the influence of climate on human conflict. *Science, 341*. http://cat-int.org/index.php/2016/06/01/isis-financing-in-2015-report-and-summary.
Imanishi, K. (1941). *Seibutsuno Sekai (The world of living things)*. KabundoShobo.
Itoh, H. (2008). *Kasai Nehan-zu to egakareta yasai ni tsuite* (Jakuchu's "Vegetable Nirvana" and vegetable painted in it), in Japanese. *Studies in Language and Culture, Graduate School of Languages and Cultures, Nagoya University, 30*(1), 3–24.
Jevons, W. S. (1865). *The Coal Question*. Macmillan & Co.
Jonsson, F. A. (2012). The industrial revolution in the Anthropocene. *The Journal of Modern History., 84*(3), 679–696.
Kelley, C. P., Mohtadi, S., Cane, M. A., Seager, R., & Kushnir, Y. (2015). Climate change in the Fertile crescent and implications of the recent Syrian drought. *Proceedings of the National Academy of Sciences of the United States of America, 112*(11), 3241–3246.
Landes, D. S. (2003). *The unbound prometheus technological change and industrial development in Western Europe from 1750 to the present* (2nd ed.). Cambridge University Press.
Latour, B. (1993). *We have never been modern* (C. Porter, Trans.). Harvard University Press.
McNeil, J. R. (2000). *Something new under the sun an environmental history of the twentieth century world*. W.W. Norton & Company Press.
Micklin, P. (2007). The aral sea disaster. *Annual Review of Earth and Planetary Sciences, 35*(1), 47–72.
Mill, J. S. (1848). *Principles of political economy*. John W.Parker.
Mill, J. S. (1874). *On nature in three essays on religion*. Henry Holt & Co.
Mirowski, P. (1989). *More heat than light: Economics as social physics, physics as nature's economics*. Cambridge University Press.
Mokyr, J. (1990). *The lever of riches: Technological creativity and economic progress*. Oxford University Press.
North, D. (1981). *Structure and change in economic history*. W.W. Norton & Company Press.
Parthasarathi, P. (2011). *Why europe grew rich and asia did not: Global economic divergence, 1600–1850*. Cambridge University Press.
Patel, R. (2008). *Stuffed and starved: The hidden battle for the world food system*. Melville House.

Polanyi, K. (1957). The economy as instituted process. In K. Polanyi, C. M. Arsensberg, & H. W. Pearson (Eds.), *Trade and market in the early empires*. Glencoe, Illinois: The Free Press.
Pomeranz, K. (2000). *The Great Divergence: China, Europe, and the making of the modern world economy*. Princeton University Press.
Pomeranz, K., & Topik, S. (2006). *The world that trade created: Society, culture, and the world economy, 1400 to the present*. Routledge.
Postel, S. (2000). Entering and era of water scarcity: The challenges ahead. *Ecological Applications, 10*(4), 941–948.
Richter, B. S. (1997). Nature mastered by man: ideology and water in the soviet union. *Environment and History, 3*, 69–96.
Riello, G. (2013). *Cotton: The fabric that made the modern world*. Cambridge University Press.
Said, E. W. (1993). *Culture and imperialism*. Vintage.
Schabas, M. (2006). *The natural origins of economics*. University of Chicago Press.
Scherer, J. A. B. (1916). *Cotton as a world power: A study in the economic interpretation of history*. Frederick A. Stokes Co.
Schmidt, J. J., Brown, P. G., & Orr, C. J. (2016). Ethics in the Anthropocene: A research agenda. *The Anthropocene Review*, 1–13.
Schumacher, E. F. (1973). *Small is beautiful—Economics as if people mattered*. Harper and Row.
Shimizu, Y. (1992). Multiple commemorations: The vegetable Nehan of Ito Jakuchu. In J. Sanford, W. LaFleur, & M. Nagatomi (Eds.), *Flowing traces: Buddhism in the Literrary and visual arts of Japan*. Princeton University Press.
Smil, V. (2011). Nitrogen cycle and world food production. *World Agriculture*, 9–13.
Steffen, W., Broadgate, W., Deutsch, L., Gaffney, O., & Ludwig, C. (2015). The trajectory of the Anthropocene: The great acceleration. *The Anthropocene Review, 2*(1), 81–98.
Steffen, W., Crutzen, J., & McNeill, J. R. (2007). The Anthropocene: are humans now overwhelming the great forces of nature? *Ambio, 36*(8), 614–621.
Steinberg, T. L. (1986). An ecological perspective on the origins of industrialization. *Environmental Review, 10*(4), 261–276.
UN Comtrade. (2016). https://comtrade.un.org/. Accessed on December 16, 2016.
UNEP and ENVSEC (2011). *Environment and security in the Amu Darya river basin*. UNEP-Grid-Arendal.
Watsuji, T. (1935). *Fûdo: Ningengakuteki Kôsatsu (Climate and culture: Observations on national character)*. Iwanami.
Werner, B. (2012). Is Earth F**ked? Dynamical futility of global environmental management and possibilities for sustainability via direct action activism. In *American geophysical union 2012 fall meeting*. http://abstractsearch.agu.org/meetings/2012/FM/EP32B-04.html.
Williams, M., Zalasiewicz, J., Haff, P., Schwa gerl, C., Barnosky, A. D., & Ellis, E. C. (2015). The anthropocene biosphere. *The Anthropocene Review, 2*(3), 196–219.
Worster, D. (1994). *Nature's economy: A history of ecological ideas* (2nd ed.). Cambridge University Press.
Wrigley, E. A. (2010). *Energy and the english industrial revolution*. Cambridge University Press.

Author Biography

Ryuichi Fukuhara is Research Fellow of the Center for the Study of the Creative Economy, Doshisha University. He holds his M.Sc. in Agriculture (Forestry) from Kyoto University in 1994 and a postgraduate certificate in Water Resources Management at the University of Jordan. He is a former Programme Officer of United Nations Environment Programme (UNEP), International Environmental Technology Center, playing a leading role in UNEP—UNESCO joint project "World Heritage inscription as a tool to enhance natural and cultural management of the Iraqi Marshlands of Mesopotamia"; the project site is inscribed as the World Mixed Heritage in 2016. Prior to that, he also served as Programmme Specialist in United Nations Educational, Scientific and Cultural Organization (UNESCO) Iraq Office, working for water and environmental issues, in particular, for the Tigris and Euphrates Rivers basin as part of the UN reconstruction programme for Iraq after the Iraqi war in 2003. His specialties include water resources and ecosystem management, and trans-boundary water issues in the Middle East, and Environmental Sound Technologies applications for water supply and sanitation. He was involved in preparing many UN's technical reports in such fields, including the UN World Water Development Report.

Chapter 4
Dimensions of Change Within the Economics Mainstream

Tadashi Yagi

1 Essential Features of the Economics Mainstream

1.1 Meaning of Efficient Resource Allocation

The efficient allocation of resources is the key guiding principle within the economics mainstream. The message of "invisible hand" is that resources are allocated efficiently in markets through the transaction of goods and services, assuming consumers seek to maximize their own utility and producers seek to maximize their own profits. Efficient resource allocation is assumed to automatically occur through market mechanisms without any human controls. In short, this key tenet of the economics mainstream implies that selfish behavior lead to a harmonious situation through market mechanisms. The economics mainstream has developed numerous mathematical models and derived various policy implications based on this assumption of efficient allocation of resources in markets; however, limitations of this principle have emerged in various real-world situations and policy contexts such as income inequality and the global financial crisis.

The meaning of efficiency is also a target of reconsideration. Profit-seeking behavior and efficiency are often seen as being connected, and this relationship has resulted in inhumane behavior such as the exploitation of human and natural resources. The concept of efficiency excludes the emotional factors that real human beings must confront. Human behavior is closely related to emotional factors such as sympathy, joy, and anger. In addition, the effects of emotional factors on human behavior depend on social structures such as culture, religion, and community. A key goal of economics is understanding human behavior and to do this we must

---

T. Yagi (✉)
Faculty of Economics, Doshisha University, Kyoto, Japan
e-mail: tyagi@mail.doshisha.ac.jp

examine how social structures affect the relationship between emotion and behavior. Efficiency is just one consideration in economic activities.

Because of this limitation of the economics mainstream, various new approaches have been pursued by academic researchers to capture the nature of the new economy. Schumacher (1992, 1993) began his argument by discussing the concept of "Right Livelihood" in Buddhism. He stressed the importance of religious and spiritual values in utilizing modern technology. This idea is far removed from the concept of efficiency in the economics mainstream.

Looking back to Adam Smith, however, we see that emotional factors were a crucial point of consideration in economics. In the next section, we revisit his argument.

2 The Theory of Moral Sentiments and Empathy

Eighteenth-century economist Adam Smith is called "the father of modern economics" and is known for the concept of the "invisible hand." This concept represents the idea that the market works to allocate resources efficiently via the price mechanism. From this great contribution to the development of economic theory, he is often regarded as a founding figure in the development of laissez-faire economic liberalism, which advocates extensive economic liberalization policies such as privatization, fiscal austerity, deregulation, free trade, and reductions in government spending in order to enhance the role of the private sector in the economy.

Laissez-faire economic liberalism dismisses the moral aspects of economic behavior, and rather, presumes that each individual behaves selfishly to maximize his or her utility. Behind this presumption is the belief that market mechanisms ultimately lead to a pre-established harmony at an equilibrium point. However, this belief can lead one to the mistaken idea that a collection of selfish individuals produces no harm in society and that consideration of morality is not necessary. What is wrong with this idea is that market mechanisms do not necessarily bring about equal income distribution.

The term "greedy capitalism" not only represents the unequal distribution of income, but also reflects the immoral behavior of economic agents. Adam Smith recognized this aspect of market mechanisms. Before writing *The Wealth of the Nation* in 1776, Smith published *The Theory of Moral Sentiment* in 1759. It is worth noting that Smith devoted much effort to revising this book until the end of his life. In all, Smith published six versions of this book, which implies that Smith viewed *The Theory of Moral Sentiment* as a serious and important work.

In his book, Smith included the concept of sympathy, which assumes that anonymous observers exist in the economy. An essential part of his theory is that economic agents always act as if anonymous observers were watching their behavior. If the behavior of an economic agent is judged by the anonymous observers as being against certain societal norms, the agent loses his or her place of trust in the society. This prevents the economic agents from behaving selfishly, and works to control reckless profit-seeking in the market.

3 Economics of Good and Evil

Smith's argument on economics started from his essential view of the market economy that moral sentiment is the basic presumption required for economic agents in the market. After his death, the parts of his theory concerning moral sentiment have been dismissed by economists until only recently, and the role of market mechanisms in promoting efficient resource allocation, somewhat unfairly, gained prominence in the economics mainstream. The lack of a moral component made it possible for economists to build mathematical models, and the technical aspects of economic analysis developed rapidly. However, the serious cost of ignoring moral sentiment in the market has become widely recognized after the global financial crisis in 2008.

Responding to the increased awareness of the need for moral sentiment, critical arguments against the standard neo-classical economic framework have been growing. Among them, Sedlacek (2012) sharply criticizes the conventional approaches for understanding the essence of the economy and notes the limitations of the conventional theories. His approach is quite different from the conventional ones. He presents mythical stories that represent the essential features of the modern economy. He states that mathematical models are a kind of story and fable, in a sense that they capture essential parts of the real world at a high level of abstraction. In the same manner, Greek mythology captures the essence of life and economy and is often used to describe what it means to lead a "good life".

Myths and fables always reflect some kind of value judgement. Similarly, even when a mathematical model is deemed value neutral, it actually reflects certain value judgements on what is good and what is evil. This is why we must discuss the nature of good an evil. In particular, it is important to consider what constitutes evil. Why did people get angry about the behavior of the financial capitalists who led the world economy into crises such as in the 1998 Asian financial crisis or 2008 global financial crisis?

In what way are they evil? The answer is that these capitalists manipulate transactions and pursue strategies to gain huge monetary benefits while ignoring the fact that other people may suffer serious harm because of their tactics. The main factor is the "degree" of their selfishness. In economic activities, a certain level of social consciousness regarding the equality of distribution is required. The degree of selfishness depends on the morality of the individual and his or her ability to have sympathy—factors that are influenced by the prevailing philosophy in a society.

Economic theory assumes humans act as "homo economicus," with no ethical requirements and only economic concerns. This has allowed economists to develop methods for mathematical modeling. But it has also prompted economists to dismiss ethical considerations in economic activities that do not fit neatly into a model. Further, 18th century philosopher Bernard de Mandeville tried to justify unethical behavior by stating his view that an evil mind serves to vitalize the economy. His idea stems from desire being a source of vitality and the existence of evil being unavoidable. The former reflects humans' innate psychological tendency for enjoying rewards; the latter reflects the biological variance in humans' innate ability to feel sympathy for others. By their nature, some persons are quite insensitive to others' sense of suffering from immoral and evil behavior. Some persons do not feel sympathy toward those who are in trouble. As long as such humans continue to possess such a wide range of innate psychological dispositions and life environments, it is natural that some individuals will behave immorally and intentionally attack others due to greed and envy.

Although we acknowledge the role of selfish behavior in vitalizing the economy and society to a certain extent, many people view the market as incapable of moderating excess selfishness. For example, the speculative behavior of the dominant financial capitalists, which led the Asian economy to crisis, could be blamed on selfish and unethical behavior. However, it is quite difficult to control the speculative behavior of the dominant financial capitalists in the market by using legal means. Given the inability to limit selfish behavior in the market itself, it may be more realistic for the government to take policy actions to redistribute income from the rich to poor.

In addition, as is analyzed by Vitali et al. (2011), the top 50 control-holders of transnational corporations have 39.78% of the total network control. This suggests that only small number of transnational corporations exert a dominant economic influence on the global economy.

Reflecting these facts, an Oxfam report issued at the beginning of 2017 demonstrated that the eight wealthiest men control the same amount of wealth as the bottom 50% of the world population.[1] Bill Gates alone has assets totalling $426 billion.

Furthermore, the assets of the wealthiest 500 people will likely be passed on through inheritance during the next 20 years, resulting in $2.1 trillion in assets being transferred to heirs, a sum larger than the annual GDP of India.

These facts make us recognize the seriousness of the negative effects of globalization on the fair distribution of wealth. Remembering that market mechanisms have no power for redistributing income, policy actions are required to remedy these problems. However, it is quite difficult for the policies of a single nation to exert influence over transnational corporation because of the difficulty of legislating common laws internationally. the most effective measure for redistribution is the progressive income tax. Atkinson (2015) proposes a drastic increase in the marginal tax rate for the highest income bracket in a progressive income tax system and notes

---

[1]See   https://www.oxfam.org/en/pressroom/.../just-8-men-own-same-wealth-half-world   (date: Febraury 27, 2017).

the importance of simultaneously implementing measures to prevent rich people from transferring income to tax havens.

However, excess redistribution will harm the incentive structure of the economy. The aspiration to become rich can act as a driving force for the poor to study and work hard. In this sense, "harmony" can be seen as the critical concept for realizing a good society. The incentives of the rich and the poor must be harmonized in society. This harmonization could be attained by the ethical and sympathetic behavior of the rich and the diligent behavior of the poor.

Thus, a key question to ask is why rich people, many of whom are generally good people, often violate social trust by behaving unethically. This dilemma is well illustrated by the issues of tax evasion and tax havens, as discussed in the following section. This question requires us to analyze the psychological structure of evil behavior.

4 The Psychological Structure of Evil Behavior

Behavioral economics has clarified aspects of the psychological structure that makes people behave irrationally but systematically. Ariely (2008, 2010) scientifically explains why people behave evilly. One interesting set of experiments described by Ariely explains the psychological barrier to evil behavior. The design of the experiments is simple. Undergraduate and MBA students at Harvard University participated in the experiments. In the first experiment, the participants are required to solve 50 general knowledge questions in 15 min. Students are required to write the answer on a worksheet, and then they must transcribe the answers from the worksheet to an answer sheet. Students receive 10 cents per correct answer. In the second experiment, the students were asked to transcribe the answers to an answer sheet on which the correct answers are printed slightly. Thus, it is possible for them to cheat and fill in the correct answers for questions they initially answered incorrectly during the transcription stage. Participants are required to submit both the worksheet and the answer sheet. In the third experiment, participants are only required to submit the answer sheet, which means that there would be no evidence for any cheating that occurred.

In the first experiment, it is impossible to cheat. Thus, this experiment gives us a true value of participants' score, which averaged 32.6 correct answers out of 50 questions. In the second experiment, the average score increased to 36.2 out of 50. In the third experiment, the average score was 35.9 out of 50. These results suggest to us that many people cheat, but only to a small degree, and that the level of cheating is independent from the degree of risk of the cheating being discovered.

More interestingly, there were surprising results in an experiment in which the students were required to read the Ten Commandments before solving the problems and were required to remember it during the experiment. No one cheated in this situation even if there was no risk of being caught cheating. This result suggests that people do not decide whether or not to cheat by comparing the risk of being caught versus the potential benefit from cheating. People decide to cheat by talking to another side of themselves in their own minds. If a person can persuade this other side of one's self in his or her mind by justifying the cheating, he or she will cheat, to the extent that the other side of his or her mind allows it to occur.

This interpretation of evil behavior has never been incorporated into neoclassical economic theory, including in areas such as the theory of tax evasion. For example, Allingham and Sandmo (1972) analyze tax evasion behavior by comparing the cost and benefits of cheating. The cost of cheating is dependent on the risk of the tax evasion being discovered and the penalty for the revealed tax evasion. Thus, to reduce tax evasion, their model would imply a policy of increasing the expected penalty for the tax evasion. However, the policy prescription derived from the experiments of behavioral economics suggests that educating people about their obligation and responsibility to pay taxes for the benefit of society is a more effective policy for reducing the tax evasion. The same logic can be applied to the issue of tax havens. An effective method for reducing the use of tax havens would be the use of messaging and propaganda describing how reducing tax burden using tax havens is immoral and shameful behavior for a good citizen. In general, it is necessary to educate rich people about how the rich should demonstrate social responsibility by referring to historical facts and lessons.

5 Capability Approach

5.1 Key Concepts of the Capability Approach

In the economics mainstream, the concepts of resources and efficiency are restricted to monetary values. For example, the definition of "the poor" is determined based on a monetary income level. This limitation is crucial for understanding the structure of poverty and inequality. In 1979 Amartya Sen introduced the concept of capability in his Tanner Lectures on "Equality of What?" to overcome this limitation, and stressed the significance of individuals' capability for leading valuable lives. The capability approach aims to respond to the following questions and concerns.

(1) What factors determine the ability for a person to achieve value from one unit of resource or money? In designing policies for constructing the welfare state, these factors should be outlined carefully. For example, one concert ticket will increase well-being of persons with disabilities, but only if the venue of the concert is accessible to them.
(2) Option value is important for an individual to improve their well-being during life. Option value is closely related to freedom of choice, such as the right to receive a good education, the right to choose one's own occupation, and the right to freedom of movement and residence. These kinds of freedom are types of capabilities.

(3) Strategies for addressing income inequality should incorporate capabilities for converting income to well-being. Monetary income transfers from the rich to the poor should be bundled with improvements in capabilities resulting from the transfer of income.

Capability depends on the social structure and should be used to maximize the value generated from one unit of money. Key factors to consider from the perspective of building capabilities include:

(i) price systems and the cost of public services;
(ii) infrastructure;
(iii) social security and safety net programs;
(iv) creation of an environment that increases the value of family relations; and
(v) education for improving life.

5.2 Policies Based on the Capability Approach and Economic Implications

People's well-being depends primarily on two factors: positive and negative happiness (Yagi 2016). Positive happiness includes positive thinking and sense of attainment. Negative happiness includes the sense of insecurity. Thus, well-being generated from one unit of income depends on the ability of a person to increase positive thinking and sense of attainment while decreasing the sense of insecurity.

Social infrastructure and the social security system play crucial roles in improving well-being by affecting positive and negative happiness. For example, the education system has a critical impact on the development of positive thinking and sense of attainment. Learning and studying improve the ability to do something and increase confidence, leading to a positive attitude about the future. By improving the ability of individuals to work and study, it becomes possible to have a sense of attainment after putting forth effort toward a goal.

Elimination of infrastructure barriers for persons with disabilities improves positive thinking and decreases the sense of insecurity. Barrier-free access allows persons with disabilities to visit various places such as museums that enrich their lives. In such cases, one unit of income earned by a person with disabilities generates a larger increase in well-being if it is accompanied by a reduction in barriers to accessing public places.

This example can also be applied to persons without disabilities in a similar manner. Transportation costs such as bus and train fares act as a kind of economic barrier to using public transportation and accessing public places. Government-subsidized fares are a public expenditure that decreases barriers and improves well-being by decreasing the cost of movement.

In this section, we discuss the economic implications of fare subsidies. Suppose that the marginal cost pricing rule is applied as the pricing rule for transportation fares. The subsidy is paid to the public transportation company, which decreases their marginal cost. The fixed cost to develop a public transportation network is quite high, while the marginal cost for each additional passenger is quite low. The typical example is a subway system. The initial cost is quite high because of the construction costs and the purchase of expensive rolling stock. In addition, it is necessary to maintain the certain number and frequency of routes according to a set timetable even when the number of passengers is small.

The economic implications of fare subsidies are described in Fig. 1. When fixed cost is high and marginal cost is almost flat, the average cost decreases as shown by the AC curve. The demand curve is given by D. The marginal cost without subsidy is given by MC_0. The marginal cost pricing rule requires that the price is set at P_0, and the quantity demanded is determined at Q_0. Since the average cost at Q_0 is AC_0, the deficit is given by the area $P_0FE(AC_0)$.

When the subsidy is introduced, the marginal cost curve shifts down to MC_1. The marginal cost pricing rule requires that the price be set at P_1, and the quantity demanded is determined at Q_1. Since the average cost at Q_1 is AC_1, the deficit is given by the area $P_1HG(AC_1)$.

Depending on the shapes of the demand and the average cost curves, it is possible that the size of deficit decreases after the introduction of the subsidy due to the decrease in the average cost. The important point is that consumers' welfare can increase because of the decrease in price and the increase in quantity demanded, without a sharp increase in deficit, when the marginal cost is constant.

It might be worth noting that the subsidy for public transportation not only improves the capacity for movement, but also invigorates the community's

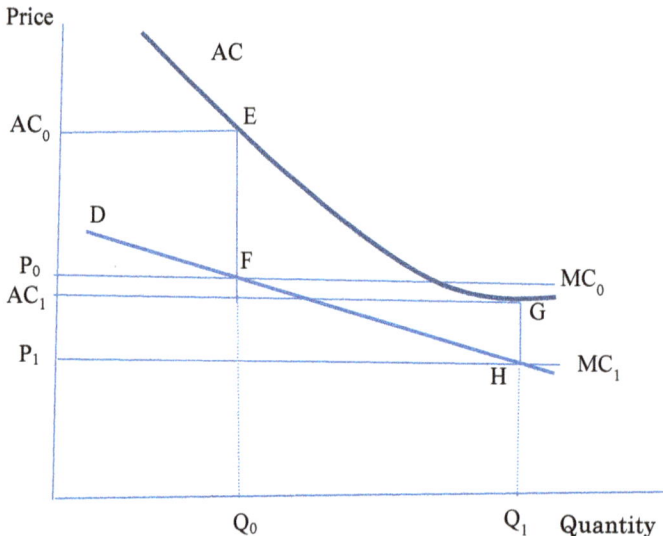

Fig. 1 Effect of subsidizing transportation fares

economy by introducing consumers into the town. This contributes to the redevelopment of the failing central downtown commercial environment.

Next, we examine education subsidies as means to improve capabilities. In particular, we discuss the impact of a voucher system in education. When considering about the effect of a voucher system on improving capability, the following aspects should be discussed carefully: (1) the properties of market equilibrium with entry competition; (2) the children who will benefit from the voucher system (i.e., lower ability children or higher ability children); and (3) the policy implications of introducing a voucher system.

First, we discuss about the properties of the market equilibrium. Not unlike the consideration of price in the market, students choose a school considering the degree of difficulty to enter the school after taking an entrance examination. Because the number of students admitted is fixed and limited, the difficulty of the entrance examination increases as the quality of the school increases. In other words, high-ability students are concentrated in high-quality schools, while the low-ability students are concentrated in low-quality schools. This kind of competition gives school managers and teachers strong incentives to improve the quality of school.

Second, we discuss the effects of a voucher system in education. A voucher is a kind of coupon ticket used for the payment of tuition fees. The government provides students a certain value of vouchers which may be used at any school in a designated area. In contrast with direct subsidies to schools, a voucher system subsidizes students pay tuition costs without distorting the market mechanism and the market equilibrium. Epple and Romano (1998) conclude that voucher systems are beneficial for high–ability students, while it is harmful for low-ability students. This result occurs because it expands the quality gap between high-quality schools and low-quality schools through the peer group effect.

On this point, we need to mention the possibility of positive correlation between parent economic status and student ability. If there is such a correlation, a voucher system has a preferentially positive effect on the students from relatively good economic environments because the supplemental education costs for improving ability could be financed by the relatively rich families themselves. Thus, implementing a voucher system possibly works to transmit income inequality across generations.

Third, we discuss the policies needed to ameliorate the problems caused by voucher systems. Before discussing these policies, we need to examine the peer group effect. If the social welfare improvement from the peer group effect is larger in a school where both high-ability students and low-ability students attend together, the widening school gap and the concentration of the same ability students decreases overall welfare by decreasing the peer group effect.

However, whether or not the concentration of the same ability students is better is also expected to depend on the efficiency of teaching. If different ability students study together, the level of teaching must be set by the teacher at the level that allows the low-ability students to understand. On the other hand, if low-ability students can learn from high-ability students in the same class, the peer group effect is expected to be large. Thus, the net effect is unpredictable.

From these discussions, it is justifiable to propose a voucher system in a school district system so that the quality gap among schools could be controlled to a certain extent, especially at the elementary and junior high school levels. Learning together in a class with various types of students benefits both high-ability and low-ability students.

When introducing a voucher system, policies are needed to counteract the potential for a widening quality gap between schools. One example would be the allocation of high-ability teachers to the low-quality schools. The important point is that we must maintain the opportunity for low-ability students to study in good-quality schools while also maintaining incentives for school managers to improve school quality. These policies are necessary to improve capabilities through the education system.

This reallocation of teachers is not easy in reality because some private schools can afford to pay more and offer far better educational environments for the high-quality teachers. However, it is possible to design a career path so that high-quality teachers who spend time in low-quality schools could receive a preference in promotions in the long run.

Finally, we will discuss the success story of Finland's education system, which is reflected by the dramatic improvement in its Program for International Student Assessment (PISA) scores. According to a report from Smithonian.com, the key factor that led to the success is the consistent quality of teachers who are highly trained in government schools and share the same national goals. Under this policy, the differences in student quality is minimized whether he or she lives in a rural village or a university town.[2]

6 Happiness Studies

6.1 Development of Happiness Studies

One of the pioneering works in the field of happiness studies is Frey and Stutzer (2010). In their work, they linked happiness and economics scientifically. For this purpose, they developed a methodology for measuring quality of life by introducing findings from psychology.

The important contribution of happiness studies is to present an alternative method for measuring utility. Psychological analysis clarified the difference between happiness and utility. For example, money can provide utility but it cannot

---

[2]See http://www.smithsonianmag.com/innovation/why-are-finlands-schools-successful-49859555/#thyzYWz8EIkyREZz.99 (Date March 1, 2017).

buy happiness. In conventional economic theory, utility is an increasing function of income. Happiness is more complex than the concept of utility.

Yagi (2016) applied the Oxford Happiness Index to measure the degree of happiness using survey data. A 29-item questionnaire was used to estimate the two principal component factors of happiness (positive and negative happiness). Positive happiness represents the sense of achievement and negative happiness represents the sense of anxiety. One interesting results of the study shows that the effect of income on increasing positive happiness is not large, but income has a strong effect on reducing negative happiness (i.e., the sense of insecurity).

In the next subsection, we discuss about the sense of insecurity in more detailed. This discussion reveals several differences between Western and Eastern philosophies. That is, the concept of happiness and the effects of feelings of insecurity are closely related to the prevailing philosophies and life perspectives in society.

6.2 The Sense of Insecurity and Happiness

The Buddhist economics advocated by Schumacher (1992) focuses on psychological aspects such as anxiety, aspirations, and emotions that direct the economic activity of humans. The differences between Buddhist and Western economics, respectively, are summarized by the seven key sets of contrasting concepts: (1) No-self[3] versus self-interest; (2) minimize losses versus maximize profits; (3) minimize desire versus maximize desire; (4) unfair markets versus fair markets; (5) less weight on entity versus importance of entity; (6) small is beautiful and less is more versus big is better and more is more; (7) gross national happiness versus gross national product.

In this chapter, we propose that the characteristics of the Buddhist economics stated above can be interpreted in Western economics. In particular, we focus on the first aspect of Buddhism, no-self, and argue that the other key characteristics follow in line with this concept.

In the Western understanding, the concept of no-self is consistent with the notion of social welfare maximization, in the sense that an individual's utility might be sacrificed to maximize social welfare. No-self is closely related to minimizing self-interest and desire. The optimal pattern of consumption in Western economics is to maximize utility, but it is low consumption in Buddhist economics. The goal of a low level of consumption is to allow people to live without great pressure and stress. This kind of philosophy is not only friendly to the natural environment, but also beneficial for overall well-being and reducing anxiety.

Mass production systems for profit maximization are rejected for various reasons in Buddhist economics. Low consumption needs to be coupled with low levels of production. Mass production systems violate the identity of workers since they

---

[3]In Buddhist teachings, supreme truth can be reached by forgetting the self.

divide labor into small pieces. Obtaining joy from work is important in modern society and decreases the stress of working.

Pursuit of a high standard of living increases anxiety caused by income insecurity. Denying this pursuit is good for decreasing the sense of insecurity, as long as the education of children is secured. The level of education predicts the state of society and quality of life in the future. Controlling one's own desires and the ability to think about society with no-self requires education since education gives people the ability to think about the many aspects of society.

In Buddhist economics, greater happiness is attained by decreasing the sense of insecurity. The sense of insecurity can be decreased by accepting a lower standard of living in material terms limiting material desires. Accepting a lower standard of living in material terms is related to the essence of the philosophy on "nonattachment" that is expressed by the saying, "you only lose what you cling to."[4]

Education is crucial for constructing a harmonious society in which the community works together for mutual benefit. A harmonious society is sustainable when the concept of no-self is present since this concept minimizes self-interest and conflicts of interests among members.

6.3 Accessibility of Resources as a Measure of Happiness

In the discussion above, we argued that happiness cannot be measured using the level of materialistic wealth. The negative side of happiness is affected by the sense of insecurity. The positive side of happiness is related to positive thinking such as the sense of attainment. In this section, we discuss accessibility and happiness for persons with disabilities.

In general, "accessibility" is defined as the design of products, devices, services, or environments for persons with disabilities; in other words, the "ability to access" and benefit from some system or entity. By improving accessibility, the well-being of persons with disabilities improves because they have a wider range of choices and freedom in life.

In the same manner, accessibility of resources is crucial for all persons, not only those with disabilities. For examples, some areas of concern for accessibility of resources include high tuition fees for schools such as universities, structural barrier to entering the market, institutional constraints on job opportunity, collusion among companies in market transactions. The reasons why the poor are unhappy relates to the accessibility of resources, especially when the accessibility of resources is constrained by income level. There are many empirically testable examples. The right of movement and the right of starting up new business are both restricted by income level. However, education is the most important example of accessibility affecting the well-being of the poor.

---

[4]The origin is not clear, but it is believed to be the words of Buddha.

Connell (2013) sharply criticized the commoditization of education in the modern economy. In principle, education should be a public resource that is accessible by all people. Education makes it possible for all people to achieve something valuable, and can allow people to be free from poverty. In this sense, education is regarded as a precious resource in producing happiness.

In reality, however, education is supplied in the market, the same as other commodities, and the accessibility of education is limited for various reasons, irrespective of individuals' willingness and desire to study. For example, the accessibility of education in Japan was reduced by the erroneous "relaxed education" policy of the central government. This educational policy reduced class hours for core subjects such as mathematics and science in the elementary and junior high school curricula. To access the limited number of university placement, students must take an entrance examination that evaluates their academic ability. The relaxed education policy places students in relatively poor family at a disadvantage in this competition because students in rich families can afford to pay for supplementary education in the private market to make up for the lost instruction time in the core subjects. Students in poor families cannot afford to pay for this.

It should be noted that the relaxed education policy had the effect of decreasing the accessibility to a good education for economic reasons. Income inequality is harmful for many reasons, in particular when it decreases the accessibility of resources such as education. Public policies should be introduced to remedy this harmful effect of income inequality. In the case of education, government subsidies to educational institutions and education vouchers have been the most important policy measures for improving the accessibility of educational resources. These measures are monetary measures. The lessons derived from the failures of the relaxed education policy tell us that the capability of accessing educational resources should be realized during the compulsory education period. By building basic academic abilities such as reading and comprehension during the elementary school period, it becomes possible for students to study subjects by themselves. Building this self-learning ability improves the accessibility of a good education for students from poor families.

Improving the accessibility of resources enhances happiness by enhancing the sense of achievement in areas such as education and business. Perceptions of fairness and equality should be based on the state of accessibility of resources, not just measured in monetary terms. It is necessary to discuss why low income is harmful. From the Buddhist economics perspective, low income is not bad in and of itself because low consumption is good for society. However, if the accessibility of resources is limited by low income, happiness can be depressed by eroding the sense of achievement. Thus, policies to counter inequality should be developed so that the accessibility of resources is guaranteed for all people. The accessibility of resources can be improved by a range of policies such as promoting fair trade, prohibiting lobbying activities, reducing barriers for new entrants to the industry, supporting small business, and eliminating unequal pay by gender, among others.

7 Issues Arising from Globalization and the Paradigm Shift from the West to the East

7.1 Structure of Conflicts in the Global Economy

The conflict between the Western world and Islamic world has grown increasingly serious, without any hopes for a resolution. To analyze the structure of the conflict at its root level, it is necessary to understand the characteristics of Christianity and Islam. According to Kikuchi (2013), the three major monotheistic religions (Judaism, Christianity, and Islam) started as religions of ruled or socially disadvantaged people, including the poor. This fact helps explain how Christianity and Islam grew rapidly to their current wide reach, and also how they are linked with wars. The ruled people had to fight against their ruler to attain the freedom. In such situations, there are strong incentives for socially disadvantaged people to cooperate because each person individually has relatively little power. Christianity and Islam played important roles for socially disadvantaged people in various areas.

The most important role has been the redistribution of income, and providing assistance to the poor and the sick. Since socially disadvantaged people make up the largest portion of society, especially in highly unequal societies, these two religions appealed to a large segment of the people in various societies. As of 2010, Christians comprised around 31.5% of the world population, and Muslims around 23.2%.[5] In total, around 3.8 billion people are adherents to either Christianity or Islam, which is a quite important fact. By definition, monotheism requires an absolute and supreme god, and the logic of the monotheistic worldview is constructed based on a single unique god. For this reason, monotheism cannot accept the god or gods of a competing religion. Otherwise, it is impossible to maintain the authority of their own god.

In considering the root structure of the conflict between Christianity and Islam, the conflicts between the ruler and the ruled, and between the rich and the poor are the crucial factors. Globalism increased the disparity between the rich and the poor, not only at the country level, but also at the global level. The relationship between the ruler and the ruled is defined not on a political level, but on an economic level. There is no endogenous mechanism for redistributing income and attaining social fairness in capitalism based on market mechanisms. "Greedy capitalism" has acted to destroy the trust between developed countries and developing countries, and between workers and capitalists. The erosion of trust enflames feelings of hostility, especially for people who are living in poverty.

---

[5]See http://www.pewforum.org/2012/12/18/global-religious-landscape-exec/.

7.2 Limitations of a Global Economy Based on Competition

Efficiency is a logical concept, while fairness is a concept that is understood by using both logical and emotional thinking. Emotional thinking is complicated in many ways. In response to stimuli, whether a person feels good or bad differs among people. Once a person feels bad, it is difficult to change this feeling by using logic. This implies that it is possible that a person gives higher weight to emotionally acceptable matters. Efficiency is not emotionally important, but fairness and equality are. In other words, efficiency improvements attained by competition are accepted logically only when they are emotionally acceptable.

If we start from the above argument, then it is possible to understand why globalism cannot be accepted by a large portion of the people in the world. It is true that the economic growth in developing countries is spurred by the transfer of technologies and foreign direct investment from developed countries, and this development improves living standards in monetary terms and convenience in life. On the other hand, the development of a monetary economy makes people's life more difficult in other areas, especially for people who are poor in monetary terms. High volatility in employment opportunities and inflation impact the lives of workers in urban area while income inequality expands. This worsens the sense of fairness, which emotionally breeds a sense of resistance to capitalism and globalism.

The worst case arises when the trust in society erodes. In a society where the efforts to build trust are neglected, the economy becomes inefficient. Workers are monitored by employers, and transactions are based on contracts. Mutual assistance cannot be expected in communities, and only the public sector is responsible for maintaining the living standards of the people. The psychological resistance for committing crime is low if people are not emotionally connected. If people are educated to believe that any actions are permitted unless the action is against the rules, there is a high cost to keep society safe and comfortable because the concept of trust is ignored. In such a society, each member seeks to maximize their own interests, tries to pinpoint legal loopholes to get an advantage, and must think about countermeasures against attacks from other members of the society. In some sense, this society can be seen as a competitive society. However, the costs to compensate for the lack of trust increase as the level of trust deteriorates. If unhappy workers are always seeking opportunities for sabotage, the monitoring costs increase without limit.

On the other hand, in an economy where trust formation is a primary concern, it is possible to reduce various kinds of cost. For example, if workers feel sympathy toward the goals of the president of the company, feel that their work contributes to the development of society, and feel that others are thankful for their contribution to society, the aspiration to work is improved. In this case, monitoring costs are not necessary, and we can expect high productivity among the workers. Workers can be creative when their aspiration for working is cultivated.

The final point to be discussed is whether the argument about can be generalized across society, and to what extent trust formation varies by layer of society. There are various social layers that exist such as race and nationality. Employers and employees belong to different layers. Even when trust formation such as a teamwork is successful within a layer, there is no guarantee that there will be successful trust formation between different layers. Thus, it is necessary to examine the reason why trust formation may not be pursued when designing the optimal strategy.

7.3 *Paradigm of the West Versus Paradigm of the East*

Although Western and Eastern philosophies have interacted with each other over their long history, as discussed by Woodhull (2016), there still exists a sharp contrast between them. The paradigm of the West is partly represented by the philosophy of Descartes, who claims that the essences of things are found by decomposing things into their constituent parts. This is called "reductionism" and contributed to the development of science. The structure of logic is deemed a core part of religion in Christianity. The logic of God is the essence of the authority in the Christian world. However, since the authenticity and justification of religion are rooted on the logic of Christianity, it became difficult to accept the different logic of other religions, which led to the religious wars against the Islamic world. Conquering other religion is justified under the logic of religion.

In contrast to the Western paradigm, the Eastern paradigm takes a more holistic approach. Eastern religions such as Shinto place less importance on the logic of religion. Harmony with nature and aesthetics are the main concerns of the Shinto religion. Because the role of logic is of less important, Shinto is flexible in incorporating aspects of other religions such as Buddhism and Christianity. In Japan, most people follow customs and habits rooted in the Shinto religion in daily life, but believe Buddhism.

The point is that the importance of harmony and aesthetics in the Shinto religion give the Japanese a sense of holistic perception and recognition. Japanese people regard trust and cooperation as the most important factors in economic activities, and economic competition is controlled so that the trust within the community and society is not harmed. There is an income redistribution system within society and the community based on the value of the Shinto and Buddhist religions. Mutual assistance within the community is a natural part of life in Japan. Merchants deem trust as the most important resource, and try to share the happiness among customers, producers, and society members. The most prominent example is the merchants of the Oumi region in Japan. There, they follow the principle of "Sanpo-yoshi," which means that economic activities should benefit all stakeholders including customers, producers, and citizens. Since trust is regarded as the most important factor in economic activities in Japan, Japanese people do not find it necessary to enter contracts. This implies that the cost of entering into contracts can be saved, and that the efficiency of transactions can be improved in the long-run.

The holistic approach allows Japanese people to grasp things from various perspectives. Seeing invisible things in the mind's eye is an important characteristic of the Japanese way of recognizing things. Reading between the lines is a basic concept when reading poems. Japanese writers have long showed their excellence in using symbols and codes in their works such as *The Man'yoshu* (the oldest Japanese anthology of poems) and *The Tales of Genji*. Noh uses quite sophisticated ways of expression in the performing arts on the stage. The simplicity in expression developed through this long literary history makes people imagine an expanded world that transcends time and physical space.

Key concepts in Eastern and Western metaphysics are summarized in Table 1. The concepts in the table were proposed by the Organization of the Age of Sage, which I classified into categories. The comparison is consistent with the discussion above about the categorization of essential differences between the paradigms in the East and West.

Differences in the importance of the self generate the sharpest contrast between the East and the West. In Eastern philosophy, the concept of "anatta" (no-self) is the ideal position of self, which leads to certain implicit and explicit rules and habits within organizations. In Eastern cultures, achieving the objective of the organization is viewed as superior to self-interest. The concept of sacrifice is more easily accepted in Eastern culture. In Eastern philosophy, it is possible for a person to attain individual objectives only through achieving the objectives of the organization. If all members of the organization believe this thinking, the costs resulting from various conflicts between member's interests could be reduced.

A key point to discuss on this topic is the incentive structure in organizations. Individual objectives provide a single person with good incentive to work hard. For an individual to work hard to meet the objectives of the organization, he or she must believe that the objective of the organization is his or her own objective. This belief can be formed over the long run through education and training in society.

The second important difference is the status of recognition. In Eastern culture, regression, not progress, is positively accepted, while only progress is given value

Table 1 Eastern and Western metaphysics

Category	Eastern society and culture	Western society and culture
Importance of self	Community orientation	Individualism
Action principle	Passive	Value activity
Thinking style	Contemplative	Encourage diligence
Stance of recognition	Accepting of what is	Seeking of positive change
Meaning of success	Hope of enjoying life through society	Hope for materialistic success
Meaning of wealth	Wealth seen as resulting from good fortune	Wealth seen as resulting from effort
Subject of cherishment	Cherish wisdom gained over years	Cherish youthful vitality
Source of value	High value on extended family	High value on material pursuits

Source Age of the Sage.org http://www.age-of-the-sage.org/philosophy/eastern_western_metaphysics.html

in Western culture. Thus, the coexistence with nature is a natural way of thinking in Eastern culture because regression toward a simpler, more natural state is easily accepted by people for the sustainability of the nature in some situations. In the Western way of thinking, nature is a subject to be conquered by human beings. Seeking positive change is not always consistent with the sustainability of the nature, and can create various kinds of costs in the long run.

Differences in the meaning of success affect the concepts of income inequality and poverty. In Western society, income level is regarded as a measure of happiness to a large extent. In Eastern society, it is believed that happiness is attained through the activities in a society, irrespective of the income level. In Eastern culture, the concept of honorable poverty (living a humble and modest life) is valued. This concept implies that a person needs more and feels more insecure as he or she has more material possessions, and that mindfulness, not possessions, is what makes a person happy.

It is necessary to discuss why poverty is equated with misery in the modern world. In a world where the monetary economy prevails, money is inevitably necessary for living. Poverty means the danger of poor living conditions because money is necessary to keep a house and buy food. Therefore, we need to consider a system in which a minimum living condition is secured. One candidate would be the provision of public housing and food. Publicly maintained minimum sanitation and public education should be guaranteed for all people of the world. For the financial sustainability of the government, the problem of explosive population growth should be resolved. Child labor should be restricted severely to allow for educational attainment.

After taking the necessary measures to address the poverty-related problems mentioned above, the importance of income transfers by the government decreases. Once minimum living conditions are guaranteed, income is not a necessary condition for improving well-being. Especially in the Eastern culture, humble living is deemed a virtue, and low income is not regarded as shame. For people to live happily, human relationships are more important than money. In Eastern society, a system that supports mutual aid and good human relationships is viewed positively, and the extended family gains high importance in the society.

In conclusion, it is meaningful to rediscover the Eastern paradigm in science, arts, and international politics. There may be some hints that help solve the problems facing modern society.

8 Innovation and Cultural Bases

What determines the value of innovation? This question contains profound meaning. Innovation is based on a new concept that allows society to move in a new direction for the future. How are such new concepts generated? Basically, new concepts are created by combining various factors that exist in a holistic way. The key point is how the various existing factors are combined. These factors may include culture, art, philosophy, technology, society, and religion. In cases where the degree of cultural diversity is rich, the possibility of creating new concepts by combining the different cultural factors increases. For example, to circle back to our earlier discussion, introducing Eastern culture into Western culture can produce new concepts such as the concept of minimalism. The concept of minimalism is closely related to Zen philosophy in the Eastern world. In Zen philosophy, "nothing" is crucial and "nothing" is equal to universe. "Nothing" is the source of creation (Suzuki 2013). In Zen dialogue, one can see much things from the simplest things. Once the unnecessary things are removed from what we can visually see, the essence of the things appears. For Westerners, decoration is important for expressing messages and intentions. In Zen philosophy, nothingness generates various meanings depending on the mind of the person. Design based upon minimalism, such as the design of iPhone, is continuously creating new meaning for the users.

With innovation, determining the value of new concepts is a more complicated issue. It is possible to propose some new concepts, but some may not be accepted by society and others may disappear after only a short period. What are the conditions necessary for the new concept to influence the society at a fundamental level? Emotional impact is a crucial factor for people affected by a new concept. Emotional impact is affected by six factors—design, story, symphony, empathy, play, and meaning (Pink 2006). Design implies that people are moved by shapes and colors, not by function. Story is a message that appeals to consumers, in contrast to argument, which does not. Symphony grasps the whole picture of the matter in the optimal manner. Empathy directly appeals to emotion and intuition beyond logic. Play brings humor to business and products. Finally, meaning tells us the purpose of the journey and suggests to us how our life should be.

In considering these questions, the quality of the cultural bases in society plays the critical role. The cultural bases include the mixture of art, technology, philosophy, and religion. These are directly related to spirituality and emotion, which are both drivers of people's behavior. For example, Japanese culture is partly based on Shinto religion and Zen philosophy, which value aesthetics, existence within the universe, and coexistence with nature as important criteria for judgment. For example, in Zen philosophy, the concept of the universe is intimately linked with the concept of void. Art is created from the void. Zen philosophers state that artistic ability is the ability to see something from unwritten things and to hear sound from silence (Suzuki 2013, 109). Musician can create music by taking in nature. Flowers, sky, mountains, sea, and stars inspire sounds to the musician whose mind is a void. By setting the mind as a void, it becomes possible for the musician to be involved in nature. Art is a kind of journey to another world. Humans recognize this world through the body, the mind and intellectual thinking. Zen philosophers argue that intellectual thinking is a kind of obstacle for this journey to another world. Artists should listen to the voice in their own minds or in their unconsciousness by placing their body into nature to enter into the other world (Suzuki 2013).

In the Shinto religion, the concept of creation is a core issue. In many Japanese Shinto shrines, various gods of creation are enshrined. Worshiping a god of creation is a ritual ceremony for expressing thanks for creative and industrial activities. Through the ceremony, it is possible to gain inspiration for new ideas and to become aware of the sacred importance of creative activities. For example, Imamiya Shirin in Kyoto Prefecture enshrines the god of textiles. This Shinto shrine is located in the town of Nishijin, where many companies in the textile industry such as weaving companies are located. Festivals and ritual ceremonies in Imamiya Shrine play a key role in activating the community of Nishijin and boosting the development of the region through the improvement of human networks.

Cultural activities, including religious festivals, can be viewed as important factors for creative activities as they reflect the spirituality behind the culture. This spirit is reflected in technological development. Technology that is highly esteemed based on aesthetic criteria has virtues not only in its design but also in its efficiency. A typical example is Fukuda Metal Foil and Powder Co., Ltd. This company was founded around 300 years ago, and has been developing new materials based on a traditional method for producing gold foil. For example, a surface treatment technique for new materials such as copper powder was developed from the traditional methods. These arguments suggest that we should deepen our understanding of the superior aspects of our own culture to design new concepts and foster innovation.

9 Diversity Through Fusion

The fusion process is an important source of cultural diversity. For example, Asian civilizations were strongly affected by European liberalism, nationalism and Marxism following the introduction of European ideologies (Delanty and He 2008). On the other hand, the level of Asian cultural influence on European culture is limited, although Zen philosophy has made inroads into various areas of European culture.

In this section, we discuss about the mechanism of fusion among countries and regions. As shown in Fig. 2, culture is closely related to politics and economics and reflects the relative power between the ruler and the ruled. In some eras, religions have been used as a tool for ruling countries, and the different religions have influenced the politics and economy of the country by affecting the ruled people, as in the example of Christianity in the Roman Empire. Religion also affects the moral sentiment and trust formation in a society or community. In Buddhist philosophy, the concept of "no-self" is crucial within organizations, and trust formation is related with "shame." Individualism is less important in Eastern countries. When Western philosophy swept into the Eastern countries, the concept of individualism affected the people's behavior, changed the rules and laws, and affected the market structure in an economy.

The cultural fusion process is complicated and profound because the power structure between the ruler and the ruled affects how different cultures are incorporated. The important point is that culture has been developing through an ongoing fusion process by which various types of culture are merged.

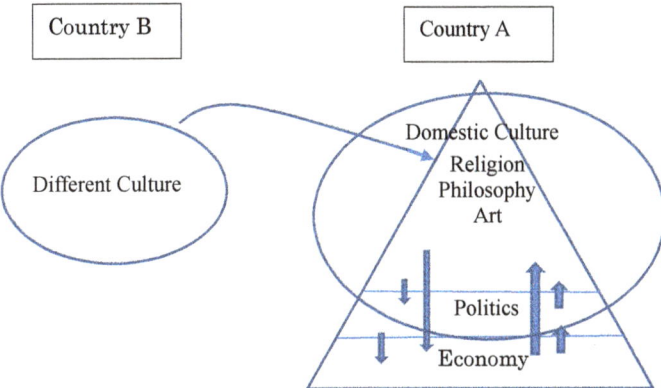

Fig. 2 Fusion mechanism among countries and regions

Diversity through fusion is accompanied by various types of societal conflicts. Different cultures may affect the economic and social structures in society, as is observed in various developing countries after the start of globalization. In these developing countries, the fusion process can potentially overwhelm and extinguish the existing culture. If a new culture dominates the existing culture while the structural changes in the economy and society are occurring, the degree of diversity may decrease. This scenario is exemplified by the standardization of culture in the global economy.

Hill (1978) empirically analyzes the colonization of culture during globalization by using the case of Thailand. He shows that the resilience of local culture can transform globalized interventions, and that the influence of prior local cultural practices remain strong.

One possible hypothesis is that the market economy and the commercialization of culture conspire to decrease the diversity of culture by dominating the local culture through the cultural fusion process. If this hypothesis is true, devising a counter-policy to preserve the local culture is important for maintaining the diversity of culture. On the other hand, it is possible that the differentiation of products and services that reflect the local culture increases their value in the market as the standardization of culture prevails. In this case, market mechanisms work to maintain cultural diversity, and public policy solutions are not necessarily needed.

One business example of the success in diversifying culture would be "amoeba" management advocated by the former president of Kyocera company in Japan. This management system creates a small team-centered organization that is characterized by accounting management at the division level, development of human resource using a management mind, and sharing the sense of participation in management with all organization members. Amoeba management is based on Japanese cultural norms, in particular that of *"toku"* (morality) that emphasizes the importance of seeing the Kyocera philosophy as a holistic entity [see Takeda and Boyns (2014)].

Contrary to the western management philosophy, amoeba management has been leading the way towards a flatter hierarchical control within organizations.

10 The Importance of Emotion and Meaning

Emotion is a crucial factor that drives people's behavior. Haidt (2012) describes the key aspects of emotion by highlighting recent developments in the research on emotion. First, we summarize these key aspects of emotion based on his arguments.

In the conventional argument, represented by Kohlberg (1969), morality is built autonomously through individuals' experiences with danger and harm during early childhood. For example, children learn how disordered behavior is unpleasant while waiting in line to swing on the playground.

Haidt expanded this argument, and contended that moral formation is influenced by cultural environments as well. In a society where individualism prevails, the range of morally unacceptable behavior is narrow. People believe that each individual has the freedom to behave as he or she wants. On the other hand, in a society where people believe that everyone is a member of society and a prosocial consciousness is viewed as being important, a wide range of morally unacceptable behavior exists.

The important point of Haidt's argument is that emotion plays a crucial role in the formation of morals. Rational reasoning comes after the emotional impact when people are faced with unpleasant or irreverent behavior. Emotional intelligence is controlled in the brain by the ventromedial prefrontal cortex (vmPFC), and rational decision making works through communication with the vmPFC. By using emotional intelligence, humans can quickly make decisions using their intuition [see Haidt (2012, p. 39)].

Based on this discussion, we can understand why emotion is crucial for forming social relationships. People cannot be persuaded by rational reasoning. First, it is necessary to appeal to emotional intelligence. Once a person is persuaded at an emotional level, they accept the rational reasoning. In this sense, the words of David Hume are appropriate: "Reason is, and ought only to be the slave of the passions" (Ainslie and Butler 2015). People often attempt to deny rational arguments if their emotional intelligence cannot accept the argument.

When communicating with other people, humans collect emotional information through various ways. In the field of evolutionary psychology, the patterns of the systems for exchanging emotional information have been studied. Cosmides and Tooby (2013) state that the shift in focus from knowledge acquisition to the adaptive regulation of behavior has brought about a new perspective in psychology. For example, faces regulate social interaction and an initial look at a human face regulates behavior by processing various information including emotional movement. Emotion-driven behavior is evolutionally attained to self-protect and mate with other members of the society.

This argument is crucial when discussing the properties of an organization. Let us pose a question. In what situation are members of an organization most emotionally sensitive? One answer would be the situation where members of the organization feel that some members behave out of self-interest. In such situations, members may feel threat or risk emotionally, even when there is no explicit evidence for the distrustful behavior. In this situation, it is hard to maintain good cooperation among members. Thus, emotional factors can be seen as determining the state of cooperation in the organization. The conflict in self-interest among members causes emotional conflict, and this could be the crucial obstacle preventing cooperation within the organization. Emotionally, members of the organization trust other members who do not care about their own self-interest and who pursue the aims of the organization with no-self. In other words, the behavior of no-self is ideal in that the behavior could be accepted emotionally be many members of the society in general.

The criticism for the behavior of acting with no-self is directed at the concept of motivation. As is discussed deeply in Sedlacek (2012), an evil mind is a kind of energy source for making effort. In many cases, no-self is linked with no effort, unless a person finds some sense of meaning in the behavior. Emotion and meaning are closely related. Meaning can also work as a source of energy for making effort due to emotional stimuli. Dirkx (2001) argues that the meanings we attribute to emotions reflect the individual's particular socio-cultural and psychic contexts, and that the process of making meaning is essentially imaginative and extra-rational. Garland et al. (2015) empirically conclude that if a person can enjoy positive features of the socioenvironmental context, which subsequently motivates values-driven behavior, then it becomes possible to engender eudemonic meaning in life. In such cases, feelings of happiness and motivation to put forth effort become consistent.

As is stressed by Berger (2011), it is important to understand the reality of meaning. The importance of meaning depends on the emotional factors perceived by an individual. A musician recognizes meaning as sound, a motion generated by the combination of waves. Waves of sound have their own meanings. Melodic progression is a type of motion, and is generated by the combinations of waves. By combining different waves, different meanings are given to motion, even when the waves themselves are the same.

In the real world, each individual behaves in an individualistic manner. Society, however, is the combination of behaviors of individuals. In music, each sound wave must be beautiful for their total collection to be beautiful. In the same manner, each individual should be motivated by beautiful meaning in their minds for society to be beautiful. The pattern of beauty, however, may vary depending on the unique patterns and combinations of individual behavior. Depending on the tradition and culture of each society, the pattern of beauty in societies differ, even when the motivation for behavior based on beautiful meanings is similar. This is the diversity in fusion.

In music, reality is interpreted through emotional perception. In the same manner, reality in logic and theory is also realized through emotional perception.

Whether or not meaning is reality depends on the strength of empathy. The important point is that the logic and theory should be constructed in such a way that meanings are incorporated that appeal to empathy.

In society, various systems are formed to cultivate empathy among members. Religious festivals are an important example. People feel the divine through sacred ceremonies and learn about morality. Through religious festival, trust is built among members, which is followed by the empathy. These traits are then beneficial to society.

In sum, it is important to consider the social systems that give people meaning and foster profound humanity and empathy. Employment systems should incorporate these properties. In the workplace, empathy should be the dominant driving force for workers to perform well, and the competition should be friendly competition based on mutual trusts. In this kind of workplace, workers can find beautiful meaning in their work.

The existence of a company should be built upon meaning that flows from the empathy in a society, not profit-seeking. Incentives based on profit-seeking will not be consistent with the interests of the members of the society in the long run. Ultimately, profit-seeking motivation decreases the sustainability of the companies in society. Public policies such as tax systems may play some role in enlightening executives of companies and tempering the effects of profit-seeking behavior. In other words, policies should be consistent with the beautiful meaning for the existence of the companies.

11 The Meaning of Mixture of Religion

What happens when a religion meets with different religions? In the 6th century, Buddhism came to Japan from India via China, Korea, and other south Asia countries. At the time, people in Japan would have been surprised at the arts and culture related to Buddhism. We can imagine that statues of Buddha and paintings related to Buddha's philosophy stimulated the creativity of the intellectual class in that era [see Stone (2003)].

Technologies were also transported from China and Korea into Japan along with Buddhism. Most importantly, new knowledge from China and Korea were mixed with the knowledge existing in Japan, which created new and different knowledge. Religion played an important role in this process. The Shinto religion in Japan deemed aesthetics to be the critically important factor in designing everything. Harmonization with nature is another essential aspect of Shinto. When combining Shinto's spirit with imported Buddhism (i.e., localizing Buddhist philosophy), sacred ceremonies, rites, festivals and rituals past down from the ancestors of the community played an important role in this process [see Breen and Mark (2013)]. One typical example is ancestor worship, which was a key feature of ancient Shinto. In Koshinto and Shinto, ancestor worship is believed to have been practiced in the Jomon Period. Ancestor worship went along with the concept of souls existing after death. On the other hand, Buddhism held that if people cultivated sufficient virtue over the cycle of rebirth, they would finally reach enlightenment and become Buddhas. The major philosophy of Shinto is the worship of nature and of the dead (animism). Shinto also emphasizes a broader understanding of human life, souls, and the gods of one's ancestors. These beliefs might have affected the style of Buddhism rituals, and creative activities in the long history of Japan [see Kuroda et al. (1981)].

The worship of ancestors cultivates morality in community and society because people believe that their behaviors are always being observed by their ancestors. Worshipping nature sharpens the sense of harmony with nature and improves the sense of aesthetics. Thus, the imported technologies developed in a different manner in Japan, and the sophistication of technologies and culture advanced in Japan. Knowledge creation originates in the communication between nature and God via ritual or ceremony. Thus, ritual or ceremony improved trust formation in the community and society because the goal of prayer was building the prosperity of the community and society. People prayed not for their self-interest but for the safety and prosperity of others in their community and society. In this manner, trust was formed, which later stimulated creative activities that are valuable for society.

12 Concluding Comments

In this chapter, we discussed the limitations of traditional approaches in economics for resolving several issues arising in a globalized society. Although the concept of efficiency has been the core principle when analyzing economic phenomena in modern economics, it has been apparent that the concept of fairness and justice are far more important concerns for most of the people in the global society.

Fairness and justice will be the major focus of scientific research in various fields such as philosophy, psychology, moral science, neuroscience, sociology, and so on. In this sense, the direction of economics will be centered around issues of humanity and spirituality.

References

Ainslie, D. C., & Butler, Annemarie (Eds.). (2015). *The Cambridge Companion to Hume's Treatise*. New York: Cambridge University Press.
Ariely, D. (2008). *Predictably irrational: The hidden forces that shape our decisions*. London: HarperCollins.
Ariely, D. (2010). *The upside of irrationality: The unexpected benefits of defying logic at work and at home*. London: HarperCollins Publishers.
Allingham, M. G., & Sandmo, A. (1972). Income tax evasion: A theoretical analysis. *Journal of Public Economics, 1*, 323–338.
Atkinson, A. B. (2015). *Inequality*. Cambridge, MA: Harvard University Press.

Berger, P. (2011). *Invitation to sociology: A humanistic perspective.* New York, NY: Open Road Media.
Breen, John, and Mark Teeuwen. (2013). *Shinto in history: Ways of the kami.* Routledge.
Connell, R. (2013). Why do market 'reforms' persistently increase inequality? *Discourse: Studies in the Cultural Politics of Education, 34,* 279–285.
Cosmides, L., & Tooby, J. (2013). Evolutionary psychology: New perspectives on cognition and motivation. *Psychology, 64,* 201–229.
Delanty, G., & He, B. (2008). Comparative perspectives on cosmopolitanism: Assessing European and Asia perspectives. *International Sociology, 23,* 323–344.
Dirkx, J. M. (2001). The power of feelings: Emotion, imagination, and the construction of meaning in adult learning. *New Directions for Adult and Continuing Education, 89,* 63–72.
Epple, D., & Romano, R. (1998). Competition between private and public schools, vouchers, and peer-group effects. *American Economic Review, 88,* 33–62.
Frey, B. S., & Stutzer, A. (2010). *Happiness and economics: How the economy and institutions affect human well-being.* Princeton, NJ: Princeton University Press.
Garland, E. L., Farb, N. A., Goldin, P. R., & Fredrickson, B. L. (2015). The mindfulness-to-meaning theory: Extensions, applications, and challenges at the attention–appraisal–emotion interface. *Psychological Inquiry, 26,* 377–387.
Haidt, J. (2012). *The righteous mind: Why good people are divided by politics and religion.* New York: Vintage.
Hill, S. C. (1978). Contrary meanings of science—Interaction between cultural and personal meanings of research in a developing country research institution. In S. S. Blume (Ed.), *Current perspectives in the sociology of science.* London: Wiley.
Kikuchi, N. (2013). *Judaism, Christianity, and Islam—The linkage of Monotheism.* Tokyo: Chikuma-shobo. Japanese.
Kohlberg, L. (1969). *Stage and sequence: The cognitive-developmental approach to socialization.* Chicago, IL: Rand McNally.
Kuroda, T., Dobbins, J. C., & Gay, S. (1981). Shinto in the history of Japanese Religion. *Journal of Japanese Studies, 7*(1), 1–21.
Pink, D. (2006). *A whole new mind: Why right-brainers will rule the future.* New York: Riverhead Books.
Schumacher, E. F. (1992). *Small is beautiful: A study of economics as if people mattered.* London: Vintage Books.
Schumacher, E. F. (1993). Buddhist economics. In H. Daly & K. Townsend (Eds.), *Valuing the earth: Economics, ecology, ethics.* Cambridge, MA: The MIT Press.
Sedlacek, T. (2012). *Economics of good and evil: The quest for economic meaning from Gilgamesh to wall street.* London: Oxford University Press.
Stone, J. I. (2003). Original enlightenment and the transformation of medieval Japanese Buddhism. No. 12. University of Hawaii Press, 2003.
Suzuki, D. (2013). *Eight lectures on Zen.* Tokyo: Kadokawa Sensho. Japanese.
Takeda, H., & Boyns, T. (2014). Management, accounting and philosophy: The development of management accounting at Kyocera, 1959–2013. *Accounting, Auditing & Accountability Journal, 27*(2), 317–356.
Yagi, T. (2016). Happiness and employment status. In K. Urakawa, K. Yonezaki, & T. Tachibankai (Eds.), *Advances in happiness research: A comparative perspective.* Tokyo: Springer.
Vitali, S., Glattfelder, J. B., & Battiston, S. (2011). The network of global corporate control. *PLoS ONE, 6*(10), e25995.
Woodhull, S. (2016). The convergence divergence dichotomy—Eastern and Western philosophy—Can the Twain Ever Meet? http://ssrn.com/abstract=2780887. Accessed May 25, 2016.

Chapter 5
Ethics of Economics in Late Stage Capitalism: Postmodern Chords

C. Edward Arrington and Grace Gonzalez Basurto

For many of us, conventional approaches to both economics and to ethics have become consummately dangerous. As many of the authors in this book point out, the rigid boundaries imposed by modern economists in answer to the question of what, exactly, is meant by economics are breaking down in our late modern, or postmodern, world. And it is so with ethics as well. Ethics—the question of how we ought to live— is in its modern economic context reduced to questions of property rights, of individual identity understood as autonomous action in markets, and of the good society as that which protects those rights and those markets. At least in the West, the actualization of economics has become synonymous with the machinations of capitalism, leaving those of us with normative claims to make about political economy at best at the margin of economics and at worst irrelevant to economics.

The crisis of the Left is a very real one indeed, and much of that crisis has to do with the struggle to find a critical wedge that might disrupt neoliberal capitalism enough to yield a space for economic voices other than conventional ones. Modern economics has not only conflated the term economics with the term capitalism (resulting in the politics of neoliberalism) but has for quite a while now reduced the human to a homogenous identity as what Dierdre McCloskey terms "that great stick of a character," *homo economicus*. Additionally, the question of distributive justice has been effaced within the web of positive law and private property rights, the social has been reduced to the market, and the meaning of human freedom has been narrowed to the scope of economistic individualism.

C. E. Arrington (✉)
Corrimal, NSW, Australia
e-mail: cearring1@gmail.com

G. Gonzalez Basurto
Kansai Gaidai University, Osaka, Japan
e-mail: ggonzale@kansaigaidai.ac.jp

But the good news in all of this is that we are beginning to experience a renascent regard for and reinterpretation of deeply rooted values about distributive justice, interpretations which see redistribution as necessary to overcome the asymmetries of wealth and the historical pathologies of economic power. Many now hold to an unflinching resolve to affirm plurivocal modes of respectful recognition of identities (see Fraser 1996, 1997).[1] Particularly in areas like post-structural feminist literature, critical social theory is alive and well in embracing what Zambrana (2013: 93) terms "the struggles of the present with the aim of contributing to dismantling systematic forms of domination". Those systemic forms are heavily brushed with modern economics as, indeed, politics and social policy are writ large in the language of capital. Unlike earlier efforts, the postmodern emancipatory energy of a renascent Left now works without the illusory comfort of a grounding in some putative, foundational normativity (e.g., a "universal pragmatics"). To paraphrase Michel Foucault, *everything* is now viewed as potentially dangerous, including foundational norms. It is the dangers of economic life, moreso than the violations of norms, which demand our attention. As Foucault (1984: 343) suggests, modern ethics has been peddling normative "solutions" as if the hard work of cultural history and emancipation might be glossed over:

> I am not looking for an alternative: you can't find the solution of a problem in the solution of another problem raised at another moment by other people. You see, what I want to do is not the history of solutions, and that's the reason why I don't accept the word *alternative*. I would like to do the genealogy of problems, of *problematiques*. My point is not that everything is bad, but that everything is dangerous, which is not exactly the same as bad. If everything is dangerous, then we always have something to do.

Despite the constrictions, contradictions, and refusals to recognize its own weaknesses and vulnerabilities, neoliberalism has colonized the political with the economic, or, better yet, with the capitalistic. Following Aristotle, if politics is colonized, so is ethics. Within that colonization, it has become precisely the role of the right-centrist politician to remind the public that this particular, neoliberal economization of their lives as citizens is not a threat to traditional values like fairness, equity, the good, and the just but is itself the medium through which these moral ends may be realized. [Never mind the facts; see Piketty 2014]. Seen in this light we see an illusion in which "unrestrained power of capital [thus] represents a progressive change" (Zambrana 2013: 109), legitimated through "ideological manipulation of normative language" (Zambrana 2013: 114), and thus critical theory is stood on its head. "Bureaucratic management replaces solidarity;" and, with that, moral comportments are translated into neoliberal evaluations of "goals"

---

[1] Of paramount importance for our analysis is Fraser's concept of participatory parity in which "some individuals and groups are denied the status of full partners in social interaction simply as a consequence of institutionalized patterns of interpretation and evaluation" (Fraser 1996: 24). In other words, participatory parity highlights the grammar of difference and the need for its recognition in order to attain social justice. Accordingly, it seeks to synthesize the politics of 'recognition', 'redistribution', and 'representation' to shed light onto the imperatives of ethical change in contemporary social relations.

and "performance" in achieving them. Human value—alone and in community with others—is administered in the name of capital's ends. Ethics must find its assigned seat in this horror movie.

As Jürgen Habermas' body of work reminds us, the roles of experts necessary to the functioning of the complex systems through which our social lives are administered has been central to late-modern life. This is very much the case in economics, particularly within the domain of financial capital and monetarist economics. Yet the gaps and discrepancies we now live with through the dialectic of systems and lifeworld (see Sayer 2001) are just as political and moral as they are economic, and the economic is not reducible to financial capital and monetarism. These gaps and discrepancies are at the core of things like the rebellious (but dangerous) current socio-political context of "post-truth," where the "facts" of expert work are seen as lacking in both legitimacy and moral-political usefulness to a populous no longer guided by the "religiosity" of the expert/priest.[2] This situation sadly highlights the dangers of an era of demagogues who capitalize on the so-called "alternative facts".

The Global Financial Crisis and the growing schism between the rich and the poor are too revealing in this context. Such exposure is vocalized in many ways, ranging from what some would consider the most uninformed and undereducated to the "elites" of the modern university and the press. It is because difference-obliterating education or difference-obliterating access to expertise has been poorly disseminated that the dichotomy between (personal) 'beliefs' and knowledge (Turner 2001) seems increasingly more acute and visible in contemporary life (i.e., through the ubiquity of social media). What emerges from this milieu of discontent is something like, in Keyes (2004) terms, an "ethical twilight zone" in which strategic success in both economics and politics is the order of the day for all, all who have caught on to the fact that the comforting little rhetoric of moral values, prosperity for all, globalization, and the right and the just no longer works, expert or no expert. Fear, trauma, disenfranchisement, Brexit, ecological crises, the Trump Effect, the rise of medievalism in religion and terrorism, far (alt)-right ultra-nationalist policies of trade, defense, racism and immigration are here—now—very real—and very "economical". The ongoing worldwide political and economic uncertainty, socio-economic inequality, and public distrust have been deemed by the head of the International Monetary Fund (in Elliot 2017) as the factors behind the current "middle-class crisis" and the surge of right-wing populism/nationalism in developed countries.

Increasingly, socio-economic unrest or discontent is also found in the developing world (i.e., Arab States, Sub-Saharan Africa, Eastern Asia) (International Labour Office 2017). For instance, in major African nations like South Africa, Nigeria, and Kenya, most of the public consider the political and economic systems to work

---

[2]A drawback from the lack of trust in expert knowledge is exemplified by the percentage of American adults on crucial topics such as climate change. Only 50% of U.S. adults agree that climate change is mostly due to human activity vis-à-vis 87% of the American Association for the Advancement of Science (AAAS) scientists (Pew Research Center 2015).

against them, benefiting only a few social groups (Wike et al. 2016). The growing social frustration and activism worldwide indicate, by all accounts, the urgent need for a new social habitus, a habitus which jettisons the constraints of oppressive and divisive modernist institutions and which embraces universal social protection systems, systems which supersede and rewrite what economics is and what it is not through a presumption in favor of the overwhelmingly neglected "99%," whose natures seem to be—in a way which perhaps shocks the dogmatic economist—something other than the "losers" who couldn't win, something more selfless, more human than the self-interest of the self-interested.

One significant and creative "economy" which seems to have somewhat broken away from the traditional, expert-driven protocols has to do with the symbolic and material conditions of the generation termed "millennials" (born between the year 1980 and 2000) as they patch something novel and curious together right under the noses of the institutionalized capitalism that has betrayed them. (And they make the capitalists very nervous indeed). The decimating social, economic, and political consequences of late capitalism and its seemingly open-ended global financial and economic crises, such as that witnessed from 2007 through 2009, have turned the millennials into a generation of "absolute beginners" when pondering their life choices and reaching traditional adulthood markers (i.e., self-sufficiency, marriage, family formation). For instance, access to stable employment, housing, and even health services[3] are contingent upon an economic mode of subjectification in which everyone is responsible for managing their own human capital to maximal effect (Fraser 2003: 168). According to the Organization for Economic Co-operation and Development (OECD, henceforth) (2016), despite being the most highly educated generation in history, young people (15–29 year-olds) worldwide navigate between unemployment and poorer-quality jobs (e.g., temporary contracts and low wage jobs) much more so than their older counterparts. Moreover, 15% of young people in high-income countries and 26% in (lower/upper) middle-income countries are not participants in education, employment, or training (NEET) (OECD 2016, International Labour Office 2015). In this regard, the new horizons of possibility and generational pushback against downward mobility embrace aspects of a "sharing" and "post-ownership" economy.[4] While the social, political, and economic organizing principles of capitalism are far from being *dépassé*, the centrality of new and perhaps more ethical economic practices (of the self) surrounding, for instance, the do-it-yourself (DIY) cottage industry movements (often caricatured in Western countries under the guise of the 'hipster' or 'fauxhemian'), are adopted by the millennials to varying degrees of socio-economic synergy, connecting the

---

[3]Prime examples of these trends are the global cities (London, New York, Tokyo), in which forbiddingly expensive residential property prices and rents are the norm. For instance, the typical London home sold for twelve times the city's average annual salary between 2002 and 2016 (The Economist 2016).

[4]These are terms that suggest alternatives ways to produce, exchange, finance, and manage resources with social and environmental aims at their core (Sahakian 2016) by engendering disruption in business/competition models and cohesion in trust-and-community building.

private and public, the local and global, the system and the lifeworld. Engulfed by digital technologies, globalization, terrorism, and economic downturn we find a metamodern[5] structure of feeling (Vermeulen and van den Akker 2010, 2015) and an ontological, epistemological, and practical "oscillation between a typically modern commitment and a markedly postmodern detachment" (Vermeulen and van den Akker 2010: 2). In a broad sense, the social relations of economic activity for the metamodern are rerouted to address discursive orders of (repressive-depressive) capitalist accumulation and economic rationality in the 20th century.

But that is just one creative and itself socially and ethically problematic example of an alternative actualization of economy; it does not stand in any sort of substantial emancipatory relation to those outside of itself and is thus of little value to critical theory. The resources necessary for the empowerment of millennials or, in a wider spectrum the global middle classes, to construct alternatives is not something shared by the vast majority of those subject to the untoward consequences of global capitalism. To begin to develop an ethical posture toward the economic world for our times, we need a broader domain of answers to the question of what is possible for us, possible in the seemingly impossible material realm of the economic, a realm which ethics can only pretend to escape at its own peril if we are to speak meaningfully and critically about our own accountability:

> Given what seems to be the inexorability of economic accounting in and throughout every aspect of human – and not only human – existence, from the base of the base to the tip of the superstructure, and given also that its operations implicate each of us in loss, cost, debt, death, and other continuous or ultimate reckonings, it is understandable that the dream of an escape from economy should be so sweet and the longing for it so pervasive and recurrent. Since it does appear to be inescapable, however, the better, that is, more effective, more profitable, alternative would seem to be not to seek to go beyond economy but to do the best we can going through...(Smith 1988: 17).

A useful starting point for "going through" economy is to draw upon William Schweiker's (1987) appeal to three classical terms, each of which refers back to a particular type of economy, of human dwelling. These terms remind us of the polysemy of the term economy, and of how much we lose by referencing it as a singularity. Schweiker (1987: 92), in the context of ecumenical theology, writes:

> [T]he conceptual polysemy of *Oikumene* prompts three interrelated areas of inquiry for ecumenical theology: dwelling as such (*oikeo*); the houses of communities in which humans dwell (*oikoi*); and human world (*oikumene*).

The particularities of various economies, as well as that which they share in common, compel us to recognize that the *meaning* of "economy" is contingent, often radically so. Part of that contingency involves the range of meanings and interpretations which accompany the ethical evaluations which follow from the fact that economic force becomes moral power when it is enacted in a world of others. Those are often, but need not be, particular others, since the consequences of

---

[5]We envision the metamodern as a useful, albeit emergent, perspective in the reconstruction of economic/ethical systems and the lifeworld in order to address issues of participatory parity.

economic force often extend to unknown others in unknown worlds. That is a fact that both immediately exposes the poverty of contractarian ethics so very common in capitalist ethics and has much to say about the inability of global capitalism to *answer* those affected by but distant from its power. [How do the unborn or the globally displaced enter into a contract, economic or social?] At its core, capitalism not only misrecognizes distal others but remains, under the cover of contractarianism and utilitarianism, morally indifferent to them just as it exploits them. Ethics, that discipline which seeks to understand moral force, now comes to betray its own normative justification, as its very terms are coopted by neoliberalism. Commenting upon Alex Honneth's work, Zambrana (2013: 96–97) explains:

> We are faced with the "perplexing predicament, Honneth argues, that in the context of neoliberalism the emancipatory meaning of individualism, equality, achievement, and intimacy revert to their opposite. In an era of deregulation and privatization, trickle-down economics and personal responsibility, international financial flows and the power of global firms, these normative achievements have become legitimizing principles for capitalist expansion.

Ethics is thus stood on its head: everything is justified to the extent that it serves capital under the cover of ethics. Zambrana (2013: 97) continues:

> Honneth writes that he is interested in "the peculiar fact that today much normative progress of the last decades has been turned into its opposite, a culture that decreases solidarity and independence, and, under the pressure of a neoliberal de-domestification of capitalism, has become a mechanism of social integration," (see Honneth and Hartmann 2006: 41).

The scope of Schweiker's reminder of the breadth of the term economy combines with Zambrana's reminder of the moral and social destructiveness of modern economic ethics which is indeed quite dangerous in the context of contemporary economics—creating the very conditions that make its own moral vocabulary part of the construction of conditions of life opposite to that which it morally professes. If that is the case, and we think that it is, the intellectual resources necessary to recover and sustain ethically meaningful economics reside elsewhere than within the conventional lexicon and discursive protocols of the disciplines of ethics and of economics. Terms like justice, rights, utility, and the good are corrupted to the point where their very use facilitates the advancement of forms of life which are opposed to them. Paraphrasing Foucault, the regimes of truth and of ethics which have constructed us are now consummately dangerous. If that is in fact the case, then novel approaches, post-liberal approaches, to the relation between economics and ethics are needed. The remainder of this paper suggests one such novel approach, a hermeneutic and interpretive approach which treats binding norms with some suspicion.

1 A Critical Hermeneutic of Economic Ethics

In his Tanner Lectures, published as *Interpretation and Social Criticism* (1987), Michael Walzer analyzes three ways of doing moral philosophy—the path of discovery, the path of invention, and the path of interpretation. These paths have their analogues in economics. [As a caveat, the extension of Walzer's work into the economic domain of concern to this paper is our work and reflective of our perspective, not necessarily Walzer's.] The path of discovery is, in our context, most evident in the naturalized ontology of a "self" possessed of a "nature" which humans did not create but in some strange way are capable of "knowing." As Walzer notes, this nature comes armed with a particular natural morality; in the case of neoclassical economics, our nature is to be economically self-interested above all else and it is perverse to behave in a manner inconsistent with that self-interested nature. From this "metaphysical" view, the grounding of an economic world does not reside in something that humans create; rather, the "discovery" is of something outside of ourselves, outside of our invention, legislation, and choice, as in our "nature."

It is not our place here to engage in an articulation of the many philosophical vulnerabilities of this "path of discovery." It is our place to say that, practically, the idea of grounding economic ethics in a moral ontology of an immutable and self-interested "nature" has failed, and failed miserably as the moral force of those possessed of enormous power to facilitate their own selfishness has wrecked both the Earth and the emancipatory possibility that others might emerge from poverty and deprivation (though the powerful always announce that they are themselves providing just such emancipatory possibilities; the King is always a good King). It is of course imperative that we care for ourselves—we are after all finite creatures who must come to terms with both survival and our own aspirations. But what we do in the name of care for ourselves is something for which we are responsible, and attributing the morality of what we do to something outside of ourselves—a nature, a God, what have you—is, for us, morally irresponsible. For most of us, though certainly not all, the destructive capacity of economic self-interest (and its terminological cousins "greed" and "selfishness") is obvious. We are responsible for that, and the "God-talk" of the path of discovery lets us bypass that responsibility—it is simply our "nature" to act as we do. Further, in our postmodern world, the Leviathan—the "Nation State" which secures our civility in the presence of our "natures"—has seen better days; neoliberalism has most assuredly butchered the role of the State as an agent of human welfare, redistribution, recognition, and solidarity. [In our neoliberal world, those who have benefited most from the *economic entitlements* of wealth and privilege (part of their "natures" we suppose) seek to slaughter the recognition of those who, presumably, live off of "entitlements" that a State welfare function might untowardly provide. They seem to forget their own "entitlements," accidents of birth, good fortune, etc.]. The current paralysis (or remaking) of the State devastatingly signifies the consolidation of plutocracies and kleptocracies the world over. The State as the guarantor of equal opportunity, fairness, and justice in society has not only acquiesced with the requirements of the capitalist classes, but has also been effectively eroded and replaced by a thinly veiled projection of parasitic entities. Interestingly, the most parasitic moment of all seems most certainly the conscious strategy of politicians who secure political advantage by endearing themselves to the wealthy through the vulgar and indeed pornographic sale of public property and public birthrights to the rentiers grown fat on such welfare. Future generations be damned. It is after all our "natures" to act so, and that appeal to "nature" is the "moral" grounds on which the thugs defend themselves.

Be that deathliness as it may, the second path, which may or may not begin at a junction with the path of discovery, requires invention, legislation, and thus emerges from humans. This is the path of invention, which Walzer (1987: 20) explains in distinction from discovery in his context of moral philosophy:

> Discovery is not itself execution; it simply points toward executive authority. But invention is legislative from the beginning, for philosophical inventors mean to invest their principles with the force of (moral) law. That is why invention is the work of representative men and women, who stand for us all because they could be any one of us.

Interestingly, Walzer selects Jeremy Bentham's moral philosophy of utilitarianism as his example of the path of invention. That is interesting to us since it is one example of how the path of invention often does have ontological origins in the path of discovery, thus taking a naturalized form; and, more importantly, it is interesting because a rather "twisted" utilitarianism occupies such a central place in modern economics. In this context, a moral world is one in which humans build institutions and ethics firmly grounded in the question of how to render economic self-interest not just consistent with but productive of a civil, good society. Along with Thomas Hobbes' *Leviathan,* utilitarianism provides the moral bedrock for economic institutions based on the superordinate priority of subjective utility and contractarian models of economic intersubjectivity designed to optimize private utility through construction of variants on markets and minimal states, each of those central to the morality announced for itself by neoliberalism. The end that is presumably sought is a civil society, with civility understood in terms of the peaceful pursuit of pleasure and avoidance of pain through markets in which intersubjective relations, and thus ethics, is strategic to its core. It is not responsive to other aspects of common life where, for example, we embrace values like solidarity, redistribution, respectful representation, fairness, goodness, preservation, etc. *unless* those values just happen to be compatible with the end of subjective utility. As we have mentioned earlier, these sorts of values are increasingly at the core of the disenchantment that many feel over globalization and its paternal cousins, neoliberalism, "naturalized" rights to private property, and commodification of nature. [An economy must do more than "grow," particularly when "growth" is financial and announced through the calculative ephemerality and malleability of accounting systems.]

Cutting through a great deal of argumentative development (and we refer the reader to Walzer for that), we seek to reject both discovery and invention as the best paths to a postliberal ethic for economics. We do that for two reasons. Like scientism and religion—the attempt to hide behind the methods of the natural sciences (or dogmatics) to provide the appearance of universality and stability to social processes—the universalistic urges of these two paths are ontologically suspect since, as Aristotle reminded us long ago (and as neo-Aristotelians, pragmatists, and postmoderns are reminding us now), human world is rightfully unstable, fluid, and not conducive to representation with models grounded in universality, stability, permanence, and simplicity. Second, these methods are cowardly *for us* now. As Walzer (1987: 21) states:

> Discovery and invention are efforts at escape, in the hope of finding some external and universal standard with which to judge moral existence. The effort may well be commendable, but it is, I think, unnecessary. The critique of existence begins, or can begin, from principles internal to existence itself.

The "principles internal to existence itself" emerge from cultures and communities, the "homes" which form both moral and economic "place" as well as particular modes for the ethical conduct of economy. One wonders, with Walzer (1987: 20), why the cosmopolitan flair for the universal emerges at all at the practical level of ethics—the "one voice" which to be "one voice" would have to be "nobody's voice":

> We do not have to discover the moral world because we have always lived there. We do not have to invent it because it has already been invented – though not in accordance with any philosophical method. No design procedure has governed its design, and the result no doubt is disorganized and uncertain. It is also very dense: the moral world has a lived-in quality, like a home occupied by a single family over many generations, with unplanned additions here and there, and all the available space filled with memory-laden objects and artifacts. The whole thing, taken as a whole, lends itself less to abstract modeling than to thick description.

Cultures and communities have, with a few exceptions, managed reasonably sustainable economies (and ethics) for themselves for quite a long time now, and many of them have managed to assimilate (or reject if needed) the economic force of Western colonialism and now postcolonialism to some meaningful degree. But, and global capital is the best example, we continue to approach these economies with the "abstract modeling" of an economy not their own, as if capitalism (which at the moral level means that the value of capital growth is superordinate to all other economic values) *should* guide us *all* through the pluralism and complexity of everything local as we seek answers to the most common moral question of all for any community—what is the right thing *for us* to do? (cf. Walzer 1987: 23). Note the *for us*; this makes the question quite different from the universalist one; that question is always relevant in contexts for particular people at particular times and places, and it is not a question easily abstracted away into the frothy domain of putative universals. Rejecting universals, we turn toward the moral virtue of *phronimos* where we find the discernment necessary to the task of economic ethics, the "post-virtue" virtue of one whose "interests" are epiphenomenal to an eminent though contingent context called *life*. The economic finds its now more modest place in the broader and multiplicitous dimensions of intersubjective experience (ethical, political, social, cultural, and spiritual). We do in fact need principles, rules, and ideas about universals, not as the suffocating constraints on ethics that they have become but as monads of energy—like feeling, empathy, anger—to keep the moral question answerable, answerable not for everyone all the time everywhere but *for us for now*. To paraphrase John Caputo (1993), *phronesis* is a way of "staying loose" under the weight of the comb-binding of the many "universals" stuck between our teeth.

While certainly the best option we have, *phronesis* has its own set of postliberal problems for those who seek to practice it in a postmodern world. Like everyone, she, like the world she inhabits, is constructed through a lexicon and a history which are, themselves, carved into the modern stone of "liberal ethics." This is what makes phronesis a post-virtue for us. The postmodern or postliberal path which she follows is already marked with the cairns of modern ethics, the very ethics she seeks somehow to keep and kick over at the same time, as, for example, when a word like "justice" sits uncomfortably on our tongues as we recall the horrors of historical "justice." This is the setting for postliberal ethics, a setting Caputo (1993: 102) remarks:

> Suppose the times are out of joint, that the gods of *arête* have flown, that we live "after virtue," or after "Being" and the gods have taken flight, or after History, or after Marxism (has - almost – ended), in times still more needy and destitute than even Heideggerrean *Denken* will allow?....Suppose, on the best heteromorphic grounds, there are in fact many prudent men, and quite a few prudent women too, too many to keep track of, too many to forge (*bilden*) a set of coherent schemata, with a certain deconstructed constellation, a kind of de-constellation, or dis-astrous constellation or configuration? Suppose instead that "events" are a disaster, a string of happenings transpiring without the benefit of a guiding star or *grand récit,* more a deconstellation than a constellation, more star wars than a heavenly sweep? Suppose an "event" is what happens, but without the big story of Being or the Spirit or Freedom to keep it in line ....
>
> Then the *phronimos* is a little lost ... Then we will require a kind of meta-*phronesis*, which means the ability to cope with, to judge among, competing and incommensurable schemata, a more radical, deconstructed *phronesis*, one that is ready to face the worst, to wade into the difficulty of factical life without the guardrails of metaphysics or ethics.

Thus the title of Caputo's book—*Against Ethics*. Note that Caputo does not abandon ethics; he simply strips it of the "guardrail" which keeps ethics away from its own refusal to stick with the original difficulty of life in the name of some God, or some analytic, or some "principle," or some "discovery" or some "invention" (to return to Walzer) presumed binding. That "sticking with" takes courage; not expertise. Ethics is about coping, not about the idea of "getting it [universally] right." What is the particular right thing *for us* to do, now, in this event?

Through Walzer and then Caputo, uncongenial twins that they might otherwise be, we can arrive at a "path" for postliberal economic ethics, a "path" under the rainbow rather than over it. That path is a somewhat radicalized variant on Walzer's path of interpretation, of critical engagement with the many perplexing and always conflicting discursive events which co-occur with other postmodern aspects of lived experience. There is no shortage of either the perplexing or the conflicting, as every morning paper we pick up reminds us to dialectically tack between, for example, a xenophobic nationalism and a patronizing neoliberalism which reduces both our economy and our democracies to that which can be processed through "the calculating machine." But beyond that, in economics, it seems that even the least expert among us have a rather robust grasp on economic life, as we usually and often tacitly read correctly the concrete material conditions of our own lives and the lives of those around us. Many who know that things are not so good suffer the "wrath" of the neoliberals for being the lazy welfare sponges that they "are." The sheer audacity of seeking "entitlements" from the "entitled"!! That *ethos* mirrors that of the working (and middle) classes, aghast at the betrayal of their own ascetic virtue; as the lion's share of returns accrue to those rentiers who pursue either the fruits of technology or the "easy" money of financial capital, privileged schooling, and "school boy" networks of politics and commerce. No wonder that hard work does *not seem to work very well now.* [At least we could stop berating those with spoonless navels].

With Walzer, we can see that ethics and economics always require interpretation, ethics because even the evocation of the principles and universals presumed "discovered" or "invented" as moral are "clear and distinct" only when left out of the concreteness of lived experience, experience much like Caputo's "de-constellation (or train wreck) of clashing claims each of which commends itself and none of which necessarily prevails. We live in the proverbial ethical cloud wherein a pluralism of "oughts" contorts and flexes behind the rainfall of "cans," with the looming specter of as-yet-unimagined horizons of possible actors waiting to speak. These all work to construct social meanings through a historical inheritance which is re-enacted every time we engage the question of "what is the right thing *for us* to do?" Indeterminate, undecidable, but no less real for that, the *meanings* that provide us with answers to that question are not just plural but infinite in scope and subject to arduous interpretive acts. In Walzer's terms, the grand decrees of intention and discovery are no different from ordinary talk about the right thing to do. That is because

> there is an infinite number of possible discoveries and inventions and an endless succession of eager discoverers and inventors ... they also fail because the acceptance of a particular discovery or invention among a group of people gives rise immediately to arguments about the meaning of what has been accepted. A simple maxim: every discovery and invention (divine law is an obvious example) requires interpretation (Walzer 1987: 26).

Put simply, meaning(s)—either enacted or as a cultural surplus—are all that we have, and meanings are born from interpretive action in the full scope of *lived* experience.

So what might this focus upon interpretation and meaning offer an ethic of economics? One direction would be to grant the expert—the economist—priority in giving the rest of us the *meaning* of economics and thus a political "context" for economic ethics. We tried that; we gave them the right to control defintions and indeed meanings. That is what gave rise to neoliberalism in the first place and, perhaps more dangerously, gave us the subsuming of economics in toto into the hermeneutical domain of [global] capitalism. Global capitalism takes on a construed meaning from economic experts in which all of the world becomes an adjective to modify capital—on the move to become what it was not, with totalizing terror and blindness to its own arrogance. This arrogance is parodied in Arundhati Roy's biting opening gambit in her book *Capitalism: A Ghost Story*:

> The Minister says that for India's sake, people should leave their villages and move to the cities. He's a Harvard man. He wants speed. And numbers. Five hundred million migrants, he thinks, will make a good business model (Roy 2014: 1).

Another approach to a post-liberal ethic of economics would be to listen—to seriously listen—to all who might have something to say. After all, each of us is an economic being; and, in a world where the moral force of the few becomes moral power over the economic lives of billions of others, all affected by global capitalism certainly have a "right" to be heard (They should be heard irrespective of that "right"). That discourse is what economic ethics *is*, and it may hermeneutically just yield the cultural surplus necessary to generate the moral resources to overcome the economic horrors that confront us. After all, economics means lived economies. We need more voices, not fewer; heterogeneous rather than singular meanings, plurivocality rather than expertise. Agnes Heller uses the metaphor of umbilical cords to give us a design for just this sort of hermeneutic (and moral) progress:

> The more heterogeneous the [social] regulations, the greater the range of options for rendering meaning; the greater the range of options for rendering meaning, the more numerous the differentiations of shared meanings, the greater the variety within the bundle of umbilical cords binding the Self to a particular world; and, the greater the variety in the bundle of umbilical cords, the more *individualized* Selves may become. Yet, as discussed, there can be cords in the bundle of single Selves which cannot be connected – or at least comfortably connected – to the meaning offered by standing [social] regulations. Selves can also seek for meaning which has not yet been 'provided', thus creating a cultural surplus (Heller 1988: 26-27).

Each of us occupies a "particular" economic world, which is, for us, the canvas on which the moral import of economic life is painted. That "particular" world is also a general one, as in our time Schweiker's distinctions across *oikeo, oikoi, and oikumene* merge into each other—the local is the global, is the glocal, is the "economy;" the private is the public and the public the private. If, with Walzer, we are to "cash in" analytics (principles, etc.) for Geertz-like "thick description," it seems that Heller's way is the best way. Put simply, the meaning of economics is the totality of all of what we come to interpret and understand about living the economic life that we do in fact live and do in fact always in some sense imagine as becoming better, more meaningful. That is the best hope that we have, the best "post-liberal" ethic, not an ethic of principle but an ethic of *listening* and *learning* and *responding* and *doing something with* the moral imaginaries of economics as embedded in the lives of those who live it. [The expert is called upon when needed, seated amongst us on perhaps Row 12 Seat 9].

More radically, it seems that we should question just as we embrace the work of those like Jürgen Habermas and Nancy Fraser who sustain faith in an egalitarian pluralism of participation in this discourse. Perhaps capital should lose its place at the table; it is, after all and by definition, committed to itself: within it capital and the capitalist morally count for more. The source of much of the death, cruelty, and destruction we have witnessed in our time follows from that *moral* and undebatable preference for the capitalist, irrespective of whatever "good" it might have done. To borrow from liberation theology and its presumption in *favor of the poor*, perhaps it is time to do something meaningful about the insidious abuses of power that have come from egalitarian notions which have provided too much cover for the selfish ones. [That is a topic for a different time].

2 Towards Harmony and Solidarity: Of Spirit?

As previously pointed out, the understanding and practice of economics has departed from the "spirit" of the home/household (*oikos*) to become the root of systemic/structural violence in contemporary social life. In Derrida's terms, they supplement one another within an equivalency of: economics in society = economy as society, in which capital growth (particularly via financial capitalism) has become the signified and the signifier (Malabou 2002). In this sense, the exchange between language and the economy as a source of fetishism and bottomless hyper-normalized violence has permeated all areas of social life, effacing the very concept of humanity. Language needs to be resuscitated, put back to good use.

While ongoing socio-economic, political, and environmental crises only highlight the limits of capitalism and capital accumulation, critical spaces for the socio-political debate are needed to openly tackle the contemporary and violent moral consequences of capital growth and accumulation. What does this mean for the expert in terms of (a) knowledge and (b) the abstraction from the everyday life of the general population? How feasible is it to imagine and seek a society of solidarity, a society where discourse, interpretation and meaning grant economic sociology a discursive priority over neoclassical "expertise"?

Against this background, we propose to "exhume" Derrida's post-linguistic sense of spirit/the spiritual[6], which, rather than a value, designates the very resource for any deconstruction and the possibility of any evaluation (Derrida 1989: 15). Spirit therefore exposes the balance of metaphysics (and the far too narrow and reductive pseudo-spirituality of modern materialism) in the name of ethics and the question of Being. Spirit in the vein of deconstruction (Derrida 1992: 953, 955) is:

> [a] sense of responsibility without limits, and so necessarily excessive, incalculable, before memory...a responsibility before the very concept of responsibility that regulates the justice and appropriateness of our behavior, of our theoretical, practical, ethico-political decisions.

---

[6]Derrida's "Of Spirit" primarily discusses and elucidates the reading of Heidegger's texts on *Geist* and the question of ethical and political responsibility.

Spirit here is neither an (Hegelian) abstract universality nor the companion of modernity. This "spirit" endeavors to overcome the Judeo-Christian metaphysical pneumato-spirituality (a "high," "nonmaterial" spirituality; see Rose 1993: 61). In contrast, the nonthingification (unnameable; prelinguistic; unarticulated) of Derrida's spirit centers on the imprint of responsibility/irresponsibility in thought and action at both authorial and expert levels. Neither has a pneumatic claim over the other.

In the current era of abject inequality, economic travails, environmental destruction, and political fractures, the re-reading of a deconstructed "spirit" becomes a rather timely endeavor and enticing possibility to galvanize the makings of the social contract in the 21st Century. To this end, the performativity of academic knowledge (and that of scholars in general) is apt to play a constitutive role in engendering re-makings and/or bringing new social worlds into being, from the ground-up (Gibson-Graham 2008). Of paramount importance here is the challenge not only to tackle the crisis of accountability of institutions, governments, and experts –seen as a triad of malice, abuse of power, and incompetence by the general public– but also to bring back a political economy that overrides and transcends the violence embedded in capitalist economics, for it threatens the very essence of human welfare/wellbeing (i.e., base-level access to shelter, health, clothing, and nourishment) (Malabou 2002). In essence, an everyday life attached to sustained intellectual and civic engagement that prioritizes the multidimensionality of human dignity beyond the modern discursive *power* of progress, freedom, and justice is not too much to ask. Nor is it more "idealistic" and "impractical" than capitalism in its ideographic forms.

Furthermore, the use of "spirit" could redirect thought and action towards a post-humanistic ethical pluralism, in which the human and *Homo sapiens* are removed from "any particularly privileged position in relation to matters of meaning, information, and cognition" (Wolfe 2010: xii), shedding anthropocentric prejudices, assumptions, and lack of elucidatory concepts of the "world" from ethical and moral values (Derrida 1989: 49–51). This approach would not only advance aspects of compassion and solidarity, but also highlight the crucial life-supporting environmental conditions currently at peril. The horizon of (post) humanity is ultimately that of irreducible responsibility and ethical alterity. The horizon of (post) economics is imaginary, for now. Spirit, harmony, and indeed ethics are not ours to tame. Start to listen.

References

Caputo, J. D. (1993). *Against ethics: contributions to a poetics of obligation with constant reference to deconstruction*. Bloomington, IN: Indiana University Press.

Derrida, J. (1989). *Of spirit*. (G. Bennington, R. Bowlby, Trans.). Chicago and London: The University of Chicago Press.

Derrida, J. (1992). Force of law: The 'Mystical Foundation of Authority. In D. Cornell, M. Rosenfeld, & D. Carlson (Eds.), *Deconstruction and the Possibility of Justice* (pp. 920–1045). London and New York: Routledge.

Elliott, L. (2017). Middle classes in crisis, IMF's Christine Lagarde tells Davos 2017, https://www.theguardian.com/business/2017/jan/18/middle-classes-imf-christine-lagarde-davos-2017-joe-biden, Accessed 20 January 2017.

Foucault, M. (1984). On the genealogy of ethics: An overview of work in progress. In P. Rabinow (Ed.), *The Foucault reader* (pp. 340–372). New York: Pantheon Books.

Fraser, N. (1996). Social justice in the age of identity politics: Redistribution, recognition, and participation. *The tanner lectures on human values.* Stanford University. http://www.intelligenceispower.com/Important%20E-mails%20Sent%20attachments/Social%20Justice%20in%20the%20Age%20of%20Identity%20Politics.pdf. Accessed 30 Sept 2016.

Fraser, N. (1997). Heterosexism, misrecognition and capitalism: A response to Judith Butler. *Social Text, 15*(3/4), 279–289.

Fraser, N. (2003). From discipline to flexibilization? Rereading Foucault in the shadow of globalization. *Constellations, 10*(2), 160–171.

Gibson-Graham, J. K. (2008). Diverse economies: Performative practices for 'other Worlds'. *Progress in Human Geography, 32*(5), 613–632.

Heller, A. (1988). *General ethics.* Oxford, UK: Basil Blackwell Ltd.

Honneth, A., & Hartmann, M. (2006). Paradoxes of capitalism. *Constellations, 13*(1), 41–58.

International Labour Office. (2015). What does NEETs mean and why is the concept so easily misinterpreted? Technical Brief No. 1, http://www.ilo.org/wcmsp5/groups/public/@dgreports/@dcomm/documents/publication/wcms_343153.pdf, Accessed 13 Nov 2013.

International Labour Office. (2017). World employment social outlook. http://www.ilo.org/global/research/global-reports/weso/2017/WCMS_541211/lang–en/index.htm. Accessed 15 Feb 2017.

Keyes, R. (2004). *The Post-truth era: Dishonesty and deception in contemporary life.* New York: St. Martin's Press.

Malabou, C. (2002). Economy of violence, violence of economy (Derrida and Marx). In Z. Dyrek & L. Lawlor (Eds.), *Jacques Derrida. Critical assessment of leading philosophers* (pp. 180–198). London, New York: Routledge.

OECD. (2016). Society at a glance 2016. OECD social indicators, http://www.keepeek.com/Digital-Asset-Management/oecd/social-issues-migration-health/society-at-a-glance-2016_9789264261488-en. Accessed 11 Nov 2016.

Pew Research Center. (2015). Public and scientists' views on science and society, http://assets.pewresearch.org/wp-content/uploads/sites/14/2015/01/PI_ScienceandSociety_Report_012915.pdf. Accessed 15 Jan 2017.

Piketty, T. (2014). *Capital in the twenty-first century.* (A. Goldhammer, Trans.). Cambridge, MA and London: The Belknap Press of Harvard University.

Rose, G. (1993). Of Derrida's spirit. In D. Wood (Ed.), *Of Derrida, Heidegger, and spirit* (pp. 56–72). Evanston, IL: Northwestern University Press.

Roy, A. (2014). *Capitalism: A ghost story.* London: Verso.

Sahakian, M. (2016). The social and solidarity economy: Why is it relevant to industrial ecology? In R. Clift & A. Druckman (Eds.), *Taking stock of industrial ecology* (pp. 205–228). Heidelberg: Springer.

Sayer, A. (2001). For a critical cultural political economy. *Antipode, 33*(4), 687–708.

Schweiker, W. (1987). To Dwell on the Earth: Authority and ecumenical theology. In W. Schweiker & P. Anderson (Eds.), *Worldviews and warrants: Plurality and authority in theology* (pp. 89–110). Lanham, MD: University Press of America.

Smith, B. H. (1988). *Contingencies of value: Alternative perspectives for critical theory.* Cambridge, MA: Harvard University Press.

The Economist. (2016). Global House Prices, http://www.economist.com/blogs/dailychart/2011/11/global-house-prices. Accessed 11 Nov 2016.

Turner, S. (2001). What is the problem with experts? *Social Studies of Science, 31*(1), 123–149.

Vermeulen, T., & van den Akker, R. (2010). Notes on metamodernism. *Journal of Aesthetics & Culture, 2,* 1–14.
Vermeulen, T., & van den Akker, R. (2015). Utopia, sort of: A case study in metamodernism. *Studia Neophilologica, 87*(1), 55–67.
Walzer, M. (1987). *Interpretation and social criticism.* Cambridge, MA: Harvard University Press.
Wike, R., Simmons, Vice, M., & Bishop, C. (2016). In Key African Nations, widespread discontent with economy, corruption. *Pew research center,* http://assets.pewresearch.org/wp-content/uploads/sites/2/2016/11/15092830/Pew-Research-Center-Development-in-Africa-Report-FINAL-November-15-2016.pdf. Accessed 15 Feb 2017.
Wolfe, C. (2010). *What is posthumanism?.* Minneapolis, London: University of Minnesota Press.
Zambrana, R. (2013). Paradoxes of neoliberalism and the tasks of critical theory. *Critical Horizons, 14*(1), 93–119.

Author Biographies

C. Edward Arrington, now retired, served as Professor of Accounting at Louisiana State University (US), The University of Strathclyde (UK), The University of North Carolina at Greensboro (US), and The University of Wollongong (Australia). He held earlier faculty positions at Arizona State University, Florida State University, and the University of Iowa. He received his DBA degree in Accounting from Florida State University, and both an MA and a BA in English from The University of Southern Mississippi. A former independent fellow of the National Endowment for the Humanities, Ed's work engages the humanities as a critical wedge to disrupt the dominance of scientistic perspectives on human disciplines like economics and accounting. His published work focuses on poststructural and critical theories and ideas as they enrich our understandings of ordinary life as it is lived under the weight of often oppressive systems. His current work includes study of the hermeneutic tensions within critical social theory, the dangers attached to an ethic of accountability; and, of particular import to this book, the idea of an economy of hospitality as an alternative to the rather "unwelcoming" economics that we practice today.

Grace Gonzalez Basurto is Assistant Professor at the College of Foreign Studies, Kansai Gaidai University. She holds Ph.D. in International Political Economy from the University of Tsukuba. She specializes in contemporary issues of urban political economy, particularly those reconfiguring the form and function of the city in the context of the knowledge/cultural economy. Her current research focuses on policy trends and frameworks of event-led regeneration and cultural branding in London and Tokyo. Her publications include "From London 2012 to Tokyo 2020: Urban Spectacle, Nation Branding, and Socio-Spatial Targeting in the Olympic City" (in London 2012 and the Post-Olympics City: A Hollow Legacy? Palgrave Macmillan, 2017) and "Asian and Global? Japan and Tokyo's Cultural Branding Beyond the 2020 Olympic and Paralympic Games" (in Asian Cultural Flows: Creative Industries, Policies and Media Consumers, Springer, forthcoming 2018). Grace has been a member of the Center for the Study of the Creative Economy at Doshisha University since October 2013.

Second Movement: 'Foundation Stones of Spirituality'

Chapter 6
The Three Foundations of Kyoto's Traditional Culture

Manami Oka

According to the Trip Advisor, Fushimi Inari Taisha was chosen in 2016 as one of the main reasons why tourists from around the world flock to the ancient capital of Kyoto. Some people may think it is puzzling that the Fushimi Inari Taisha outranked Kiinkakuji and Kiyomizudera. Fushimi Inari Taisha is not registered as a World Heritage Site even though it is the center of worship for the thirty thousand or more shrines scattered throughout the country. Mt. Inari is regarded as the very spot where the local deity descended according to oral tradition.

Fushimi Inari Taisha actually is a relatively modest shrine. Some say one has the sense that he or she is entering a numinous dimension. Tourists from around the world have commented that they experienced "the sacred" as they passed through the myriad vermilion pillars (Fig. 1).

Unfortunately, few of these tourists have much understanding about the ancient Hata clan that first envisioned this sacred space. The Hata were *toraijn* (ancient immigrant kinship groups) that immigrated to Japan. They include people of Korean and Chinese origin.

Ten years ago I wrote a book on making a sacred pilgrimage by exploring the numinous dimensions of Kyoto. (Oka Manami, *A spiritual pilgrimage of Kyoto* Tokyo: PHP, 2005) I used the following photo of the pillars that decorate the path of the famous shrine. I initially became interested in this pilgrimage site because of its connections with the Hata clan. The fact that tourists choose to explore this sacred space reveals a change in their perception of Japan. Kyoto is becoming a spiritual center for those interested in a more introspective journey.

Translated by Jonathan Augustine, Associate Professor, Ryukoku University, Faculty of Science and Technology, Kyoto, Japan.

M. Oka (✉)
Representative of Research Institute of the History of Journalism and Culture in Kyoto LLC, Kyoto, Japan
e-mail: manami-oka@syd.odn.ne.jp

Fig. 1 Senbon Torii (vermilion red torii gateways) ©Fushimi Inari Taisha

In this essay we would like to take three different perspectives that could help illustrate Kyoto's cultural foundations. First, we would like to adopt the standpoint that above all Kyoto is a "city of wood" or at least it used to be. Surrounded by mountains on the North, the West and the East, the city has always enjoyed an abundance of fuel. The quality of Kyoto's wood and wood products is also related to the more than sufficient amount of rainfall it enjoys. Most of the sacred temples and shrines are located along the outskirts within the mountains. Recently, "trees" have become associated with carbon reduction which is the surest way to reducing global warming.

The second perspective which we have briefly alluded to is the viewpoint of immigrant kinship groups such as the Hata. In 2016 a special exhibition was held to commemorate the 20th anniversary of the normalization of the Japanese-Korean relationship which was crucial in the formation of ancient Japanese identity. In 2017 the city of Kyoto is scheduled to host o joint project to promote peace between East Asian nations. The Hata who originally immigrated from Silla introduced what was considered cutting-edge technology, religion, philosophy and law to the ancient Yamato court which was trying to establish itself based on continental models. Their contributions in these areas led to the construction of capitals in Nara, Nagaoka and Kyoto.

The third perspective, which we would like to consider, has to do with the women of Kyoto and their feminine culture. The women of Kyoto have traditionally been considered modest and sociable. They are capable of being firm and assertive as we shall see from around the Muromachi period about 680 years ago. It is thought that as the locus of power shifted away from the nobility and the warrior class gained more authority, women began to participate actively in commerce. Some women also formed guilds through their work as artisans. It is remarkable that even while raising children they were able to assert themselves in a society traditionally dominated by men. The role of women and their contribution in the field of traditional crafts can unveil a spirit that has been hitherto forgotten.

1 The Three Mountains of Kyoto

In 794 Emperor Kanmu declared in an imperial edict that this land has mountains that are as beautiful as the sleeves of *kimono*. Since the mountains form a protective barrier, the name of this land should be altered from "the land that stands behind the Heijo capital of Nara" to "the land that is surrounded by mountains that resemble a castle wall." This proclamation established the paramount importance of the three mountains of Kyoto for posterity. The Heian capital, which has a history expanding over one thousand years, has not declined even after the modern capital was moved to Tokyo. In fact, Kyoto served as the host city for The League of Historical Cities (LHC).

In addition, the two major rivers, the Kamo River in the East and the Katsura River in the West have played significant roles. Since the Yayoi period, the land along these rivers formed large plots of farmland where numerous archeological findings have been excavated. In the surrounding hamlets the collecting and selling of firewood for fuel was one of the chief occupations. The women in their villages known as *Oharame* organized themselves in groups, and the firewood that they sold in the capital was used for fuel as well as household items which could be found in temples, shrines and tea houses. Kitayama cedar was considered particularly valuable and served the needs of various classes of people (Fig. 2).

The high quality of Kyoto's water is another factor that we must not fail to consider. Vegetables, *tofu, yuba, namafu* as well as *sake* and Yuzen culture would not have been possible without the ideal quality of Kyoto's water. Prof. Kusumi Harushge of Kansai University's Department of Mechanical Engineering has proven that underneath the city of Kyoto there is an enormous lake the size of Lake Biwa. He has named this "The Giant Water Basin of Kyoto". A special program produced by NHK on the ancient capitals of Asia has also taken up the topic of Kyoto's plentiful supply of water as serving the cradle of civilization (Fig. 3).

The local hills near these mountain ranges also served an important role. The villagers entered these hills to collect firewood, but the hills were protected to maintain high standards of conservation while being accessible. Since Japanese gardeners used the mountains as part of the background for their artistic layout, they often enter the hills to cut and prune the vegetation to suit their aesthetic sensibilities. People were accustomed to the mountains of Kyoto that were neatly trimmed for centuries. However, 150 year ago during the Meiji period the state nationalized the forests including those that belonged to the temples. At the time

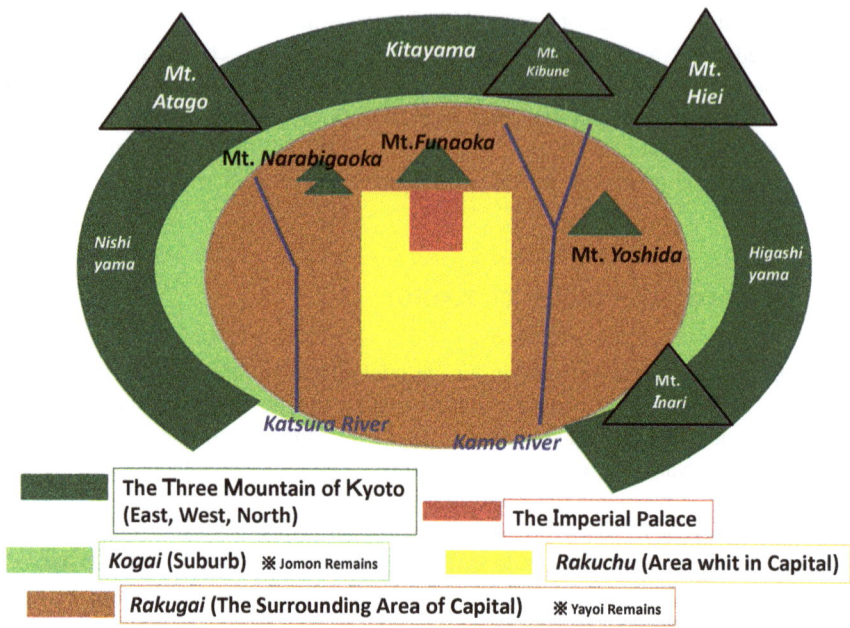

Fig. 2 The division of Kyoto into *Rakuchu*, *Rakugai* and *Kougai*

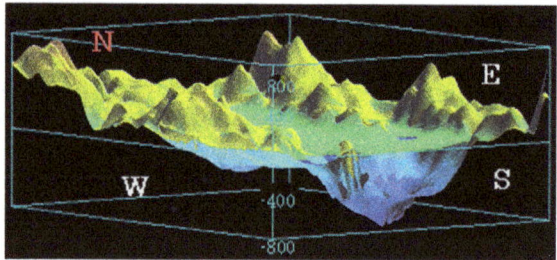

Fig. 3 Simulation of Kyoto's water basin. © Prof. H. Kusumi KANSAI UNIV

people were not permitted to enter the hills to cut trees or collect firewood. This nationalization and monopolization of fossil fuel made it difficult for people to rely on collecting the wood in the forests for a livelihood. The Japanese red pines that decorated the mountains of Kyoto vanished and were replaced by chinquapin and Japanese oak. Since people noticed that the mountains were becoming brown and losing its lushness, in 2007 Prof. Tetsuo Yamaori organized a panel to discuss the role of Kyoto's forests as an essential aspect of traditional culture. (The Council of Kyoto's Traditional Culture and Forestry) (Fig. 4).

There is now considerable attention placed on the protection of forests and the scenic views at the grass roots level. The local villages' relation to the city of Kyoto can be characterized by the harmonious relationship of man and nature. Through various seminars and conservation activities, I felt that the people of Kyoto were

6 The Three Foundations of Kyoto's Traditional Culture

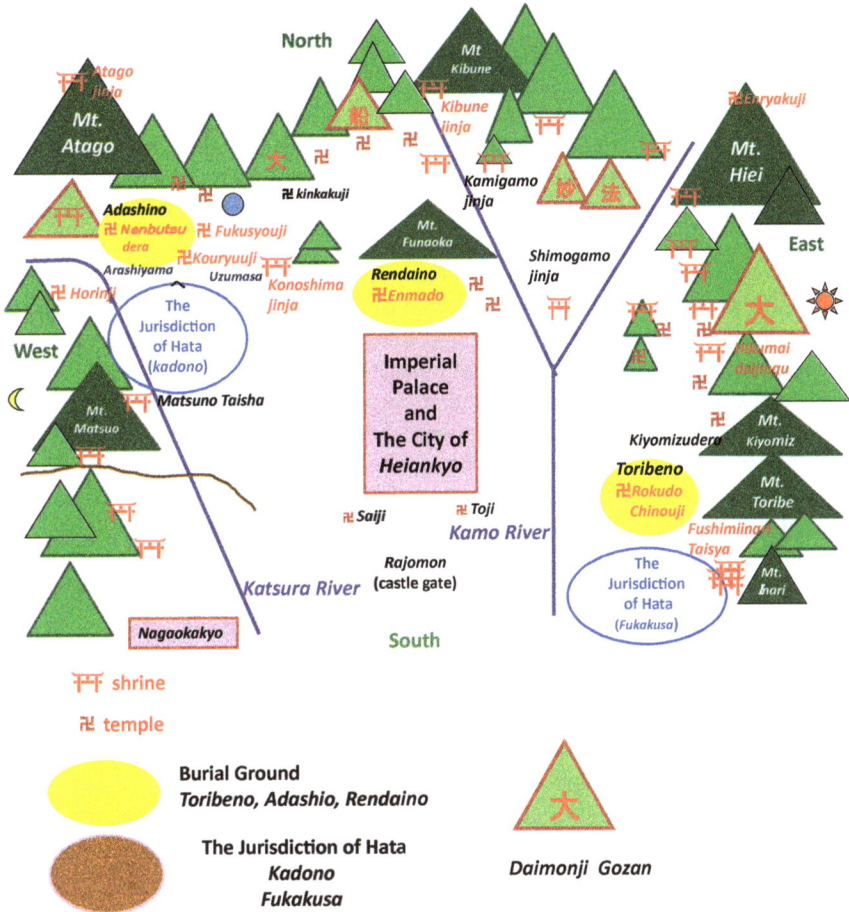

Fig. 4 Map of Kyoto city

very much concerned about the fate of the three surrounding mountains. The city has attempted to harmonize the role that commerce and conservation plays in the natural environment.

The mountains around Kyoto have served as the sacred abode of the gods and the buddhas. The mountains were also believed to be the entrance into the other world. The Shinto religion was able to thrive by coalescing Buddhism as it was adopted by the imperial court. Gradually an original religious ideology emerged by coalescing Shintoism with Buddhism.

There are numerous temples and shrines erected in pilgrimage sites in the mountains of Kyoto such as on Mt. Hiei and Mt. Atago. Mountain deities are venerated in Enryakuji where monks had prayed for the protection of the nation since the Heian period. On Mt. Atago in the West, a lesser known deity is worshiped to protect the city against fire. Kyoto has suffered numerous fires in the past.

Since the houses are not spaced far apart, fires were dreaded more than anything. Even today ordinary households and traditional restaurants paste protective charms to prevent fires.

There are special sites in Kyoto associated with water in the North, the West and East. One of the most famous World Heritage sites, Kiyomizudera, has a waterfall called Otowa no taki. Buddhist practitioners can be seen performing austerities in this waterfall. The dragon deity which is associated with the waterfall merges with the Buddhist goddess of mercy (*kannon*).

The dragon deity, the source of the Kamo River, is also worshiped in *Kibune* Shrine. The tree in the Kibune forests grow faster than in other areas. Prof. Kenichi Takada of Regeneration of Forests Support Center (NPO) has indicated that the tree in the *Kibune* area grows faster than in other Areas.

Ancient sources have noted this peculiar phenomenon and it has been discovered that water trapped in large rock formations underground can be confirmed. In the West, Matsuno Taisha worships both mountain and water deities. The water that is collected from the Kamenoi is believed to possess sacred properties and is excellent for producing high quality *sake*. Even before the founding of the Heian capital, the Hata clan built a shrine to worship the local deity (Fig. 5).

Since ancient times, many people have held the belief that after death the spirit returns to the mountains. The Buddhist notion of paradise generally corresponds to Christian notions of heaven. However, in Buddhism the spirit is subjected to trials by Enma who is the Daoist King of hell. Afterwards, the spirit enters the sixth hell which is called *Rokudo*.

One should note that Enma is the fifth judge of the ten officials of hell. His role is to decide which level of hell the souls of the sinners are going into. Buddhism adopted this Daoist influence and modified the continental ideas so that Enma alone subjects the spirit to scrutiny rather than the ten officials of hell. The sinners are sent into the cycle of rebirth to become another being such as a hungry ghost, a human or a heavenly being. This cycle of rebirth is repeated until the spirit can enter the Pure Land and achieve enlightenment (Fig. 6).

During the early Heian period, three burial spots were designated at the foot of the three sacred mountains in Toribeno (on the foot of Mt. Toribe in the East), Adashino (on the foot of Mt. Atago in the West) and Rendaino (on the foot of Mt. Funaoka in the North). Perhaps, this is related to the legend of the Lord Ono no Takamura. He is thought to have entered the realm of hell through a well in Rokudo Chinnoji on the foot of Mt.Toribe. After serving King Enma at night he is believed to have returned through a temple called Fukushoji which was on the foot of Mt. Atago.

In Rendaino there was a statue of King Enma that Ono no Takamura sculpted. Since he had been an official that managed burial, he played a cosmological role as an official who served both realms. These mountains with their burial grounds and temples served as popular centers of worship in Kyoto as is evident in these legends (Fig. 7).

The Festival of Samhain which Halloween is based upon can be traced back to the ancient Celts. They believed that the spirits of the ancestors would return on the

Fig. 5 a *Reiki no Taki* (*Matsuno Taisha*); **b** *Kamenoi* (*Matsuno Taisha*). © matsunoo

31st day of the tenth month. The gates of the underworld would be opened on this day and the Celts would hold a fire festival to celebrate New Years eve. Afterwards, people would take home the embers of the fire and light their ovens to ward off evil. There are surprising similarities with the Bon festival. In the beginning of August, an important ritual is performed to welcome ancestors. They then believe that they can spend several days with their ancestors. Afterwards on August 16th, these ancestors are led to the fires which are burning on the mountains and sent off to the

Fig. 6 a The well *Ono no Takamura* descended into © Rokudo chinnouji; **b** *Ono no Takamura* © Rokudo chinnouji; **c** *Enma Daio* © Rokudo chinnouji

other world. At this time, the three mountain ranges are lit up to represent the Chinese characters signifying the five piles of the bonfires of Kyoto. Everybody gazes the pictograms representing "grandeur", "mysticism", "a boat", and "the entrance to the shrines (*torii*)" as they engage in prayer. During World War, this ritual was performed during the day. People were seen wearing white T shirts so as not to attract the attention of American bombers.

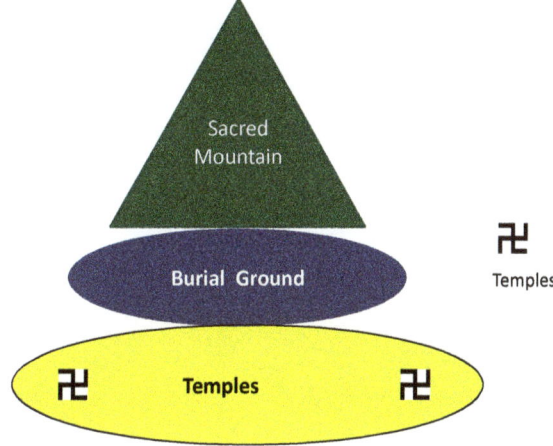

Fig. 7 The cosmology of the burial ground *Toribeno, Adashino, Rendaino*

Japanese sun worship is well-known throughout the world. Since the sun rises in the East, believers erected a miniature version of the Ise Shrine which is dedicated to the Goddess of the sun and food. The *Amida* Buddha's paradise is believed to be located in the West according to Buddhist dogma. When one observes the "*Yamagoe Amidazu*", one can observe *Amida* accompanied by heavenly deities crossing over the Western mountains. One used visualize this painting as part of one's aesthetic training. In the Eastern Mountains aesthetic training involving the worship of rising sun and at the end of the day the Western mountains were venerated. This process of rising and setting signified life and death (Fig. 8).

2 The Hata Clan's Technical Expertise in Ancient Japan

Kyoto's economy has been sustained by artisans who have created the art of Nishijin weaving, Yuzen dying, Kiyomizu pottery, Kyoto dolls and Japanese lacquer and architecture is famous throughout the world and need not be translated for non-Japanese people to understand what they are referring to. In fact, their roots can be traced back to the Hata clan who immigrated and settled in Kadono (the western section of Kyoto) and Fukakusa (the southern section of Kyoto) in the later half of the 5th century.

In Arashiyama one can witness impressive architectural mounds and sites. It is one of the most famous tourist destinations and one can witness their technical expertise. To deal with frequent flooding the Kadono River which is the present day Katsura River, the Kadono branch of the Hata clan constructed a dam called Kadono Oi to divert the flow of the river. In the late 5th century this project was carried out on an unprecedented scale. The Hata also diverted the flow of the river by filling in dirt to create an artificial island. Vast amounts of plots of farmland were created by irrigation. This process increased water flow in the Medieval period. In

Fig. 8 Yamagoshi Amida zu (Amida Coming over the Mountain). (This image may not be reprinted or reproduced in any form, in whole or part, without the expressed written permission by the Kyoto National Museum.)

fact, the irrigation canals of the Katsura River still rely on them to this very day. Arashiyama is also supplied by similar facilities that the Hata clan built in ancient times (Figs. 9, 10 and 11).

The Oi River (present day Kadono River) also had dams.(*Kadono Oi*) Today, the upper reaches of the Togetsu Brige that forms the most of famous landmark of

6 The Three Foundations of Kyoto's Traditional Culture

Fig. 9 *Kadono Oi Arashiyama.* ©Manami Oka

Arashiyama are called "Oi River" The upper stream of the river which everybody is familiar with is the "Katsura River".

In *Dujiangyan* in Sichuan which is well-known for its World Heritage Site one can observe that the same irrigation methods were employed. This shows that the Hata clan introduced the latest technology to the Yamato court (Figs. 12 and 13).

The Hata clan also erected a bridge across *Arashiyama* called *Togetsu* Bridge which has become one of the most popular tourist's spots in Kyoto today. The bridge was important for the Hata clan because it led to a road where the *Kokuzo* Bodhisattva is thought to await worshipers. The name of the temple is Horinji. The path was formerly known as Hourinji Bridge after the temple that possesses the precious statue. The statue was believed to protect artisans and when children become thirteen, they pray for wisdom. In fact the two shrines are believed to be inhabited by deities who protect the bridge itself.

The head of Hata clan was called Uzumasa. This location was known as "the Hollywood of Japan" because there was a movie studio. There is also a famous statue of the *Miroku* (Maitreya) Bodhisattva in Koryuji which is the oldest temple in Kyoto built by the Hata clan. Carl Jaspers praised the statue as the ideal state of man. Since it is made from a rare pine that only exists in Korea, scholars have concluded that the statue was made in Korea. The statue closely resembles the golden Maitreya that is registered as the 83rd national treasure of South Korea today. The *Nihon Shoki* lists an entry describing an incident in which an envoy from the Prince Shotoku presented a Buddhist statue to Hata no Kawakatsu who was a Hata official. Kawakatsu built Hachiokadera (Koryuji*)* and installed the statue of Maitreya in 603.

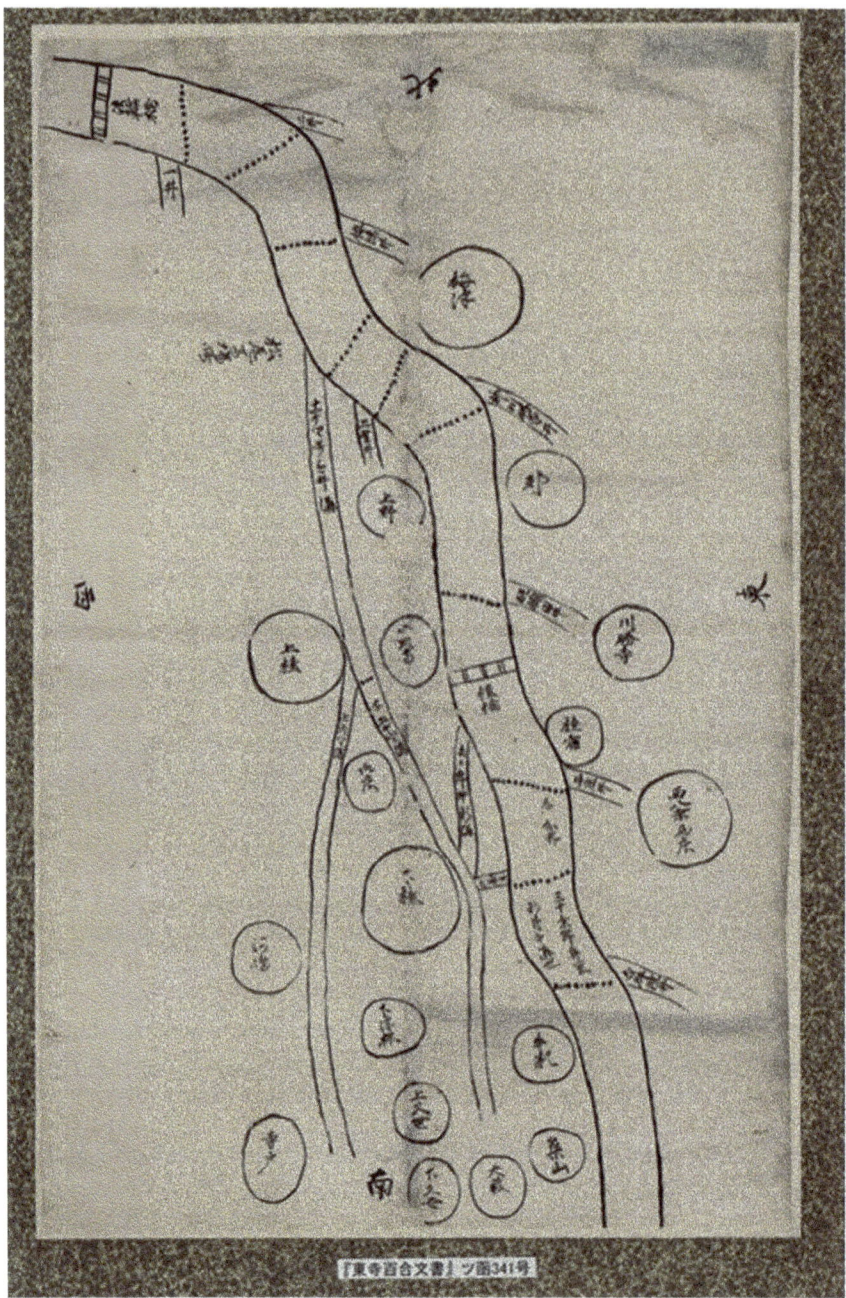

Fig. 10 *Katsuragawa Yosui* (*Rakusai Yosui*) from the *Toji Hyakgou Monjyo*. *Source* website of Kyoto Institute, Library and Archives, "Kyo no Kioku Archive"

Fig. 11 The map of *Arashiyama*. Reference source of Kyoto Research Institute of the History of Journalism and Culture in Kyoto LLC

Historians have speculated whether this Hata official was Uzumasa who supposedly worked under the Prince Shotoku regime from the late sixth to seventh century. Koryuji retains the very first national treasure of Japan to this very day.

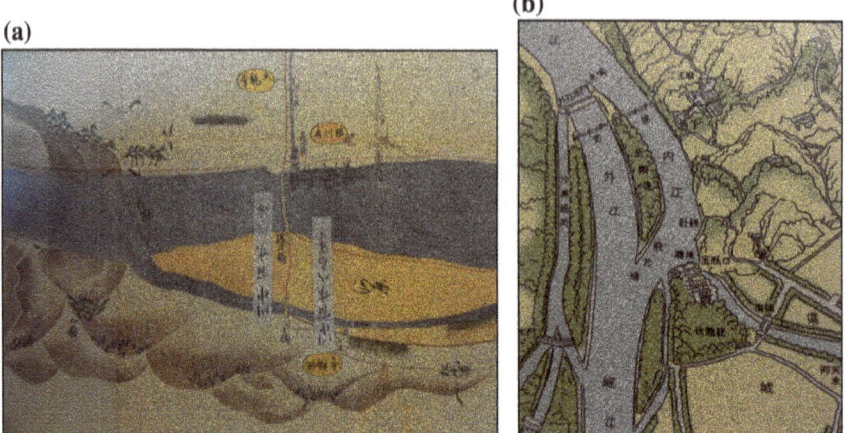

Fig. 12 The map of ancient *Arashiyama* and *Dujiangyan*. **a** The map of Old Arashiyama (Around the Middle of the Edo Period). In Kyoto Institute, Library and Archives; **b** The Map of Dujiangyan. *Rakusai Yosui* (*Ichinoiseki*) *of Saga Arashiyama*. © Kyoto Prefecture

The bodhisattva Maitreya is believed to reappear 5.6 billion years after the death of the historical Buddha and this deity was the center of worship in ancient Silla. This powerful Korean state supplanted the other two kingdom of Paekche and Koguryo at the end of the seventh century. The rulers established a new Buddhist folk tradition.

The tradition of referring to aristocratic officials who excelled in leaning, morality, martial arts and music as incarnations of Maitreya *(Miluxianhua)* was widely practiced. This was called "Silla Faran" and the practice was debated as a political issue in Silla.

The *Nogaku* tradition initially began from *Kagura*(an ancient form of sacred music and dance)which was supposed to be performed exclusively for the gods. Zeami is often identified as the founder during the Muromachi period but the tradition can be traced back to Hata no kawakatsu. The *Fushi kaden* (zeami) and The *Myoshuku shu* (Zenchiku Konparu) also list him as the founder. Prince Shotoku supposedly ordered 66 of these programs to be performed to insure the peace and prosperity of the state. There are oral traditions that link Hata no Kawakatsu's descendants to the founders of *Sarugaku* that became known as *Konparu ryu* as well as to the *Gakunin* of Shitenoji. There is plenty of evidence that identifies the Hata as the immigrant kingship group that helped solidify the role of these theatrical arts while simultaneously acting as the religious leaders. It is important to note that the Hata clan was more concerned with increasing production rather than gaining political ascendancy. It is not surprising to see that they worshiped the gods associated with industry.

The Hata clan also started weaving and sericulture which became the leading industries in Kyoto later known as Nishijin ori and Yuzen zome. Today one can observe that the Nishijin ori organization dedicated the impressive stone steps in the

Fig. 13 *Togetsu* Bridge *Arashiyama*. © Manami Oka

Kaiko no Yashio of the Konoshimajinjya. This sacred shrine is also known for its sacred fountain which is enshrined by a three-legged *torii*. This peculiar *torii* is shaped like this so that worshipers can approach it from three sides. Since water was

Fig. 14 a A three legged Torii (*Konoshima Shrine*) © Manami Oka; **b** The *KaikonoYashiro* in *Konoshimajinja*. © Manami Oka

regarded as the most sacred commodity in an agrarian nation, it is not surprising to find monuments erected in dedication to the source of life itself (Fig. 14).

Fushimi Inari Shrine which Hata no Irogu originally built worshiped the god of rice. Rice was the main food staple in most Asian countries at the time. During the Edo period the warrior class's salaries were calculated in rice. In the *Yamashiro no Kuni Fudoki*, it is recorded that when Hata no Irogu was practicing archery, he shot an arrow at a rice cake (*Mochi*) as a target. But before the arrow could reach the target, the rice cake transformed itself into a swan and flew away. Since the swan eventually landed on Mt. Inari and rice sprouted from the spot, a shrine was erected called Inari. Irogu was known to have been a prosperous farmer and the deity mentioned above was worshiped by the Hata clan for generations afterwards.

During the middle of the sixth century during Emperor Kinmei's reign, the emperor had a dream that seemed to indicate that the court would economically prosper if he employed a man called Hata no Otsuchi. Since Kinmei discovered a man in Fukakusa who was a merchant, he promoted him to the Minister of Finance. The Hata branch who resided in Fukakusa were well-known as famers and merchants and were wealthy enough to attract the attention of the imperial court. Thus, the two branches of the Hata clan eventually merged in the capital walls during the Heian period. Some scholars have pointed out that Hata no Kawakatsu's residence was located in the Shishinden that is located within the imperial castle. The Hata clan's involvement in various industries even after hundreds of years since they settled in Kyoto is intriguing. When the capital moved to Tokyo, there was concern about Kyoto's economy, so the traditional industries evolved from pottery to producers of ceramics which became associated with "cool japan" abroad. This flexibility seems to resemble the Hata clan's adaptability. Hata clan played the vital role of linking continental culture with the new evolving culture of the islands.

3 The Women of Kyoto and Feminine Culture

The dramatist Bakin Takizawa remarked that the merits of Kyoto can be seen in its women. During the Heian period it was not surprising that the most attract women flocked to the capital. But the extraordinary attributes of the women of Kyoto have more to do with their economies and productive capacity. By the Muromachi period the *Ritsuryo* system had collapsed and the power had shifted away from the nobility to the Ashikaga warrior clan. Commoners were freed from their obligatory duties. Now that they were outside the *shoen* land holdings. People could focus on commerce. The influence of Chinese *Chan* gave birth to Japanese Zen culture. Around this time the traditional Japanese room (*washitsu*), and tea culture occurred because of the new freedom commoners gamed.

Nogaku is made up of *Noh* and *Kyogen* which are two separate sub-genres. *Noh* that was first developed by Zeami evokes the mystical world of *Yugen*. *Kyogen* is a more satirical comedy. In *Kyogen* servants can make fun of their masters and the wives can also complain about their husbands. By using commoners' language, *Kyogen* allured people to tear down class barriers. Sennojo Shigeyama, who is the master of *Kyogan Okuraryu*, indicates that the roots of Kyoto women can be located in the expressions of medieval *Onnagata* actors which was performed by men (Fig. 15).

She predicts her husband's unfaithful behavior and takes appropriate actions against him. In *Kyogan* they were depicted as being extremely clever and were often described by an archain phrase *wawashi* which meant they were skilled at outwitting men. These "*wawashii* Kyoto women" were portrayed in a humorous lively manner in *Nanajyuichiban syokunin Utaawase* during the Muromachi period. In a dialogue that forms the subtext of the play, 142 professions are narrated and analyzed. Of these 34, approximately 24% were women artisans. Among them were weavers, dyers and seamstresses, and their skills have been handed down through the centuries. There were also peddlers and merchants who sold and were involved in the making of *sake*, rice cakes and various kinds of fish. There are streets called Shimodachiuri and Kamitachiuri where the merchants gathered together to conduct their daily business (Fig. 16).

Kyoto women were not necessarily the elegant aristocratic type, but were active in the city as spirited merchants and artisans. Women formed guilds from around this period.

The *Oharame* are particularly known for carrying bundles of twigs on their head from Ohara which they sold along the way. Needless to say, the *Katsurame* were from Katsura. They sold *ayu* that they caught in the Katsura River on their way to Kyoto. The *Shirakawame* also attracted attention in local sources as flower sellers. They even entered the imperial palace at times (Fig. 17).

In a sense these women inherited the Hata clan's entrepreneurial spirit. On the surface the women of Kyoto can be seen as soft-spoken, but they were quite skilled in running their business. There are numerous sources showing these women engaged in similar professions for centuries.

Fig. 15 A medieval women performed by male *Kyogen* actor. © M.Mabuchi

Fig. 16 Women artisans during the medieval period. **a** *Hataori Konkaki*, an image of weaver and dyer; **b** *Kumishi Nuimonoshi*, an image of a seamstress; **c** *Sakana Uri*, an image of a fish seller; **d** *Sake Tsukuri*, an image of a brewer. From the text *Nanajuichiban Syokunin Uta Awase* in the National Diet Library

Fig. 17 A women peddler from the *Jidai Festival* in Kyoto. **a** *Oharame*; **b** *Katsurame*; **c** *Shirakawame*. © M. Mabuchi

At the production center of the Nishijin Brocade which was an excellent article for sale of Kyoto, many women artisans worked. They succeeded to a traditional technique to a daughter from a grandmother to mother. And they balanced housework and child care with work. For many artisans and merchants the work place and home were shared space. The women who played the role of both artisans and merchants had a special advantage with regards to communication.

One of the women whose family has been in the business for centuries commented that the women of Kyoto work really hard raising kids while taking care of business and domestic affairs. These responsibilities is simply taken for granted. Another woman who inherited a weaving business remarked. In Kyoto people are both artisans and merchants. I cannot afford to engage in irresponsible behavior. There is a saying in the family that we have tried to honor. "Righteous behavior proceeds profit".

One of the most famous architectural examples of Kyoto is the *Kyomachiya*. Oddly enough, it is referred to as "the resting spot of the eel" (*Unagi no nedoko*). Since the house itself is extremely narrow. In fact from the outside these structures look as if they are a single house since the spaces between the entrances are extremely narrow. This is a prime example of Kyoto's local culture which has little to do with the courtly ideal. The women who spent a great deal of time in kitchen were called *okudosan* since they worked on handicrafts during the day while taking care of their children. The men's role in these houses was quite ambiguous under these peculiar circumstances.

Since the women were constantly pressed for time, they had to make sure that their household businesses would not fall apart. Perhaps that is why the maxim of which emphasizes "sincerity when dealing with clients and customers" was passed down through the generations. The women who lived through this era had to make a conscious effort to maintain their femininity which is perhaps why the women of Kyoto have become famous throughout Japan.

When I wrote a book about the women of Kyoto, I interviewed women of various professions such as an innovator in the industry of *kimono*, an artist of *kyonui* (traditional embroidery) who worked in companies who produced the famous brands of Europe such as Hermes and Dior. I spoke to an architect of *kyomachiya* and an elderly woman who had been *geiko*, I also had the opportunity to interview a proprietress of a traditional Japanese restaurant, a Buddhist priest, a poet and an art producer. Women who held important positions in the media and artisans who paint traditional lacquer were also consulted and featured prominently in my book.

A common idea that links all these women together is the notion of *en* and the mystical sense that "we are basically allowed to exist in the world through the mercy of the gods and buddhas". The notion of *en* has formed a communal ethos in japan. It often transcends the rigid boundaries that are imposed by the elite section of society. The notion that "we are allowed to live" has roots both in the Shinto and Buddhist traditions that developed in the mountain environment of Kyoto.

As we have seen, the women of Kyoto have transmitted spirit of Hata craftsmanship.

In fact recently it is evident that the number of women working in traditional craft industries is increasing. These women offer hope because their knowledge of the household and workplace offer fresh insights. Perhaps, the women of Kyoto will create the next generation of outstanding artisans that are respected throughout the world.

In conclusion, we can see the role that nature plays in the three perspective that we adopted. Surrounded by mountains on three sides, the woods of Kyoto play a vital role in reducing CO_2. The continental culture has the potential of cultivating peaceful relations among East Asian nations. The cultural contributions that the women of Kyoto have made offer wisdom and promising prospects for the future.

Author Biography

Manami Oka is a historical non-fiction writer on the history and culture of Japan and also the representative of Research Institute of the History of Journalism and Culture in Kyoto LLC.

She was born in Kyoto and is a graduate of Kyoto Notre Dame University, Department of English Language and Literature She has a wide range of experience in the media industry in her past career, through her position as a news caster for the Japan broadcast corporation (NHK) station, and as a producer and director of television programs relating to Kyoto. She has been awarded for her work from the Agency for Cultural Affairs of the Japanese government.

Now, as an expert on the ancient history of Japan and culture of Kyoto, she delivers lectures at various levels, from the local community to high schools and universities. She also serves on committees of Kyoto municipal and prefectural government which deals with issues such as tourism, environment, and culture. She is the writer of many books including *A Spiritual Pilgrimage of Kyoto* (2005) (in Japanese).

Chapter 7
Supplement for Chapter 6: The Wisdom of Traditional Kyoto Culture

Tadashi Yagi

As the consequences of globalization, reductionist philosophy and excessive individualism are being traced back to the development of certain Western ideals, Eastern values which are deeply rooted in its historical tradition are being reconsidered. These ideals were first developed in India and made their way into the ancient capitals of Nara and Kyoto via China and Korea. Zen is a good example of this cultural importation. Manami Oka's essay explores how the Eastern intellectual trends developed historically while situating the role of Kyoto culture in a global context. Oka investigates how the city as a whole confronted and adapted to continental influence. Throughout its history, Kyoto has benefited from its natural surroundings. Much of its cultural development was born out of the wisdom that people gained through their adoration of nature. In sharing their natural resources, the people of Kyoto have tried to consider what they should and should not do.

The religious festivals that were performed in Buddhist temples and shrines enhanced the wisdom that was gained through single-minded nature worship. They also functioned as a link between commerce and aristocratic culture while forming the identity of the local people.

The Yasurai festival of the Imamiya shrine is a good example of a procession that is intended to ward off pestilences. Through these activities, the local people increased their awareness towards various diseases that were circulating at the time. The shrine also promoted the Tanabata festival that benefited merchants who specialized in designing elaborate clothing The merchants expressed their gratitude toward the gods by producing gifts that were submitted as offerings These

---

Some thoughts on Manami Oka's Essay This chapter is supplement for M Oka, The Three Foundations of Kyoto's Traditional Culture (Translated by Jonathan Augustine, Ryukoku University, Faculty of Science and Technology, Kyoto, Japan).

T. Yagi (✉)
Faculty of Economics, Doshisha University, Kyoto, Japan
e-mail: tyagi@mail.doshisha.ac.jp

merchants were able to gather together and humbly perform the prescribed rituals of worship.

One idea that can be promoted from Kyoto is the importance of transmitting specialized aesthetic skills. The Kyoto artisans have managed to develop a productive system that emphasizes coexistence with nature. Due to the influence of logical positivism and an overemphasis on individualism, nature began to be viewed as something to be conquered around the time of the industrial revolution. Since religion started to be viewed as something unscientific, its importance diminished in the local community and "the individual" became estranged. Fortunately, the merchants and artisans of Kyoto maintained their traditions because they were faithful to the wisdom that their ancestors had accumulated. They understood that they could not afford to be distracted by short-sighted individualistic goals. Some of the traditions of Kyoto may seem to be unscientific, so it is necessary to examine why these customs and traditions have survived despite the flux in the social fabric of Japanese society.

Oka has analyzed the role of women as transmitters of culture and wisdom within the local community. They are responsible for instructing children about ethics and morality and have frequently introduced important innovations. When devising a division of labor, the women of Kyoto have chosen to play an active role outside of the household. Their success often resulted from altering the status quo.

Recently, people have begun to examine the role that diversity plays in the process of creation. Men and women are biologically different so they are inspired to create unique forms of art. Drawing on feminine inspiration, the women of Kyoto have definitely enhanced the creative process. It is not an exaggeration to say that the women of Kyoto have cultivated profound knowledge that they accumulated through the ages and have applied it to business. The concept of *en* plays an essential role in bringing people together. Also, the recognition that the individual is fortunate because basically he or she is "allowed to live in this world" gives one a sense of consolation and humility. The wisdom of such trust and humility are some aspects of wisdom that Kyoto could offer the world today.

Chapter 8
Listen to the Stone—Searching for Spiritual Harmony in Polyphonic Coexistence

Stomu Yamash'ta

1 Being Now

In my hometown of Kyoto I am furthering my life as a musician as I reach seventy years of age, with activities involving the instrument made of sanukite. For some thirty years, I have had a dialogue with the stone (sanukite) made instruments and been absorbed in an enquiry into the music of stone. There has been a steady and calm flow of time for me as I listen to the voice of the stone and at the same time communicate with it.

In all the energy of nature, the universe generated from the Void coexists here and now in the actual world of earth in which stone and human beings live together as the result of miraculous phenomena woven through eternal time. Repeatedly, my creative works are all within the series of dialogue. My way of expression is based on training and liberal arts.

Reflecting on the day when I encountered the stone, my way of expression based on my musical sensibility with musical knowledge which I had cultivated in America, Europe, and Japan for forty years was to compose and perform by myself. However, by this everything was completely shattered and made for a second start from scratch.

The cause of my failure originated in the work of my mind itself. To seek expeditiously a result, interlocution with sanukite was not enough. The method I

Translated by Toshifumi Uemura, Japan Lutheran College, Tokyo, Japan.

S. Yamash'ta (✉)
Center for the Study of the Creative Economy, Doshisha University, Kyoto, Japan

Sound Core Co., Ltd., Kyoto, Japan
e-mail: info@sound-core.jp

© The Editor(s) 2018
S. Yamash'ta et al. (eds.), *The Kyoto Manifesto for Global Economics*,
Creative Economy, https://doi.org/10.1007/978-981-10-6478-4_8

adopted was to pursue the expression of Western music in the basis of my self-expression with which I was convinced to create music. Having a firm belief to succeed as I did in the past, the stone music must have been procured social recognition. However, this mental work, or way of thinking could not be applied to sanukite. Although the first five years were truly a severe trial, with this precious experience this struggle has brought me to a different dimension of thinking and divergent style of expression. I have learned a lot from this stone.

To put it simply, that is to live slowly and gently. "Let's make a dialogue at ease without haste and feel that we live together."

Stone lives far much longer than human beings in this earth, universe, and the realm of nature. It tells us that hitherto the abstruse is filled within. Both sanukite and human beings were born from the incidence of Miracle, the Creation, the phenomenon of the universal mundane. In the total balance between mysterious cosmic power and natural power, we are to live and let live peacefully.

The sound of stone could awaken us to know that the invisible world of wave or undulation and our visible material existence are linked through the marvelous energy of sound. Hearing a 'voice' of stone, our hidden intuition and of the muse have generated and perceived space and time ad infinitum in the cosmos and nature. Sanukite gives me this creative power and possibility.

Now let's start the story of this precious stone, sanukite.

2 Sanukite, the Miracle Stone (from the Records of Mr. Maeda Hitoshi,[1] Founder of the Instrument)

Sanukite is called Sanuki-stone and made of bronzite, a type of lava with glasslike characterstics. Almost thirteen million and five hundred thousand years ago, lava flowing forth from the northern part of the central tectonic line of southeast Japan became a layer of Sanukite. One of the most unusual stones in the world, it is distributed around Sakaide, Kanayama, and Kokubudai of Kagawa Prefecture.

When the first humans came to reside in the Japanese Archipelago, this stone was intimately involved in their lives, both for hunting animals and protecting themselves as they lived in the forest. It is said that stone tools were also used as knives, axes, and arrowheads from more than twenty thousand years ago.

At the same time, these ancient people would take these stones—with their beautiful reverberations—and purposely sound them together to enjoy the rhythms as well as relay messages. In short, these stones and humans have had a long association with each other.

---

[1]Dr. Hitoshi Maeda (1929–2008) was born and lived in Shikoku, around Sanuki area. Yamash'ta has made a new approach to associate through Buddhism to create a new direction for the stone's music. During over twenty years, Dr. Maeda and Yamash'ta were fully devoted to support each other to develop the spirit of Sanukite.

This stone was initially described by Dr. Naumann, a geologist from Germany invited by Tokyo Imperial University in 1874. He brought it to the University of Munich, where a Dr. Weinschenk named it sanukitee at the academy in 1891.

In the 5th century B.C. Confucius told us that Li established the order of the heavens and earth and that music brought harmony to the world. Although the music of Emperor Wǔ Wáng, in the Zhou Dynasty, had some beauty, he did not feel it had achieved goodness. Confucius again taught Yan Hui that the tunes of Cheng were the cause of licentious. At the same period in Greece, Plato stated, "Without lyrics, music should not be allowed. The sound itself is not music, but it is nothing but the cries of animals." Such comments show us that, even more than 2000 years ago, philosophers had their own music theory. Music originating from sounds gradually came to express the feelings of human beings and it has developed in accordance with humans and their culture.

Many stories of music related to emperors appear in ancient Chinese history. One example is from the era of Three Sovereigns and Five Emperors (mythological rulers of ancient China of —Fu-xi, Shen-nong, Huang-di, etc.), when the Yellow River civilization came about five thousand years ago.

The Li-ji (or Book of Rites, one of the Five Classics) said, "All modulations of the voice spring from the minds of men. When the feelings are moved within, they are manifested in the sounds of the voice; and when those sounds are combined so as to form compositions, we have what are called airs. Hence, the airs of an age of good order indicate composure and enjoyment. The airs of an age of disorder indicate dissatisfaction and anger, and its government is perversely bad. The airs of a state going to ruin are expressive of sorrow and troubled thought. There is an interaction between the words and airs of the people and the character of their government." This is one of the characteristics of Eastern culture explaining 'the path of ancient wise kings' in the Four Books and Five Classics of Confucianism.

In the era of ancient Chinese Yin 3500 years ago, the sounding stone, qing (ancient Chinese chime) was used for li-yue (Chinese ceremony and music, the fundamental precept of Confucianism) as a component of ba-yin (eight kinds of ancient Chinese musical instruments—a gong, soil whistle, hand drum, etc.). Qing was classified into several types. Yu-qing (made from jade) was used by an emperor, and it was shaped to be semicylindrical or trapezoidal (the base is almost a straight line) in the Yin period. It was already in the Zhou period (1050–256 B.C.), however, when the dimension of five sides was prescribed and the size was decided.

Bian-qing was hung with twelve stones (tones) in a single file, and over time, it evolved into one to which was added four stones for a total of sixteen stones hung to two upper and lower steps. Te-qing, which was used for the court music of ancient China, had one stone; the first tone (same as a sound of the lah), huang-zhong. In the Analects of Confucius, the sound of the stone is mentioned as follows, "The Master was playing the stone-chimes, during the time when he was in Wei."

Subsequently, the stone-instrument evolving through the eras of ancient China was recorded on the Zhou-li or Li-ji as "the most curious and precious instrument in the Zhou Period." And Volume 19 of Yue-ji of Li-ji said, "The sounding-stones give out a tinkling sound, as a summons to the exercise of discrimination. That discrimination may lead to the encountering of death. When the ruler hears the sounding-stone, he thinks of his officers who die in defense of his frontiers."

Thus, the characteristics bequeathed by the sound of stones to the human heart are enumerated, and the thoughts of the ancients attributed to qing are remembered.

Qing had been given an important position as an instrument of the music performance from Yin period; however, it began to decline with the development of the bronze musical instrument before long, finally to disappear in the Tang Period. The gong with a wooden stick had evolved into the bell like qing in the middle of Zhou Dynasty (B.C. 900–800), and the times moved on to the period of Fu-zhong, the bell with 36 protrusions made by Mr. Fu (recorded on the Zhou-li). Hence, the over 2200 years of history–from the Yin to Tang Period—of musical instruments made of stone came to a close.

Probably because a naturally occurring material giving off beautiful tones was not produced or it was overshadowed by the gorgeous Fu-Zhong, the history of qing was over by the Tianbao era of the Tang Dynasty (A.D. 750s).

The musical stone-instrument "qing" was made in ancient China, and seven tone were born from the ancient pentatonic scale; gong, shang, jue, zhi and yu. The name of twelve-tone was recorded on the Zhong-yue at the scene of the questions and answers between Jing-wang, the King of Zhou and Ling-Zhoujiu, the secretary of the court music (B.C. 522). In addition, the original form of today's musical scale was established 2500 years ago, and the twelve tones were sorted into two groups. In this way, the tone of the Yin or Yang based on huang-zhong or da-lu was specified. With the ancient orderly music, I was surprised by the mysterious power of the sounds as follows:

- Gentle sounds to make an infant sleep;
- Sounds to let young people dance with the exciting rhythm of a festival drum or bell;
- Music to bring back memories of a hometown or nostalgia for childhood;
- Sounds to recall a heart of mercy and love during a hymn or prayer.

The mysterious power of sound can but surprise us.

In this way percussion instruments made of stone were highly treasured in ancient times. Now in the 21st century, I play the instruments made of Sanukite from Kanayama, Shikoku Island, Japan. The vibratory characteristics of Sanukite have wide ranges of frequency distribution from low sound ranges to high sound ranges.

The sounds produced by Sanukite contain frequencies that are not capable of being heard by humans. Those sounds higher than the hearing range have frequencies exceeding 500,000 Hz. Dr. A. Tomatis (France) and other scholars mentioned in their papers that high-frequency sounds work effectively even in small amounts to promote brain activities and improve concentration.

In recent years the effects of tonal components have been highly recognized worldwide. An increasing number of people use sound effects to seek possible reactions to living organisms in such a way as to help soothe feelings, grow plants and vegetables by exposing them to music, or make wine and "sake" to music.

3 Revive Tradition and Creation on Sound Spirit

The reason for the use of the word "revive" comes from a heartfelt, deep desire for "blessings" and "hope" for the future of humanity.

In the society and environment of the 21st century, we generally live in dependence on digital technology. In collecting and analyzing a massive amount of data, both natural and social changes are both predicted and planned for coping with these. The future of our society can generally be predicted based on what I call Big Data, which reminds me of the movie "2001—A Space Odyssey" directed by Stanley Kubrick as well as Apollo 11's landing on the Moon in 1969. The Apollo program was one of the American space development programs. This remarkable event was televised live to the national television audience of the United States and to the world. As the result, it gave huge hope to people all over the world. Man's challenge through science technology introduced a new ways of thinking about value. At that time, by witnessing the historical moment, young people all over the world including me caught a glimpse of the future image of mankind and sensed a huge hope to realize a world that had only been a dream

Around that time, as for musical art, electronic sound was introduced and a new musical expression, Avant-garde music, started to be explored by musicians around the world.

In the 1970s electronics were introduced into all the fields of music and drastically changed music styles.

In the 1980s, as electronic technology progressed, the music industry flourished worldwide. Over one and a half centuries, the advance of scientific technology saw improvements progressing from phonographs to analog recording devices such as SP and LP records and cassette tapes and then on to compact discs (CD). Especially with the emergence of the CD technology, the transition from analog to digital accelerated and a new era of digitalization arrived.

One important thing to remember is that the electronic music instrument known as the "synthesizer" was developed in the late 1960s. The invention of this instrument transformed its music expressions and changed music styles and forms significantly.

In 1970s Reggae music was born in a call for a return to ethnic culture, while Punk music arose raising an objection to ethnic cultures and traditions. There was a wide variety of music expressions based on different ideas and principles.

In the late 1970s virtual music, such as Fusion and Cross-over, started by adapting electronic technology. Music expressions based on fusions of different musical genres, such as Classical, Jazz and Rock, transcended ethnical and national boundaries and represented a new concept of human values.

In 1980s Pop music evolved as a developed form of Fusion. Pop music was fueled by video technology and consequently Pop culture started.

After the collapse of the Berlin wall in Germany, the 1990s started with the breaking out of the Gulf War. With national liberation movements and destruction of the old regime, this new era changed the fundamental direction of the music scene from Ideal Expressionism to Recreational Activities. Employing a sampling technique and digital devices, most of the artistic expressions and art works created in the late 19th and the 20th centuries were commercialized with digital technologies and distributed to society as entertainment products. This was the dawn of a consumption of culture for the entertainment business.

Now in the 21st century, life in human society is mostly digitized and systemized. Achieving better social functioning with a higher efficiency and creating a more physically enriched world seem to be the goals to be attained. From now on, digital technology will keep on developing and evolving faster and faster. However, will this digital technology really lead us to an ideal world and bring happiness? The important thing is the fact that we human beings exist in such a mysterious world, consisting of the "non-existence" of such as intangible, immaterial phenomena and the "existence" of physical substances.

In this world, miraculous energy emerges from the Void, an infinite vacuum world that has no absoluteness or perfection. This energy creates both "non-existence" and "existence": universe and phenomena are considered as "non-existence" as they are immaterial, and "existence" means all things material. Is it truly possible to digitize this ever-changing world completely? While living with continuously changing phenomena and existences, how can we human beings harmonize with nature and establish an interacting relationship with it? I would like to contemplate this and seek out possibility and direction from a musician's point of view.

Based on my perception as a musician, I would like to give an example: "Sound" that is created with electronics. This is a sampling technology. Wave motions and wave lengths of digital sound sources created by electronic technology differ from those of natural sound. The important thing is that the digital sound source (digitized sample) becomes a major cause that unifies human thought orientation and creativity as it weakens them. This indicates a decline in multidimensional thinking and originality, which implies a non-diversified world where cultural diversity will disappear. This situation could weaken the human five senses and deny the necessity of developing a sixth sense. If human beings do not appreciate the sensibility gained from miraculous phenomena and instead choose a life based on rationality for virtual reality, it is not so difficult to imagine what kind of society this would lead to in the future.

Music serves as one of the elements of human happiness. Musical expression is one of the greatest and most valuable objectives that humans have acquired. One other is mathematical expression. Music and mathematics—what they have in common is that they provide methods to seek the links between universe, nature, and man spiritually by the laws of universe and nature.

Exploring the artistry of music requires us to be our natural selves. It is essential to catch the wave motion and wavelength of sound in nature. The essence of sound has nothing to do with economic success or popularity.

With my above-mentioned philosophy, now in Kyoto, I am exploring a new culture, combining elements of religion, art, and science. Historically they are just three separate subjects having different standpoints. They have been treated independently. However, for the future of human beings and sustainability of society, it is essential to unite religion, art, and science through dialogue.

Based on this thinking, I have worked on many music projects mainly in Kyoto for the 21st century. I started with the "Kyoto 21C Millennium", a festival. On December 31, 2000, for the first time in many winters, the traditional Kyoto fire festivals were held all together. The giant bonfire of Daimonji, the shape of the character Dai meaning large or great, was lit with the eternal flame of Mt. Hiei. Mt. Kurama's and other fire festivals were also held. These fire festivals were held with the intent to inherit the spirit of Kyoto.

I was the general artistic director of the project. The concept of the festival was the "revival of traditional spirit". The culture of Kyoto is characterized by the spirituality established from polytheism. Respect for harmony and order between man, material things, nature, and the universe represents coexistence. This shows the mandala perspective of the world.

Over 1200 years, the culture of Kyoto has been a repetition of creation and revival. For this reason, many traditions and heritages remaining in Kyoto today are the living evidence transcending time. It is marvelous that Kyoto has a traditional culture with memories of fusing Eastern and Western cultures. People, objects, or matters keep on evolving with the times. The millennium festival was held to reaffirm the philosophy of linking the past and present. The result was many responses from all over Japan and the world that were filled with interest, admiration, and anticipation. At present, Kyoto enjoys the respect of people around the world as a world-famous cultural city, for which it is truly grateful.

In 2001, I introduced my music "Listen to the Future" at the opening ceremony at Nijo Castle, a world heritage site where the last Shogun made a declaration for the modernization of Japan.

In 2004, I performed KUON-SHIKI/sound memorial at the lecture hall of Myoshinji Temple. KUON-SHIKI is the "offering ceremony for sound" that I created, based on my knowledge gained through a three-year study of Buddhism and Buddhist music at the main "dojo", a Buddhism training monastery, of Toji Temple in Kyoto after ceasing all my music activities overseas and returning to Japan.

In 2005 I completed "Echo." The music was based on "Saga", a myth and legend handed down the Viking culture of Iceland. It was produced with modern Icelandic dialects and performed with an Iceland children's choir. In June 2005, at the Théâtre du Châtelet and Maison de la Culture du Japon in Paris, France, "On-Zen" had it worldwide premiere. Since then, for 11 years, "On-Zen" has been held both in Kyoto and France. Now, "On-Zen" has become an annual ceremony jointly performed with Shinto at the lecture hall of the Daitokuji Temple initiated by Zen master Myoho Takada.

"On" means "Otodama (sound spirit)". The mysterious energy of sound leads us to a world harmonized with universe, nature, man, and stone.

Zen teaches Nothingness. Nothingness means ultimate truth, virtue and beauty. It is said that all living things, all beings, and all reality are of the truth, virtue, beauty and blessing coming out of Nothingness. The ceremony with the fusion of

On and Zen is to wish for world peace. At On-Zen, I serve as artistic director and performer of the musical instrument made out of stone called Sanukite.

As I approach the end of this Chapter, I would like to write about a shrine ritual, the "Orihime Tanabata Festival," which was revived in August, 2015. The center of the festival is Orihime-no-Ohkami enshrined in Murasakino, Northern Kyoto. Orihime-no-Ohakami is a protectorate goddess of textile craftsmen and has been worshiped by people liveng around Murasakino, Nishijin as a goddess for artistic skill and creativity. Historically, Nishijin is an area where weavers and their families live together. The "kimono" woven by those skilled craftsmen is called Nishijin-ori, which has become one of the most valuable kimonos in Japan. However, in modern Japanese society, due to changes in lifestyles, the kimono became a formal dress only for special occasions. As a result, the Nishijin society has shrunk significantly. The uniqueness of Nishijin-ori is the handwork depending on artisan's senses and skills. Each process in the procedure is handled by a specialist; thus, it takes much time to make one kimono. This production system with low rate of productivity is clearly contrary to the principle of efficiency that today's society espouses.

In the past, a festival brought people prosperity, blessing, and harmony. If the festival ceases, the relationships within society would also be lost. The Chief Priest, Mr. Sasaki of Imamiya Shrine, explained the situation to me and said, "The Shinto priest serves for society to relate with shrine."

This is why I restarted the festival to revive Orihime Tanabata. I contributed to the festival as an art director with Sanukite.

At both the On Zen ceremony and Orihime Tanabata Festival, the Sanukite stone plays an incredibly important role. The sound and resonance of stone continue to give inspiration and peace not only to myself but also so many related people. The stone begins to talk to us: "Enjoy your life to the utmost and promote harmony with nature. Calmly and slowly.... Feel it in your heart, respect the order of the universe and love the world."

Shift to a new era with harmonious feeling and look at the sky, mountains, rivers, sea, trees and others, as one.

I am not sure how long I can pursue my life of music. However, I live with great joy and happiness now in Kyoto. This is the city created by many great predecessors, covering a period of 1200 years. Every day I feel that Kyoto is the embodiment of peace and the benevolence of compassions emerging from a "crystallization of hearts" of those who have lived there.

Thinking back on what I went through, the wonderful experiences I had in the United States and Europe for 20 years have surely helped establish my present situation. The world encountered with a variety of senses through music was truly surprising. My musical expressions are from something unknown. It might be from a holy spirit; it may be a sense of creativity with a combination of unconsciousness and inspiration. This must be the source of my activities. Various rhythms and prosodies of every human being have enriched our society.

Living in the 21st century, we seem to be losing diversity in society with the development of digital skills. As a result, the global society shows a tendency to emphasize the economy as the seat of our primary values. What we are to seek is a real cultural combination of the East and the West. Harmonizing and integrating both analogue and digital ways of thinking is necessary to open a new door to 'the super analogue world'.

Our lives are created with both "Enishi," or relations, and "Yui," or combination. To feel a sense of this principle, the active work of the natural heart is required. The heart is a mirror of life. The more one polishes it, the more it shines, which brings one to the world of beauty. Nature tells us to live beautifully, and, as a result, this can be our precious heritage for beauty. Humans are interlinked with the energy of the abundant Nothingness and infinite beauty.

Closing this chapter, I will conclude it with my decision to keep up music and art activities for the rest of my limited life. This stems mainly from the essence of 'Polyphony' as taught to me by the dialogue with my stones.

'Polyphony' is the essence of the ecological scheme, namely the word that represents the world of multiple sound tracks generated by activities in nature. Scientifically, this continuously circulates. In other words, we call it *Kanzeon*, bodhisattva of mercy and salvation. In Nirvana, sutras teach that mountains, rivers, grass, trees, and all things have the Buddha nature in them.

In the 21st century, digital technology occupies most of our daily lives. The same thing is true in the musical world. That is to say, we hear through virtual sound technology, which actually only imitates real sound. However, the most important factor is the polyphony, which essentially circulates in nature and requires music with impromptu inspiration and innovation to coexist in harmony.

When digital sound, with its virtual reality covers the earth, it implies that the natural world itself will disappear. It is crucial to rethink what it means to live as a human being with nature. For this reason, I want to suggest understanding polyphony in a new way to know better the world of analog.

Chapter 9
Zero and Emptiness (Vacuum/Void) in Physics and Chemistry

Kazuyoshi Yoshimura

In this chapter, I will explain what the absolute zero and the absolute emptiness (vacuum/void) are in the fields of quantum physics and chemistry. At first one likely believes that there is nothing—no particles at all—in the vacuum state. Is it correct? The importance of this question even extends to other fields, including philosophy and religion. To answer this question, we must examine the history of modern physical sciences since the early 20th century. Here, I will discuss quantum physics and chemistry, especially solid-state quantum physics and chemistry.

A vacuum is defined as a space entirely devoid of matter, in which there are no particles. However, in Albert Einstein's theory of relativity, energy (E) and mass (m) are equivalent and can be interconverted. Thus, energy can produce matter, and vice versa, according to

$$E = mc^2, \qquad (1)$$

where c is the speed of light (Einstein 1905a). Therefore, the vacuum, even with the absence of particles, should correspond to a full of particles behind it if there is huge energy in it. This is the remarkable result from Einstein's classical physics (mechanics), which was discovered and published early in the 20th century.

K. Yoshimura (✉)
Department of Chemistry, Graduate School of Science, Kyoto University, Kyoto 606-8502, Japan

Research Center for Low Temperature and Material Sciences, Kyoto University, Kyoto 606-8501, Japan

International Research Unit of Integrated Complex System Science, Kyoto University, Kyoto 606-8501, Japan

International Research Unit of Advanced Future Studies, Kyoto University, Kyoto 606-8502, Japan
e-mail: kyhv@kuchem.kyoto-u.ac.jp; yoshimura.kazuyoshi.8e@kyoto-u.ac.jp

In quantum physics (mechanics), which was also developed early in the 20th century, and has become central in all the sciences, how do we deal with the vacuum state?

In quantum physics, elementary particles should be represented as matter waves, as proposed by de Broglie (1923). These are particles that also behave as waves. de Broglie's idea of wave-particle duality is analogous to the quantum theory of light proposed by Max Planck and Einstein at the start of the 20th century (Planck 1900; Einstein 1905b).

Niels Bohr developed his model of the atom based on de Broglie's concept (Bohr 1913). In the Bohr model, electrons in an atom can be described as standing-wave states of de Broglie waves, leading to the discrete energy levels of electrons in the atom. Subsequently, this way of quantizing energy was developed independently by Erwin Schrödinger and Werner Heisenberg as wave mechanics (Schrödinger 1926) and matrix mechanics (Heisenberg 1925), respectively. These two superficially different theories were found afterward to be essentially equivalent, and are known as quantum mechanics, leading to the first quantization of the discrete energy of electrons (particles) in atoms and materials (Dirac 1930). Here, the most widely used and important equation, which represents the motion of electrons, is the Schrödinger wave-equation

$$i\hbar\frac{\partial}{\partial t}\varphi(\mathbf{r}, t) = H\varphi(\mathbf{r}, t) = \left\{-\frac{\hbar^2}{2m}\left(\frac{\partial^2}{\partial x^2} + \frac{\partial^2}{\partial y^2} + \frac{\partial^2}{\partial z^2}\right) + V(\mathbf{r})\right\}\varphi(\mathbf{r}), \quad (2)$$

where $\hbar$ is the Planck constant, $V(\mathbf{r})$ is the potential energy, t is time and $\mathbf{r}(x, y, z)$ is space. H is the Hamiltonian, which is the operator by which the eigenvalue of the total energy, E, can be obtained in operating H on wave function, φ (Schrödinger 1926). In the left-hand term, the energy can be expressed as the first derivative of the wave function φ with respect to t, whereas the energy can be derived as the second derivative of φ with respect to $\mathbf{r}(x, y, z)$ in the right-hand term. Therefore, time and space are not treated equally in the Schrödinger equation. This fact does not appear to satisfy Einstein's theory of relativity (Einstein 1905c), and was considered as a big problem in quantum mechanics early in the 20th century, although quantum mechanics had contributed much to solving many scientific problems. Paul Dirac solved this problem in 1928 in his famous relativistic quantum theory of electron waves in his genius and creative way which nobody else could hit on (Dirac 1926a, 1930). The Dirac equation is written as

$$i\hbar\frac{\partial\varphi}{c\partial t} = H\varphi = -i\hbar\alpha \cdot \left(\frac{\partial}{\partial x} + \frac{\partial}{\partial y} + \frac{\partial}{\partial z}\right)\varphi + \beta mc\varphi, \quad (3)$$

where α and β are matrices as

9 Zero and Emptiness (Vacuum/Void) in Physics and Chemistry

$$\alpha_1 = \begin{pmatrix} 0 & 0 & 0 & 1 \\ 0 & 0 & 1 & 0 \\ 0 & 1 & 0 & 0 \\ 1 & 0 & 0 & 0 \end{pmatrix}, \alpha_2 = \begin{pmatrix} 0 & 0 & 0 & -i \\ 0 & 0 & i & 0 \\ 0 & -i & 0 & 0 \\ i & 0 & 0 & 0 \end{pmatrix},$$

$$\alpha_3 = \begin{pmatrix} 0 & 0 & 1 & 0 \\ 0 & 0 & 0 & -1 \\ 1 & 0 & 0 & 0 \\ 0 & -1 & 0 & 0 \end{pmatrix} \text{ and } \beta = \begin{pmatrix} 1 & 0 & 0 & 0 \\ 0 & 1 & 0 & 0 \\ 0 & 0 & -1 & 0 \\ 0 & 0 & 0 & -1 \end{pmatrix}$$

Both the time and space parts of equation are treated equally: they are represented as first derivatives of φ with respect to t and $\mathbf{r}(x, y, z)$. Dirac's theory explained all the physical properties of electrons properly for the first time, with a half-integer spin quantum number of 1/2 and a g-factor of 2, leading to the spin magnetic moment of the electron being 1 μ_B, where μ_B is the Bohr magneton. Although Dirac's relativistic quantum mechanics achieved great success in unifying quantum mechanics and Einstein's theory of relativity, the solution of Dirac's equation resulted in another big problem. Here, the solution of the Dirac's equation can be written as eigenvalue E of Hamiltonian H as

$$E = \pm\sqrt{p^2c^2 + m^2c^4}, \tag{4}$$

where p is the electron momentum. The positive solution corresponds to the energy of electrons. However, the meaning of the negative solution was not understood at the time, and was extensively discussed because the theory was considered otherwise elegant and correct (Dirac 1926a). Eventually the negative solution was found to correspond to the energy of positively charged electrons, called positrons, rather than to electrons with negative energy (Dirac 1926a). This result had a huge influence on physics, especially high-energy physics, because it implies the existence of antiparticles and antimatter corresponding to particles and matter, respectively. Therefore, a vacuum contains particles and the same number of antiparticles such as electrons and positrons, respectively. The concept of pair annihilation of particles and antiparticles or of matter and antimatter also arose from this finding. If a particle meets its antiparticle, they disappear through pair annihilation. In fact, when a positron meets an electron in some material, they disappear and a gamma ray is emitted,

$$e^+ + e^- \rightarrow h\nu \ (\gamma - ray). \tag{5}$$

This phenomenon is called electron-positron annihilation (or simply called positron annihilation) and is used in applied sciences such as material science, to investigate the defects in materials (Brandt and Dupasquier 1983; Schultz and Lynn 1988). The lifetime of a positron in a material depends on the material's defects, such as vacancies, dislocations and voids. Thus, when a particle meets an antiparticle, a high-energy vacuum is created.

Pair creation of particles and antiparticles is also an important concept. A particle and an antiparticle can be created from a high-energy vacuum,

$$Vacuum + h\nu \ (high \ energy) \rightarrow e^+ + e^-. \tag{6}$$

In quantum electro-dynamics (QED), vacuum breaking has been extensively discussed (Landau and Lifshits 1934; Hubbell 2006). This phenomenon is not out of the ordinary in QED, although high energies on the order of at least mega-electronvolts (10^6 eV:1 eV corresponds to about 10^4 K) are required to break a vacuum. Furthermore, antiprotons have recently been produced at CERN (Martin et al. 2016).

The most extreme example of vacuum breaking and pair creation is the Big Bang at the beginning and the initial stages of the Universe more than 100 billion years ago (Alpher et al. 1948; Weinberg 1977). At the Big Bang the Universe was just like the size of the tip of a sewing needle at extremely high temperatures of $\sim 10^{32}$ K at 10^{-44} s and $\sim 10^{29}$ K at 10^{-38} s, and in the eons since, the Universe has cooled to its present temperature of 3 K (Penzias and Wilson 1965). In the 3 min after the Big Bang, all the matter in the Universe was created by pair creation and spontaneous symmetry breaking according to the Big Bang theory (Weinberg 1977).

In quantum physics how are the creation and annihilation of matter and particles treated? Quantum field theory is introduced to creation and annihilation in the second quantization theory in which the field itself is quantized (Dirac 1930; Sakurai 1994). The most important concept is that the creation and annihilation conjugate operators, a^+ and a, play important roles in the framework of quantum field theory. The particle state, φ_n, with n particles is represented as $\varphi_n = |n\rangle$ or $\langle n|$, where $\langle\,|$ is the bra vector and $|\,\rangle$ is the ket vector, and $\langle\,|$ and $|\,\rangle$ together are called bracket vectors in Hilbert spaces and are conjugate with each other. This notation was introduced by Dirac (1930) and is called the Dirac formalism. In this notation, the vacuum state $\varphi_V = \varphi_0$ is defined and expressed as

$$\varphi_V = \varphi_0 = |0\rangle. \tag{7}$$

If a^+ and a operate on $\varphi_V = \varphi_0 = |0\rangle$, the results are

$$\begin{cases} a^+ |0\rangle = |1\rangle = \varphi_1 \\ a |0\rangle = 0 \end{cases}, \tag{8}$$

If a operates on $\varphi_1 = |1\rangle$, the state returns to the vacuum as $a |1\rangle = |0\rangle = \varphi_V$. More generally, where a^+ and a operate on $\varphi_n = |n\rangle$, the results are

$$\begin{cases} a^+ |n\rangle = \sqrt{n+1}\,|n+1\rangle \\ a |n\rangle = \sqrt{n}\,|n-1\rangle \end{cases}, \tag{9}$$

which means that the state $\varphi_n = |n\rangle$ becomes $\varphi_{n+1} = |n+1\rangle$ or $\varphi_{n-1} = |n-1\rangle$ after the operation. Thus, we can obtain the next formula algebraically as

$$\langle n|a^+ a|n\rangle = \langle n|a^+ \sqrt{n}|n-1\rangle = n\langle n|n\rangle = n, \tag{10}$$

where $\langle n|n\rangle = 1$ is the orthonormality of the wave function in quantum mechanics. Therefore, a^+a is the number operator, by which the number of particles in the system can be obtained.

Quantum field theory was developed to describe the subatomic scales of physics, as in elementary particle physics and solid-state physics, it has been adopted to explain the early Universe just after the Big Bang by astrophysicists and high-energy physicists, such as Steven Hawking (Hawking 1988). At the beginning of the Universe, creation and annihilation may have occurred frequently at the horizon of the Universe, leading to the theory of cosmic inflation (Sato 1981; Guth 1981).

The concept of a vacuum involving the creation and annihilation operators is easier to understand and apply to solid-state sciences, such as solid-state physics and chemistry. Elementary particles are classified as fermions and bosons, which follow the quantum statistics of the Fermi-Dirac distribution (Fermi 1926; Dirac 1926b) or the Bose-Einstein distribution (Bose 1924), respectively. The most important differences are that the quantum spin number of a fermion is a half-integer and that of a boson is an integer, and that in the two-particle state, the wave function of fermions changes sign, whereas that of bosons does not. These differences lead to Pauli's exclusion principle for fermions (Pauli 1925): no two fermions can occupy the same quantum state simultaneously in a system. Bosons do not follow this law, so Einstein suggested that bosons should form what is now called the Bose-Einstein condensate (BEC), in which all the bosons assume the lowest energy state at low temperatures (Einstein 1925). An example is the superfluidity of liquid helium-4 at 2.2 K (London 1938). Helium-4 has an atom number of 2 and has two protons and two neutrons (atomic mass of 4), leading to its quantum spin number of zero, therefore, helium-4 is a boson. In a BEC, if bosons are treated as de Broglie particle waves, the bosons move in phase (Landau 1941; Bogoliubov 1947). In quantum field theory, the bosonic state in a BEC can be expressed by the second quantization method as (Landau 1941; Bogoliubov 1947)

$$\begin{cases} |n\rangle = \dfrac{(b^+)^n}{\sqrt{n!}} \varphi_V = \dfrac{(b^+)^n}{\sqrt{n!}} |0\rangle, \\ b^+ b \varphi_n = b^+ b|n\rangle = n \end{cases} \tag{11}$$

where b^+ and b are the creation and annihilation operators for bosons, and b^+b is the bosonic number operator. The bosons are at the lowest energy represented in this formula.

The gas or liquid state of fermions, such as electrons, can be written as (Landau and Lifshitz 1980)

$$\phi_F = \prod_{k \leq k_F} a^+_{-k\downarrow} a^+_{k\uparrow} \varphi_0 = \prod_{k \leq k_F} B^+_k \varphi_0 = \prod_{k \leq k_F} B^+_k |0\rangle, \tag{12}$$

where $\uparrow$ and $\downarrow$ represent the up and down spins of electrons, respectively, k is the wave number (the momentum $\boldsymbol{p}$ of the electron is written as $p = \hbar k$ with $\hbar = h/2\pi$), k_F is the Fermi wave number, and $B^+_k = a^+_{-k\downarrow} a^+_{k\uparrow}$ is the pair creation operator for an electron-pair with $-k \downarrow$ and $k \uparrow$. Hereafter, we use electrons as a typical example of fermions. This state of the electrons in Eq. (12) corresponds to Pauli paramagnetic metals, in which electron pairs with opposite wave number vectors and opposite spins as $-k \downarrow$ and $k \uparrow$ are contained in the vacuum state and fill energy levels up to the Fermi energy, $E_F = \hbar^2 k_F^2/2m$ (Pauli 1927; Kittel 1953; Ashcroft and Mermin 1976). This behavior arises from Pauli's exclusion principle (Pauli 1925, 1927).

How to explain correlation effects between electrons in the metallic and Pauli paramagnetic state? How to understand the insulating state of electrons is going to be this metallic and Pauli paramagnetic state? The Hubbard Hamiltonian is important for answering these questions (Hubbard 1963).

$$H = -t \sum_{\langle i, j \rangle, \sigma} \left(a^+_{i,\sigma} a_{j,\sigma} + a^+_{j,\sigma} a_{i,\sigma} \right) + U \sum_{i=1}^{N} a^+_{i\uparrow} a_{i\uparrow} \cdot a^+_{i\downarrow} a_{i\downarrow} \tag{13}$$

Here, t is the value of the transfer integral, U is the strength of the onsite Coulomb interaction, σ is spin $\uparrow$ or $\downarrow$, and i and j represent the atomic sites to which the electrons belong. The electron momentum $p = \hbar k$ is $\sim \hbar k_F$, because the electrons with $k \ll k_F$ are confined within the Brillouin zone and cannot move. The first term describes the energy gain when the electrons move from sites i to j. The second term describes the energy loss due to the Coulomb repulsion when electrons with $\uparrow$ and $\downarrow$ spins occupy the same site i. Therefore, when $t > U$, an electron can move from site i to j, leading to the metallic electronic state in the Hubbard model. When $t < U$, an electron cannot move, leading to the insulating electronic state in the Hubbard model. Creation and annihilation are again important for discussing and explaining the metal-insulator Mott transition (Hubbard 1963; Mott 1949).

If the exchange interaction between electrons is ferromagnetic, and exceeds the Stoner condition, the Fermi liquid system is in the itinerant ferromagnetic state (Stoner 1938), which is a typical example of a collective state (mode) of electrons. Stoner theory is mean field theory applied to the itinerant system. The magnetic moments of ferromagnetic materials are mainly due to the electron spins. At finite temperature and even at low temperatures, the magnetic excitation, which is spin excitation, is called magnon excitation and is important for understanding magnetic properties, including their origin. The Holstein-Primakoff model well describes magnetic magnon excitations, which are virtual bosons, like energy quanta in quantum mechanics (Holstein and Primakoff 1940). In magnon theory, the total spin operator, S_x, S_y and S_z, which give the amplitudes of spin components when they operate on the wave function, φ, are described by the bosonic creation and annihilation operators, b^+ and b for magnons as

$$\begin{cases} S_+ = S_x + iS_y = \hbar\sqrt{2s}\sqrt{1 - \dfrac{b^+b}{2s}}\, b \\ S_- = S_x - iS_y = \hbar\sqrt{2s}\,b^+ \sqrt{1 - \dfrac{b^+b}{2s}} \end{cases} \qquad (14)$$

and

$$S_z = \hbar(s - b^+b), \qquad (15)$$

where S_z is the projection of spin to the quantized axis, z, and S_+ and S_- are spin-raising and -lowering operators. Thus, the magnetically excited state can be expressed by introducing and utilizing virtual bosons like energy quanta in the magnetic state. The spin-wave state corresponds to that with magnons created in the system. When a magnon is created, the magnetization is lowered by $\hbar$ in S_z, decreasing the magnetization in ferromagnetically ordered state. Finally, n magnons are excited, and the spin projection to z, $\langle S \rangle$, becomes

$$\langle S \rangle = S_z \varphi = \hbar\{s - (b^+b)^n\}|0\rangle_B, \qquad (16)$$

where $|0\rangle_B$ is the vacuum state of bosons (magnons), which is the state with no magnons. Spin-wave (magnon) thoery gives $T^{3/2}$ dependence of the magnetization in ferromagnets at low temperatures, which agree well with many experimental results (Kittel 1953; Ashcroft and Mermin 1976; Holstein and Primakoff 1940; Holtzberg et al. 1964). The magnons are elementary spin excitations and are also treated as virtual (pseudo-) bosons, leading to the magnon BEC state at low temperatures, which was found in some antiferromagnetic compounds under magnetic fields (Nikuni et al. 2000; Nawa et al. 2011). Therefore, the creation and annihilation of particles are also important in solid-state physics.

In an itinerant-electron (metallic) system, spin excitation becomes so important that it is treated as self-consistent renormalization (SCR) of spin fluctuations to the magnetic free energy, to exceed the Stoner mean field theory (Stoner 1938) and the dynamical mean field theory, called the random phase approximation (RPA) theory with no mode-mode coupling of spin fluctuations (Murata and Doniach 1972). Moriya and Takahashi have developed the SCR theory of spin fluctuations for itinerant-electron magnetic systems (Moriya and Kawabata 1973; Moriya 1979, 1981, 1985, 1987; Takahashi and Yoshimura 2012; Takahashi 2013). The definitions of spin fluctuations, $\langle S^2 \rangle = \langle S^2 \rangle_T + \langle S^2 \rangle_{Z.P.}$, which are magnetic excitations and band fluctuations in itinerant-electron magnetic systems, are

$$\begin{cases} \langle S^2 \rangle_T = \dfrac{6}{N_0^2} \sum_q \int_0^\infty \dfrac{d\omega}{\pi} n(\omega) Im\chi(q, \omega) \\ \langle S^2 \rangle_{Z.P.} = \dfrac{3}{N_0^2} \sum_q \int_0^\infty \dfrac{d\omega}{\pi} Im\chi(q, \omega) \end{cases}, \qquad (17)$$

where $\langle S^2 \rangle_T$ is the thermal spin fluctuations, $\langle S^2 \rangle_{Z.P.}$ is the zero-point spin fluctuations, q is the wave vector of the spin fluctuation ($\hbar q$ is the momentum of the spin fluctuation), ω is the frequency of the spin fluctuation ($\hbar\omega$ is the energy of the spin fluctuation), N_0 is the number of magnetic atoms in the system, and $Im\chi(q, \omega)$ is the imaginary part of the dynamical magnetic susceptibility as a function of q and ω. Furthermore, $n(\omega)$ is the bosonic factor, namely the boson number operator written as

$$n(\omega) = b^+ b\varphi(\omega). \qquad (18)$$

The difference of $\langle S^2 \rangle_T$ from $\langle S^2 \rangle_{Z.P.}$ is only the presence of $n(\omega)$. Moreover, $Im\chi(q, \omega)$ is usually written by the following double Lorentzian formula as

$$Im\chi(q, \omega) = \dfrac{\chi(0,0)}{1 + q^2/\kappa^2} \cdot \dfrac{\omega \Gamma_q}{\omega^2 + \Gamma_q^2}, \qquad (19)$$

where κ and Γ_q represent the q- and ω(energy)-width of the spin fluctuation spectrum, and κ^2 corresponds to the inverse susceptibility, $1/\chi$. In the SCR theory, κ and Γ_q are important spin-fluctuation parameters for expressing magnetic quantities, such as the ferromagnetic transition temperature, called the Curie temperature, T_C, and the temperature dependence of the magnetic susceptibility above T_C (Moriya and Kawabata 1973; Moriya 1979, 1981, 1985, 1987; Takahashi and Yoshimura 2012; Takahashi 2013; Takahashi and Moriya 1985). The SCR theory of spin fluctuations, which is the mode-mode coupling theory between different wave q-vectors of spin fluctuations, has explained many experimental magnetic properties of the itinerant ferromagnets and antiferromagnets, for example, the low Curie temperature T_C in itinerant-electron systems and the dynamical measurements of spin dynamics in itinerant magnets (Moriya 1979, 1981, 1985, 1987; Takahashi and Yoshimura 2012; Takahashi 2013; Takahashi and Moriya 1985; Yoshimura et al. 1987, 1988).

After providing quantitative evidence for the SCR theory in 1985 (Takahashi and Moriya 1985), Takahashi assumed that Eq. (20) is valid even in explaining magnetic properties at finite temperatures (Takahashi 1986). He has developed his theory of spin fluctuations for several decades and has obtained some more important results by assuming that total spin fluctuations, namely, the total square amplitude of the local spin fluctuation, are constant and conserved even in the itinerant system as (Takahashi and Yoshimura 2012; Takahashi 2013; Takahashi 1986).

$$\langle S_{loc}^2 \rangle = \langle S_{loc}^2 \rangle_T + \langle S_{loc}^2 \rangle_{Z.P.} = const., \tag{20}$$

Equation (20) is naturally satisfied in the localized moment system. Takahashi assumed the Eq. (20) is valid even in an itinerant system, although that is not intuitive in the itinerant system. By using the relation deduced from the Eq. (20), the magnetic properties at finite temperatures can be reproduced and explained (Takahashi 1986; Yoshimura et al. 1999; Ohta and Yoshimura 2009; Yang et al. 2013; Imai et al. 2014). This allows the unification of the itinerant-electron magnetism (Takahashi and Yoshimura 2012; Takahashi 1986, 2013; Moriya and Takahashi 1978) between the Pauli paramagnetic weak limit (Moriya and Kawabata 1973) and the localized-moment limit, even in the metallic state (Anderson 1959). Again the creation and annihilation of pseudo-particles and spin excitations (i.e., spin fluctuations) are important in explaining itinerant-electron magnetism.

In the next section, superconductivity is discussed, which is another typical example of a collective mode of electrons in solid-state physics. Superconductivity was discovered by Onnes in 1911 in metallic Hg (Onnes 1911), and described in the 1957 Bardeen-Cooper-Schrieffer (BCS) theory of superconductivity by utilizing second quantization methods, such as the quantum field theory of quantum mechanics (Bardeen et al. 1957). There have been many developments in this field including the remarkable discovery of high-T_c cuprate (T_c is the superconducting critical temperature) by Bednorz and Müller in 1986 (Bednorz and Müller 1986). Next, BCS theory (Bardeen et al. 1957) is discussed to demonstrate the importance of the creation and annihilation of pseudo-particles in explaining the behavior of collective electrons.

In BCS theory (Bardeen et al. 1957), the BCS electronic state is considered as

$$\varphi_\theta - \prod_k \left(u_k + \exp(i\theta) v_k B_k^+\right)\varphi_0 = \prod_k \left(u_k + \exp(i\theta) v_k B_k^+\right)|0\rangle. \tag{21}$$

Here, B_k^+ and B_k are the bosonic creation and annihilation operators of the electron pair, as in Eq. (12), which are expressed as

$$B_k^+ = a_{-k\downarrow}^+ a_{k\uparrow}^+, \quad B_k = a_{k\uparrow} a_{-k\downarrow}, \tag{22}$$

The electron pair is called a Cooper pair in superconductivity. Furthermore, u_k and v_k are parameters, that are related by

$$u_k^2 + v_k^2 = 1, \tag{23}$$

$$u_k = \begin{cases} 0 & (k \ll k_F) \\ 1 & (k \gg k_F) \end{cases}, \quad v_k = \begin{cases} 1 & (k \ll k_F) \\ 0 & (k \gg k_F) \end{cases}, \tag{24}$$

where $exp(i\theta)$ in Eq. (21) is the phase factor in the phase description of the wave function. The superconducting state is assumed to be the BEC state of Cooper pairs of electrons, where the Cooper pairs have the phase θ, so that they move in phase in the superconducting BEC state with the same value of $exp(i\theta)$.

The BCS Hamiltonian is (Bardeen et al. 1957)

$$H = \sum_{k,\sigma} \left(\frac{\hbar^2 k^2}{2m} - \frac{\hbar^2 k_F^2}{2m} \right) a_{k\sigma}^+ a_{k\sigma} - \frac{g}{V} \sum_k{}' \sum_l{}' B_k^+ B_l, \qquad (25)$$

where the first term is the relative kinetic energy compared with the Fermi Energy, E_F, the second term is the interaction between the Cooper pairs, g/V is the strength of their interaction per volume, and $\sum'$ is the summation of the wave vector, k or l, near k_F. By Eq. (25) operating on the BCS state of Eq. (21), we obtain the relative energy compared with the non-superconducting (normal) state. When g is positive, the interaction between the Cooper pairs is attractive, and the superconducting state is stabilized. In the BCS theory, this positive interaction is attributed to the electron-phonon (energy quantum of lattice vibration) interaction. In other words, the phonon scattering of the electrons is the origin of the attraction of the Cooper pairs. Therefore, in the second term of the Eq. (25), when the electron pair with wave vector l is scattered by the phonon to become the electron pair with wave vector k, the system gains the energy of g per V (Bardeen et al. 1957). However, the Hamiltonian in Eq. (25) cannot be solved because it includes the many-body problem. Therefore, BCS theory can be modified to give the mean field theory via the one-body approximation as

$$H_m = \sum_{k,\sigma} \left(\frac{\hbar^2 k^2}{2m} - \frac{\hbar^2 k_F^2}{2m} \right) a_{k\sigma}^+ a_{k\sigma} - \sum_k{}' (\Delta^* B_k + \Delta B_k^+) + \frac{V}{g}|\Delta|^2, \qquad (26)$$

where H_m is the Hartree-Fock-Gor'kov Hamiltonian (Gor'kov 1959). The superconducting gap energy Δ and its conjugate Δ^* are introduced, where Δ can be written as:

$$\Delta = \frac{g}{V} \sum_k{}' \langle \varphi_\theta | a_{k\uparrow} a_{-k\downarrow} | \varphi_\theta \rangle = \frac{g}{V} exp(i\theta) \sum_k{}' u_k v_k. \qquad (27)$$

The second term can be written with one bosonic creation or annihilation operator in Eq. (26), whereas the term is given by the product of two operators in Eq. (25). The third term of Eq. (26) is a correction of the mean field approximation.

Bogoliubov produced the formalism of the diagonalization of the BCS mean field Hamiltonian (Bogoliubov 1958). He introduced the Bogoliubov transformation, $a \to \alpha$, as

$$\begin{cases} a_{k\uparrow} = u_k \alpha_{k\uparrow} - v_k e^{i\theta} \alpha_{-k\downarrow}^+ \\ a_{k\downarrow} = u_k \alpha_{k\downarrow} + v_k e^{i\theta} \alpha_{-k\uparrow}^+ \end{cases}. \qquad (28)$$

Then, the mean field Hamiltonian can be transformed to the following diagonalized form (Bogoliubov 1958)

$$H_m = \Omega_0 + \sum_k E_k \left(\alpha_{k\uparrow}^+ \alpha_{k\uparrow} + \alpha_{k\downarrow}^+ \alpha_{k\downarrow} \right). \tag{29}$$

with

$$\Omega_0 = \sum_k 2\xi_k v_k^2 - \sum_k{}' 2u_k v_k |\Delta| + \frac{V}{g} |\Delta|^2. \tag{30}$$

Here, ξ_k and E_k are defined as

$$\xi_k = \frac{\hbar^2 k^2}{2m} - \frac{\hbar^2 k_F^2}{2m} \tag{31}$$

and

$$E_k = \left(\xi_k^2 + |\Delta|^2 \right)^{1/2}. \tag{32}$$

Therefore, Ω_0 is the energy of the superconducting state, and two pseudo-fermions called Bogoliubov pseudo-particles, represented by $\alpha_{k\uparrow}^+ \alpha_{k\uparrow} + \alpha_{k\downarrow}^+ \alpha_{k\downarrow}$ in Eq. (29), appear with the gap energy $|\Delta|$ when the Cooper pair breaks (Bogoliubov 1958). The Bogoliubov pseudo-particles here are electrons, which form the Cooper pair itself. This is a real property of the superconductivity elucidated by the BCS theory (Bardeen et al. 1957; Gor'kov 1959; Bogoliubov 1958).

The formalism of the BCS mean field theory should be valid even in High-T_c cuprate (Bednorz and Müller 1986; Wu et al. 1987) and iron pnictides (Kamihara et al. 2006, 2008) superconductors, as well as other strongly correlated electron superconductors, such as heavy-fermion superconductors (Steglich et al. 1979) and organic superconductors (Lebed 2008), although the mediation mechanism of Cooper pairs may be different from that of BCS theory (Anderson 2013; Nagaosa and Lee 1990; Moriya 2006; Pines 2013). In high-T_c cuprates, microscopic experiments have shown that the magnetic excitations were crucial (Imai et al. 1993), leading to the possible mechanism involving magnetic interaction-mediated Cooper pairs (Anderson 2013; Nagaosa and Lee 1990; Moriya 2006; Pines 2013). BEC of fermion pairs was also discovered in liquid He3, which is the discovery of the superfluidity of fermion liquid He3 (Osheroff et al. 1972), and has become more and more important in quantum physics. Therefore, the concept of vacuum and the creation and annihilation of the particles is also important for understanding superconductivity, which is a phenomenon of BEC of fermion pairs.

The concepts of zero and vacuum in quantum physical sciences were discussed in the second quantization method of quantum field theory. The vacuum or emptiness with no particles but with huge energy is equivalent to the state with a lot of particles and antiparticles. The creation and annihilation of particles and antiparticles are important concepts and their operators are convenient, essential tools in modern quantum physics. By utilizing and modifying this concept with the pseudo-particles, such as magnons, spin fluctuations, Bogoliubov pseudo-particles, we can explain the solid-state sciences, such as BEC, itinerant electron magnetism and superconductivity including high-T_c exotic superconductors. Particle creation and annihilation are also important in understanding the origin of the Universe, for example, through Big Bang and cosmic inflation theories. I hope and believe that the concept of the vacuum that I have discussed here is important even in other fields.

Acknowledgements The author would like to thank Stom Yamash'ta for encouraging him to write this chapter with valuable discussion.

References

Alpher, R. A., Bethe, H., & Gamow, G. (1948). The origin of chemical elements. *Physical Review, 73*, 803–804.
Anderson, P. W. (1959). New approach to the theory of superexchange interactions *Physical Review, 115*, 2–13; Localized magnetic states in metals. *ibid., 124*, 41–53 (1961).
Anderson, P. W. (2013). Twenty-five years of high-temperature superconductivity—A personal review. *Journal of Physics Conference Series, 449*, 012001/1–10; Resonating valence bonds: A new kind of insulator?. *Material Research Bulletin, 8*, 153–160 (1973).
Ashcroft, N. W., & Mermin, N. D. (1976). *Solid state physics* (Harcourt, Orlando).
Bardeen, J., Cooper, L., & Schrieffer, J. R. (1957). Theory of superconductivity. *Physical Review, 108*, 1175–1204.
Bednorz, J. G., & Müller, K. A. (1986). Possible highTc superconductivity in the Ba–La–Cu–O system. *Zeitschrift für Physik B Condensed Matter, 64*, 189–193.
Bogoliubov, N. N. (1947). On the theory of superfluidity. *Journal of Physics (USSR), 11*, 23–32.
Bogoliubov, N. N. (1958). *Nuovo Cimento 7*, 794; A new method in the theory of superconductivity. I, II, III. *Soviet Physics JETP, 34*, 41–55 (1958).
Bohr, N. (1913). On the constitution of atoms and molecules. *Philosophical Magazine, 26*, 1–24; *ibid., 26*, 476–502 (1913); *ibid., 26*, 857–875 (1913); Atomic Structure. *Nature, 107*, 104–107 (1921); *ibid., 108*, 208–209 (1921).
Bose, S. N. (1924). Plancks Gesetz und Lichtquantenhypothese. *Zeitschrift für Physik, 26*, 178–181.
Brandt, W., & Dupasquier, A. (1983). *Positron solid-state physics* (North-Holland, Amsterdam).
de Broglie, L. (1923). Waves and quanta. *Nature, 112*, 540; *Annales de Physique* (Paris), *3*, 22 (1925).
Dirac, P. A. M. (1926a). On the theory of quantum mechanics. In *Proceedings of the Royal Society of London A, 111*, 405–23; The quantum theory of the electron. *ibid., 117*, 610–624 (1928); Quantized singularities in the electromagnetic field. *ibid., 133*, 60–67 (1931); Relativistic quantum mechanics. *ibid., 136*, 453–464 (1932); *Mathematical Proceedings of the Cambridge Philosophical Society, 30*, 150–63 (1934); *ibid., 35*, 416–418 (1939).
Dirac, P. A. M. (1926b). On the theory of quantum mechanics. In *Proceedings of the Royal Society, Series A, 112*(762), 661–77.
Dirac, P. A. M. (1930). *The principle of quantum mechanics.* Oxford University Press.

Einstein, A. (1905a). Ist die Tragheit eines Korpers von seinem Energieinhalt abhangig? *Annalen der Physik, 323*(18), 639–641. (Weinheim: Wiley-VCH Verlag).
Einstein, A. (1905b). Über einen die erzeugung und verwandlung des lichtes betreffenden heuristischen gesichtspunkt. *Annalen der Physik, 17,* 132–148.
Einstein, A. (1905c). Zur elektrodynamik bewegter körper. *Annalen der Physik, 17,* 891–921.
Einstein, A. (1925). Quantentheorie des einatomigen idealen Gases. *Sitzungsberichte der Preussischen Akademie der Wissenschaften 1,* 3.
Fermi, E. (1926). Sulla quantizzazione del gas perfetto monoatomico. *Rendiconti Lincei* (in Italian) *3,* 145–149; *On the quantization of the monoatomic ideal gas* (trans: Zannoni, A.) (1999).
Gor'kov, L. P. (1959). Microscopic derivation of the ginzburg-landau equations in the theory of superconductivity. *Soviet Physics JETP, 9,* 1364–1367.
Guth, A. H. (1981). The inflationary universe: A possible solution to the horizon and flatness problems. *Physical Review D, 23,* 347.
Hawking, S. (1988). *A brief history of time.* Bantam Dell Publishing Group.
Heisenberg, W. (1925). Über quantentheoretische Umdeutung kinematischer und mechanischer beziehungen. *Zeitschrift für Physik, 33,* 879–893.
Holstein, T., & Primakoff, H. (1940). Field dependence of the intrinsic domain magnetization of a ferromagnet. *Physical Review, 58,* 1098–1113.
Holtzberg, F., McGuire, T. R., Methfessel, S., & Suits, J. C. (1964). Ferromagnetism in rare-earth group VA and VIA compounds with Th_3P_4 structure. *Journal of Applied Physics, 35,* 1033–1038.
Hubbard, J. H. (1963). Electron correlations in narrow energy bands. In *Proceedings of Royal Society A276,* 238–257; *ibid., A277,* 237–259 (1964); *ibid., A281,* 401–419 (1964).
Hubbell, J. H. (2006). Electron positron pair production by photons: A historical overview. *Radiation Physics and Chemistry, 75,* 614–623. and references therein.
Imai, M., Michioka, C., Ohta, H., Matsuo, A., Kindo, K., Ueda, H., et al. (2014). Anomalous itinerant-electron metamagnetic transition in the layered $Sr_{1-x}Ca_xCo_2P_2$ system. *Physical Review B, 90,* 014407/1–6.
Imai, T., Slichter, C. P., Yoshimura, K., & Kosuge, K. (1993). Low frequency spin dynamics in undoped and Sr-doped La_2CuO_4. *Physical Review Letters, 70,* 1002–1005; Imai, T., Slichter, C. P., Yoshimura, K., Kato, M., & Kosuge, K. (1993). Spin-Spin correlation in the quantum critical regime of La_2CuO_4. *Physical Review Letters, 71,* 1254–1257.
Kamihara, Y., Hiramatsu, H., Hirano, M., Kawamura, R., Yanagi, H., Kamiya, T., et al. (2006). Iron-based layered superconductor: LaOFeP. *Journal of the American Chemical Society, 128,* 10012–10013.
Kamihara, Y., Watanabe, T., Hirano, M., & Hosono, H. (2008). Iron-based layered superconductor $La[O_{1-x}F_x]FeAs$ (x = 0.05–0.12) with T_c = 26 K. *Journal of the American Chemical Society, 130,* 3296–3297.
Kittel, C. (1953). *Introduction to solid state physics.* Wiley.
Landau, L. D. (1941). The theory of superfluity of helium. *Journal of Physics (USSR), 5,* 71–90, *Physical Review, 60,* 356–358 (1941).
Landau, L. D., & Lifshits, E. M. (1934). Production of electrons and positrons by a collision of two particles. *Physikalische Zeitschrift der Sowjetunion, 6,* 244–257.
Landau, L. D., & Lifshitz, E. M. (1980). *Statistical physics, part 2.* Pergamon: Oxford.
Lebed, A. G. (Ed.). (2008). *The physics of organic superconductors and conductors.* Springer Series in Materials Science (Vol. 110). Berlin: Springer.
London, F. (1938). The λ-Phenomenon of liquid Helium and the Bose-Einstein degeneracy. *Nature, 141*(3571), 643–644.
Martin, C. T., Perillo-Marcone, A., Calviani, M., & Muñoz-Cobo, J.-L. (2016). CERN antiproton target: Hydrocode analysis of its core material dynamic response under proton beam impact. *Physical Review Acceleration and Beams, 19,* 073402/1-12.
Moriya, T. (1979). Recent progress in the theory of itinerant electron magnetism. *Journal of Magnetism and Magnetic Materials, 14,* 1–46.
Moriya, T. (1981). *Electron correlation and magnetism in narrow-band systems.* Springer.

Moriya, T. (1985). *Spin Fluctuations in Itinerant Electron Magnetism*. Springer Series in Solid-State Sciences 56. Berlin: Springer.
Moriya, T. (1987). A unified picture of magnetism. In H. Capellmann (Ed.), *Metallic magnetism*. Berlin: Springer.
Moriya, T. (2006). Antiferromagnetic spin fluctuation and superconductivity. In *Proceedings of the Japan Academy Series B, 82*, 1–16; Moriya, T., & Ueda, K. (2003). Antiferromagnetic spin fluctuation and superconductivity. *Report on Progress in Physics, 66*, 1299–1341; Moriya, T., Takahashi, Y., & Ueda, K. (1992). Antiferromagnetic spin fluctuations and superconductivity in high-T_c oxides. *Journal of Magnetism and Magnetic Materials, 104–107*, 456–460; Moriya, T., Takahashi, Y., & Ueda, K. (1990). Antiferromagnetic spin fluctuations and superconductivity— A possible model for high T_c oxides. *Journal of the Physical Society of Japan, 59*, 2905–2915.
Moriya, T., & Kawabata, A. (1973). Effect of Spin Fluctuations on Itinerant Electron Ferromagnetism I & II. *Journal of the Physical Society of Japan, 34*, 639–651; ibid, *35*, 669–676 (1973).
Moriya, T., & Takahashi, Y. (1978). Spin fluctuation theory of itinerant electron ferromagnetism— A unified picture. *Journal of the Physical Society of Japan, 45*, 397–408.
Mott, N. F. (1949). The Basis of the Electron Theory of Metals, with Special Reference to the Transition Metals. *Proceedings of the Physical Society* (London) *A62*, 416–422; Metal-Insulator Transition. *Reviews of Modern Physics, 40*, 677–683 (1968).
Murata, K. K., & Doniach, S. (1972). Theory of magnetic fluctuations in itinerant ferromagnets. *Physical Review Letters, 29*, 285–288.
Nagaosa, N., & Lee, P. A. (1990). Normal-state properties of the uniform resonating-valence-bond state. *Physical Review Letters, 64*, 2450–2453; Lee, P. A., & Nagaosa, N. (1992). Gauge theory of the normal state of high-T_c superconductors. *Physical Review B, 46*, 5621–5639.
Nawa, K., MichiokaI, C., Yoshimura, K., Matsuo, A., & Kindo, K. (2011). Magnetic phase diagram of alternating chain compound $Pb_2V_3O_9$. *Journal of the Physical Society of Japan, 80*, 034710/1-7.
Nikuni, T., Oshikawa, M., Oosawa, A., & Tanaka, H. (2000). Bose-Einstein condensation of dilute magnons in $TlCuCl_3$. *Physical Review Letters, 84*, 5869–5871.
Ohta, H., & Yoshimura, K. (2009). Anomalous magnetization in the layered itinerant ferromagnet LaCoAsO. *Physical Review B, 79*, 184407/1–5.
Onnes, H. K. (1911). The superconductivity of mercury. *Communication from the Physical Laboratory at the University of Leiden, 122*, 124.
Osheroff, D. D., Richardson, R. C., & Lee, D. M. (1972). Evidence for a new phase of solid He3. *Physical Review Letters, 28*, 885–888.
Pauli, W. (1925). Über den Zusammenhang des Abschlusses der Elektronengruppen im Atom mit der Komplexstruktur der Spektren. *Zeitschrift für Physik, 31*, 765–783.
Pauli, W. (1927). Uber Gasentartung und Paramagnetismus. *Zeitschrift für Physik, 41*, 81–102.
Penzias, A. A., & Wilson, R. W. (1965). A measurement of excess antenna temperature at 4080 Mc/s. *Astrophysical Journal Letters, 142*, 419–421; A measurement of the flux density of CAS A at 4080 Mc/s. *ibid., 142*, 1149–1154 (1965).
Pines, D. (2013). Finding new superconductors: The spin-fluctuation gateway to high Tc and possible room temperature superconductivity. *Journal of Physical Chemistry B, 117*, 13145–13153.
Planck, M. (1900). Zur theorie des gesetzes der energieverteilung im normalspectrum. *Verhandlungen der Deutschen Physikalischen Gesellschaft, 2*(17), 237–245.
Sakurai, J. J. (1994). *Modern quantum mechanics* (revised edition, Addison-Wesley P. C. Inc.).
Sato, K. (1981). First-order phase transition of a vacuum and the expansion of the Universe. *Monthly Notices of Royal Astronomical Society, 195*, 467.
Schrödinger, E. (1926). Quantisierung als eigenwertproblem. *Annalen der Physik, 79*, 361–376; An undulatory theory of the mechanics of atoms and molecules. *Physical Review, 28*, 1049–1070 (1926).
Schultz, P. J., & Lynn, K. G. (1988). Interaction of positron beams with surfaces, thin films, and interfaces. *Review of Modern Physics, 60*, 701–779.

Steglich, F., Aarts, J., Bredl, C. D., Lieke, W., Meschede, D., Franz, W., et al. (1979). Superconductivity in the presence of strong Pauli paramagnetism: $CeCu_2Si_2$. *Physical Review Letters, 43,* 1892–1896.
Stoner, E. C. (1938). Collective electron ferromagnetism. *Proceedings of the Royal Society A: Mathematical, Physical and Engineering Sciences 165,* 372–414 and Collective Electron Ferromagnetism II. Energy and Specific Heat. *ibid., 169,* 339–371 (1939).
Takahashi, Y. (1986). On the origin of the curie-weiss law of the magnetic susceptibility in itinerant electron ferromagnetism. *Journal of the Physical Society of Japan, 55,* 3553–3573.
Takahashi, Y. (2013). Spin fluctuation theory of itinerant electron magnetism. *Springer Tracts in Modern Physics, 253.* Berlin: Springer.
Takahashi, Y., & Moriya, T. (1985). Quantitative aspects of the theory of weak itinerant ferromagnetism. *Journal of the Physical Society of Japan, 54,* 1592–1598.
Takahashi, Y., & Yoshimura, K. (2012). *Itinerant electron magnets and spin fluctuations* (1st ed., Uchida Rokakuho, ISBN4-621-07307-9).
Weinberg, S. (1977). *The first three minutes: a modern view of the origin of the universe* (Basic Books, New York, updated with new afterword in 1993, ISBN 0-465-02437-8).
Wu, M. K., Ashburn, J. R., Torng, C. J., Hor, P. H., Meng, R. L., Gao, L., et al. (1987). Superconductivity at 93 K in a new mixed-phase Y-Ba-Cu-O compound system at ambient pressure. *Physical Review Letters, 58,* 908–910.
Yang, J., Chen, B., Wang, H., Mao, Q., Imai, M., & Yoshimura, K. (2013). Magnetic properties in layered ACo_2Se_2 (A = K, Rb, Cs) with the $ThCr_2Si_2$-type structure. *Physical Review B, 88,* 064406/1–9.
Yoshimura, K., Imai, T., Kiyama, T., Thurber, K. R., Hunt, A. W., & Kosuge, K. (1999). ^{17}O NMR observation of universal behavior of ferromagnetic spin fluctuation in the itinerant magnetic system $Sr_{1-x}Ca_xRuO_3$. *Physical Review Letters, 83,* 4397–4400.
Yoshimura, K., Mekata, M., Takigawa, M., Takahashi, Y., & Yasuoka, H. (1988). Spin fluctuations in $Y(Co_{1-x}Al_x)_2$: A transition system from nearly to weakly itinerant ferromagnetism. *Physical Review B, 37,* 3593–3602.
Yoshimura, K., Takigawa, M., Takahashi, Y., Yasuoka, H., & Nakamura, Y. (1987). NMR study of weakly itinerant ferromagnetic $Y(Co_{1-x}Al_x)_2$. *Journal of the Physical Society of Japan, 56,* 1138–1155.

Author Biography

Kazuyoshi Yoshimura is Professor of Graduate School of Science of Kyoto University since 2002. He is also Director of Research Center for Low Temperature and Material Sciences, Kyoto University since 2013, Director of International Research Unit of Integrated Complex System Science, Kyoto University since 2015, a research member of International Research Unit of Advanced Future Studies, Kyoto University since 2015 and Vice Director of Agency for Health, Safety and Environment, Kyoto University since 2016.

Professor Yoshimura received PhD in engineering from Kyoto University in 1987. Since then, he has held teaching positions in Faculty of Engineering, Fukui University from 1986 to1988 and in Department of Chemistry, Faculty of Science, Kyoto University from 1988 to present. He has been studying Magnetism and Superconductivity in transition-metal compounds and alloys consistently. He is currently a research member of the Center for the Study for the Creative Economy at Doshisha University.

Chapter 10
Supplement for Chapter 9: Impression and Comment on "Zero and Emptiness (Vacuum Void) in Physics and Chemistry" by Kazuyoshi Yoshimura

Stomu Yamash'ta

I would first like to confess my surprise regarding the complexity and continuity of scientific exploration of the essential properties of the universe, beginning in the 15th century, that is, since medieval Europe. Scientists have struggled with conceptual conflicts underlying our scientific under-standing of the universe for five hundred years. They have faced various obstacles, such as from religious parties, during the pursuit of truth regarding the essence of the universe, and these obstacles have been difficult at times. The reliability of the current science is therefore based on the continuous, intense efforts of scientists over centuries.

I am well-aware of these harsh experiences of scientists throughout history, because I am an artist in the field of music, and I appreciate the similarities between the histories of music and science. Artists in the field of music have struggled to uncover real-world truths, while maintaining harmony between nature and mankind, as the supreme objects of art. In this essay, however, I do not focus only on religion as on obstacle for the development of science and arts, but rather explore the mutual interactions between them.

During the latest half century, the sciences, especially the fields of astronomy and astrophysics, have progressed drastically. The understanding and awareness of the solar system and Milky Way have deepened enormously. In particular, the exploration of the beginning of the universe has brought us the concept of "this

---

This chapter is supplement for K. Yoshimura, Zero and Emptiness (Vacuum/Void) in Physics and Chemistry (Translated by Tadashi Yagi, Faculty of Economics, Doshisha University, Kyoto, Japan).

S. Yamash'ta (✉)
Center for the Study of the Creative Economy, Doshisha University, Kyoto, Japan

Sound Core Co., Ltd., Kyoto, Japan
e-mail: info@sound-core.jp

universe" and "other universes". This new concept indicates the possibility of the parallel existence of the multiple universes.

We once had a similar concept "this world" corresponding to the solar system in Japan in the 1940s. People believed that there existed another universe referred to as the netherworld or the great beyond. This belief can be re-interpreted in the context of the recent hypothetical understanding of the black hole, where the surfaces of the universes are faced and may be contacted.

The intuitive understanding of people around 50 years ago included comprehension of the existence of multiple universes; this maybe because the concept made it possible to interpret the things that happening consistently in the real world. The important point is that people in that period had an intuition that there may be multiple universes, and modern people are losing this intuition, irrespective of scientific developments. Put another way, we are currently failing to recognize the real world and non-real world in a philosophical sense.

To revitalize the intuition of modern people with respect to the concept of multiple universes, it is important to reset the current consciousness and will of people, and to sharpen the sensitivity that mankind is innately endowed with as a consequence of the long process of evolution. In other words, we need to improve the ability to conceptually recognize the state and order of the world. Without an improved ability to grasp the hidden logic of the world, the substantial and rapid scientific developments will result in further disconnect between scientific knowledge and man's recognition of the universe. Prof. Yoshimura's manuscript provides important insight into this issue.

"Life and death" is the eternal theme for mankind and is linked to similar themes, such as "existence and non-existence", "this world and that world", and "this universe and other universes". Throughout humanity's long history, mankind has devoted tremendous efforts to seeking the truth behind these themes. In particular, a crucial question relates to the beginning of matter and life during the long journey of eternal change. "How and why did the universe begin?" This has been a deep question for humans.

In Eastern philosophy such as the philosophy of Buddhism, the concepts of "Zero" and a "Vacuum void" have been important for understanding the beginning of the universe since ancient times. The mathematical concept of "0 (Zero)" was invented in ancient India, and translates to "expand", "hollow", and "void". The original root of zero in Buddhism, originated around 2500 years ago in India, was "Shana (emptiness: "Kuu" in Chinese)" indicating that the truth lies in the non-real and the emptiness.

Importantly, both "Zero" and "Vacuum void" were invented in ancient India. At 2100 years before the present, 400 years after from the birth of Buddhism, it was transferred to China, and subsequently transformed based on Chinese culture. Buddhism was then transferred to Japan in 538. Chinese culture was instrumental in the spread of Buddhism. A monk named Xuanzang had a key role in transferring Buddhism to Japan. His most important contribution was bringing the Heart Sutra to Japan.

The heart of the teaching of Buddhism is based on recovering naturalness. The Heart Sutra is the scripture that describes this aim. The principles and the laws of nature are demonstrated as follows. The body is material, and spirit is the non-real existence. The way to receive the non-real existence is to perceive the non-real world via the body and the four mental functions, that is, consciousness, will, sensitivity, and thinking. The Heart Sutra states that "there is no coming and going in this world of emptiness, there is no uncleanness and cleanness, there is no increase and decrease".

Based on this statement, it is possible to link the original meaning of "0 (Zero)" and the astrophysical concept of a "Vacuum void". Yoshimura's paper states that the phenomenon of the vacuum void is the swelling limit of eternal energy, and it is empty. Similarly, the Heart Sutra grasps the essence of the void as the state of impermanence and the heart of the energy that generates everything in the real world. Real existence is generated from an oracle and is not shaped intentionally.

Man perceives this deep meaning of real existence by enhancing the four mental functions after experiencing the suffering of life. The Heart Sutra states that it is possible to escape from this suffering by understanding the principles and laws of nature, that is, the "Vacuum void" and "0 (Zero)". By understanding this teaching in Buddhism, man can open his mind to the universe, grasp the naturalness of this world, and recover the original form of man, without imprisonment by self-interests, which have negligible value in the universe.

Naturalness is attained in the state where the body and mind are synchronized with the principle and laws of the universe. In this state, man can express himself uniquely, and the expression generated from the individualistic personality gains supreme wisdom and strength. This liberates one's mind and body, and can provide a sense of real security from the heart.

In the synchronized state, one's mind is free from the past and the future, as well as from existing value and knowledge. This is the essence of naturalness. Religious meditations including prayer for Buddha and gods, is important as a means to reach to the oracle. This journey began in India and developed through synthesis with Chinese culture. However, it is not clear how such a beautifully developed Buddhism took root in Japan, and I will explore the underlying factors.

It was 538 when Buddhism was introduced to Japan; at the time, people worshiped the old Shinto, which translates to the way of gods, and originated from the worship of nature. The old Shinto subsequently developed to the its current form. Shinto is a unique religion, and the center of the faith is "four spirits for one soul". One soul refers to the source of energy in the universe, and four spirits means that the soul appears in the forms of "Aratama (the vicious aspect of gods, i.e., savage souls)", "fire"; "Nigimitama" (tranquil god), "water"; "Sakitama (god who bestows happiness upon people)", tree; "Kushimitama (soul of auspiciousness)", metal and material. All of these factors merge together into to form four spirits and consequently, the soul.

I will explain the above argument in more detail. According to the Shinto religion, the soul is expressed by the four voices, or spirits, of the soul's energy. To experience the "miracle" of life and our connectedness to all creation and the special power of nature, we must however empty the soul of these energies, both positive and negative. Creativity and creation lie in the void that remains—as with quantum physics, according to Zen and Shinto, the closer we come to 'nothingness', the closer we come, paradoxically, to the source of infinite energy, the center of creation, and the miracle of life. As in quantum physics, this infinite power lies beyond the point at which the concentration of energy is greatest, at both the nano-level of atoms and the macro-level of the universe. This is the ultimate destiny of a collapsing star and the massive energy involved in its creation and life. It is equally the power from which original creation was derived, that is, a "singularity,"—a point with no substance.

This power of nothingness is the ultimate quest of enlightenment, and the source of miracles.

The idea of the outward "diffusion" of the four spirits, is based on letting go, rather than force. This can otherwise be expressed as non-attachment. As soon as we utilize energy to push thoughts or energy sources away, we again fill our souls with this energy, rather than emptying it. We remain attached, or anchored, in the pragmatic, everyday world of material objects, experience, and intention.

The idea of creating a "vacuum" in the soul simply means, leaving nothing behind. Similiar to a vacuum cleaner that sucks up dust from the carpet via attraction by pumping out air to produce a partial vacuum, the void is the ultimate end-point of all matter. This is the ultimate goal of the outward diffusion of the four spirits—to achieve oneness with the void and to find our soul, the 'singularity'.

The experience of "diffusing the four spirits outwards" is ultimately one of bliss, or enlightenment and connectedness with the creative forces of the cosmos. Within the philosophical framework in ancient times, this connectedness was expressed as a miracle attributed to the gods or as representations of forces of inspiration and grandeur, beyond understanding.

In the modern world, the process is the same, as it is a fundamental property and source of humanity. However, our explanations have changed over time and are informed by new knowledge. Still, the concept of a miracle persists. Some indeed attribute this to a god or a transcendent connection beyond the natural world. Others seek a scientific understanding. However, the path, namely, the diffusion of the four spirits outwards, remains the source of miracles that we can experience. One can thus connect with the miracle of the cosmos, that is, creation.

Based on the concept of the soul, gods have been regarded as objects of dread owing to the potential for natural disasters, as well as objects of blessing. It has been believed that all disasters are consequences of the arrogance of man. The ceremony for blessing is aimed at expressing thanks to the god of nature. Interestingly, evil is not regarded as "bad", but rather as "yin (negative energy)" and is called Aratama, and good is regarded as "yang (positive energy)" and is called Nigimitama. Destiny and fortune are referred to as Sakitama, and miracles are called Kushimitama and are regarded as the power of the diffusion of the four spirits outward, or an even number; and are also regarded as the power of vacuums of the soul, and an odd number.

The above described concept has been considered the essence of life in Japan from an ancient period even before the arrival of Buddhism. It might not be a particularly difficult transition for Japanese people with the recognition on gods to coalesce on the fundamental philosophy of Buddhism. Evidence for this includes the combined ceremonies for Shinto and Buddhism.

Time flows like a rolling stone, and sociality evolves or changes. However, the universal truth of Buddhism including the ontology, impermanence, self-lessness, five senses, spirit and body, and origin, has been invariant. Throughout its 1500 years history, prayer for Shinto and Buddhism in combination has continued. In modern Japan, this prayer continues, with some modification. I am taking some roles in this.

After reading the manuscripts of Prof. Yoshimura repeatedly, I can confirm that the supreme object of man's activities, including science, religion, and art is the salvation of mankind, that is, a dialogue with nature, despite differences in methodologies, structures and styles among these activities. The universe, nature, spirit, material objects, non-material entities, existence, and non-existence all exist and continually evolve.

The essence is, however, the "Void".
Everything is related to Nothing.
It's a miracle story is in the wonder of the world.

I would like to express my deep respect and appreciation for the sincere attitude toward research activity and the spirit of inquiry. Thanks again for the precious proposal.

Chapter 11
Next Civilization and Spirituality

Tadao Takemoto

1

Advancement of miraculous information and communication technology has enabled us access instantaneously to the comprehensive knowledge web as if we could possess Buddha's "All-knowing Awareness (*Sarva-jña-jñāna* in Sanskrit)", but this fact has paradoxically driven us to raise an essential question; how could this godlike means of "communication" contribute to the "communion (*musubi* in Japanese)" of human beings? We communicate, yes, but to commune for what?

"For humanism" was what the American democracy instructed us to follow as postwar Japan's new societal norm after the World War II. Mixed folk dance was a new and eye-opening experience for us as we were not allowed to hold hands of the opposite gender in public. Our communion then was forced to be extended particularly towards the horizontal direction; whereas, our vertical axis that was derived from our divinities (*kami*) as described in the Japanese mythology, deviated from our history, being condemned and regarded as unscientific. Although Japanese had had a sense of communion with the "invisible" world since time immemorial, such a connection to the spiritual root was cut out. Japan is not an exceptional case. All old Asian kingdoms and empires were destined to lose their identical roots. Thus, we might interrogate again as follows; *Is possible a communion without a transcendental axis*?

Having said that, Japanese older generations—I am also one of them—could manage to keep such a "correspondence" for 30 or 40 years after the World War II. There occurred a little symptomatical incident recently. In Sensou-ji temple in

---

Translated by Ryuichi Fukuhara, Doshisha University, Kyoto, Japan.

T. Takemoto (✉)
Professor Emeritus of Tsukuba University, Tsukuba, Japan
e-mail: takeo.tadamoto@gmail.com

© The Editor(s) 2018
S. Yamash'ta et al. (eds.), *The Kyoto Manifesto for Global Economics*, Creative Economy, https://doi.org/10.1007/978-981-10-6478-4_11

Asakusa, one of the most touristic place in Tokyo always crowded by visitors from all over the world, there remained a modest praying hall "*Yōgō-dō*" (Hall of Epiphany) undisturbed close to the main street. This sort of place was found quite commonly at many Shinto shrines and Buddhism temples in Japan, and those who wanted to make a wish were used to stay there to pray for several days, often up to "Three seven-days", that is 21 days. As shown in many mythologies of temples and shrines since Japan's middle-age, there comes the goddess of mercy, *Kannon,* holding a sacred gem on her hand at the fulfilment day. Auspicious! A sterile woman miraculously will have a baby. Yōgō-dō was however relocated to the backyard of the temple in order to widen space in front of the main street for the Brazilian Samba Carnival, which was initiated by the local administration to attract more tourists. Since then, the manifestation of Kannon has been replaced by the voluptuous Amazons dancers...

This case does not necessarily mean that there is no longer a field to commune with the invisible world in Japan. We have myriads of Buddhist temples and Shinto shrines even now although these religious places are no longer the main premise to have a session with such world, as we just see the Asakusa case.

Fortunately, we Japanese still maintain our traditional culture such as Noh or Haiku, which are not only popular but also highly sophisticated as the means of contemporary creation by drawing up from the quarry of our identified roots. These arts are irreplaceable to keep communion with "*hi-gan* (*that world*)", which literally means "another riverside" in Japanese. A tea ceremony's room, surrounded by skyscrapers, hypostasizes the timelessness in serenity. Pure modus vivendi of this kind is very rightly referred by Parisians to as "*l'art de vivre* (the art of living)"; it is often forgotten that the place for living need not to be in this world, though.

Through a cup of tea or a flower, "Now" can be related to "the wholeness of the time being"—in-between life and death; even the Western world finally came to recognize the importance of such a field, consequently shifting their attentions to the Japanese norm. In comparison to the fact that martial arts and Ikebana were easily accepted by the West, Zen Buddhism was very hard because it required to accept some sort of irrationality beyond dualism against completely the Cartesian thought, the golden rule of the Western civilization. It was desperately controversial whether or not the West could accept the essence of Zen in the 1960s. The more shocking Tibetan Buddhism was introduced thereafter, which disclosed that the reincarnation was not superstitious but *real*. At least the Western civilization was thereby re-interrogated. The very point the Eastern and Western civilizations were faced to know was how to reincorporate the invisible world into this one, and what would be the core principle to do so.

"Conflicts in *Jambudvipa*[1]" in Buddha's words has now intensified across different nations, religions and ethnic groups in many parts of the world. Policy measures do not suffice to resolve conflicts and to realize peace in harmony, so it is

---

[1] *Jambudvipa* literally refers to "the land (*dvipa*) of Jambu trees", as envisioned in the cosmologies of Hinduism, Buddhism, and Jainism, which is the realm where ordinary human beings live.

then imperative for everybody to renovate fundamentally each person's perspective on the world, as some sages have unveiled 1000 years ago. This new perspective should not be trapped in an endless loop of dichotomizing; on the contrary, it has to envision integrating infinite dichotomized matters into the oneness. How should this new perspective be like? I dare to shed light on it in the following section.

2

The human civilization witnessed the highly spiritual periods at least three times over history; distinguished sages appeared independently but simultaneously in each period. Those who appeared in the first period around 500 BC were Buddha, Lao Tzu, Zoroaster, Jeremiah, Plato and others; the period called "Axial age" by Karl Jaspers. In the second period, Saint Francesco in the 12th century and Hōnen in the 13th century realized a correspondence towards the *hi-gan*, and many distinguished monks and priests followed. The third period started in the 1930s when genius visionaries like Albert Einstein, Carl Jung and André Malraux turned up in the West while Rabindranath-Tagore and Daisetzu Suzuki represented the profound Asian spirituality in the East. This last period also opened the first dialogue between the Western and Eastern elites, as seen in the Circle of Eranos, which was established in 1933.

It may be difficult to imagine now how fanatically the existentialism was supported after the World War II, making old wisdoms fall into obscurity. To consider everything as existing on crevasses between "the self" and "the other" and to call it "*l'absurde*", that was in fact overwhelmingly more influential to interpret the tragic 20th century when "the Satan had resurged in the form of the atomic bombs and the gas chambers". Vatican warned against the epidemic of existentialism but in vain. Jean-Paul Sartre, the originator of the idea, received an enthusiastic welcome by Japanese media. The philosophy regarded simply as *object* a tree's root exposed on the ground and cried "How it is hideous!". It looked certainly more tenacious than the Japanese sensibility which found the sign of every life from just a stone to a dry branch. In such an ideological storm, it was only Hideo Kobayashi, a famous Japanese literary critic, who expressed his distrust by voicing "what a cold-blooded thinking it is!". His opinion on a little newspaper's column was not widely known, but it was the best summary of genuine and unvoiced Japanese opinions concerning this existential thought.

Words of Zen master Dōgen in the 13th century, the second period in the above-mentioned, could primarily confirm Kobayashi's claim. Dōgen, the founder of Sōtō Zen school, argued on time theory in the fascicle of "*Uji* (Time Being)", well known to be an extremely esoteric discourse, of *Shōbōgenzō*; there he reveals that "Time", "Being" and "Self" constitute nothing but *Oneness*. It is to say; I am not sitting on the bench of a park, staring indifferently at the root of a tree outside. "Being and Time" are inseparable from the whole Existence and whole world [In each time exists Whole Existence-World.]* Time is not coming, it is not flowed down. "Now" is interlinked with twenty four hours of a day, being not distinct [Now must make unity with twelve hours] (Eihei 2007). The Self of Being Now is same to one who climbed up a mountain one day; and the Self who climbed up a mountain one day is same to one who lives at this just moment in a golden palace. If so, it means time is neither flying away nor coming up...

Dōgen's writings are too elaborated to succinctly summarize, and his discourse indeed defies our common sense on time. He deliberated, *"Were time to cease to exist, so mountains and oceans would cease to exist."* While Henri Bergson regarded time as *"la durée pure"*, Dōgen recognized "for the time being" was inseparable with "each event for the time being". Moreover, I being—"Self" was not inseparable with the wholeness of time and space as interconnected by "for the time being". It is noteworthy that the time theory of Zen Buddhism, which affected on Martine Heidegger, is not only speculative but experimental for real. The theory teaches us that "Self" for the time being, that is "Being now", contains the wholeness of time and space may be comparable to Buddha's "Divine ear (*dibba-sota*)", that is, clairaudience as well as "Divine eye (*dibba-cakkhu*)". clairvoyance to see others' karmic destinations. It makes possible to see a continuum from the past to the future. Prevision and precognition thereby will not be impossible. One might foresee a not-so-distant future event through a precognitive dream. Ever since Sigmund Freud founded psychoanalysis, the precognitive dream becomes part of science. Theoretically speaking, it should be possible to predict the distant future at a macro level if possible for the near future at a micro level. As Dōgen said, time does not fly but is just here. "Self" is not outside the flow of time but certainly embedded inside by "Being Now"; furthermore, it is already there and the invisible will necessarily become visible.

The next civilization will have to take a new direction to restore such clairvoyance. It should intuit a whole vision by "Being now". Archeology has uncovered that Paleolithic men held that kind of intuitions for the wholeness that included both visible and invisible realms. Of course, it was not because they ate psychedelic mushrooms to see hallucination. Moreover we should avoid such folly to confuse the awakening of Zen with the hallucinatory effects by drugs. That reminds me of when I visited my Zen master Daisetzu Suzuki at Enkaku-ji temple in Kamakura around 1960, if I remember correctly. He had received many fan letters from beatniks in the United States and picked up one of them to read it to me. "I heard one might view a chair as a golden lion after the Zen enlightenment. If so, I can experience the same when I do drugs". My master then told me "it is totally wrong though". The 90-year-old Zen master, with soft eyes under the lobster's tentacle-like eyebrows that were considered the long-lived feature in the East, smiled and continued, "I replied that the enlightenment should be something to fundamentally transform the whole world."

Did Daisetzu make a grandiose claim? I assume that this problem has already been concluded though. As I mentioned earlier, those who believe the reincarnation have increased in parallel to that regular churchgoers are decreasing. I would appreciate not to misunderstand what I am saying; I do not judge it is right or wrong. The old era of the worship for the absolute Holiness—lasted for 2000 years—has been drastically transforming to the new era where the sacred and the profane are not rigorously dichotomized but this continued field constitutes "spirituality".

In May 2016, the leaders of the G-7 summit visited the Ise Grand Shrine, the central place of Shinto, representing the spirituality of relativeness between *kami* (divinities) and surrounding forests. In the inner sanctuary of Naikū of the Ise Shrine, Arnold Toynbee found "the holy universal to any religion" and André Malraux became convinced in his maximum ecstasy that "Ise and Einstein's relativity theory would converge" (Malraux 1967). In terms of relating the spirituality of Shinto and the holiness of Christianity, the most implacable approach that could be ever be taken may be summarized by Olivier Clément, a famous French mystic, for both Catholic and Greek Orthodox, as follows;

Shinto is the most opened perspective towards the Transcendence

From the Western point of view, it may be more important to tend towards the absoluteness of the Transcendence represented by Jesus Christ; on contrary in Japan, we can say the essence lies in this perspective per se, which Lao-tze may have called "Tao". Here culminates probably a dialogue between the East and the West.

3

If the Occident had arrived to recognize unification of the opposites as *field* and to accept to call it *spirituality*, except some special cases like Hermeticism, it was done neither through theology nor religion but through natural science. To speak out without a fear of being mistaken, "the interpenetration of two spheres of material and spiritual" described in "Flower Garland Sutra (*Avatamsaka Sutra*)" has been gradually realized since the last century, particularly after the 1930's, the third period I referred to earlier in this chapter, by the synchronic developments of both natural sciences and humanities going beyond barriers between the universe and a mankind, this world and the *hi-gan*, in order to find over the continuity, correspondence and even "back and forth". The brief chronology of these developments is as follows.

- The first significant event was in 1905 when Einstein presented his "Special Theory of Relativity", and Jung's "*Studies in word association*" followed next year. Einstein, a great physicist, was also known as a mystic who believed "*The most surprising thing is that the universe has certainly a meaning*", as he told Malraux in Princeton. On the other hand, Jung the pathfinder of depth psychology finally recognized that "Collective Unconsciousness" would attain the "Cosmic Unconsciousness", as suggested by Daisetzu Suzuki.

- Einstein visited Japan in 1922 and stayed for 53 days. He highly appreciated the Japanese arts, finding in the Japanese scroll painting of the Middle Ages "free focus" similar to his own "space-time continuum" view on the universe. He also pointed out the "true reality" including even *the hi-gan* within such painting as "Amitabha's descending" and "the Waterfall of Nachi".

- From the mid 1920s, as quantum physics had been coming to the forefront of the natural sciences, the Western intellectuals' classical static Cartesian-Newtonian world view started a landslide shift to another one that the understanding would be intensified by seeing the universe as dominated by "chance" and "absurdity", always fluid, and indifferent to human beings. Thus, with its rebound, they were tempted to the Asian world view of "Void" and "Impermanence". It was in the same year that young Malraux made this wise remark: "In the very center of the Occidental Civilization reigns a metallic realm of *l'absurde.*" (*The Temptation of the Occident*, Malraux 1926)

- Niels Bohr and Einstein supported this view of the Void at the fifth Solvay international Conference on Electrons and Photons held in 1927, when *Bardo Thodol* (Tibetan book of the Dead) was firstly published in English. In the preface of this, Jung declared to interrogate scientifically to the Death. The awakening from division to unity will arose in all different cultural areas, increasing attentions to Japanese view on things. In the increased importance of Japanese visions.

- In 1928, Sergey Eisenstein, director of *"Battleship Potemkin"*, shocked with Japanese Kabuki transplanted to the Moscow stage (Act 4 Scene 4 "Vacating the Manson" of *"Chusingura"* was played there), which led him to develop his famous "Theory of contrapuntal montage" in his visual expression. Japanese theatrical plays generally do not split the stage and the audience. "Self" seeing the stage is part of space-time continuum in the theater including audiences. Furthermore, this continuum that corresponds and channels to the invisible world eventually provoked an "avant-garde" furor in Paris and New York through Noh and Japanese movies (for example, *Uegetsu* directed by Kenji Mizoguchi that won the Silver Lion Award for Best Direction at the Venice Film Festival in 1953).

- Werner Heisenberg, who introduced the Uncertainty Principle, had won the Nobel Physics Prize in 1933. This quantum concept of "uncertainty" decisively made the "Irrational" of human minds more acceptable. One year before, Joseph Banks Rhine established a Parapsychology Lab at Duke University in order to pioneer research on interactions between material and mind.

- In the same period, Daisetzu Suzuki and his colleague introduced *the Gandvyuha Sutra* to the Western World (Suzuki and Idzumi 1934–1936). It is the last chapter of *the Svatamsaka Sutra* that describes the constitutive Buddhism perspective of transcendental interpenetration and interdependence of all the time and beings. This sowed a seed of the coming encounter between the Western Science and the Eastern thoughts. Later in the 1960s, this perspective on the universe flabbergasted an American theoretical physicist Geffrey Chew, who is known by his bootstrap theory of the strong interactions with the S-matrix approach proposed by Heisenberg in 1943. Fritjof Capra's bestseller *"The Tao of Physics: An Exploration of the Parallels Between Modern Physics and Eastern Mysticism"* if asserted with striking parallels that the modern physics and the ancient wisdom lead undoubtedly to the same verities (Capra 1975).

- Wolfgung Pauli, the 1945 Nobel winner for Physics, and Jung, who presented the synchronicity hypothesis in the foreword of the English translation of the "*I Ching*", co-authored "*The Interpretation of Nature and the Psyche*" in 1955, which revolutionarily highlighted non-dichotomy between material and spiritual worlds based on Jung's architype and synchronicity theory.

I think the above is enough to compare, and would like your forgiveness that I could not dig deeper here. Anyway, I will appreciate if readers can have a glance at how the approaches to the world of "psi" has been deepened even through the hardest science of modern physics. Since then, academic exchanges between the two spheres have been going on; Japanese Society of Psychosomatic Medicine was established in 1959, the very daring and magnificent International Colloquium "Science et Conscience organized by France Culture in Cordoba in 1979, and Japan-France International Colloquium "Sciences et Symboles—Les Voies de la connaissance" followed 5 years later in Tsukuba University in Japan. Such developments are carried through to the present.

The consequent discussions called "From Cordoba to Tsukuba" highlighted "implicate and explicate order" coined by American theoretical physicist, David Bohm. This is an ontological concept for quantum theory; the "implicate order", also referred to as the "enfolded order", is seen as a deeper and more fundamental order of reality. In contrast, the "explicate" or "unfolded order" includes the abstractions that humans can normally perceive. According to the theory, the material and spiritual worlds exist in the framework of both implicate and explicate orders in the universe. It was already known that the conscience has a function activating on the brain *non-locally*. From here on, an American neuroscientist Karl Pribram and Bohm co-developed the holonomic brain theory, which is a model of human cognition that explains the brain's deep structure as fundamentally holographic. This idea fascinated intellectual pioneers in the 1970–80s, and we, "Tsukubist" named by Yves Jaigu, the organizer of the Cordoba Colloquium, were one of those so that we were inspired to organize our own colloquium as mentioned before.

"Implicate and explicate order" theory might look too extravagant to public, but not to us. When I read "*Implicate and Explicate Orders of the Universe and the Role of Consciousness*" presented by Bohm in Cordoba, I intuitively recalled the rock garden of the Ryōan-ji temple in Kyoto. Later when we brought the big photo panel of this garden to him in London, he said "I know this garden. Hideki Yukawa took me there, and said to me that this was your perspective of the universe". I felt a little pity that my intuition was not so unique, but impressed with that my idea was reaffirmed.

4

It is my affirmation that the art is an indispensable function to revive our existence in the fundamental wholeness, including the implicate order. The next civilization will be an era that resurrection of such function stronger than in any other epochs ever seen. More than Japanese themselves did, Claud Lévi-Strausse, a very rigorous anthropologist, believed in the continuity of Paleolithic "Jōmon Spirit" represented in the famous "Flamboyant-style potteries".

The fundamentalism does exist not only in Islam but also in the democratic world in the name of individualism. We should not forget it. The world had changed radically when the Asian supreme values, *annata* in Pali or "non-self" was replaced by individualism. The world needs to inevitably change once again. For that, we must learn how to live in "Being now", converging towards the wholeness. This prospect is a field like a vast mirror without any frame, where is no distinction between certainty and fortuity, even between life and death. The prospect also could reflect the future life as well as the previous life as Gautama Buddha saw through.

My discourse may look so ridiculous, but at least the Japanese spirituality rather constituted through not ridiculing such a thought. The first example I can refer to is the oldest chronicle "*Kojiki*", in the introduction of which reads "*Kami* (divinities) entered and went out both of the invisible *Yū* (幽) and visible *Ken* (顕) world". In the 15th century, Noh play, shaped by Zeami, perceived this "shores" of the same life were in the in-line continuum. Noh drama unfolds in such a way that a monk representing "self" are traveling between the two worlds by seeing the manifestation of the ghost. This is why this sort of Noh style is called "*Mugen Noh* (Supernatural Noh)". Other might call it "*Ōkan Noh* (Correspondence Noh)", which I assume more appropriate.

Two hundred years later, it was Matsuo Bashō who sublimed this correspondence in poesy for nature.

Furu ike ya/kawazu tobikomu/mizu no oto.

The old pond, ah!/A frog jumps in/The water's sound! (translated by Suzuki 1959)

This haiku has become the most famous one because it could illustrate that "Self" could prove the wholeness by listening to "Being now" represented by the water's sound in a moment. Kindly noted that sound of "the sound of the water's sound" should be "*oto*" before our conceptual thinking begins to function. In general translation, "Oto" in Japanese means "sound" but it is not translatable in the real sense of the term since the Western logos divides an "oto" into "sound" and "noise". John Cage nonetheless invented his "musique concrète" when he listened to the lecture by Daisetzu Suzuki in Hawaii and got his satori "*Oto is oto*, nothing else".

There is a field where noise and sound, creation and created are not yet divided; where forms and sounds remain undifferentiated and melted completely. Distinguished artists could perceive the existence of such field since ancient times. When Su shi, a great literate of the Sung Dynasty, saw Wang Wei's famous shan-shui painting, he inscribed "I savor his painting within poesy, I view his poesy within painting." Great French poet, Victor Hugo, who left thousands of drawings, said "*la poésie peinte*" (painted poesy). Furthermore, it was symbolist poets in 19th century, the dawn of the era of non-existence of God, who captured such a field of "correspondence" most vividly. Arthur Rimbaud had grapheme-color synesthesia; his sonnet "Vowels" starts with "*A black, E white, I red, U green, O blue* ...". As for Baudelaire, who entitled that poem so significantly *Correspondance*, so he sings; *"The Nature is a Temple where living pillars / let occasionally leak vague paroles. / ...Perfumes, colors and sounds respond alternatively."*

Olivier Messiaen, the 20th century's composer, in his Kyoto Prize award lecture, reminisced: "Since my childhood, whenever I listened to music, pictorial shapes came to my mind."

These undifferentiated fields were regarded "Symbolistic" in the 19th century. Baudelaire continues in the last part of the same strophe; *"The man traverses it (nature) through the forest of symboles."* That is to say, the secret of nature could be seized by an auto-substitution of perception, in other word, by figurative means of *"It is like …"*

The West spirit has been preoccupied by how to attain the "Eternity" in opposition to "Being now (*l'immédiat*)". Only Victor Hugo, a visionary terrible, could break through in the 19th century. Kindly remember Hugo is not only the author of *"Les Misérables"*, but also wrote the trilogy collection of poems *"La Légende des siècles"*. One of his unfinished poems shocked a great painter of the 20th century, André Masson. The poem reads;

A stone stands on the green hill (…)

Every night, before dawn, the stone

Gets off the hill and goes to drink in a stream.

It sounds wired but not *surréaliste* (Masson did not like being called "surrealist", by the way). Similar to Zen Master Dōkai of Mount Taiyo instruction to his disciples as,

The verdant mountains are constantly moving on, and the Stone Maiden, in the dark of night, gives birth to Her Child.

As far as we see nature, this poem depicts the scene as Victor Hugo saw within a vision "la Réalité Intérieure", so might say Malraux with his *L'Intemporel* (Malraux 1976). In such a sense that Einstein made remarks on "Amitabha's descending, the Irrational would naturally take place. Amitabha with twenty-five attendants will would for a dying monk. The hi-gan is no longer figurative nor symbolistic, but "Being now".

That is to say, the transfiguration could take place in some fields. Mary of Magdalene did not realize resurrected Jesus for the reason that he appeared in the similitude of a gardener carrying a spade. Thomas, one of the Twelve, said, "Unless I see the nail marks in his hands and put my finger where the nails were, and put my hand into his side, I will not believe" (John 20: 24–25), while other disciples believed immediately the resurrected Jesus appearing as a pilgrim of Emmaus with a different outlook.

While western exegesists have distressed over the interpretation of these events, Japanese, who invented Noh, are not naturally surprised too much. For example, a brinewoman passing by a travel monk on the beach is uncovered to be the ghost of the favorite mistress of an exiled prince (in Noh play *Matsukaze*). Another example can be taken from the Noh play *Atsumori*, in which a man blowing a blade of grass appears in front of a military commander of the winning *Genji* clan, then the winner realized that the man was the avatar of Atsumori, the young deceased of the losing *Heishi* clan, whom he killed.

Correspondence Noh is generally diptych; the protagonist called "*Shite*" portrays an avatar such as a brinewoman or a grass whistler in the former part, and plays the true characters of these avatars in the latter part. Which is which? Does *Shite* play as a human or a ghost? In a sense, Shite plays both roles without any distinction. Life and death are opposed to each other due to resentment at the outset, and both will be reconciled to present one field as a whole. The reason why the ghost of *Atsumori* appeared in front of the winner of Genji was he entered the monkhood and was travelling for the repose of Atsumori's soul. Thus, as feeling of resentments disappears; the theatrical space of Noh, which has intrinsically no separation between the stage and the seats, will sublime to be integrated as "true reality" in the higher dimension.

Were it played by Noh, the Resurrection of Jesus Christ, the very sacred focus of Christianity, would have revealed its meaning more clearly. The gardener with a spade and the pilgrim at Emmaus, who could be played by *Mae-shite* (ante-protagonist), will constitute the former part of the play; and when played by *Ato-Shite* (post-protagonist), they are revealed to be the avatar of Jesus Christ, in the latter part.

Our reasoning scarcely accepts that human reality is consisted with both of the life including death and the death including life. Perhaps no one could understand it better than a genius, Rembrandt van Rym. His masterpiece "Pilgrims at Emmaus", by placing light and dark on the same plane, admits and admires the miracle of the Resurrection of the Savior. In a room of the Louvre, by setting the glorious transfiguration of the traveler Jesus in front of disciples in astonishment, the European civilization implies "Oui" to that miracle through the most mysterious beauty.

5

The stone already has come down the green hill and become the Buddha statue. An old woman gave a prayer to it with her body and soul. A skinny guy like an ascetic was about to pass by but was stunned by her praying. He saw that she intoned subvocally and innocently, and understood in a flash, "This is what I am missing!"

The guy is Stomu Yamash'ta, a percussionist. He started his professional career in the United States and created a furor in London and Paris with his revolutionary rock-style performance, and then came back to Japan. The great success however got him to ask himself; could everything be OK like this? Then he entered the Tō-ji in Kyoto, the head temple of the Esoteric Shingon Buddhism sect. He lived cloistered 2 years there as an ascetic trainee, and made up his mind to be a monk. Despite that, the superior monk of the temple admonished him to have a mission that he should bloom the flowers of the sounds in the real world. His three-year monkhood thus came to an end. It was right after his return when Stomu Yamash'ta encountered Sanukite.

Sanukite rocks (sanukitoid in the lithological term) are an andesite characterized by orthopyroxene as the mafic mineral, andesine as the plagioclase, and a glassy groundmass, which are considered to be metamorphosed from the mantles in 13.5 million years ago. Sanukite stones had been used since the Paleolithic period in Japan, and it was also in use to decorate the surface of the *kofun* tombs (the keyhole-shape/mound megalithic tumuli tomb in ancient Japan) such as *Hashihaka-kofun* in Nara for an unknown person of an exalted rank; so, those *kofun* tombs were gleaming back under the sunlight. Sanukite were used as well for alarming or ceremonial purposes since it could sound the metallic high tones when drummed. Stomu Yamash'ta was apprenticed to Hitoshi Maeda, who first made the music instruments of Sanukite, and was fascinated to the mystical power of stone sound that could activate the human brain with its more than two-minute resonance including inaudible high frequency waves more than five hundred thousands Hz. He found a new path of his musical activity with Sanukite, but beset from all sides for 2 years. Based on the Western musical principle, Yamash'ta believed the music was self-expression, but this was not the case to play with the stone. Since then, he had been suffering from no known disease like hell, and finally he in the pits met by chance the above-mentioned old woman praying for the stone Buddha statue.

Stomu Yamash'ta looked back, "My attitude toward the stone that contained 13.5 million year memories was impolite with hindsight." His teacher's foresight, "The Sanukite stone will tell you all", has been proved true. "From that moment, I became able to hear the grandeur of the memorial vibrancy", as he confessed emotively at the Japan-France colloquium held in Ise on March 2014. On that occasion, the further experiential results were shown to us. He had played Sanukite in water to vibrate water, and its vibrations made marble-like patterns of the ink-stick on the water surface, then the patterns were carefully transferred to an absorbent silk fabric, one of dying techniques inherited in Kyoto 1000 years ago. Finally, those fabrics were used for fusuma sliding doors of Nyoze-in subtemple of Myōshin-ji temple in Kyoto, where Zen novices practice actually *zazen*, being surrounded by marvelously visualized *oto*, thus participating in "Being Now" associated with "the whole world".

It is unforgettable that Olivier Clément, whom I referred to already earlier in this chapter, said at the International Colloquium in Tsukuba in 1984 as follows; "There exists an epiphanic transcendence, and the human body can become part of it. We call it that we feast the cosmic sacraments". Here comes the era when the supernatural is to be contemplated in relation to the universe. Now that we recognize with wonder and fear that artificial intelligence may be exceeding human's intellectual capacity, this will be a new and dignified definition of human existence.

Earlier in this article, we have briefly reviewed accelerating correspondences between the discoveries in natural sciences and humanities in the past century. In my view, the greatest findings in natural sciences and humanities in the 20th century are DNA and Jung's architype respectively; both share a commonality of inheritance of the original types—although the architype does not follow causality but acausality called in Buddhism "*In-nen (Nidana)*". His architype theory drove Jung out of the academia but later has appraised him as the apotheosis of modern humanities.

Irrationality of Zen Buddhism and uncertainty of quantum theory face each other in concord. Bashō said "composing haiku is like stretching the gold", that is, to read a continuum of the world. Just for the time being is the wholeness of time as the quantum-scale objects have the wave-particle duality. Until 50 years ago, physics

Fig. 1 "Six Persimmons" by Mu qi in the 13th century (located at Ryoko'in subtemple of Daitoku-ji temple, Kyoto, Japan)

Fig. 2 "Separation of light and darkness", part of the cupola of the creation at St. Mark's Basilica, Venetia, the 13th century

had only dealt with the existential time after the "Time being" called Big Bang. In all the ancient civilizations of the East and the West, "not to be" was originally considered as "normal" but "to be" as abnormal. This was the actual state in ancient China as Zen master Dongshan Liangjie portrayed in *Song of the Precious Mirror Samadhi* that "normal and abnormal interacts, interpenetrates and rotates." *Muqi*, a famous painter of the Southern Sung Dynasty, embodied this concept in his masterpiece drawing "*Six Persimmons*" (Fig. 1), which Malraux called "*la confidence du monde*". The so-called "Genesis Mosaics" on the plafond of St Mark's Basilica in Venetia depict a spectacle with God's word of "Let there be light" that a red sphere representing "light" is going to separate from a dark blue one representing "darkness" (Fig. 2) as if it were a huge amplification of Muqi's wash drawing.

The question is to know how something could come up from nothing? The Western civilization, from Plato to Heidegger, had to wait during 2300 years until they started to address this question without thinking of the Creator. For us, the Eastern people, it is from "normal" that was born from "abnormal". The Western architects have placed the garden of Katsura-Rikyū (Katsura Imperial Detached Palace) in Kyoto in opposition to the style of the Versailles Palace in which is cumulated the architecture of symmetry, commonly prevailing over the whole Eurasian continent. You will enter there through a low-lintel gate, and be taken breath away when looking at a "dewy path" running diagonally towards the major space of the garden. I should not say more for those who have never been there, but I would like to add one thing that "there is a clue to transform the world".

Should living every day in such unusual atmosphere help approach the mystery of the origin of the universe, the Japanese garden would have another significance. Professor Yoichiro Nambu, Nobel physics laureate in 2008 for the discovery of the mechanism of spontaneous broken symmetry in subatomic physics, mentioned "Japanese culture finds beauty in asymmetry rather than in perfect symmetry. As I grew up in such a cultural setting, I could notice the existence of symmetry breaking". This breaking in subatomic should not be just a little seam opened if the origin of the universe lies there. One day Daisetzu Suzuki made audiences laugh by his answering to the question about the birth of the universe. His answer was, "It is because something moved a little bit in the nowhere". This might not be contradictory to Nambu's symmetry breaking theory.

The future of human civilization will go toward the creation of such domain inseparable empirically. As science and technology has become one and only reality for modern humans, we are very materialists more than we think. Thus, a narrow definition that reproducible phenomena are only evidential scientific facts has been widely accepted as a common sense. In contrast, irrational phenomena have been occurring on many people, and they are neither recurrent nor constant. Even some of those phenomena could relativize life and death. Raja Rao, Indian guru who is also a novelist and scientist, once revealed to Malraux as follows. "Why are the Western people likely to *dramatize* the door between life and death?" He then continued "Death is the path to the light."

Death will disappear as far as one may enter the pass alive. In the same sense that Christianity would not come into existence without the Resurrection, Buddhism could not exist without Samadhi. "One experience *Ikkyō*", says Dōgen. That is to say, "Have an experience". Experience means human verities. When we cease to admit the superiority of science and technology over humanity, then the next civilization will be emerging. Incipient light can be seen on the horizon. Finally, since millenary Kyoto can exhibit the truth that "the world exists because we take part in it", and has to be responsible for the next millennium as the heart of an ever-present "spiritual culture" by manifesting "Being Now".

References

Capra, F. (1975). *The Tao of physics: An exploration of the parallels between modern physics and eastern mysticism*. Berkeley, California: Shambhala.
Eihei, D. (2007). *Shōbōgenzō—The treasure house of the eye of the true teaching: A trainee's translation of great master Dōgen's spiritual masterpiece* (Hubert. N, Trans.). California: Shasta Abbey Press.
Malraux, A. (1926). *La Temtation de l'Occident (The Temptation of the West)*. Paris: Grasset.

Malraux, A. (1967). *Antimémoires (Anti-memoir)*. Paris: Gallimard.
Malraux, A. (1976). *La Métamorphose des dieux* (Vol. 3). Gallimard, Paris: L'Intemporel.
Suzuki, D. (1959). *Zen and Japanese culture*. New York: Pantheon Books.
Suzuki, D., & Idzumi, H. (1934–1936). The Gandavhuna Sutra criticaly edited (in Sanskrit). The Sanskrit Buddhist Texts Publishing Society, Kyoto, Japan.

Author Biography

Tadao Takemoto is Professor Emeritus of University of Tsukuba, ancien professeur invité de Collège de France. Tadao Takemoto, born in 1932 comes from a descendant family of samurai class since the 9th century. He majored in French Literatures at Tokyo University of Education and then continued at Pantheon-Sorbonne University. He practiced Zen Buddhism under the guidance of two Zen masters, Shin'ichi HISAMATSU and Daisetzu SUZUKI. In 1974, as he was an eyewitness of André Malraux's enlightenment inspired by the cascade of Nachi and the sanctuaire of Ise, he spread the significance of this very rare revelation all around the world. He was a translator for Her Majesty Empress Michiko's choices poems waka Sé-oto Le chant du gué into French, published by Éditions de Signatura, Paris. He was the main organizer of the two important international colloquia to promote transcendental dialogues between the East and the West; "Les Voies de la Connaissance" at Tsukuba University in 1984 and "Dialogue des Racines contre Racines" at Ise, Japan in 2014. He is the author of many books and theses in Japanese, French, English and other European languages.

Chapter 12
Spirituality as the Source of Human Creativity: Insights from India

Akio Tanabe

1 India in Transition

India is in the midst of tremendous change. Since the second half of the 1990s, there is a conspicuous process of deepening of democracy in India, that is, increasing participation of more diverse population in public activities.

I would like to argue in this chapter this movement towards 'vernacular democracy' is supported by the affirmation of diversity based on the ethico-spiritual value of ontological equality. By 'vernacular democracy', I mean a form of democracy embedded in the vernacular lifeworld, the formation of which involves both the vernacularization of democratic politics and democratization of social relationships. It is my contention that spirituality, as a way of life in pursuit of one's worth in a search for one's essence of being, is the foundation for creative formation of vernacular democracy in India. Indian thought tells you that the essence of many diverse beings is one and equal, and it is through the many beings that we can recognize the one. It is in relation to the One being as the source of human creativity that people can affirm and celebrate the Many that manifest as diversities while being connected as a whole.

A. Tanabe (✉)
Graduate School of Arts and Sciences, University of Tokyo, Tokyo, Japan
e-mail: tanabe@anthro.c.u-tokyo.ac.jp

2 Ontological Equality as the Basis of Socio-ecological Ethics

For some time, the study of India in general has concentrated on the aspects of 'hierarchy of status' and 'dominance of power'. It is undeniable that hierarchy and dominance play important roles in Indian society. I, too, took part in debates over these aspects of Indian society at the beginning of my graduate studies. However, as I treaded along my path of research, I began to sense the importance of another, perhaps more profound, value that has supported the socio-political integration in India, namely 'ontological equality'. Ontological equality is equality or oneness of all beings at the level of being or existence which, though philosophically, religiously and spiritually orthodox in Indian tradition, remains a socially 'subalternate' value as opposed to the hegemonic values of hierarchy and dominance (Gregory 1997).

Ontological equality is the idea that the Absolute, while transcending all beings, is at the same time immanent, permeating each being in the world. This means that all beings—whether human or non-human, alive or non-alive—are equal at the ontological level, as their spiritual essence is one and the same. The source of ontological equality is based firmly in *spiritual* exploration and ideation in India. This is expressed in the 'Great Words' (*mahāvākya*) of the Vedas in such phrases as 'I am Brahman' and 'Thou art That'.[1] In India, this idea is not only orthodox, but has also expanded into many forms, and is a popular idea that is widely shared. In the history of India, this idea has been expressed not only in the Vedas but also in various other forms, such as in Buddhism and Bhakti movements. However, although this idea has attracted many scholars and intellectuals in the field of Indology, less attention has been paid on its social and political implications.

I believe one of the best aspects that Indian thought has to offer humanity is the value of 'the ontological equality'. Japanese tradition has accepted the idea of ontological equality through Buddhism (Kamimura 2007). It first came into Japan in the form of the idea of *Tathāgatagarbha* [the Buddha-nature], which pronounces that there is potentiality for all people to become realized, as the Buddha-nature is present in all regardless of status. This then developed into the idea of *Hongaku* [inherent enlightenment], that we are all innately and intrinsically endowed with the pure knowledge of *satori*. This idea has been important in Japan for affirming the intrinsic value of the world and life thereof—not withstanding the popular understanding of Buddhism in the West as being pessimistic and world denying.

It is important to stress here that the idea of ontological equality is not limited to the religious domain in a narrow sense. It has the potential of becoming a common cultural resource for us to conceptualize a new kind of public philosophy, where we

---

[1]The "Great Words" are words that evince the highest principle of identifying Brahman with Atman in the Upanishad (sacred Hindu treatises). These are conventionally identified as the following four: "Consciousness is Brahman," "This Atman (the true Self) is Brahman," "I am Brahman," and "Thou art That".

can affirm the value of diversity in the world. What I am imagining is a new public philosophy based on ontological equality that makes possible the flourishing of social and cultural diversity. I believe that diversity is one of most important values in today's global world, alongside liberty and equality. In what ways is the socio-cultural diversity connected with the value of ontological equality?

3 The Logic of Tetralemma for Coexistence of Diversity

I would like to explain this by taking up the Indian logic of tetralemma (*catuṣkoṭi*) that goes beyond the logic of excluded middle, and allows the co-existence of A and non-A (Yamauchi 1974; Kioka 2014). Against the 'law of excluded middle' in western philosophical tradition, classical Indian logic accepts the 'middle', namely 'both A and not-A' and 'neither A nor not-A'. In the real-life situation, diverse beings exist in relation to each other—one reflecting and containing the other (Izutsu 1989: 54). The logic of tetralemma grasps the world of mutual dependency, rather than the world of division and exclusion.

Most articulately expressed by Nagarjuna (c.150–c.250 CE), the four logical possibilities of tetralemma—(1) A (affirmation); (2) not-A (negation); (3) 'both A and not-A' (both); and (4) 'neither A nor not-A' (neither)—express the logic in the world of relative truth (*saṃvṛti-satya*). These are all negated in the face of the Absolute Truth (*paramārtha satya*), which is beyond the four logical possibilities of relative truth. In other words, it is the very existence of the Absolute (*śūnyatā* or 'emptiness' in case of Nagarujuna)—that is, the level of what I call 'ontological equality'—which makes the coexistence of A and not-A possible. If there is Absolute Truth beyond the relative world, A and not-A can coexist as relative truths with both reflecting the Absolute Truth in relative ways.

The point will be made clearer, if we compare Indian logic with Western logic. According to standard western logic, A is A. It cannot be 'both A and not-A' nor 'neither A nor not-A'. It has to be 'either A or not-A'. This means that A and B (that is to say, not-A) must fight over truth and existence. Either A or B will be the Master, and the other must be subjugated and become a Slave. This western logic finds expression in the Hegelian formulation of history and philosophy, where history is seen as a fight for recognition. To recognize another's superiority is to recognize him as the Master and the self to be the Master's Slave. According to Kojève, a Hegelian, 'History will be completed at the moment when the synthesis of the Master and Slave is realized, that synthesis that is the whole Man, the Citizen of the universal and homogeneous State' (Kojève 1969: 44). Here, diversity must be denied in order to reach the final truth.

However, in the world of Indian logic, A and not-A can coexist along with many other diversities. In fact, the Absolute or ontological equality can find its expression in the world only in the form of diversity. The totality of the One expresses itself in the Many that are interdependent and mutually reflect and contain each other.

This principle of life allows the existence of diversity where various beings share and participate in the world together.

Such idea, in fact, is not limited to India. It is a universal idea that finds resonance in Japan as well as in Europe. Let me quote Gille Deleuze as an example.

> Opening is an essential feature of univocity. ... Only there does the cry resound: 'Everything is equal!' and 'Everything returns!'. However, this 'Everything is equal' and this 'Everything returns' can be said only at the point at which the extremity of difference is reached. A single and same voice for the whole thousand-voiced multiple, a single and same Ocean for all the drops, a single clamour of Being for all beings: on condition that each being, each drop and each voice has reached the state of excess (Deleuze 1994: 304).

This quotation from *Difference and Repetition* seems to me as if it describes the vibrancy of what I call 'vernacular democracy' in India, where there is a clamor of diverse voices mingling and interacting with each other to form an inseparable whole. It is at the extremity of difference and diversity that ontological equality can be recognized. And it is based on this ontological equality that there can be thousand-voiced clamor of multiplicities.

4 Transformation Toward Vernacular Democracy

Now let me go on to explain what I mean by vernacular democracy. 'Vernacular' has two meanings: (1) everyday language; and (2) according to the people's mode of living. Vernacular democracy is actualized through people's creative mediation of their everyday language and mode of living with democratic values, ideas and institutions. Through the development of vernacular democracy, democracy becomes more embedded in people's lives, and at the same time, existing social relationships and cultural values are questioned and transformed from democratic perspectives.

Such move towards vernacular democracy was made possible with the deepening of democracy where there is increasing participation of wider population. Today, there are diverse social groups and individuals, including dalits (so-called 'untouchables') and adivasis (indigenous tribals), religious minorities, women, the poor and the new middle classes, all participating in new ways and becoming much more active in India's political and economic life (Neyazi et al. 2014).

These diverse groups of people have been referred to as 'subalterns' who are characterized by Gayatri Spivak as people without voice (Spivak 1988). When development led by state elites was the most important political agenda in Independent India, subalterns were objects or recipients of development and education, and not active agents in the public arena. Today, however, the subalterns are raising their voices. If the definition of subaltern is people without voice, then we could say that there are hardly any subalterns in India today. This, however, does not mean that subalterns have grown to become free and autonomous citizens through development and education, as modernization theorists would have hoped.

Disparities and discrimination based on class, caste, gender, religion, and so on, still exist. But at the same time, it is precisely by means of these multiples axes of difference that the diverse social groups maintain their unique positions and have their voices heard from diverse positionalities, as their political agency increases. Subaltern voices in the vernacular are mediated and represented by various organizations, institutions and technologies in India today. It is only when vernacular voices are mediated by various democratic means that they are ensured a place in the public sphere. In turn, democratic conditions involving participation of diverse actors are made possible by vernacular voices attaining political presence.

5 Redefining Caste from Below: Local Politics and Intercaste Relationships

I will give you an ethnographic example from my field in Orissa (Tanabe 2007). Until the beginning of the 1990s, factional politics centered on the dominant caste was very active in rural Orissa. The situation changed, however, after the 73rd and 74th amendments to the constitution in 1992, which stipulated the devolution of power to local self-governments and rigorous reservation measures for the marginalized sections of society. Scheduled Castes (SC), Scheduled Tribes (ST), Other Backward Classes (OBC) were granted reservation quotas in accordance with the population ratio, and women one third of the seats.

Social change is accompanied, as Spivak says, by 'functional change in the sign system' (Spivak 1985: 330). That is to say, even if the same words and categories are used, their meanings can be shifted. A functional change in the sign system leads to change in how meanings are assigned to social relationships and cultural values. Democratization promotes the possibilities of such social change, since through democratization, hitherto marginalized people come to participate in debates and negotiations over meanings of social relationships and cultural values, and new meanings are added from different perspectives.

In my interviews, I tried to find out whether the process of democratization and social change at the local level was bringing about a new vision of society presented by the lower castes. When I asked the lower caste village representatives about why they decided to stand as candidates as ward members, many of them said they did so in order to do some 'work (*kāma*)' as 'service (*sebā*)' and 'duty (*kartabya*)', 'for the ward,' 'for the people,' and 'for the development of the village'. These words, such as work, service and duty are often used to talk about caste division of labor in the locality, and are also often heard in religious discourses. The village representatives' words sounded like clichés to me at first.

Later, however, I came to realize that they were innovative applications of popular idioms to give readily cognizable but original significance to the new patterns of political practice in local society. This realization came when I heard another traditional term employed in the new context. The lower castes talked about 'shares (*bhāga*)' to demand equal rights of access to the state resources. For example, one person explained to me the mechanism for the distribution of the state's resources in gram panchayat as follows: '[The government budget] is given ward wise. Work comes to the wards one by one. In our hamlet, the work of road paving came in that manner.... Everything is distributed according to quota [he used the English word here]. Large wards gain more according to their 'share'. Everything is like that'. I had already learned through my research on 18th century 'system of entitlements' in the region that the products of the local community were distributed to entitlement holders according to their 'shares' (Tanabe 2005). So I was surprised to hear the same term being used after such long lapse of time. However, there was a shift in the meaning of the term. In the 18th century, the shares differed according to the duty performed; but in contemporary usage, it is implied that the shares should be distributed fairly and equally. In this way, the term 'shares' that was part of the system of division of labor by caste, is now used to assert fair and equal rights for all. The lower castes creatively draw on terms such as 'duty', 'service', and 'share' to assert a new ideal of democratic local governance. By employing terms based on existing social relations and cultural values that must be accepted by all as legitimate, they were in fact criticizing the politico-social relationships centered on the dominant caste and trying to present a new vision of democratic relationships in local society (Tanabe 2007).

We can understand the process of social transformation through reinterpretation of discourse rooted in local society as a process of establishment of vernacular democracy, where the ideas and institutions of democracy are talked about in the vernacular and practiced in people's everyday lives as diverse groups participate in politics. Cultural resources of discourses, ideas, practices and institutions that enable diverse people to live and cooperate with each other are historically accumulated in all societies, though in different ways. For democracy to become firmly rooted in local society, it is necessary to draw upon such vernacular cultural resources, while critically overcoming their unequal and undemocratic aspects, and connect them with democratic ideas and institutions. Such development of vernacular democracy is possible by the exercise of cultural-political agency of people through their participation in political processes.

6 Politics of Relationships

The rise of the subaltern voices is, of course, not limited to village politics. We are now witnessing a huge, widening space for the subalterns to explore new opportunities for asserting their agency and seeking life chances. The process of empowerment of the subalterns in which they acquire vernacular voice and subjectivity in public is concomitant with the process of penetration of the state and the capital into the everyday lifeworld. Here, of course, the picture does not have only the bright side. There are also new kinds of exclusion and oppression. Here we find both a potentiality and a threat for a new kind of democracy for sustainable and inclusive development.

Conventional politico-economic systems are based on ideas and institutions of proprietary rights and representative democracy. These notions, however, disembed, abstract and objectify partial aspects of human life and its relationship to the world. I suggest that promoting sustainable and inclusive development involve questions of not only how to satisfy individuals' needs to 'own' and who has the right to 'represent' communities, but also how and what kind of 'relations' human beings can have with other human and non-human beings. I refer to the politics pertaining to the latter 'politics of relationships'. Politics of relationships play an important role in the newly emerging vernacular public arena in contemporary India, where different people with diverse positions, interests and values have begun to raise their voices, and participate in public negotiation processes to critically assess and attempt to improve their relationships, and therefore their own standings, vis-à-vis other human and non-human beings.

Let me give an example from my case study of bauxite mining projects and their opposition movements in the Niyamgiri hills of Orissa (Tokita-Tanabe and Tanabe 2014). This region faces serious political struggles over the use and distribution of natural resources, as well as questionings over what course of politico-economic and socio-cultural development the region should take. This region also forms a part of what is called 'the red belt' where Maoists are often active.

The Niyamgiri hills of southwest Orissa are rich in biodiversity and are inhabited by the Dongria Kondh, who worship the peaks of the Niyamgiri Hills as the home of Niyam Raja, the God of Law. The soil of the hills is also rich in bauxite which attracted Vedanta Resources, a multinational mining and metals company headed by an Indian businessman, Anil Agarwal, whose headquarters are in London. Vedanta's mining project in the Niyamgiri region is clearly opposed by the local people and people's movements. Gandhian people's movements play a significant role in people's movement in Orissa. They inherit Gandhi's philosophy of non-violence, and philosophy and activism of the Gandhian socialist, Rammanohar Lohiya (1910–1967), and conduct campaigns against industrial development by organizing public demonstrations and protest meetings and through their writings. In an interview, they stressed that the pressing question is, not only about displacement and environmental pollution, but whether limited water resources should be used for agriculture or for industry. They stressed that it is the very relationship between human and nature which is at stake here. There is also a new generation of social movement activists who use the Internet and new media to disseminate information about the problems in Niyamgiri. For instance, a filmmaker and activist, Surya Shankar Dash, made a documentary film called 'Sham Public Hearing: The Real Face of Vedanta' and uses YouTube as a media to reach people globally. Dash not only makes videos himself but also sometimes uses video images taken by the Dongria Kondh. He said to me in an interview, 'I give Dongria Kondh people old video cameras to shoot what is happening around them. I place them in YouTube so that the world can see what the truth is. If the Maoists give them guns, I give them cameras—to shoot not the enemy but the reality around them'

(4 August 2010). The new generation of people's movement activists, like Dash, combines YouTube, DVD showings, public gatherings and demonstrations to link localities, towns, and cities all over India, as well as different parts of the world, constructing a global network of groups and organizations interested in common issues. In this way, the problem of Niyamgiri has become known worldwide, and there are now global anti-Vedanta movements over the Niyamgiri issue by human rights and activist groups, including Survival International and Amnesty International.

The local tribal people extend their socio-political agency by being connected to the networks of urban Indian and overseas social activists. Such movements call for dialogue and negotiation between various stakeholders. That is to say, they are creating new vernacular public arena beyond the channels provided by existing political parties and the system of representative democracy.

The Orissa state government initially concluded an agreement with Vedanta Resources regarding the mining of bauxite in the Niyamgiri Hills in October 2004 (Sahu 2008). However, in 2010, the Ministry of Environment and Forest, Government of India, set up a committee led by N.C. Saxena and ordered a detailed investigation into the effects that bauxite mining in Niyamgiri will have. The report that the committee submitted to the Ministry on August 16, 2010 pointed out that mining in the region would have serious consequences and was highly problematic (Saxena et al. 2010). On August 24, 2010, the Ministry of Environment and Forests announced that it rejected earlier clearance to Vedanta's mining project in accordance with the Saxena Report. Against these moves by the Government of India, the Orissa state government (which is run by the Biju Janata Dal [BJD] and not the Indian National Congress of the central government at that time) retaliated, saying that Orissa's industrialization and economic development were being hampered by the central government. Orissa's Chief Minister, Naveen Patnaik, criticized the central government's decision as being detrimental to Orissa and the interests of its tribal population. BJD accused the Congress Party of political intervention, and especially that of Rahul Gandhi, who visited a village near the Niyamgiri Hills on August 26, 2010, two days after the rejection of permission. In his speech, Rahul referred to a tribal youth who said that his people worship the Niyamgiri hills as their deity and said, 'That is your dharma. My dharma is that every voice, including that of the poor and adivasis should be heard. ... Development means that every citizen of India develops... Our government in Delhi, our PM, Sonia-ji will fight for development and to give you a voice'. In this way, there are conflicts between political parties over the permission to mine in the Niyamgiri Hills, and each party is playing political games in trying to get support from various social groups. People's movement activists welcomed the fact that the mining project was suspended, but expressed displeasure at the fact that the political parties were using the issue as tools for extending their influence.

In April 2013, the Supreme Court decided that Vedanta's bauxite mining must have the permission of gram sabhas (village councils) of the area to go ahead with its activities. The gram sabhas and specialist observers appointed by the Supreme Court would determine whether or not to permit the mining plans after deliberating upon the cultural and religious rights of the tribals and forest dwellers (including the right to worship Niyamgiri as a deity) before reporting to the Ministry of Environment and Forests. All twelve gram sabhas in the region unanimously rejected the mining project.

In India today we see that the political process has come to acquire complex interactions between the state and society, party politics and non-party politics, the elite and the subaltern, and the religious and the secular. With the rising voice of the forest-dwelling population, the Forest Rights Act of 2006 for the first time recognized the rights of the inhabitants to live and utilize the forest, making compromises to proprietary rights of the state. Also, the court recognized, in line with the recent policy of devolution of power, the rights of self-determination of the local people, which has come to relativize the power based on representation that used to be the ideal model of the modern nation state. This does not necessarily mean that India is falling to a populist rule, since specialist knowledge and opinion are also consulted upon, while respecting the people's will, as we see in the employment of Saxena Report. It is also worth noting that religion and belief, which used to be seen as belonging to the sphere of the private or the community under secularism, have been given a more public place and consideration, as we see in Rahul Gandhi's speech and the Supreme Court's decision regarding the right to worship Niyamgiri as a deity. In this way, we see a process by which vernacular forms of life and values, and democratic and public institutions are brought together and combined.

7 Beyond Excluded Middle Towards 'Negotiative Coexistence': In Between Law and Life

7.1 State of Exception: Between Law and Life

So, how are we to locate this space of vernacular democracy and politics of relationships in today's world? Following Agamben, I suggest that we see it as a space 'between law and life' (Agamben 2005). Law is concerned with the relationship between the sovereign state and individual-citizens with equal rights. But in India, the 'individual-citizen' is in fact a minority category. India is a country where 22% of the entire population live below poverty line (2011–2012),[2] 18% of the urban population live in slums,[3] 25% are Scheduled Castes and Scheduled Tribes,[4] 40–50% are Other Backward Castes, 20% belong to various religious minorities,[5] all of

---

[2]Reserve Bank of India, https://www.rbi.org.in/scripts/PublicationsView.aspx?id=15283, accessed on 9th February 2015.
[3]Slums in India: A Statistical Compendium 2011, http://nbo.nic.in/Images/PDF/Slum_in_india_2011_english_book_23_May_12.pdf, accessed on 9th February 2015.
[4]Census of India 2011, http://www.censusindia.gov.in/, accessed on 9th February 2015.
[5]Census of India 2011, http://www.censusindia.gov.in/, accessed on 9th February 2015.

whom require special attention as exceptions to the rule. With such a vast number of the population as exceptions, law can only have an official status in the nation and cannot function with efficacy. Thus there is a vast space which is beyond the rule of law.

This does not mean, however, that there is no working of state power in this space. It is not the law but the working of governance that claims to provide for the various needs of the diverse groups of people (Chatterjee 2004). This is how the power of governmentality penetrates deep into the people's lifeworld. However, the lifeworld in India is too complex and heterogeneous to be governed in a uniform way. The workings of governance remain at best fragmentary and unstable. It is also a space that is rife with corruption and political maneuverings. The scattered and fragmented workings of power become resources for people to utilize in ad hoc ways. This aspect of Indian political life is often discussed in terms of its 'ungovernability', where the society is said to be too chaotic and the government too inefficient (Kohli 1990). However, the labelling of Indian society as 'chaotic' is based on legal or official perspectives where civil society with individual-citizens is seen as the norm. From such a perspective, India is far behind. If development and democracy can only be realized by the emergence of citizen-individuals as the majority population, India still has a long way to go. However, what we are witnessing in India today is rapid economic development and deepening of democracy, where there is no rule of law but vibrant clamors of diverse voices. How is this possible?

7.2 Principle of Life as a Subalternate Logic

What is happening is that a plethora of subaltern voices has begun to play an increasingly larger role. In politics, the presence of lower castes—Other Backward Classes (low castes excluding Scheduled Castes and Scheduled Tribes) from the 1980s and Scheduled Castes (ex-untouchables) from the 1990s—in party politics is prominent, and has expanded into non-party politics, such as the people's movements. I do not have space to discuss the economic aspects of this change, but I believe that we should pay more attention to the significance of the expanding informal sector where the subalterns play significant roles as both producers and consumers (Tanabe 2017). Subalterns used to be seen as 'marginalized people without voice', but as I have already mentioned, this does not mean that they never had any voice. Their voices are in the vernacular, as opposed to the official language of elites; and they are raising their voices today with the opening up of the space of vernacular democracy.

What is the most important principle in vernacular democracy in India? I would like to suggest that it is the 'principle of life' where diversity of life forms are given due space based on the value of ontological equality. In simple terms, it is the spirit of sharing and coexistence in accordance with the logic of tetralemma. While the hegemonic values of status and power—combined today with the idea of civil legality and capital efficiency—place different persons and beings in the logic of hierarchy and inclusion/exclusion, it is notable that Indian society has not abandoned the subalternate values that is concerned with providing source and place of livelihood for each being.

In a village in Orissa, where I stayed in the early 1990s, the often used phrase for negotiation by the service castes for demanding more payment from the dominant caste patrons was 'How can we eat with this?' or 'How can we survive with this?' It was interesting for me that while there were clear hierarchical intercaste relationships in the village, this did not mean that the lower caste people just kept quiet. They made persistent demands on their patrons about what was expected of them to keep them alive. In the Niyamgiri issue, while the mining company offered the Khond people some money and employment as compensation for displacement, the concern of the Khond people, as well as those who supported them, were how the Khond people will maintain themselves in the low lands once they were displaced from the forest environment in the hills.

7.3 The Contemporary Space Between Law and Life

In today's world where the state power and the global capital penetrate deep into the lifeworld, we cannot simply celebrate the subalternate logic of sharing and coexistence. However, we should also note that we cannot simply repeat the same teleological prescription of the Enlightenment to transform the subalterns into individual-citizens. What we must do first is to discern and understand the situation in which the non-elite subalterns, who actually form the majority of the world population today, are placed. In describing this place as the space between law and life, I would like to point out not only the arbitrary usage of power by the state as Agamben does, but also how the people who occupy and live in this space utilize the scattered and fragmented resources to open up new opportunities and create new relationships, albeit with much instability and risk.

Especially, I have paid attention to the process in which this subalternate logic of sharing and coexistence is attempting to find a place in the emerging vernacular democracy and the politics of relationships in the expanding lifeworld where democratic politics and market economy have become a part of the everyday. In the context of India today, we can say that the democratization process is not a process by which subalterns learn to become individual-citizens, but a process whereby subalterns become socio-political agents who utilize whatever resources that have become available to them in order to seek better life chances and create life forms in the new lifeworld. I have tried to show how vernacular democracy and politics of relationships are the means by which subalterns are emerging as socio-political agents.

This process is by no means without frictions and conflicts. As capital and governance penetrate the far corners of the world, natural and human resources useful for these forces are exploited and expended, and those that are useless or inhibiting are marginalized or evicted. A case in point is the predicament of the Dongria Khond, who are pressurized to relocate in order for the ground to be cleared for the digging of bauxite. Here we see the logic of excluded middle. However, the workings of governance and capital do not function in a homogenous, empty space, at least in India, and are inevitably meshed in complex relationships and crosscutting interactions between diverse sections involving the tribals, NGOs, people's movement organizations, government bodies, political parties, media and the global corporations. In this process, there is an emergence of hybrid and heterogeneous public arena where diverse elements belonging to the global and local, urban and rural, elite and subaltern, interact, giving rise to new connections, friction and vibrancy. Here, there are chances of sharing the fruits of development and negotiating with others to obtain one's place thereof, as well as risks of losing one's livelihood and being excluded through division and violence.

In this way, in the sphere between law and life, there are workings of both kind of logic, namely, the logic of excluded middle that divides and chooses one while excluding the other, and the logic of tetralemma that allows diverse elements to share and negotiate. It also means that there are workings of both the hegemonic values of status and power combined with the principle of civil legality and capital efficiency, on the one hand, and the subalternate values of survivability of diverse forms of life through sharing, on the other. Here, this dynamic process involves serious socio-political, economic and ideational negotiations and conflicts that are full of potentiality and risk.

8 Conclusion

India's potentiality lies in the affirmation of diversity based on the spiritual value of ontological equality. It is true that there is severe discrimination and inequalities India till this day, and these problems indeed need to be rectified. However, the solution is not simply to provide the same rights and income for all. The aim of social life and democracy is to offer each person the possibility of leading a life that one deems worth pursuing. The value of ontological equality sees human beings not in terms of equivalence but as diverse and singular manifestations of the One. Ontological equality is firmly based in the *spiritual* value of seeing oneness in all beings. This oneness is also recognized, in the spiritual exploration and ideation in India, as the source of diversity, dynamism and creativity of humanity. From this perspective, we can view India as an arena where diverse colors come together and share space of participation, rather than as a gradation of different shades of grey (Nancy 2008: 57–58).[6]

It is my contention that the vibrancy in democratic politics and market economy in today's India is the results of bringing out the potentiality of colorful diversity. It is the diverse people in society who enable the vibrancy, not the state or the market which are the institutions that support the people's agency. The spiritual value of ontological equality is the foundation of such diversity-affirming democracy and economic development. The principle of ontological equality seeks to find the universal unity within the manifestations of diversity, and such unity emerges precisely in the interaction between diverse beings.

In the end, I would like to reiterate my suggestion that the movement towards 'vernacular democracy' that has become conspicuous since the second half of the 1990s is a historically ground-breaking movement supported by the subalternate value of ontological equality and the logic of tetralemma that affirms diversity. The idea of democracy in modern times is undoubtedly a worthy quest. But has it not become somewhat reductive and limited by sticking to claims for representative democracy or deliberative democracy? Put differently, can one provoke the current consensus on the idea of modern democracy by posing it instead as *a profound problem of the failed inclusion of the subaltern democratic imagination*? Subalterns are not conceptually passive to the high discourse on democracy nor are they merely voting blocs shaped by narrow local interests. Rather, a reflexive ethnography reveals a different and alternate universe of ideas, principles and practices that cuts into core beliefs about representative and deliberative democracies.

Deepening of democracy in contemporary India is a process of formation not of a homogeneous civil society, but of a heterogeneous public arena where diverse elements belonging to elite and subaltern, modern and traditional, rational and religious, interact in the space between law and life, giving rise to new potentialities and risks. It is also a way in which more diverse sections of population finds a place in securing one's livelihood and participation in socio-economic life of contemporary India. Although many economists and media pay attention only to the flamboyant achievements of India's large business houses which are engaged in export-oriented production with foreign direct investment, we should not forget that the real story of India's current economic development would be incomplete if the more basic engine of economic vibrancy is ignored. The real substance of India's economy lies with many and diverse small-sized firms, manufacturing units, entrepreneurs and enterprizes, through which the ordinary and subaltern people

---

[6]Jean-Luc Nancy says, 'The democratic rule, the power of the people, is the power first to defeat the order and then, for all and everyone, to take charge of the infinite opening thus brought to light. To take charge of this opening means to make possible the finite inscription of the infinite. This fundamental choice—it must be repeated, it is the choice of an entire civilization—results in the inevitable annulment of the general equivalence, which is the indefinite perpetuated instead of the inscribed infinite, which is indifference instead of affirmative difference, tolerance instead of confrontation, grey instead of colors' (Nancy 2008: 57–58).

increasingly take part in economic activities in pursuit for better life (Yanagisawa 2014; Vaidyanathan 2014; Tanabe, 2017). At the heart of the dynamism of contemporary India lies increasing participation of more and more diverse people in the public arena (Neyazi et al. 2014).

Vernacular democracy is a creative way and process of imagining a world where both diversity and equality can stand together. This movement takes the form of politics of relationships where there is a constant negotiation as regards the relationships between human and human, and human and nature.

Questions of how to combine representation and participation, achieve both diversity and equality, and imagine a future that takes into account a sustainable relationship between human and nature, are important agendas not only for India, but also for the entire world. The diverse and multi-layered dynamism of democratic politics in India may indeed appear chaotic from the viewpoint of civil society and the law. But I would like to see here a potentiality of formation of a new kind of democracy where the diverse people of India are reaching out for their voices to be heard in spite of the conflicts and exclusion involved. The new kind of democracy does not stop at achieving freedom of individuals. It aims at the coexistence of diversity of beings and the ontological equality of all, that is to say, a world where all human and non-human beings are secured a place.

References

Agamben, G. (2005). *State of exception* (K. Atell, Trans.). Chicago: University of Chicago Press.
Chatterjee, P. (2004). *The politics of the governed: Reflections on popular politics in most of the world*. New York: Columbia University Press.
Deleuze, G. (1994). *Difference and repetition* (P. Patton, Trans.). New York: Columbia University Press.
Gregory, C. A. (1997). *Savage money: The anthropology and politics of commodity exchange*. Amsterdam: Harwood Academic.
Izutsu, T. (1989). *Kosumos to Abchikosumosu: Toyo Tetsugaku no tameni (Cosmos and anticosmos: For eastern philosophy)*. Tokyo: Iwanami Shoten.
Kamimura, K. (2007). *Bagavaddo Gita no Sekai: Hindukyo no Kyusai (The world of Bhagavad Gita: Salvation in hinduism)*. Tokyo: Chikuma Shoten.
Kioka, N. (2014). *Aida wo Hraku: Renma no Chihei (Opening the 'in-between': The horizon of lemma)*. Kyoto: Sekai Shisosha.
Kohli, A. (1990). *Democracy and discontent: India's growing crisis of governability*. Cambridge: Cambridge University Press.
Kojève, A. (1969). *Introduction to the reading of Hegel: Lectures on the phenomenology of spirit* (J. H. Nichols, Jr., Trans.). New York: Basic Books.
Nancy, J.-L. (2008). *Vérité de la démocratie*. Paris: Galilée.
Neyazi, T. A., Tanabe, A., & Ishizaka, S. (Eds.). (2014). *Democratic transformation and the vernacular public arena in India*. London: Routledge.
Sahu, G. (2008). Mining in the Niyamgiri Hills and tribal rights. *Economic and Political Weekly, 43*(15), 19–21.
Saxena, N. C., Parasuraman, S., Kant, P., & Baviskar, A. (2010). *Report of the four member committee for investigation into the proposal submitted by the Orissa Mining Company for*

Bauxite Mining in Niyamgiri. Government of India: Submitted to the Ministry of Environment & Forests.
Spivak, G. C. (1985). Subaltern studies: Deconstructing historiography. In R. Guha (Ed.), *Subaltern studies IV: Writings on South Asian history and society* (pp. 330–363). New Delhi: Oxford University Press.
Spivak, G. C. (1988). Can the subaltern speak? In C. Nelson & L. Grossberg (Eds.), *Marxism and the interpretation of culture* (pp. 330–363). Urbana: University of Illinois Press.
Tanabe, A. (2005). The system of entitlements in eighteenth-century Khurda, Orissa: Reconsideration of 'caste' and 'community' in late pre-colonial India. *South Asia: Journal of South Asian Studies, 28*(3), 345–385.
Tanabe, A. (2007). Toward vernacular democracy: moral society and post-postcolonial transformation in Rural Orissa, India. *American Ethnologist, 34*(3), 558–574.
Tanabe, A. (2017). Conditions of 'developmental democracy': New logic of inclusion and exclusion in globalizing India. In M. Mio & A. Dasgupta (Eds.), *Looking beyond the State: Changing forms of inclusion and exclusion in India*. London: Routledge.
Tokita-Tanabe, Y., & Tanabe, A. (2014). Politics of relations and the emergence of the vernacular public arena: Global networks of development and livelihood in Odisha. In T. A. Neyazi, A. Tanabe, & S. Ishizaka (Eds.), *Democratic transformation and the vernacular public arena In India*. London: Routledge.
Vaidyanathan, R. (2014). *India Uninc*. Chennai: Westland Ltd.
Yamauchi, T. (1974). *Rogosu to Renma (Logos and lemma)*. Tokyo: Iwanami Shoten.
Yanagisawa, H. (2014). *Gendai Indo Keizai: Hatten no Engen, Kiseki, Tembo (Contemporary Indian economy: The origin, trajectory and prospect of development)*. Nagoya: Nagoya University Press.

Author Biography

Akio Tanabe is a Professor at the Graduate School of Arts and Sciences at the University of Tokyo. He specialises in anthropological and historical research of South Asia, with an emphasis on caste and religion; democratisation and social change; and South Asian paths of development. His publications include articles in *American Ethnologist, Modern Asian Studies* and *South Asia, Caste and Equality: Historical Anthropology of Local Society and Vernacular Democracy in Eastern India* (in Japanese) (University of Tokyo Press, 2010) and as co-editor *The Challenges of a Diverse Society: Contemporary India* Vol. 1 (in Japanese) (University of Tokyo Press, 2015), *Human and International Security in India* (London: Routledge, 2015), *Democratic Transformation and the Vernacular Public Arena in India* (London: Routledge, 2014), *The Tropical Humanosphere in Global History: Beyond the Temperate Paradigm* (in Japanese) (Kyoto University Press, 2012), *The State in India: Past and Present* (New Delhi: Oxford University Press, 2006), *Dislocating Nation-States: Globalization in Asia and Africa* (Kyoto University Press and Trans Pacific Press, 2005) and *Gender and Modernity: Perspectives from Asia and the Pacific* (Kyoto University Press and Trans Pacific Press, 2003).

Third Movement: 'The Dynamic of Creativity'

domestic market; (N5) degree of customer orientation; (N6) buyer maturity; (N7) labor relations; (N8) hiring flexibility; (N9) financial maturity; (N10) venture capitalism; (N11) availability of new technology; (N12) capability to accept technology; (N13) size of subcontractors; (N14) quality of subcontractors; (N15) unique competitiveness; (N16) global logistics management; (N17) production process maturity; (N18) marketing expertise; (N19) innovation capability; (N20) level of competency in science and engineering research institutes; (N21) investment in R&D; (N22) industry-academia collaboration and technology transfers; (N23) governmental purchases of cutting-edge products; (N24) availability of science and technology personnel; (N25) patents; (N26) development of human resources; (N27) corporate social responsibility; (N28) telecommunications technology; (N29) capability to develop and utilize technology; (N30) technological assets; (N31) proficiency of technical work force; (N32) green technology; (N33) capability for sustainable development; (N34) capability to mitigate pollution; and (N35) business-friendly environmental regulations.

Applying principal factor analysis and cluster analysis, these 35 indicators are classified into the following four clusters:

- (C1) sustainable capability (N1, N5, N7, N8, N10, N12, N23);
- (C2) basic infrastructure capability (N2, N3, N11, N22);
- (C3) primary activity capability (N4, N6, N13); and
- (C4) innovation capability (N15, N19, N20).

The Spearman rank correlations between WCY and NQCI for 18 selected countries were 0.896 (for 2005), 0.806 (2007), 0.879 (2008), 0.922 (2009), and 0.888 (2010), suggesting high statistical correlation between the two indexes. From this, Cho et al. (2014) conclude that the main factors that determine national competitiveness are innovation capability and infrastructure capability for innovation. Supporting this conclusion, the United States, Germany, and Japan are ranked relatively high in these measures for all years. In contrast, other countries, such as China and Russia, which are ranked lower, have a need for the government to play a greater role in strengthening quality competitiveness and implementing industrial modernization.

1.3 Policies for Promoting Innovation

There are five main policy methods for promoting innovation: the public subsidy system for R&D at universities or public research institutions; public subsidies to private companies through venture capital, industry clusters, and access to public research centers; and the education system for cultivating the human resources necessary for R&D. A typical example of the first policy is the National Science Foundation (NSF) in the United States. A prominent example of the second is the Small Business Innovation Research (SBIR) program, which aims to foster private sector commercialization of funded R&D projects. Although some studies, such as those by Wessner (2000), expect a low probability of commercialization, there are various advantages to promoting innovation in an economy (Link and Scott 2009).

The SBIR program is designed to promote private R&D through direct governmental support. Initially this program was run by the NSF, and in response to the success of the initial program, the Small Business Innovation Development Act of 1982 (P. L. 97–219; hereafter, the 1982 Act) was enacted. This act states that the objectives of the program are to stimulate technological innovation, use small business to meet federal R&D needs, foster and encourage participation by minorities and disadvantaged persons in technological innovation, and increase private sector commercialization of innovations derived from federal R&D investments.

SBIR awards are given in three phases. In Phase I, awards are less than $100,000 over a six-month award period and given for the purpose of promoting firms that have high potential scientific and commercial ideas. In Phase II, awards range up to $750,000 over two years. These awards are directed to the firms that are evaluated highly in Phase I, and are expected to develop their research into a commercially viable product, process, or service. These Phase II awards of public funds are sometimes augmented by private funding. Phase III does not involve SBIR funds, and additional outside finance is required for moving their product, process or service into the marketplace.

Eleven federal agencies currently participate in the SBIR program, including the Environmental Protection Agency, the National Aeronautics and Space Administration, and the National Science Foundation, as well as the Departments of Agriculture, Commerce, Defense, Education, Energy, Health and Human Services, Transportation, and Homeland Security. The SBIR program has several advantages. First, SBIR remedies market failure in developing socially valuable R&D. Social value and market value are not always equal, and R&D products that have lower market value will not receive adequate investment, even when their social value is high. Second, SBIR contributes to increasing the diversity of products and services. In the market, products or services directed to minor market segments are not provided because of their small market size. Initial investment funds for such small markets are rarely available in financial markets, but SBIR subsidizes this initial investment for businesses in small-scale markets.

Now, let's turn our attention to the effects of the SBIR program. Link and Scott (2009) hypothesize that commercialization is more likely when there are outside private investors (i.e., private investors other than the firm winning the SBIR award or its principals) participating in the SBIR project. They expected that better decisions are made through the market with its superior information, which guides venture businesses in a better manner than a program such as SBIR. Through econometric analysis, they concluded that the likelihood of commercialization primarily depends on market demand and access to financial markets, rather than technical issues. The results of their analysis show that the probability of commercialization is substantially higher when outside private investors finance a Phase II SBIR project. The paper concludes that there is considerable room for improving the performance of the SBIR program in regards to its commercialization goals. The average expected probability of commercialization could be improved by modifying the program. For instance, steps to improve predictions about marketability would increase available information about the probability of commercialization of SBIR Phase II projects, which would bolster the SBIR program overall.

Contrary to Link and Scott (2009), Yamaguchi (2015) demonstrates the effectiveness of SBIR empirically by using data from the pharmaceutical industry. According to Yamaguchi's research, 77% of total sales in the venture pharmacy industry in 2012 (which accounts for 17% of the total pharmaceutical industry) is attributable to companies that were awarded SBIR Phase I funds. In the entire US pharmaceutical industry, 18.3% of companies receive awards from the SBIR program, and the total sales amount of SBIR companies is about threefold that of companies not receiving awards.

1.4 Innovation Hubs

Recently, the concept of the "innovation hub" has been gaining attention. In this concept, the city represents a city acts as information and human network hub of knowledge and know-how that promotes innovative products and services in the market. The typical example of an innovation hub is the European Technology Platform (ETP) included in the Seventh Framework Program (FP7). FP7 was an EU research and development program that was active from 2007 to 2013, and assisted in all phases of innovation process. In particular, the ETP is a network hub where researchers and engineers gather and exchange information related to R&D.

The ETP includes the following activities: developing industry-focused strategic research and innovation agendas; encouraging industry participation in the EU's framework program for research and innovation; promoting networking with other ETP programs to expand the range of open innovation; expanding international cooperation; and launching public–private partnerships under the program. The ETP commission plays the role of information hub and takes on coordination responsibility in R&D. Consultation about implementing R&D projects is another important role provided by the innovation hub.

A similar concept is used in the UK. The UK government aims to build a complex web of technologists and scientists, businesses, financiers, consumers, universities, skilled workers, public agencies, government agencies, and other institutions that interact in various ways to promote innovation. A key focus of their economic policy is making Britain a global hub for innovation, based on the idea that all innovations depend on the combination of three factors: new knowledge, resources, and market connections. As noted by Andersen et al. (2011), these factors can be attained through dynamic networks and systems of public and private organizations, including intermediary institutions.

In the UK, direct public support for innovation is provided by building the right regulatory institutions and policy environment. One form of support considered effective leveraging the purchasing power of public sector organizations. Public procurement operates to create new markets by offering greater scale for new products and demonstrating their advantages. Regulatory mechanisms such as operational standards and market-based incentives such as tax breaks are also used.

An outstanding example of an innovation hub in the UK is the Financial Conduct Authority (FCA). This organization, which is accountable to the Treasury and Parliament of the UK, is funded entirely by fees assessed to firms on their financial activities. One of the FCA's areas of activity is enhancing the integrity of the UK financial system. This innovation hub enables the promotion of new businesses by introducing innovative financial products and services to the market. Further, the FCA establishes and offers the most appropriate form of support for organizations that meet its eligibility criteria by providing genuine innovation, consumer benefit, and background research, while also demonstrating the need for support.

The essential function of an innovation hub is the coordination of the various types of businesses and ideas through information collection. This coordinating role is not normally attained through market mechanisms, given that market failure is common for these services without specific supports. Thus, leadership from a public authority or an alliance of companies is needed to perform the necessary coordination. Whether or not a company invests in an innovation hub depends on the cost–benefit ratio. To consider how effective an innovation hub might be, the central issue to examine is why open innovation is important. The obvious main reason is that innovation helps firms meet their need for the proper mix of various types of global technologies with a company's own unique, internal technology. Even when a company's internal technology has little market value by itself, it might be possible for it to gain market value when combined with technologies developed by other companies. The core aim of coordination, therefore, is to find an appropriate company to help improve the value of a company's original technology.

1.5 Innovation Community

The concept of an "innovation community" is developed from the idea that innovation should be pursued with the goal of improving society, not profit seeking. Professor Ikujiro Nonaka, regarded as a pioneering researcher in innovation theory, advocated this concept at the Topos Conference. The concept on the innovation community is closely related with Maslow's hierarchy of needs, which places human needs in a pyramid with basic physiological needs at the base and progressively works upward to safety, love/belonging, esteem, and self-actualization (Maslow 1943). As the consumer market matures, the willingness of consumers to pay more for their needs increases as the type of product or service shifts from basic necessities to self-actualization. Thus, the value of innovation in the market increases as innovation begins to connect with consumers' desire for self-actualization. In other words, consumers feel happiness from social relationships, harmony with nature, and spirituality in a fully mature society. Community enhances the development of needs and cultivates the foundation for understanding innovation. This implies that the value of innovation is increased by enriching the quality of the community to which a person belongs.

A related concept is Communities of Innovation (CoI). This concept is based on the idea that the feasibility of sustainable innovation can be improved by organizing a community so that its members assume total financial, administrative, and operational control. The key point that distinguishes such a community from a conventional community is the organizational control of environmental sustainability and social development. In this regard, employment and education are crucial matters.

The Aga Khan Foundation is a good example of a CoI. This organization has implemented innovative developments by organizing communities since 1970, coordinating several agencies and thousands of volunteers. The Aga Khan Foundation is regarded as a model of participatory rural development that combines development principles with a community's specific context and needs in flexible manner. As described by Lee and Cole (2003), another example of a CoI is the Linux operating system, which has been developed in an open-source manner that involves coordination and collaboration across the boundaries between firms. The use of a CoI made it possible to assemble talented people from various geographical and professional areas. This type of organization is also enabled by the Internet and Web-based technologies.

The theoretical foundation for the effectiveness of innovation communities and CoIs is explained by the model developed by Berliant and Fujita (2008). Their paper examines the mechanism of knowledge creation based on the assumption that knowledge is created through the interaction of people with different sets of knowledge. That is, diversity helps to enhance knowledge creation. As time passes, the subsection of knowledge possessed by all members increases, and the productivity of knowledge creation declines. To avoid this decline in the productivity of knowledge creation, a system or place for attracting newcomers to the community is necessary. Thus, non-exclusive social capital and social relationships are more desired when seeking to promote knowledge creation (Putnam 1993, 2000).

Knowledge creation by expanding human networking is now progressing via online social networking services (SNS). SNS act as a kind of CoI in the sense that various talented people from diverse areas collaborate with each other via the Internet. NPOs engaged in innovation are another type of CoI that have ideas for society. SNS work effectively by collaborating with well-organized NPOs because knowledge creation via SNS can be controlled and targeted towards achieving the specific social objectives that are the focus of the NPO's activities.

Weinberg et al. (2013) developed the notion of an organization based on the principle of collaboration. Their paper attempts to answer questions about the allocation of responsibility for social media within organizations, the governance of activities, and structural changes in response to the rapid development of SNS. The paper argues that the organizational structure should be complemented by a collaborative community in response to market demands, and that social media can effectively facilitate and support such a collaborative community. It is worth noting that the utilization of SNS strengthens the social stance of the organization, which leads to the creation of a social business.

CoIs are expanding in various ways. For example, CoIs perform the core parts of knowledge creation through the exchange of ideas in various fields and provide management capacity as projects are executed. Whether a project becomes successful depends on the social value of the innovation it introduces. When the social value of an innovation is low, support from multiple fields becomes harder to guarantee and the outlook for the project worsens.

A more difficult point to consider is the market value of innovation. High social value does not necessarily guarantee high market value, especially when the innovation in question is needed by people in lower income classes. People in lower income classes often cannot afford to purchase certain products or services, even when the social value of the product is clear. One example of this is robots to care for the elderly. Many elderly people require care in daily life and the need for such care is especially high for elderly persons without family and social connections. Thus, the market value of innovative products or services depends on the supply and demand structure for each specific product or service.

In extreme cases, the market for an innovative product or service is nonexistent when the equilibrium price of the product/service is below the zero-profit level. Even when the product/service has high social value, private companies cannot enter such a market because there is no guarantee of long-term sustainability. For example, training and educational service for persons with disabilities are important for the advancement of any society that values social inclusion, in which persons with disabilities and elderly individuals are treated as equal members. However, such services are not easily sustained due to high costs on the supply side and affordability issues on the demand side.

1.6 Social Business

Social businesses may provide a potential solution to the problems mentioned above. A social business is designed and operated so that the company is sustainable without outside subsidies or donations. The difference between a regular business and a social business is in their primary purpose. While regular businesses hold profit maximization as their primary purpose, social businesses aim to achieve certain social objectives such as the alleviation of poverty. Social business differs from NGOs in the sense that a dependence on fundraising is not required.

Yunus et al. (2010) suggest new business models in which stakeholders take a role in maximizing social value instead of shareholders, using the case of Grameen Bank as an initial example. Grameen Bank loans money to over 7.5 million poor people to help them escape from poverty. While conventional bankers were reluctant to consider poor people as potential customers, Grameen Bank made small loans that were sufficient to finance income-generating businesses such as rice-husking and buying/selling milk cows, goats, cloth, and pottery without requiring collateral.

The most interesting feature of this model is how it creates an incentive system for repayment, and as a result, the Grameen Bank has a repayment ratio of about 98.4%. Building this incentive system for repayment without collateral is the most important innovation in the Grameen business model. Solidarity lending is a cornerstone of micro loans (Discussed in greater detail on Grameen Bank's website; http://www.grameen-info.org/), where each borrower is required to belong to a 5-member group. Although repayment responsibility rests solely on the individual borrower, each borrower's behavior is watched by members of the group so that each borrower behaves responsibly and none encounter problems with repayment. Without using formal joint liability, Grameen Bank succeeded in keeping repayment rates high using only a penalty system of terminating further credit to a group in which a member defaults.

Wilson and Post (2013) examine how social businesses are designed such that they can effectively combine social and economic missions. They conclude that a hybrid business model that includes both profit-seeking and social value creation is the most promising from a sustainability perspective. They suggest the importance of creativity derived from the social value-seeking process, which then may be applied to the profit-seeking business.

It would be worth attempting to describe the characteristics of social businesses by focusing on the relationship between income distribution and profit level for each income segment. It is well known that actual income distribution can be approximated by a lognormal distribution (Salem and Mount 1974). The density function of a lognormal distribution is defined by the following equation:

$$f(x) = \frac{1}{\sqrt{2\pi}\sigma x} e^{-\frac{(\ln x - \mu)^2}{2\sigma^2}},$$

where x is income, μ is the mean of the lognormal distribution, and σ is the standard deviation of the lognormal distribution. Figure 1 depicts the shape of the density function of the lognormal distribution for the case where $\mu = 0$, $\sigma = 1$. In Fig. 2, we assume a convex profit rate functions for each income segment. This assumption reflects the case where the profit rate increases in a convex manner as the income group being targeted increases. In other words, we assume that the profit rate attainable would be high if the product or service is targeted to a high-income group and low if targeted to a low-income group. The most typical example is the profit rate of hotels, where the profit rate per guest in a luxury hotel is far higher than that in a cheap hotel. The density function of income distribution represents the number of customers for each income segment by multiplying by the total population. Then, the total profit of the product or service for each income segment is given by multiplying the density function and profit rate per customer. This is described by Fig. 2 when the total population size is 1.

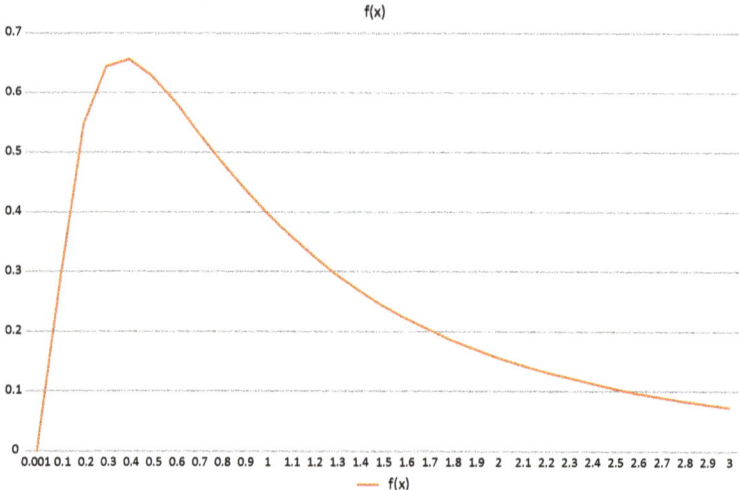

Fig. 1 Lognormal distribution

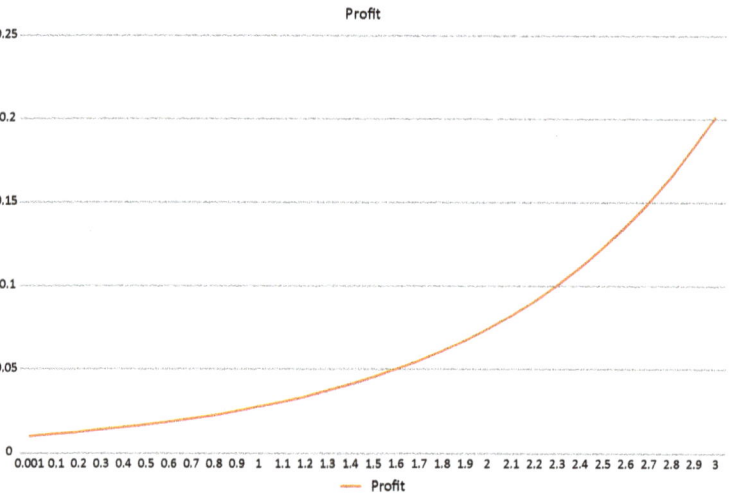

Fig. 2 Profit for each segment

Figure 3 suggests why it is difficult for social businesses to be sustainable. The essential reason is the non-linear profit rate function by income class. Social businesses are mainly targeted to lower income groups; thus, the profit rate is usually quite low and the profit received is usually below sustainable levels.

The implication derived from this discussion is the importance of creating products and services that are consumed by middle- or high-income groups as a by-product of the main target of sales to low-income groups. One example of this is travel packages that use unused rooms or houses—this idea can initially be targeted to low-income groups but scaled to middle-income groups if the added value is

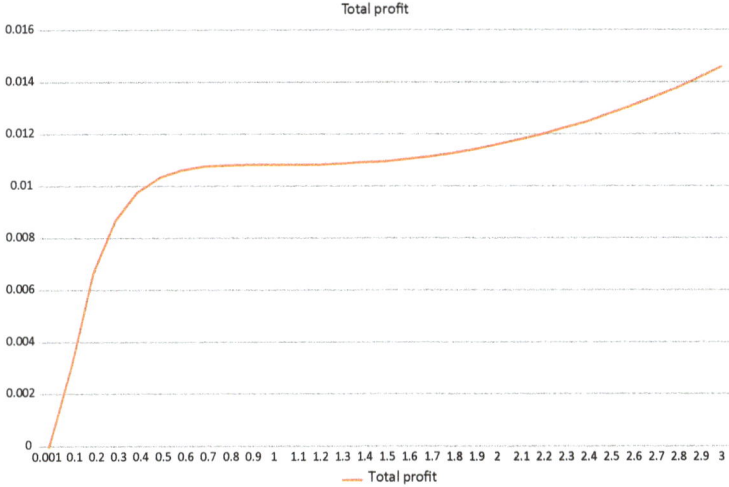

Fig. 3 Total profit

appropriate. Creativity plays an important role in designing and creating this additional value.

As discussed by Sonne (2012), financial limitations are another major source of difficulties for social businesses. To overcome this limitation, some financial innovations are needed such as microfinance, local business incubation, and micro-venture capital systems. A factor that helps ensure a financing project is successful are systems used for decreasing the information gap between banks and entrepreneurs. As is discussed in the above case of the Grameen Bank, microfinance uses a 5-member system for collecting information and maintaining repayment incentives. Rural business incubation has been demonstrated by organizations or systems such as the Grassroots Innovation Augmentation Network (GIAN), UnLtd India, and the Honeybee Network (a database of rural inventions) in India. The rural innovation incubator Villgro, based in Chennai, Tamil Nadu, in southern India, is a GIAN-type organization that focuses on the incubation process of commercializing enterprises by formulating and refining business plans to attract potential investors. Villgro's main advantage is its information network of local innovation technology, which can be used to assist businesses helping the poor.

2 Understanding Creativity

2.1 The Essence of Creativity

To discuss the creative economy, it is necessary to discuss what creativity itself is. Intuitively, creativity is cultivated by the accumulation of high-quality emotional experiences and knowledge. Feeling the beauty of nature, enjoying art performances, and viewing sophisticated paintings are some examples of such high-quality emotional experiences. Emotion is deemed as the main driving engine for the creativity.

However, the essence of creativity has until now been seen as an extremely difficult subject of debate. This difficulty is evident in the fact that even those who have succeeded once in a creative project have no guarantee that they will be able to do so again. More than a few scientists have looked back on the genesis of their major discoveries and seen in them as "the work of God." As Bonting (2006) points out, the role of God in creation was in fact explicitly debated until the early nineteenth century, but when science and theology diverged, creativity came to be understood as the process for extracting order from chaos. This holds true not only for the natural sciences but for the social sciences as well. For example, the economic theory of general equilibrium can be understood as a theory that perceives a chaotic economy and, through the process of theoretically explicating the existence of a market-clearing price that arises simultaneously in multiple markets, brings the order that exists in economic activity to light.

Since ancient times, both Eastern and Western cultures have explained the wellspring of creativity through the common proverb that "necessity is the mother of invention." This proverb tells us that if a problem clearly exists, the process of searching for a solution to that problem will generate creativity. This fundamental mechanism of creativity has not lost its importance in the present day. However, because our basic needs have largely been met in today's society, opportunities for creativity to arise through this mechanism have decreased. Most creativity today takes the form of locating a problem that can be neither seen nor sensed in the chaos of a situation, bringing order to that problem, and then presenting the solution to society.

According to Isaacson (2011), on the day the Macintosh computer was released, a reporter at *Popular Science* asked Steve Jobs what sort of market research he had done, and Jobs replied by asking, "Do you think Alexander Graham Bell did market research when he invented the telephone?" He meant that consumers don't know what they want until someone shows it to them. To locate a need, then, is the same as identifying a problem from chaos. This requires a well-honed sensibility. Once a true need has been identified, the possibility arises that the product created to meet that need will have market value. In other words, creative products often have difficulty attaining market value because people either do not need the solution generated by the product or they do not recognize that they need it.

Even if we define creativity as the process of extracting order from chaos, however, we cannot characterize creative activities within society unless we understand the factors that determine which problems are selected from chaos and what type of order is envisioned. For example, the process by which the understanding of the natural world transitioned from a geocentric theory to a heliocentric theory involved a complex interaction between intellectual and social structures. These intellectual structures are defined by interconnected systems of social customs, rules, morals, and ethics, and the social structures are defined by the interconnected frameworks of religion, art, and science of that time. The divergence of religion and science is thought to have weakened religion's role as an underlying societal factor, but, in reality, systems of social customs, rules, ethics, and morals can be said to represent the unconscious regulation of the society by religion. For example, Japanese people unconsciously employ concepts from Japan's Shinto religion through their perception that gods inhabit nature when they find meaning in life. Additionally, the very same Japanese who unconsciously believe Shinto concepts also employ Buddhist beliefs in their understanding of death. The nature of the self and relations with others is also determined by the underlying societal factors.

These factors impact creativity by influencing how people select problems and seek order. For instance, Isaacson asserts that Steve Jobs was strongly influenced by the minimalism of Zen Buddhism, and as a result sought elegant rather than extravagant design. Emotionally powerful films, meanwhile, draw their strength from the synthesis of universal themes and local idiosyncrasies. Idiosyncrasies bring change and difference to these stories, while universality allows them to attract a global audience. By communicating new discoveries that contribute to our understanding of humanity, films gain individuality and market success. It is the reexamination of society's underlying factors and the interconnections between them that allows for these new discoveries.

New creative products also influence lifestyles and social structures. By advancing communication and changing the way information is used in daily life, the iPhone has changed our lifestyles and our very society. Through the medium of the smartphone, social media has influenced the quality of communication, human relationships, and even the relationship between the state and its citizens; it has also dramatically impacted the creative activities that occurred after the development of the various SNS. Creative products that fundamentally transform society instigate a chain of new creation. When underlying societal factors change, it becomes possible to discover new problems and propose new types of order. When understandings of humanity change, the type of order people seek and the solutions they propose also change.

As the discussion up to this point has indicated, the essence of creativity is the extraction of order from chaos, and the nature of the problems selected and the order sought are influenced by underlying societal factors. Additionally, because creative products can alter these factors, they can lead to the genesis of new creative products. This implies that a deepening understanding of the underlying societal factors is essential to sustain creativity.

Creative products that bring social change greatly impact daily life. Yet, humans inherently tend to adapt to their environment. Since this tendency is not believed to bring about transformative activity, it is necessary to identify the factors that provoke people to transform society. In addition, when analyzing the mechanisms of socially transformative action, it is not enough to identify the people at the center of the transformation; we must also identify the other participants, and the relationships between them. This is often complicated and difficult. Mumford (2002) proposes the following four conditions for social innovation.

1. Social change requires active information exchange between like-minded individuals.
2. Ideas for social change must be profitable and achievable at low cost through currently existing systems.
3. On top of foundational support from the target group, elite support is also necessary.
4. Societal acceptance of social change requires effective propagation of information.

Mumford's inquiry into the cognitive processes of the leaders who serve as central actors in change reveals that they are the same as those employed in the ordinary creative process: problem discovery, information collection, concept formation, and idea creation. He proposes the following three theses in relation to leadership.

1. Leaders actively collect information on social problems.
2. Leaders identify constraints to problem resolution as well as strategies for avoiding these constraints.
3. Leaders' process of reexamining methods for achieving social change adheres to an interactive and integrative model that enables leaders to gain support and improve problem-solving methods.

In addition, by analyzing one of history's most prominent social innovators, Mumford extracts the following eight principles for success in the creative activity of social change.

1. Experience is important when locating problems whose resolution requires social change.
2. Experience allows people to evaluate the significance of problems and the possibility of new ideas.
3. By building on experience and selecting original ideas and methods, it is possible to achieve change that shatters existing ideas.
4. Problems should be broken down into a limited number of manipulatable essential elements, and a method for improving these elements proposed.
5. The proposed method of resolving the problem should be practicable and should lead to long-term progress.
6. It is important to communicate the fact that social change will bring short-term benefits at a relatively low cost. A strategy for attaining necessary funds should be elucidated on a practical level.
7. Effective means of information exchange should be established so that socially transformative ideas can penetrate society.
8. Ideas should be presented for creating new social systems and rules through social change, as well as for restructuring current social relationships.

While the above insights include a mixture of practical and theoretical aspects, they provide many hints for understanding the essence of the creative activity of social change, in which many actors participate and influence one another.

2.2 The Lineage of Creativity Research

Albert and Runco (1999) introduce seven approaches to studying creative ability, which are listed below.

1. The mystical approach
2. The pragmatic approach
3. The psychodynamic approach
4. The psychometric approach
5. The cognitive approach
6. The social-personality approach
7. The confluence approach

Each approach is summarized below.

1. The Mystical Approach

Adherents to this approach argue that the genesis of creativity lies in inspiration from a muse. In addition, they believe the mystical wellspring originates in the introspective activities of the artist, and that "demonic voices lurking in the heart" bring about creation. The unscientific nature of this approach has undeniably been an obstacle for creativity researchers attempting to gain knowledge from scientists.

Ghiselin (1985) has studied the mystical nature of creativity from a scientific perspective. For example, he suggests that sustained introspective contemplation is an important condition for inspiration. In the East as well, the scientific study of creativity has continued uninterrupted for many centuries. Zen philosophy can be viewed as one attempt to understand creativity scientifically. According to Legate (1981), the word "Zen" originates from the Sanskrit term dhyāna, meaning meditation, which was transliterated by the Chinese as zenna and then shortened to zen. Zen was brought from India to China during the Tang dynasty (618–905) by Daruma Daishi, and took root there. According to Zen teachings, zazen meditation leads to a state of "no-mind" and heightened concentration, flooding the body with energy and enabling flashes of inspiration.

The fact that this method has taken root globally can be interpreted as evidence that its effectiveness in heightening creativity has been confirmed through experience, it is a method to which a scientific basis can be attributed. Compton and Becker (1983) report that people with extensive experience in zazen meditation have higher Personal Orientation Inventory (POI) scores than those with less experience. This suggests that the creativity drawn out by Zen does not merely rely on mysticism, but rather has a scientific basis.

2. The Pragmatic Approach

Edward De Bono's theory of increasing creativity through "lateral thinking," which is not bound by preconceptions but rather approaches problems from a variety of angles, is representative of the pragmatic approach. However, this approach has scant theoretical basis and is only meaningful from a practical perspective. De Bono proposes methods such as using the four "po" words (hypothesis, suppose, possible, and poetry) to come up with ideas, and becoming adept at using the "six thinking hats" (white for data-based thought, red for intuitive thinking, yellow for positive thinking, black for critical thinking, green for creative thinking, and blue for process control). These diverse approaches to thinking, he suggests, will trigger creativity. Beginning in the 1950s, other thinkers also proposed methods such as brain storming and analogy, and starting in the 1980s, some suggested that creativity could be heightened by stripping away mistaken conventional notions. These ideas are limited by their lack of substantial theoretical basis and evidence of effectiveness.

3. The Psychodynamic Approach

This is the first scientific approach to creativity from a theoretical basis. As discussed in Freud (1964) and Blass (2006), the basic concept of this approach is that creativity is the expression of subconscious desires, including the drive for knowledge acquisition. Later, Kris (1952) proposed the theory of adoptive regression, asserting that the creative process consists of two stages. In the first stage, ideas that are repressed within the consciousness well up when sleeping or in dream-states, and in the second stage, these ideas are adapted to reality. However, other research suggests that conflicts in the subconscious cause fixated and repetitive ideas, blocking creativity. These approaches are difficult to substantiate through case studies, and over time mainstream psychology has moved away from them.

4. The Psychometric Approach

When studying the creativity of geniuses such as Leonardo da Vinci and Albert Einstein, obtaining experimental evidence is difficult. In response to this challenge, Guilford (1950) proposed using commonplace items such as books to calculate scores on a "divergent thinking" scale. This "psychometric approach" spread as a method of measuring creativity in ordinary people. Using the same concept, Torrance (1974) proposed the Torrance Tests of Creative Thinking , which use simple verbal and non-verbal tasks to measure divergent thinking and problem-solving ability. The test assesses fluency, flexibility, originality, and elaboration through tasks such as:

- asking questions (e.g., making up as many questions as possible about a given image);
- product improvement (e.g., proposing ways to improve a given toy to make it more fun to play with);
- unusual uses (e.g., proposing unconventional ways to use a box full of cardboard); and
- circles (e.g., combining circles to make a variety of shapes, and giving each one a name).

While this test has the benefit of providing a simple method for assessing creativity in ordinary people, critics have asserted that the creativity it tests is self-evident and that it is inappropriate for certain fields. In response, attempts are being made to increase the sophistication of the tasks. A more fundamental criticism is the items being measured (fluency, flexibility, originality, and elaboration) may not capture the elements of creativity. According to this line of thinking, creativity cannot be measured solely on the basis of how different a person is from the general population, and therefore the elements of creativity and the standards by which it is measured must be clearly defined.

Some have proposed a method in which the creativity of task solutions is evaluated by multiple people, and a consensus evaluation formed. However, many unresolved issues remain, including the essential question of whether understanding the creativity of ordinary people is the first step in understanding the creativity of geniuses.

5. The Cognitive Approach

The cognitive approach aims to understand the mental representations and processes of creative thinking. Two methods are used, one which studies human subjects and one which employs computer simulations. In the first category, Finke et al. (1992) have proposed the "genoplore" model, which divides creative thinking into two phases, generative and exploratory. In the generative phase, an individual forms mental representations called "pre-inventive structures," which promote creative discovery. In the exploratory phase, the individual generates a range of creative products by repeatedly attempting to give material form to these mental representations within the context of practical constraints. The cognitive approach is unique in that it sees the cognitive process by which an individual understands a particular reality as dependent upon knowledge; this knowledge becomes the foundation for a process of analogy formation and transformation that leads to new creations.

Methods employing computer simulations are useful in demonstrating creative processes. They have been used to recreate the processes leading to the discovery of scientific principles and to create jazz improvisations by inputting performance rules into a program.

6. The Social-personality Approach

This approach analyzes the influence of personality on creativity by examining the personality traits of creative people. For example, research by Barron and Harrington (1981) indicates that independent decision-making, self-confidence, attention to complexity, aesthetic orientation, and love of danger are linked to creativity. Related research analyzes the important role of self-actualization in motivating creative activity, and concludes that when an environment supporting creative activity exists, this motivation produces excellent results.

Amabile (1983) asserts that the motivation to create exists as an inherent human desire, and Sternberg and Lubart (1992) indicate that evaluation of creativity by others creates additional motivation to create, invigorating intellectual activity.

Research by Simonton (1994) and others on the societal factors that encourage creative activity indicates the importance of cultural diversity.

7. The Confluence Approach

The cognitive approach focuses on individual cognitive processes, while the social-personality approach excludes consideration of the problem of mental images; as such, both illuminate only one aspect of creativity. Sternberg (1985) made the first attempt to clarify the entire picture by elucidating the interconnections between various factors that determine creativity, known as the confluence approach. Sternberg views individual differences in cognitive process as reflections of personality differences, and has studied the connections between personality traits and the cognitive processes that influence creativity. The processes examined include techniques for connecting multiple ideas, patterns of identifying similarities and differences, aesthetic differences, differences in motivation, and understandings of societal norms.

To link cognitive processes with creative processes, it is also necessary to develop skills, knowledge, and abilities appropriate to creative activity. In practical terms, this means the development of problem discovery skills, problem solving skills, and the ability to sustain creative activity. Knowledge is also necessary for differentiating creative ideas from existing ones, avoiding problems, and solving problems.

Csikszentmihalyi (1988) proposes the concept of a creative system comprised of individuals, domains, and fields. Individuals turn existing information in the domain into new concepts by using cognitive processes, individual background, and motivation. The field is made up of people who participate in the domain and who evaluate new ideas. Let us take painting as an example. Painters form a group, encounter landscapes that stimulate their creativity, and engage in creative activities. In this case, the painter is the individual, painting is the domain, and the salon where art critics and sellers gather is the field. Creativity is understood as the product of an anomaly or discord in the system. For example, the Impressionists were at first regarded as heretics and their work repeatedly rejected from salons, but they formed associations with other like-minded painters, and a new system was created.

Sternberg and Lubart (1996) have proposed an "investment theory" that is related to the confluence approach. Although the idea of "buying low and selling high" takes place at a stage preceding evaluation of work, the process of presenting ideas with latent potential for development, adhering to them even while encountering early resistance, and popularizing them to improve their evaluation is considered a creative activity.

Investment theory leads to the idea that six resources are necessary for creative activity: intellectual ability, knowledge, thinking style, personality, motivation, and environment. In particular, the first three intellectual resources enable an individual to discover problems. Then, by considering them from a new perspective, the individual can move beyond the framework of existing ideas, determine which new ideas have high latent value, and consider the context in which a new idea can be communicated to other people.

Confluence approaches like those described above have enabled broad and deep understandings of creativity.

3 The Role of Codes, Icons, and Symbols in Creative Process

3.1 Definition of Code, Icon and Symbol

The basic definition of code is "a system of symbols, letters, or words given certain arbitrary meanings, used for transmitting messages requiring secrecy or brevity" (Random House Dictionary). An efficient way of transmitting messages would be sentences that explains all the information. All the members of a society can share messages from sentences if they share a common. Code is used to share messages among only the members of the specific group in which the secrecy behind of the code is common knowledge. In the creative process, code is important for sharing information among the specific group while preventing members of other groups from knowing it.

The basic definition of symbol is "a word, phrase, image, or the like having a complex of associated meanings and perceived as having inherent value separable from that which is symbolized, as being part of that which is symbolized, and as performing its normal function of standing for or representing that which is symbolized" (Random House Dictionary).

Code and symbol have special roles in condensing meaning and concept by linking to myths or stories. In particular, myths deliver various natural and religious mysteries and represents deep philosophy.

3.2 Celebrations and Creativity: The Roles of Code, Icon, and Symbols for Creative Activities

During celebrations, such as festivals and similar holidays and events, codes and symbols are used effectively to deliver myths and stories to the people, and provide justification for the celebration. The continuation of old traditions and clarification of the identity of the culture is done by using codes and symbols.

The myths and stories behind festivals are important for people in directing creative activities. Creation has long been viewed as the work of God, and the will of God has been delivered through myth and stories. In celebrations and festivals, science has been deemed as less important for explaining the mysteries of nature. In the creative process, these factors have stimulated creators in evoking ideas.

In the next subsection, we discuss about the points mentioned above by introducing the Tanabata festival of Japan. This festival is based on two legends. The first concerns Hikoboshi (the Cow Herder) and Orihime (the Weaving Princess), and the other is based on the story of the Swan Maiden. The outline of the former legend is as follows. Hikoboshi and Orihime fell in love, and got married. They were so happy living together that they forget to work hard. God became angry and he split them apart by a river through the universe, and permitted them to meet only once every year on July 7. This day commemorated the Lantern Festival (Bon) under Japan's old (lunisolar) calendar. This is a day when the ancestors come home. The original meaning of "Tanabata" is the day when people welcome ancestors. In addition, an event named "Kikkoden" has been held on the same day to pray for the improvement of craftsman skill. The latter legend is called "Hagoromo", and several variations of the story exist.

The key point is that the legends reflected the various types of messages included in the stories. Since the story had been passed down orally, the variations of messages reflected the different cultures of the area. Oral tradition is closely related with the emotions of the speakers, implying that the message can vary according to the emotional state of the speakers. Despite of the wide variations in the stories, the common message that run through the legend can be transferred by "code" and "symbol." By using these, the core message of the legend can appeal to the people. In case of "Tanabata," the code would be "universe," as represented by "Orihime star," "Hikoboshi star," and "Milky Way," and the symbol is "cloth." The code "universe" represents eternity, and the "cloth" symbolizes creativity.

The legend of "Tanabata" conveys the message that the eternal cycle of life is governed by cosmic law, and stresses the existence of absolute law that man cannot violate. Throughout the cycle of life, creation is a gift from the gods. The festival makes the people recognize these concepts, and provides them with the opportunity to express thanks to the gods for giving creative activities. The ritual in the festival is a means for transforming creative activity into sacred activity, and gives eternal value for creative activities. In other words, the festival works as a means for generating respect for the creative activities of people, and functions as a system for unifying the community and society. This is a reason why the legend and the festival have been passed down through many generations.

3.3 Code, Icon, and Symbol as a Means of Transferring Tacit Knowledge

Code, icon, and symbol work to convey condensed information in a concise manner. Thus, communication via code, icon, and symbol contains a wide variety of stimuli depending on the situation. For example, some specific colors convey a certain meaning depending on the situation. The combination of colors could act as a code. The simplest example is the color combination of the *misanga* (good-luck bracelet). The combination of blue and red implies the desire to win in a fight.

In transferring tacit knowledge, code, icon and symbol are used to select the people to whom the knowledge could be transferred. In the process of contemplation, there are many decision points. For decision making, some rules are necessary, and sometimes the rules are hidden through code, icon, and symbol. Selection of a color combination is the simplest example of a code and the subsequent transfer of tacit knowledge to the people who understand the code.

In contrast with knowledge transfer via an explicit manual, tacit knowledge is transferred via the transfer of logic rules and ways of thinking. This method of knowledge transfer has some advantages in knowledge creation and allows for flexible responses to unexpected events because the main part of the knowledge transfer is the rule or way of logic construction, rather than explicit knowledge. This type of knowledge is applicable in various manners. For example, in the Noh performance world, there exists no manual for costume combination. Noh performers learn the rules and logic of selecting the combination of costume through long training and experience. This logic is applicable to new performances, and the best combinations could be derived from this received knowledge.

Code, icon, and symbol are used to transfer information relating to logic. In Noh performance, various kinds of icons are used to transfer information and messages. The combination of icons is used to express messages. For example, "The Well Head" (Izutsu) is one of the most famous performances in Noh. In this performance, the well head is used as the main icon that acts as a mirror that reflects the past, present, and future. In addition, the well expresses the internal thoughts of the lady, and the lady can communicate with a man in another world through the well. Each accessory is given some meaning, and the combination of accessories expresses a certain message. The example of Noh illustrates the role of icon in transferring tacit knowledge and messages in creative activities.

The transfer of logic and ways of thinking by using code, icon, and symbols makes it possible for us to grasp things in a holistic manner because logic is constructed by linking various factors and elements. In another way, this holistic recognition makes it possible for us to evaluate stimuli or information received from outside. The process of evaluating information or stimuli is quite important for creative activities. Code, icon, and symbol are used to limit the volume of information, and allow us to focus on the essential factors of the logic construction and creative activities. Through this process, one can expand the imagination and link the information with emotion, and promote creative thinking. A simple example is a radio drama. The lack of visual information promotes the emotional sensitivities to dialogue and sound, and stimulates the imagination to visualize the world behind of the drama.

3.4 Anomalies Systematically Occur from Social Systems

War, revolution, riot, and revolt are regarded as anomalies in history. The point is that these anomalies arise systematically from social systems. One typical example is the appearance of Nazis before the World War II, and their process for gaining power in Germany. It is a kind of anomaly in history in the sense that most of the society became pro-war, and people were psychologically infected by the fascist beliefs. This drastic movement in Germany, as led by Adolf Hitler, used icon, code, and symbol to generate a collective hysteria in a society. The swastika was used as the symbol of Nazism, and represented the superiority of the Aryan race. The question remains: how could Hitler gain power by using this icon? The collective hysteria that occurred in Germany is regarded as an anomaly in history. However, this resulted from social contradictions in the process of economic development. Icon, code, and symbol are used to control the emotional movement of people living with these social contradictions. Anxiety or anger felt by the people were used to attract dissatisfied people to the Nazi party. Icon, code and symbol were used to generate such emotions through sharing of a common ideology.

Nazism is one of the worst example of this kind of anomaly, but it shows how an anomaly can systematically occur in the development of the economy, and icon, code, and symbol played an important role in guiding the emotions of the people.

3.5 Qualia, Collective Intelligence, and Tacit Knowledge: The Case of the Victory of Donald Trump

The example of Nazism can be generalized by introducing the concepts of qualia and collective intelligence. Qualia is a kind of emotional system. As Rolls (2014) explains, primary reinforcers generate feeling of "rewards" or "punishment" in response to stimuli; secondary reinforcers generate various complicated emotion such as anger or joy in combination with a given knowledge set. This implies that emotions respond to stimuli in different ways depending on the knowledge accumulated through an individual's experiences, which varies among individuals. Thus, the emotion generated from certain stimuli also varies among individuals. Since intelligence is linked with emotion in decision-making and behavior, subjective intelligence varies among individuals.

Collective intelligence is formed through the integration of the varying subjective intelligence of members of a society. Nishigaki (2013) defines collective intelligence as "the intelligence that dwells in the herd of a living organism," and, more narrowly, as "the intelligence generated through the knowledge exchanges among people via internet." In particular, it is necessary to stress that collective intelligence is different from the intelligence of experts. A typical example is the Fukushima nuclear power accident. In this example, the intelligence of experts concerning safety was not correct, and the accident happened. On the other hand, there were many people who were wary of the dangers of the nuclear power plant.

Another example is the victory of Donald Trump in the 2016 presidential election in the United States. Many experts predicted that Democratic candidate Hilary Clinton would win for various reasons. However, the actual results of the election can be regarded as the collective intelligence on the best leader for the United States. This example is quite important for understanding the essential reliability and the meanings of collective intelligence.

As is discussed above, the decision making and behavior of people are strongly dependent on emotional intelligence formed through the accumulation of experiences during one's lifetime. It is possible that the experiences faced by the experts are quite different from those of other ordinary people in the globalized economy. Roughly speaking, emotional intelligence is affected by a desire based on self-interest. In addition, logical thinking is affected by emotions that reflect their desires.

Collective intelligence reflects the shared emotions of a large portion of the people. Anger and fear about unemployment resulting from globalization generated negative emotions toward globalization and the free trade system. The victory of Mr. Trump in the 2016 election reflects the emotion of a large part of the people in the United States.

References

Albert, R. S., & Runco, M. A. (1999). A history of research on creativity. *Handbook of Creativity, 2*, 16–31.
Amabile, T. M. (1983). The social psychology of creativity: A componential conceptualization. *Journal of Personality and Social Psychology, 45*(2), 357.
Andersen, B., Brinkley, I., & Hutton, W. (2011). *Making the UK a global innovation hub: How business, finance and an enterprising state can transform the UK*. Big Innovation Center Working Paper, September 2011.
Barron, F., & Harrington, D. M. (1981). Creativity, intelligence, and personality. *Annual Review of Psychology, 32*(1), 439–476.
Berliant, M., & Fujita, M. (2008). Knowledge creation as a square dance on the Hilbert cube. *International Economic Review, 49*(4), 1251–1295.
Blass, R. B. (2006). A psychoanalytic understanding of the desire for knowledge as reflected in Freud's Leonardo da Vinci and a memory of his childhood. *The International Journal of Psychoanalysis, 87*, 1259–1276.
Bonting, S. L. (2006). Spirit and creation. *Zygon, 41*(3), 713.
Cho, I., Lee, K., Park, H., Park, M., & Kim, J. K. (2014). Development of an index for evaluating national quality competitiveness based on WEF and IMD compiled indices. *Quality Innovation Prosperity, 18*, 73–92.
Compton, W. C., & Becker, G. M. (1983). Self-actualization and experience with Zen meditation: Is a learning period necessary for meditation? *Journal of Clinical Psychology, 39*, 925–929.
Csikszentmihalyi, M. (1988). Society, culture, and person: A systems view of creativity. In R. J Sternberg (Ed.), *The nature of creativity*. Cambridge: Cambridge University Press.
Finke, R. A., Ward, T. B., & Smith, S. M. (1992). *Creative cognition, theory, research and applications*. Cambridge, MA: MIT Press.
Freud, S. (1964). *Leonard Da Vinci and the memory of his childhood*. New York; : Norton. (Original work published in 1910).
Ghiselin, B. (1985). *The creative process: A symposium*. LA: University of California Press.
Guilford, J. P. (1950). Creativity. *American Psychologist, 5*, 444–454.
Isaacson, W. (2011). *Steve Jobs*. Wydawnictwo: Insignis.
Kris, E. (1952). *Psychoanalytic exploration in art*. New York: International University Press.

Landry, C. (2000). *The creative city: A toolkit for urban innovators*. London: Earthscan.
Legate, J. J. (1981). Zen and creativity. *The Journal of Creative Behavior, 15*(1), 23–35.
Lee, G. K., & Cole, R. E. (2003). From a firm-based to a community-based model of knowledge creation: The case of the Linux kernel development. *Organization Science, 14*(6), 633–649.
Link, A. N., & Scott, J. T. (2009). Private investor participation and commercialization rates for government-sponsored research and development: Would a prediction market improve the performance of the SBIR programme? *Economica, 76,* 264–281.
Maslow, A. H. (1943). A theory of human motivation. *Psychological Review, 50,* 370–396.
Mumford, M. D. (2002). Social innovation: Ten cases from Benjamin Franklin. *Creativity Research Journal, 14,* 253–266.
Nishigaki, T. (2013). *Shugochi to wa Nannika-Netto Jidai no 'Chi' no Yuku (in Japanese)*. Tokyo: Cyuko-Sinsho.
Pink, D. (2005). *A whole new mind*. New York: Riverhead Books.
Putnam, R. D. (1993). *Making democracy work: Civic traditions in modern Italy*.Princeton: Princeton University Press (K. Jyunichi, Trans. 2001). *Tetsugaku Suru Minshushugi-Dento to Kaikaku no Shimintekikozo*. Tokyo: NTT Shuppankai.
Putnam, R. D. (2000). *Bowling alone*. New York: Simon & Schuster (Y. Shibanai, Trans. 2001). *Kodokuna Bowling-Beikoku Community no Hokai to Saisei*. Tokyo: Kashiwa Shobo.
Rolls, E. (2014). *Emotion and decision making explained*. Oxford: Oxford University Press.
Salem, A., & Mount, T. (1974). A convenient descriptive model of income distribution: The gamma density. *Econometrica, 42,* 1115–1127.
Simonton, D. K. (1994). *Greatness: Who makes history and why*. Guilford Press.
Sonne, L. (2012). Innovative initiatives supporting inclusive innovation in India: Social business incubation and micro venture capital. *Technological Forecasting and Social Change, 79,* 638–647.
Sternberg, J. R. (1985). Implicit theories of intelligence, creativity, and wisdom. *Journal of Personality and Social Psychology, 49,* 607–627.
Sternberg, J. R., & Lubart, T. I. (1992). Buy low and sell high: An investment approach to creativity. *Psychological Science, 1,* 1–5.
Sternberg, J. R., & Lubart, T. I. (1996). Investing in creativity. *American Psychologist, 51,* 677–688.
Torrance, E. P. (1974). *Torrance test of creative thinking*. Lexington, MA: Personnel Press.
Weinberg, D. B., de Ruyter, K., Dellarocas, C., Buck, M., & Keeling, D. I. (2013). Destination social business: Exploring an organization's journey with social media, collaborative community and expressive individuality. *Journal of Interactive Marketing, 27,* 299–310.
Wessner, W. C. (2000). *The small business innovation research program: An assessment of the department of defense fast track initiative*. Washington, DC: National Academy Press.
Wilson, F., & Post, J. E. (2013). Business models for people, planet (& profits): Exploring the phenomena of social business, a market-based approach to social value creation. *Small Business Economics, 40,* 715–737.
Yamaguchi, E. (2015). *Innovation Seisaku no Kagaku*. Tokyo: Daigaku Shuppan.
Yunus, M., Moingeon, B., & Lehmann-Ortega, L. (2010). Building social business models: Lessons from the Grameen Experience. *Long Range Planning, 43,* 308–325.

Chapter 14
Trust, Not Competition, as a Source of the Creative Economy

Stomu Yamash'ta and Tadashi Yagi

1 Introduction

In a society, trust is a crucial factor for efficient cooperation and transactions. Without trust, cooperation is impossible and to prevent cheating the cost of transactions becomes too high. In this sense, it is important to examine the mechanisms of trust formation in a society. These mechanisms have not been fully studied in a field of economics. Despite this, the importance of trust in economic activity is recognized by many researchers, including Zak and Knack (2001). They examine the conditions under which a society generates trust between members, and then derive the relationship between trust and economic growth.

In this paper, we further develop the work of Zak and Knack by considering the relationship between trust, happiness, and inequality. In pursuing this aim, the concept of social capital plays a central role. The pioneering work of Coleman (1990, Chap. 12) roughly defines social capital as the capital created when the relationships among people change in ways that facilitate action. The definition of social capital has been developing with the accumulation of research. There are primarily two conceptual types of social capital: external bridging and internal bonding. As an example of the former, Portes (1998, p. 6) defines social capital as the ability of actors to secure benefits by virtue of membership in social networks or other social structures. As an example of the latter, Putnam (1995, p. 67) defines

---

S. Yamash'ta
Center for the Study of the Creative Economy, Doshisha University, Kyoto, Japan

Sound Core Co., Ltd., Kyoto, Japan
e-mail: info@sound-core.jp

T. Yagi (✉)
Faculty of Economics, Doshisha University, Kyoto, Japan
e-mail: tyagi@mail.doshisha.ac.jp

social capital as the features of social organization such as networks, norms, and social trust that facilitate coordination and cooperation for mutual benefit.

Petrou and Kupek (2008) argue that social capital is the source from which the quality of social interactions is generated. The level of social capital in a society is determined by the degree of social and organizational trust. Yip et al. (2007) empirically show that higher levels of social capital have positive effects on happiness and that the level of trust affects health and well-being through the pathways of social networks and social supports.

Bjonskoy (2003) and Gundelach and Kreiner (2004) derive similar results by using cross-national data. The key point for our analysis here is that these prior studies show a positive correlation between happiness and trust level via the formation of social capital. In the literature, social capital is shown to have two roles: promoting income growth and stability for persons with low incomes, and increased security for persons with high incomes. At the level of the firm, a flat hierarchy, trust, and team-based enterprises may improve performance when operating in a wider trust-limited economic and organizational environment. However, over-investment in social capital increases transaction costs for the community.

In this chapter, we introduce a study by B'enabou and Tirole (2011) in which trust formation behavior is explained theoretically, and a study by Yagi (2017) in which the relationship between trust and happiness is empirically examined by using the data compiled in a research project funded by the Japan Society for the Promotion of Science (JSPS) in 2014. The dataset contains survey data from five countries (Japan, US, UK, France, and Germany) on respondents' levels of happiness and trust, in addition to data on various personal attributes and characteristics.

The results of the analysis show that higher levels of trust in society increase positive happiness, such as feelings of attainment, and decrease negative happiness, such as feelings of anxiety or anger. This trend is similar across all five of the countries, but there are some differences in the degree to which trust affects positive and negative happiness. For example, the effect is stronger in Japan than in the United States. These results have various implications for our understanding of the importance of trust in society. Because trust is formed through moral behavior, these research results suggest that there are some incentives for individuals to "invest" in morals to increase the positive benefits to society as a whole.

As discussed in Chap. 3, the concept of "no-self" is important for trust formation in a society or organization.[1] Simply put, a person who acts only for a society or organization without pursuing self-interest is believed to be "honest" and "fair." Such a person is trustable for many because he or she has no incentive to cheat others. The point is that the concept of "no-self" is the opposite of the concept of pursuing self-interest. Yet, "self-interest" is regarded as the driving force for people to make efforts. The concept of "no-self" is pro-equality, while the concept of

---

[1] In Chap. 3, the essential interpretation of the concept of "no-self" is given. In this chapter, it may improve understanding to restrict the concept to a narrower and more superficial meaning by defining "no-self" to mean that self-interest is not pursued seriously.

"self-interest" is anti-equality. In this sense, trust formation and economic growth may be more or less inconsistent. In this chapter, we examine this issue in detail.

The organization of the chapter is as follows. To clarify the theoretical foundation of the empirical analysis, Sect. 2 examines the behavioral structures through which individuals invest in morals. Section 3 explains the empirical analysis and discusses the implications of the empirical results. Section 4 discusses the issue of income inequality and its implications, and Sect. 5 explains how trust derived from the "no-self" concept is the best way for improving competitiveness. Section 6 concludes the paper.

2 Behavioral Structure of Investment in Morals

The mechanisms through which trust is built in a society are worth investigating. In this section, the incentive structure to pursue the building of trust in a society is examined. Morals are an important factor for generating trust. If each agent behaves opportunistically, it is hard to believe in others and trust cannot be formed. However, the behavior for investing in morals is not simple and we must analyze the behavioral structure of this pathway for building trust.

B'enabou and Tirole (2011) examined this problem by building a mathematical model. In their three-period model, individuals are each endowed with the initial moral stock A_0. This initial moral stock is a function of the innate ability for empathy given to the individual. It is assumed that individuals can expect their innate moral level to be high at probability p, and low at probability $1 - p$. In period 0, individuals determines whether they invest in morals ($a_t = 1$) or not ($a_t = 0$). Thus, the moral stock at period 1 is determined by $A_1 = A_0 + a_0 r_0$, where r_0 is the rate of return on the investment in morals. At the start of period 0, the agent receives a signal about whether his or her level of altruism is high or low (H or L). At period 1, individuals infer their true innate ability for empathy from the actual investment behavior for morals in period 0 at probability $(1 - \rho)$. $\hat{\rho}$ denotes an individual's prior belief about "what kind of person" he or she is and the individual's future belief about his or her innate ability for empathy is given by $\hat{v} \equiv \hat{\rho} v_H + (1 - \hat{\rho}) v_L$.

The optimization problem is formulated as follows:

$$\max_{a_0 \in \{0,1\}} \{-c_0^k a_0 + \lambda V(v_k, v_k, A_0 + a_0 r_0) + (1 - \lambda) V(v_k, \hat{v}(a_0), A_0 + a_0 r_0)\},$$

where c_0^k is the investment cost, V is a value function, and λ is the probability of remembering one's true valuation of V in period 1. $1 - \lambda$ can be viewed as the malleability of beliefs through actions. By solving this problem, B'enabou and Tirole derive the following results. First, people invest in morals as their own belief in their true ability for empathy becomes more malleable. Second, people tend to invest more in morals as the cost of investment decreases and the return on the investment increases. Third, people tend to invest more in morals when the initial moral stock is higher (i.e., the innate ability for empathy is higher).

Trust is formed through the interrelationships between members of society and social capital is accumulated through trust formation. Since investment in morals by members of a society determines the trust level in the society as a whole, the optimal level of investment by individuals and the socially optimal level of investment diverge when the innate ability for empathy differs among individuals.

For an individual who views the return on moral investment as being small (i.e., a small value of rA_0), a decision to make no investment is optimal. However, this behavior erodes overall social capital and decreases the level of trust in society. In other words, there must be some mechanism to encourage low-empathy individuals in a society to make an investment in morals.

An important point to stress is that opportunistic behavior is not the same as illegal behavior, and the law is not an efficient tool for preventing opportunistic behavior. Contracts are a method for avoiding the damage from opportunistic behavior by other parties, but the transaction costs are high, which makes contracts an unrealistic option in community relationships.

With this in mind, we examine the factors that prevent members of a society from behaving opportunistically. A key mechanism for achieving this is increasing the initial endowment of moral ability A_0, which is partly determined by innate ability, but is possibly increased by moral education within the family or community during childhood. Nishimura et al. (2015) show that basic types of moral behavior (e.g., "Do not lie," "Be kind to others," "Follow the rules," "Study," etc.) are formed in the family during childhood and affect individuals' earning potential in the labor market. According to Nishimura et al. (2015), individuals with disciplined morality earn $7183 more than individuals without disciplined morality. This difference can be interpreted as the return on investment for moral formation in the family.

B'enabou and Tirole (2011) assume that moral investment is voluntarily determined by individuals, but in reality, the initial level of morality is formed within the family forcibly and independently from an individual's optimal choice. A high initial value of morality affects the investment decision positively in the later period and the level of moral stock increases as time passes.

It should be borne in mind that the decisions made by individuals are affected by the level of social trust via the rate of return on moral investment. In other words, the rate of return for moral investments may be higher in a society with a high level of trust. Individuals will not rely on trust within society if the trust level is believed to be quite low. For example, the importance of contracts is higher in the United States than in Japan. One interpretation is that people do not rely on trust when conducting transactions in the United States and instead use contracts as a tool for preventing immoral behavior. In contrast, people in Japan more often rely on trust without the use of contracts, which reduces transaction costs. In Japan, whether an individual is judged to be a person of high morals affects the evaluation of the person by others in the market.

The discussion above suggests that moral investment behavior differs among countries and societies depending on the level of trust. A low level of trust can lead to a self-perpetuating cycle in moral investment behavior, where low trust begets opportunistic behavior and low investment in morals, which lowers trust even further. However, the return on moral investment might not be restricted to economic benefits. The level of trust in a society may affect the happiness of individuals directly without passing through economic channels. Trust within communities may enrich people's lives, increase the sense of security, relieve anxiety, or alleviate feelings of loneliness.

Finally, we must discuss a point of view that is absent in the analysis of B'enabou and Tirole (2011). Not only does empathy affect team building in organizations, so does the social process itself. The effects of these is most prominent in organizational affairs where empathy is captured into collective action. In addition, in a situation in which society has high sub-group trust, but an overall aggregate framework of non-trust may be one that is often observed. It is necessary to examine how trust formation is altered in multi-level subgroups when overall trust is not attained. Moreover, it is worth mentioning that the moral investment of business organizations is increasingly enforced by wider (shareholder) pressure to pursue moral (organic, sustainable, non-exploitative) goals.

In the next section, we examine the relationship between trust and happiness empirically, and test the theoretical implications.

3 Trust and Happiness

In conventional economics, happiness was excluded from academic examinations. One reason for this was that many believed happiness to be subjective and not amenable to objective measurement. Frey and Stutzer (2002) challenged this topic scientifically, and the many researchers have followed their approach by developing measurements of happiness. Tachibanaki (2015) presents the advancement of scientific analysis on happiness and reveals various important facts about how people feel happiness by using comparable data from five countries (Japan, US, UK, France, and Germany).

In this section, we discuss the relationship between trust and happiness. Trust is a kind of social capital and is formed following the accumulation of efforts spent forming trust. Intuitively, we know that a person cannot be happy if he or she is isolated from society. To live together in a society, trust is indispensable. This is the basic relationship between the trust and the happiness.

In addition, another key relationship between the trust and the happiness is observed in the work place, especially in creative activities. A person feels happiness when he or she achieves something important, or creates new things. To achieve something in a workplace, trust between members is crucial. Friendly competition among colleague brings about good results and achieves important things. In the workplace, colleagues do not listen to the opinion of a person who is unreliable because people guess that his or her opinion reflects personal interest rather than the organizational interest. On the other hand, a person who is reliable can attract colleagues and receive help from them when needed, allowing him or her to accomplish important things. In this kind of situation, people feel happiness.

Yagi (2017) examined the relationship between trust and happiness by using micro-level data collected from a nationwide Internet survey in five countries (Japan, US, UK, France, and Germany). The surveys were designed and implemented during 2012–2013 for a research project sponsored by the JSPS that investigated the socioeconomic determinants of subjective well-being. The surveys captured ample information about individuals' subjective assessments of their own well-being, personal traits, demographic and socioeconomic status, and perceived neighborhood characteristics, all of which are useful for examining the relationship between trust and happiness. The approach for data collection is in line with previous research such as Oshio and Urakawa (2012).

The survey contained a question about feelings of trust. Specifically, the survey asked about the degree of trust in others with the question: "How much do you trust people?" In addition to this question, the survey also includes other questions on the level of trust with specific people and groups in society. The objects of trust included family, friends, community, society, and so on. Using factor analysis, we isolate three principal factors: "community activity," "ease of consultation," and "community security," which are listed in Table 1.

Table 1 Factor analysis on level of trust in society

	Able to consult	Crime anxiety	Community activity	Meeting neighbors
Frequency of meeting your neighbors	−0.258	0.004	0.288	0.654
How many neighbors do you meet?	−0.234	0.009	0.399	0.631
Community activities	−0.161	0.011	0.622	0.298
Sports activities	−0.167	0.005	0.589	0.094
Volunteer activities	−0.132	0.020	0.729	0.058
Consulting neighbors	0.488	0.035	−0.199	−0.470
Consulting family	0.588	−0.090	0.020	0.019
Consulting relatives	0.662	−0.049	−0.053	−0.050
Consulting friends	0.633	−0.038	−0.047	0.009
Consulting doctors or consultants	0.560	0.028	−0.096	−0.083
Consulting teachers	0.479	0.092	−0.155	−0.109
Victim of crime	0.045	0.537	0.029	0.029
Noticed graffiti	−0.009	0.726	−0.020	0.041
Group of teenaged boys making noise	−0.021	0.781	−0.021	0.056
Illegally parked cars	−0.007	0.625	0.021	0.027
Far from the nearest police station	−0.030	0.200	0.002	−0.064

Source Yagi (2017)

Helliwell and Putnam (2004) show that spiritual belief and social capital have some effect on happiness. Social capital includes high levels of social trust and high levels of institutional or organizational trust (Petrou and Kupek 2008). Cross-country data also indicates a high correlation between social capital and happiness (Bjonskov 2003; Gundelach and Kreiner 2004). In short, the empirical results are consistent with the results given in the previous literature.

As is shown in Fig. 1, the effect of trust on positive happiness is dominant. While there could be some correlation between the level of trust and certain personality traits such as neuroticism or disagreeableness, the regression analysis includes personality variables to control for the effect of personality on positive happiness. Conscientiousness has the strong effect on positive happiness. According to Roberts et al. (2014), conscientiousness plays a role in most of the major domains of life and predicts higher achievement in education and work outcomes, and occupational attainment. It is a personality trait that reflects enduring, automatic patterns of thoughts, feelings, and behaviors. These properties

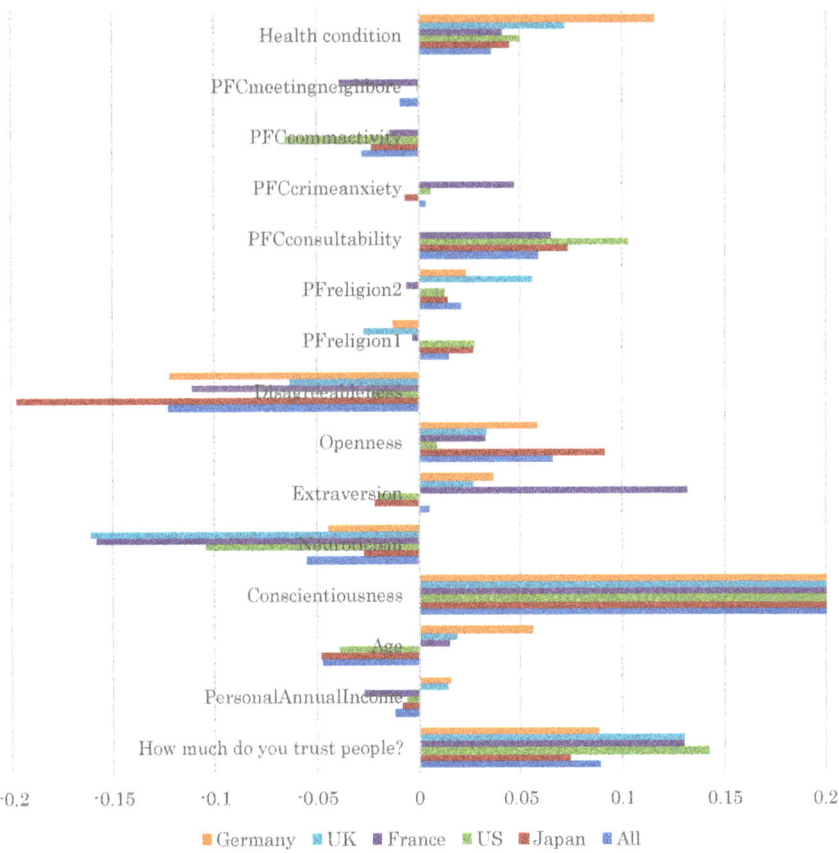

Fig. 1 Effect of trust on positive happiness. *Source* Yagi (2017)

promote positive efforts to attain goals. In addition, Shanahan et al. (2014) suggest that there is a positive relationship between conscientiousness and health. Health condition is found to strongly affect happiness, as predicted by Petrou and Kupek (2008).

The results show that the trust captured by the question "How much do you trust people?" has a strong positive effect on positive happiness. This result is common across all five countries. It is interesting that trust has the strongest effect on positive happiness in the United States. The principal factor "PFC consultability (able to consult)" has the second strongest positive effect on positive happiness, excluding the impact of personality effects.

It is worth noting that the trust variable has a stronger effect on positive happiness than annual income, with this tendency common across all five counties. It must be asked: why does the trust variable have a stronger effect than income? One possibility is that there is a strong correlation between the trust variable and income. However, the correlation coefficient between the trust variable and income is only 0.11, which is not particularly strong. The results therefore give us some important implications for the meaning of trust. Most importantly, a person can feel happy if he or she can trust other people, regardless of income level. Whether a person can trust others is more important than whether one is rich.

Because positive happiness represents feelings of attaining something important, the results imply that trust is necessary for attainment. To attain something, cooperation is necessary. That is, a person who is successful in maintaining cooperation can attain his or her objective and, as a result, feels positive happiness.

Finally, the effects of religion on positive happiness are not straightforward, but they are generally weak and the direction of the effect differs among the five countries.

Figure 2 shows the results of the multivariate regression analysis on the effect of trust on negative happiness after controlling for the effects of personality. Negative happiness represents feelings of anxiety, sadness and so on. The results of the analysis show that increasing trust (as captured by the question, "How much do you trust people?") decreases feelings of negative happiness. In contrast, the trust has a weaker effect on positive happiness. Overall, the effects of trust and income are similar. That is, income is also important for decreasing feelings of anxiety. The principal factor of "community activities" also decreases feelings of negative happiness. It is not easy to interpret the results for the principal factor of "ability to consult," which appears to increase feelings of negative happiness. One interpretation is that a person who feels anxiety or sadness needs someone with whom to consult. Similar to the results for the positive happiness, religion does not significantly decrease feelings of negative happiness.

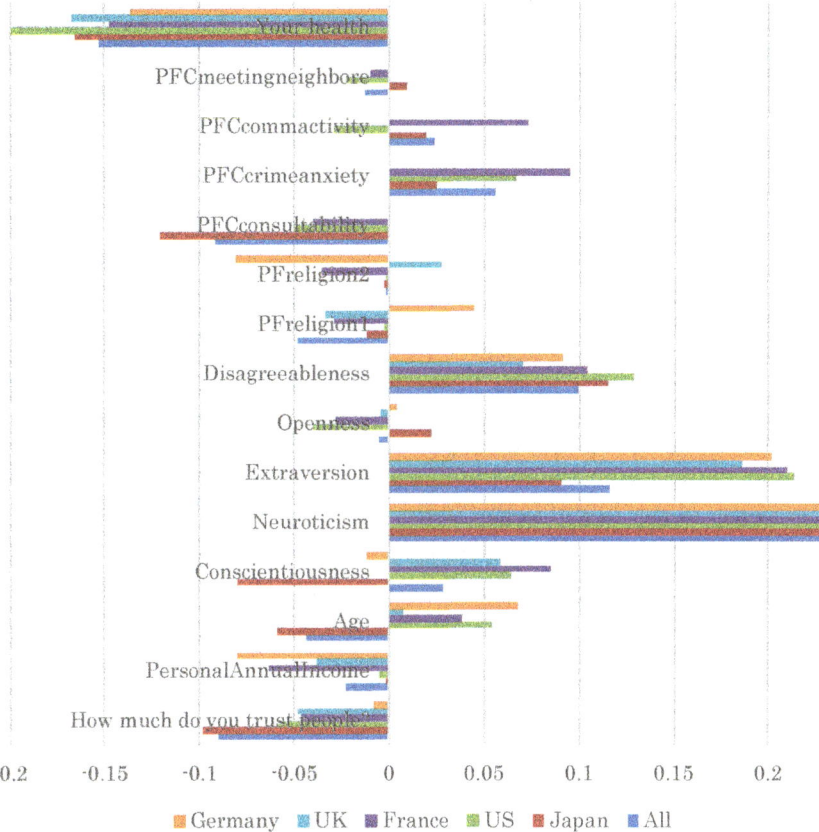

Fig. 2 The effect of trust on negative happiness. *Source* Yagi (2017)

4 Trust and Inequality—Trust-Consistent Self-interest

The concept of "no-self" is important for trust formation in a society or an organization, while "self-interest" is regarded as the driving force for people to put forth effort. In this sense, the relationship between trust formation and inequality must be examined carefully.

To tackle this problem, we consider the concept of "trust-consistent self-interest." This issue has been discussed in various contexts in numerous studies over the years such as Berg et al. (1995), Lyons and Mehta (1997), and Bocian et al. (2016). Berg et al. study trust and reciprocity including the repeat game reputation effect. Lyons and Mehta examine the role of trust in facilitating efficient exchange relations when agents are vulnerable to opportunistic behavior. Bocian et al. examine how trust is affected depending on whether or not cheating arises from self-interest by using a psychology approach.

The concept of "trust-consistent self-interest" does not allow for the pursuit of self-interest if the behavior does not appeal to moral sentiments, as discussed by Smith (1761). In his writing, Smith stresses that sympathy plays a role in determining how the actions of others are judged. Concretely, we judge the action as just if we sympathize with the affections that brought about the action, and unjust if the opposite. In this section, we propose several criteria for evaluating the pursuit of self-interest using the concept of "trust-consistent self-interest," as listed below.

1. First-order criteria: Pursuing self-interest is allowed if it is necessary to attain the basic needs for living.
2. Second-order criteria: Pursuing self-interest is allowed if it brings about Pareto improvement, that is, if it improves a person's own well-being without harming the well-being of other people.
3. Third-order criteria: Pursuing self-interest is allowed if it improves the average well-being all other people in society.
4. Fourth-order criteria: Pursuing self-interest is allowed if adheres to the moral sentiment of members of society.

The order of these criteria reflects the degree of social concern. When self-interest is consistent with societal interest, self-interest can be viewed as acceptable in a society. Using these criteria, we can evaluate whether a behavior builds trust in society.

For example, we can evaluate the behavior of an international company that receives high profits from globalization. As discussed in Atkinson (2016), income inequality in developed countries such as the U.S., U.K. and Japan are worsening as globalization increases. Atkinson shows that the richest 1% of the population earns around 25% of the total income in the U.S., and 15% in the U.K. In this example, as long as the company's business improves the average well-being of the members of society where it operates, the company's behavior can be regarded as trustworthy. However, tax havens, child labor, unfair contracts with low wages, and low payments for intermediate products by using strong negotiating power are practices that are not aligned with moral sentiments.

The key point is whether the market has some mechanism for identifying companies whose behavior runs counter to moral sentiment. For this purpose, the price mechanism is not helpful because consumers want to buy products and services at the lowest price possible unless he or she believes in or follows pro-social ethics such as, for example, free range eggs, coffee and forest products from sustainable agriculture, or textiles from companies not associated with exploitative child labor practices in developing countries.

The only way to control immoral behavior is to appeal to the moral sentiments of consumers through various kinds of media such as mass media and SNS. Trust in the society will be eroded if the behavior of the company is contrary to the moral sentiment of the people in the society, and it is through this mechanism that companies will be selected in the market.

According to prior research such as Ariely (2010) on deterring immoral behavior, the most effective way to prevent fraud is to appeal to the internal emotions of a person. Individuals can commit fraud, even when it is against the law, if they can justify their behavior to themselves. On the other hand, many individuals will be unwilling to commit fraud, even when the fraud will be never discovered, if they feel some psychological cost for committing the fraud. In this sense, criticism via various kinds of media decreases the immoral behavior of companies.

Extreme inequality erodes the trust of people in a society because excess profits imply the exploitation of various kinds of resources and causes negative feelings based on their moral sentiment. The erosion of trust in society could cause a decline in the efficiency of the economy because of the decline in work incentive and weakening cooperation in a society or an organization. In addition, lack of trust causes some people to commit crime because they can justify the crime to themselves, and thus society becomes unstable.

It is true that the policies available for controlling immoral behavior are limited, unless new laws are enacted. For example, some have advocated for international cooperation to restrict the use of tax havens, but the effectiveness of this approach has been limited. The most promising policy for maintaining trust in society is to increase the marginal tax rate on the highest income bracket, as proposed by Atkinson (2016). This policy discourages people from seeking excess profits, and the tax revenue gained could be used to enhance the well-being of ordinary people.

In practical terms, however, the richest have the financial resources to employ the best lawyers and accountants to ensure they minimize their tax liability. In addition, it is necessary to examine the relative effectiveness of policies on the taxation of income versus the taxation of wealth. In general, taxation of wealth is not easy to implement when income is taxed because taxation on the same income source twice is often prohibited. The exception to this is the estate tax and other taxes on inheritance. By raising the tax rate on estate transfers, it is possible to decrease the transmission of inequality over generations.

5 Trust and Cooperation in an Organization

In conventional neoclassical economic theory, altruistic behavior is only assumed to occur with family members or siblings, and altruistic behavior toward others is assumed non-existent. The empirical and experimental studies, however, show some evidence for the existence of altruistic behavior toward others in the real economy [see Forsythe et al. (1994)]. Bolton and Ockenfels (2000) examine the factors that drive altruistic behavior by formulating the equity, reciprocal, and competitive (ERC) theory. These previous studies are limited to simple cases where the relationships between the people examined are not complicated. The relationships among people within an organization is more complicated because the interdependency is complicated. Because of the complicated interrelationships among organization members, it is unrealistic to assume that people can simply seek an advantage by behaving strategically using a game theory framework.

DeScioli and Krishna (2013) criticize the ERC model because it assumes only self-interest, and stress the importance of the social preference theory, which focuses on social psychology, including interpersonal altruism, fairness, reciprocity, and inequity aversion.

An organization's culture is a critical for predicting the state of cooperation. For example, a leader with a clear vision and a non-hierarchical management style can build a culture of cooperation. In this case, the organization can be competitive and act in the interest of the organization as a whole.

In this book, we introduce the Buddhist concept of "no-self" for explaining stable organizational structures. The concept of "no-self" is important for forming trust in an organization. A person with "no-self" has a big advantage in gaining trust from other members of the organization because the members can believe that the person's behavior is not strategic and is done for the benefit of the organization. Once organization members feel that a person's behavior is strategically pursing self-interest, it is hard for the members to believe the person because of his or her intention and purpose cannot always be predicted.

Having "no-self" is a robust and optimal way of behaving in an organization because trust can be formed easily and cooperation within an organization can be attained smoothly. On the other hand, a person who is seen as pursuing his or her own self-interest cannot form trust among the members, and will find it hard to gain cooperation.

According to the research on an R&D engineering organization by Nakata (2017), it is shown that many R&D organizations regard the "no-self" character of engineers as an important element when hiring. Since R&D is produced in a team, behavior based on self-interest could be an obstacle to cooperation. Once the members of the team believe that an idea is based on self-interest, the members will hesitate to accept the idea because they believe that it would not be optimal for attaining the team's objective.

The question is what system incentivizes members of the organization to behave in a "no-self" manner. Basically, it is necessary to teach the virtue of the "no-self" concept to the members of the organization repeatedly. In addition, fair treatment of members and a long-run evaluation system are necessary for the system to be sustainable. If members of the organization believe that behaving in a "no-self" way is the best way for attaining long-run self-interest, the behavior should be consistent with the incentives of members and sustainable in the long-run. This system promotes trust formation and cooperation, and improves the efficiency and competitiveness of the organization.

The conventional approach has focused on analyzing the bonus structure in R&D organizations, which is viewed by many as the most effective method for understanding the behavior of an engineer. Holmstrom (1989) shows that the cost of providing an engineer with bonuses increases as the size of the organization increases due to the difficulty of identifying the portion of the contribution attributable to any one person. This implies that setting up a bonus structure is not an effective way to improve the productivity of an engineer.

Hirshleifer and Suh (1992) and Jensen (1993) explain why it is difficult to construct a bonus structure for improving the productivity of engineers by focusing on reverse innovation or downsizing during heightened competition. On the other hand, Lerner and Wulf (2007) concludes empirically that long-term evaluations of R&D engineers are the best way to identify an engineer's contribution toward improving the R&D productivity and to compensate them accordingly. The results of these studies are consistent with the idea that the trust derived from the "no-self" concept is the most important source of competitiveness.

6 Conclusion

This chapter discusses the mechanisms of moral formation, which act as the source of trust in society and in organizations. It then investigates the effect of trust on happiness. The findings suggest that moral investment behavior differs among countries and societies depending on the level of trust. Furthermore, there may be a self-perpetuating cycle in terms of low trust leading to less moral investment behavior. However, the return on moral investment might not be restricted only to economic factors. Trust in society may also affect the happiness of individuals directly without passing through economic channels. Trust in a community may enrich peoples' lives, improve the sense of security, relieve anxiety, and remedy the sense of loneliness.

Lastly, we introduced the concept of "no-self" as the best way of forming trust. Having "no-self" allows members of an organization to cooperate. In this sense, pursuing self-interest is not the best way to improve the productivity of an organization, and economic analysis based on pursuing self-interest does not capture the essential mechanism of cooperation within an organization.

References

Ariely, D. (2010). *The upside of irrationality: The unexpected benefits of defying logic at work and at home*. New York: HarperCollins.
Atkinson, A. B. (2016). *Inequality—What can be done?*. Cambridge, Massachusetts: Harvard University Press.
B'enabou, R. & Jean T. (2011). Identity, morals and taboos: Beliefs as assets, *The Quarterly Journal of Economics, 126*, 805–855.
Berg, J., Dickhaut, J., & McCabe, K. (1995). Trust, reciprocity, and social history. *Games and economic behavior, 10*(1), 122–142.
Bjonskov, C. (2003). The happy few: Cross-country evidence on social capital and life satisfaction. *Kyklos, 56*, 3–16.
Bocian, K., Baryla, W., & Wojciszke, B. (2016). When dishonesty leads to trust: Moral judgments biased by self-interest are truly believed. *Polish Psychological Bulletin, 47*(3), 366–372.

Bolton, G. E., & Ockenfels, Axel. (2000). ERC: A theory of equity, reciprocity, and competition. *American Economic Review, 90,* 166–193.
DeScioli, P., & Krishna, S. (2013). Giving to whom? Altruism in different types of relationships. *Journal of Economic Psychology, 34,* 218–228.
Forsythe, R., Horowitz, J., Savin, N. E., & Sefton, M. (1994). Fairness in simple bargaining experiments. *Games and Economic Behavior, 6,* 347–369.
Frey, B., & Stutzer, A. (2002). *Happiness and Economics.* Princeton, NJ: Princeton University Press.
Gundelach, P., & Kreiner, S. (2004). Happiness and life satisfaction in advanced European countries. *Cross-Cultural Research, 38,* 359–386.
Helliwell, J. F., & Robert, D. P. (2004). The social context of well-being, *Philosophical transactions—Royal Society of London series B359 biological sciences,* 1435–1446.
Hirshleifer, D., & Suh, Y. (1992). Risk, managerial effort, and project choice. *Journal of Financial Intermediation, 2,* 308–345.
Holmstrom, B. (1989). Agency costs and innovation. *Journal of Economic Behavior & Organization, 12,* 305–327.
Jensen, M. C. (1993). The modern industrial revolution, exit, and the failure of internal control systems. *Journal of Finance, 48,* 831–880.
Lerner, J., & Wulf, J. (2007). Innovation and incentives: Evidence from corporate R& D. *The Review of Economics and Statistics, 89,* 634–644.
Lyons, B., & Mehta, J. (1997). Contracts, opportunism and trust: Self-interest and social orientation. *Cambridge Journal of Economics, 21*(2), 239–257.
Nakata, Y. (2017). Report on productivity of Japanese software engineer and the effect of work compensation—Comparative study among U.S., Asia and Europe-, Information-Technology Promotion Agency, Japan.
Nishimura, K., Junnich, H., Tadashi, Y., Junko, U. (2015). Basic morality and social success in Japan. *Journal of Informatics and Data Mining, 1*(1):6, 1–10, (available from: http://datamining.imedpub.com/archive.php).
Oshio, T., & Urakawa, K. (2012). Neighborhood satisfaction, self-rated health, and psychological attributes: A multilevel analysis in Japan. *Journal of Environmental Psychology, 32*(4), 410–417.
Petrou, S., & Kupek, E. (2008). Social capital and its relationship with measures of health status: Evidence from the Health Survey for England 2003. *Health economics, 17*(1), 127–143.
Portes, A. (1998). Social capital: its origins and applications in modern sociology. *Annual Review of Sociology, 24,* 1–25.
Putnam, R. D. (1995). Bowling alone: America's declining social capital. *Journal of Democracy, 6,* 65–78.
Roberts, B. W., Lejuez, C., Krueger, R. F., Richards, J. M., Hill, P. L. (2014). What is conscientiousness and how can it be assessed? *Developmental Psychology, 50*(5), 1315.
Shanahan, M. J., Hill, P. L., Roberts, B. W., Eccles, J., & Friedman, H. S. (2014). Conscientiousness, health, and aging: the life course of personality model, *Developmental Psychology, 50*(5), 1407.
Smith, A. (1761). *Theory of Moral Sentiments* (2nd ed.). London: A. Millar.
Tachibanaki, T. (2015). *Advances in happiness research.* Tokyo: Springer.
Yagi, T. (2017). Moral, trust and happiness-Why does trust improves happiness? *Journal of Organizational Psychology,* 17: forthcoming.
Yip, W., Subramanian, S. V., Mitchell, A. D., Lee, D. T., Wang, J., & Kawachi, I. (2007). Does social capital enhance health and well-being? Evidence from rural China. *Social Science and Medicine, 64,* 35–49.
Zak, P. J., & Knack, S. (2001). Trust and growth. *The Economic Journal, 111,* 295–321.

Chapter 15
Creative Organizations

Tadashi Yagi

1 The Organizational Theory Approach to Creativity

The organizational theory approach to creativity examines the types of structures and cultures that heighten creativity. Ever since the mid-eighteenth century, when Adam Smith revealed the benefits of the division of labor, economists have considered it desirable for each person to faithfully fulfill his or her assigned task so as not to disturb the order of the organization as a whole, just as if they were parts of a machine. However, while the division of labor enables workers to improve their efficiency by increasing their knowledge and skills within one limited area, it also renders comprehension of the entire production system difficult, leading to a decline in ability to respond to irregularities and environmental changes.

Critics have noted the importance of forming decentralized organizations capable of responding swiftly to a range of environmental changes, rather than hierarchical ones that issue orders and regulations in a centralized manner. Within this context, some have noted that the ability of members in an organization to make decisions and act autonomously within a network plays a key role in promoting creativity within the organizational structure (see Williams and Yang 1999). In particular, as the pattern of innovation changes from gradual knowledge creation to revolutionary knowledge creation, several attributes of network organizations gain importance: autonomous participation, sharing of goals and values, distributed and open systems, duplication of members, redundancy, and leeway (see Kikuchi 2009). Along with these attributes, an openness to the external world enables knowledge creation in response to the increasingly complex and sophisticated problems that accompany abrupt environmental changes.

T. Yagi (✉)
Faculty of Economics, Doshisha University, Kyoto, Japan
e-mail: tyagi@mail.doshisha.ac.jp

© The Editor(s) 2018
S. Yamash'ta et al. (eds.), *The Kyoto Manifesto for Global Economics*,
Creative Economy, https://doi.org/10.1007/978-981-10-6478-4_15

The problem is that in some cases, members of an organization resist innovation on a psychological level. In organizations that have historically offered long-term employment, workers seeking stable jobs tend to reject change. When this type of psychological barrier exists, it is easy to fall into thinking patterns that confuse goals with methods. Change is obstructed when workers forget the real purpose of the organization and instead aim only to follow current rules. Frequently, workers who were content with the old structure fear a loss of status under the new structure and form a contingent that is resistant to change. A more serious situation arises when individuals who prioritize short-term personal profit over the preventing the demise of the organization secretly obstruct change even when it is obvious that the organization has reached a dangerous state, and change is unavoidable. Such a situation renders change impossible and leads to the destruction of the organization. In some cases, blame is directed not at the organization but at its members who are unable to respond to change. Yet even in this type of situation, major personnel changes implemented through mergers and acquisitions or other techniques can revive a project if it has significant latent potential.

It is a mistake to assume that traditional hierarchical organizations have nothing to offer in terms of promoting creativity. These organizations obstruct creativity when bureaucratic and conservative administrators create an atmosphere in which creativity is not valued, but they can be highly effective if they affirm valuable creative activities while maintaining the discipline of the organization, thereby improving the overall efficiency of decision making. In decentralized organizations, there is no guarantee that decisions that are appropriate for one division will be optimal for the organization as a whole. For that reason, when deciding whether to undertake organizational reform to promote creativity, it becomes necessary to consider in detailed and practical terms the pros and cons of both options.

It is necessary, then, to elucidate the types of groups and processes within which creative activities occur, and to consider how their work impacts intra-organizational relationships. For example, if one department is developing a new product, it is necessary to assess that department's cooperation with other departments developing competing products, as well as to consider the standing of the individuals who control that cooperative relationship. Within an organization, creative activities frequently compete with existing activities. It is therefore important to carefully design organizational structures and remuneration systems so that creative activities are not impeded, even when the interests of various members of the organization clearly diverge.

To increase individual creativity, organizations must create an atmosphere in which freedom is permitted, clarify the steps involved in creative activities, and implement training in creative thinking patterns. However, insofar as original thinking patterns can lead to unique creative products, the effectiveness of training is not clear. Furthermore, it is important to form groups where individuals can engage in frequent discussion and debate; promote the formation of networks inside and outside the organization; and continuously bring information about changes in the outside world, as well as external stimulation, into the organization. Recent research has indicated the importance of corporate social responsibility (CSR) programs in furthering these efforts (see Kikuchi 2009). The goal of CSR is for the company to contribute to society, but by engaging in CSR projects, workers develop social awareness and gain perspectives that help them identify problems, conceive of new plans, and understand emerging societal needs, which contributes to the company's creative development. Therefore, while moral education and CSR training of workers may not appear directly related to creativity, they play an important role in enhancing social perspectives, which in turn nurtures creative ability.

Determining remuneration for creative products is an important problem to address within organizations seeking to promote creativity. It is necessary to consider the degree to which creative accomplishments stem from the contributions of individual members versus from the organization itself. An iconic example of this issue is the patent lawsuit brought by former Nichia Corporation employee Shuji Nakamura over the production methods for LEDs, blue laser diodes, and other inventions. The main point of contention was how to calculate a reasonable price for product licensing and the value of Nakamura's contributions. The product licensing price was based on multiple factors, which included not only on Nichia Corporation's sales, but also on the estimated sales of other companies. Specifically, the prices took into account Nichia Corporation's sales, the estimated market share of other companies, estimated license royalty rates, and Nakamura's level of contribution. In addition, because total sales covered the period starting with commercialization and extended throughout the term of the patent, it was necessary to forecast the company's future sales. Estimating Nakamura's contribution was also extremely complicated because it was necessary to assess things such as the feasibility of substituting other technologies and the compatibility of LEDs with mass production technology.

In contrast, a different approach starts from the premise that it is impossible to calculate an individual's actual contributions. Instead, remuneration can be set by designing a range of incentive structures, such as the following:

(1) Value creative activities and provide motivation for engaging in them.
(2) Value creative activities and provide motivation for supporting them.
(3) Create structures that do not obstruct creative activity.
(4) Create structures in which creative-activity chain reactions can occur.
(5) Create structures that promote cooperation on creative activities.
(6) Provide motivation to create environments that encourage creative activity (such as increased staff diversity, exchanges with outside personnel, etc.).

When considering these incentive structures, it is necessary to clearly identify the essence of competition and complementarity. In practical terms, mechanisms can be designed so that rewards are determined in a manner similar to a tournament (see Chen et al. 2012).

2 Organizations and Knowledge Creation

To clarify the discussion at this point, let us limit our consideration of creativity to knowledge creation. According to surveys of research on the mechanisms giving rise to knowledge creation, early discussions mixed the terms "knowledge" and "information" (see Nonaka et al. 2006). Dretske (1981) defines the two terms as follows: Information is that commodity capable of yielding knowledge, and what information a signal carries is what we can learn from it (Dretske 1981, p. 44). Knowledge is identified with information produced (or sustained) belief, but the information a person receives is relative to what he or she already knows about the possibilities at the source (ibid, p. 86).

Simply cobbling together information does not result in knowledge. Knowledge creates new value, and the magnitude of that value depends greatly on the workings of the organization that creates the knowledge. Nonaka (1994), Nonaka and Takeuchi (1995), and Nonaka et al. (1996) divide the organizational process of creating value from knowledge into four steps: socialization, externalization, combination, and internalization. Together, they call these steps "SECI." The concept of "tacit knowledge" plays an important role in this process. Polanyi (1966) divides knowledge into "tacit" and "explicit" forms; he defines tacit knowledge as "tradition, inherited practices, implied values, and prejudgments." Tacit knowledge is based on experience or intuition, and is difficult to express in words. Nonaka argues that the process of forming tacit knowledge is an important feature of Japanese knowledge creation, and has used the SECI model to explicate the intra-organizational knowledge formation process known as "knowledge resonance." He has also clarified the "knowledge-enabling conditions" necessary for the SECI model to function effectively, which are organizational intent, autonomy, redundancy, change, and diversity. Further, he argues that knowledge creation takes place in five phases: sharing of tacit knowledge, concept creation, concept justification, prototype creation, and knowledge transfer.

The accumulation of experience through on-the-job training is a typical example of tacit-knowledge formation within companies. Workers acquire know-how and insider techniques by observing more experienced workers and accumulating experience, even if this information is not written in a manual. This type of tacit-knowledge formation constitutes socialization. Tacit knowledge is transformed into explicit knowledge through the process of externalization. Metaphors play an important role in this process. In the combination process, newly created explicit knowledge combines with existing explicit knowledge to form additional explicit knowledge. Finally, explicit knowledge is internalized through the activities of the organization, creating new tacit knowledge.

Thus, for tacit knowledge to be created, cognitive processes and transformative processes must repeat in a circular pattern. Cognitive processes are essential to socialization processes. By sharing approaches to assessing a phenomenon, it becomes possible for individuals to share their understanding in a social context. Knowledge then enters the expression phase, enabling broader interpretation and application. Finally, by combining tacit knowledge with various types of explicit knowledge, new knowledge is created internally.

Nonaka defines the space where this knowledge-creation process takes place—which has tacit knowledge at its core—as the "site," and positions it as an important concept within knowledge creation systems at Japanese companies. One characteristic of tacit knowledge transmission at these sites is mastery through experience. In the world of Noh, a form of classical Japanese masked theatre that maintains high artistic value to this day, almost no written guidelines are said to exist.[1] Despite the fact that hundreds of types of masks, costumes, and small props exist, no text tells actors which to use in any one of 200-some plays. This can be interpreted as evidence that manuals are obstacles to absorbing logic through experience; furthermore, many pieces of knowledge cannot be written down—and these are often the most important pieces. Once an actor masters the logic of how plays are classified, he or she can select the correct combination of mask, costume, and props without consulting a manual. To accurately master this logic, the student must accept harsh and repeated criticism from the head of the Noh theatre school where he or she is studying. However, the teacher does not necessarily reveal the right answer. If students do not develop the ability to arrive at the right answer on their own, they will not be able to apply the logic correctly. Without this logic, it is impossible to select the appropriate combination of mask, costume, and props out of the hundreds of potential combinations, but a student may do so if he or she is able to apply the logic correctly.

Tacit-knowledge formation at the site is not easily accomplished; it is a cooperative undertaking that demands both parties to "move to the same beat." The goal is that an unspoken mutual understanding will develop between the people who make up the site. The ability to move to the same beat is a sign that one has become a true site-member. This is because members are expected to understand the tacit rules of the site, and the ability to move to the beat is necessary for making the cooperative work of the site flow smoothly and harmoniously. Members of the team that makes up the site are expected to share a goal and ideology, and each member is expected to understand his or her role, to a certain extent, without being told what to do by the leader. If all members share this spiritual unity, efficient knowledge creation becomes possible, as does the mutual understanding and refinement of certain types of knowledge that cannot be expressed in words.

For members to move to the same beat, they need to understand the essence of the logic that underlies team decision making, which requires accumulated experience. They must recognize the differences between team decisions and personal decisions, and understand the reason for these differences. Understanding these differences leads to mastery of team logic. Here, too, experience is an important concept. Simply memorizing written rules does not lead to mastery of this logic. By mastering team logic through experience, it becomes possible for team members to instantly arrive at shared decisions in response to various changing conditions.

---

[1]From an interview with the Noh instructor Haruhisa Kawamura (August 14, 2013).

Let us examine the role of the site by considering the example of a company's R&D division. A member proposes a new development concept and shares knowledge about the technical features of the development concept, which creates a shared understanding of how it will change the quality of the product. With this shared knowledge as a base, members exchange individual knowledge among themselves, creating new knowledge within the site. New knowledge is created with particular efficiency when friendly competition exists between members. If one member creates something, other competitive members are stimulated to create something different. This chain of stimulation and creation invigorates the team's creative activities and leads to successful R&D activities based on a shared ideology and vision. However, when competition is hostile, sharing knowledge, including tacit knowledge, becomes difficult and high creative productivity cannot be expected.

Nonaka's theory is built around knowledge creation using tacit knowledge and it has received much praise, but also much criticism. For example, Bereiter (2002, pp. 175–179) not only argues that Nonaka fails to explain the mechanism of new knowledge creation, but also claims that Nonaka does not explain the process by which understanding of knowledge is deepened. Gourlay (2006) rejects the SECI model itself and asserts that tacit and explicit knowledge are created through different types of creative activities.

Within the context of intensified global competition and relentless demands for wage cuts in response to price wars, emphasis is shifting from a closed innovation style, in which most R&D takes place at an expensive, centralized research center within a company, to an open innovation style, which effectively incorporates R&D from outside the company, primarily through the use of venture capital. As the style of knowledge creation shifts from a model involving only members of the organization to one involving cooperation with people outside of the organization, the concept of moving to the same beat (assuming each organization has its own unique beat) obstructs mutual understanding and becomes a source of friction between organizations. In addition, as the fluidity and multinational composition of work forces increase, work styles that emphasize cooperation and modesty lose their meaning within the organization and may even die out. In multinational groups whose members have different cultural backgrounds, the process of converting tacit knowledge to explicit knowledge becomes difficult. In particular, when members have weak critical thinking skills and poor ability to express their ideas due to a lack of clear reasoning ability, it is not possible to develop a shared decision-making logic, and therefore tacit knowledge within the team does not lead to knowledge creation.

Preciously, knowledge creation through "knowledge resonance" was once typical in Japanese companies. However, as globalization accelerates, the environment is changing in such a way that these processes no longer function well, and Japanese companies are therefore losing their competitive edge in knowledge creation. People have ceased to value the processes of tacit-knowledge formation developed over the years and have lost sight of the essence of these processes; thus, knowledge creation continues to stagnate. The original meaning of tacit knowledge is mastery through experience and sharing of ideologies, goals, and logic. If these processes greatly improve the efficiency of creative activities, then it is meaningful to consider whether they should be continued in some form, even within globalized organizations.

3 Theory of Resonance Field and Creativity

Contrary to the criticism of Nonaka's SECI model, Yamaguchi (2016) redevelops the concept of "space" to the concept of a "resonance field" to explain the mechanism of innovative creation. He stresses that the market value of innovation stems not only from technology innovation, but also from emotion innovation and management innovation. When innovation is accompanied by a paradigm shift, new markets emerge. The typical example of such a paradigm-shifting innovation is the smartphone. This paradigm shift was brought about through an emotional innovation that has changed the lifestyle and communication style of people around the world, including the use of services such as social networking services (SNS).

Yamaguchi argues that paradigm-shifting innovations are nurtured in a resonance field that is defined by the place of the emergence and stimulated by the interaction among people with different knowledge and experiences. This resonance field can be sustainable if the evaluation system in an organization is consistent with interdisciplinary interaction among researchers. When the objective of an organization is restricted to narrow goals and short-term achievements in R&D, interdisciplinary interaction between researchers may be avoided to save time and focus on the more immediate goals. Paradigm-shifting innovation is only brought about through risky R&D investment with low probabilities of success. Static paradigm innovation is expected to be less risky, but the rate of return is low and decreasing over time.

In the long run, an organization's objective should be the attainment of paradigm-shifting innovation, otherwise the organization will shrink from the decreasing rate of return from R&D investment. Thus, the organizational strategy in R&D is to design a system for increasing the probability of success for R&D investments achieving paradigm-shifting innovation.

One potential strategy for achieving this goal is strengthening the role of creative director, as illustrated by the example of Steve Jobs. The role of creative director is to select promising research and then to combine different research projects after reflection on the expected social impact. A laissez-faire style attempt to create a resonance field may fail in the short term because the matching of researchers is random and the probability of creating good matches is low without coordination.

In addition, successful matching may not occur or continue for long periods because the stimuli generated from the match will not continue once the differences in knowledge among researchers decrease. In the next section, we discuss the sustainability of matching theoretically.

4 Theoretical Explanation on the Sustainability of Resonance Fields

4.1 Cognitive Diversity and Creativity

One of the important criticism of Nonaka's theory of knowledge creation centered on tacit knowledge is the weak foundation of the knowledge creation mechanism. In this section, we consider a detailed mechanism of knowledge creation within organizations and explain about the sustainability of the resonance field theoretically. The theoretical examination makes it possible to clarify the conditions in which a resonance field is successful.

Berliant and Fujita (2008, 2009, 2011) assume that knowledge is created by the interaction of people who have different knowledge, and the scope of knowledge creation depends on the amount of common knowledge shared by the people. In their model, the knowledge creation mechanism is quite simple. They assume that the source of knowledge creation is the diversity among people and the negative aspects of diversity in knowledge creation are assumed away. As the amount of common knowledge in a group increases, Berliant and Fujita predict that the productivity of knowledge creation within a group decreases; therefore, partnerships for knowledge creation should be changed to increase the diversity of knowledge among the members of the group.

Shin et al. (2012) examine the micro-foundation of the knowledge creation mechanism by focusing on cognitive diversity within an organization. Cognitive diversity includes processes such as processing information, combining different ideas, and accepting ideas of those with different perspectives. Cognitive diversity has both positive and negative effects on team creativity. The positive side includes the stimulation of inspiring new ideas when members who have different ideas work together; the negative side includes conflicts about the ideas among team members. In the worst case, team members cannot talk together because of the looming threat of conflict from sharing differing ideas with members who have different cultural or philosophical values. For this reason, leadership is regarded as an important factor for successfully combining team diversity and team creativity. The roles of leaders on a team include transforming different cultures and philosophies into common ones shared by members of the team, and developing members' creative self-efficacy for individual creativity.

Thus, the efficiency of team creativity depends on the effectiveness of the leadership in the team and the level of cognitive diversity on the team. Shin et al., however, does not discuss the emotional effects of cooperation among members. Trust is the main resource for building emotional relationships among members. If trust is not strong among members, it is hard to overcome the differences in ideas and philosophies, and team productivity would be low.

The trust among members depends on the reward system in the team. If the reward is proportional to the contribution, it is natural that all the member will insist on demonstrating the value of their own contributions and fight for the realization of their own ideas. In this case, cognitive diversity may decrease team creativity. Because of this, the reward systems for improving team creativity should be examined. Competition and cooperation are important alternatives to consider when designing a reward system. Chen et al. (2012) concludes that intergroup competition enhances cohesion, which leads to an improvement in group creativity, and reward systems based on group competition motivate group creativity. Although this paper provides us with experimental evidence concerning the relative effectiveness of reward systems for group creativity, a dynamic mechanism of knowledge creation is present in situations where group members can choose whether they join or depart from the group. In the next section, we discuss the dynamic system of knowledge creation based on Yagi (2015).

4.2 Dynamic Mechanism of Knowledge Creation

In this subsection, we discuss about the dynamics of knowledge creation by using the model employed by Yagi (2015). In Chen et al., the membership of the group is exogenously fixed, and the effect of the wage system on group creativity is analyzed. Problems with this approach arise when decisions on whether members stay in the group is endogenously determined depending on the marginal productivity of each member's creative activity. Berliant and Fujita (2008) assume that the productivity of creative activity depends on the portion of common knowledge shared by the group. In the initial stage of collaboration, the portion of the common knowledge is small, especially when creative diversity is large. However, as the time passes, the portion of common knowledge increases within the group. Thus, the team productivity decreases as time passes. This process is clearly demonstrated by the example of musical groups such as the Beatles, who find success and then break up; this superstar effect is similar within the academic field, as discussed by Azoulay et al. (2010).

First, we describe the knowledge creation process of a research group and illustrates the nonlinear effects of collaboration among researchers. The quality of innovation created by the group is described by several factors (denoted by e_i) such as theoretical background, skills, experiences, know-how, etc. The linear characteristic equation of the co-creation process is defined as

$$Q(\lambda e_1, \lambda e_2, \lambda e_3, \ldots, \lambda e_n) = \lambda Q(e_1, e_2, e_3, \ldots, e_n), \tag{1}$$

where Q is the quality of innovation created. If the quality function is specified by the linear combination of elements,

$$Q(e_1, e_2, e_3, \ldots, e_n) = a_0 + a_1 e_1 + a_2 e_2 + a_3 e_3, \ldots, a_0 e_n, \qquad (2)$$

The quality of innovation will increase linearly as the number of talented researchers in the group increases.

On the other hand, the nonlinear characteristic equation of the co-creation process is defined as

$$Q(\lambda e_1, \lambda e_2, \lambda e_3, \ldots, \lambda e_n) = \lambda^t Q(e_1, e_2, e_3, \ldots, e_n), t > 1. \qquad (3)$$

It is possible to consider a specification that exhibits nonlinear characteristics when there are multiple combination of quality elements:

$$Q(e_1, e_2, e_3, \ldots, e_n) = \prod_{i=1}^{n} a_i e_i \qquad (4)$$

The analysis aims to ascertain whether the quality of innovation increases nonlinearly as the number of talented researchers in the group increases.

Before examining the knowledge creation process, it is important to have an intuitive understanding of nonlinearity, which we can illustrated by again looking at the case of musical groups. Connolly and Krueger (2006) and Strobal and Tucker (2000) argue that there is a skewed distribution of revenue from music album sales. This finding is in line with the "superstar effect" proposed by Rosen (1981).

Based on Eq. (4), we can write the following:

$$Q(e_1, e_2, e_3, \ldots, 0, \ldots, e_n) = \prod_{i=1}^{n} a_i e_i = 0. \qquad (5)$$

Equation (5) shows that with the presence of a subpar element, the overall quality of the innovation created is severely affected, even reduced to zero in the extreme case.

Because of the nonlinear property in the creation process, the quality of the knowledge creation process of a group is dependent on the nature of the interactions among members such as the degree of idea exchange and the competition within the group. Groups made up of members with unequal status easily foster rivalries. On the other hand, groups with members who have relatively equal status form highly creative and productive teams. These groups can be successful as a result of the free exchange of ideas, which leads to the nonlinear effects of good collaboration.

This point is described by the following formulation. Suppose that the quality of innovation is represented by

$$Q(e_1, e_2, e_3) = A(p(e_1; h)e_1)^\alpha e_2^\beta e_3^\gamma, \qquad (6)$$

where e_i is the i-th elements that determines the quality of innovation, and α, β, and γ are the weights of each element. Let $p(e_1; h)$ be the probability of success in innovation depending on the state of the relationship among members in group h. The nonlinear effects of good collaboration emerge when there is mutual cooperation in a group, increasing the probability of successful innovation.

Let $k_{ie}(t)$ denote the knowledge stock of individual i at time t. As human capital matures, knowledge creation within the group decreases for two reasons: decreasing differences in knowledge among members and reduced flexibility for accepting the differences of knowledge creation. The knowledge accumulation function can be written as

$$\frac{dk}{dt} = f(k_i)\phi(\omega \sum_{j \in M} d(k_i - k_j)) + g(k_i)\phi((1 - \omega) \sum_{j \notin M} d(k_i - k_j)). \qquad (7)$$

Here, f represents the degree of flexibility in accepting differences of knowledge creation and is a decreasing function of k, and ϕ is an increasing function. Let g be the knowledge creation that arises from collaborating with a non-member, assuming that it is an increasing function of k. Let $k_i(t)$ denote the vector of knowledge of member i at time t and let $\omega(t)$ denote the portion of time spent with the members of the group.

The members control the portion of time they spend working together so as to maximize their creative output in terms of quality, subject to the dynamic equation of knowledge capital k. The objective function is represented by Eq. (8) and the dynamic equation of knowledge is shown by Eq. (9). We assume that the time discount rate is zero, with equal weight given to each time period to simplify the model:

$$Max_\alpha \int_t^T Q(k_i(t) : k_j(t))dt \qquad (8)$$

s.t. $$\frac{dk}{dt} = f(k_i)\phi(\omega \sum_{j \in M} d(k_i - k_j)) + g(k_i)\phi((1 - \omega) \sum_{j \notin M} d(k_i - k_j)). \qquad (9)$$

The Hamiltonian for this problem is given by the following equation:

$$H = Q(k_i(t)) + \lambda \left[f(k_i)\phi(\omega \sum_{j \in M} d(k_i - k_j)) + g(k_i)\phi((1-\omega) \sum_{j \notin M} d(k_i - k_j)) \right] \quad (10)$$

The optimality conditions are given by Eqs. (11) and (12), as follows:

$$\frac{\partial H}{\partial \omega} = \lambda[f(k_i)\phi'(\omega \sum_{j \in M} d(k_i - k_j)) \cdot (\sum_{j \in M} d(k_i - k_j))$$
$$- g(k_i)\phi'((1-\omega) \sum_{j \notin M} d(k_i - k_j)) \cdot (\sum_{j \notin M} d(k_i - k_j))] = 0 \quad (11)$$

$$\frac{d\lambda}{dt} = -\frac{\partial H}{\partial k_i} = -\frac{\partial B_i}{\partial k_i} - \lambda[f'(k_i)\phi(\omega \sum_{j \in M} d(k_i - k_j)) + f(k_i)\phi(\omega \sum_{j \in M} d'(k_i - k_j))$$
$$+ g'(k_i)\phi((1-\omega) \sum_{j \notin M} d(k_i - k_j)) + g(k_i)\phi((1-\omega) \sum_{j \notin M} d'(k_i - k_j))] \quad (12)$$

The transversality condition is given by

$$\lim_{x \to T} \lambda(t)k(t) = 0. \quad (13)$$

As long as λ is positive, the optimality condition (11) implies that the optimal time share ω is determined at the point where the following equation is satisfied:

$$f(k_i)\phi'(\omega \sum_{j \in M} d(k_i - k_j)) \cdot (\sum_{j \in M} d(k_i - k_j))$$
$$= g(k_i)\phi'((1-\omega) \sum_{j \notin M} d(k_i - k_j)) \cdot (\sum_{j \notin M} d(k_i - k_j)). \quad (14)$$

Because ϕ' is a decreasing function, the left-hand side of the equation is a decreasing function of ω, while the right-hand side is an increasing function of ω. The left-hand side can be considered the marginal productivity of within-group knowledge creation (MPI) and the right-hand side measures the marginal productivity of outside group knowledge creation (MPO). Note the relationship between k_i and the optimal level of ω. To illustrate this, we take the first derivative of the left- and right-hand sides with respect to k_i. The first derivative of the left-hand side is given by

15 Creative Organizations

$$\frac{\partial f(k_i)\phi'(\omega \sum_{j\in M} d(k_i - k_j)) \cdot (\sum_{j\in M} d(k_i - k_j))}{\partial k_i}$$

$$= f'(k_i)\phi'(\omega \sum_{j\in M} d(k_i - k_j)) \cdot (\sum_{j\in M} d(k_i - k_j))$$

$$+ f(k_i)\phi''(\omega \sum_{j\in M} d(k_i - k_j)) \cdot \omega \sum_{j\in M} d'(k_i - k_j) \cdot (\sum_{j\in M} d(k_i - k_j))$$

$$+ f(k_i)\phi'(\omega \sum_{j\in M} d(k_i - k_j)) \cdot (\sum_{j\in M} d'(k_i - k_j))$$

(15)

The derivative of the right-hand side with respect to k_i is

$$\frac{\partial g(k_i)\phi'((1-\omega) \sum_{j\notin M} d(k_i - k_j)) \cdot (\sum_{j\notin M} d(k_i - k_j))}{\partial k_i}$$

$$= g'(k_i)\phi'((1-\omega) \sum_{j\notin M} d(k_i - k_j)) \cdot (\sum_{j\notin M} d(k_i - k_j))$$

$$+ g(k_i)\phi''((1-\omega) \sum_{j\notin M} d(k_i - k_j)) \cdot (1-\omega) \sum_{j\notin M} d'(k_i - k_j) \cdot (\sum_{j\notin M} d(k_i - k_j))$$

$$+ g(k_i)\phi'((1-\omega) \sum_{j\notin M} d(k_i - k_j)) \cdot (\sum_{j\notin M} d'(k_i - k_j))$$

(16)

Because f is a decreasing function of k_i and g is an increasing function of k_i, the MPO curve shifts upward as k_i increases, while the MPI curve shifts downward k_i increases, as shown in Fig. 1. Therefore, one can conclude that the optimal amount of time spent collaborating within the group decreases. This suggests that the research group breaks up when the shared knowledge stock of its members rose.

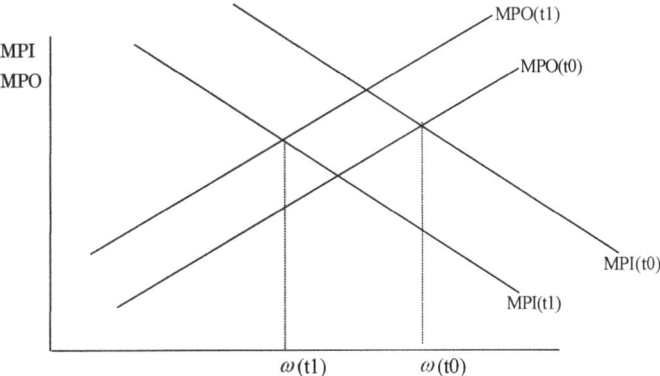

Fig. 1 Value of co-creation within and outside the group

4.3 Implications for the Sustainability of a Resonance Field

As the proportion of common knowledge among members increases, the efficiency of knowledge creation decreases because of a corresponding decrease in the amount that members can learn from one another. Yet, at the same time, the benefits of collaborating with non-members increase because the gap in knowledge increases as each member's knowledge capital increases. This mechanism is reflected in the upward shift of the MPO curve. For these reasons, the optimal portion of the time spent in collaboration with non-members increases.

An important implication of the model in this section is that the incentives for collaborating within a team tend to decrease as the knowledge of each member is shared over time. The findings of this section may be applied to the practice of human resource management in firms. For example, company executives may decide to employ the same personnel so as to maintain continuity within the company or to increase staff turnover as a way of fostering a more competitive spirit in employees.

This model also revealed the conditions conducive to successful innovation through collaboration. A harmonious environment in which team members can trade ideas freely and engage in fair play fosters creativity, leading to innovation. This finding will be useful for businesses when planning the organizational structure of the company's R&D division. In particular, this study will be useful for businesses in deciding on a flat or hierarchical structure for the research team. Our findings imply that an overly strong initiative on the part of an individual team member in the R&D process may potentially deteriorate the collaboration effect among researchers.

Lastly, the analysis illustrated the importance of diversity during the process of knowledge creation. The nonlinear effects of superstar collaboration emerge in a team made up of talented individuals who each possess unique specialist knowledge or expertise. By putting to use diverse sets of skills and knowledge, talented innovators can achieve successful innovation in a team, and the value of the innovation and new knowledge increases nonlinearly as the talent of members of the team increases.

4.4 Creative Diversity and Reward Systems in Dynamic Settings

In the previous discussion, we examined how a member of a group behaves in a creative group with a dynamic setting. The above model implicitly assumes a group competitive tournament with individual piece-rate pay. Musical groups compete in a market, but the reward system is individual piece-rate pay, especially when copyright income accrues to the composer and song writers. When the reward system discussed by Chen et al. (2012) is applied to business organizations, the endogenous member formation is assumed away.

In reality, superstars are recruited for teams, and then the superstar leads the new team in its creative activity. In the process of a group competitive tournament, the quality of team members is evaluated, and some members spin off to increase their own market value. In particular, the talented superstar in the group can easily decides to break away from the group, and the team creativity becomes unstable from the changes in team membership. Cohesion of the team is vulnerable in a long run, as shown by the case of music group break-ups. Group members' psychological bond is endogenous, and depends on the reward system in place. Equal rewards strengthen the cohesion of the team and team creativity improves in the short run. However, this equal reward system has a negative effect on the long-run team creativity because of the increased probability that the superstar of the team breaks away from the group to pursue greater rewards.

5 Concluding Comments

In the course of the discussion with Prof. Hill, the editor of the book, we reached some important conclusions related with organizational creativity. In particular, from his writings drawing from research studies of the Australian Research Council's Center of Excellence on Research Policy which he directed in the early 1990s and as a researcher and policy consultant throughout Asia since 1965, Prof. Hill claims that the following messages from the observations of almost all of Asia's modern R&D/innovation development.

The followings are the comments from Hill. The most important observations are these:[2]

1. What matters is the significance of not only tacit knowledge, but of direct inter-subjective relationships in transfer of this knowledge. Indeed, we found personal mobility of scientists was the most significant platform for transfer of knowledge and innovation—not literatures, not internet. I studied this in nation-wide research in Australia, and then, with some colleagues, across over 10,000 scientists across Asia.

   I developed the idea that there was a 'New Order of Science' based on these principles, published initially (and appropriately for our own project) in Japan after a talk I gave in 1992 (reference below). What was then interesting was that I had drafted a further article and had it hanging around in my Center for Research Policy —by now, with further empirical support, but as a draft. A couple of English academics came by and I gave it to them for interest. Next thing, I found they had passed it on to Marilyn Strathern, Social Anthropology Professor at Cambridge who was Editor of the International 1995 Anthropology Yearbook. She decided to include my draft as a lead article in the Yearbook. And I didn't even try. (reference, also, below).

---

[2]See Chapter 29.

2. No matter what structures you set up, personal networks are at the heart of an innovation moving from research in an academic or research institution to industry. I studied this in both survey and in-depth case study across a large number of situations. The worst thing a university can do is to set up a liaison unit where the non-expert tries to carry an idea across to industry. Then, you have a zero-sum game. With no prior network, no transfer (at least generally); but if there is a network of relations—both ways—transfer happens easily ... network spiderwebs are best. But the people talking have to understand each other at a technical level and communicate at an inter-subjective level.
3. People matter. The key to success is to find the good guy and bring them in.

BUT ... then, there are a few organization things that matter, i.e.: a leader with vision, a team-based organization—reinforced as a basic management priority, but with maximum decentralized autonomy whilst maintaining leader control over core concerns. I say this on the basis of not only research, but also the practical experience of doing it in both a research institution and the UN.

As an example from my UN responsibilities, as a UNESCO organization, we had limited funding but a creative mandate. (I was fully responsible as both UN Ambassador and Regional Field Director. I needed to raise around $4 million in external funds beyond the UN funding each year to do the job.) I built cross-disciplinary teams; encouraged communication across them on projects and ideas; ensured the team-leader also 'shared' rather than acted as a hierarchical arshhole; met with them a lot—in particular to explore our mandate and new things we could do; BUT: provided a coherent vision (which we talked about and shared) and maintained control over central decisions, e.g.: funding opportunities, policy, and relations with government. I did of course keep a close eye on how things were going, but left the on-going decisions to the teams though I made sure each member had the skills to do their job (including sending them off for training if necessary). Worked like a charm. All of this is reported in formally published UNESCO Annual Reports by the way. If you have any interest, I will send you the final wrap-up at the time I left—which, was, of course, endorsed by the General Conference.

This was the UN, where most organization was buried in bureaucracy. Indeed, as I am sure I must have told you, I was commissioned by the Director-General to reform and decentralize the entire UN Agency globally in 2000. What I found I needed to deal with was not one but two organizations. At field level we 'managed change and uncertainty'. At Headquarters, they 'administered an illusion of certainty'—hence the need for allegiance to bureaucratic security. (I knew this directly as, whilst engaged in reform over a two-year period, I was based not only in Indonesia but also in the Director General's Cabinet with a team, so very directly engaged with the HQ Bureaucracy. I had Assistant Director-General status there for the job, so a fair bit of clout.)

Apart from some major structural reform, my central idea was to implement a vision: this new organization had to be concerned to support the field, not just focus on central bureaucratic controls and processes. Lots of associated actions, e.g.:

changing authorities so that the Field Directors called the shots in their country(ies) rather than Headquarters; changing promotion criteria to include field experience; changing field missions from HQ, previously basically, tourist missions to preach to the Government—into a month-long requirement to build networks and abide by what the Field Director was doing, etc.

Basically, I used pretty similar principles as I outlined earlier about organizing my UN Office in running my Research Institute, and it worked.

In both cases, my job was to turn the institution into a creative and responsive social organization.

4. Contemporary application-oriented research organizations need to be open to the outside research world, not secretive or closed. Patenting concerns are a death-knell to new creative invention. But, the organization must be fast on its feet. The best model was a highly productive research organization which brought in research groups from a number of industrial companies, ranging in size from 3 to 20. But, all internal communication was open and shared. Openness to and from the external research world was encouraged, not constrained. Any innovation a company group came up with inside the Research Institution, even having learnt from the others, then had 6 months to get the patents in place, and after that, the innovation was open to all inside the organization to develop.
5. The most common problem with Research Hubs, Science Parks, etc. is lack of open interaction between the members. Most often they are real estate ventures. And inter-organization communication is discouraged. These fail. Building open research communication within the Science Parks is what matters, and this requires a lot of work to convince the (normally secretive) commercial companies involved.

What works very well is providing space in a single large room for young entrepreneurs to develop their product but talk with all the other guys + to have people coming by to help them along with the skills they need to get their product to market. Inter-subjective!

Taiwan's main national research organization also used to have a policy that anyone developing a good idea, was free to take it out to create a company with no debt to the national system which gave the person the opportunity. I have not checked what they do now.

References

Azoulay, P., Graff Zivin, J. S., & Wang, J. (2010). Superstar Extinction. *The Quarterly Journal of Economics, 125,* 549–589.
Bereiter, C. (2002). *Education and mind in the knowledge age.* Mahwah, NJ and London: Lawrence Erlbaum Associates.
Berliant, M., & Fujita, M. (2008). Knowledge creation as a square dance on the Hilbert cube. *International Economic Review, 49,* 1251–1295.

Berliant, M., & Fujita, M. (2009). Dynamics of knowledge creation and transfer: The two person case. *International Journal of Economic Theory, 5,* 155–179.

Berliant, M., & Fujita, M. (2011). The dynamics of knowledge diversity and economic growth. *Southern Economic Journal, 77,* 856–884.

Chen, C. X., Williamson, M. G., & Zhou, Flora H. (2012). Reward system design and group creativity: An experimental investigation. *The Accounting Review, 87*(6), 1885–1911.

Connolly, M., & Krueger, A. B. (2006). Rockonomics: The economics of popular music. *Handbook of the Economics of Art and Culture, 1,* 667–719.

Dretske D. (1981). *Knowledge and the flow of information.* Cambridge, MA: MIT press.

Gourlay, Stephen. (2006). Conceptualizing knowledge creation: A critique of Nonaka's theory. *Journal of Management Studies, 43*(7), 1415–1436.

Kikuchi, F. (2009). Six views for innovation science—1st view: Social, recognition, and organizational view. *ntelplace* No. 114, June 2009.

Nonaka, Ikuo. (1994). A dynamic theory of organizational knowledge creation. *Organization Science, 5*(1), 14–37.

Nonaka, L., Takeuchi, H., & Umemoto, K. (1996). A theory of organizational knowledge creation. *International Journal of Technology Management,* 11(7–8), 833–845.

Nonaka, I., & Takeuchi, H. (1995). *The knowledge-creating company: How Japanese companies create the dynamics of innovation.* Oxford university press.

Nonaka, I., Von Krogh, G., & Voelpel, S. (2006). Organizational knowledge creation theory: Evolutionary paths and future advances. *Organization studies, 27*(8), 1179–1208.

Polanyi, M. (1966). *The tacit dimension.* London: Routledge.

Shin, S. J., Kim, T.-Y., Lee, Jeong-Yeon, & Bian, Lin. (2012). Cognitive team diversity and individual team member creativity: A cross-level interaction. *Academy of Management Journal, 55*(1), 197–212.

Strobal, E. A., & Tucker, C. (2000). The dynamics of chart success in the UK pre-recorded popular music industry. *Journal of Cultural Economics, 24*(2), 113–134.

Rosen, S. (1981). The economics of superstars. *The American economic review, 71*(5), 845–858.

Williams, W. M., & Yang, L. T. (1999). Organizational Creativity. In R. J. Sternberg (Ed.), *Handbook of creativity* (pp. 3–15). New York: Cambridge University Press.

Yagi, T. (2015). Nonlinear effects of superstar collaboration: Why the beatles succeeded but broke up. *Applied Economic and Finance, 2*(2), 103–111.

Yamaguchi, E. (2016). Why Japanese innovation declined?—The crisis of technology led Japan (in Japanese), Chikuma Shinsho.

Fourth Movement: 'Building the Kyoto Platform for Change'

Chapter 16
A Self-similar Dynamic Systems Perspective of "Living" Nature: The Self-nonself Circulation Principle Beyond Complexity

Masatoshi Murase

> In the world of action, we know that it is disastrous to treat animals or human beings as if they were stocks and stones. Why should we suppose this treatment to be any less mistaken in the world of ideas? Why should we suppose that the scientific method of thought—a method which has been devised for thinking about inanimate Nature—should be applicable to historical thought, which is a study of living creatures and indeed of human beings?
>
> Arnold Toynbee
>
> "A Study of History: Illustrated" p. 33,
>
> Portland House, New York, 1988

Globalization brings about benefits and wonders; it has allowed us to solve single-value problems, but it can increase the potential risks of "systemic problems," leading to system-wide disruptions. Our efforts to solve problems often cause further problems, beyond our expectations. What can we do to protect against such emerging systemic problems? We now need a *Copernican revolution* for paradigm shifts in our cognition. We should apply the same "systemic forces" that generate the "systemic problems" in the first place. We can fight *like with like* in trying to cope.

How can we do this? Let us think about nature as it is. Nature is full of self-similarities, known as "fractals," in which particular characteristic patterns of structures appear successively at descending or ascending scales so that their parts, at any scale, are similar in shape to the whole. A seemingly complex fractal nature has been fully understood on its own terms in the form of simple rules.

M. Murase (✉)
Yukawa Institute for Theoretical Physics (YITP),
Kyoto University, Kyoto, Japan

International Research Unit of Advanced Future Studies (IRU-AFS),
Kyoto University, Kyoto, Japan
e-mail: murase@yukawa.kyoto-u.ac.jp

The present paper extends the idea of fractals from the *self-similar static structures view* to the *self-similar dynamic processes view* essential to "living" systems in order to explore simple principles beyond complexity. The only assumption is as follows: *Simple principles of complex "living" dynamics can be deduced from the demand that the underlying principles should be self-consistent, regardless of the scale with which we are concerned. It is the self-nonself circulation principle that governs the complexity of life.*

1 Emerging Self-consistent Life Philosophy: Toward a Creative Approach to Emerging Problems

> Hardly a concept, a notion or word is more ambiguous than "life". Thus definitions serve only as sectored limitations, such as philosophical, biological or physiochemical distinctions, which inherently produce a loss of meaning. At the moment, the theories of cognitive science of living systems culminate in the proposition that the cognitive process is tantamount to the process of life. The history of philosophical approaches towards the concept of life confirms this conception that rational man who is constantly confronted with life, cannot distance himself from life. It is always life that happens to him, with him, through him. The experience of life, therefore, is neither pure recognition of self nor merely reaction to outside stimuli.
>
> Franz-Theo Gottwald
> "Life—A Problem Inherent in the Research Context" pp. 25–26
> World Scientific, Singapore, 2002

Due to complex interactions among humans, societies, economies, and many other organizations, our world is more global than ever; thus, it looks like a huge "living" system involving systems nested within systems. Owing to such "self-nested hierarchies" in our world, most of our major problems, such as energy, financial security, the environment, education, and even science issues, cannot be understood in isolation (Zolli 2012, Murase 2008a; b, 2016; Murase et al. 2017) and are often referred to as "systemic problems" (Capra and Luisi 2014).

Indeed, these problems seem to be very complex; therefore, it has been difficult to find solutions. What is worse, extensive efforts to solve these problems have often led to the emergence of additional problems due to the chain of hidden causation (Meadows 2008). The realization of such "emerging problems" has consistently been one of the most challenging issues in various disciplines. These problems have been discussed in the framework of "emergent diseases" and "aging" in the life sciences (Murase 1996). They are often called "side effects" or the "risk-to-benefit ratio" in medical sciences (cf. Pitot 1986), "trade-off effects" in evolutionary developmental biology (Gilbert and Epel 2009), and "neg-emergence" in the study of "death" (Aguilar 2009; Capra and Luisi 2014).

Despite the resulting complexity, once these individual problems are considered as different aspects of a single whole, such seemingly contradictory issues can become totally understandable, as they can be integrated into a single coherent framework. This is the integrationists' approach, or a holistic approach, in contrast with the reductionists' approach (see Sect. 2).

Situations of this kind are truly relevant to understanding the question "What is Life?" From a conventional materialistic or reductionist view, life can be decomposed into many different kinds of material elements, but it is still difficult to understand life as a whole. Contrary to this traditional approach, we have taken a self-similar dynamic systems view of life, by which we increasingly try to understand life as a dynamic "living" system involving communicative "living" subsystems (Murase 1992, 1996, 2000, 2008a, b, 2011, 2016; Gottwald 2002).

"Life" should not be an object to be distinguished from an external observer, but the creative circulatory processes linking the subject and object to construct new dimensions that cannot be predicted or defined in advance (Izutsu 1975; Valera et al. 1991; Almanspacher and Dalenoort 1994; Murase 2000, 2008b; Bateson 2002). Such creative circulation processes are referred to as self-nonself (or endo–exo) circulation on the basis of the claim that "life" must be understood based on "life itself" in a self-consistent way (Murase 2000).

A full understanding of our present-day problems now requires nothing less than a new conception of life itself. A "self-similar dynamic systems perspective" is necessary to explore the basic principles, irrespective of the scale of "living" nature considered. It is the "self-nonself circulation principle" originally given by Murase (2000) that could govern the emergent complexity typical of life.

2 Beyond the Limits of Western Scientific Thinking: Toward a Holistic (or Integrationist) Approach to Life

Charles Richet (1900) emphasized the general phenomenon, "The living being is stable. It must be in order not to be destroyed, dissolved or disintegrated by the colossal forces, often adverse, which around it. By an apparent contradiction it maintains its stability only if it is excitable and capable of modifying itself according to external stimuli and adjusting its response to the stimulation. In a sense it is stable because it is modifiable—the slight instability is the necessary condition for the true stability of the organism."

Walter B. Cannon

"Organization for Physiological Homeostasis"

Physiological Review, Vol. IX No. 3, 399 (1929)

The centuries-old problem of "What is Life?" has not been solved satisfactorily, despite advanced studies of Western science (Schrödinger 1967). This is probably not because we lack a complete knowledge of components, such as molecules, organelles, cells, or organs, at different hierarchical levels of life necessary for the reductionist approach of Western science. Instead, this is probably because we lack a holistic view that integrates fragments of knowledge at different hierarchical levels into a coherent framework essential to the integrationist approach of Eastern philosophy (Murase 1996, 2000, 2008a; Gottwald 2002).

Indeed, Western science has succeeded in progressively characterizing "nonliving" material things based on a reductionist approach. However, there is likely a serious problem if we apply the same approach to "living" systems, without questioning its reliability in these extreme cases (Toynbee 1988). Here, we should realize the presence of a two-fold problem: it is a serious problem that we hardly question the reliability of the Western scientific framework within the framework itself, in addition to the overarching problem of "What is Life?"

Let us, therefore, think about the basic principles of a reductionist approach typical of Western science, and identify "emerging problems" inherent to this approach related to its applicability to a living system. These problems are mutually interrelated with each other, as usual for "systems problems."

1. Life Beyond Materials

Using a reductionist approach, we have increasingly characterized the detailed "nonliving" components of "living" systems. Indeed, we are far too familiar with the traditional reductionist view that requires identifying elements at different levels of biological organization and understanding the relationships among different levels. On the basis of traditional reductionism, however, we cannot understand the difference between "living" and "nonliving" things because both are equally made of material molecules.

In other words, there appears to be a very sharp distinction between "nonliving" parts and a "living" whole; thus, it is very difficult to explain how a "living" whole emerges from "nonliving" parts. Relating to this sharp distinction, we can identify three different kinds of problems to be solved:

(a) The first problem must be the origin-of-life problem, namely, how prebiotic materials began to exhibit life as a whole. To develop a new theory for the origin of life, Murase (2011) assumed that life's origin and subsequent evolution represent the *continuous complexation* of initially non-living—yet highly interacting—entities, and therefore simple principles could govern a great diversity of dynamic phenomena at any instance and at any level of the highly interacting entities (see Sect. 4).

(b) The second problem is simply the reverse of the first one. Based on the assumption of continuous complexation, we can identify the unique principles essential to the origin of life by investigating the dynamic organization—involving both structures and processes—typical of present-day life, which will be explained in some detail (see Sect. 3).

(c) The third must be categorized as a counter-problem of the origin-of-life problem (Murase 1996). What are the origins of disease, aging, and death, typical of present-day life? How do specific characteristics, such as disease, aging, and death, emerge from "living" processes? Murase (1996) proposed a theory of aging as an intra-individual evolutionary process driven by *natural selection* (Darwin 1859) and *self-organization* (cf. Kauffman 1993). Recently, the death of a living system has been described in terms of "neg-emergence" (Aguilar 2009; Capra and Luisi 2014). Indeed, Murase (1996) suggested that the process of aging toward death could be seen as a progressive process corresponding to the destruction of emergent properties at various levels of the entire organism (see Sect. 5).

2. Limits of a Dichotomous Perspective

The reductionists' approach assumes that there is a strict dichotomy between the "perceiving" subject (or endo) and "perceived" object (or exo), and that both are independent of each other (see Izutsu 1975; Almanspacher and Dalenoort 1994). Such assumptions, however, appear to be violated in the field of particle physics. Remember "Heisenberg's uncertainty principle" in modern physics. It became clear that observing a particle also perturbs the particle, and we cannot avoid the essential "uncertainty" regarding the state of the particle. The only way to make progress in our understanding is to predict the outcome of experiments statistically.

Surprisingly, similar problems have appeared in the "living" world due to complex interactions within systems, between systems, and beyond systems (Murase 1992; Meadows 2008; Scharmer 2009; Zolli 2012; Murase and Murase 2014; Doidge 2015). For example, in "fractal" structures involving self-similarity, the particular characteristic patterns appear successively at descending and ascending scales, where their parts are similar in shape to the whole at any scale to the observer. It is possible to extend this fractal notion of self-similar static "structures" to self-similar dynamic "processes" essential to "living" systems.

A self-nested "living" systems perspective can eliminate the serious difficulty in resolving problems concerning uncertainty because there is already uncertainty from the beginning. There is no sharp distinction between individual parts and an integrated whole, for both are "living" systems. We should now consider that there is no sharp distinction between the "perceiving" subject and "perceived" object, for we are both spectators and actors in the world (see Sect. 6).

3. Violations of Reproducibility Principles

Owing to the traditional dichotomy mentioned above, Western scientists have generally assumed that the outputs of an object in response to a particular input by a subject are consistent under identical conditions, known as the *reproducibility principle*.

Does this principle still hold in life? The answer is definitely "no." To understand life itself, we have to identify not only the "elements" of the organism, but also the "elementary processes" within the organism, between the organisms, and beyond the organism. Only then can normal states, disease states, and even senescent states be clearly interpreted in terms of "dynamic changes" in elementary processes as well as *plastic changes* in the elements (Murase 1996).

Even in constant external environmental conditions, organisms are continually subject to "intrinsic instability" at any level and scale (cf. Cannon 1929). It therefore must be emphasized that "transients" and "instabilities" are essential and advantageous to life because changes in the environment, regardless of whether they are constant or not, are important for successful adaptation, learning, and evolution.

In this sense, the reproducibility principle is not completely true; that is, we should not always expect that any biological system will show the same responses to the same stimuli (Murase and Murase 2013a, b).

4. Toward a Complementarity Perspective

Relating to the traditional dichotomy of a subject or an object, we are very familiar with the dichotomy between "yes" and "no" with regard to any given statement. Contrary to this dichotomy perspective, there is an alternative *complementarity* perspective typical of Eastern philosophy, which is surprisingly similar to *Niels Bohr's complementarity principle* in modern physics (Bohr 1985). It actually suggests that opposites are not mutually exclusive, but merely complementary to one another because they are thought to be different aspects of the same wholeness.

The complementarity perspective strongly suggests that there is no clear distinction between subject (or self) and object (or nonself). It is, therefore, the self-nonself (or the subject-object) circulation that must be a fundamental dynamical process in diverse "life" phenomena, as there is no definitely isolated subject nor clearly separated object.

The rest of this paper will deal with this self-nonself circulation theory in some detail on the basis of *continuous complexation* from the origin of life to the emergence of cognition in humans, and even to the origin of aging.

3 The Dynamic Nature of the Intercellular and Intracellular Society

> Every cell must eat, communicate with the world around it, and quickly respond to changes in its environment. To help accomplish these tasks, cells continually adjust the composition of their plasma membrane and internal compartments in rapid response to need.
>
> Bruce Albers et al.
> Molecular Biology of The Cell, p. 695,
> Garland Science, New York, 2015

1. A Body as an Intercellular Society

Our bodies develop as clones derived from a single fertilized cell with progressive cell division and differentiation of structure and function. The body is composed of two different kinds of cells: dividing cells, like skin cells and liver cells, and nondividing cells, such as nerve cells and muscle cells.

Figure 1 shows a schematic illustration of how our body is realized as a nested hierarchical "society," that is, an intracellular society within an intercellular society.

Individual cells, both dividing and nondividing, have complex intracellular societies (see right panel of Figs. 1 and 2). It is interesting to realize the self-similarity: there are also parallels between the intercellular society within a human body and the human society in an ecological system.

2. The Intracellular Society: The Endocytic-Exocytic Cycle

For a long time, the adult nervous system was considered "static" based on its inability to generate new nerve cells through cell division; accordingly, the plasma membrane of nerve cells was dismissed as a passive, permeable barrier. This static view was far from the truth. We are now acknowledging the "dynamic" view that neurons undergo remarkable changes in morphology during early childhood as well as late adulthood in response to environmental stimuli (Doidge 2015). The plasma membrane not only plays a dynamic role in intracellular signaling (Rothman 1985), but also undergoes continuous cycles of endocytosis and exocytosis, as illustrated in Fig. 2.

A small part of the plasma membrane is continually internalized in the process of endocytosis and it is conversely added to the cell surface in the process of exocytosis (Dautry-Varsat and Lodish 1984; Bretscher 1987). These dynamic cellular processes are responsible for the remarkable adaptability of nerve cells to environmental stimuli, but such dynamic processes are, of course, not determined by immediate gene instructions. Instead, they are driven by the coordinated activity of

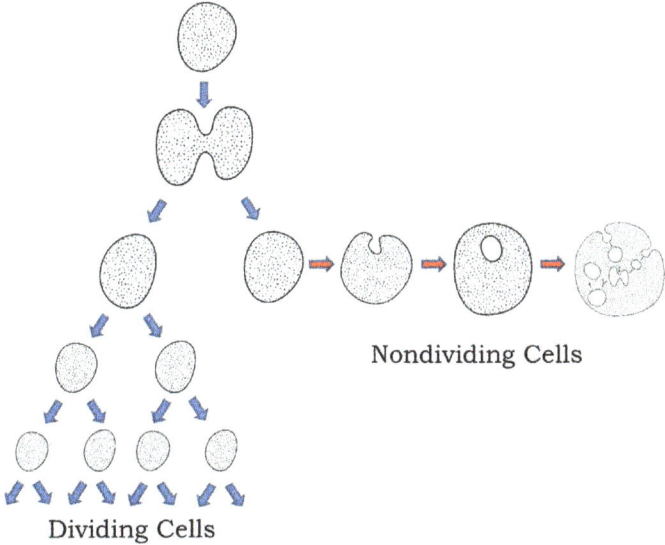

Fig. 1 A body as an intracellular society within an intercellular society. Our body is composed of two different classes of cells: dividing and nondividing cells. Those cells are a clone of a single fertilized cell (shown at the top) subjected to successive cell division and cell differentiation. Although the complex intracellular society is only illustrated in the right panel, any cell has its own intracellular society

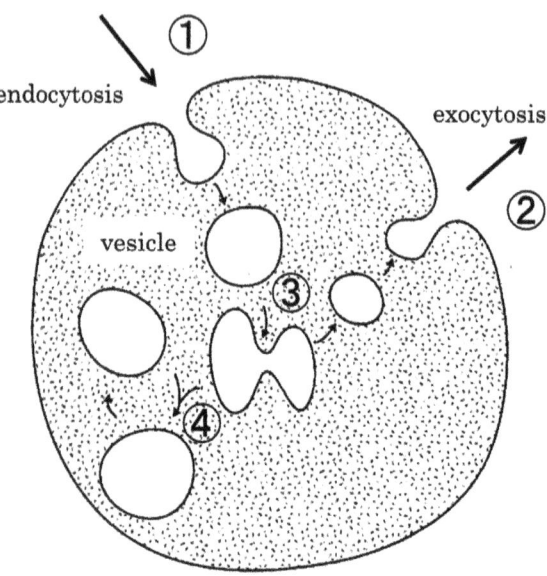

Fig. 2 The dynamic characteristics of a living cell. Four different processes are represented: *1* the uptake of external molecules by endocytosis, *2* the secretion of molecules by exocytosis, *3* the budding of transporting vesicles, and *4* fusion of different vesicles

a complex metabolic network, since metabolic proteins serve as the main machineries of molecular recognition and catalysis and also determine the shape and structure of the cell.

Figure 2 summarizes the dynamic characteristics of a cell (cf. Rothman 1985), including four main processes: (1) the uptake of external molecules by endocytosis, (2) the secretion of molecules by exocytosis, (3) the budding of transporting vesicles, and (4) fusion of different vesicles.

3. The "Self-Nonself (or Endo–Exo) Circulation Theory"

Reviewing most dynamic living phenomena, Murase (2000) proposed the "Self-Nonself (or Endo–Exo) Circulation Theory" of life. This theory can abstract the cyclic membrane processes of endocytosis and exocytosis involving the budding and fusion of vesicles (see Fig. 2).

Figure 3 illustrates how the "Self-Nonself (or Endo–Exo) Circulation Theory" can describe the dynamic nature of a living cell summarized in Figs. 1 and 2.

From a self-nested systems perspective, it is possible to assume that the simple principle of "continuous complexation" could govern not only the evolution of life, but also the origin of life (Murase 2011). It is the self-nonself circulation principle that can govern a great diversity of dynamic phenomena at any instance and level of highly interacting entities, including initially non-living, yet highly interactive, entities providing a basis for the origin of life (see Sect. 4).

4. Intracellular Protein Metabolism

After the astonishing discovery of the self-templating structure of DNA molecules (Watson and Crick 1953), the "central dogma" was proposed, asserting that all

Fig. 3 The "Self-Nonself (or Endo-Exo) Circulation Theory." This theory can abstract the cyclic membrane processes of endocytosis and exocytosis involving the budding and fusion of vesicles

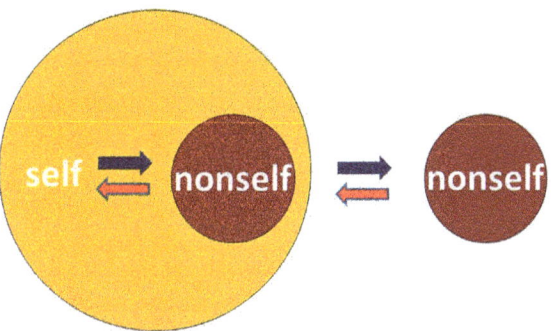

amino acid sequences are determined by DNA base sequences (Crick 1958). Newly synthesized proteins do not exist in the form of chains; instead, they exhibit self-folding to become "subunits." Several of these subunits exhibit self-assembly to form macromolecular structures. This process of self-assembly occurs on the basis of information contained in the subunits themselves.

Figure 4 shows how macromolecules are formed step by step from the information stored in DNA. It was originally considered that all of the information necessary for folding and subsequent self-assembly can be traced back to the "genetic" information in the form of DNA sequences. This leads to the gene instructionist view of life, in which the development and even aging of living organisms are thought to be fully determined by gene instructions.

Such a "gene-centric" view of life turned out to be too simplistic and even inaccurate for the following reasons (cf. Sporns 1994; Murase 1996).

(a) Not all proteins and amino acids are specified by genetic codes. Some antibiotics in bacteria (Cavalier-Smith 1991) and amino acid neurotransmitters in higher organisms (Bloom 1981) are synthesized entirely by enzymes. Although the enzymes themselves are directly encoded by genes, the products of these enzymes are not.

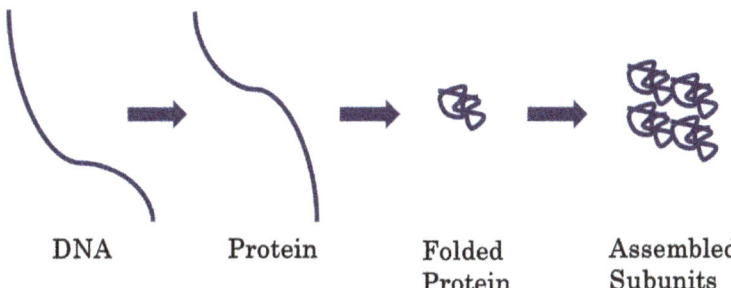

Fig. 4 DNA sequences determine amino acid sequences of a protein. The resulting protein is self-folded within the information of amino acid sequences. The properly folded proteins act as "subunits" to form macromolecules

(b) Some newly synthesized proteins, indeed, contain the information necessary for proper folding and subsequent self-assembly within their amino acid sequences. Others, however, require interactions with sophisticated enzymes referred to as "molecular chaperones" (Craig 1993; Agard 1993).

When interactions with different kinds of proteins are taken into account, both the fate of subunits and the final conformations of macromolecules are no longer immediately controlled by gene instructions, just as the fate of cells and the final form of the body are not totally controlled by immediate gene instructions, but are generally determined by cell–cell interactions known as inhibition, induction, or competition. In this sense, "epigenetic" information is thought to reside not only in proteins themselves, but also in noncovalent protein–protein interactions. This can explain the origin of "emergence."

(c) In addition to the self-nonself circulation process and the biogenesis of newly synthesized proteins based on genetic and epigenetic information, we should realize the dynamic nature of the intracellular society, which would provide us with deep insights into understanding how our society could work efficiently.

Let us consider supramolecular components of intracellular society, such as enzymes, cytoplasmic filaments, and membranes. They are not generated as single molecules connected by covalent bonds, but form a hierarchical organization by the noncovalent assembly of many subunits, as mentioned above. Such macromolecules are not "permanent" structures; they undergo continuous "disassembly" into small subunits and "reassembly" into large macromolecules (see Fig. 5).

Unlike the covalent bonds that connect subunits of fixed structures, noncovalent protein–protein interactions between subunits can reversibly form and break. Therefore, the function of multisubunit assemblies can be easily controlled by adding or removing subunits. For this reason, a single protein does not necessarily have a predetermined function. Instead, its function emerges only when the final combination of all of individual components is determined, as in the case of gene regulatory proteins. New functions arise by slight changes in the combination of multiple subunits among the limited pool of molecules.

Therefore, this combinatorial control has great advantages for both the evolution and development of complex living organisms.

(d) The dynamic nature of intracellular molecules is more than this. In fact, the self-assembled macromolecules are frequently recognized by other proteins to form much more complex assemblies, and these complex assemblies then serve as new recognition targets by separate proteins, and so on.

Actually, such protein–protein interactions are essential to the biogenesis of plasma membranes, including vesicles named lysosomes and endosomes, the secretion of molecules by exocytosis, the uptake of external molecules by endocytosis, the catalytic activity of enzymes, the formation of gene regulatory proteins, the budding and fusion of transport vesicles, the dimerization or oligomerization of

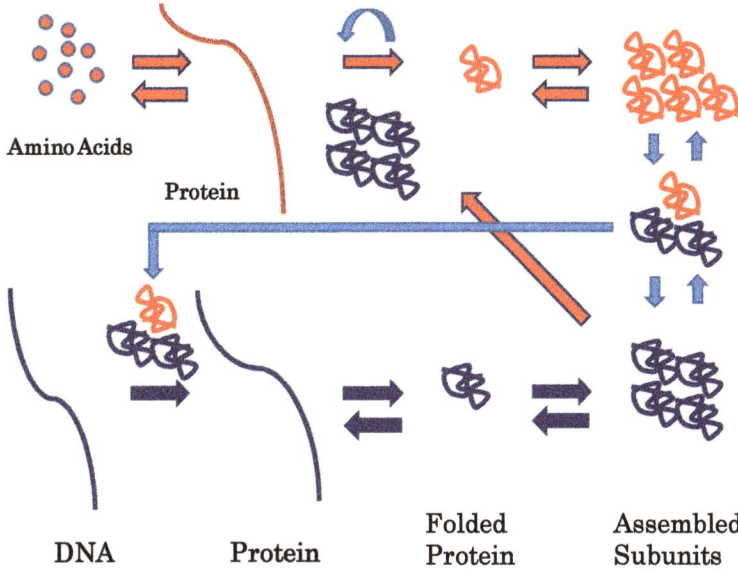

Fig. 5 Intracellular dynamic interactions among constituent molecules, such as DNA, amino acids, proteins, subunits, and macromolecules

cell surface receptors in signal transduction, viral envelope assembly, and many other biological functions.

(e) There now arises the mysterious relationship between individual component parts and an emerging whole. We are realizing that a portion of genetic information exists at the level of DNA sequences, but we are also learning the importance of epigenetic information in the form of protein–protein, subunit–subunit, or macromolecule–macromolecule interactions. Necessary information for the emerging whole system involves emergent processes.

This suggests that the identity of life must be ascribed not only to the constituent components, but also to dynamic processes. To understand life itself, in other words, we have to specify not only the elements, but also the elementary processes within the organism, between the organisms, and beyond the organism.

Figure 5 shows a schematic representation of how proteins and subunits form by intracellular dynamic interactions among constituent molecules, such as DNA, amino acids, proteins, subunits, and macromolecules. We used to think about the world with respect to time elapsed, where cause is assumed to precede effect, as shown in Fig. 4. This is related to the gene-centric view that biological structure and function must be directly controlled by immediate gene instructions. We now understand the alternative view that simultaneities must be considered. This is a comprehensive or a field-like view, in contrast to a cause-and-effect or an arrow-like view.

If we consider particular molecules as "self," and many other molecules as "nonself," then intracellular dynamics of different molecules can be realized as self-nonself circulation processes.

4 The Origin and Evolution of Life by Means of Self-nonself Circulation

> Can matter organize itself? In other words, can beings come into the world without parents, without ancestors? Here is the question to resolve.
>
> Louis Pasteur, 7 April 1864
> Cited From: Origins of Life: The Central Concepts, p. 3
> Jones and Bartlett Publishers, Inc., Boston, 1994

Studying the origin of life requires a radical shift in our perceptions from a Western scientific view useful for explaining the "nonliving" material world to a holistic view adequate for dealing not only with present-day life under evolution, but also with the globally interconnected world-wide living system as a whole.

Traditionally, studies on the origin of life have focused on self-replicating units, either one-dimensional polymers (Eigen and Schuster 1979; Cech 1986; Gilbert 1986; von Kiedrowski 1986; Tjivikua et al. 1990; Kauffman 1993; Joyce and Orgel 1993) or three-dimensional vesicles (Morowitx et al. 1988; Luisi and Varela 1989; Bachmann et al. 1992), but not both. Because there were no interactive processes between the two different hierarchical levels, such as polymers and vesicles, most studies have failed to explain how initially nonliving entities show continuous complexation, ultimately leading to the origin of life.

Murase (2011) assumed that there are both random polymers and membrane-bounded vesicles. Polymers are future candidates for self-replicating genetic systems that evolve by natural selection (Darwin 1859); whereas vesicles or "endo-systems" (Wassenaar 1994) or "selves" have their own boundary membranes that can contain micro-environments favorable for polymers, as these are isolated from the external environment or "exo-world" (Wassenaar 1994).

Murase (2011) proposed a new paradigm of "self-nonself (or endo–exo) circulation," describing the interactive processes between two different hierarchical levels, such as the self or endo-system and the nonself or exo-world. A principle of self-nonself circulation would govern the origin and evolution of life, and would also explain the dynamic organization typical of present-day life (Murase 1996, 2000, 2008a, b).

Figure 6 illustrates how a self (or a closed endo-system) not only shows a distinct identity from the open environmental nonself (or the exo-world), but also undergoes evolution by mutation and "weak selection" in the context of a combination of elements. A self (or a closed endo-system) can maintain its identity, as it has boundaries that isolate internal materials from the nonself (or the exo-world).

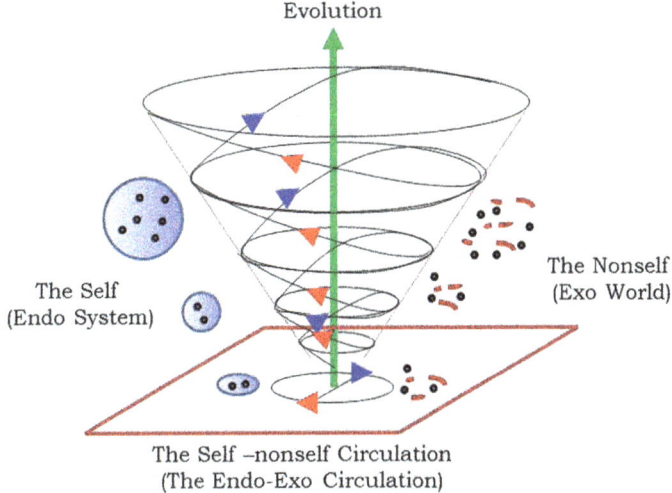

Fig. 6 Evolution of a closed endo-system by means of self-nonself (or endo–exo) circulation

Suppose that such a self (or a closed endo-system) is subject to formation–deformation cycles, as shown in the lower panel—that is, the boundaries are broken, allowing the entry of new elements from the nonself (or the exo-world), and then they are resealed. At each cycle, the closed endo-system does not retain the same composition as it had previously, but instead evolves in a spiral fashion, as shown in the upper panel. This interactive process between the self (or the endo-system) and the nonself (or the exo-world) is referred to as self-nonself (or endo–exo) circulation.

What mechanisms initially drive the self-nonself (or endo-exo) circulation on the prebiotic Earth? We should realize that there are two very different kinds of molecules: some molecules readily forming linear polymers upon dehydration (Usher 1977) and other molecules spontaneously aggregating to create closed vesicles upon hydration (Hargreaves et al. 1977; Hargreaves and Deamer 1978). Thus, dehydration-hydration cycles (Deamer and Barchfeld 1982; Deamer and Fleischaker 1994) can be one of the plausible mechanisms of the endo-exo circulation, by which many different kinds of polymers and vesicles are alternately generated and degenerated. Such drying-wetting cycles must have occurred in the prebiotic environment, particularly at intertidal zones, just as today (Deamer et al. 1994). Although emphasis was placed on the encapsulation of various solutes by closed vesicles (Deamer and Barchfeld 1982), this evidence suggests that the dehydration-hydration cycles would drive the self-nonself (or endo-exo) circulation.

Figure 7 shows the co-evolution of polymers and vesicles by self-nonself (or endo-exo) circulation, driven by drying-wetting cycles. Such cycling environments are initially required as the external "drive" (see the bottom panel).

Polymerization is driven during the dehydration phase; vesicles tend to fuse into multilayered structures that could trap solutes within single membranes or between

Fig. 7 Co-evolution of polymers and vesicles by self-nonself (endo–exo) circulation, driven by drying-wetting cycles

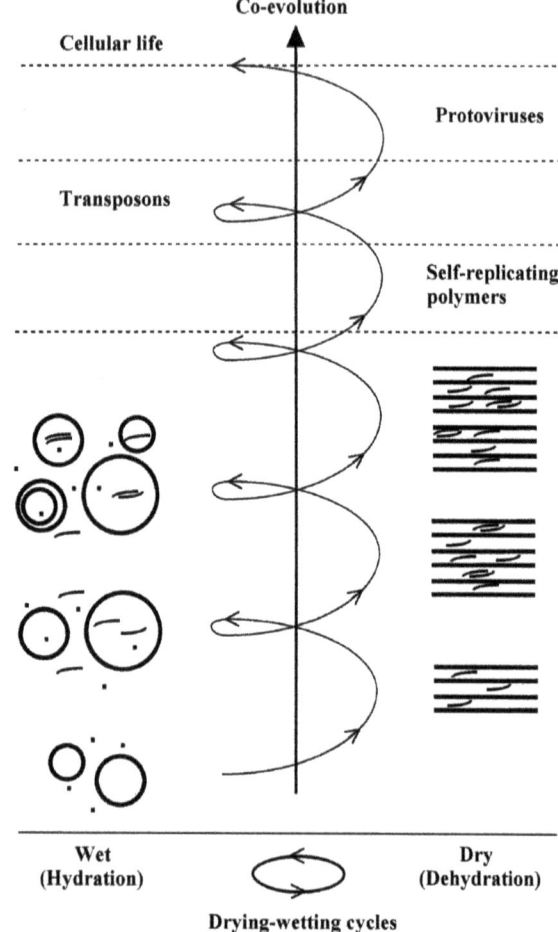

alternating membranes, thereby bringing a variety of molecules into close contact with one another (see the middle panel on the right side).

Here, membranes are indicated by circles (on the left side) or straight lines (on the right side). Polymers and monomers are represented by curves and dots, respectively. Via intermolecular interactions, the molecules might be weakly selected at any instance.

Upon hydration, many kinds of polymers and vesicles would be produced. Some vesicles could encapsulate nearby solutes, including polymers. There may, of course, be some amount of truncation selection in which vesicles that develop weak membrane structures are removed for maintenance. In this sense, selection would occur at any level of the hierarchy. During another round of dehydration, the encapsulated pre-existing polymers would have an ordering effect on other encapsulated monomers because they could serve as "templates" to direct replication effectively in a narrow space of multilayered structures (Deamer and Barchfeld 1982).

Upon rehydration, many different vesicles are formed again from multilayered structures, some of which would enclose the solute molecules including original templates and several copies. The first self-replicating polymers, transposable elements, and protoviruses would be driven to co-evolve before the autonomous cellular life (see the top panel). Note that self-replication is the derived character of the self-nonself (endo-exo) circulation. The origin of autonomous cellular life can be defined by the events that an autonomous system of self-nonself (or endo-exo) circulation would arise to take over.

As described in Sect. 3 (see Fig. 2), endocytic–exocytic cycles emerge as autonomous self-nonself circulation processes typical of present-day life. Molecular dynamics, such as the encapsulation of pre-existing molecules and protein–protein interactions, can be realized as intercellular dynamics (see Fig. 1) and intracellular dynamics (see Figs. 2 and 5).

5 The Origin and Evolution of Aging

> Aging is a puzzling phenomenon for the theory of evolution by natural selection. The basic intuition of Darwin was that adaptation could be explained by the enhanced survival rates of individuals with heritable attributes that fostered survival and reproduction. ... So how does it happen that evolution has so frequently produced organisms with survival and reproductive rates that decline with adult age?
>
> Michael R. Rose
>
> Evolutionary Biology of Aging, p. 3
>
> Oxford University Press, Oxford, 1991

Many thousands of different molecules are organized into a complex molecular metabolic network. As one progresses from small subunits to large macromolecules in this hierarchical organization, the functions that the large macromolecules can perform become more remote from those specified by immediate gene instructions and hence more elaborate and flexible. We thus see that adaptive cellular behavior emerges out of the coordinated activity of the complex network of molecular metabolism.

As long as this complex network operates effectively, the cell—independent of whether it is dividing or differentiated—can continually adapt to environmental changes. However, at the same time, this complex network is always subject to the threat of collapse to a short-circuit "catastrophe," leading to selfish behavior, as in the case of the hypercycle (cf. Eigen and Schuster 1979), because it is impossible to avoid dynamic variability.

We can begin by considering how natural selection operates at the level of molecules within a single non-dividing cell (Murase 1996, 2008b). A "normal" intracellular environment is shown in Fig. 8a. Here, a number of different circles are used to denote a variety of molecules in different states of synthesis and degeneration. Together, they form a dynamic stable state. All cell molecules in a dynamic intracellular environment are possible targets of mutation and natural selection. Although the endocytic–exocytic cycles and many other vesicles are omitted for simplicity, we should remember that a dynamic intracellular society is maintained due to self-nonself circulation.

Targeted molecules, which become non-degenerative in nature, may begin to accumulate within the cell. This situation can be seen in Fig. 8b, which shows a single molecule that changed from ○ to ■ by mutation or external influences. The resultant deformed molecule causes nearby normal molecules to become abnormal and, in doing so, acts very much like a kind of intracellular "cancer." Eventually, the accumulation of abnormal molecules destroys the cell. This process is the origin of all neurodegenerative disorders.

Of course, structural variability can give rise to additional variability in the resulting dynamics. Even without any structural variability, however, dynamic variability can still arise. Just as structural components or "elements" are exposed to random variation, self-organization and natural selection, dynamic processes or "elementary processes" may be also subject to variation, self-organization and natural selection, independent of whether structural variability is present or not.

To understand this possibility, let us consider membrane-bound proteins, such as the amyloid precursor protein (APP) of beta-amyloid (Murase 1996). Like other macromolecules formed from many subunits, the plasma membrane is not a permanent structure; it is continually removed and added by endocytic–exocytic cycles, by which APP is recycled back to the plasma membrane. Some APP is

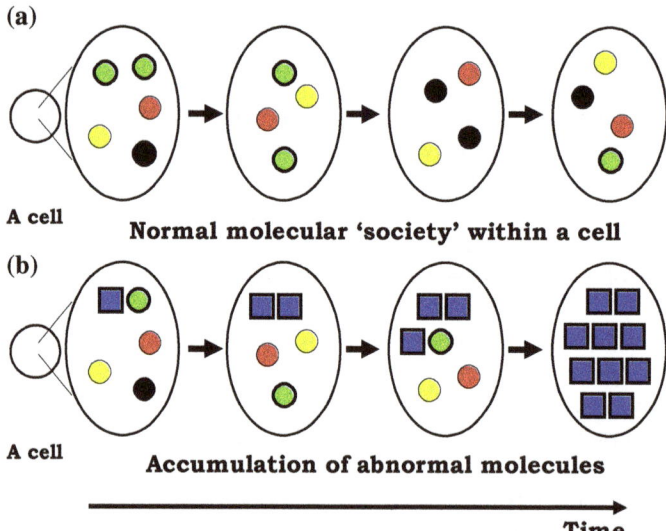

Fig. 8 Molecular society within a single non-dividing cell in **a** normal and **b** abnormal cases. Open circle and filled square denote normal and abnormal molecules, respectively

further affected by the endosomal–lysosomal pathway and ends up in lysosomes, where it is degraded by proteases for the recycling of amino acids. Here, self-nonself circulation plays important roles during the recycling of the plasma membrane and of amino acids.

Such recycling not only maintains a steady-state distribution of membrane components essential to the homeostasis of a cell, but also coordinates the cellular processes responsible for the cell's adaptability to its changing environment; it provides a potential short-cut to selfish dynamics in the absence of structural variability.

These selfish dynamics, in turn, may trigger structural variability or the formation of denatured proteins. Then, denatured proteins begin to accumulate because the dynamic processes, like structural components, are further subject to random mutations, self-organization, and natural selection. Consequently, there are different ways in which structural and dynamic variability arise, as suggested by studies of defects in intracellular protein trafficking.

Now, it is clear that self-nonself circulation is a double-edged sword. On the one hand, such dynamical processes can generate the dynamic steady states necessary for the maintenance of life itself; on the other hand, they can result in shortcuts to selfish dynamics, leading to "aging" or "disease" states. We therefore consider both benefits and wonders, despite potential risks that develop only after time delays. Situations of this kind must be the same as those in our living world. Our efforts to solve social problems often cause further problems, beyond our expectations. Independent of the scales of systems, systemic problems always exist; we are surrounded by benefits and wonders, but we are also individually subject to health and disease from within.

In Sect. 6, let us consider how our perception works and fails to work in the context of self-nonself (or subject-object) circulation.

6 The Emergence of Dynamic Patterns: Visual Illusion

> Art and cognition have always stood as two convex mirrors each reflecting and amplifying the other.
>
> Robert L. Solso
> Cognition and the Visual Arts, p. xiiv
> The MIT Press, London, 1993

We have often been confronted with opposition or contradictions. A typical example given by Roger Penrose is known as the Penrose impossible triangle, as shown in Fig. 9 (Left). He created this image in 1958. Inspired by this illustration, Richard Gregory made a real model in 1967 (see Gregory 1998) as illustrated in Fig. 9 (Right).

This seems to be a compatible contradiction. How does this happen? When we see a three-dimensional object, it is projected onto a two-dimensional retina. We lose information along the depth dimension. Rotating the object, we see quite different structures, as shown in the top, middle, and bottom panels. Only when we observe the object from a certain orientation does the impossible triangle appear. This suggests that seemingly conflicting results are compatible when hidden variables or missing dimensions are considered.

Much more complex phenomena are found in phantom sensations. Even for a static visual stimulus, dark squares can appear and disappear endlessly, as illustrated in Fig. 10. The visual illusion in this case can be understood in the following three steps.

First, there is a combination of *local activation with lateral inhibition*; local activation is simply from the incident light and lateral inhibition is the inhibition of neighboring retinal cells. When a retinal cell is excited by light, it inhibits its neighbors (see right panel of Fig. 10). Thus, a cell at the intersection has a greater number of illuminated surrounding neighbors than a cell in a white corridor and is inhibited more strongly than a corridor cell. As a result, a dark square appears.

Next, let us consider the opposite case, as illustrated in Fig. 11.

Besides the neurons that respond to light, there are also neurons that can respond to darkness. These opposing neurons also show lateral inhibitions; therefore, intersections appear to be bright.

Finally, let us consider how the visual illusion disappears. Please look at Fig. 12. When lateral inhibition occurs along an inclined line upon phantom dark squares,

Fig. 9 Roger Penrose impossible triangle (Left) http://en.wikipedia.org/wiki/File:Penrose_triangle.svg. A Real model made by Richard Gregory (Right). The same object shows different structures depending on the orientation

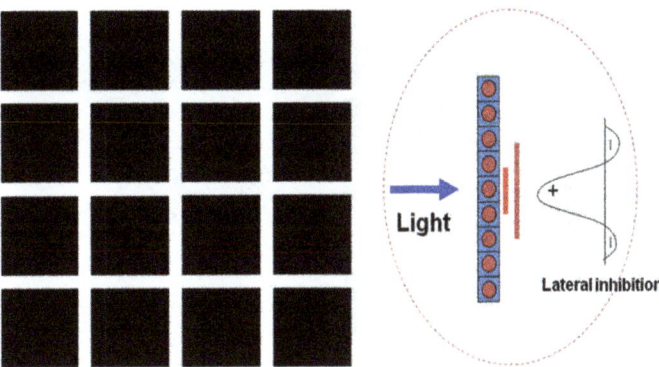

Fig. 10 Visual illusion. Dark squares appear at the intersections of the white corridors. A schematic illustration of the retinal neural net is shown on the right. A retinal cell excited by light inhibits its neighbors

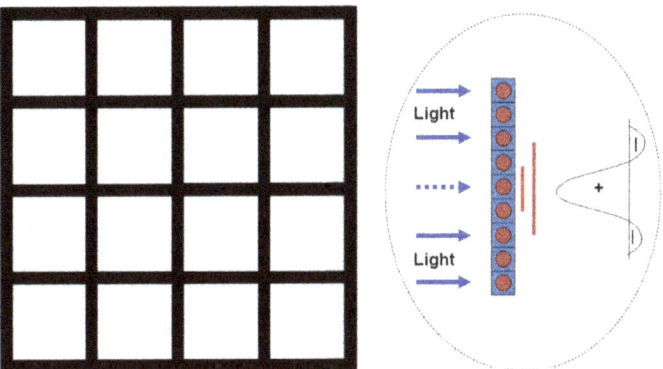

Fig. 11 Visual illusion: bright squares appear at the intersections of black corridors. A schematic illustration of the retinal neural net is shown on the right. A retinal cell excited by darkness inhibits its neighbors

the squares disappear. Neurons therefore respond not only to the real stimulus, but also to their own outputs. This means that there is no clear distinction between the real object and the pseudo object. Interestingly, when white ellipses are drown, the dark square disappears at the central intersection, although the dark squares are still observed in the other intersections of the white corridors. Our perception, therefore, creates phantom sensations.

Again, it is clear that the self-nonself (or subject-object) circulation, which is necessary for understanding the outside world, has the potential to lead to phantom sensations.

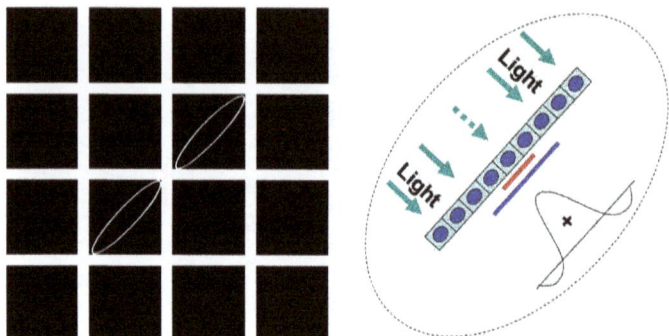

Fig. 12 Visual illusion: The dark square disappears at the central intersection when white ellipses are drown, while the dark squares are still observed in the other intersections of the white corridors. A schematic illustration of the retinal neural net is shown to the right. A retinal cell excited by darkness inhibits its neighbors

7 Discussion

> The crisis of our time isn't just a crisis of a single leader, organization, country, or conflict. The crisis of our time reveals the dying of an old social structure and way of thinking, an old way of institutionalizing and enacting collective social forms.
>
> C. Otto Scharmer
>
> Theory U: Leading from the Future as It Emerges, p. 2
>
> Berrett-Koehler Publishers, Inc., San Francisco, 2009

From "Emerging Self-consistent Life Philosophy" in Sect. 1 to "The Emergence of Dynamic Patterns: Visual Illusion" in Sect. 6, we have discussed six different topics. The present situation seems similar to the famous story about *six blind men and the elephant*.

In this story, the individual men had quite different impressions of the same animal, interpreting it as a wall, a snake, a spear, a tree, a fan, and a rope. Each of these answers described a different part of the same animal. It was not a question of which answer was correct and which was not. The real question must be: "By considering complementary perspectives, how do we acquire an improved understanding within limited constraints?"

Lessons learned from this famous story provide deep insights into the "truth" beyond complexity.

1. Realization of the Two-Fold Problem

Unexpected interrelations among different human and nonhuman systems (Zolli 2012) result in a huge "living" Gaia system involving systems nested within systems, referred to as "self-nested hierarchical systems." Most major problems in our present age have been poorly understood because they are "emerging systemic problems" (cf. Capra and Luisi 2014). How could we understand and solve these emergent problems?

Situations of this kind are truly relevant to attacking the question "What is Life?" Despite advanced studies in science and technology, we hardly understand "life" as a whole, and so we have failed to develop medical therapies effective against emergent diseases, such as cancer (cf. Brock et al. 2009). Remember the two-fold problem (described in Sect. 2): it is a serious problem that we hardly question the reliability of the Western scientific framework within the framework itself, in addition to the general problem, "What is Life?"

In attacking the two-fold problem, we should realize that it can be solved in a self-consistent manner; life will always be a process of cognition, and living systems are cognitive systems (Murase 2000; Gottwald 2002). The present paper showed that the simple principle of self-nonself circulation could be deduced from the demand that the underlying principles should be self-consistent, regardless of the scale with which we are concerned. Once we have realized such a self-consistent theoretical framework, it becomes possible to understand most emerging problems as follows.

2. What is a Crisis?

Although our world is full of emerging systemic problems, most ultimately must be seen as different facets of a single crisis, like the story of *six blind men and the elephant*.

What is a crisis? It must be a crisis of our perceptions (Scharmer 2009; Capra and Luisi 2014). This is good news—if we can change our perceptions with respect to the "living" world, it will be possible to recognize emerging problems and thus to let them disappear, just like visual illusion (see Fig. 12).

3. What is Cognition?

As there is a crisis of our perception, let us examine the problem "What is Cognition?" We are familiar with the Western scientific view that there is a very sharp distinction between the perceiving subject and perceived object. However, when we try to understand our cognitive process, the lack of a clear distinction between subject and object is a serious issue; we are both spectators and actors in the world at the same time.

As illustrated in Fig. 13, the only way to understand the problem "what is cognition?" is to construct a new framework involving both the perceiving subject and perceived object in a circulating manner. Here, induction and deduction, represented by two different arrows, correspond to endocytosis and exocytosis in the case of cellular dynamics (see Fig. 2).

A "self-nonself circulation" process would operate not only during the developmental history of an individual human, including aging, but also during the evolutionary history of life itself as well as cognitive function, as all of these are undoubtedly products of the continuous actions of life in the world and, simultaneously, unavoidable reactions (Murase and Murase 2013a, b, 2014, 2015; Murase et al. 2017).

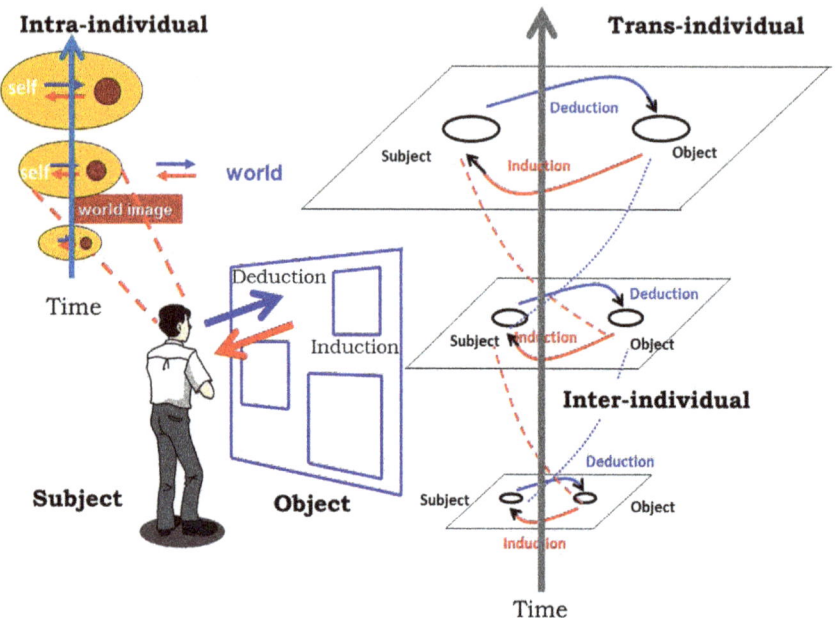

Fig. 13 How we recognize the outside world

4. Integrationists' Approach: Fighting Like with Like

For the development of an integrationists' approach, we should not consider opposing views as mutually exclusive, but instead as complementary. In this way, we should not consider "emerging problems" as inherently bad, for there must be complementary aspects of the problems that lead to good outcomes.

Figure 14 summarizes the wholeness within us, around us, and beyond us. Due to self-nested hierarchical structures, relationships between subjects and objects appear everywhere, within the subjective world as well as the objective world.

It is, therefore, possible to use the same "systemic forces" that generate the "systemic problems" in the first place to attack problems. In trying to cope, we can fight *like with like*.

5. Emerging Problems as Perceptive Illusions?

Section 6 deals with visual illusion. Indeed, we have demonstrated the recognition of dark squares at the intersections of white corridors in Fig. 10. However, when white ellipses are placed near the center, as in Fig. 12, we realized that the visual illusion could be more or less suppressed in that area.

This experience is instructive in three ways with respect to dealing with "emerging systemic problems" in our world.

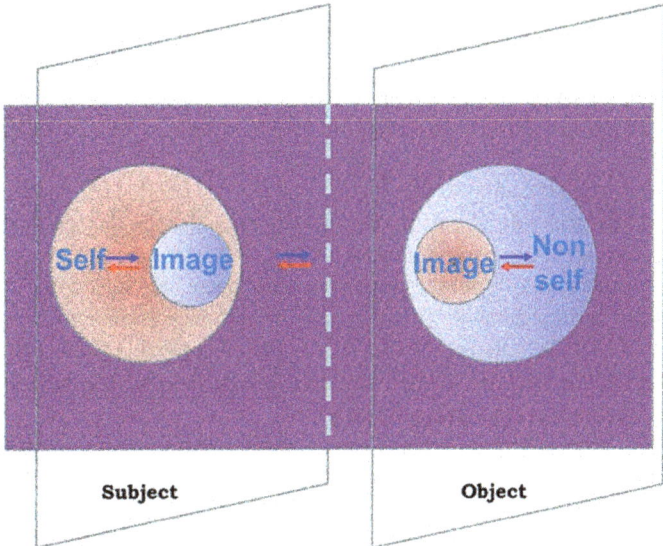

Fig. 14 Self-nested dynamics

(a) We human beings must be considered parts of "systemic problems." Just as a visual illusion does not exist without a perceiving subject, emerging systemic problems are not possible without thinking human beings. Intensive efforts to deal with emerging problems may be useless and even harmful, as these additional efforts may result in further emerging problems. Instead of adding additional "forces," it may be useful to "pull down" the forces that already exist.

(b) We already know that a visual illusion will appear independent of subjects. As long as an observer is present, it is impossible to avoid a visual illusion. Similarly, as a person is considered a part of "systemic problems," even if the person is replaced by another person, such problems cannot be solved (cf. Meadows 2008).

(c) We have shown that a visual illusion can disappear, even if a perceiving subject is operating. A visual illusion disappears only when we modify different structures, apart from locations that exhibit the illusion. The problems of our world may disappear not by dealing with the problems themselves, but by changing quite different systems structures.

8 Conclusion

It is clear that a very simple principle of self-nonself (endo-exo) circulation could govern not only present-day living cells, but also the origin of life, the emergence of aging, cognition of the outside world, and even visual illusions. This means that we are self-nested hierarchical systems.

Based on this principle of self-nonself (endo-exo) circulation, we have to consider both nature and nurture, and not one or the other. They are linked together and inseparable via dynamic processes, such as circulation. Such endless circulation between nature and nurture—or between self (or endo) and nonself (or exo) in the terminology of Murase's theory—gives rise to the emergence of new systems. It is the new systems that account for both creative and destructive features of life. The latter can be defined as systemic problems.

Our world, involving humans and surrounding environments, is full of complexity. What is Complexity? It has often been characterized by unpredictability, diversity, contradictions, and opposition. Actually, we have failed to understand how minor events can lead to sudden "emerging successes," leading to miraculous advances in science and technology or "abrupt disruptions," such as global financial crises and unexpected consequences, even without natural disasters or human errors (Bak 1996).

What can we do to resolve such emerging systemic problems? We now need a *Copernican revolution* for paradigm shifts in our cognition. We should apply the same "systemic forces" that generate the "systemic problems" in the first place. We can fight *like with like* in trying to cope. Paradoxes involving contradictions and opposition must be the source of creative problem-solving, as they cause emergent problems.

Acknowledgements This work was supported by the *International Research Unit of Advanced Future Studies, Kyoto University* and by *JSPS, KAKENHI: Grant-In-Aid for Challenging Exploratory Research No. 26560136*. This work was also supported by the *Future Development Funding Program of Kyoto University Research Coordination Alliance*.

References

Agard, D. A. (1993). To fold or not to fold. *Science, 260*, 1903–1904.
Aguilar, A. L. C. (Ed.). (2009). *What is death?*. Rome: Ateneo Pontificio Apostolorum.
Albers, B., Johnson, A., Lewis, J., Morgan, D., Raff, M., Roberts, K., et al. (2015). *Molecular biology of the cell* (6th ed., p. 695). New York: Garland Science.
Almanspacher, H. & Dalenoort, G. J. (1994). Inside versus outside. Berlin: Springer
Bachmann, P. A., Luisi, P. L., & Lang, J. (1992). Autocatalytic self-replicating micelles as models for prebiotic structures. *Nature, 357*, 57–59.
Bak, P. (1996). *How nature works: The science of self-organized criticality*. New York: Springer.
Bateson, G. (2002). *Mind and nature: A necessary unit*. Cresskill: Hampton Press Inc.
Bloom, F. E. (1981). Neuropeptides. *Scientific American, 245*(4), 148–168.

Bohr, N. (1985). Light and life. In A. P. French & P. J. Kennedy (Eds.), *Niels Bohr* (pp. 311–319). Cambridge: Harvard University Press.
Bretscher, M. S. (1987). How animal cells move, *Scientific American, 257*(6), 70–76
Brock, A., Chang, H., & Huang, S. (2009). Non-genetic heterogeneity—A mutation-independent driving force for the somatic evolution of tumours. *Nature Reviews Genetics, 10,* 336–342.
Cannon, W. B. (1929). Organization for physiological homeostasis. *Physiological Reviews, 9,* 399–431.
Cech, T. R. (1986). A Model for the RNA-catalyzed replication of RNA. *Proceedings of National Academy of Sciences, 83,* 4360–4363.
Capra, F., & Luisi, P. L. (2014). *The systems view of life: A unifying vision.* Cambridge: Cambridge University Press.
Cavalier-Smith, T. (1991) The evolution of cells. In S. Osawa & T. Honjo (Eds.), *Evolution of life: Fossils, molecules, and culture.* Tokyo: Springer, pp. 271–304
Craig, E. A. (1993). Chaperones: Helpers along the pathways to protein folding. *Science, 260,* 1902–1903.
Crick, F. H. C. (1958). On protein synthesis. *Symposia of the Society for Experimental Biology, 12,* 138–163.
Darwin, C. (1859). *The origin of species by means of natural selection* (Reprint ed.). New York: Prometheus Books.
Dautry-Varsat, A., & Lodish, H. F. (1984) How receptors brinbg proteins and particles into cells. *Scientific American, 250*(5), 52–58
Deamer, D. W., & Barchfeld, G. L. (1982). Encapsulation of macromolecules by lipid vesicles under simulated prebiotic conditions. *Journal of Molecular Evolution, 18,* 203–206.
Deamer, D. W., & Fleischaker, G. R. (1994). *Origins of life: The central concepts.* Boston: Jones and Bartlett Publishers Inc.
Deamer, D. W., Mahon, E. H., & Bosco, G. (1994). Self-assembly and function of primitive membrane structures, pp. 107–123. In S. Bengtson (Ed.), *Early life on earth.* New York: Columbia University Press
Doidge, N. (2015). *The brain's way of healing: Stories of remarkable recoveries and discoveries.* UK: Penguin Books.
Eigen, M., & Schuster, P. (1979). *The hypercycle: A principle of natural self-organization.* Berlin: Springer.
Gilbert, W. (1986). The RNA world. *Nature, 319,* 618.
Gilbert, S. F., & Epel, D. (2009). *Ecological developmental biology: Integrating epigenetics, medicine, and evolution.* Sunderland: Sinauer Associates Inc.
Gottwald, F.-T. (2002). Life—A problem inherent in the research context. In H.-P. Dürr, F.-A. Popp, & W. Schommers (Eds.), *What is life? Scientific approaches and philosophical positions* (pp. 25–37). Singapore: World Scientific.
Hargreaves, W. R., Mulvihill, S., & Deamer, D. W. (1977). Synthesis of phospholipids and membranes in prebiotic conditions. *Nature, 266,* 355–357.
Hargreaves, W. R., & Deamer, D. W. (1978). Liposomes from ionic, single-chain amphiphiles. *Biochemistry, 17,* 3759–3768.
Izutsu, T. (1975). The interior and exterior in Zen Buddhism. In *Correspondences of man and world,* A. Portmann, R.Ritsema, & E. J. Brill. Leiden: Eranos Yearbook 1973
Joyce, G. F., & Orgel, L. E. (1993) Prospects for understanding the origin of the RNA world, pp. 1–25. In R. F. Gesteland & J. F. Atkins (Eds.), *The RNA World.* New York: Cold Spring Harbor Laboratory Press
Kauffman, S. A. (1993). *The origins of order: Self-organization and selection in evolution.* New York: Oxford University Press.
Luisi, P. L., & Varela, F. J. (1989). Self-replicating micelles: A chemical version of a minimal autopoietic system. *Origins Life and Evolution of Biosphere, 19,* 633–643.
Meadows, D. H. (2008). *Thinking in systems: A primer.* Vermont: Chelsea Green Publishing.
Morowitx, H. J., Heinz, B., & Deamer, D. W. (1988). The chemical logic of a minimal protocell. *Origins Life, 18,* 281–287.

Murase, M. (1992). *The dynamics of cellular motility*. New York: John Wiley & Sons.
Murase, M. (1996). Alzheimer's disease as subcellular 'cancer'—The scale-invariant principles underlying the mechanisms of aging. *Progress of Theoretical Physics, 95*(1), 1–36.
Murase, M. (2000). *Life as history: The construction of self-nonself circulation theory*. Kyoto: Kyoto University Press.
Murase, M. (2008a). Endo-exo circulation as a paradigm of life: Towards a new synthesis of Eastern Philosophy and Western Science. *Progress of Theoretical Physics Supplement No. 173*, 1–10
Murase, M. (2008b) Environmental pollution and health: an interdisciplinary study of the bioeffects of electromagnetic fields, *SNSAI. An Environmental Journal for the Global Community, No. 3*, 1–35
Murase, M. (2011). The origin and evolution of life by means of endo-exo (or self-nonself) circulation. *Viva Origino, 39*(1), 7–10.
Murase, M. (2016) Challenging from the Advanced Future Studies. *Journal of Integrated Creative Studies*, No. 2016-018-d
Murase, M., & Murase, T. (2013a). Constructive cognition: Extension of self-nonself circulation theory. *Journal of Quality Education, 5*, 29–51.
Murase, M., & Murase, T. (2013b). Investigating polluted environment adaptation syndrome based on structuralism: A perspective of self-nonself circulation theory as a unified theory of life. *Japanese Journal of Clinical Ecology, 22*, 80–91.
Murase, M., & Murase, T. (2014). Structuralism revisited: On the basis of self-nonself circulation theory. *Journal of Quality Education, 6*, 27–43.
Murase, M., & Murase, T. (2015). Synchronization of arts and sciences: The essence of mind and problem of education. *Journal of Quality Education, 7*, 1–28.
Murase, M., Murase, I., & Murase, T. (2017). Towards the origin of learning and playing: From the perspective of self-nonself circulation theory. *Journal of Quality Education, 8*, 1–29.
Pitot, H. C. (1986) *Fundamentals of oncology: Third edition, Revised and expanded*. New York: Marcel Dekker, Inc.
Gregory, R. L. (1998). *Eye and brain: The psychology of seeing* (5th ed.). Oxford: Oxford University Press.
Rose, M. R. (1991). *Evolutionary biology of aging*. Oxford: Oxford University Press.
Rothman, J. E. (1985). The compartmental organization of the Golgi apparatus. *Scientific American, 253*(3), 84–89
Scharmer, C. O. (2009). *Theory U: Leading from the future as it emerges*. San Francisco: Berrett-Koehler Publishers Inc.
Schrödinger, E. (1967). *What is life?*. Cambridge: Cambridge University Press.
Solso, R. L. (1993). *Cognition and the visual arts*. London: The MIT Press.
Sporns, O. (1994). Selectionist and instructionist ideas in neuroscience. In O. Sporns, & G. Tononi (Eds.), *Selectionism and the brain*. San Diego: Academic Press, pp. 3–26
Tjivikua, T., Ballester, P., & Rebek, J. (1990). A self-replicating system. *Journal of the American Chemical Society, 112*, 1249–1250.
Toynbee, A. (1988). *A study of history: Illustrated*. New York: Portland House.
Usher, D. A. (1977). Early chemical evolution of nucleic acids: a theoretical model. *Science, 196*, 311–313.
Varela, F. J., Thompson, E., & Rosch, E. (1991). *The embodied mind: Cognitive science and human experience*. Cambridge: The MIT Press.
von Kiedrowski, G. (1986). A self-replicating hexadeoxynucleotide. *Angewandte Chemie (International ed. in English), 25*, 932–935.

Wassenaar, J. S. (1994) Circular causality and the Human self-organized endo-exo interface, pp. 331–346. In H. Atmanspacher, & G. J. Dalenoort (Eds.), *Inside versus outside*. Berlin: Springer

Watson, J. D., & Crick, F. H. C. (1953). Molecular structure of nucleic acids: A structure for deoxyribose nucleic acid. *Nature, 171,* 737–738.

Zolli, A. (2012). *Resilience: Why things bounce back.* New York: Simon & Schuster.

Author Biography

Masatoshi Murase is Associate Professor of Yukawa Institute for Theoretical Physics at Kyoto University. He is also Director of Research Promotion Strategy Office at The International Research Unit of Advanced Future Studies of Kyoto University. His research topics are meta-biology, life theory, theoretical biology, constructive recognition, semantics theory, environmental biology, theory of aging, emergent disease, origin, and evolution of Life.

Prior to the appointment at Kyoto University, he was chair researcher at Tokyo Metropolitan Institute of Gerontology from 1985 to 1992. He received a PhD degree from the University of Tokyo, Graduate School of Pharmaceutical Sciences in 1987. Positions held overseas include a period of a postdoctoral fellow in the Physiology Department at Duke University Medical Center from 1987 to 1988, and visiting associate professor in the Department of Mathematics at University of California at Davis from 1990 to 1991.

Chapter 17
'Sacred Silence'—The Stillness of Listening to Humanity

Stephen Hill

1 Embarking on the Journey

To truly engage with our shared humanity requires bringing others—even from across widely different cultural worlds—into our very self. We must truly listen—*suspend the noise* of our own inner dialogue of consciousness that otherwise gets in the way. It is here and in our immediate social world that our meanings and culture are formed, not elsewhere.

Here too lies the power of transformation. The term I use is 'global localism'—building action within local communities and then finding ways to link these to other communities and ultimately the world as a whole. I develop this concept further in Chap. 18 following.

Our first task is to bridge 'diversity', to bring others *into* our local world, our 'commonality' where we can share and generate our group strength.

Our second task is then to employ this community-focused cultural center to 'bridge' and empower others' 'diverse' cultural worlds.

This action strategy is a variant on the well known adage, 'think global, act local', an idea originally formulated by Patrick Gedes, an English town planner from the early 20th Century (Barash 2001).

In this Chapter I will demonstrate why 'global localism' matters, but particularly through case studies drawn from direct experience rather than as an abstract philosophic argument.

The core message however is 'listening'—across cultural difference—the basis of bridging our personal and local domain with the world as a whole. In later chapters I explore the consequences more broadly.

S. Hill (✉)
University of Wollongong, Wollongong, Australia
e-mail: sthill@uow.edu.au

2 The Power of Linguistic Silence

As outlined in the Preface to this book, one of the two platforms for the creation of the current Kyoto International Symposium Series and consequent book was collaboration between Rano Sianturi and the local Indonesian NGO, 'Sacred Bridge', which he inspired, supported and directed, and myself, providing support from UNESCO. We had a very close relationship, even naming the organization together, as it was clear their mandate was directly what UNESCO needed to do, use culture, music and performance to *heal* children caught in conflict or trauma. Philippe Delanghe, our UNESCO Culture Specialist, and the Jakarta Office team, provided enthusiastic support. Local professional musicians and performers volunteered and provided continuous, highly creative, and caring support.

What we did together was particularly important as response to the trauma of orphaned children from the immensely destructive Tsunami that hit Aceh, Indonesia, at 8.00 am on Sunday 24th December, 2004. Most of the children had lost not only their direct family but also many other relatives and friends. Around them, 38,000 other children had died.

In one school in the village of Ulee Lheue on the shores of Banda Aceh, only four percent of their friends were left when the children came back to class some time later. Their entire school had been destroyed along with much of the city and its people. Up to 80 percent of the 273,000 people thought to have lost their lives from the Tsunami across the whole Indian Ocean region came from Aceh.

When the children came from the orphanages to our program they were silent. They were scared. For example, when a thunderstorm broke one afternoon, they were absolutely terrified. It reminded them of the Tsunami that had carried away their whole family and previous life.

We did not seek to bring them out through counseling—apart from being affectionate and caring. Instead, in our general program healing the trauma of children caught up in conflict or trauma, we *engaged* the children in musical expression, even getting them to construct their own percussion instruments. They 'spoke' with each other through music, even introducing new participants to the group by playing music to each other (just, simple drums) rather than by talking. They *shared* with each other through artistic expression—including creating joint 'posters of peace' when we were dealing with cross-group conflicts, for example, between children caught up in Christian-Moslem conflict or involved in Jakarta street gangs.

Our collective enterprise between UNESCO and *Sacred Bridge* was a quest to 'heal', to bring peace between people across their diversity and differences, and within the inner self of each. To create a 'culture of peace', very much a core objective of UNESCO.

Healing came through suspending the language in consciousness of hate, division or trauma, and *sharing* the trans-cultural language of music and performance across what otherwise was a cultural divide, or separation from the participants' own human spirit and power. In this way, music could take them to the door of the sacred, for this is what our *shared* humanity is, and open it for them to explore.

What *Sacred Bridge* was capturing was *the power of linguistic silence:* holding still the noise of our own inner dialogue so that we can *hear,* share with others who may even seem very different.

The criterion test is … it worked!

The same can happen through mime, performance, dance. A while ago I spent some time with a famous classical dancer from Solo, Indonesia, Sardono Kusumo. He was working with the Dyak tribes-people of Kalimantan. They had heard about the city life of the United States. But they could not understand how a people could live in a world without trees. Sardono told me that he took a group of Dyak dancers to New York. They wanted to dance and to see people from New York dance so that they could understand.

The cross cultural understanding
that can be reached through linguistic *silence*[1]

3 Crossing the Culture Divide to the Other

3.1 Sacred Silence

Indeed to truly understand and communicate across very different cultures, we need to take 'silence' a step further, to suspend the noise of our learned inner dialogue that otherwise gets in the way. To be 'silent' so we can hear. For it is here that our own surrounding culture—and its barriers—are embedded. We need to *listen* not to intervene, but to understand.

This is Sacred Silence, the stillness of listening to humanity,
the focus of this Chapter.

3.2 Lessons from the Jungle

I will give you a dramatic example of how important this is.

On the 8th January 1996 one of my Jakarta-based UNESCO colleagues for whom I was directly responsible, Martha Klein, was abducted by Free Papua

---

[1]This idea is strongly reflected in Buddhist philosophy. I refer in particular to the 2000 year old Mahayana Buddhist teaching, the Vimalukirti Sutra, on 'nonduality—perception without reference to subject and object, self and other, specifically, Chap. 9. Manjusri, the Bodhisattva of Wisdom, challenges Buddha's disciples to explain 'dualism and non-dualism'. Several try through verbal explanation. Finally a disciple, Saliputra, as response, remains silent. For Manjusri, this was the answer (O'Brien 2015).

Movement (OPM) warriors at the village of Mapnduma in the remote Highlands of Indonesia's West Papua.

Crossing the cultural divide between the modern world and the tribal world was basic to negotiations to get Martha and her fellow hostages released, unharmed.

Martha had taken an eight day trek with her partner Mark van der Val, a consultant to WWF[2] and UNESCO. Her trek was part holiday and part of her UNESCO responsibility to monitor Indonesia's Lorentz National Park which we were preparing for World Heritage status.

Along with 14 other hostages, five of whom were from Europe, she was swept up in a raid by 200 armed tribesmen and taken off into the jungle.

Martha had just discovered she was pregnant.

The OPM's intention was to bargain with these 'white noses' as they called the foreigners, to bring to world attention Indonesia's exploitation and repression of the Papuan people, and ideally to secure West Papuan independence.

I was unexpectedly caught in the beam of the headlight of a fast approaching juggernaut from around a corner in my UN road I had thought was quite safe. I suddenly was confronted by the fact that my own actions were important in getting Martha and Mark and the other hostages out without being murdered or injured.

I was therefore deeply involved in negotiations as the Representative of the United Nations, reporting every day to the UN Security Council. I could not be on the front line of negotiations in the jungle as politically this situation was seen as an internal issue of the State, Indonesia. The United Nations had to stand at a distance, as did National Embassies of all international hostages—the UK, the Netherlands and Germany. We brought in the International Red Cross, the ICRC, to conduct direct negotiations whilst I, representing the UN, along with WWF, the Indonesian Military, and Embassies whose nationals had been abducted, formed the negotiation teams.

It took another 128 days before we secured Martha's release. Two of her fellow Indonesian hostages were murdered at the last minute, another story filled with the most extraordinary covert and political intrigue.

This was a dramatic saga, with negotiations complicated considerably by the distance between the culture of the modern world from which Martha had been extracted, and the tribal culture of the West Papuan people.

I do not intend to tell this story here in any detail. It is, for anyone interested, the subject of my recent e-book, '*Merdeka*', the Indonesian word for freedom or independence. Hill (2014), republished as a substantially revised and updated hard copy edition as '*Captives for Freedom*' by the University of Papua New Guinea Press, 2017 (Hill 2017).

Instead I will take you, the reader, into some of the negotiations and the critical role played by crossing a wide cultural bridge. We did not always understand the other side of the chasm we were crossing. The drama was being played out in a very remote jungle environment and often we simply did not know what was happening

---

[2]The 'World Wildlife Fund for Nature'.

—and with people whose cultural way of doing things was equally remote to the modern world which we came from.

After the first couple of weeks of the crisis we completely lost contact with the abductors. Previous scheduled radio contact, or 'scheds', suddenly stopped. Military trackers could not find where they were. We thought the rebels, or freedom fighters, were playing 'hard ball' and refusing to communicate. As it turned out, the problem was that the person with the radio had been informed by a local priest that the military might attack and had headed off into the jungle to escape. He took the radio with him and was now entirely separated from the group. The abductors had no radio.

Finally, we re-established contact.

At the front end of our negotiations in the field was a doctor, Ferenc Meyer, representative of the International Red Cross. I talked with Ferenc the next day when he got back to Jakarta.

What he told me was that he was taken 400 m from his helicopter, directed to sit on the edge of a 100 m deep ravine, and found himself surrounded by a large number of naked tribesmen coated in pig-fat to keep out the cold, dressed in koteka or penis sheaths,[3] feathers and war paint, armed with spears, bows and arrows, and the occasional gun. His situation was designed to be seriously intimidating.

Meyer was confronted by the OPM junior leader, Titus.

Meyer described him as very tough. Titus stared at Meyer for a good two minutes and then said,

What do you want me to wear? T-shirt or penis sheath?

Meyer, momentarily taken aback, then replied,

That is your choice, whether you choose to wear traditional or modern clothes, not mine.

And after a short pause,

But I have three T-shirts to give you if you are cold.

Perhaps sitting on the edge of a 100 m ravine surrounded by a naked rebel army dressed in penis sheaths and carrying spears and rifles sharpened Meyer's focus.

But his was the correct answer to the test and allowed further communication to be pursued. Meyer had said two things that resonated with the OPM cause and tribal values, 'You are the people who have the right to choose', and 'I come to bring you a "gift" not to take something'.

---

[3]Penis sheaths are universal male fashion amongst tribal Papuans, covering only their reproductive organ. They are formed from a collected root crop gourd that can come in an enormous variety of long but erratic shapes and sizes, and are worn to protect (or perhaps to emphasise) one's private parts. They are held at an erectile angle by a thin strand of fibre or thread attached around the man's waist. Size of the koteka does not necessarily represent status, but occasion. Short koteka are worn when working in the fields, long koteka in ceremonies.

Ferenc responded in the same way when he later achieved access to the leader of the OPM group that captured the hostages, Daniel Kagoya. Daniel said to Ferenc on initial contact,

What are you coming here to take away, the hostages?

Meyer replied,

I do not come to take away anything. I come to give you these (packages of food and supplies). You will give me the hostages when you decide.

These two issues, gifts and offer of choice, became the core of the subsequent series of tests that Meyer confronted. Each time, passing the test led to a further stage in the negotiation, or a higher level of OPM leader who he could subsequently consult.

Earlier in negotiations I had failed to cross this same cultural bridge.

I believed that letters appealing for release of the hostages from the top dignitaries in the world would influence the abductors to see that they had attracted high level international attention, but now needed to release the hostages to maintain their credibility and global concern for their cause within this modern world.

Together with the UN Coordinator in Indonesia, Jan Kemp from UNDP, I spent an entire night until dawn over many cups of coffee and a fax machine organizing for letters to be sent to the rebels from the Secretary General of the United Nations, the Director-General of UNESCO, the Archbishop of Canterbury ... *and the Pope*.

We considered the Pope's letter would have enormous power as the leader of the jungle OPM who had given the instruction to capture the hostages had previously been a Seminarian under the tutelage of Catholic Bishop Munninghoff.

The letters all mirrored international humanitarian values and the universal condemnation of taking hostages, for example, as in the words of the UNESCO Director General, Federico Mayor,

The taking of hostages is condemned throughout the world, whatever the circumstances and whatever the purpose.

But we had made a fundamental error.

The way the OPM interpreted the letters from the religious leaders, the Pope and the Archbishop of Canterbury, whose appeals we regarded as our 'best shot', was a total surprise.

Bishop Munninghoff, Kwalik's previous religious mentor, travelled into the jungle and read the Pope's letter to Kwalik directly. The rebel leader listened attentively to the Bishop's report. He then observed that the Pope expressed concern about the plight of the hostages, but said nothing about the troubles faced by the Papuan people. This brought discussion of the Pope's correspondence to an end. It would appear that Kwalik interpreted the Pope's intervention as a misdirected moral directive rather than a positive sign of international attention.

It was also reported to us that the letter from the Archbishop of Canterbury had been dealt with in a curiously Papuan way. The Deputy OPM leader who received it, Daniel, looked at the letter, held it in one hand as if weighing it, and said,

On this side I have this letter, and on the other, the hostages. This (the letter) weighs almost nothing.

He then threw the letter away.
I had not truly 'listened'.

4 Listening to the Past

4.1 The Legacy of Humanity

When the 'self' is separated from the other, the self no longer derives its being from the way in which it refers to the other, just from within the already established world views and prejudices of its own separation from others, separation from *their* cultures and meanings.

In other words inter-subjective understanding and connection is 'welcoming the other' into one's own self—for this is how deep our own culture is embedded.

But, we must *silence our own cultural language of consciousness,* and 'listen', to lay down the 'welcome mat' for truly sharing[4].

'Sacred Silence'
The source of sharing across cultures and mutual empowerment!
The rewards of cross cultural understanding are not just set in the present.

The richness of humanity has been formed over thousands of years. Indeed, each of us stands today at the intersection between the cultural history that formed the meanings within which we now participate, and the contemporary cultural diversity that both challenges and enriches our connection to humanity as a whole. C. Wright Mills talked of situating our disciplined reflections on society at this intersection as '*The Sociological Imagination*' (Mills 1959). We must pay attention to both dimensions.

We cannot participate in past cultures but we can certainly learn from them.

Conserving the past, the best of humanity's achievements—both physical and intangible, as in traditional cultural practices, as well as nature's spectacular and sustaining diversity, is the objective of UNESCO's World Heritage Program. To maintain and cherish our collective 'memory of the world'.

Here, I will only note the consequence of not being able to interrogate past cultures ... of not being able to *listen* to the past because all memories have been lost.

To destroy the past either through careless abandonment or conscious strategy has an equivalent impact on society as the burning of books – erasing alternatives to the current order and its ideology. Without alternatives, the ideology and power of the current governing regime becomes unassailable, an expression of totalitarianism. Limitations on freedom to question and to express criticism invariably follow. 'Humanity' is impoverished.

---

[4]For development of this phenomenological perspective, see Lévinas (1969) and Hill (1995).

The destruction by the Afghan ruling Taliban regime in March 2001 of the Buddhist Statues of Bamiyan is a terrible example.

The Statues were built in the 6th Century on the Silk Road, historically a caravan route that linked the markets of China with those of the Western world. Bamiyan was the site of several Buddhist monasteries, a thriving center for religion, philosophy and art. Fifty three meters and 36 m tall respectively, the Statues were the largest standing Buddha statues in the world, their bodies carved from the surrounding sandstone cliffs. The Bamiyan Statues along with their wider environment were a declared UNESCO World Heritage Site.

Against enormous international opposition, including from their Arab neighbors, the Taliban elite destroyed the Bamiyan Statues because they had declared them 'idols' to be removed according to Islamic teaching.

The Director General of UNESCO at the time, Koichiro Matsuura, called the destruction,

... a crime against culture. It is abominable to witness the cold and calculated destruction of cultural properties which were the heritage of the Afghan people, and, indeed, of the whole of humanity. (ABC 2001)

Although the majority of the people of Afghanistan at the time that the Taliban dynamited the Statues were Muslim, many had embraced their multicultural past and were appalled. The destruction of the Bamiyan Buddhas became a symbol of oppression and a rallying point for subsequent freedom of religious expression.[5]

4.2 Cultural Resilience Against Totalitarian Regimes

My own direct experience in Indonesia demonstrated the disempowerment to a society that follows from regime *control and censorship* of alternative cultural expression.

However, I saw the process in reverse—the dawning of cultural freedom with the fall of President Soeharto's dictatorial regime in May 1998.

I was there, watching the Revolution on the streets and the 'awakening' that followed.

Indeed, Jill, my wife, and I had to escape our house – in a largely Chinese suburb – through the mobs, fires and looting whilst the noise of what were called Probowo's Ninjas could be heard approaching - at 2.00 am when even our employed 'satpans', or house guards, had decided it was too dangerous and changed out of their uniforms and run off down the street.

I subsequently evacuated everyone else from my UN staff and families, but needed to stay as a UN representative. (Moussa, our International Administration Officer insisted also on remaining in Jakarta to watch events unfold first-hand.) So I was in the front row to watch the revolution drama evolve over the next week – even

---

[5]See 'Buddhas of Bamiyan' in *Wikipedia* for a good summary of this event (Wikipedia 2015).

went to the Indonesian Parliament to talk with the rebelling student movement people – until the Islamic youth attack force arrived and I had to get out through a quite confronting crowd.

During Soeharto's 32 year 'New Order Government', censorship was severe, news was entirely centralized and broadcast 13 times a day from Jakarta through the provinces where no investigative news reporting capacity was allowed to exist[6]. Education was by rote learning not questioning. And the peoples' voice was silent apart from those few dissidents who risked 'disappearance' or at minimum, incarceration, if they protested. A good friend of mine was Principal of the most advanced High School in Jakarta. He went to a police station simply to enquire why one of his students had been arrested. It was twelve months later before he walked out.

Within our UNESCO Office, we noticed immediately after May 1998 however, that the people quite literally started to rise as it were from a long slumber. Day by day through the week of protest and killings that heralded the ousting of President Soeharto, the Press became more open, throwing off the shackles of censorship that had previously silenced their voice of critique. Increasingly from there on, we noticed that the village communities developed a voice and an empowered commitment to take their destinies back into their own hands. Previously they had been acquiescent and silent.

It was in this new context that our own UNESCO Office, bringing in collaboration with UNICEF, was able to lead a whole new approach to basic education across Indonesia—fundamentally involving local communities and creative learning and questioning within the classroom.

The stimulus was a mission I took with other Heads of UN Agencies in Indonesia at the height of the 1997 Asian Economic Crisis. We wanted to see what was happening in the very poorest villages of provincial Indonesia in order to know what our priorities should be.

Everywhere, even in the very poorest of communities, parents told me that they would do anything to keep their kids in school. But they did not really understand what schools did or how to be engaged themselves. Meanwhile the schools were teaching by rote learning and were tightly controlled from Jakarta.

I initiated the program, 'Creating Learning Communities for Children' or 'CLCC', in late 1998. We employed three key principles, community engagement, decentralized management, and opening up the classroom to creativity, interaction, and questioning rather than rote learning.

We did not just ask parents to meetings, we trained them to participate and do things for the school, as, in most cases, they had never known how to engage with the school before. It was like a separate hidden world for them.

---

[6]I mounted a nation-wide program to develop freedom of media and expression immediately after the revolution, capitalizing on the new opportunity. We helped change the law within 9 months. We also developed and trained an independent network of 32 radio stations across the nation capable of investigating and reporting local news.

We worked with government to convert a previously highly centralized national system (down to how many pencils were sent to a remote village in West Papua) into nationally decentralized school-based management. It was a lot of work and required raising rather a lot of funding from sources other than UNESCO.

The program took off like a wild fire—from the roots of the communities themselves. The people were now ready and they *wanted* the new creative freedoms for their children's future. Parents wanted their kids to be in one of our CLCC schools. Teachers would even try to move to new areas to be involved.

The new decentralized system is now in place—for 42 million children across the whole country. We provided the ideas, training and organization, and I had a team working directly within the Ministry of Education. But we were simply responding to an enormous and driving demand from the local communities.

It could not have happened under the totalitarian control of the previous New Order Government.

But the transformation of basic education across all Indonesia was based on the principle of *listening*—to the voice of the people. And assisting the government to decentralize basic education so that this voice could be heard more clearly.

4.3 The Eternal Flame of Culture

Additionally, it is worth observing that the peoples' need for human empowerment of their culture is likely to be burning away unnoticed while the totalitarian regime is in power. Even the boot of totalitarian repression cannot extinguish the flame.

Two examples, one from Timor Leste, and one from Mongolia, again, both from my direct experience.

In Timor Leste, 25 years of Indonesian rule had left the Timorese traditional 'Sacred Houses' in ruins and disconnected from village life. This was a conscious strategy of the Indonesian Government.

Timor was then freed from Indonesian rule following the peoples' vote for Independence in September 1999, but amidst an orgy of orchestrated and bloody violence by militia acting on behalf of Indonesia's military. The generals had strong economic and military interest in *not* allowing Timor's Independence. The politics behind what was a continuingly festering legacy of Soeharto's previous dictatorial control were complex. I had access to a lot of inside information. But I will not digress to talk about this now.

I moved quickly to establish a 'satellite' UNESCO Office in Dili, Timor's capital, and initiated a number of programs to assist Timor's new development priorities.

In response to a request from the incoming transitional government, we rebuilt two of the most important of Timor's traditional 'Sacred Houses'. Philippe Delangue, our Culture Specialist, played the central role in this project. Here, I just wish to make a single observation.

Each of the Sacred Houses and their ceremonies was the center of the networks of kin through the whole country.

The people celebrated at the first of the rebuilt Sacred Houses, spending somewhere near $(US) 16,000 on the food, an enormous amount for a very very poor community. But the people who came from across Timor took food back to their kinship networks across the whole country, to share symbolically in the new freedom of religious expression. The Sacred House was central in helping to rebuild the integrity of the nations' people and their cultural connectedness.

Indeed, Xanana Gusmao, President at the time, told me personally, that he applauded this initiative and regarded the recapture of the 'intangible' cultural heritage of Timor Leste, the traditions, cultural practices, kinship networks and meanings, as a key priority for him. Without recapturing and understanding this it was difficult for him and the nation to envision what its future should be. Indeed it was UNESCO's support of Timorese culture that was most significant in the country's decision to join UNESCO as one of its first international priorities, just 3 months after Independence was declared.

In Mongolia, Buddhist Temples were either destroyed or allowed to remain derelict under communist rule until Gorbachev's reforms in the Soviet Union were carried across to the regime of Mongolia from 1992 onwards, then the communist based government fell in a democratic election in 1996.

Immediately, as I found on a UN mission I took shortly thereafter, a very poor people found the finances and labor to start to rebuild the temples, adorn the temples' sacred statues in gold leaf—to recapture their past culture.

Human culture and meaning is so powerful
it can even resist decades of repression
and then regenerate

4.4 Cultural Diversity—A Basis for Human Survival

Beyond the direct relation between destroying the ability to *listen* to the past and totalitarian regimes, there is perhaps an even more important consequence of losing our ability to interrogate and live in continuity with our past cultures.

It is the loss of connection to both present and historic diversity that confronts us with the very real question of human survival beyond the twenty-first century.

In the biological world, there is ever increasing diminution of diversity of staple food crops through the commercial control most powerfully of the multinational corporation, Monsanto. As I observed in Chap. 2, its patented seeds have been genetically altered to be resistant to Monsanto's own weed killer, 'Roundup'. This allows Monsanto to not only make enormous profit from its herbicide, 'Roundup', but also from the only seeds that can resist its poison. Farmers who buy Monsanto's patented 'Roundup Ready Seeds' are required to sign an agreement not to save the seed for re-planting, or to sell the seed to other farmers. They must buy new seed every year. Monsanto belligerently protects their patents over these seeds right down to small time farmers and stores in remote and poor developing countries. Now, even the biological ability of the purchased seeds to regenerate has been compromised by further genetic manipulation by Monsanto. Control of the biodiversity of humanity's main staple crops is firmly in the control of a single corporation (Bartlett and Steel 2008).

The consequence for humanity's very survival if confronted by an unexpected attack by a mutation of predatory insects or other pests could cause massive starvation across the globe.

The same lesson applies to loss of diversity of human culture under the command of globalism. Very basic lessons for human survival may be lost with forgotten cultures of the past, or 'exotic' species of culture that have so far remained relatively untouched by modern civilization, as in still tribal societies.

However, to 'listen' to the diversity of our shared cultural past requires *silence*, to avoid the 'noise' of imposing our own cultural interpretation on what has gone before.

An example of the problem of cultural *noise* in listening to the past can be found with the European Renaissance and the translation of ancient Greece's classical culture into the context of evolving 'ways of seeing' that were developing in the 15th and 16th Centuries in Europe.

Renaissance literally means 'rebirth', the generally acknowledged parent of which in the European Middle Ages was the fall of Constantinople in 1453 and the subsequent carriage of ancient Greek literature to Europe by the Byzantine scholars who were expelled out of the city. What the sudden discovery of a whole previously hidden set of ancient texts presented was *alternatives*, alternatives to the whole assumed stock of classics and classically-inspired traditional knowledge and wisdom of the Middle Ages, alternatives to the rule of truth that the Christian Church commanded as *the* arbiter of understanding and social order of the day.

The trigger of discovery that 'fired' the Renaissance worked because *the time was right*. The society had rediscovered the past and was seeking to *listen* – to learn from it.

However, scholars and leaders of thought were seeing the past through new eyes, listening through ears tuned to the sound of their present culture.

The world of the Renaissance did not simply copy and reproduce ancient Greek and Roman architecture and thought. Rather, it *digested* the classics into their modern civilization, and thereby changed the original meaning to fit the idea of the time.

The aesthetics of ancient Greece were those of human engagement. The perspective of the large Greek statues of the Parthenon in Athens, for example, are distorted mathematically so that the proportions look right to the human observer from a 1.7 meter-above-the-ground vantage point. Such precise distortion of proportion involved a complex series of mathematical transformations.

The Renaissance architects and sculptors however could not tap into the ancient Greek mathematics for this knowledge had been lost. Rather, they were guided by the new 'liberating' philosophy of Francis Bacon that sought knowledge by direct disciplined observation rather than by what religious decree declared to be true.

The 'new' philosophy focused attention on the mathematical order of the thing itself rather than the mathematics of proportion as seen from the vantage point of a human being.

Consequently, reproduction of the classics abided by quite new assumptions of the relationship between the human and their physical world.

Baconian science located the person *outside* their world. Greek science had the person firmly at the center. Now, the observer's position was less important than the order of the system itself, a totally different philosophy to that which guided the ancient world. But nobody noticed how fundamental was the change (Hill 1988, pp. 49–50, 2010). And it was now set firmly into the physical world that surrounded their immediate experience.

The 'noise' of their present culture got in the way. And 'the person' was pushed out of the center of the universe.

In the late 18th Century European industrialism followed. The person and their labor was now a cog in a physical machine that produced 100 times faster than individual human action could deliver. External control of the person. Efficiency ruled over human empowerment. The shape of humanity's subsequent history followed (Hill 2010, pp. 109–136).

Silence in consciousness is basic to truly listening to the past.

Furthermore, the description of this previous historic period of transformation, the "Renaissance", was not invented until this time of nineteenth century industrialization. The contemporary cultural environment of change, immensely accelerated into daily life by industrialization, made people look backwards at change that had happened before.

Again, people listened to history through the filter of their culture's present voice. Perhaps through the noise of 'change' they could not see the lessons of 'continuity' clearly enough … back to the heart … the person at the center.

5 The Sacredness of Humanity

By not listening to the past, efficient economic development, invention, and interest of those in control was fostered through the world's post-18th century industrialization enterprise. But a deep connection to our very humanity as the center of our vision was lost in the noise.

What constitutes our 'humanity' is not a global collection of alienated and disempowered individuals, spread in their billions across the globe, obeisant to, and separated by, the power, the economically inspired exploitation, of others, and the marginalization of all cultures and meanings apart from those who are in power.

Rather, 'Humanity' is what we *can* be as a human race, empowered, fulfilled individuals, whose own identity and meanings are deeply woven into caring and sharing with others across our separate cultural worlds. A people who have learnt from their past and can share across boundaries of apparent difference. A people who can live together, understand each other and accept difference. Who can live in peace through a continuous quest for mutual empowerment and inner fulfilment.

To quote Nobel Prize Laureate, Aung San Suu Kyi from Myanmar:

The true development of human beings involves much more than mere economic growth. At its heart there must be a sense of empowerment and inner fulfilment. (UNESCO 1995)

> *The depth of humanity is what is 'sacred',*
> *entitled to reverence or respect*

6 Humanity and Survival

6.1 The Noise of Fear

We should not relax in the light of this realization in the belief we still have some time to respond. In this year, 2017, humankind as a whole, and the essence of our 'humanity' is at terrible risk! I sketched some key dimensions of this risk in Chap. 2.

Finding how to assert, then 'manage', our collective 'humanity' within our current globalized world, a central goal of this book, is not only something we should cherish, but a basic precondition for our very survival past the twenty-first century as I argued in my Chap. 2.

To quote from my book, *The Tragedy of Technology:*

> The horizon of daily life is alternatively shaded by the darkest of technologically-produced clouds and illuminated by the brightest of technologically produced sunshine. In the interests of ever-expanding capital accumulation, and with the "hubris" of Icarus, human kind flies towards this horizon, precariously close to the sun that is both source of power and destruction. (Hill 1988, p. 1)

The technological power that now is held in the paranoid control of the very few is strong enough to annihilate the human race entirely through nuclear war within, as a worst case scenario, 30 min—even as the result of human error within the nuclear war machine. As I demonstrated in my Chap. 2, this *has almost happened* several times over the last 35 years.

Potential global conflict has emerged from within the culturally formed paranoia of separate groups wishing to preserve their own cultural ways because others' 'humanity' cannot be trusted whilst *'we'* have the power to do something about it. Each fears that the *'others'* may seek to take *'our'* valued ways from us, such as 'The American Dream', and subject *'us'* to the command of *'their'* ideology and culture.

Alternatively, *'they'* insist that *'their'* culture is the only way for all. And *'they'* have the power to annihilate *'us'* if *'we'* seem a threat to *'their'* culture and way of life, or will not convert to *'their'* way. Even direct invasion of another society for their land, resources or people is about fear—that *'we'* will not have enough unless we conquer *'them'*.

Its all about 'us' and 'them'. *Separation* from our shared humanity.

Religious belief can be the most basic dividing line. It expresses the ultimate horizon of the group's perception of their own humanity and destiny—likely to be unnegotiable. A particular religious institution *can* offer a genuine path to the values of a fully shared humanity, but humanity is intrinsically ecumenical, as therefore, is our spirituality. Ideological separation is the platform for political and aggressive self-preservation that underlies most current wars and threats. Assertion or belief in absolute legitimacy of the proponents' particular take on a religion may well be at the core, as presently is the case with the terrorism of ISIS. Even the killing, rape and exploitation of others can be not only excused, but encouraged … the ultimate denial of our shared humanity.

Separation produces fear or exploitation of the other. Separation.

Unfortunately, it appears that those whose minds are deeply embedded in the bunkers of fear or exploitation do not realize that they too will be destroyed.

The nuclear war scenario in the Cold War period of the 1960s to the 1990s was assigned to the strategy of 'Mutual Assured Destruction' the acronym for which was 'MAD'. Highly appropriate. Unfortunately, the insanity of MAD still hovers over the head of humanity's survival today. With a countdown of … 30 min to Midnight … and the total extinction of humanity by our own hand.

6.2 The 'Noise' of Globalism

Beyond these immediate nuclear threats, we also confront the erosive economic interests of increasingly powerful and monopolistic global corporations, exploding single corporate demands across the very fabric of cultural diversity and resilience of the world's differing societies. Even remote traditional cultures are now likely to be obeisant to the symbols of power and the economics of demand these corporations now control.

The presence and symbolism of a single coca cola bottle or a Macdonald's logo within a society for which this is alien but by its exotic difference, to be valued, can start to disassemble the very roots of the society's previous cultural meanings and resilience.

A friend working in Papua New Guinea some years ago observed to me:

In the early development of the Bougainville Copper Mines, young Papua New Guineans were employed straight out of a timeless tribal society into the copper mines of Bougainville. With their entry into a money economy, they purchased Western consumer products and took them home to their villages. The symbolic wealth power of alien artifacts, such as clothes, radios and watches that they could present as 'bride prices' stood in stark contrast to the 'normal' traditional exchange gifts of pigs, cassowaries and tribal artifacts. The symbolic power of gifts was directly associated with acquired status and exchange-induced obligations.

The effect therefore of young men entering the money economy through the Bougainville Copper Company was to deeply penetrate and erode the traditional structures of authority, obligations, status and cultural meaning of the indigenous society. (Hill 1988, pp. 74–75)

Modernist 'cultural' invasion can alter the fabric of *economic relations* so fundamentally that the people are dragged out of their traditional sustainable productive ways into a modernist economy where they become dependent and disenfranchised.

In the Kingdom of Tonga during the 1970s, a bakery commenced the baking of bread for the first time in the capital city, Nuku'Alofa. The demand was initially very small from a people whose staple diet was taro, coconuts and fish, and only one sack of imported flour was used a day.

Twenty years later, when this observation was drawn to my attention, the demand was hundreds of times higher. Bread symbolized modern food, and presaged Kentucky Fried Chicken, Macdonalds and so on, that arrived through Asia and the Pacific with advertising campaigns that consciously asserted high budget symbols. With improved roads across the island Tongatapu, a product of development assistance, access to the capital became considerably easier, and people started to come to town to purchase bread. Children from schools were now buying bread for lunch rather than eating traditional foods. The need to purchase a staple commodity that cannot be produced from local resources has required villagers to enter the cash economy, so many young people (particularly) congregated in the town looking for work that the modernizing elements of the economy could not yet provide adequately. But meanwhile the unemployed were eating bread rather than traditional foods.

Traditional relations and obligations of village life were thus being eroded with each new loaf of bread that was baked. Because of the low level of wealth of the nation, the flour that was imported was of the lowest quality that could be obtained, and whilst rich in starch, was very poor in nutritional ingredients. Diet-related health problems started to accelerate, all because, as one senior Tongan official observed, 'the people had got used to buttered bread.' (UNESCO-SPEC 1987)

As in this Tongan example, a development strategy that focuses on everything *but* culture, may produce a result in an 'accidental culture', that concurrently *weakens* the society's ability to act autonomously and envision its future development objectives.

Examples from traditional or village-based societies show the erosive power of globalism in high relief.

More insidious is the power of globalism on the cultural life of those living in modern societies. For, we live in a 'New Age' where the global deeply penetrates into one's very subjective world everywhere.

In a modern society, these same symbols 'command' our 'coolness', social acceptance, and the 'meaning' implied by our consumption of specific branded food and fashion products we purchase, in other words, our values in relating to others. As a result they command our economy.

The consequence is more serious than we often recognize. To the extent that our human values, meaning and culture are 'commanded' from outside rather than formed within our immediate subjective world, we are limited in our ability to participate autonomously in our society and culture.

The survival of our 'humanity'
is threatened by the noise of fear and economic greed.

7 The Hidden Grammar of Culture

To understand how this *noise*, this 'external' cultural command from global fear and commercialism, has such power, we need to reflect for a moment on what culture is.

Many associate 'culture' with the 'arts', opera, music, painting—creative expression. This is not wrong, just limited in understanding the power and ubiquitousness of culture.

Instead, *our* culture is *our* 'design for living' (Kluckhorn 1951) expressed in the guiding commands of the norms, values, and expectations of our own social world that allow us to orient our life and action, and appreciate what it all means… why we do things.

This 'design for living' is fashioned collectively. It is constituted 'organically' over time, and passed on to new generations according to what has been proven to 'work'. A culture's 'design for living' is fashioned out of peoples' need to orient their own individual actions – at every moment of consciousness – in terms of both the social world they inhabit, and the meanings this social world attributes to action that allows the collectivity, and the individual, to survive. (Hill 1988, p. 91)

As anthropologist Clifford Geertz points out,

The drive to make sense out of experience, to give it form and order, is evidently as real as the more familiar biological needs: the organism cannot live in a world it is unable to understand.[7]

Even though we may participate in the social worlds of multiple personal identities, mother, sister, musician, Buddhist, community leader, salaried employee (Sen 2006) … within our own consciousness and dealing with others, we synthesize *a* culture, a design that works for *our* world and its meaning including acting in different ways in different social contexts. The self is a narrative unity.

---

[7]See Geertz (1968). I had the privilege to meet and share a speaking platform with Clifford Geertz in Jogjakara, Indonesia, when we were both speaking about the importance of cultural heritage. He was the master—of understanding Indonesia's range of traditional cultures. One of his previous papers on tribal rituals became the tribal community's 'manual' when their previous rituals had been forgotten. They used Geertz's publication to reconstitute their traditional ceremonies.

But as the phenomenologists tell us, we construct meaning through *action within our 'world within reach'*[8], in subjective relations with others, in socially producing together, in direct sharing .... in our *local* world. *Our culture is not produced elsewhere.*

This has very important implications for the action strategy we might develop as a product of the present book. I will return to this later.

A child grows from within this direct subjective world, laying down the underlying structures of consciousness for later understanding before they deal with the world beyond their direct subjective relations with their immediate parents and others.

Even throughout this early development the child confronts 'external' worlds and symbols. Your six year old son is likely to *insist* with tears, that you *must* go out to Macdonalds tonight to have a coca-cola and hamburger because of what they have seen on TV, what their friends tell them, or because Macdonalds are offering a whole new set of miniature plastic dinosaurs.

What is presented to our consciousness from the world outside our direct subjective world has the form of an 'ideal type', i.e.: received 'passively', its meaning remaining unpacked. It therefore has the power to 'command' rather than foster responsive communication. We must fit this 'ideal type' into our own way of understanding but cannot open it to see what its meanings are and were at source. These external symbols simply become fitted in, invisibly and as 'command', into the development of the child's understanding of meaning and their own culture, into their socialization 'grammar'. Like a cyst or even a tumor within our living social body.

As adults, our own culture is therefore hidden. Our structures of meaning are buried in consciousness. Worlds and symbols beyond our subjective life remain unpacked but somehow made sense of within our 'world within reach'. Culture is our underlying 'grammar' for life expression .... NOW.

A fish, swimming in the ocean, has no idea of what water is and how important to its life, until it suddenly finds itself stranded on dry land as the tide goes out. The ocean is its whole world, not needing to be questioned.

Culture surrounds and nurtures us in the same way. As its simplest definition, culture is 'the way we do things around here'. Meanings that are not opened up, just *lived.* We only really notice it when we confront a very different cultural world to which we must respond.

Herein lies the culturally destructive power of globalism.
We don't notice its command!

---

[8] I personally had the chance to share in research and the exploration of phenomenological views of the self and the socialization of consciousness with Thomas Luckman, both in Wollongong where he spent a 6 month mission in my Sociology Department in 1977, then in Constanz, Germany in 1979, where I worked with him on my own sabbatical leave, including living with him in his apartment just over the border in Switzerland. I had the privilege of walking across the border between Switzerland and Germany each morning, debating ideas about phenomenology. Needless to say, I learnt a great deal. See Schutz and Luckman (1974), Hill (1988, 1995, pp. 92–97). Development of my own theoretical approach to personal identity and action was derived from a major empirical study I conducted of 1300 scientists under commission from the Australian Academy of Science (Hill et al. 1974a, b; Hill and Howden 1974).

But by closing others out, the richness and resilience of our own cultural world is diminished.

As observed earlier, when the 'self' is separated from the other, the self no longer derives its being from the way in which it refers to the other, just from within the already established world views and prejudices of its own separation from others, separation from *their* cultures and meanings. In other words inter-subjective understanding and connection is 'welcoming the other' into one's own self—for this is how deep our own culture is embedded. But, we must *silence our own cultural language of consciousness,* and 'listen', to lay down the 'welcome mat' for truly sharing[9].

'Sacred Silence'
The source of sharing across cultures and mutual empowerment!

8 Global Localism

We actively form our culture within our immediate subjective world.

Empowerment starts in the same place, within our 'local' world. For it is here that humanity's strength resides. Our quest is then to build what I call 'global localism'[10], capturing the power of the local where meaning is constituted, our immediate and subjective relationships and culture, and exploding our connectedness at this human level across the global human world.

Virtually all development focused programs we ran out of our UNESCO Jakarta Office and which really worked, focused on assisting the community at local level to take power for themselves. This often required helping them to see a new vision, training so they could handle the tasks required, mentoring, securing the power of their local voice within the external governance system, and of course providing core funding to get things started.

'Sacred Silence' was our starting point. Listen to the people rather than impose a design imported from elsewhere. Progressive handing over of responsibility was critical—ultimately to the point where all decisions about how funding would be used were in the hands of the local community, not us. And, of course, we paid

---

[9]For development of this phenomenological perspective, see Lévinas (1969) and Hill (1995).

[10]Originally, I used the phrase 'New Localism' to describe the dynamic we had observed from a comprehensive research program we conducted across all areas of science and its organization from within the Australian Research Council Centre of Excellence, the Centre for Research Policy, at the University of Wollongong which I founded and directed in the early 1990s. A particular focus was on contemporary scientific knowledge construction and communication. See Hill and Turpin (1994, 1995). The parallel idea of 'Global Localism' as a basic concept for social change is developed in Hill (2010, pp. 272–278). It was based in particular on a subsequent decade of UNESCO programs we ran through the UNESCO Office, Jakarta: experience is reported in UNESCO Annual Reports of the Jakarta Office, 1995–2005. UNESCO, (2004 and 2005) I spoke about the global localism dynamic with NGO *Sacred Bridge*, in Jakarta in 2012 (Hill 2012).

attention to 'sustainability'. My usual first question of a new project was 'what will happen next?' once our intervention is completed.

We could then use the initial target community as a model to network and expand to other communities. As I noted earlier, I have called this approach to societal transformation, 'Global Localism'.

At heart was the idea that the people created the new meaning associated with their empowerment themselves—within their own local world. And then we use this base for more global expansion of the idea.

In Chap. 18 when developing the idea of 'community', I present a detailed case study to demonstrate how this approach works in practice. It is the story of 'greening' an urban village in Jakarta, Banjarsari. For now, I will focus primarily on the power and importance of 'listening'—noting however that, as with the case of Banjarsari, the idea of global localism provides the context for stimulating and managing *global* cooperation.

9 Action for Mutual Understanding and Sharing on a World Level

In general, we live out our daily lives in separate 'local worlds' where our own meanings and culture reside, but share beyond this only minimally in a global world across many other local cultures. Whilst we live this way, we are disempowered within a globalized world of external control.

But, we must remember how powerful the peoples' *own* cultural meanings are, even, as demonstrated in the case studies of Indonesia and Mongolia, able to persist underground for many years of repression from the State, but then regenerate when the totalitarian 'lid' to freedom of cultural expression is finally lifted.

Local culture is the power house for global change. We just have to grasp this power.

An action strategy follows—focusing change and empowerment at local levels, but then using this base to spread the strategy across others' 'local' worlds, which the people inhabit—right across the globe.

Building bridges across these worlds is fundamentally dependent on *sacred silence*, as demonstrated in the *West Papuan Hostage Negotiation Case*.

Banjarsari provides a model of empowering a community—*by listening to and supporting their local voice,* then spreading the idea across other communities.

Sacred Bridge's interventions with children in conflict or trauma situations extends the idea, in this case, starting at the boundaries that separate people from each other, or from themselves. Both approaches deserve support as core strategy.

At government level, *all* policy, whether it be economic, transport, immigration, defense or anything else, needs to include the *culture dimension.*

The alternative unintended consequence of an 'accidental culture' was shown in the *Case Study of the Kingdom of Tonga* which I presented earlier.

Equally, the unintended consequence of destruction of local traditional cultures and the security of their social meanings from culturally insensitive economic development was shown in the *Case Study of Bougainville.*

The people may be dragged into the modern world, but as weakened supplicants, not empowered participants. The power of their cultural strength has been undermined, not bridged.

Policy here is both *explicit* and *implicit.*

In the case of economic policy for example, impact on local culture and community empowerment is implied and needs to be taken into account in planning economic strategy.

In the case of social policy, local community engagement and understanding must be included quite explicitly. Policy needs to be based on 'listening' and community engagement that is genuinely open rather than directed to secure an outcome that government has already decided. Bring *sacred silence* into governance.

At heart of *all* policy and organizational action is this single cultural idea .... 'Sacred Silence', suspending the 'noise' and 'listening', then applying this core vision to *everything* from political and implementing CEO decisions to the role of the office cleaner.

This is not a fantasy, but a quite practical approach to organizational change. Focus on the meanings, the culture, and its transformation needs to be around a single clear vision. It will produce both empowerment of the participants, greater sharing of contribution to their joint enterprise, and as a consequence, even greater efficiency. This was basic to the approach I used when commissioned by the Director-General of UNESCO to 'reform and decentralize' the entire UN Agency globally back in the early 2000s (UNESCO 2000a, b, c; Hill 2001). At heart was addressing the problem of changing the organization 'culture' and 'listening'.

Finally, the 'noise' of daily life, of political, social or economic conflicts across *boundaries* we, the people, have inherited or constructed, must be addressed.

International protocols such as can be agreed within United Nations deliberations, can set reference standards and penalties. A framework of enforced expectations. These are important.

But, ultimately, change must focus down on education and in particular, creating opportunities to truly *share* and *cooperate* across boundaries that otherwise separate us.

Again, the *Sacred Bridge* model offers a great starting point, the power across boundaries of *linguistic silence.* Add to this learning from and maintaining *silence in consciousness in order to listen to the past,* and *sacred silence,* listening, truly *listening across social and cultural worlds.*

Basic to world peace is the idea of including these as fundamental objectives of education across our many worlds. This was the founding principle of UNESCO's Constitution forged by international agreement in 1945, "since wars begin in the minds of men *(sic),* it is in the minds of men that the defenses of peace must be constructed".

'Sacred Silence': the stillness of listening to humanity

References

ABC. (2001). *News*. U.N. confirms destruction of Afghan Buddhas, 12 March. http://abcnews.go.com/International/story?id=81406&page=1#.UA4FSrQe5TI.

Barash, D. (2001). *Peace and conflict* (p. 547). UK: Sage Publications.

Bartlett, D. L., & Steel, J. B. (2008). Monsanto's harvest of fear, *Vanity Fair,* May. http://www.vanityfair.com/politics/features/2008/05/monsanto200805.

Geertz, C. (1968). Ethos, world view and the analysis of sacred symbol. In A. Dantes (Ed.), *Every man his way* (p. 314). Englewood Cliffs, New Jersey: Prentice Hall.

Hill, S. (1988). *The Tragedy of Technology—Human Liberation vs. Domination in the Late 20th Century.* London; Winchester, MA: Pluto Press; Unwin Hyman (Hardback), December 1988 (Published simultaneously in Paperback through Pluto Australia).

Hill, S. (1995). The formation of identity as scientist. *Science Studies,* 8(1), 53–72; republished from original 1979 article by invitation and with review editorial by John Ziman.

Hill, S. (2000a). UNESCO decentralization reform, In *Presentation to the Regional Consultation of National Commissions,* European Group, Bled, Slovenia, 9 June.

Hill, S. (2000b). UNESCO decentralization reform, In *Presentation to the Regional Consultation of National Commissions,* Sub-Saharan African Group, Windhoek, Namibia, 29 June.

Hill, S. (2000c). UNESCO decentralization reform, In *Presentation to the Regional Consultation of National Commissions,* Asia-Pacific Group: Tashkent, Uzbekistan, 11 July.

Hill, S. (2001). Managing uncertainty—survival instructions for life in the field, In *Lead Presentation to the UNESCO Roundtable Seminar on Field Practice, 31st General Conference of UNESCO,* Paris, France, 27 October.

Hill, S. (2010). Ways of seeing—Science and technology within their cultural setting, invited chapter. In A. Jain (Ed.), *'Science and the Public', Section: 'Science in Society'* (pp. 252–280). New Delhi: Sage. Volume in Series: 'Civilization, Philosophy, Science and Culture', (Series Editor: Prof. P. Chatapadhyaya).

Hill, S. (2012). Harnessing the power of culture for sustainable development and community empowerment, Address to *Sacred Bridge,* Jakarta, 3 March (available from the author).

Hill, S. (2014). *Merdeka—freedom, jungle hostages and flying pigs.* Sydney: Perceptric Press, (available as an e-book on Amazon).

Hill, S. (2017). *Captives for freedom—Hostages, negotiations and the future of West Papua,* Port Moresby: University of Papua New Guinea Press, 2017.

Hill, S., Fensham, P., & Howden, I. (1974a). *The making of professional scientists.* Canberra: Australian Academy of Science, Monograph No. 7.

Hill, S., Fensham, P., & Howden, I. (1974b). *The future education of scientists.* Canberra: Australian Academy of Science, Monograph No. 8.

Hill, S., & Howden, I. B. (1974). Adult socialisation: A theory and its application to PhD training in science, Chapter 28, In D. Edgar (Ed.), *Sociology of education: Australian readings* Melbourne: Angus and Robertson.

Hill, S., & Turpin, Tim. (1994). Academic research cultures in collision. *Science as Culture,* 4(20), 327–362.

Hill, S., & Turpin, T. (1995). Cultures in collision: The emergence of a new localism in academic research, Chapter 7, In M. Strathern (Ed.), *The uses of knowledge: Global and local relations. The reshaping of anthropology,* Volume 1—Shifting Contexts, London: Routledge.

Kluckhorn, C. (1951). The concept of culture. In D. Lerner & H. D. Lasswell (Eds.), *The policy sciences.* Stanford, California: Stanford University Press.

Lévinas, E. (1969). *Totality and infinity—an essay on exteriority* (trans: Alphonso Lingis). Pittsburgh, Duquesne University Press, (original French edition, 1961).

Mills, C. W. (1959). *The sociological imagination.* London: Oxford University Press.

O'Brien, B. (2015). 'Vimalukakirti Sutra—the Dharma Door of Nonduality'. http://buddhism.about.com/od/mahayanasutras/a/The-Vimalakirti-Sutra.htm.

Schutz, A., & Luckman, T. (1974). *The structures of the lifeworld.* (trans: Richard M. Zaner and H. Tristram Engelhardt (Jr). London: Heineman.
Sen, A. (2006). *Identity and violence: The illusion of destiny issues of our time.* New York: W.W. Norton.
UNESCO. (1995). *Aung San Suu Kyi, quoted at the start of the education chapter in UNESCO's 1996–2001 medium-term strategy.* Paris: UNESCO.
UNESCO-SPEC. (1987). *Meeting Report of the UNESCO-SPEC High Level Regional Meeting on 'Policy and Management of Science and Technology for Development in the South Pacific Region',* Apia, Western Samoa, 16–19 March, Australian National Commission for UNESCO May, Appendix.
Wikipedia. (2015). Buddhas of Bamiyan. https://en.wikipedia.org/wiki/buddhas_of_bamiyan.

Chapter 18
'Community': Platform for Sustainable Change

Stephen Hill

1 From Roasted Barley to Instant Noodles: The Lesson of Ladakh

Ladakh, or "Little Tibet" is a remote region on the Tibetan plateau. Politically, a part of India, the culture of the Ladakhis is more that of Tibet. In the mid 1970s it was still a community of self-supporting farmers living in small, scattered settlements in a high desert. Little had changed for many generations.

Although natural resources were scarce, the people had developed a remarkably high standard of living. In traditional Ladakhi culture, basic needs such as food and clothing were provided from a variety of crops and the few animals needed for the community—without money. In an intricate and long-established web of human relationships, all labor was given free when it was needed as was food and clothing. Houses were built out of what was there, mud and stone. The Ladakhis worked at a relaxed pace, and only for four months of the year, allowing them time to create beautiful architecture, art and jewelry. The people had no need for money so had very little.

Film maker Helena Norberg-Hodge visited Ladakh in 1975. Whilst being shown the remote village of Hemis Shukpachan, she observed that all the houses were especially large and beautiful so asked her guide, Tsewang, where the poor people lived. He looked confused and then finally replied, "we don't have any poor people here" (Norberg-Hodge 1999).

Then the Indian Government decided to open up the region to development, to connect it into the Indian and global economy.

S. Hill (✉)
University of Wollongong, Wollongong, Australia
e-mail: sthill@uow.edu.au

© The Editor(s) 2018
S. Yamash'ta et al. (eds.), *The Kyoto Manifesto for Global Economics*,
Creative Economy, https://doi.org/10.1007/978-981-10-6478-4_18

The outside global world invaded, helped along the path by international development assistance agencies—all, with 'the best of interests', for the externally determined 'welfare' of the Ladakh people. The Ladakhis were not asked.

Just twenty years later things had changed dramatically.

Visions of global consumerism and value had taken over. Food was now imported from the Indian plains, while local farmers who had previously grown a variety of crops and kept a few animals for self-sufficiency were now encouraged to grow cash crops—and thus were dependent on huge transportation networks, oil prices and fluctuations in international finance. Building traditions gave way to "modern" methods and materials—concrete, steel and plastic unable to be produced locally, whilst traditional building materials were left untouched. Under command of the global economy now, the Ladakhis needed money. Previously virtually irrelevant, they now needed money to compete for the scarce imported staple food supplies and building materials. Tourists came—with, as far as the Ladakhis were concerned, vast wealth in money and clothes that reflected the new 'modern' culture they should aspire to. Clothes now needed to show, as in the globalized world, status and separation—and had to be purchased using money. And, because they noticed the wealth of tourists, for the first time, the people started to feel "poor".

Most importantly, local economies were crumbling as they were overwhelmed by the externally controlled economy of global corporations. Along with this, the people were losing the sense of security and identity that builds from deep long-standing connections to people, *local* community and place. A community-based sense of identity was being replaced by money-led symbols of individual worth. Women, previously strong and outgoing, were now becoming unsure and desperately concerned with their appearance and being 'modern'. The Ladakhis were starting to seriously question who they are as their life sped up, mobility increased, competition for scarce paying jobs increased, and political representation within the new centralized structures increasingly divided communities that previously worked together in tolerant cooperation without dispute. Ethnic and religious differences took on a political dimension causing bitter enmity unheard of before.

The Ladakh *community* is collapsing, replaced by competitive individual isolation and unhappiness. They used to live in a coherent cooperative society and were content. Now they live in a global economy, alienated from each other and the value of their local community.

All within twenty years.

As Helena Norberg-Hodge observed in the late 1990s, the people were so embarrassed to serve her as a valued guest with roasted barley ngamphe, local traditional food, that they had to find enough cash to purchase and serve instant noodles instead. They now must compete according to the globalized rules of being fashionable. Inequality and the consumer culture of the global economy now lives amongst the Ladakhis when it never did before (Norberg-Hodge 2009).

2 The Transformative Power of 'Community'

What we see in Ladakh is a prism through which the global development light of the world's last three centuries is intensely concentrated into one eighth of this time. The resulting spectrum is the same. Growth of our globalized and industrialized economy, and its penetration into the very crevices of life in the 21st Century, has not brought the shared welfare for all that many economists predicted, as I demonstrated in Chap. 2. Outside traditional communities such as the Ladakh, we have just had more time to progressively adjust.

2.1 Learning from Traditional Communities and the Past

Where does our *humanity* lie when we allow the consequence of massive inequity to destroy or marginalize fellows in our human society, to destroy their food rights in the interests of global capital, to tear apart their communities?

The answer is shown in a quite beautiful example of how wealth itself does not necessarily reflect the human heart and spirit of community.

> In June 2002, Masai tribespeople from a remote Kenyan village donated 14 cows to the United States when they heard of the 9/11 terrorist attacks on New York and Washington. Cattle are sacred for the Masai, valued above all possessions. Their gift was the highest expression of regard and sympathy. Dressed in red robes and jewelry, they handed over the cows to the Deputy Head of the US Embassy in Kenya, carrying banners that declared, "To the people of America, we give these cows to help you" (BBC 2002).
>
> The people have no running water, electricity or telephones. But their human compassion reached across the world to a people far more wealthy than themselves.
>
> The cattle, by the way, were sold in Kenya and the money transferred to assistance for victims of 9/11 in New York.

It is not just *level* of wealth. We can learn about caring, a sense of community... our *humanity*—even across global boundaries—from the very poor, from the values of traditional communities. What matters is *care*, a fundamental human condition of relationship and community.

As the Ladakh community collapsed, so too did mutual relationships of cooperation and care. But the Masai community, though very poor, were able to retain their cultural and community integrity, and reach across the world to offer care.

We have much to learn from even the most fragile of communities now confronting the firing line. But, globalization is directly associated with the *extinction* of traditional cultures and the shaping of their local 'place-centered' cultures into increasing globalized uniformity—as demonstrated in the opening Ladakh case.

These societies, with millennia of ability to survive, have critical *human* lessons to offer our modern world in facing our 21st Century future, as is demonstrated in the Masai example I spoke of above, and the case of West Papuan tribes people, of whom I spoke in Chap. 17 and depict in more detail in my own latest book, 'Merdeka'.

So, as we lose the 'wisdom of the ages' we also lose alternative human ways of doing things that could be very important in dealing with contemporary life and the imminent threats that hang over it.

As demonstrated in the presentation Mme Chau Sun Kérya made to our formative Kyoto 2 Symposium in 2015, the history and cultural legacy of Cambodia's Angkor also offers us important lessons about the physical, intellectual and spiritual inspiration to be drawn from understanding historic community (Kéreya 2015). Angkor was the largest urban complex in pre-industrial society, with one million inhabitants or 0.1% of the entire world population, a complex supportive irrigation system and a rich culture. It lasted six centuries into the European Middle Ages.

But their culture provides us lessons for our future *NOW*.

It is significant, as I observed in Chap. 17, that those who wish to assert their own unyielding ideology or fundamentalist religious doctrine in the present so often seek to destroy these historic legacies, reminders of an alternative past. The Taliban blew up the Bamayan Buddhas in Afghanistan, and Islamic State (ISIS) is now destroying historic monuments across Iraq (ABC 2001; Wikipedia 2014). ISIS regards pre-Islamic artefacts as relics from the 'period of ignorance', Jahiliyah: archaeology reveals spiritually significant objects of the past, attracting the possibility of idol worship which is strictly forbidden in Islam (Shubert 2015).

Extinction of the past is a formula for contemporary unquestioned repression. Loss of 'exotic' cultures and communities—both from the past and in the present, is potentially of equal concern for human futures as is the loss of endangered species of flora and fauna for our physical survival.

2.2 Tapping the Resource of Our Humanity

We are losing valuable knowledge about alternative ways as each one of these communities is absorbed into the consumer-focused society mandated by a globalizing economy.

More importantly, world society now confronts fundamental threats to our very survival, as demonstrated already with the takeover of all seed control by concentrated US based corporate interests—discussed in Chap. 2. The global economic paradigm is certainly not going to fix these problems for our *human* future, having created the problems in the first place. Indeed, as with collapsing societies or corporations from a sociological perspective, most are *frozen* into what worked to get them to their position of power in the first place, and they cannot adjust to a totally different paradigm whilst the world around them is undergoing a fundamental transition (Hill 1980, 2010).

We cannot continue to drift any longer in obeisance to the transnational corporation-driven global economy, but must take *command* over our future.

The *only* source of power to do this lies at the depths of what our humanity is, how it is most powerfully expressed in our shared community, and how we can tap this enormous resource.

But, industrialization and development of a global economy has captured us into a prison of our own making.

Our global economic system has been good over the last 250 years at tapping and embedding into 'systems', physical resources like steam, then oil, gas, energy, minerals, systems of production, transport and communication ... and supplicant human labor—starting with the late 18th century development of the factory system that made labor one hundred times more productive through specialization and a central power source for the machines. But meanwhile we became entangled in the 'system' (Hill 1988, pp 111–136). Even humanities' scientific creativity was captured in support of further economic progress or its military defense.

As a result, sustainability of our human 'community' has been lost in a globalized and ownership-concentration-based race for profit. In the 21st Century we must now pay serious attention to tapping the resource of our very basic humanity. If our humanity is to survive, it is our humanity that must call the shots—the basic message of this book.

As Thomas Piketty observes, "the market and private property should be the slave of democracy rather than the opposite" (Fries 2014; Piketty 2014).

Following Piketty's observation, we need to start examining a society's welfare from 'the other way around', i.e.: from the community and its people first rather than from the requirements of its wider global economic framework. But, beyond Piketty, there is much more to see, and to achieve, in terms of the quality of life and human empowerment than just democratic parity.

To paraphrase and extend Piketty, then, "capitalism and markets should be the slave of democracy *and the welfare of our shared human community,* rather than the opposite."

Amatai Etzioni fashioned an enlightened path in this direction as far back as the 1980s in exploring the role of values in economics. Etzioni pointed to the role of the 'social capsule' otherwise interpreted as the 'community', and 'moral choices' in economic decision (Etzioni 1988). The debate within economic and sociological theory has followed, in particular reflecting on 'action theory' (Etzioni 1996; Beckert 2008; Lehman 2008). There is further to go as we must move beyond theory to re-formed social action in the light of the immediate and present danger to humanity.

2.3 *The Need for Community as the Reference Point in Economic Action*

We need a new economics but with a different paradigm of values.

Its base has to be, as Piketty implies, Etzioni theorises, 'happiness research' promotes as alternative in measuring welfare (Tachibanaki and Yagi 2015), and Norberg-Hodge identifies at a local level, our *humanity,* human community and meaning within our communication, shared vision and interaction with each other.

Sense of community "is a feeling that members have of belonging and being important to each other, and a shared faith that members' needs will be met by their commitment to be together" (McMillan and Chavis 1986)—strengthened by ritual, myths and symbols (Shamai 1991). The *social capital* of the community—from which all can draw—embodies the specific processes among people and organizations, working collaboratively in an atmosphere of *trust*, that lead to accomplishing a goal of *mutual social benefit* (Kreuter et al. 1997).

What lies at the heart of the human drive to community is the need, as social animals, to *belong*, to have an anchor of meaning that allows people to act, to share, to feel appreciated or loved—certainly *included* ... to have a personal identity that others reinforce.

2.4 The Quality of Community

The quality of community is determined by factors that intrinsically cannot be easily quantified, such as meaning, sympathy, and in particular the significance of spirituality to full human sharing and achievement within community. The person within the community cannot find their own humanity without participating in the community's shared meanings. Religion and religious ritual such as is presented in the On Zen sacred music performances of Stomu Yamash'ta can reveal what is hidden—right back to the very source and origins of community and therefore our basic shared humanity. Our Kyoto initiative is therefore closely linked with both the performance and reflections on the meaning of On Zen.

If the community's inherited values are destroyed, the community and its people are at serious risk even of survival. This is not an imaginary proposition but quite real with the tragedy that happened in Cambodia in the not-too-distant past to the ancient capital of Angkor. By tracing the history and recent development of the Angkor World Heritage site in Cambodia in the first place and following the Aboriginal and Japanese cases as well, Kyoto Symposium 2 explored the implications of destruction and restoration of the sacred sites for the community's identity—history, tradition and culture—the fundamental constituents that enable the community and its people to exist with a true sense of 'belonging' and quality in human relationships. Reviving 'Angkor' is reviving human meaning otherwise lost.

Human community and culture is a continuously evolving tapestry, woven out of our interactions with each other. But, our interactions in the 21st Century are caught within a web of economics driven demands.

2.5 The Quality of Connectedness

Whilst the strength of human community lies in direct sharing, its breadth is far wider.

Whilst our personal identity and values are cast within the immediate subjective world to which birth introduces us, our 'humanity', that is connectedness with others, extends as far as our consciousness of others. Our humanity extends as far as the point where we draw boundaries around who is included and who is excluded from who *I* am.

In a pre-industrial European village, or tribal society where the limits of collective contact were probably around 150 people, these were the limits of understanding and inclusion of others.

But, as industrializing systems increasingly dominated over the last 240 years this world has expanded, and along with this, our reference points of our humanity (Hill 1988). In a 21st Century world joined by globalized communication, the limits now extend to *all* humanity.

We may well draw the shawl of exclusion around us to deny the humanity of others who are remote from our direct life world and seem 'different' or a threat. But any one of these 'excluded' could enter our personal subjective world, given global communication and travel, immigration and refugee arrival. And then, we have a choice—reject this person as part of *our* humanity, or include them.

Rejection denies our wider humanity and the connectedness of all. We may not like them or their particular expression of belief. But, that's not the point. They are still part of the shared humanity from which we draw our identity and nurture of *human* meaning.

Immediately, there is a lesson we must learn from remote indigenous societies. My own direct experience of remote tribal people includes the Highland tribal groups of West Papua, Indonesia. An outsider, including foreigners from a world of which the locals had no experience or understanding, would be included *if* they proved they could be trusted. A ceremonial meal in which all shared meant they would thereafter be friends for life, protected by the tribe, as family, against anyone from outside who may wish to hurt them (Hill 2017, p. 52).

2.6 Quality of Community: Its Essence in Meaning

The *quality* of community, and therefore its strength as a human force, is therefore fundamentally based on its strength of shared *meaning*—demonstrated most powerfully within the daily lives and culture of indigenous tribes such as those of West Papua.

Whether in traditional or modern society however, the basic message is the same. We learn, we create, we *live* this shared meaning in our *direct subjective experience*, not elsewhere.

Referring now to our present modern world in particular, where we live with change rather than millennia old traditions, it is here that people are empowered to act collectively as a force for change. It is here that the highest of our spiritual values, our vision of our ultimate humanity, come to rest. Not out there in an abstract globalized economic world (Hill 1988, pp 90–95, 1995).

Played out in practices, norms, values, taboos, rituals … language, 'the way we do things around here', this meaning is housed in and expressed through our *culture*. Played out as a 'grammar' for the language of daily life, we are rarely all that conscious that we are living within this 'meaning design'. I spoke of this in Chap. 17.

The main point I need to emphasize here however is that global economic practices, objects and consumerism symbols (e.g.: Coca Cola or Macdonalds) may penetrate this world of daily life, but they have no meaning unless absorbed and drawn into the person's subjective world and re-interpreted to fit—or the world of subjective meaning adjusted so that the external symbols *can* fit.

But it is by this very externality that these symbols of globalization have power … 'ideal types' that cannot be opened up. This is classically shown in the way traditional tribal societies seek to understand 'Western' products suddenly thrust upon them from outside their cultural world, for example in the 'cargo cult' of Papua New Guinea seeking to attract 'cargo', that is, American refrigerators, canned foods, coca cola, and so on, through constructing landing strips to attract 'cargo' in the same way they constructed a 'trap' for cassowaries in their normal jungle world (Hill 2017, pp 119–120; Lawrence 1964; Worsley 1968; Cochrane 1970; Steinbauer 1979).

Things are not all that different in our own modern world, just less noticeable against the background of continuous consumer-promotion noise. The consumer objects stand *inside* our world of meaning beaming out powerful *external* messages for normative behavior ("Buy me! Others will see you as a Great Man"). But they remain constituted from outside—from the global economy—not from inter subjective experience and meaning. The meanings from outside are backed by a continuous flow of advertised significance to the person-as-consumer. Globalism's vehicle for control … *inside* our own subjective domain.

Movements such as *'Local Futures'* led by Helena Norberg-Hodge, are seeking to escape this external global economic control over community, our inter-subjective world and local economies. For it not only the consumer 'objects' and 'symbols' that penetrate, it is the grammar that stands behind—in the global economy's *systems*. Based on her experience with the Ladakhis, Norberg-Hodge is working towards popularizing and implementing a focus on building and sustaining *local* economies against the destructive winds of globalization (Local Futures 2017).

2.7 Community and Place

At the core of the *Local Futures* vision of community is 'place'. Here, at local level, the richness of human sharing exists because it is housed in the *local* environment where people live, produce, interact, create, and share the meaning together of their collective world directly, subjectively and continuously.

Location of itself does not give a sense of place. Rather it is "a piece of the whole environment which has been claimed by feelings" (Gussour 1979). As demonstrated by the Ladakhis, their sense of place encompassed their whole lives. Their economy was drawn from it.

Equally, a local 'community' may not serve the needs of *all*, providing an empowering sense of belonging. Some may remain stigmatized or isolated within the wider whole.

'Community' needs to be seen as *an inter-subjective collective*. 'Place' provides a context for this inter-subjective collective to be expressed more fully and immediately.

2.8 Elective Community

However with the march of the global economy through the last two hundred and fifty years over every aspect of the world's production, consumption, and relationships, the depth of our relationship to *place* has been seriously eroded—as it was so suddenly for the Ladakh people.

In the 21st Century, the tendency of a global economy driven society is for people to live in cities or urban sprawls where they may not even know their neighbors. Work is elsewhere, possibly requiring hours of commuting every day. Social life is formed through *networks of common interest* that spread across potentially very wide territory. And lives are individuated and anonymized, our status within the society communicated to others by symbols—cars, clothes, size of house—that stand for who we are in a world largely made up of strangers. We live a 'systemized life' in a world organized by 'systems'—both technological and social—where control of these systems remains largely elsewhere (Hill 1988). As demonstrated earlier, the pace and structure of our lives is driven by a small number of transnational global corporations. Essential to the global economy is growth. The consequence is the drive for systematization to spread and penetrate more deeply into every aspect of life that can be turned into a consumption target.

Consequently, as 'place-based' communities erode, community is likely to be expressed as *'communities of interest'* spread as networks across the social and geographic landscape rather than centered in place.

These are 'elective communities' linked together by factors such as religious belief, occupation, ethnic origin, sexual orientation, or hobby-based groupings. A sense of selfhood and identity forge the conceptual space within which non-place forms of community can be understood (Hoggett 1997): "this is the group to which *I belong*". But communities of interest cannot provide the depth of coherent subjective reinforcement and strength of a place-based community. Instead they provide *a range of communities* to which we can identify, and identities from which our self, as the prism for these beams of light, constructs our own overall personal identity and knowledge about how to act in a globalization-dominated society. Depth of belonging is intrinsically fragmented.

2.9 Cyber Communities

A new development of the 21st Century is 'cyber-communities', linking of people through internet based networks such as Facebook, Linked-in, and Twitter, where others are known only via electronically mediated information they provide not by full inter-subjective communication and understanding. Hence, for example, a pedophile may well present himself as a teenage girl on internet to build trust and to groom the real teenage girl towards a physical meeting. Without personal contact, no one knows. Value is measured by how many 'friends' or followers one has—but most are anonymous, certainly not people you spend time with in a subjective context.

Electronically mediated communication cannot replace inter-subjective dialogue: it is good for providing information or orders, not good for genuine sharing or negotiation. In no way is electronically mediated communication a *replacement* for inter-subjective relationships. As example, business organization, Forbes, conducted a survey of senior executives on their reaction to video-conferencing and other virtual internet-mediated meetings versus face-to-face meetings. The results were clear.

> Business executives overwhelmingly agreed (eight out of ten) that face-to-face meetings were not just preferable but *necessary* for building deeper, more profitable bonds with clients and business partners and maintaining productive relationships with co-workers. Eighty five percent of those preferring face-to-face meetings then said they build stronger more meaningful relationships. Seventy-seven percent said the personal meeting gave them the ability to "read" another person, and seventy five percent reported that it provided greater social interaction (Forbes 2009).

Nevertheless, whilst recognizing this limitation, internet communication offers a force for change. I will come back to this in my later Chap. 21.

2.10 Space and Boundaries

Whether it be conceptual or physical space, communities have boundaries that distinguish who is included and who is not (Cohen 1982, 1985) Within this space, *identity* of the community has to be reinforced, revivified, ritually shared. Activities that bring the community together and reinforce its identity—such as festivals, celebrations, rituals, voluntary community group meetings—empower the community and its coherence from within. Without revivification—particularly in the shared 'rituals' of daily life and communication—the community strength of identity will steadily disappear along with the shared commonality that brought the community together or defined it in the first place. I spoke of the re-energizing of kinship networks across the whole of Timor Leste in Chap. 17 through the return of ritual. Our rebuilding the peoples' Sacred Houses, trashed under Indonesia's previous rule, brought people together from across the entire island. Carrying home food from the ritual feast to their own villages and families brought back their previous cultural network and connectedness.

Guarding the boundaries of community space then matters for community cohesion. Arguably, the most powerful dynamic in bringing a community together is a common external threat across these boundaries where all must work together internally to deal with it. This could be a threat, for example, of hostile legislation to the elective gay community, or a threat to a local neighborhood that turns a 'collective' of strangers who happen to live near each other into a *community* to fight this threat.

This was particularly the case with the violence evoked at the time of the fall of President Soeharto in Indonesia in May 1998.

> Orchestrated and violent mobs erupted through the city and the local communities drew their people together at the boundaries to protect themselves. The local people from my own UN staff would not stay in the office, or remain in a safe place, but instead went back to their community to build its protection together.

A similar dynamic developed in my own experience in the early 1970s when living in Glebe, an inner city suburb of Sydney. An urban environment largely of old terrace houses, it had a mixed inner city population—pensioners, students, motor bike gang members, tenants who had lived there for decades, a sprinkling of young middle class people like myself moving into renovate and live in old houses close to the central city.

> The NSW State Government had decided however that Sydney should be a city of commuters – living in the outer suburbs, with expressways radiating out from the Central Business District, the CBD, cutting deeply through the inner city suburbs – regarded as slums to be destroyed – and out to the suburbs. Already they had started to demolish houses in the path – using what we called the 'missing tooth' effect, pulling down adjoining terrace houses to those from which people did not wish to move, leaving unsupported precarious side walls that could well collapse into vacant blocks of rubbish and rats. Glebe was destined to be cut into three, separated by deep expressway culverts, destroying any street life and a burgeoning village atmosphere of small shops and cafés.

> As a young sociologist I could not help but try to do something about it. Particularly as it was designed to destroy my own community.

> Collectively, we developed a non-violent protest movement and fought the bulldozers and demolitions, creating as much public media impact as we could. Finally, we managed to get the leader of the NSW Labor Union Movement, Jack Mundie, to assist us. He declared what came to be known as a 'Green Ban' on the demolitions and expressway construction – preventing any unionized labor to be involved. The Government developers had nowhere to go.

> We won the battle and saved the suburb, and along with this, other inner city suburbs of Sydney also destined to be destroyed in the path of expressways or other forms of neighborhood-destructive development 'progress'.

But what was left behind in Glebe was more. For a genuine new *place*-based community had been forged in the process, where people across totally different age, class and interest groups started to interact, share and care for each other within the same physical neighborhood. We built a *community!*

In jest I talked in my subsequent sociology classes of the need to develop a 'portable sewerage smell machine'. That is, an 'external' problem that could be transported in and would get the locals together to confront it as a group, and thereby build a community. Then, the 'sewerage smell' machine would move on to help build other communities.

The lesson of 'forming community' around a common purpose and in particular, against external threat across the borders of this community, remains. This is based on our shared humanity. What matters is having and continuously reinforcing a strong *common* purpose.

However, globalization and its current economic base *assume out* the highest of humanity's aspirations and learning—our inherited and experienced deeper humanity and spirituality that should be our guide in forging common purpose. For these values are sacrificed on the altar of individualistic short-term economic self-interest and indicators of apparent welfare such as GDP and income that are but weak shadows of human welfare and empowerment.[1] Instead, global economics is, day by day, tearing this humanity apart whilst it is intrinsically unable to fix the mess it has put us in.

2.11 Dynamic of Change

My case study of Glebe may show a community in evolution in a modern urban setting. But this community was developing *within* globalization, not separate from it. Daily lives of all within the Glebe community of the time were deeply embedded in a globalized economic system. If this globalization force of separation and anonymization tips the balance, the salience of 'local' community is almost certain to erode.

Boundaries of 'community' today are highly permeable and therefore different from those of an isolated traditional society. We *cannot* return to the romanticized idea of living entirely within a *local* place-based economy and society for we are already deeply embedded in globalization. We can no longer hope to overwhelm the dynamic of the global economic by confronting it directly with what has to be a fantasy, a global return to local economies and societies alone. Instead we need to explore a dynamic that will work.

Our task is to deal with this dichotomy between community and global economics. But, instead of asserting one side of what is an oppositional dynamic—global versus local—we need to think in dialectic terms that reflect the historic and on-going *inter*-action between the two.

The 'thesis' of 'society' has forged its 'antithesis', global capitalism—'the globalized economy'—in the course of the last 250 years of globalized

---

[1]A delightful exception is the tiny Kingdom of Bhutan where an indicator of "Happiness" replaces the standard indicators of welfare measured by GDP. See also the emerging field of the "The Economics of Happiness" (Tachibanaki and Yagi 2015).

industrialization and consumerism. The antithesis is now the new thesis of the 21st Century and is forging its own 'antithesis', the need for a 'new community' or society … to recreate humanity lost.

The point of a dialectic dynamic is that the 'antithesis' is forged *out of the thesis*, not as a separate contradiction. Therefore, the 'project' is to identify the weaknesses within the 'thesis' and it own values, and use these as entry point for change … assertion of the new thesis.

The strength of a change program therefore lies in *asserting* our *humanity—human connectedness and care*—in every interaction, organization and vision—*within* the global economic system. The starting point is where our humanity is strongest—in regenerating the power and vision of inter-subjective community—in our "*Being Now*", a central philosophy of our Kyoto Symposium Series and the current book.

3 Grasping Our Future

3.1 The Wider Power of Community

The model that Helena Norberg-Hodge and others propose, that is, return to *place-based community* and local economy, is valuable (Trainer 2012). For it is here that strength of human meaning can be created comprehensively in direct inter-subjective relationships, and an alternate economic framework for a community-centered society can be anchored.

But from the start it is critical to not deal in stereotypes—local versus global, for the 'local' has permeable boundaries to the global, hence the dynamic of the dialectic relationship I suggested earlier.

The concept of 'Glocalism' appears attractive as it provides the bridge (Hong and Song 2010; Visser 2015).[2] However, the valence of 'Glocalism' is primarily determined *within* the global economic, that is, referring to the adjustment of products for local markets within an overall global productive enterprise. Our project is to establish an empowered human inter subjectivity and collective humanitarian vision at the core of *all* globalized economics … as with my earlier quote from Thomas Piketty, 'the other way around'. For this reason I prefer the expression I have used for 20 years now, "Global Localism"—focusing on the 'local' as the node for the inter-subjective collective, but then expanding this model and influence globally.[3]

---

[2]"Glocalism's" origins in the 1980s derive from the Japanese word 'dochakuka', which means "global localization", a marketing strategy originally referring to a way of sadapting farming techniques to local conditions: See Visser (2015).

[3]See Chap. 17, Footnote 11.

The 'local' is therefore at the center of strategy. *Meaning* is grounded in *inter-subjectivity*.

Expression of inter-subjectivity in *all* aspects of life and experience is most comprehensively available in an economically self-sufficient community such as Helena Norberg-Hedge champions. So, at the core of transformation there needs to be attention to retaining or building economic self-sufficiency at local community level.

> For example, in a *city* environment, Kyoto's urban emphasis on small individual trader enterprise is an instructive example.
>
> In urbanized communities that have lost or never developed a small-scale local 'village' design, it is valuable to promote small-scale and locally focused enterprise such as, for example, farmers markets, networked local shops, restaurants, and street markets, local industries and crafts (eg: ceramic kitchen ware, woodworking, herbal products, and so on).
>
> Even better, it is valuable to promote collective local enterprise and self-sufficiency, as through city-based 'community' farms and gardens, and enterprise workshops.

The local economy-based self-supporting community is the 'node' for transformation to which all other action needs to refer—where 'community' is at the center of 'economy' rather than the other way around.

3.2 Expanding Influence Beyond the Local Community—Towards "Global Localism"

Attention to local community empowerment is not enough. As I have already argued, local community boundaries are porous. Every one of these rural or urban communities is connected into the global economy and power structures in some way or another. They cannot be disconnected from the wider economic and administrative system without consequence.

> A somewhat quaint example of seeking to disconnect the 'local' but failing was an eccentric shop owner with a significant passing trade at the top of the escarpment south of Wollongong, Australia, close to where I live. His shop was adjacent to a highway out into the Southern Highlands of NSW. Around 10 years ago he got sick of continuous fights with bureaucrats over various licenses and conditions, and after months of plastering anti-government signs and placards over his shop windows, finally decided to secede from the Commonwealth of Australia, formally declaring his pie shop an independent Sovereign State.
>
> All the local authorities had to do was turn off the electricity and the new 'nation' fell to its knees.

Turning this same lesson the other way around, that is, towards the expansion of the power for change from source *at local community level*, we have to recognize that "the role that community-based organizations can play in economic revitalization will continue to be limited ... by economic actors, trends, and policies that are beyond the control of any one neighborhood" (Cordero-Guzman and Auspos 2006).

Consequently, whilst local communities can take action to build up their own local community strength and economy—centered around 'place', we cannot stop there. We have to build the connections back into the global economy, but on the communities' terms ... not the other way around. This is the essence of the idea of 'global localism.'

I have many case studies I could refer to from experience. But there is space for only one, the "greening" of the polluted urban village of Banjarsari in South Jakarta, Indonesia. I mentioned it in passing in my previous Chap. 17.

The program grew out of several years of scientific research the UNESCO Jakarta Office had been doing on the urban pollution of *Pulau Seribu*, Jakarta Bay's 'Thousand Islands'. My marine science staff had been monitoring pollution levels for 10 years before I arrived, and year-by-year the pollution was demonstrably getting worse. So far, UNESCO was only monitoring and reporting the problem.

So, we had a look at what was happening and how we might change things.

> Apart from uncontrolled industrial pollution, we realized that much of the destruction of the Bay was a result of very careless environmental practices of the people who lived in the city. They used their waterways basically as convenient vehicles for disposal of their rubbish – 1400 cubic meters of garbage thrown into the city's 13 river systems then flowed into Jakarta Bay each day, enough to cover a football stadium field up to several meters.
>
> *Every day!* Plastic bags and drink bottles could be found tens of kilometers out into the islands. Travelling out to the more remote islands by boat you could see a clear line of scum and rubbish perhaps 30 kilometers from shore.
>
> Potentially recyclable organic waste was dropped into the convenient river, now closer to serving as a sewer than a source of water, to be carried away. As it decomposed in the Bay, this organic waste threatened to suffocate corals and other marine organisms along with the fish life that depended on them.
>
> We confronted little interest from the city planners. Serious environmental concern was not yet on the agenda of the Indonesian Government whilst still under the control of Soeharto's New Order Government, the priority of which was maintaining dictatorial control over the will and empowerment of the people in the interest of the elite.
>
> So, instead of continuing to measure the problem we decided to do something about it – but at the level of local communities, source of much of the problem. Seventy percent of the waste that flowed into Jakarta Bay was organic. It came from the communities. They could use it and even make money out of it.

I can only give a brief sketch of what we did and the results now without losing the flow of the book as a whole.

> We started *in* Jakarta Bay with island communities. They were destroying their own environment quite directly by careless waste management practices as well as unsustainable harvesting of fish resources through bombing the reefs and cyanide fishing, poisoning the water to stun the fish.
>
> In our initial strategy we brought together local fishermen with scientists, teachers, journalists, NGOs, fishing officers and resort owners to launch our 'Save Pulau Seribu' Initiative. This was in 1996. Our focus was on education – showing the fishermen simple techniques for monitoring the health of their own reefs, and how they could make income out of recycling waste – including through worm farming, and then selling compost.

A key feature for our subsequent work after getting the local island communities involved was to bring in school children from all over Jakarta to see, to educate them about the islands, the sensitivity of the island ecologies to Jakarta pollution, and practical things the children could do themselves, eg: recycling paper and worm farming.

Our next phase was to work with local markets in the city. In a demonstration project in Bintaro Traditional Market with local sellers, buyers and managers, we showed they could not only save 30 percent of their waste but also make money out of it. As we expanded the program to other markets, we were able to show that up to 40 percent of waste could be saved ... and used for profit.

The school children who had been out to the islands now became our 'ambassadors' to go to the markets to explain recycling to the stall holders and distribute pamphlets. One school, Pondok Labu High School, undertook to rid the school of paper waste, and started making money for the school through selling recycled paper. This school then challenged all other schools in Jakarta to do the same thing in a contest. The message started to spread.

Then we moved into three demonstration communities. Banjarsari was the key focus, a relatively poor urban village, shadowed by expressways, pollution, and the noise of city life on the south side of Jakarta. We established a community waste recycling center and went from there. We were blessed with two champions, one inside my Office, Senior Program Assistant Ibu Nuning Wirjoatmodojo, and Ibu Bambang Wahono from the village, the 70 year old daughter of Dutch-era farmers, who as matriarch of Banjarsari's environmental development, became our main trainer.

We went well beyond running training courses, and built community commitment through a three-pronged strategy: establishment of a community-based environmental management committee to take decisions and lead the village initiative; provision of technical inputs to improve the collection of waste; and most important of all, development of income-generating activities out of the waste recycling process.

Initially we targeted income generation through selling compost, primarily to middle-class urban dwellers with gardens. But then with the 1997 collapse of the Indonesian economy, this market dried up.

In cooperation with the village leaders we changed the strategy to *using* the compost to grow plants for sale – in particular pot plants to be hired out to office blocks and malls, and herbal products.

We focused young people on paper recycling. But, we went a step further and brought in a consultant from Japan to show them origami that would be popular in Tokyo. Now, Banjarsari kids were selling their recycled paper directly to the Department Stores of Tokyo. And the teenagers took on their own initiative to recycle kerosene cans as office garbage bins, painted brightly with cartoons with an ecological message. The first day the young people took them out onto the main street into the city adjacent to the village, Jalan Fatmawati, a French tourist stopped and put in an order for several hundred to take back and sell in Europe At a cost of around Rp10,000 ($US1.50 at the time) the teenagers were selling them at Rp75,000 each, a tidy profit.

Meanwhile, we started to use the village as a demonstration site for training more widely. By 2001, five years after we started, the village was conducting 21 external training programs a year.

I set up a partnership with the Boy Scouts Movement of Indonesia (with several million members). The movement sent scouts to Banjarsari for training and then to become trainers across the country. And we convinced the Navy to establish 'Green Kampongs' in the villages that were adjacent to their Naval Bases across Indonesia's many islands.

Meanwhile Banjarsari village became one of the main demonstration sites we developed for community leaders and students. Banjarsari was receiving 210 official visitors per year by 2005, not just from us, but as a result of wider knowledge that had been broadcast more generally, primarily through person-to-person contact. They were receiving so many visitors that intending visitors had to register on a waiting list.

The Governor of Jakarta then declared Banjarsari as an official ecotourism site of the city. External recognition reinforced the community's pride in their collective enterprise. And, they were earning income!

The village is now 'green', quite literally a garden paradise in what was a low income polluted urban village. The most visible sign of transformation is its foliage. Located almost underneath but adjacent to a toll road as well as one of the main routes to the city from the south, the hot, polluted, jostling, crowded thoroughfare of Jalan Fatmawati, one has only to walk 100 meters down the side road of Jalan Banjarsari. You enter a new world of green leafy streets, color coded bins for recycling, every house fronted by potted plants even springing from reused tins or bottles – thriving on a mix of salvaged topsoil and locally made compost. Many of the plants are labeled with their name plus traditional medical uses.

As journalist Djuna Ivereigh reported in Jakarta's magazine, *Island Life* in 2003,

Where space is tight, racks are stacked up for 'verticulture',

recalling a verdant Hanging Gardens of Babylon.

One extraordinary house is quite literally a four story tropical jungle, twice winning Jakarta's Award for Best Garden House. The owner told me it takes 2 h a day to water her house.

The ambience of the village now includes roadside restaurants, tiny convenience stores, travelling musicians, and pushcart VCD sellers. The streets are made of paving stone rather than asphalt or cement—adding a park-like atmosphere as well as serving the practical purpose of allowing rainwater to penetrate through the cracks thus reducing the risk of flooding during the torrential rain season.

The village houses a central paper recycling facility primarily where youth are engaged, a village medicinal garden *Tanaman Obat Keluarga* on what was previously a vacant lot, and a community hall. These serve as concentration points for village activity. Several small businesses have been established marketing traditional medicinal and herbal products. The older women of the village have established a traditional medicine based practice providing free medical treatment to local scavengers and the very poor who are associated with their community. Now, as from 2004, local medical support is complemented by an aliphatic doctor offering mainstream treatment as well.

The power to change came from the local community. The project took off when the people saw they could produce something useful together, *listened to their community,* and remembered the traditions of their parents and grandparents, i.e.: *listened to the past.* Banjarsari now is having an influence across many other communities. The commitment of children and youth have been important in spreading the message.

Kampung Banjarsari demonstrates the power of global localism and 'listening'.

4 Conclusion: The Social Paradigm: "Global Localism"

As I presented in Chap. 17, my position here is based on the power of individual action, and the power of inter-subjective *community*. For *meaning* is constructed within our 'world within reach', in subjective relations to others, in socially producing together, in direct sharing ... in our *local world. Our culture is not produced elsewhere!*[4]

Wider social empowerment starts in the same place, within our local world. For it is here that *humanity*'s strength resides.

"Our quest is then to build 'global localism', capturing the power of the local where meaning is constituted, our immediate and subjective relationships and culture, and exploding our connectedness at this human level across the global human world."

Concentrated attention on helping the local community to transform itself can then be turned into wider application through using this community as base for networking, training, mentoring and inspiring others.

The *human* focus is at local level. Its application is *global*—hence, global localism. It is the power of community that is then determining economic benefit.

References

ABC. (2001). U.N. confirms destruction of Afghan buddhas. *News*. March 12. http://abcnews.go.com/International/story?id=81406.
BBC. (2002). Kenyan Masai donate cows to US. *News*. World Edition, June 3. http://news.bbc.com.uk/2/hi/Africa/2022942.stm.
Beckert, J. (2008). The road not taken: 'The moral dimension' and the new economic sociology. In discussion forum. Twenty years of the moral dimension. Towards a new economics. *Socio-Economic Review, 6*(1), 135–173. https://doi.org/10.1093/ser/mwm021.
Cochrane, G. (1970). *Big men and cargo cults*. Oxford: Clarendon Press.
Cohen, A. P. (1982). *Belonging: identity and social organisation in British rural cultures*. Manchester: Manchester University Press.
Cohen, A. P. (1985). *The symbolic construction of community*. London: Tavistock.
Cordero-Guzman, H. & Auspos, P. (2006). Community economic development and community change. In K. Fulbright-Anderson & P. Auspos (Eds), *Community change: Theories, practice and evidence*. The Aspen Institute: Roundtable on Community Change. Washington D.C.: The Aspen Institute (Chapter 4, p. 249).
Etzioni, A. (1988). *The moral dimension: Towards a new economics*. New York, NY: Free Press.
Etzioni, A. (1996). *The new golden rule: Community and morality in a democratic society*. New York, NY: Basic Books.
Forbes Insights. (2009). *Business meetings—The case for face-to-face*. http://images.forbes.com/forbesinsights/StudyPDFs/Business_Meetings_FaceToFace.pdf.
Fries, L. (2014). Thomas Piketty: The market and private property should be the slaves of democracy, interview with Thomas Piketty, May 30. *The Real News Network*. www.truth-out.org.news/item24041-thomas-Pikketty-the-market-and-private-property.
Gussour, A. (1979). (artist). quoted in P. Lewis, *Defining sense of place* (p. 40). In P. Prenshaw & J. O. McKee (Eds.), Mississippi: University Press of Mississippi.

---

[4]See Chap. 17, Section 7.

Hill, S. (1980). Economic and industrial transformation: The waves of social consequence from technological change. In G. Dow & P. Boreham (Eds.), *Work and inequality* (Vol. 1). Melbourne: Macmillan.

Hill, S. (1988). *The tragedy of technology—Human liberation versus domination in the late twentieth century*. London: Pluto Press.

Hill, S. (1995). *The formation of identity as scientist*. 8(1), 53–72—republished from original 1979 article by invitation and with review editorial by John Ziman.

Hill, S. (2010). Ways of seeing—science and technology within their cultural setting, invited chapter in Ashok Jain (Ed.), Science and the public. Section: Science in society, Sage, New Delhi, 2010: Volume in Series: *Civilization, philosophy, science and culture* (pp. 252–280) (Series Editor: Prof. P. Chatapadhyaya).

Hill, S. (2017). *Captives for Freedom: Hostages, negotiations and the future of west papua*. Port Moresby: University of Papua New Guinea Press.

Hoggett, P. (1997). Contested communities. Section 1 in P. Hoggett (Ed.), *Contested communities. Experiences, struggles, policies*. Bristol: University of Bristol. Policy Press. http://press.uchicago.edu/ucp/books/book/distributed/C/bo13443099.html.

Hong, P., & Song, I. H. (2010). Glocalization of social work practice: Global and local responses to globalisation. In I.H. Song (ed). *International Social Work, 53*(5), 656–670.

Kéreya, C. S. (2015). Being now—community, humanity and the sacred: Angkor. Presentation to the Kyoto 2 symposium, *Being Now—Community, Humanity and the Sacred: Platform for a New Economics*, Doshisha University, Kyoto, June 7.

Kreuter, M., Lezin, N., & Koplan, A. (1997). National level assessment of community health promotion using indicators of social capital. *WHO/EURO working group on evaluating health promotion approaches*, 21 January, p. 2: quoted in A. A. Anderson & S. Milligan. Social capital and community building. In K. Fulbright-Anderson & P. Auspos (2006) (Eds.), *Community change: Theories, practice and evidence*, The Aspen Institute: Roundtable on Community Change, WHSH. Washington D.C.: The Aspen Institute (Chapter 1, p. 22).

Lawrence, P. (1964). *Road belong cargo: A study of the cargo movement in the Southern Madang District, New Guinea*. Melbourne: Melbourne University Press.

Lehman, E. W. (2008). The Moral Dimension and the Action Frame of Reference lessons for sociologists, *Socio-Economic Review, 6*(1), 131–173. https://doi.org/10.1093/ser/mwm021

Local Futures. (2017). *Economics of happiness*. International Society for Ecology and Culture. http://www.localfutures.org/.

McMillan, D. W., & Chavis, D. M. (1986). Sense of community: A definition and theory. *Journal of Community Psychology, 14*, 6–23.

Norberg-Hodge, H. (1999). Consumer monoculture: The destruction of tradition. *Global Dialogue, 1*(1), 70–77 (Summer).

Norberg-Hodge, H. (2009). *Ancient futures: Learning from Ladakh for a globalizing world*. San Francisco: Sierra Club Books. converted into a film sequel, Local Futures.

Piketty, T. (2014). *Capitalism in the twenty-first century* (A. Goldhammer, Trans.). Cambridge MA & London: Belknap Press of Harvard University Press.

Shamai, S. (1991). Sense of place: An empirical measurement. *Geoforum, 22*(3), 348.

Shubert, A. (2015). CNN. *How ISIS controls life from birth to foosball*. April 21, 2015. http://edition.cnn.com/2015/04/21/middleeast/isis-documents/index-html.

Steinbauer, F. (1979). *Melanesian cargo cults: New salvation movements in the south pacific* (M. Wohlwill, Trans.). St. Lucia, Queensland: University of Queensland Press.

Tachibanaki, T. & Yagi, T. (2015). (Eds). *Advances in happiness research: A comparative perspective. Creative economy series*. Tokyo: Springer Publishing.

Trainer, T. (2012). De-growth: Do you realize what it means? *Futures, 44*, 590–599.

Visser, W. (2015). *Glocality: Thinking global and acting local in CSR*. http://www.waynevisser.com/blog/glocality.

Wikipedia. (2014). *Buddhas of bamiyan*. https://en.wikipedia.org/wiki/Buddhas_of_Bamiyan.

Worsley, P. (1968). *The trumpet shall sound: A study of cargo cults in Melanesia* (2nd ed.). New York: Schocken Books.

Chapter 19
Evolution of Community and Humanity from Primatological Viewpoints

Juichi Yamagiwa

1 Phylogenetic Model of Primate Sociality

Until recently, most social scientists regarded "society" as a human-specific feature based on culture and language. Although some cultural anthropologists incorporated evolutionary theory (Darwin 1871) into the historical view of human societies (Morgan 1877), this work led to discrimination between primitive and advanced societies and was criticized as promoting colonialism and racism (Boas 1911). Consequently, evolutionary theory has primarily been applied to non-human animals. Natural scientists in the first half of 20th century avoided the treatment of animal consciousness and society as being similar to those of humans.

In the late 1940s, just after the Second World War, Kinji Imanishi, a Japanese ecologist, and his students at Kyoto University started field work to study animal sociology in Japanese deer, horses, and captive rabbits. They enjoyed reading Ernest Thompson Seton and called themselves Setonians. Unlike most Western zoologists who strictly avoided anthropomorphism, they identified and named each individual observed, as did Seton in his books. Imanishi thought this method was essential for illustrating social interactions among individual animals (Imanishi 1957). After investigations of several mammalian species in the wild, he and his students chose Japanese macaques as subjects for a study on animal society. They tried to habituate macaques by feeding them sweet potatoes, wheat, and soy beans, and were eventually successful at several sites, such as Koshima and Takasakiyama. They focused their field studies on the social structure and cultural behavior of Japanese macaques.

The first monograph on Japanese macaques was published in 1954 in a book titled *The Monkeys of Takasakiyama* (Itani 1954). Junichiro Itani described their

---

J. Yamagiwa (✉)
Kyoto University, Yoshida Honmachi, Sakyo, Kyoto 606-8501, Japan
e-mail: yamagiwa.juichi.4m@kyoto-u.jp

social structure, including a linear dominance ranking, leadership system, and kin relationships. Initially, habituation and the naming of individual macaques for identification were criticized as improper anthropomorphism by Western zoologists. They asserted that assigning macaque behaviors to individual names promotes misleading comparisons between animal and human behavior. After 60 years, however, many Western zoologists now use this method to conduct field work on non-human animals and to analyze social interactions.

The first generation of Japanese primatologists thought that social structure was not a mere reflection of individual survival or reproductive strategies, but reflected a norm of species-specific sociality. Reconsidering the sociality and cultural behavior of non-human primates may lead to an understanding of the evolutionary pathway leading to the formation of families and the unique sociality of humans. Imanishi (1961) defined the human family as having four unique characteristics: incest taboo, exogamy, community, and division of labor between the sexes. He considered that primitive forms of incest taboo, exogamy, and division of labor were already established in non-human primates. Only community, in which two or more different social units support each other via frequent interactions, was a potential novel characteristic of human societies. As suggested by Levi-Strauss (1949, 1956), a human family may not arise spontaneously but emerges from marriage and always interact with other neighboring families.

Itani (1977) postulated a phylogenetic model of primate social evolution. Based on fossil evidence, the first primate species appeared 65 million years ago and was a small nocturnal and arboreal mammal, similar to most prosimians. He regarded the original form of primate society as an elemental (solitary) society, which he called 'equipotent' (Fig. 1). The first stable social units attained by primates were monogamous, and these units were observed in both nocturnal and diurnal species. Elemental and monogamous species are characterized by a lack of sexual dimorphism[1] in body mass. Higher primate social structures diverged from the monogamous type in various directions by differentiation in the modes of inter-individual tolerance, which converged on two extremes, namely, female-bonded and female-dispersal. The female-bonded society is typically observed in *Cercopithecus* monkeys, including Japanese macaques, in which females remain in their natal groups for their whole life and associate with female kin. The female-dispersal society is typically observed in Hominidae, including all great apes, in which females disperse from their natal groups before maturity. Itani challenged Jean-Jacque Rousseau's *Discourse on the Origins and Foundations of Inequality among Men* (Rousseau 1754) with this primate model. Rousseau planned to consider human society through an examination of its original state in the 18th century, at which point the sociality of non-human primates had never been considered. Itani tried to reconsider Rousseau's insights in the light of scientific knowledge on

---

[1] The condition where the two sexes of the same species exhibit different characteristics beyond the differences in their sexual organs.

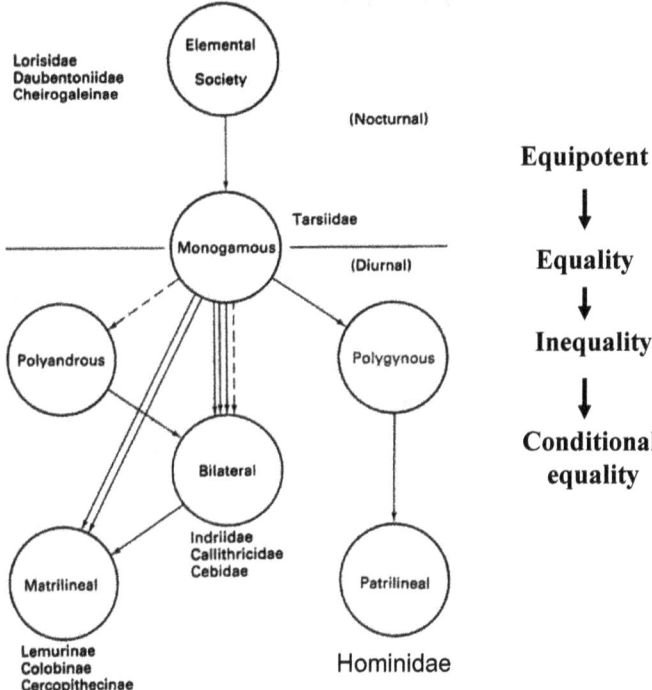

Fig. 1 Basic social units and the possible directions of their evolutionary trends. Modified from Itani (1977, 1988). Solid lines indicate high probability, while broken lines uncertain (Itani 1984)

non-human primates in the 1980s. Itani divided the principles of non-human primate sociality into equality and inequality (Itani 1988). In contrast with Rousseau, who expected that human inequality in the civilized state was derived from equality in the natural state, Itani proposed that societies of non-human primates developed from the original state of equality to fundamental inequality and subsequently to conditional equality. The inequality principles, based on the recognition of strong-weak or superior-inferior, developed with increasing group size from a monogamous society. They function to avoid conflicts between competitive individuals by forming stable dominant/subordinate relationships in group-living primates. The equality principle was founded on the negation of the inequality principle. Itani used the term "conditional equality," which involves an implicit agreement for achieving peaceful co-existence within groups. Itani considered food sharing and prolonged play in great apes as good examples of conditional equality, and predicted that this behavior emerged in the linage of great apes and expanded into human society.

2 Socio-ecological Model of Primate Sociality

Western primatologists defined social relationships as observable social interactions among group members (Hinde 1976) and as investments benefiting the individuals involved with high predictability (Kummer 1978). Prolonged social relationships require information on past interactions with partners (Aureli and Schaffner 2002), and emotional states are important for the integration of these interactions (Cords 1997; Aureli and Whiten 2003). Their perspectives were based on socio-biological predictions that natural and sexual selection lead to behavioral innovations to increase individual reproductive success. In primates, offspring production is more costly to females, owing to their roles in pregnancy, delivery, and caretaking until maturation, than to males (Trivers 1972). Female reproductive success depends heavily on environmental conditions (e.g., nutrition and security), while male reproductive success depends on their accessibility to fertile females. Based on arguments on factors influencing group formation in non-human primates and examinations of several models using field data, Sterck et al. (1997) proposed the socio-ecological model of primate groups (Fig. 2). It predicts that food distribution and predation pressure constitute major factors shaping female gregariousness, which attracts males to join groups. Social factors, such as infanticide or sexual coercion by males, function to increase male reproductive success and promote female associations with males for protection. Habitat saturation may lead to competitive regimes, resulting in various social relationships within and between groups. Both ecological and social factors explain phylogenetic inertia and environmental conditions shaping social structures and features of primate species.

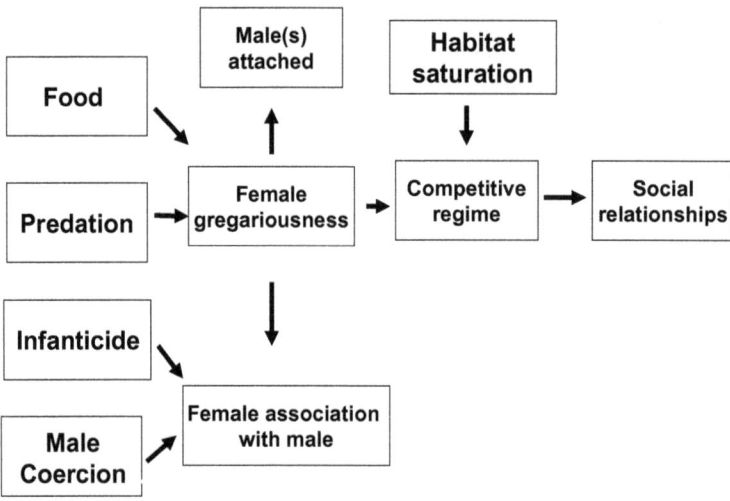

Fig. 2 Socio-ecological model of nonhuman primates. Modified from Sterck et al. (1997)

The best example of the role of ecological factors in this model is the social structure of baboons (Barton et al. 1996). Anubis baboons inhabit woodlands in East Africa, where fruit is available and large carnivores roam. Intense competition over food promotes alliances among females, and high predation pressure leads to the association of females with males for protection. These conditions promote a multi-male and multi-female social structure. Hamadryas baboons inhabit grasslands with lions. A low level of feeding competition over vegetative foods leads to a reduction in female gregariousness and the enclosure of females by males, but strong predation pressure leads to alliances among males. These conditions promote a multi-level society with a one-male and multi-female troop structure. Chacma baboons inhabit mountainous grasslands. These areas lack predators; accordingly, alliances among males are not necessary and the baboons form small groups consisting of one male and multiple females. Field studies on primates in various habitats mostly support this model.

Although phylogenetic and socioecological models do not completely explain variation in non-human primates (Janson 2000), we can find common social features in great apes that are expected to be linked to those of human ancestors (Yamagiwa and Basabose 2014). Adding to these models, primatologists have identified various social features of great apes that reduce the perceived gap with humans, such as cultural behavior (Goodall 1986; McGrew 1992; Nishida 1987), self-medication (Huffman 1997), food sharing (McGrew 1975; Nishida et al. 1992), elaborate hunting (Boesch 1994; Stanford 1996; Uehara 1997), prudent alliances or intervention in agonistic interactions (Ihobe 1992; Kuroda 1980; Nishida 1983; Sicotte 1995; de Waal 1982; Watts 1995; Yamagiwa 1992), and extended sexual behavior in various social contexts (Furuichi 1987; Kano 1989; Nadler 1981). It will be useful to construct the ancestral state of the human family and community based on great ape social features.

3 Food Sharing as the First Driving Force for the Evolution of Human Sociality

Hunting has been regarded as the main driving force in human evolution (Bartholomew and Birdsell 1953; Cartmill 1993). However, in the 7 million year period since the human clade[2] diverged from the last common ancestor (LCA) with chimpanzees, meat consumption increased 2.5 million years ago and distinct hunting tools, such as spears, first appeared about 0.5 million years ago (Foley and Gamble 2009). Gathering and sharing plant foods may have constituted the major dietary behaviors in the early two-thirds of human evolutionary history.

---

[2]A monophyletic group of organisms that consists of a common ancestor and all its lineal descendants, and represents a single branch on a phylogenetic tree.

Unlike in humans, sharing foods is rarely observed in nonhuman primates because food resources are limited, increasing conflicts among conspecifics. For example, when a male Japanese macaque notices a dominant male approaching while feeding, he takes his hand off the food and exhibits a grimace. This facial expression looks like a human smile, but indicates fear and subordination. The dominant male stares at him with his tail up and usurps the food. This prevents agonistic interactions over food. Japanese macaques usually recognize their dominance ranks within troops and behave accordingly.

In great apes, however, dominant individuals do not always supplant food or feeding places from subordinates. Subordinate chimpanzees and bonobos occasionally approach the dominant possessors of food and overtake them. Meat and plants are frequently shared among community members, and food sharing involves trade for social commodities, such as grooming, coalition building, and sexual access (McGrew 1975; Nishida et al. 1992; Boesch and Boesch-Achermann 2000). Food sharing is observed in all African apes and is usually accompanied with diverse behaviors, such as begging, displacement of feeding spots, resistance of possessors, stealing, offering, and retrieving (Yamagiwa et al. 2015).

A phylogenetic analysis of food sharing found two distinct trends (Jaeggi and van Schaik 2011). First, food sharing among adults is only observed in species that exhibit food sharing with offspring. Second, food sharing among adults is observed in particular linages within a phylogenetic tree, such as great apes and small New World monkeys (Feistner and McGrew 1989; Price and Feistner 1993; Huck et al. 2004). Based on phylogenetic trends in food sharing, we can determine the unique history of primate evolution. Food sharing emerged in species due to the slow maturation of offspring e.g., in great apes, or high fecundity (twin or triplet births) with communal breeding, e.g., in small New World monkeys. Food sharing among adults developed in species that share foods with offspring, and these species acquired alternative benefits of social commodities. Finally, only one species (*Homo sapiens*) expanded food sharing to non-kin individuals and outside groups. Food scarcity and risky habitats may have promoted the expansion of our ancestors outside of tropical forests.

Food sharing in humans occurs in a wide variety of contexts. The behavior is expected when an individual collects more food than they require. Collected foods are usually brought to camp, shared, and eaten with colleagues. We use foods as a social tool and for communication. We decorate feeding places with tables, chairs, dishes, cups and bottles, table cloths, and other accessories unique to each culture. We use various costumes and table manners according to each tradition, but the basic style of food sharing is common across cultures.

When and how did basic patterns of food sharing unique to humans emerge and develop in human evolutionary history? Bipedalism, the first human-specific feature, appeared 7 million years ago in woodlands, and was gradually elaborated, with increasing function in transporting foods (Lovejoy 1981). Dispersed foods and high predation pressure in open land may have forced early hominids to select safe feeding places for immature individuals. Adult individuals changed association patterns with daily fission-fusion for gathering, transporting, and sharing foods with their offspring, and exchanged information in limited safe places, which led to information centers, central places for foraging, and home bases (Isaac 1978; Potts 1984; Marlowe 2006; Aureli et al. 2008). Frequent food sharing may have improved nutritional conditions and thereby increased fecundity, which in turn may have promoted cooperative breeding and food sharing. High-quality foods, such as nuts and underground tubers, were also exploited using tools for provisioning and sharing (Wrangham and Conklin-Brittain 2003; Wood and Strait 2004). Food transport and sharing mediated by bipedalism probably led to the first human foraging revolution, which enabled an increase in intellectual ability and improved their socio-ecological conditions in open land.

4 Foraging Revolution and Life History Strategy

Outside the tropical rain forest, human ancestors faced two major risks for survival, food scarcity and high predation pressures. The tropical rain forest provides great apes a variety of fruits and leaves throughout the year and high tree stands for the avoidance of large terrestrial predators. Bipedalism probably evolved as a solution to the former issue and human life history traits probably evolved in response to the latter risk.

Life history is expressed as a schedule of development and reproduction within a life cycle. Life history parameters, such as gestation length, prenatal and postnatal growth rate, weaning age, age to first reproduction, inter-birth interval, and life span, vary in an allometric fashion with body size (Read and Harvey 1989; Charnov 1991, 1993; Purvis and Harvey 1995). Ecological factors influence the life history traits of primates in various ways (Kappeler et al. 2003). High mortality rates are associated with a high growth rate in primates (Janson and van Schaik 1993). Primates living in more unpredictable habitats have higher birth rates and earlier ages at first reproduction (Ross 1998).

Social structure is also related to life history traits. Group-living primates are classified into female-bonded species and female-dispersal species (Wrangham 1980). Most nonhuman primates form a group in which females remain during their entire lives. They usually associate with female kin and form coalitions with these coalitions in agonistic contexts. Cooperation and support of female kin influence female reproductive success. On the other hand, female great apes usually leave their natal groups before maturity and spend their reproductive lives without related females. Social relations with males or unrelated females are important for their reproductive success. Female-dispersal species tend to have a higher age at first parturition and longer inter-birth interval than those of female-bonded species (Yamagiwa et al. 2014). Lactational amenorrhea prevents ovulation, and a delay in weaning increases the inter-birth interval (Taylor et al. 1999). Great apes have slower life history traits than those of female-bonded species because they receive little aid for infant care from kin and require longer times for caretaking. Life history traits of great apes are not related to body weight (Table 1). Gorillas are the

Table 1 Life history traits of great apes and modern humans

Species	Adult female body mass (kg)	Neonatal mass (kg)	Endocranial volume (cm^3)	Gestation length (Day)	Age at weaning (Year)	Age at menarche (Year)	Age at first molar emergence (Year)	Age at first reproduction (Year)	Inter-birth interval (Year)	Potential reproductive span (Year)	Maximum life span (Year)
Orangutan	37.8	2	346	260	7	12	3.5–4.6	15.6	8.5	43	58.7
Gorilla	95.2	2.1	433	255	4.1	9	3.2	10	4.4	42	54
Chimpanzee	35.4	1.8	356	225	4.5	12	3.1–4.1	13.3	5.5	28	53.4
Bonobo	33.4	1.4	326	240	4.5	8.5		14.2	4.8	26	50
Modern human	45.5	3.3	1212	270	2.8	16	4.7–7.1	19.5	3.7	26–32	85

Source Robson and Wood (2008), Humphrey (2010), Marlowe (2012), van Schaik and Isler (2012), Yamagiwa et al. (2014)

heaviest of the great apes, but start reproduction at the earliest age and have the shortest inter-birth interval. Orangutans show the slowest life history traits. All great apes show faster life history traits in captivity than in the wild (Yamagiwa et al. 2014). Nutritious foods and security may promote their rapid life history traits in captivity.

Human life history is characterized by a mixture of rapid and slow traits. The neonatal weight of human babies is largest among species in Hominidae (great apes and humans). Human babies wean earlier, but begin reproduction later than great apes. Humans also have the shortest inter-birth interval. Early weaning and the end of suckling enable mothers to resume ovulation, reducing the inter-birth interval. This increases fecundity, compensating for the increased mortality outside of tropical forests. In non-human primates, weaning tends to occur when infants reach about 33% of the adult body weight (Charnov and Berrigan 1993) or when the first molar erupts (Smith 1992). Under these assumptions, the weaning age would be 5–7 years, far older than the actual weaning age. Apparently, our ancestors transitioned to rapid population growth by early weaning, despite its high risks, such as infant mortality and morbidity from infectious and parasitic diseases that retard growth and development (Martines et al. 1994; Kennedy 2005). This feature probably evolved in open land areas with high predation pressure, as observed in non-human primates (Ross 1998; Janson and van Schaik 1993). Human babies wean early, but cannot consume hard foods using milk teeth; accordingly, the childhood period in which soft foods should be provided by elder individuals emerged in human evolutionary history.

Human babies have higher birth weights, but earlier weaning times than those of great apes. Heavy weights mean large body fat deposits that function as insurance for the developing brain (Cunnane and Crawford 2003). Just before birth, fat deposition on the human fetus accounts for 90% of its weight gain (Battaglia and Meschina 1973). Therefore, human brain evolution depended on an abundant, reliable, and nutritious food supply for a long period during pregnancy and after birth.

The second foraging revolution occurred during the period from 2.5 to 1.8 million years ago, with the first sign of an increase in hominid brain size following the emergence of stone tools and increased meat consumption (Foley and Gamble 2009; Prat et al. 2005). The dietary innovation of collecting high-quality foods, including meat, preceded encephalization[3] and promoted a division of labor between the sexes for foraging.

The third behavioral (foraging evolution) shift may have preceded the final increase in brain size to the level of modern humans. The increase in meat consumption and cooking using fire may have contributed to the supply of more energy to the brain by improving food quality and digestibility (Aiello and Wheeler 1995; Wrangham 2009). Evidence from fossils and their remains shows a gradual increase

---

[3]Defined as the brain mass relative to an animal's total body mass and used as an indicator of the level of intelligence.

in the use of tools and fire for processing animal tissues by *Homo erectus* (Shipman and Walker 1989; Goren-Inbur et al. 2004; Berna et al. 2012). Complex diets and social life increased following an increase in brain size (Jerison 1976; Clutton-Brock and Harvey 1980; Milton 1981; Dunbar 1996). These life history strategies unique to the *Homo* clade probably promoted the division of labor between the sexes and the formation of the family, the basic reproductive unit of humans (Wrangham 2009; Hrdy 2009).

Increased brain size led to the allocation of energy to rapid brain growth and a delay in somatic growth. Delayed maturation coinciding with the increase in brain size has been estimated from patterns of dental development (Smith 1994). Such changes in life history traits resulted in the emergence of childhood and adolescence, unique to humans. The long dependency period required cooperative breeding and pair bonding, while risky environments strengthened kin-based alliances among males. The completion of brain development permits energy expenditure to somatic growth, which occurs during the adolescent growth spurt at 12–16 years old (Leigh and Shea 1996; Leigh 2001; Gurven and Walker 2006). The adolescent growth spurt may cause many problems in human children. The problems that occur after early weaning and during the adolescent growth spurt required alloparental care and facilitated cooperation within and between groups, which probably led to a new organization of human society. Bipedal walking resulted in difficult delivery, and humans acquired menopause and extended life spans to assist in the reproduction of the young generation. These features of human ancestors led to the formation of families and communities for communal breeding and resulted in enhanced empathy and sympathy among adults.

Why did human brain size increase? Several hypotheses have been examined to explain this pattern. For example, frugivorous primates have greater memory requirements, including memories of the time and place of particular fruiting trees, than those of folivorous primates (Clutton-Brock and Harvey 1980), and primates feeding on embedded foods need more imaginative ability than that of primates feeding on visible foods (Gibson 1986). However, differences in these properties are not correlated with differences in brain size. Only the mean group size is positively correlated with the ratio of the neocortex size to other parts of the brain. This is called the "social brain hypothesis," which proposes that social complexity is the driving force for increases in brain size (Dunbar 1996). Extrapolating from correlation between brain size and group size for a range of species, the brain size of modern humans fits a group size of 150, consistent with the average band size of modern hunter-gatherers.

The last behavioral shift (foraging evolution) was the adoption of agriculture and the domestication of animals to produce nutritious and digestible foods; this occurred around the beginning of the Holocene. These remarkable innovations in human-specific foods promoted settlement and the formation of communities, which led to systematic activities to improve life history strategies in *Homo sapiens*. However, life history traits unique to humans, such as early weaning, late eruption of molar teeth, delayed somatic development, short inter-birth interval, and long post-reproductive period, were already present before the emergence of agriculture.

5 Communal Care and the Emergence of Human Families

The large brain of modern humans (three times larger than that of gorillas) requires a basal metabolic rate of more than 20%, compared to 13%, on average, for non-human primates, but there is no evidence for an increase in basal metabolism due to an enlarged brain. Aiello and Wheeler (1995) compared organ mass and the shape of the rib cage among humans, non-human primates, and *Australopithecus afarensis* and hypothesized that this dilemma can be explained by energy compensation via a reduction in gut size. Since gut size is associated with diet and the digestibility of food (Milton 1986; Martin 1990), the increase in meat consumption and cooking with fire may have contributed to an increased supply of energy to the brain by improving food quality and digestibility (Aiello and Wheeler 1995; Wrangham 2006, 2009).

Bipedalism, the first known human-specific characteristic, functioned in the efficient collection of disperse foods and promoted food carrying and sharing. High predation pressure in grasslands increased the mortality of immature individuals and required an increase in group size and fecundity in early hominids. Such changes in life history traits may have promoted early weaning to shorten the inter-birth interval. Provisioning and increased animal foods in the diet preceded encephalization, which was associated with a delay in somatic growth. Early weaning and delayed maturation required cooperative breeding and a multi-level social structure based on monogamous families and strong alliances among families. Cooking and the control of fire strengthened pair bonding and promoted the division of labor between the sexes. The provisioning of weaned infants and immature individuals during a long dependency period resulted in strong empathy, sympathy, and prosociality by cooperative breeding.

The great apes show compassion and empathy for injured or distressed individuals (Boesch 1992; O'Connell 1995; Flack and de Waal 2000). However, most cooperative activities in non-human primates are limited to kin or individuals within the same group, and the other-regarding behavior of chimpanzees is mostly based on maximizing individual fitness (Jansen et al. 2006; Vonk et al. 2008; Yamamoto and Tanaka 2010; Silk and House 2011). By contrast, humans participate in a wide range of activities that benefit others, including non-kin individuals, and they show regard for the welfare of those who are poor, sick, or elderly. The emergence of these prosocial behaviors occurred after the divergence of chimpanzees and humans, and possibly after a distinct increase in brain size.

Female dispersal from natal groups is shared among great apes, but social organization exhibits a distinct difference among species with respect to male dispersal (orangutans and gorillas) or philopatry[4] (chimpanzees and bonobos). Male orangutans tend to disperse over a wider range compared to the dispersal range of female orangutans (Singleton and van Schaik 2002; Knott et al. 2008;

---

[4]The tendency of an organism to stay in or habitually return to a particular area, most commonly its birthplace, to breed.

Morrogh-Bernard et al. 2011), while male gorillas tend to remain near the range of their natal groups or to breed in their natal groups (Robbins et al. 2004; Bradley et al. 2004; Stoinski et al. 2009; but see Inoue et al. 2013). Recent isotopic and genetic analyses of fossil hominids predict trends toward female dispersal and male philopatry (Copeland et al. 2011; Lalueza-Fox et al. 2011; Vigilant and Langergraber 2011). Based on these comparisons, the LCA may have lived in a medium-sized group with a one- or multi-male and multi-female social structure characterized by a strong tendency for female transfer between groups and a weak tendency for male philopatry. They also exhibited a minor sexual dimorphism in body mass, with females showing no overt signs of estrus. Large climatic changes in the late Miocene forced the LCA to expand from tropical forests to open lands, including fragmented forests, woodlands, and savannas (Reed 1997; Elton 2008). The dispersed food resources and high predation pressure in the new environments constituted the driving force for provisioning and early weaning. Increased brain size led to the allocation of energy to rapid brain growth and caused a delay in somatic growth. Such changes in life history traits resulted in the emergence of childhood and adolescence, unique to humans. Adolescence includes the long period (10–18 years for girls and 12–21 years for boys) of postpubertal growth in modern humans, and teenage girls and boys remain immature in terms of socio-cultural knowledge and experience (Schlegel and Barry 1991; Kaplan et al. 2000; Bogin 2009). The adolescent growth spurt may cause many problems for human children, who start to have various social interactions outside their families in complex societies. The long dependency inherent to these periods required cooperative breeding and pair bonding, while risky environments strengthened kin-based alliances among males. Cooking and the control of fire increased the digestive ability and expanded the dietary range of hominids (Aiello and Wheeler 1995; Wrangham 2009). Reductions in the time and energy spent on food processing and consumption allowed them to expand their social interactions. The prevalence of provisioning and food sharing in adulthood enabled the development of reciprocity and prosociality, possibly leading to the creation of a multi-level community structure consisting of families, as observed in modern foragers' societies (Chapais 2011; Foley and Gamble 2009). This social structure might have increased the resilience of the *Homo* clade to severe conditions in the new environments and led to their first steps out of Africa.

Modern humans live in communities consisting of several families. Human sociality, supporting this multi-level structure, is characterized by reciprocity, prosociality, and prolonged identity to a community (Yamagiwa 2015) (Fig. 3). Until recent civilization and urbanization, frequent food sharing and communal breeding contributed to the maintenance of community structure. A long childhood enabled hominids to extend apprenticeships to learn complex social interactions, and the recent emergence of speech and language may have enabled hominids to extend their post-reproductive period. Menopause and the extension of the post-reproductive period may have emerged recently, contributing to the increased survival of immature individuals and overall population growth (Gaspari and Lee 2006; Bogin 2009). The development of speech and language and other cultural

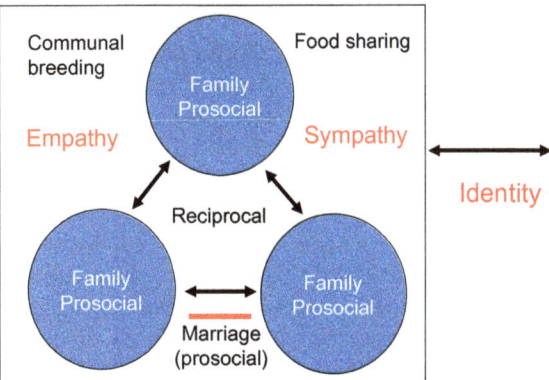

Fig. 3 A community structure of humans

innovations played important roles in shaping this remarkable life history trait unique to modern humans.

6 Sexual Features and Family Formation

Sexuality varies among primate species. Human sexuality is not the standard of non-human primates and is derived from a special feature that is strongly connected with human sociality. A typical example of a trait related to primate sexuality is the swelling of sexual skins. In some primate species, estrous in females is associated with the swelling of the sexual skin on the buttock region and a color change to pink or red. This conspicuous sign attracts males and invites copulation. However, the swelling of sexual skin is not a universal feature of primates. Phylogenetic trends in this feature suggest that it emerged at least five times independently during evolution (Dixon 1983). In the clade of Hominidae, only chimpanzees and bonobos show this feature, and humans lack sexual skin.

Like humans, female primates generally show a menstrual cycle. In the middle of the cycle, ovulation occurs. Drastic changes in two hormone types cause ovulation. In rhesus macaques, estrogen increases to reach peak levels and decrease rapidly when ovulation occurs (Gordon 1981). In turn, progesterone gradually increases. Estrogen may increase sexual attractiveness and copulation, both of which are decreased by progesterone. However, copulation occurs after a decrease in estrogen; accordingly, hormones are not the only factor influencing the occurrence of copulation in primates (Enomoto 1978).

Swelling of the sexual skin is a good signal of female estrus, but it does not indicate the precise time of ovulation. In pig-tail macaques, swelling grows as estrogen increases and reaches a maximum when ovulation occurs, but it does not shrink with an abrupt decrease in estrogen (Eaton and Resko 1974). Therefore, males copulate with and inseminate females after ovulation, although these copulations do not lead to fertilization.

A good example of this mismatch is Japanese macaques (Enomoto 1978; Takahata 1980). Copulation increases with increasing estrogen and occurs most frequently on the day of ovulation. However, this increase is caused by female invitations. Invitations by males occur far before and after ovulation. Therefore, estrous signs in females, including swelling of sexual skins, may not be a reliable sign of ovulation, but may attract many males by their prolonged duration.

Squirrel monkeys do not show distinct estrus signs (Wilson 1977). Females usually refuse invitations by males for copulation, except on the day of ovulation, when both females and males positively invite each other. For primate species without distinct estrus signs, invitations by females are an important trigger for the occurrence of copulation. Otherwise, males do not recognize female estrus or try to mount females. Additionally, females refuse mounting by males, leading to frequent unsuccessful mating.

The presence or absence of estrus signs in females is strongly linked with the social structure of non-human primates (Kappeler and van Schaik 2004). Monogamous pairs rarely show swelling of sexual skins. Species that exhibit swelling always form multi-male groups. Male copulatory ability is also related to social structure. Males of species that form multi-male groups have a larger testis weight relative to body weight than that of species with monogamous or single-male groups (Harcourt et al. 1981). Sperm competition in species with multi-male groups probably led to higher sperm production (larger testis size) than that of monogamous or single-male species. The ratio of testis weight to body weight in human males (0.06%) is intermediate between those of chimpanzees (0.28%) with promiscuous mating and gorillas (0.01%) with single-male mating. This has implications for whether human ancestors had a promiscuous mating system with increased monogamous features without signs of estrous or a single-male mating system with increased promiscuity.

Reproductive and social features of modern humans are a mosaic of features shared with great ape species (Table 2). Sexual dimorphism in body mass and strong alliances among males are shared with chimpanzees, the lack of external signs of estrus is observed in orangutans and gorillas, a prolonged consortship and intensive paternal care are observed in gorillas. How did this combination of features evolve in humans?

In great apes, swelling of the sexual skin is strongly linked with a promiscuous mating system. Orangutans and gorillas with no or faint swelling have short and long consort periods in mating, respectively (Galdikas 1981; Fossey 1982). Sillen-Tullberg and Moller (1993) performed a phylogenetic analysis of the relationship between monogamous mating systems and visual signs of ovulation in non-human primates and concluded that a lack of ovulatory signs is more likely to promote monogamy than vice versa. These findings suggest that the overt swelling of sexual skins observed in chimpanzees is a derived feature that evolved after the divergence of the human clade. The LCA may have had a society with a monogamous or polygynous social structure in which sexual dimorphism was low and females did not show visual signs of ovulation.

Table 2 Social features and mating strategies of great apes and modern humans

Species	Social structure	Dispersal/philopatry	Sexual dimorphism in body mass	Mating system	Sign of estrus	Paternal care	Infanticide
Orangutan	Solitary	♂♀ dispersal	2.2	Temporal consort	None	None	None
Gorilla	Unimale or multi-male polygyny	♀ dispersal, ♂ dispersal/philopatry	1.6	Prolonged consort	Faint swelling (only immature)	Frequent	Occasional
Modern human	Multi-leveled with families	♂♀ dispersal/philopatry	1.2	Prolonged consort	None	Frequent	Occasional
Chimpanzee	Multi-male and multi-female	♀ dispersal, ♂ philopatry	1.2	Promiscuous	Exaggerated swelling	Rare	Occasional
Bonobo	Multi-male and multi-female	♀ dispersal, ♂ philopatry	1.3	Promiscuous	Exaggerated swelling	Rare	None

Source Mitani et al. (1996), Furuichi and Hashimoto (2002), Lindenfors (2002), Harcourt and Stewart (2007), Utami et al. (2009), Marlowe (2012)

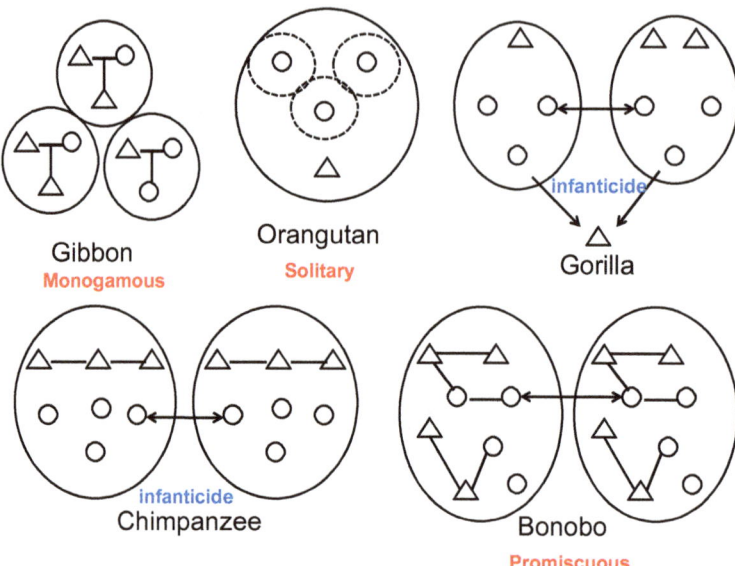

Fig. 4 Social structure of apes

Social structures of apes are highly diverse (Fig. 4). Gibbons form a monogamous social structure and are characterized by minor sexual dimorphism in body mass and territoriality. Orangutans are solitary with large sexual dimorphism. Gorillas form cohesive and polygynous troops with large sexual dimorphism and no territoriality. Chimpanzees and bonobos form multi-male and multi-female troops with moderate sexual dimorphism. Sexual dimorphism of modern humans is similar to that of chimpanzees, but human social structure is based on monogamy. However, the human social structure is not similar to the monogamy observed in gibbons or multi-male and multi-female structure of chimpanzees. Instead, humans exhibit a multi-level structure according to family and community (Chapais 2011).

Modern humans universally form families as the basic social component and several families form a community. Individuals frequently move among families and communities, but they usually maintain relations with the family or group from which they emigrate. The formation of a new family involves the combination of two families through marriage (Levi-Strauss 1949; Murdock 1949). The multi-level community is not found in ape societies. Why and how did human ancestors develop such a complex society?

Early hominids may have developed this kind of social system in which more than two social units are associated with each other. The marked ecological differences corresponding to cold and dry weather forced early hominids to advance into open lands, and food carrying and sharing combined with bipedalism probably increased the advantage of associations among social units, rather than dispersal (Fig. 5). The main features of human sexual behavior developed under these

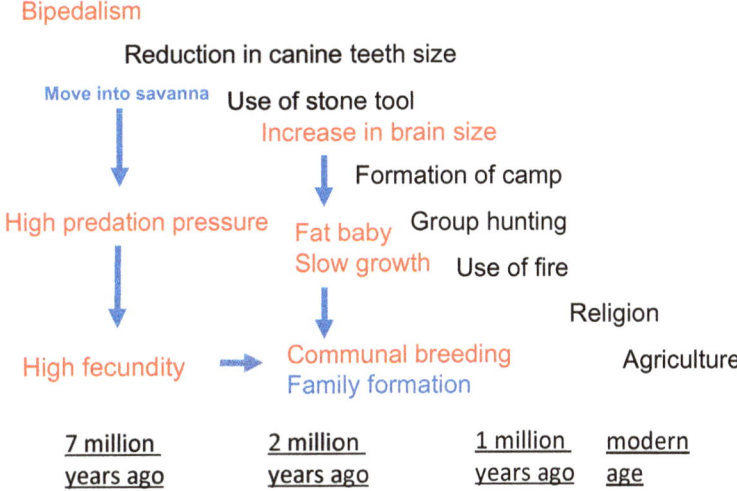

Fig. 5 Emergence of human-specific features

ecological and social conditions. Human sexual interactions tend to be hidden from the public and invitations for copulation are usually made in private. Unlike bonobos (Kuroda 1980; Kano 1992), humans do not frequently use sexual behavior in other social contexts, such as greeting or appeasement. The expansion of a male's sexual interest and increased female receptivity may produce greater flexibility and variety in sexual interactions, which may contribute to the establishment of individual mating patterns. These characteristics of human sexual behavior enabled early hominids to maintain prolonged consorts of a particular pair in the multi-male and multi-female social system.

Incest taboo is also a universal feature of human sexual activity characterizing the human social system. It is based on incest avoidance, which is observed extensively in non-human primates and even in other mammals (Itani 1977; Pusey and Packer 1987; Wilson 1975). Two behavioral tendencies contribute to incest avoidance in non-human primates. One is the difference in dispersal from the natal group between the sexes. Since only males tend to leave their natal groups before maturity and stay for a short period in a group in matrilineal societies, inbreeding rarely occurs in mother-son, sibling, and father-daughter dyads (Sugiyama 1976; Kuester et al. 1994). Frequent female transfer also results in a low rate of inbreeding in patrilineal societies (Furuichi et al. 1998; Nishida et al. 2003; Harcourt and Stewart 2007). In some species, aggression by conspecifics forces individuals to emigrate, while in others, sexual attraction among extragroup members accelerates the rate of transfer (Butynski 1982; Dunbar 1984; Henzi and Lucas 1980; Sugiyama 1976). However, the proximate cause of dispersal is difficult to determine because age, time, and the process of dispersal vary within species (Pusey and Packer 1987).

Another behavioral tendency is rather psychological or related to social memories. Even when sons remain in their natal groups after maturity in matrilineal societies, copulation between males and their mothers is rare. Based on a detailed study of mating partnerships in Japanese macaques, Takahata (1982) reported that copulation in mother-son, sibling, uncle-niece, and aunt-nephew pairs was avoided. Mating avoidance with conspecific kin has been observed in other primate species (e.g., red colobus: Starin 2001; baboons: Alberts and Altmann 1995; langurs: Sterck et al. 2005).

Copulation in mother-son pairs is also rare in the great apes (Pusey 1980; Harcourt and Stewart 2007; Kano 1992). In gorillas, copulation tends to be avoided in father-daughter pairs (Stewart and Harcourt 1987). It is not necessary for these males to be biologically related to daughters; an affinitive relationship between a male and young female may be sufficient for the avoidance of copulation. Alexander (1970) reported that copulation was avoided in a male-female pair in which the male took care of the female during her childhood. Kuester et al. (1994) monitored pairs of Barbary macaques and found that mating avoidance may occur when more than 3% of daytime is allocated to intimate caretaking lasting 6 months, irrespective of biological paternity. This implies that incest avoidance is fostered by intimate social relationships at immaturity, even in nonhuman primates. Human families are not totally based on biological kin relations, but are constructed based on cognitive relationships through caretaking after birth.

The incest taboo in human societies was potentially created and elaborated for multiple functions derived from incest avoidance in non-human primates. Like gorillas, early hominids may have used psychological incest avoidance to regulate individual dispersal from natal groups. As suggested by Levi-Strauss (1949), a male could offer his female kin to another male outside his family, simply because he is inhibited from forming a sexual relationship with her. The early hominids may have connected incest avoidance with outbreeding and invented the incest taboo and exogamy as a custom or an institution.

The multi-level social system including several families expanded group flexibility and reinforced alliances among families. Among nonhuman primates, *Hamadryas* baboons living in grasslands form a unique multi-level society in which small polygynous groups aggregate to form a large band or troop and females transfer among groups within bands. The lack of competitive food resources in grasslands may prevent females from forming kin-based coalitions, and the high predation pressure may lead to frequent associations and alliance formation among males of different polygynous groups (Barton et al. 1996). Adding to these ecological factors, sexual coercion, including infanticide, may have promoted cooperation among kin-related leader males of different groups and facilitated a modular society (Grueter et al. 2012). When early hominids extended their range into open land, they may have faced the same problems as those of *Hamadryas* baboons, promoting a multi-level social system (Fig. 6). However, unlike early *Hamadryas* baboons, early hominids had many infants owing to their high fecundity and large brains. The increasing need for communal care with increasing brain size and slow somatic growth resulted in larger communities supported by higher cognitive abilities with empathy and other regarding behavior. No overt sign of estrus and

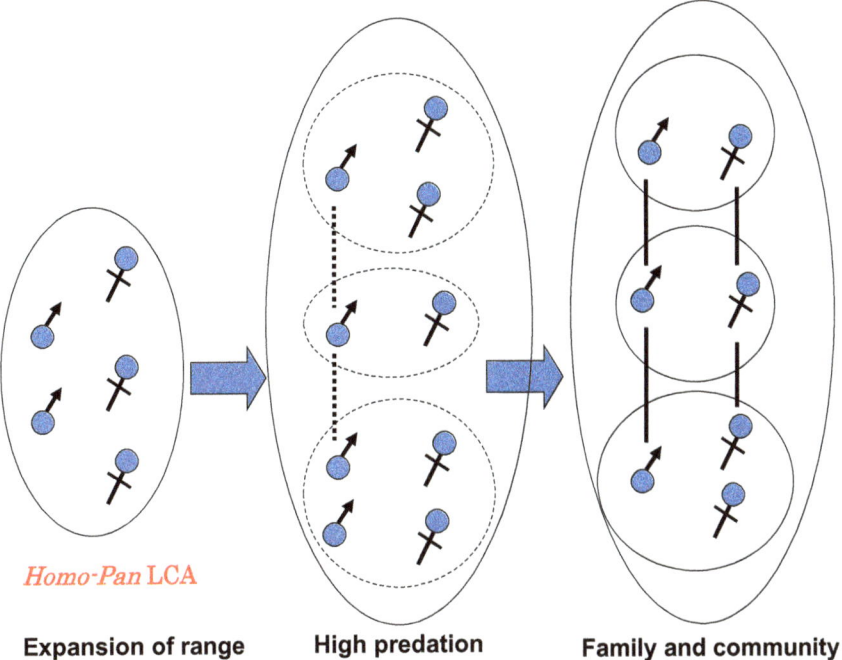

Fig. 6 Human ancestral society

incest taboo enabled males and females to coexist in large groups with continuous family formation.

7 Modern Problems Derived from Evolutionary Trends in Human Sociality

Primatology predicts that human sociality is deeply rooted in the common social features of great apes. However, our ancestors developed new social features outside the tropical rain forest, after their divergence from the LCA. A risky niche fostered prosocial and reciprocal behaviors through provisioning, food sharing, and cooperative breeding, resulting in a human community constituting several families. The human community has also been maintained by enhanced empathy and sympathy among group members, producing a strong identity with a community.

The resilience of human sociality enabled our ancestors to expand their range to include all habitats on the planet. Modern humans (*Homo sapiens*), born in Africa 200,000 years ago, appeared in the Middle East 100,000 years ago, and then advanced to Asia, Australia, Europe, and recently to the American continent. The human population gradually increased with the expansion of habitats, but its density remained constant as long as hunting and gathering dominated. At the dawn of agriculture 12,000 years ago, the estimated human population was only 6–8 million.

However, the production and stock of foods accelerated human population growth. Since the Industrial Revolution and the Information Revolution, the human population has now reached 7 billion. The social system and features inherited from our ancestors hardly fit our modern society and large population. The recent development of new communication systems, such as the internet and smartphones, and the increased mobility of humans and materials have rapidly changed the social structure and relationships among humans. People who live in big cities do not rely on family and community, but spend most of their time seeking individual benefits. Policies with economic priority expand differences in social status and quality of life. Globalism accelerates the movement of goods and people across borders, and civil wars produce huge numbers of refugees seeking safe places. To stop these trends, we should construct a new community with social priority, individual human security, diversity, freedom, and equality. Moreover, we should reconsider our evolutionary history and the path toward human sociality to determine the direction of our future society.

A good example for reconsideration with respect to our social features is violence, which is a major problem in today's world. However, there are many misunderstandings about violence. In order to understand the nature of violence, we have to examine its evolutionary origin, from the viewpoint of primatology and anthropology.

Gorillas were, until recently, regarded as the most violent animals since their discovery by Western explorers in the middle of the 19th century. This perception was mostly shaped by the chest-beating behavior displayed by mature males, which was regarded as a prelude to explosive attacks, when gorillas encountered the explorers. *King Kong*, the classic movie made in 1933, used gorillas as a model and projected the general image of gorillas at that time. In the latter half of the 20th century, pioneering field work on mountain gorillas indicated that chest-beating has multiple meanings, including play invitation, courtship, excitement, and curiosity (Schaller 1963; Fossey 1983). It took 100 years for people to understand the peaceful nature of gorillas.

We can find a similar case with respect to human violence. Most people still imagine that our ancestors survived owing to the violent behaviors of excellent hunters and fighters in our evolutionary history. In the 1950s, just after the Second World War, the hunting hypothesis was proposed by cultural and physical anthropologists (Bartholomew and Birdsell 1953; Dart 1953). *Australopithecus africanus*, which lived approximately 2.3 million years ago, started to use tools made from animal bones for hunting and even for fighting among groups (Dart 1953, 1955). The famous movie *2001: A Space Odyssey*, directed by Stanley Kubrick, clearly reflects this hypothesis. At the beginning of the movie, when ape-men (probably *Australopithecus*) lived in the savanna, a rectangular monolith from space landed, providing inspiration for the ape-men. One of them picked up a large bone from a giraffe and started to use it for hunting. He succeeded and became the leader of his group. He later found another way to use this tool. When his group encountered another group of ape-men at a watering hole, he attacked them with this tool, killing one and successfully chasing the others away from the watering hole. This event was regarded as the origin of sin, leading to the birth of wars in the movie. The majority of people around the world still believe this sort of story, in which hunting inevitably led to the development of weapons to enforce order in our competitive world.

However, this scenario is incorrect, and fossil evidence and socio-ecological theory on primate social evolution do not support the "hunting hypothesis" (Brain 1981). In 7 million years of human evolutionary history, distinct hunting tools, such as spears, first appeared 0.4–0.5 million years ago (Thieme 1997; Foley and Gamble 2009), while evidence for violence with weapons among humans appeared very recently, around the emergence of agriculture (Hart and Sussman 2005). War, even hunting, is not human nature. For most of human evolutionary history, being hunted as a prey, rather than hunting, appears to constitute a major factor influencing human sociality, as observed in non-human primates (Sterck et al. 1997).

These misunderstandings were caused by confusing aggression between species with aggression within species. Predation and hunting are based on interspecific aggression, and their purpose is to efficiently prey on animals for eating. Aggression within a species is derived from competition over food, resting places, or mates. When competitors exhibit moderate or reduced competition, the need for fighting is reduced and the aggression occasionally results in stronger bonds for coexistence via reconciliation and consolation (de Waal 2006).

Why and how did violence emerge and increase during the evolution of humans? We can now consider about the evolutionary pathway leading to violence, which was not accompanied by hunting or weapons until recently (Fig. 7). Strong empathy and identity with the community enabled human ancestors to expand their habitats to include risky environments. However, the emergence of language and food production (agriculture and animal domestication) led to the development of such emotional traits for the protection of communities and land tenure. Investment and the stock of production yields promoted strong coalitions among people within a community and increased hostility between communities, eventually resulting in violent interactions.

These assumptions lead us to conclude that violence is not human nature, but an artificial product resulting from strong empathy and community identity for surviving in risky habitats being combined with new communicative and productive abilities. A phylogenetic analysis of the incidence of lethal violence suggested that human violence is deeply rooted in the great ape lineage (Gomez et al. 2016). The incidence of lethal violence in humans is 6 times higher than the average in mammals (0.3% of deaths attributable to violence from a member of the same species among all deaths) at the origin of our species (2%), but the rate is already high (2.3%) in the common ancestor of primates and tree shrews. The higher rate of violence compared with other mammals can be attributed to the increases in group living and territoriality (Gomez et al. 2016). Violence gradually increased in primates from those that are solitary to those exhibiting group life, with increasing

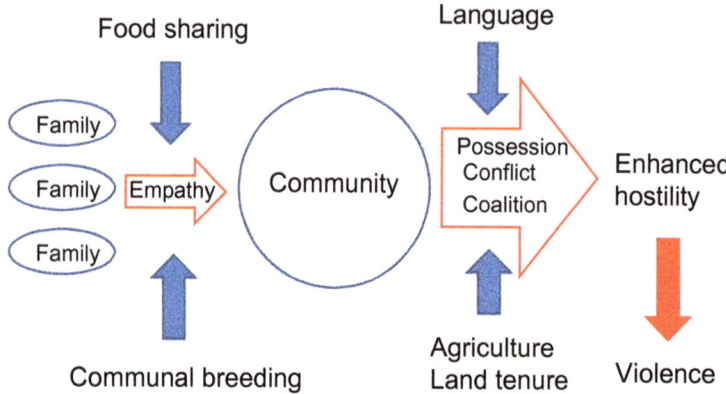

Fig. 7 Evolutionary pathway to increased violence in human society

aggressive interactions between groups to compete for resources. The rate in paleolithic people was steady, but it increased by about 8–15 times 3000 and 500 years ago before declining in contemporary populations (from 100 years ago). A comparison between chimpanzees and modern hunter-gatherers also indicates a similar level of intergroup aggression (Wranghm and Glowacki 2012). These statistical analyses suggest that cultures exhibiting food production and technology may constitute the main cause of enhanced violence among humans.

A distinct decline in violence in recent years implies that the modern legal system and technology prevent the occurrence of violence. However, empathy and sympathy, which we have developed in our evolutionary history, have not yet been applied across cultural or religious borders. Violence still has strong negative effects on human relationships at various levels of human societies. To reduce violent interactions and to recover peaceful relationships, we should reconsider the origin of violence and the appropriate use of our social features that developed during our long evolutionary history.

Acknowledgements This paper was prepared for the "Kyoto Manifesto" organized by Prof. Tadashi Yagi, Prof. Stephen Hill, and Mr. Stomu Yamashita. I would express my sincere thanks to the organizers for taking on the challenge of addressing worldwide problems related to community, humanity, and spirit. I also thank all of the trackers and villagers in and around Kahuzi-Biega National Park (Democratic Republic of Congo) and Moukalaba-Doudou National Park (Republic of Gabon) for their kind assistance and hospitality during my field work on gorillas.

References

Aiello, L. C., & Wheeler, P. (1995). The extensive-tissue hypothesis: the brain and the digestive system in human and primate evolution. *Current Anthropology, 36,* 199–221.

Alberts, S., & Altmann, J. (1995). Balancing costs and opportunities: Dispersal in male baboons. *American Naturalist, 145,* 279–306.
Alexander, B. K. (1970). Paternal behavior of adult male Japanese monkeys. *Behaviour, 36,* 270–285.
Aureli, F., & Schaffner, C. M. (2002). Relationship assessment through emotional mediation. *Behaviour, 139,* 393–420.
Aureli, F., Schaffner, C. M., Boesch, C., Bearder, S. K., Call, J., Chapman, C. A., et al. (2008). Fission-fusion dynamics: New research frameworks. *Current Anthropology, 49,* 627–654.
Aureli, F., & Whiten, A. (2003). Emotions and behavioral flexibility. In D. Maestripieri (Ed.), *Primate psychology: The mind and behavior of human and nonhuman primates* (pp. 289–323). Cambridge: Harvard University Press.
Bartholomew, G. A., & Birdsell, J. B. (1953). Ecology and the proto-hominids. *American Anthropologists, 55,* 481–498.
Barton, R. A., Byrne, R. W., & Whiten, A. (1996). Ecology, feeding competition and social structure in baboon. *Behavioral Ecology and Sociobiology, 38,* 321–329.
Battaglia, F. C., & Meschina, G. (1973). Foetal metabolism and substrate utilization. Foetal and neonatal physiology. In *Proceedings of Sir Joseph Barcroft Centenary Symposium* (pp. 382–395). Cambridge: Cambridge University Press.
Berna, F., Goldberg, P., Horwitz, L. K., Brink, J., Holt, S., Bamford, M., et al. (2012). Microstratigraphic evidence of in situ fire in the Acheulean strata of wonderwork cave, Northern Cape Province, South Africa. *Proceedings of the National Academy of Sciences of the United States of America, 109,* E1215–E1220.
Boas, F. (1911). *The mind of primitive man.* New York: Macmillan.
Boesch, C. (1992). New elements of a theory of mind in wild chimpanzees. *Behavioral Brain Sciences, 15,* 149–150.
Boesch, C. (1994). Cooperative hunting in wild chimpanzees. *Animal Behaviour, 48,* 653–667.
Boesch, C., & Boesch-Achermann, H. (2000). *The chimpanzees of the Taï forest: Behavioural ecology and evolution.* Oxford: Oxford University Press.
Bogin, B. (2009). Childhood, adolescence, and longevity: A multilevel model of the evolution of reserve capacity in human life history. *American Journal of Human Biology, 21,* 567–577.
Bradley, B. J., Doran-Sheehy, D. M., Lukas, D., et al. (2004). Dispersal male networks in western gorillas. *Current Biology, 14,* 510–513.
Brain, C. K. (1981). *The hunters or the hunted?.* Chicago: The Chicago University Press.
Butynski, T. M. (1982). Harem-male replacement and infanticide in the blue monkey (*Cercopithecus mitis stuhlmanni*) in the Kibale Forest, Uganda. *American Journal of Primatology, 3,* 1–22.
Cartmill, M. (1993). *A view to a death in the morning: Hunting and nature through history.* Cambridge: Harvard University Press.
Chapais, B. (2011). The deep social structure of humankind. *Science, 331,* 1276–1277.
Charnov, E. L. (1991). Evolution of life history variation among female mammals. *Proceedings of the National Academy of Sciences USA, 88,* 1134–1137.
Charnov, E. L. (1993). *Life history invariants: Some explorations of symmetry in evolutionary ecology.* Oxford: Oxford University Press.
Charnov, E. L., & Berrigan, D. (1993). Why do female primates have such long lifespans and so few babies? Or life in the slow laned. *Evolutionary Anthropology, 1,* 191–194.
Clutton-Brock, T. H., & Harvey, P. H. (1980). Primates, brain and ecology. *Journal of Zoology London, 109,* 309–323.
Copeland, S. R., Sponheimer, M., de Ruiter, D. J., et al. (2011). Strontium isotope evidence for landscape use by early hominis. *Nature, 474,* 76–78.
Cords, M. (1997). Friendships, alliances, reciprocity and repair. In A. Whiten & R. W. Byrne (Eds.), *Machiavellian intelligence II* (pp. 24–49). Cambridge: Cambridge University Press.
Cunnane, S. C., & Crawford, M. A. (2003). Suvival of the fattest: Fat babies were the key to evolution of the large human brain. *Comparative Biochemistry and Physiology Part A, 136,* 17–26.

Dart, R. A. (1953). The predatory transition from ape to man. *International Anthropological and Linguistic Review, 1,* 201–217.
Dart, R. A. (1955). Cultural status of the South African Man-Apes. Annual Report for the Smithsonian Institution. (1955). *317-338.* Washington: Government Printing Office.
Darwin, C. (1871). *The descent of man and selection in relation to sex.* London: Murray.
De Waal, F. (1982). *Chimpanzee politics.* London: Jonathan Cape.
De Waal, F. (2006). *Primates and philosophers: How morality evolved.* Princeton: Princeton University Press.
Dixon, R. A. (1983). Observations on the evolution and behavioral significance of "sexual skin" in female primates. *Advances in the Study of Behavior, 13,* 63–106.
Dunbar, R. I. M. (1984). *Reproductive decisions.* Princeton: Princeton University Press.
Dunbar, R. I. M. (1996). The social brain hypothesis. *Evolutionary Anthropology, 6,* 178–190.
Eaton, G. G., & Resko, J. A. (1974). Ovarian hormones and sexual behavior in *Macaca nemestrina. Journal of Comparative and Physiological Psychology, 86,* 919–925.
Elton, S. (2008). The environmental context of human evolutionary history in Eurasia and Africa. *Journal of Anatomy, 212,* 377–393.
Enomoto, T. (1978). On social preference in sexual behavior of Japanese monkeys (Macacafuscata). *Journal of Human Evolution, 7,* 283–293.
Feistner, A. T. C., & McGrew, W. C. (1989). Food sharing in primates: A critical review. In P. K. Seth & S. Seth (Eds.), *Perspectives in primate biology* (Vol. 3, pp. 21–36). New Delhi: Today and Tomorrow Printers and Publishers.
Flack, J. C., & de Waal, F. B. M. (2000). 'Any animal whatever': Darwinian building blocks of morality in monkeys and apes. *Journal of Consciousness Studies, 7,* 1–29.
Foley, R., & Gamble, C. (2009). The ecology of social transitions in human evolution. *Philosophical Transactions of the Royal Society of London B: Biological Sciences, 364,* 3267–3279.
Fossey, D. (1982). Reproduction among free-living mountain gorillas. *American Journal of Primatology* (Suppl 1), 97–104.
Fossey, D. (1983). *Gorillas in the mist.* Boston: Houghton Mifflin.
Furuichi, T. (1987). Sexual swelling, receptivity and grouping of wild pygmy chimpanzee females at Wamba, Zaire. *Primates, 20,* 309–318.
Furuichi, T., Idani, G., Ihobe, H., Kuroda, S., Kitamura, K., Mori, A., et al. (1998). Population dynamics of wild bonobos (Pan paniscus) at Wamba. *International Journal of Primatology, 19,* 1029–1043.
Furuichi, T., & Hashimoto, C. (2002). Why female bonobos have a lower copulation rate during estrus than chimpanzees? In: C. Boesch, G. Hohmann, & L. F. Marchant (Eds.), *Behavioral diversity in chimpanzees and bonobos* (pp. 156–167). New York: Cambridge University Press.
Galdikas, B. M. F. (1981). Orangutan reproduction in the wild. In C. E. Graham (Ed.), *Reproductive biology of the great apes* (pp. 281–300). New York: Academic Press.
Gaspari, R., & Lee, S.-H. (2006). Is human longevity a consequence of cultural change or modern biology? *American Journal of Physical Anthropology, 129,* 512–517.
Gibson, K. R. (1986). Cognition, brain size and the extraction of embedded food resources. In J. G. Else & P. C. Lee (Eds.), *Primate ontogeny, cognition and social behaviour* (pp. 93–103). New York: Cambridge University Press.
Gomez, J. R., Verdu, M., Gonzalez-Megias, A., & Mendez, M. (2016). The phylogenetic roots of human lethal violence. *Nature, 538,* 233–237.
Goodall, J. (1986). *The chimpanzees of gombe.* Belknap: Cambridge.
Gordon, T. P. (1981). Reproductive behavior in the rhesus monkey: Social and endocrine variables. *American Zoologist, 21,* 185–195.
Goren-Inbur, N., Alperson, N., kislev, M., Simchoni, O., Melamed, Y., Ben-Nun, A., et al. (2004). Evidence of hominid control of fire at Gesher benot Ya'aqov, Israel. *Science, 304,* 725–727.
Grueter, C. C., Chapais, B., & Zinner, D. (2012). Evolution of multilevel social systems in nonhuman primates and humans. *International Journal of Primatology, 33,* 1002–1037.

Gurven, M., & Walker, R. (2006). Energetic demand of multiple dependents and the evolution of slow human growth. *Proceedings of the Royal Society B, 273,* 835–841.
Harcourt, A. H., Harvey, P. H., Larson, S. G., & Short, R. V. (1981). Testis weight, body weight and breeding system in primates. *Nature, 293,* 55–57.
Harcourt, A. H., & Stewart, K. J. (2007). *Gorilla society: Conflict, compromise and cooperation between the sexes.* Chicago: The University of Chicago Press.
Hart, S., & Sussman, R. (2005). *Man the hunted: Primates, predators, and human evolution.* New York: Westview Press.
Henzi, S. P., & Lucas, J. W. (1980). Observations on the inter-troop movement of adult vervet monkeys (*Cercopithecus aethiops*). *Folia Primatologica, 33,* 220–235.
Hinde, R. A. (1976). Interaction, relationships and social structure. *Man, 11,* 1–17.
Hrdy, S. B. (2009). *Mothers and others: The evolutionary origins of mutual understanding.* Cambridge MA: Belknap Press.
Huck, M., Löttker, P., & Heymann, E. W. (2004). The many faces of helping: Possible costs and benefits of infant carrying and food transfer in wild moustached tamarins (*Saguinus mystax*). *Behaviour, 141,* 915–934.
Huffman, M. A. (1997). Current evidence for self-medication in primates: A multidisciplinary perspective. *Year Book of Physical Anthropology, 40,* 171–200.
Humphrey, L. T. (2010). Weaning behavior in human evolution. *Seminars in Cell & Developmental Biology, 21,* 453–461.
Ihobe, H. (1992). Male-male relationships among wild bonobos (*Pan paniscus*) at Wamba, Republic of Zaire. *Primates, 33,* 163–179.
Imanishi, K. (1957). Social behavior in Japanese monkeys, *Macaca fuscata. Psychologia, 1,* 47–54.
Imanishi, K. (1961). The origin of human family: From a viewpoint of primatologie. *Ethnological Studies, 25,* 119–138. (in Japanese).
Inoue, E., Akomo-Okoue, E. F., Ando, C., Iwata, Y., Judai, M., Fujita, S., et al. (2013). Male genetic structure and paternity in western lowland gorillas (*Gorilla gorilla gorilla*). *American Journal of Physical Anthropology, 151,* 583–588.
Isaac, G. (1978). The food-sharing behavior of protohuman hominids. *Scientific American, 238,* 90–108.
Itani, J. (1954). *The monkeys at Takasakiyama.* Tokyo: Kobunsha. (in Japanese).
Itani, J. (1977). Evolution of primate social structure. *Journal of Human Evolution, 6,* 235–243.
Itani, J. (1984). The evolution of primate social structures. *Man (N.S.), 20,* 593–611.
Itani, J. (1988). The origin of human equality. In M. R. A. Chance (Ed.), *Social fabrics of the mind* (pp. 137–156). London: Lawrence Erlbaum Associates.
Jaeggi, A. V., & van Schaik, C. P. (2011). The evolution of food sharing in primates. *Behavioral Ecology and Sociobiology, 65,* 2125–2140.
Jansen, K., Hare, B., Call, J., & Tomasello, M. (2006). What's in it for me? Self-regard precluders altruism and spite in chimpanzees. *Proceedings of the Royal Society of London. Series B, 273,* 1013–1021.
Janson, C. H. (2000). Primate socioecology: The end of a golden age. *Evolutionary Anthropology, 9,* 73–86.
Janson, C. H., & van Schaik, C. P. (1993). Ecological risk aversion in juvenile primates: Slow and steady wins the race. In M. E. Pereira & L. A. Fairbanks (Eds.), *Juvenile primates, development and behavior* (pp. 57–74). Oxford: Oxford University Press.
Jerison, H. J. (1976). *Evolution of the brain and intelligence.* New York: Avademic Press.
Kano, T. (1989). The sexual behavior of pygmy chimpanzees. In P. G. Heltne & L. A. Marquardt (Eds.), *Understanding chimpanzees* (pp. 176–183). Cambridge: Harvard University Press.
Kano, T. (1992). *The last Ape: Pygmy chimpanzee behavior and ecology.* Stanford: Stanford University Press.
Kaplan, H., Hill, K., Lancaster, J., & Hurtado, A. M. (2000). A theory of human life history evolution: Diet, intelligence, and longevity. *Evolutionary Anthropology, 9,* 156–185.

Kappeler, P. M., Pereira, M. E., & van Schaik, C. P. (2003). Primate life histories and socioecology. In P. M. Kappeler & M. E. Pereira (Eds.), *Primate life histories and socioecology* (pp. 1–23). Chicago: Chicago University Press.

Kappeler, P. M., & van Schaik, C. P. (2004). Sexual selection in primates: Review and selective preview. In P. M. Kappeler & C. P. van Schaik (Eds.), *Sexual selection in primates: New and comparative perspectives* (pp. 3–23). New York: Cambridge University Press.

Kennedy, G. E. (2005). From the ape's dilemma to the weanling's dilemma: early weaning and its evolutionary context. *Journal of Human Evolution, 48*, 123–145.

Knott, C. D., Beaudrot, L., Snaith, T., et al. (2008). Female-female competition in Bornean orangutans. *International Journal of Primatology, 29*, 975–997.

Kuester, J., Paul, A., & Arnemann, J. (1994). Kinship, familiality and mating avoidance in Barbary macaques, *Macaca sylvanus*. *Animal Behaviour, 48*, 1183–1194.

Kummer, H. (1978). On the value of social relationships to nonhuman primates: A heuristic scheme. *Social Structure Information, 17*, 697–705.

Kuroda, S. (1980). Social behavior of the pygmy chimpanzees. *Primates, 21*, 181–197.

Lalueza-Fox, C., Rosas, A., Estalrrich, A., Gigli, E., Campos, Paula F., García-Tabernero, A., et al. (2011). Genetic evidence for patrilocal mating behavior among Neandertal groups. *Proceedings of the National Academy of Sciences of the United States of America, 108*, 250–253.

Leigh, S. R. (2001). Evolution of human growth. *Evolutionary Anthropology, 10*, 223–236.

Leigh, S. R., & Shea, B. T. (1996). Ontogeny of body size variation in African apes. *American Journal of Physical Anthropology, 99*, 43–65.

Levi-Strauss, C. (1949). *Les Structures Elementaires de la Parente*. Paris: Presses Universitaires de France.

Levi-Strauss, C. (1956). The family. In H. L. Shapiro (Ed.), *Man, culture and society* (pp. 261–285). Oxford: Oxford University Press.

Lindenfors, P. (2002). Sexually antagonistic selection on primate size. *Journal of Evolutionary Biology, 15*, 595–607.

Lovejoy, C. O. (1981). The origin of man. *Science, 211*, 341–350.

Marlowe, F. W. (2006). Central place provisioning: The Hadza as an example. In G. Hohmann, M. M. Robbins, & C. Boesch (Eds.), *Feeding ecology in apes and other primates* (pp. 359–377). Cambridge: Cambridge University Press.

Marlowe, F. W. (2012). The socioecology of human reproduction. In: J. C. Mitani, J. Call, P. M. Kappeler, R. A. Palombit, & J. B. Silk (Eds.), *Evolution of primate society* (pp. 467–486). Chicago: The University of Chicago Press.

Martin, R. D. (1990). *Primate origins and evolution*. London: Chapman and Hall.

Martines, J., Habicht, J., Ashworth, A., & Kirkwood, B. (1994). Weaning in southern Brazil: Is there a "weaning's dilemma"? *Journal of Nutrition, 124*, 1189–1198.

McGrew, W. C. (1975). Patterns of plant food sharing by wild chimpanzees. In S. Kondo, M. Kawai, & A. Ehara (Eds.), *Contemporary Primatology; Proceedings of the 5th International Congress of Primatology, Nagoya*, (pp. 304–309). Basel; New York: S. Karger.

McGrew, W. C. (1992). *Chimpanzee material culture*. Cambridge: Cambridge University Press.

Milton, K. (1981). Distribution patterns of tropical plant foods as an evolutionary stimulus to primate mental development. *American Anthropologists, 83*, 534–548.

Milton, K. (1986). Features of digestive physiology in primates. *News in Physiological Sciences, 1*, 76–79.

Mitani, J. C., Gros-Louis, J., & Richard, A. F. (1996). Sexual dimorphism, the operational sex-ratio, and the intensity of male competition in polygynous primates. *The American Naturalist, 147*, 966–980.

Morgan, L. H. (1877). *Ancient society*. London: MacMillan & Company.

Morrogh-Bernard, H., Morf, N., Chivers, D., & Krützen, M. (2011). Dispersal patterns of orang-utants (*Pongo* spp.) in a Bornean peat-swamp forest. *International Journal of Primatology, 32*, 362–376.

Murdock, G. P. (1949). *Social structure*. New York: The Macmillan Company.

Nadler, R. D. (1981). Laboratory research on sexual behavior of the great apes. In C. E. Graham (Ed.), *Reproductive biology of the great apes: Comparative and biomedical perspectives* (pp. 192–238). New York: Academic Press.

Nishida, T. (1983). Alpha status and agonistic alliance in wild chimpanzees (*Pan troglodytes schweinfurthii*). *Primates, 24*, 318–336.

Nishida, T. (1987). Local traditions and cultural transmission. In B. B. Smuts, D. L. Cheney, R. M. Seyfarth, R. W. Wrangham, & T. T. Struhsaker (Eds.), *Primate societies* (pp. 462–474). Chicago: University of Chicago Press.

Nishida, T., Corp, N., Hamai, M., Hasegawa, T., Hiraiwa-Hasegawa, M., Hosaka, K., et al. (2003). Demography, female life history, and reproductive profiles among the chimpanzees of Mahale. *American Journal of Primatology, 59*, 99–121.

Nishida, T., Hasegawa, T., Hayaki, H., Takahata, Y., & Uehara, S. (1992). Meat-sharing as a coalition strategy by an alpha male chimpanzee? In T. Nishida, W. C. McGrew, P. Marler, M. Pickford, & F. B. M. de Waal (Eds.), *Topics in primatology, vol 1: Human origins* (pp. 159–174). Tokyo: University of Tokyo Press.

O'Connell, S. M. (1995). Empathy in chimpanzees: Evidence for theory of mind? *Primates, 36*, 397–410.

Potts, R. (1984). Home bases and early hominids. *American Scientist, 72*, 338–347.

Prat, S., et al. (2005). First occurrence of early Homo in the Nachuku formation (West Turukana, Kenya) at 2.3–2.4 Myr. *Journal of Human Evolution, 49*, 1008–1012.

Price, E. C., & Feistner, A. T. C. (1993). Food sharing in Lion Tamarins: Tests of three hypotheses. *American Journal of Primatology, 31*, 211–221.

Purvis, A., & Harvey, P. H. (1995). Mammalian life history evolution: A comparative test for Charnov's model. *Journal of Zoology, 237*, 259–283.

Pusey, A. E. (1980). Inbreeding avoidance in chimpanzees. *Animal Behaviour, 28*, 543–552.

Pusey, A. E., & Packer, C. (1987). Dispersal and philopatry. In B. B. Smuts et al. (Eds.), *Primate societies* (pp. 250–266). Chicago: The University of Chicago Press.

Read, A. F., & Harvey, P. H. (1989). Life history differences among the eutherian radiations. *Journal of Zoology, 219*, 329–353.

Reed, K. (1997). Early hominid evolution and ecological change through the African Plio-Pleistocene. *Journal of Human Evolution, 32*, 289–322.

Robbins, M. M., Bermejo, M., Cipolletta, C., et al. (2004). Social structure and life history patterns in western gorillas (*Gorilla gorilla gorilla*). *American Journal of Primatology, 64*, 145–159.

Robson, S. L., & Wood, B. (2008). Hominin life history: Reconstruction and evolution. *Journal of Anatomy, 212*(4), 394–425.

Ross, C. (1998). Primate life histories. *Evolutionary Anthropology, 6*, 54–63.

Rousseau, J.-J. (1754). *Discourse on inequality*. Marc-Michel Rey.

Schaller, G. B. (1963). *The mountain gorilla: Ecology and behavior*. Chicago: University of Chicago Press.

Schlegel, A., & Barry, H. I. I. I. (1991). *Adolescence: An anthropological inquiry*. New York: Free Press.

Shipman, P., & Walker, A. (1989). The costs of becoming a predator. *Journal of Human Evolution, 18*, 373–392.

Sicotte, P. (1995). Interpositions in conflicts between males in bimale groups of mountain gorillas. *Folia Primatologica, 65*, 14–24.

Silk, J. B., & House, J. B. (2011). Evolutionary foundations of human prosocial sentiments. *Proceedings of the National Academy of Sciences, 108*, 10910–10917.

Sillen-Tullberg, B., & Moller, A. P. (1993). The relationship between concealed ovulation and mating systems in anthropoid primates: A phylogenetic analysis. *American Naturalist, 141*, 1–25.

Singleton, I., & van Schaik, C. P. (2002). The social organization of a population of Sumatran orang-utans. *Folia Primatologica, 73*, 1–20.

Smith, B. H. (1992). Life history and the evolution of human maturation. *Evolutionary Anthropology, 1*, 134–142.

Smith, B. H. (1994). Patterns of dental development in homo, australopithecus, pan, and gorilla. *American Journal of Physical Anthropology, 94*, 307–325.

Stanford, C. B. (1996). The hunting ecology of wild chimpanzees: Implications for the evolutionary ecology of Pliocene hominids. *American Anthropologists, 98*, 96–113.

Starin, E. D. (2001). Patterns of inbreeding avoidance in Temminck's red colobus. *Behaviour, 138*, 453–465.

Sterck, E. H. M., Watts, D. P., & van Schaik, C. P. (1997). The evolution of female social relationships in nonhuman primates. *Behavioral Ecology and Sociobiology, 41*, 291–309.

Sterck, E. H. M., Willems, E. P., van Hooff, J. A. R. A. M., & Wich, S. A. (2005). Female dispersal, inbreeding avoidance and mate choice in Thomas langurs (*Presbytes thomasi*). *Behaviour, 142*, 845–868.

Stewart, K. J., & Harcourt, A. H. (1987). Gorillas: Variation in female relationships. In B. B. Smuts et al. (Eds.), *Primate societies* (pp. 155–164). Chicago: The University of Chicago Press.

Stoinski, T. S., Vecellio, V., Nagaboyamahina, T., Ndagijimana, F., Rosenbaum, S., & Fawsett, K. A. (2009). Proximate factors influencing dispersal decisions in male mountain gorillas, *Gorilla beringei beringei*. *Animal Behaviour, 77*, 1155–1164.

Sugiyama, Y. (1976). Life history of male Japanese monkeys. In J. S. Rosenblatt, R. A. Hinde, E. Shaw, & C. Beer (Eds.), *Advances in the study of behavior* (Vol. 7, pp. 255–284). New York: Academic Press.

Takahata, Y. (1980). The reproductive biology of a free-ranging troop of Japanese monkeys. *Primates, 21*, 303–329.

Takahata, Y. (1982). Social relations between adult males and females of Japanese monkeys in the Arashiyama B troop. *Primates, 23*, 1–23.

Taylor, H., Vazquez-Geffroy, M., Samuels, S., & Taylor, D. (1999). Continuously recorded suckling behavior and its effect on lactational amenorrhoea. *Journal of Biosocial Science, 31*, 289–310.

Thieme, H. (1997). Lower Palaeolithic hunting spears from Germany. *Nature, 385*, 807–810.

Trivers, R. L. (1972). Paternal investment and sexual selection. In B. Campbell (Ed.), *Sexual selection and descent of man, 1871–1971* (pp. 136–179). Chicago: Aldine-atherton.

Uehara, S. (1997). Predation on mammals by the chimpanzees (Pantroglodytes). *Primates, 38*, 193–214.

Utami, A. S., Mitra, S. T., Goossens, B., James, S. J., Knott, C. D., Morrogh, B. H. C., van Schaik, C. P., & van Noordwijk, M. A. (2009). Orangutan mating behavior and strategies. In: S. A. Wich, A. S. Utami, T. M. Setia, & C. P. van Schaik (Eds.), *Orangutans: Geographic variation in behavioral ecology and conservation* (pp. 235–244). New York: Oxford University Press.

Van Schaik, C. P., & Isler, K. (2012). Life-history evolution. In: J. C. Mitani, J. Call, P. M. Kappeler, R. A. Palombit, & J. B. Silk (Eds.), *Evolution of primate society* (pp. 220–244). Chicago: The University of Chicago Press.

Vigilant, L., & Langergraber, K. E. (2011). Inconclusive evidence for patrilocality in Neandertals. *Proceedings of the National Academy of Sciences of the United States of America, 108*, E87.

Vonk, J., Brosnan, S. F., Silk, J. B., Henrich, J., Richardson, A. S., Lambeth, S. P., et al. (2008). Chimpanzees do not take advantage of very low cost opportunities to deliver food to unrelated group members. *Animal Behaviour, 75*, 1757–1770.

Watts, D. P. (1995). Post-conflict social events in wild mountain gorillas (Mammalia, Hominoidea). 1. Social interactions between opponents. *Ethology, 100*, 139–157.

Wilson, E. O. (1975). *Sociobiology: The new synthesis*. Cambridge: Belknap Press of Harvard University Press.

Wilson, M. I. (1977). Characterization of the estrous cycle and mating season of squirrel monkeys from copulatory behaviour. *The Journal of the Society for Reproduction and Fertility, 51*, 57–63.

Wood, B., & Strait, D. (2004). Patterns of resource use in early homo and paranthropus. *Journal of Human Evolution, 46*, 119–162.

Wrangham, R. W. (1980). An ecological model of female-bonded primate groups. *Behaviour, 75*, 262–300.
Wrangham, R. W. (2006). The cooking enigma. In P. Ungar (Ed.), *Early hominid diet: The known, the unknown, and the unknowable* (pp. 308–323). New York: Oxford University Press.
Wrangham, R. W. (2009). *Catching fire: How cooking made us human*. New York: Basic Books.
Wrangham, R. W., & Conklin-Brittain, N. L. (2003). The biological significance of cooking in human evolution. *Comparative Biochemistry and Physiology Part A, 136*, 35–46.
Wranghm, R. W., & Glowacki, L. (2012). Intergroup aggression in chimpanzees and war in nomadic hunter-gatherers: Evaluating the chimpanzee model. *Human Nature, 23*, 5–29.
Yamagiwa, J. (1992). Functional analysis of social staring behavior in an all-male group of mountain gorillas. *Primates, 33*, 523–544.
Yamagiwa, J. (2015). Evolution of hominid life history strategy and origin of human family. In T. Furuichi, J. Yamagiwa, & F. Aureli (Eds.), *Dispersing females: Life history and social strategies in male-philopatric species* (pp. 255–285). Tokyo: Springer.
Yamagiwa, J., & Basabose, A. K. (2014). Socioecological flexibility of gorillas and chimpanzees. In J. Yamagiwa & L. karczmarski (Eds.), *Primates and cetaceans: Field research and conservation of complex mammalian societies* (pp. 43–74). Tokyo: Springer.
Yamagiwa, J., Shimooka, Y., & Sprague, D. S. (2014). Life history tactics in monkeys and apes. In J. Yamagiwa & L. karczmarski (Eds.), *Primates and cetaceans: Field research and conservation of complex mammalian societies* (pp. 173–206). Tokyo: Springer.
Yamagiwa, J., Tsubokawa, K., Inoue, E., & Ando, C. (2015). Sharing fruit of Treculia africana among western gorillas in the Moukalaba-Doudou National Park, Gabon: Preliminary report. *Primates, 56*, 3–10.
Yamamoto, S., & Tanaka, M. (2010). The influence of kin relationship and reciprocal context on chimpanzees' other-regarding preferences. *Animal Behaviour, 79*, 595–602.

Author Biography

Juichi Yamagiwa is the 26th President of Kyoto University. He is a world-renowned researcher and expert in the study of primatology and human evolution. He was awarded Doctor of Science from Kyoto University in 1987. After holding positions at the Karisoke Research Center, Japan Monkey Center, and Primate Research Institute Kyoto University, he has been Professor of Graduate School of Science at Kyoto University since 2002. He was Dean of Graduate School and Faculty of Science from 2011 to 2013 and has been a member of the Administrative Council of the University from 2012 to 2013. Dr. Yamagiwa has also served as President of International Primatological Society from 2008 to 2012, and as the Editor in Chief of Primates, a quarterly peer-reviewed scientific journal of primatology published by Springer Science+Business Media from 2010 to 2014.

Dr. Yamagiwa's passion for fieldwork research frequently made him travel to Africa, such as Rwanda, Republic of the Congo, and Gabonese Republic, where he discovered an abundance of new findings related to gorillas, through his unique viewpoint of evolution.

Chapter 20
Eminent Otherness: Toward an Economy of Hospitality

C. Edward Arrington

1 Introduction

> For of the three powers known in the State as the Power of the Army, the Power of external Alliance and the Power of Money, the money-power might well become the most reliable instrument of war, did not the difficulty of determining its real force stand in the way of its employment.
>
> Immanuel Kant, "Perpetual Peace: A Philosophical Sketch
>
> We are all responsible for everyone else – but I am more responsible than all the others.
>
> Alyosha Karamazov in Fyodor Dostoevsky's *The Brothers Karamazov*
>
> *To welcome a friend is splendid, to welcome a stranger sublime.*

Humans have the capacity to transform the world for moral purpose. That is economics at its moral core; activity designed to enhance the material conditions indicative of the good life, to move from the actual given to the possibly better, and to do so with and for ours*elves* and with and for *others*. We work together or apart, we share the world as constructed by others, and we are responsible for far more than our own welfare simply because our economic products shape the lives of others, just as the products of others construct our own lives. To return to Kant, the "real force" of economic power is often ephemeral, difficult to locate, but always subject to the question of its relevance to others. This essay seeks to nudge our understanding of economic life closer to a hermeneutical horizon where hospitality and welcoming might provide the scope for understanding economic responsibility in a new ontological and moral key, a key in which the damage that we do might be lessened and the good we seek enhanced.

C. E. Arrington (✉)
Corrimal, NSW, Australia
e-mail: cearring1@gmail.com

Modern economic thought, particularly after it turned its back on political economy and divorced itself from normative questions, shares with many other social science disciplines a preference for parsimony as it works to "tame" uncertainty and chance. We can glimpse with Stephen Toulmin how the ambiguity and uncertainty out of which we living breathing humans do in fact construct our lives and ourselves as historical beings in community with others is not so easily tamed, despite the epistemic and scientistic "virtues" that have turned our humanity away from the humanities, a turning we must remedy:

> We can reconcile the twin legacies of the exact sciences and the humanities only by a change of direction; and, for that, we must first see clearly how the agenda of "modern thought" over-reached itself. By now, it will be clear that we need to balance the hope of certainty and clarity in theory with the impossibility of avoiding uncertainty and ambiguity in practice. But the received view of Modernity rested not only on the Quest for Certainty and the equation of Rationality with a respect for formal logic: it also took over the rationalists' belief that the modern, rational way of dealing with problems is to sweep away the inherited clutter from traditions, clean the slate, and start again from scratch (Toulmin 1990: 175).

At the core of Toulmin's critique stands Modernity's agenda. That "received view" plays itself out in modern economics through a range of attributes of relevance to this essay. Among those attributes are (1) the effacement of the history of political economy, both in theory and in practice, in favor of an economics of the simple, the "scientific," the "model," and the "rational"; (2) an elevation of the self and its interests to the apex of values as each of us becomes a "moral monarch"; (3) a gloss over the difficulty of pursuing harmony, equilibrium, and peace; (4) a similar gloss over the particularities of the local and the contingent; and, (5) a preference for a morality of norms and rules grounded in subjective utility rather than a morality of intersubjective life, prudence and praxis. Alike with moral philosophy, there is a "thinness" about all of this that leaves out too much of living, breathing, experience; too much of "the world," its moral richness and its complexity:

> This world has lots of good qualities. But one of its drawbacks is a tendency to narrowness on certain questions. And one of the most marked sites of this narrowness was in moral philosophy. The narrowness concerns more than just the range of doctrines considered, though it also consists of that. But, more fundamentally, it has restricted the range of questions that it seems sensible to ask. In the end, it restricted our understanding of what morality is. I have tried to sum this up by saying that Anglo-Saxon moral philosophy has tended to see morality as concerned with questions of what we ought to do and to occlude or exclude questions about what it is good to be or what it is good to love (Taylor 1996: 3).

That "tendency to narrowness" is just as true for contemporary economic thought as it is for moral philosophy. As Taylor notes, one casualty of such narrowness is the demise of inquiry into what it is good for us to be and good for us to love. Harmony and harmoniousness come to mind. But harmony has too often been romanticized and simplified within what some term "the metaphysics of presence," an unfortunate thing since approaching the genuinely harmonious requires sticking with what John Caputo terms "the original difficulty of life," a difficulty certainly strikingly obvious in contemporary economic life:

The point is to make life difficult, not impossible – to face up to the difference and difficulty which enter into what we think and do and hope for, not to grind them to a halt. Indeed, it is the claim of radical hermeneutics that we get the best results by yielding to the difficulty in "reason," "ethics," and faith," not by trying to cover it over. Once we stop trying to prop up our beliefs, practices, and institutions on the metaphysics of presence, once we give up the idea that they are endowed with some sort of facile transparency, we find that they are not washed away but liberated, albeit in a way that makes the guardians of Being and presence nervous.... Curiously enough, the metaphysical desire to make things safe and secure has become consummately dangerous (Caputo 1987: 7).

Under the cover of "science," modern economics, particularly in the US and in its capitalistic garb, has not "faced up" to this difficulty. It sought a "positive" economics as it jettisoned questions of norms (except for those like efficiency and property rights that it is fond of). It divorced itself from its birth-mother political economy and reduced what it means to be a person to what Dierdre McCloskey terms that "great stick of a character," *homo economicus*. It narrowed the Aristotelian scope of human rationality and indeed human nature to the pursuit of self-interests. It gave communication and political life over strictly to strategic rationality and strategic discourse, rendering human intersubjectivity an exercise in "how to win." In this strategic world, intersubjectivity and ethics take only those forms which "benefit" the relevant parties in their "exchange" of increments to self-interest, with private property rights and liberty understood as the freedom to pursue subjective utility maximization as the key "moral" accoutrements to economics. To the extent it bothers with welfare economics at all, and in a post-Keynesian world it doesn't bother much, it has relied upon welfare arguments adapted from Wilfredo Pareto (to whom Mussolini gave a medal as "the father of Fascist economics" and whom Karl Popper referred to as "the theoretician of totalitarianism"). This sort of economics seems rather indifferent to a world it helped create, a world ravaged by unbridled greed, indifferent at best and biased at worst to questions of economic justice, incapable of reconciling some putative economic "progress" through "growth" to the ever-expanding gap between the rich and the poor (see Piketty 2014), and, perhaps worst of all, at the brink of murdering that most gifted phenomenon of all, that tiny little sliver of cosmic "splendor" we call the Earth. The notion of economy has become consummately dangerous; a big part of the problem, not of the solution. We don't even have the economic words to deal with this.

In this essay, I will not be bound to modern economic thought and will raise different sorts of issues and questions. I will adopt a phenomenological and hermeneutic perspective focused on ordinary life, the "to and fro" of our breath, our sustenance, our language, our sociality, and our self-understandings. With a casual relation to the work of Emmanuel Levinas, and with a flirtatious glance toward non-Western ideas, I follow the idea of an economy grounded in a *for-the-other* **hospitality** rather than a *for-the-self* competitiveness. I do not offer a practical, implementable "system" or "structure" for such an economy; I offer ideas to help us *think* differently and, through those ideas, to *act* differently.

2 A Hospitable Economy

> A well formulated approach to the future ... does not depend on finding ways to quantify and extrapolate current trends: that we may leave to enthusiastic weather forecasters, stock exchange chartists, or econometrists. Rather, the questions are, "What intellectual *posture* should we adopt in confronting the future? What eye can we develop for significant aspects of the years ahead? And what capacity do we have to change our ideas about the available futures? (Toulmin 1990: 2).

I am suggesting here that the idea of a presumption of hospitality provides one such valuable intellectual posture as we answer Toulmin's questions. Certainly, recent events suggest that hospitality hardly registers in economics, politics, ethics, and the sovereign State, where competition, survival (and thus death), winning, jingoism, "border control," and neoliberal promotion of selfishness are ubiquitous, as is the hate-riddled "post-truth" autocratic (or indeed plutocratic) politics of recent emergence. These ideas are embedded in some old ones. Thomas Hobbes gave us a moral ontology grounded in a self-interested nature that, unchecked, inevitably leads us into conflict and war. Immanuel Kant viewed perpetual peace (and thus harmony) as derivative of something akin to Hobbes state of human nature but "a crossing over" from it. Of most relevance to this paper, the ongoing politics of the *border* defines the state and the market by counting those within and discounting those without, by the granting of rights and freedoms to some and granting silence (or worse) to others. We seem to be living and breathing the antithesis of [Kantian] hospitality; that is, "... the right of the stranger not to be treated with hostility when he arrives on someone else's territory" (Kant 1795/1970: 105). Those strangers are both inside and outside of the border, citizens though they may be.

Yet this notion of hospitality as the refusal of hostility has some corollary in the idea of a transactional economy governed by competition and strategic modes of interaction. If, for example, it was possible to presume, experientially, a transaction between those of equal competence and power, with each oriented toward the satisfaction of his/her preferences through trading, then the absence of intersubjective "hostility" seems a reasonable assumption. If, as it usually does, this sort of interaction transpires between those of unequal competence with asymmetries of power, then that economy is *not* hospitable. The exercise of power over others for one's own benefit is certainly a "hostile" act since "power" is never called upon without its object, that "who" or "what" it targets and that "who" or "what" it acts in the name of. But the power goes much further. A transaction takes in a broader context than a context formed by the "subjects" who enact it—the "thing" of trade, the commodified thing, which is of course an embodiment of so very many other "things" that may be produced and appropriated in a manner "hostile" to them—the earth, those who labour, unborn others, innocent victims of history, and plants and animals all come to mind. Do they all deserve hospitality, a presumption in their own favor that would open the door for them?

Hospitality, as a welcoming, is a welcoming *into* something, an inside, a home, a premises, a place which is always and already identified, owned, an asymmetrical market of what is *not* of the stranger who is welcomed in; that is to say, into an economy. The one who offers hospitality is the one who welcomes the stranger *into* that which is *not* the stranger's. As Leung and Stone state, quoting John Caputo, "[A]ny act of hospitality contains within it the trace of asymmetries of power, 'the welcome of the guest, is a function of the power of the host to remain master of the premises'" (2009: 196). This calls forth the question of justice as it bears upon the legal questions of property as, for example, over the question of retributive justice with regard to the violence that defines the history of the *acquisition* of private property and rights to it. Thus, as with the writing of both Jacques Derrida and Emmanuel Levinas, the "host" is always and already implicated in the guilt of history that surrounds the presentistic question of the *border* (ownership, statehood, citizenship, etc.). That guilty implication does no damage to the imperative of hospitality; rather, it reminds us of the difference between a "pre-ethical" obligation to unconditional welcoming and the factical life within the historical, ethical, and political space of an economy within which the inhospitable governs unless and until hospitality pays off *for me*.

This raises both the ontological question of universalism and the ethico-political question of cosmopolitanism. There is a rather strange aporia at work in the hospitality of welcoming *into* a home presumed universal, an incontrovertible "harmony" of all with all. But a universal home is no one's home, no *bordered* place about which hospitable welcoming can be "hosted"; a universal economy of welcoming would have no place, no goods, no "home." It may emerge from a harmony of something spiritual, something "noneconomic" which all are presumed to share and of which none are the author/owners, but then the necessary move to "linguistify" that which is universal is deconstructed from the outset by the quite simple fact that there is no language—and thus no economy—which can "deliver the goods" independently of history, despite the relentless urge to "purify" danger. This is the core issue in the postmodern cultural politics of difference, of resistance to the idea that ways of living, ways of believing, ways of economizing, can be contained within the modern cosmopolitan ideal that we are all, somehow, of the same and that such sameness (any sameness) provides the knowable key to "harmony." Harmony certainly can be, but it cannot stand outside of the local ecologies (and economies) which give it a history and which seek to enact it as part of their own unfolding through time. It is not "pure," not of a "post-human" claim to something that is both human and transhistorical, though the history of religion anxiously and always advances that claim.

Within the anthropological and historical context which Toulmin so aptly describes, I wish to speak of an economy of hospitality, not of a transcendental idea of hospitality:

> Once the significance of "traditions" and "forms of life" is conceded, of course, one must abandon Descartes' move in the *Discourse on Method*, in which he required us to ignore traditional ideas in favour of ones whose "clarity and distinctness" to all reflective thinkers made them cultural universals. The questions, whether people in all cultures and epochs

have access to the same neutral "basic conceptual framework" equally; and, if so, to what extent and in what respects, is a question of fact that we can face with intellectual honesty only if we are ready to take anthropology and history seriously (Toulmin 1990: 189).

This puts us right at the doorstep of E.F. Schumacher's desire for the "welcoming" and the "harmony" which attaches to local economy, the small, hospitable economy where "neighbours" (human and nonhuman) interact. This stands in contrast to the "universalization" of something like a "global economy" which seeks saturated markets and assumes that somehow the value of efficient growth is exempt from the issues that would be raised by anthropological (or cultural) difference. In that global world, in E.F. Schumacher's words, "[N]either buyer nor seller is responsible for anything but himself" (Schumacher 1973: 44). Hospitality in this economy is at best a shaking of hands before the fighting begins; and, at worst, a luring into the hollowed-out lair of exploitive enactments of power by one over the other, even if such enactments yield a rather orgiastic self-aggrandizement of exhaustion, something like the heavy-breathing terminus of a sporting match. The fittest win, and winning is everything. This ethic piously announces itself in the name of "human nature," a term which stops conversation and seems to ignore the "better angels" of our natures, angels with equally valid claims to our putative "nature". It is just that the warrior-like appeals to our animalistic "natures" oriented toward survival/death seem to have dominated, but such is the way of phallocentric reason. [In any case, whatever our "natures" might be, as reflective and moral beings we always have the capacity to refuse those "natures"; they do not control us, nor is it necessarily desirable to act in a manner consistent with them.] Given the disharmonies and destructions of modern economics, we need, to recall with Toulmin, "a change of direction" in our intellectual attitudes. This essay now turns toward a few modest ideas about just such a change of direction.

Following Paul Ricoeur and many others, we can understand "welcoming" as a necessary, almost pre-ontic, condition without which the trust essential to *any* nonviolent mode of intersubjectivity (and speaking and listening are the best examples) would be impossible. At the outset, welcoming is a given. This welcoming, this originary hospitality exists *sans* justification, hospitality-as-hospitality, as the *there is* of hospitality, as the prelinguistic, pre-existence existing of a thing (often a human) outside of whatever use we may have our eyes on putting the thing to (use as economic, as social, as ethical, as political, as religious, as spiritual, as spoken; ad infinitum). "There is"—anonymous and impersonal, *without* our always construed "identities" and "desires" to deform it:

> Let us imagine all beings, things and persons, reverting to nothingness. One cannot put this return to nothingness outside of all events. But what of this nothingness itself? Something would happen, if only night and the silence of nothingness. This indeterminateness of this 'something is happening' is not the indeterminateness of a subject and does not refer to a substantive.... This impersonal, anonymous, yet inextinguishable 'consummation' of being, which murmurs in the depths of nothingness itself we shall designate by the term *there is*. The *there is,* inasmuch as it resists a personal form, is 'being in general' (Levinas 1989: 30).

To name it only because we have no choice but to name it if we are to write at all, "there is" stands at the door—un named, un known, un speakable, Ur elemental, immune to *our* urge to name, to know, to speak. The "there is" standing in front of us is the first and most profound moment of harmony. It is not a harmony derived from our language—*That is* rather than *There is,* the *naming* of things (even God)— not derived from our interests, rationalities, ethics, desires, and sociality or our "use" of the *there is*. The "there is" informs a hospitality that is *exactly opposite* from the hospitality of modern economics which always requires that we "know" the other at least well enough to know whether there is "something in this relationship for me." It is in this way that I will speak, with Levinas, of the "elemental," the precondition of the unconditional, the presence out of which imaginary moments of economy turn into real ones. Those moments emerge from an unjustified hospitality, a welcoming of that about which we know nothing and for which we have no "use," no "instruction" to give in the right and proper and good and true modalities of economic life together, no "principles," no "values," no "faith" that would tie the knot of harmony without recognizing the givenness (and the toxicity) of the rope and its reciprocity. In Jacques Derrida's terms, that harmony begins with a respect at the core of what is about to emerge as a "violence" of metaphysics, of the speaking of. … The widow, the orphan, the corpse simply stand in front of us to be either in or out of the hospitality that we "control" through the power of recognition (or killing). These are elemental things which we transform as economy and to which we attach economic ideas. Relatedly, and usually we are silent about this, they are also the things that make an economy even possible, and the things that "make economy possible" are to be protected from unbridled economy lest we lose the possibility of an economy at all.

3 The Elemental

3.1 *Economics and Enjoyment*

Within the scope of freedom, to be human is to enjoy the ability to transform one's world rather than to live in its givenness. We are *homo faber*, the maker of things, and that making begins with an economic imaginary in which the idea of living differently is made manifest in acting upon things in a manner which does, in fact, change the world. But the things on which we act are not, first, economic things; they become economic once we "economize" them, once we enact a kind of economic violence on them, once we come to kill what they are in their givenness. That is the very meaning of the economic as we turn things into enjoyment and alimentation. As John Sallis notes in commenting upon Levinas,

> … the very essence of enjoyment is "the transmutation of the other into the same." Thus, the introduction of enjoyment as the properly human relation to things serves, in the end, only to reconstitute, even if at a more concrete and comprehensive level, the determination of this relation [as] … to comport oneself to an object is to appropriate the object, that is, to

cancel its otherness and affirm its sameness with oneself. As in eating. As if, contrary to what Heidegger's analysis ... shows, things could not withhold themselves from appropriation. As do, for instance, the sky and the earth. And perhaps even everything elemental in—or at the limit of nature (Sallis 1998: 156).

To paraphrase Sallis as he continues, the key question then becomes whether the proper human relation to the world is reducible to enjoyment, to the economic? Can we suspend alterity—particularly the radical alterity of the "there is"—for the sake of interiority (ourselves and our enjoyment)? To answer yes is to relegate ethics to a branch of economics; ethical questions become questions simply of *how* we "enjoy" other things, how we find them "useful" (or not). To answer yes is to also embrace much of modern economic doctrine, where intersubjectivity is rationalised through the lens of a reciprocity of "self-interests," where mutual enjoyment is the only legitimate basis for relations with others, a "harmony" of a rather different (but dominant nonetheless) color, the color of moral monarchs who decide for themselves what is (and should be) enjoyable *for them, for now*. Rather paradoxically, it is as if we can instrumentalize others just as they instrumentalize us (there is much work to be done on this instrumentalization of the other who is the one who instrumentalizes us; but, that is for another time).

3.2 Enjoyment and the Elemental

In the sense formed above, economic life has a context that doubles back from enjoyment to the *l'il y a,* to the *there is*. Life is enjoyment. The doubling back is rather reflective inasmuch as we come to recognize that economic life; that is, our ability to transform, possess and enjoy, catches us in a hermeneutical circle whereby the things which we enjoy are interpretable as that which is *not* economic but as that which makes the very idea of actualising the economic imaginary possible. Though we transform (and enjoy) them, they are not "ours" so much as we are somehow "theirs," dependent at the very level of the possibility of being "dispossessed" from economy just as we work to "dispossess" the noneconomic thing of its noneconomicness. Life constantly remind us, in Levinas' words, that "Every relation or possession is situated within the nonpossessable, which envelops or contains without being able to be contained or enveloped. We call it the elemental" (Levinas 1961: 104, as cited in Sallis 1998: 159).

Our time is one in which the elemental conditions of the very possibility of a meaningful life are easily ignored as they are economized at their very origin in discourse. Neoliberalism is good at that, as was Marx in his own, more constructive, way. Everything is first and foremost a candidate for enjoyment (for economy). Enjoyment is of course at the core of living well, and of happiness. What I want to suggest is that the idea which motivates this paper—the idea of an economy of hospitality—depends upon a hermeneutical posture which recognizes and extends the obvious, an axiology grounded in economy dispossesses us of respect for our dependence on the elemental, on that which cannot be possessed, on that which "welcomes" us as an act of hospitality. That hospitality provides a grounding for how we might interpret ourselves as economic beings differently, more sustainably, more ethically, and more enjoyably. That same welcoming that we sense from the elemental is a welcoming that we ourselves might initiate toward the elemental, including other persons, the Earth, space, and time.

3.3 Air and the Earth in a Welcoming Economy

Air is a welcoming, a gift from the cosmos which is elemental to the very possibility of an economy. In the infinite range of the cosmos, a tiny, tiny little atmosphere offers us the possibility of life, a welcoming which we, mistakenly, treat not as elemental and permanent but as an economic commodity, as something to be "priced," not as something essential to the very possibility of living and thus of enjoyment. This economistic opportunity (and tragedy) is new in the scope of human time. This cosmic gift, this **elemental** welcoming beyond all welcomings, is not "ours," it simply "is," just as we, through it, are made possible. As Mitchell Verter states, "[I] think Buddhadasa (1996, p. 38) is correct in the claim that 'Throughout our lives, we have been thieves. We have been stealing things that exist naturally—in and belonging to nature—namely, the conditions *(sankhara)*. We have plundered them and taken them to be ourselves and our possessions'" (Verter 2013: 237). This elemental perspective is antithetical to the John Locke-inspired perspective of the Earth as placed under the dominion and control of humankind. That notion is central to modern economics which, because of its view of "value" as derived from an ontology of subjectivity, *necessarily* means that the axiology of economic life is not just anthropocentric but private—radically subjective—as well. Economists may gesture toward "other" dimensions of value, but rarely bother to point out if, and why, such "values" place limits on the "utility" of those elemental conditions on which the values are overlaid. That is not surprising; they can't possibly do that and hold on to the foundation of their economics—a "self" who values things because of the contribution they make to private "utility." The elemental here becomes just, in Levinas terms, a "second copy of the 'I'. As elemental, as nonpossessable even as we possess it, this sense of the Earth stands no longer as an object of my economic interests but as something "gifted," something not to be accounted for according to a value calculus of my creation, yet gifted in my enjoyment. Beyond that looms another, paradigmatically profound question— not my "use" of the gift but my responsibility/responsiveness to it. That is the key question, *for us*, now.

3.4 Breath as the First Welcoming from Others

[I read this week that canned air from the Blue Mountains of Australia is being sold in China.] Breathing, itself elemental, provides two metaphors for an economics of hospitality. The first is the total passivity, the displacement of control, of the substantive self in respiration:

> ... breathing is a transcendence in the form of opening up. It reveals all its meaning only in the relationship with the other, in the proximity of a neighbor, which is responsibility for him, substitution for him. That pneumatism is not nonbeing; it is disinterestedness, excluded middle of essence, besides being and nonbeing (Levinas 1981: 181)

Breathing provides a second metaphor, one of welcoming ourselves, others, and the Earth as historical neighbors. For the most part, we inhale the same air as all who have come before us, and we exhale that same air for both all who will come after and for the Earth on which we live. Breathing, that activity which is the uninterrupted fluidity of life, of knowing that who we are emerges from an emptiness of self, an empty space through which the air and the history of all who breathe and all who will breathe are who we are—the respiratory ontic at the origin of all experience. We don't "control" our breathing any more than we "control" the air. Neither is a "propertied" thing. That which is shared so intimately with the neighbour can only be a first moment of welcoming, of no wilful choice and of no coercion, of no distancing, no control, no reciprocity, no exchange, no expectation, no will, no promising just a vitality of the giftedness of that infinitesimal plate of possibility, of living, within the infinite scope of an otherwise unbreathable airless cosmos, that is, a hospitality within a universe of the inhospitable. We are, in short, always and already assimilated into an "involuntary" economy where self/other binaries dissolve into the very possibility of an economy to begin with. That is what gives "ethics", in its broadest sense, a place to govern economy.

3.5 Childbirth as a Welcoming Economy: The Bread from One's Own Mouth

Here I rely upon Emmanuel Levinas' use of maternity as a metaphor for the unwilled hospitality of the imperative that one, "take the bread from one's own mouth" in "welcoming" the radically other. This is a dangerous metaphor inasmuch as many have critiqued Levinas' use of the feminine and maternity as a continuation of the androcentric philosophical tradition (see Rosato 2012). Levinas writes:

> In proximity the absolutely other, the stranger whom I have "neither conceived nor given birth to," I already have on my arms, already bear, according to the Biblical formula, "in my breast as the nurse bears the nursling." He has no other place, is not autochtonous, is uprooted, without a country, not an inhabitant, exposed to the cold and the heat of the seasons. To be reduced to having recourse to me is the homelessness or strangeness of the neighbour. It is incumbent upon me (Levinas 1981, p. 91).

It is through this metaphor that an economics of intention; of, for example, pursing one's "interests," even at the cost of not caring for the other, yields to a pre-ethical, pre-choice, obligation that is neither willed nor intended; it is simply given. It is the obligation to a "pre-conscious" givenness of hospitality. In Levinas' terms, the "preoriginal here does not have to get its origin in the present of appearing" (Ibid.) In this sense, hospitality becomes, like air, elemental, pre-ontic.

Clearly, the crises *of* place of the contemporary refugee and her place within an economy—any economy—is quite salient today. The neoliberal West makes this a political and economic question already; that is, one of the primary "political" questions is economic—what can the "refugee" *take from* or *contribute to* an economy which putatively "belongs" to the locals of the West? That *taking from* or *contributing to* finds its moral compass in the same place that everything about Western economy finds it—in an axiology of contributions to the "self-interest" of those who are already inside. The refugee stands at the obstetric border to become either alive within our *oikos*, our "home," or exiled/dead.

3.6 The Hospitable Self: A Caring Before all Caring

Michel Foucault's work is relevant to any conception of the self inasmuch as his entire *oeuvre* is given over to how modern Western "disciplines," like economics, depend upon particular and contingent conceptions of the self, of what it means to be a person. These "identities" and "self-understandings" emerge from radically contingent "truth games" that carry with them ubiquitous and polymorphic dangers. Economic identity is one such contingent conception. As Foucault remarks:

> My objective for the past twenty-five years has been to sketch out a history of the different ways in our culture that humans develop knowledge about themselves: economics, biology, psychiatry, medicine, and penology. The main point is not to accept this knowledge at face value but to analyze these so-called sciences as very specific "truth games" related to specific techniques that human beings use to understand themselves" (Foucault 1988: 17–18).

One of the four major types of "technologies of the self" which Foucault engages is technologies of production, which "… permit us to produce, transform, or manipulate things" (Ibid., p. 18). These technologies of production have historically yielded conceptions like human nature as self-interested; human values as egocentric and limited to utility preferences for private wealth; the human as a maker of things, concern for others as derivative from a governing concern with the self; an egoistic conception of rationality, and many others. But the "hospitable" self responds to the needs of the other not in a hierarchical and economically "rational" way, the way of "me" but as an ontological or indeed preontological fact, a "given" antecedent to all moral, political, social, and economic judgment and thereby antecedent to all discourse and all other modes of intersubjectivity. The "productivity" of the Other is irrelevant here; and, once welcomed, this Other may or may not become "productive" within the economic modalities of technologies of the self. The Other is known by no name, of no known "benefit" to us. Her benefit is no part of the pre-ethical question. She is welcomed.

3.7 Sociality: The Intimacy of Hospitality and the Affairs of Ordinary Life

To return to childbirth, a hospitality of the self is, in certain systems of thought, first and pre-natal a welcoming of history, of the souls of others, into presence. That hospitality is present to the newborn child, as one who without even showing a face is greeted by a community, by those of family for example who stand available, stand ready, without reciprocity, to give the gift of identity, of consciousness, of knowing, understanding, doing, loving, dying, and on and on. In modern economics, this entire process is simply ignored—a self, fully formed in its interests, its preferences, its talents, and its value simply appears out of nowhere, out of metaphysics, to enter into the "phenomenal field" of an economy. There is no "accounting for" that self, nor for the responsibilities of others for this "other," no assumption about a "village" necessary to the child; there is just a bundle of preferences. The *easy* route is to just skip it; that is, just posit a self who just falls out of the sky, a moment of unspoken metaphysics wherein modern economics is indifferent to giving an account of a "self" at all. (Ironically, then, the economic self has no "identity," is indeed as McCloskey notes a "great stick of a character").

A hospitable society is one which renders distinctions like the home, the community, and the whole inhabited earth irrelevant to the question of welcoming, of hospitality to the most faceless of strangers; and, to note, that includes the variety of "facelessnesses" that cohere within the selves who are closest, most loved, most known to us—the weaknesses, the sicknesses, the poverty, the namelessness of the orphan, the deadliness of the suffering *of those with us*. To borrow a metaphor from Agnes Heller, our ethical task is to grow as many "umbilical cords" of meanings as we can, each of them, like the universe itself, coursing and crossing in infinite routes of possible connectedness. Sometimes connections don't appear, and sometimes they are disconnected. But, the very possibility of shared (or any other) meaning depends upon an originary posture of welcoming, a welcoming most obvious in the very act of speaking. That hospitality is the necessary originary moment of sociality, including economics.

3.8 Language: The Intersubjective Elemental

It is in and through the act of "saying" that the birth of ethics explodes on the scene. To "say" to an other or to listen to an other is to first recognize the profound claim of the other upon us; and, second, to enact the ethical relation of trust; that is, in "saying" and more importantly in "listening" one accepts, as an act of moral faith, that the originary moment is one of trust, and care, a "welcoming" of the significations of others as an act of hospitality. An economics of nothing but strategic discourse, a discourse of competition to "get one's way," renders this somewhat profane but is nonetheless just as dependent on welcoming as is any other discourse. That is simply to say that even in strategic communication there must reside some moral ontology of trust and welcoming. It is quite simply a necessary act of faith if communication is to be possible at all.

4 Of Other and for Other: The Very Possibility of a Self

It seems incontrovertible to me that we "selves," even those constricted "selves" assumed to be couriers of a panchrestic identity of their own "interests," would certainly and rationally prefer to always be welcomed wherever we go. More mildly, we usually detest the inhospitable *for ourselves* though we often "rationally" and perhaps "ethically" construct the inhospitable *for others*. We often "don't like them;" they have "nothing to contribute" to us. That lack of hospitality may be both moral and rational. Some—some who we *know*—are within lived experience socially and reasonably unwelcome, though their numbers are perhaps rightfully far fewer than we usually imagine with our jingoisms, racisms, sexisms, and numerous other social pathologies. But the question before this essay has to do with an ***originary*** sense of "other" which at the origins of intersubjectivity simply *is*, is *simply* Other, un(known) and who binds us to hospitality *sans* regard for all the things of practical life. As Redler, commenting upon Levinas, notes, this originary sense is preontological:

> The face of the Other is frailty and demand. It demands, it asks something of me, it is a request, an authority, though not a force. The deposition of the sovereign "I" of self-consciousness is its responsibility for the Other, whom I cannot humanly refuse. The ontological condition is undone in this human, spiritual or ethical uncondition (Redler 2000).

Seán Hand (1989) notes that, for Levinas and consistent with this view, we understand that "knowledge cannot take precedence over sociality" (p. 4). This is a key to understanding this paper. Modern economics is based on a gloss over the sociality necessary to the very idea of a self, irrespective of what sort of identity economics chooses to speak of (rational, self-interested, productive, etc.). From whence emerges this "self"? The sociality that "gifts" identity its content is missing, unarticulated. Most importantly, *any* sociality (and thus any "self") is completely dependent upon originary acts of hospitality, with a welcoming into the full scope of identity and community for that which is first (like me) faceless, without identity, and whose face now simply "at the door" exceeds all ideas of the other *in me*. That applies to each of us—rational self-interested beings perhaps—who would have no *cogito*, no identity economic or otherwise, no "interests" at all, without the unconditional, originary hospitality of others. It is only through the gift of hospitality from others that we escape the aporia of an economic self who cannot account for its self (its interest, knowledge, abilities, etc.). That giftedness is unconditional, largely unwilled, and emerges from all that is elemental to the very possibility of a liveable economy. The *for the self* is epiphenomenal to the *for the other;* in Hand's terms, "to be oneself is to be for the other," a clear inversion of the modern temporal order of economic subjectivity (and practicality). We *are* due to the unconditional hospitality of others.

5 Conclusion

I would suggest in closing this essay with a very practical view that the need for a post-rational economics is now evident and urgent. Having grounded modern economic thought in both the fictive notion of an autonomous self, driven by a hyper-subjective morality of self-interests as well as an instrumental view of the elemental, we find ourselves at a point where the "Received View" is betrayed by the facts and is indeed dangerous. Poverty and wealth are moving further apart, as, to recall Kant's comments on the power of money at the outset of this essay, "[T]hose who have a lot of [money] never fail to defend their interests" (Piketty 2014: 577). And, again recalling Kant, this "most reliable instrument of war" (that is, money) conceals its power and indeed its terror. The most formidable displacement of human beings in at least 70 years is now met not with hospitality but with an economism and egoism gone mad. Climate change is dismissed by so many of those who pull the levers of economic and political policy, and by some self-interested thugs who are "business leaders." They now pillage the Earth because it *pays* to do so and they *can* do so, just as they and their predecessors pillage other persons.

Much of our economic world is mad because it fails to recognize not just the morality at stake but the economics as well. What does it take to preserve an enjoyable and sustainable economy? With regard to economic being, each of us had nothing to contribute until we were welcomed through the hospitality of sociality. Our understandings clearly embrace the value of things other than their value as economic goods, though the powers-that-be are doing all that they can to crush the economics of caring for the arts, the humanities, and the social space for learning and experiencing such value. The "self" contains multitudes, good and goods far richer than we imagine.

Though eminent hospitality is offered here as an idea; and, though an economics of hospitality may seem unworkable to many, I would ask in turn, how "workable" is the current system? To approach each other hospitably seems less dangerous than approaching each other strategically, and an axiology of value, particularly human value, can do much better than this. Hospitality is also likely to be more economically productive, as the waste of human capacity through indifference and rejection seems far more "inefficient" than the alternative.

In an invigorating and much needed recent work, Rutger Bregman's *Utopia for Realists and How We Can Get There* reminds us to that new ideas can genuinely change the world—"Ideas, however outrageous, have changed the world, and they will again. 'Indeed,' wrote Keynes, 'the world is ruled by little else.'" (Bregman 2016, p. 250, reference is to Keynes 1936, last paragraph). My critics might view the ideas here as "utopian" and "unrealistic," a view which Bregman terms "… simply a shorthand way of saying they didn't fit the status quo" (Ibid., p. 262). Bregman continues with a piece of advice for all of us who might seek new ideas as practical horizons, horizons like what we imagine as an economy of hospitality:

> … cultivate a thicker skin. Don't let anyone tell you what's what. If we want to change the world, we need to be unrealistic, unreasonable, and impossible. Remember: those who called for the abolition of slavery, for suffrage for women, and for same-sex marriage were also once branded as lunatics. Until history proved them right (pp. 263–264).

This world does have many good things about it. The economic world, of a piece with the moral world, has ample more of those good things than modern economics can accommodate. Much of what is good about the world is either unknown to us or blocked from us. The realization of the "good things" of the world seem, to me, to be best served by hospitality, not by an originary question like "Of what use is the other to me (us)?" The point is *not* to offer some putative "solution" to modern economy. There is no "solution," if by that one means a "lever" which we just need to pull to set economy right. Things are much too complex for that, and the moral force of an economy grounded in global capitalism and self-interest will not simply roll over and die because of some "better" idea. Perhaps the "fine tuning" of our hospitality will breathe life into a practical, sustainable, but as yet imaginary key, a way of economic world-making, and a new kind of harmony:

> When the lute-tuner strikes the *kung* note [on one instrument], the *kung* note [on the other instrument] responds, when he plucks the *chiao* note [on one instrument], the *chiao* note [on the other instrument] vibrates. Now [let us assume that] someone changes the tuning of one string in such a way that it does not match any of the five notes, and by striking it sets all twenty-five strings resonating. In this case there has as yet been no differentiation as regards sound; it just happens that that [sound] which governs all musical notes has been evoked.
>
> From *Huai-Nan Tzu*, as cited in LeBlanc 1985.

References

Bregman, R. (2016). *Utopia for Realists and how we can get there* (trans: Manton, E.). London, Bloomsbury Publishing.
Buddhasa, B. (1996). *Mindfulness and breathing: A manual for serious beginners* (trans: Bhikku, S.). Somerville, MA: Wisdom Publications.
Caputo, J. (1987). *Radical hermeneutics: Repetition, deconstruction, and the hermeneutic project.* Bloomington and Indianapolis: Indiana University Press.

Foucault, M. (1988). Technologies of the self. In L. Martin, H. Gutman, & P. Hutton (Eds.), *Technologies of the self: A seminar with Michel Foucault* (pp. 16–49). Amherst, MA: The University of Massachusetts Press.
Hand, S. (1989). *The Levinas reader* (p. 1989). Oxford: Basil Blackwell Ltd.
Huai-Nan, T. (1985). As cited in Charles LeBlanc (trans.). *Huai-Nan Tzu: Philosophical synthesis in early Han thought: The idea of resonance (Kan-Ying) with a translation and analysis of chapter six*. Hong Kong: Hong Kong University Press.
Kant, I. (1795/1970). Perpetual peace. In D. Reiss (Ed.), *Kant's political writings* (pp. 93–130). Cambridge: Cambridge University Press.
Keynes, J. M. (1936). *The general theory of employment, interest and money*. London: MacMillan.
Leung, G., & Stone, M. (2009). Otherwise than hospitality: A disputation on the relation of ethics to law and politics. *Law and Critique, 20,* 193–206.
Levinas, E. (1961). *Totalité et Infine: Essai sur L'extériorité*. The Hague: Martinus Njhoff Publishers.
Levinas, E. (1981). *Otherwise than being or beyond essence* (trans: Lingis, A.). The Hague/Boston/London: Martinus Nijhoff Publishers.
Levinas, E. (1989). There is: Existence without existents. In S. Hand (Ed.), *The Levinas reader* (pp. 29–36). Oxford: Basil Blackwell.
Piketty, T. (2014). *Capital in the twenty-first century* (trans. Arthur Goldhammer). Cambridge, MA and London: The Belknap Press of Harvard University.
Redler, L. (2000). Open, empty and other. *Contemporary Buddhism, 1*(1), 77–89. doi:10.1081/14639940008573722.
Rosato, J. (2012). Woman as vulnerable self: The trope of maternity in Levinas's otherwise than being. *Hypatia, 27*(2), 348–365.
Sallis, J. (1998). Levinas and the elemental. *Research in phenomenology, 28*(1), 152–159.
Schumacher, E. (1973). *Small is beautiful: Economics as if people mattered*. New York: Harper & Row.
Taylor, C. (1996). Iris Murdoch and moral philosophy. In M. Antonaccio & W. Schweiker (Eds.), *Iris Murdoch and the search for human goodness* (pp. 3–28). Chicago and London: The University of Chicago Press.
Toulmin, S. (1990). *Cosmopolis: The hidden agenda of modernity*. New York: The Free Press.
Verter, M. (2013). The flow of the breath: Levinas mouth-to mouth with Buddhism. In F. Garrett & S. Mattice (Eds.), *Levinas and Asian thought* (pp. 225–239). Pittsburgh, PA: Duquesne University Press.

Author Biography

C. Edward Arrington, now retired, served as Professor of Accounting at Louisiana State University (US), The University of Strathclyde (UK), The University of North Carolina at Greensboro (US), and The University of Wollongong (Australia). He held earlier faculty positions at Arizona State University, Florida State University, and the University of Iowa. He received his DBA degree in Accounting from Florida State University, and both an MA and a BA in English from The University of Southern Mississippi. A former independent fellow of the National Endowment for the Humanities, Ed's work engages the humanities as a critical wedge to disrupt the dominance of scientistic perspectives on human disciplines like economics and accounting. His published work focuses on poststructural and critical theories and ideas as they enrich our understandings of ordinary life as it is lived under the weight of often oppressive systems. His current work includes study of the hermeneutic tensions within critical social theory, the dangers attached to an ethic of accountability; and, of particular import to this book, the idea of an economy of hospitality as an alternative to the rather "unwelcoming" economics that we practice today.

Chapter 21
Building the Harmony of Humanity

Stephen Hill

1 Introduction

1.1 Overview

'Listening to the Harmony of Humanity' returns to the observation by Hugh Mackay with which we started the Introduction in this book, "We used to live in a society, now we live in an economy." It has been my intention thereafter throughout each of my chapters to build a case that explores the dimensions of a *new* paradigm for economic-oriented action in order to reverse the capture of our humanity into subservience to the demands of an enormously powerful global economic regime.

This Chapter therefore builds on the two previous Addresses I delivered at the Kyoto 1 and 2 Symposia in 2014 and 2015 and the consequent Chaps. 2, 17 and 18 throughout this book. Together these works establish the societal platforms of communication and 'listening' particularly across cultures, and 'community', the *expression* of our humanity at a collective inter-subjective level where culture, meaning and transformative social force are created.

My present Chapter seeks to complete the picture—expanding to humanity as a whole, to seek ways of retuning the disharmony caused by the current economic paradigm, to build *harmony* at a wide societal level—using these earlier lessons. Humanity can only acquire its ultimate strength and resilience through *harmony* across apparently disharmonious cultures and meanings—sympathetic vibration, each (human) source stimulating its surroundings to vibrate on the same wavelength. At its highest level of cohesion, mutual empowerment and inspiration, humanity reaches its sacredness.

The need for radical change is urgent.

S. Hill (✉)
University of Wollongong, Wollongong, Australia
e-mail: sthill@uow.edu.au

As in a *Faustian Bargain* which I introduced in Chap. 2, society has achieved apparently unlimited knowledge and worldly pleasure as a result of the current economic paradigm. Since the late 18th Century, technologically fed economic growth has powered industrialization and development globally along with many social benefits. But it sold its soul to the (metaphorical) Devil, that is, bargained away *human* values and spirituality for the sake of economic efficiency and its guiding essential doctrine.

The Devil, as with Faust, claims back these benefits after a limited period of time. We have reached this limit as Kenneth Boulding foresaw and summarized in 1973: "Anyone who believes that exponential growth can go on forever within a finite world is either a madman or an economist." (Boulding 1973).

The limit however does not just lie in the physical world that sustains humanity, but in the progressive takeover of social and governmental action and choice by highly concentrated global economic interests as I demonstrated in Chap. 2. More insidiously, these very forces designed to 'liberate' economic freedom are increasingly paralyzing society's ability to respond.

The 'warming' of the environment has been accompanied with the 'freezing' of humanity's ability to respond.

1.2 An Agenda for Change

An Agenda for Change however will not come from directly confronting the global economic 'system', or for that matter the theory that guides it. They are too powerful. Instead, change has to come from exposing and attacking the weaknesses within the system, to work to assert human values *within* the system, and build practical actions based on our humanity from individual to global policy levels.

It is a core objective of our Kyoto Symposia Series and this Book to raise public consciousness of what to do. But change must come from the people as well as their influence over government action and policy.

My agenda for change therefore starts with exploring the 'grammar' that lies behind both its technological and economic expressions in everyday life, that is, the unseen background assumptions and hidden constraints. Specifically, technological *systems* have progressively surrounded and set the pattern of human interaction, culture and meanings, where the person is subject to the systems rather than free. Economic *systems* which both underscored and were produced by technological systems, and *progress*, are themselves based on the simplest but most destructive of human values, that is selfishness, greed, envy and, as Citizen Kane demanded in the Orson Wells movie ... more, MORE, **MORE***!* Price sets value, as value only exists in exchange, where money is the arbiter.

These underlying values of capitalist competition intrinsically result in continuous change. Joseph Schumpeter argued that innovations resulting from capitalist competition and its underlying values make old inventories, ideas, technologies, skills and equipment to become obsolete leading to perpetual change, what he describes as "a gale of creative destruction" (Schumpeter 1942). Consequently, "old industries mature, wither and die, often leaving jobless workers immiserated and filling whole regions with depressed ghost towns" (Vinsel 2016).

However this change is the surface phenomenon of the deeper grammar of the system that lies beneath, which remains intact but exercising an increasingly tight grip on social relationships, values and human enterprise. *Economic* value rules, the *systems grammar* it evokes increasingly over-ruling human community, now on a global scale. Joseph Schumpeter thus describes capitalism as a "gale of creative destruction" (Schumpeter 1942). Schumpeter ultimately saw the demise of capitalism as a consequence economically. My own position is that even more deeply, capitalism's increasingly pervasive *systems*—with their progressive enframement of human *community*, potentially destroy the very social processes from which recovery would be possible.[1]

As in psychiatric analysis, if we can change the *frame* we change its *expression* of humanity's values and life experience. This is my own *social-based* starting point for critique.

2 The Assumptions of Economic Knowledge

Even against the clear counter-evidence such as I demonstrated in Chap. 2, the assumption of the universal benefit of economic growth persists. It is the focus of the policies of virtually all governments of the world. What should be a 'means' to national society's benefit is regarded and presented, in economic growth, as an 'end'.

More philosophically or social analysis centered economic thought such as that provided by Amitya Sen, who traces, for example the relation between social identity and economics, is honored, as even by a Nobel Prize. But, the deeper philosophic presentations, such as of the significance of basic human values, remains outside most mainstream interest or journal acceptance (Sen 2007).

Instead, a 'scientific' approach has swept across the post-Keynesian economic doctrine. But, as Theodore Roszak reminds us, economics has only become scientific by becoming statistical, whilst,

> At the bottom of its statistics, sunk well out of sight, are so many sweeping assumptions about people like you and me – about our needs and motivations and the purpose we have given our lives. (Roszak 1973)

Econometrics rules. It is played out primarily by the US elite—Chicago, Berkley, Harvard and other elite campus economics aficionados. Specific relationships between economic analysis and single human values may well be identified as demonstrated, for example, in Chap. 14 of this book, Stomu Yamasht'a and

---

[1] I have developed this 'enframement' argument comprehensively in Hill (1988).

Tadashi Yagi's 'Trust Not Competition as Source of the Creative Economy', analysis that opens up useful social issues to explore.

However, in general, viewed through the eyes of a sociologist, the assumptions about people and society that underlie the equations of econometrics, remain, in general, too simple, atomistic within an intrinsically holistic social environment. The danger of research which does not also explore wider concerns as context for econometric conclusions about society, is presentation of a 'scientific' appearance of authority—using the expressions of mathematical certainty to represent the *unmathematically describable* complexity of a holistic person and their community relationships (Lutz 1990).

Whilst knowledge of the physical laws of the cosmos may well be represented in mathematical terms, knowledge of people, the meanings by which they live, their subjective engagement with the essential community within which they live and derive their own meaning ... *cannot* be reduced to mathematical equations. The phenomenon is *holistic*, not reducible to an atomistic analysis—without serious danger of error or caricature.

Indeed, whilst there is an increasing number of exceptions such as Doshisha University's Center for the Study of the Creative Economy, 'scientific' calculable economics in general has traditionally treated as either noise or factors to be eliminated, such human aspirations as for creativity, generosity, brotherly and sisterly cooperation, natural harmony, and self-transcendence which form the humanity of those millions who lie beneath the quantified statistical surface.

As Ed Arrington and Jere Francis observe, the discipline of Accounting has followed the same path ... "accounting—like so many other social sciences—has announced itself as a sociocratic discipline that claimed scientific knowledge and professional talent to administer human lives in the name of social efficiency and economic progress" (Arrington and Francis 1993).

This does not mean that disciplined and reproducible social analysis knowledge cannot exist. It simply means that alternative methodologies need to be applied.

Unfortunately, the 'system' produced by a *scientistic* approach to 'knowledge performance' now also rules in our institutional world.

Most universities, certainly in Australia, the academic environment within which I live, now apply KPI's, "Key Performance Indicators", to analysis of new knowledge performance, therefore career opportunity, and even to funding from government for their institution as a whole. KPIs favor mainstream journals and their citation *counts* (Hill and Turpin 1995; Hill et al. 1994).

Intrinsically the wider and more open and untargeted exploratory concept of knowledge is sidelined. Mainstream economics journals follow the mainstream of current ideas and seek to excel. Challenge to the fundamental paradigm by which both the mainstream journal survives with reputation, and the universities measure their performance, and therefore, their access to funding ... cannot be accepted.

The assumption persists that knowledge quality can be measured by mathematized indicators.

Our knowledge base for *response* to the current crisis with world economies is therefore increasingly captured in the same 'system' of abstraction. Humanity's problem is watching the world collapse around us, knowing we must do something, but not being able to act, caught as we are in the current 'grammar' of economic life, captured within the cherished capsule of self-centered interest, the *basis* of our current globalized economic world. Meanwhile the depth to which we may descend as a global society is largely obscured by the appearance of continuing economic benefit ... unfortunately however, to the few, not the majority. And it is these few who rule.

3 The Grammar of Daily Life

To explore the dynamic that powered this Faustian Bargain, I will go back to starting points in recent history, the invention of technologically driven capitalism.

In this we can see more clearly—in its early formative stage—what has become the technological and economic *'grammar'* of today.

As with grammar in language, we can assert and play with the ideas *within* our grammatical structure, but unless we ultimately confront the assumptions of the underlying grammar that lies behind and constrains our expression, we do not confront the cultural assumptions we are living by and which control our thinking and consciousness.

Our first entry point for change therefore is to be aware of and then attack the underlying 'grammar' of industrialization and the economic assumptions that lie unnoticed in the background, but 'frame' the 'language' of our daily experience.

3.1 Technological Knowledge 'Systems'

All human history is a product of the context from the past into which current action is cast.

Western 19th Century industrialization could not have occurred without the preceding conceptual leap of Francis Bacon two centuries earlier that declared reality and the dynamics that guided its properties could only be revealed as an 'objective' property, separated from the subjectivity of the person as witness—a total contradiction to the previous Greek understanding of the cosmos as in relation to the person, the observer (Hill 2010). This changed not only *the way of seeing* the world around us and how we could use it, but more fundamentally, the way we could intervene to produce together. The way was laid open for the entry two centuries later of the machine age, where production, as powered by Boulton and Watt's Steam Engine, allowed the factory system to operate one hundred times faster than could be achieved by individual labor and be seen as a legitimate and profitable form of human organization—*external* to the person (Hill 1988, p. 50).

Further, the 'idea' of technology as controlling 'system' for human labor and interaction rather than 'tool' of human purpose arose out of the previous pre-18th century concept of the automata as a play thing—when Jacques de Vaucanson displayed his quite magical 'mechanical duck' to the French Academy of Science in 1740, and, based on its ingenuity, was appointed by Cardinal Fleury, Prime Minister of France to be the Inspector Silks, then was responsible for several inventions behind the Jacquard Loom and early European factory 'system' production (Hill 1988, p. 47).

It was at this point in European history that 'technology' graduated from its previous role and value as a 'tool' under human control to an external 'system' into which human labor had to fit.

> The philosophy of Francis Bacon expounding the legitimacy of 'external' observation and action rather than person-centred philosophy, as with the ancient Greeks, undelay the transformation of the technological 'idea'.

> Legitimation and direction for industrialized development was subsequently provided by the idea developing within its own associated context of Adam Smith, and the early economists who pointed to a new individual interest-based concept of economic activity. Adam Smith published his economic work in 1776, 36 years after de Vaucanson's proud display of his mechanical duck, and just 22 years before Boulton and Watt brought the first steam-powered factory to life, and thereby heralded the Industrial Revolution.[2]

The new industrialized society of the West took off. It was spawned and subsequently fed by the continuing interaction between idea and applied (technological) knowledge that was now unconstrained by religious or traditional ideological impediments.

As with all social processes, the ways in which we must deal with and benefit from our environment of productive relations interacts with the meanings we attribute to it and to our interactions—our culture.

New systems of production and related interactions in the early 19th Century and beyond transformed the peoples' cultural environment, their world of meaning. In turn, the evolving 'systems' of economic production and advantage interacted with and were built on these cultural transformations.

> Ultimately, the progressive development of 'technological systems' – factories, railways, urbanization … interacted with and benefitted economically from the increasing anonymization of 'the subjective person'. Meanwhile, technological 'systems' increasingly invaded and set the context for daily life – how we worked together, where we lived, how we interacted socially, our identities, and the *meaning* of our engagement with wider society.

Over the last half-century, internet has followed the same dynamic of enframement.

> *Facebook* offers the appearance of personal communication, but counts friends in numbers contacted via computer.

---

[2]See, for example, Adam Smith, "It is not from the benevolence of the butcher, the brewer of the baker that we expect our dinner but from their regard to their own self-interest." (Smith 1973, 2008).

Dating sites reveal only what the person wishes to show, not their subjective reality, so a 50 year old male pedophile can pretend to be a young girl ... or, boy.

A 'charming' predator on the aged can pretend to be a caring investment advisor.

Meanwhile, 'truth' (or 'alternative facts') and, as under President Trump in the US, a fundamental shift in policy, can be conveyed within the 140 characters that a 'Tweet' makes possible via Internet.

At a global level, economic investments now are ruled by algorithms rather than 'too-slow' personal decision.

Our life world is surrounded, watched, measured, programmed, communicated, controlled increasingly by the command of internet-based *systems*.

Our future promises increasing take-over of human labor and care by robots – as I demonstrate in my Chap. 25.

The march of technological-economic systems therefore continues to *penetrate* and anonymize our personal and social life worlds. Just in the last 50 years—the period when I have been watching and writing about technology and society—the 'march' has turned into a 'race' ... with the subjective person and their intrinsic power disappearing under the fast-running anonymized crowd. (That 'other' race, the 'human race' is at stake! I will come back to this.)

In this context of increasing anonymity, the 'anonymized' person must find a way of symbolizing their *human* worth to both themselves and others—else their identity and reason to act loses all meaning and therefore purpose. One cannot rely on direct personal inter-subjectivity any more. Hence the frame for our culture and its meanings is increasingly being set from outside, from the 'systems' that surround us—and are now deeply penetrating into our subjective freedoms.

Increasingly, as industrial capitalism developed, a market-conscious economic elite recognized that, by *manipulating this cultural environment*, they could sell more products, make more money, and increase their own elite advantage. The ideological legitimation of self-interest based economics meant they did not even need to be sneaky about doing this. It worked. And the increasingly socially and psychologically informed marketing/advertising fellow-traveller to capitalist-based economics took off.

> Indeed, the social invention of fashion, associated obsolescence and consumer credit to empower spending powered escape from the economic downturn of the Great Depression of the early 1930s. Basically, the Western economic system had started to ground to a halt because production had reached its limit. The people were not purchasing enough. (Hill 1988, p. 190)

Social organization based on 'society' therefore steadily morphed over the last two-and-a-half centuries into an 'economy' as the guiding force for social relations, social values and objectives, government policy and popularity ... but, at the same time, increasing anonymization of the subjective person.

The 'subjective person' is sold, not lived. Image, fashion, relative status as represented in external symbols rule. Community in general has disappeared under suburbanized living arrangements—whilst 'objectified image' allows 'identity' within this system. An intrinsically vacuous sense of self—the feeding ground for further economic exploitation … and economic 'growth'.

Technological 'systems' now form the underlying 'grammar' within which daily life is lived—where anonymization and objectification rule, and the person is living *within* not independently of 'the system'. Human community is increasingly eroded and along with this, our ability to respond and take back control.

3.2 The Grammar of Economics—Premise for Paralysis to Change

Consequently, human beings have become "slaves to their own financial and corporate creations" (Schweiker 1993).

As Teri Shearer argues, whilst the world's trade and free markets continue to expand, the influence of highly centralized control in economic activity is increasingly pervasive over the wealth and sovereignty of nation states, the fortunes of corporate entities and the people they employ, and the social wellbeing of individuals.

> But at the same time that market forces exert a greater discipline over our individual and collective lives, we find ourselves increasingly unable to control, direct, confront, or challenge the system that supports them. (Shearer 2002)

More insidiously, the demand of the global economic marketplace on human values serves to extinguish the qualities we need in order to respond. Contained within the 'grammar' of the global economic system, as Maynard Keynes applauded,

> Economic progress is obtainable only if we employ those powerful human drives of selfishness, which religion and traditional wisdom universally call us to resist. The modern economy is propelled by a frenzy of greed and indulges in an orgy of envy, and these are not accidental features but the very causes of its expansionist success." (Schumacher 1973, p. 18)

To which E.F. Schumacher adds,

> If human vices: such as greed and envy are systematically cultivated, the inevitable result is nothing less than a collapse of intelligence. A man driven by greed or envy loses the power of seeing things as they really are, of seeing things in their roundness and wholeness, and his very successes become failures. If whole societies become infected by these vices, they may indeed achieve astonishing things but they are increasingly incapable of solving the most elementary problems of everyday existence. (Schumacher 1973, pp. 15–16)

Meanwhile, human faith and *trust* have no place in the marketplace. Legally enforceable contractual relations rule.

4 Recovery from the Devil's Bargain

Consequently, growth-based economics is not a solution, but the problem.

Our capture into the 'system' and co-opted disempowerment, are our most basic problems. Under the (metaphorical) Devil's command, the dynamics of a society we used to create and inhabit have been sacrificed to the rule of economic demand, as reflected in the quote we took from Hugh Mackay in the Introduction to this book, "We used to live in a Society. Now we live in an Economy." (Mackay 2007).

We have been fundamentally weakened as a society in our ability to respond.

As with exploring the grammar that lies behind language, or our culture, ability to affirm freedom within the economic-technological grammar of daily life requires we are first aware of the grammar's cage—most evident in watching the consequences of breaking the rules, or 'seeing' from 'the other way around'.

Our first action then is to *confront* these two grammars in all of our action, i.e.: reconstruct technologically-based and economic systems and design to fully include the autonomous human rather than require their acquiescence and subservience to economic 'efficiency' per se. To build and empower community at every level.

Directly related, we must recapture the intrinsic social power that can be delivered by a society that understands and is empowered.

5 Community and Harmony—Platform for Transformation

5.1 Capturing the Power of Community

There are so many implications of seeking to reverse domination of our human context by current economics doctrine and constraints. But they are all to do with the need to affirm, design for, set policy for, apply economic activity for … creation, strengthening, using for productive and social enterprise … immediate face-to-face relationships of *human community*. It is here that meaning is created, culture lives, people can be resilient and act collectively as a force for change. It is here that the highest of our spiritual values, our vision of our ultimate humanity, come to rest. Not out there in an abstract globalized world, but *here and now*.

Whilst the strength of human community lies in direct sharing, its breadth is, however, far wider.

As I demonstrated when speaking of 'global localism' in Chap. 18, whilst our personal identity and values are cast within the immediate subjective world to which birth introduces us, our 'humanity', that is connectedness with others, extends as far as our consciousness of others. Our humanity extends as far as the point where we draw boundaries around who is included and who is excluded from who *I* am.

There are powerful examples of how this wider humanity comes home within our contemporary globalized world.

> The first is former US President John Kennedy, visiting Berlin in the midst of the Cold War with the Soviet Union on June 26th 1963. The 'Wall' was in place, separating the German city between those free to express their ideas and participate without restriction in community life (West Berlin) and those who could not (East Berlin). Kennedy's speech evoked the clarion call,

> "Freedom is indivisible, and when one man is enslaved, all are not free." … "All free men, wherever they may live, are citizens of Berlin, and, therefore, as a free man, I take pride in the words 'Ich bin ein Berliner.'" "I am a Berliner" or citizen of Berlin. (Kennedy 2017)

> Kennedy eloquently expressed—in the context of a short speech, in just 140 characters, the length of a 'tweet' these days, the dominant communication style of current US President Trump, the solidarity of the world's people against the denial of freedom represented by the Wall. The statement was embraced and mirrored worldwide. 'Humanity' embraced inclusion.

> The second example derives from the writings of Alan Moorehead, major popular writer of 20th Century history, with books such as 'Gallipoli', 'The Blue Nile', 'African Trilogy', 'Eclipse', famous and applauded war correspondent during World War II. On visiting Belsen Concentration Camp amongst the first Allied troops to reach the Camp, Moorehead's reaction was:

> Why? Why? Why has it happened? This is timeless and the whole of the world and all mankind is involved in it. How did we let it happen? (Moyal 2014)

In the realpolitik of current national interests there will continue to be tests of the worthiness of immigration across national borders for the host nation and safety from covert operations by external terrorists. For the sake of our inclusion into the wider sphere of humanity however these tests must remain at the boundaries rather than the center of judgment of inclusion.

Canada, is taking the current lead in change towards 'inclusion'—committing almost one billion Canadian dollars in humanitarian, development and security assistance in response to the Syrian crisis, re-settling over 28,000 Syrian refugees urgently, a government program complemented by numerous private citizens providing personal support (Canada 2016).

This does not necessarily mean disadvantage for the host nation. OECD concluded in 2014 for example,

> Immigrants are thus neither a burden to the public purse nor are they a panacea for addressing fiscal challenges. In most countries, except in those with a large share of older migrants, migrants contribute more in taxes and social contributions than they receive in individual benefits. (OECD 2014)

Our 'humanity' therefore implies not only connectedness, but also responsibility for inclusion and protection—as with the values of the West Papuan tribes I spoke of in my Chap. 17. This strategic attitude enriches rather than threatens the local national society. Wherever we draw boundaries of exclusion there will be conflict and loss of our connectedness to our humanity.

The reality of globalization is that we are irrevocably moving towards a totally multicultural world. This is the humanity of our future whether we like it or not.

5.2 Harmony—Both Strategy and Objective

'Humanity' is therefore about HARMONY across apparently disharmonious cultures and meanings—sympathetic vibration, a source stimulating its surroundings to vibrate on the same wavelength.

Harmony represents integrity of connectedness—coherence or concord. At the level of cross-cultural expression we are likely to see the strains and comfort of 'others' harmonies differently according to our own domain of meaning. We have learnt to see and hear in a different way. As with the admission of others into our own world, we have to *see* more broadly, to *hear* more broadly, to *understand* more globally.

Harmony and Humanity are close partners.

> What constitutes our 'humanity' is not a global collection of alienated and disempowered individuals, spread in their billions across the globe, obeisant to, and separated by, the power, the economically inspired exploitation, and 'systems', of others, and the marginalization of all cultures and meanings apart from those who are in power.
>
> Rather, 'Humanity' is what we can be as a human race. Empowered, fulfilled individuals, whose own identity and meanings are deeply woven into caring and sharing with others across our separate cultural worlds. A people who have learnt from their past and can share across boundaries of apparent difference. A people who can live together, understand each other and accept difference. Who can live in peace through a continuous and collective quest for mutual empowerment and inner fulfillment.[3]

To quote Mahatma Gandhi:

> Our ability to reach unity in diversity will be the beauty and the test of our civilization (Gandhi 1925)

Immediately, we connect with the expression of our humanity in music and the affirmation of relationship beyond the words of consciousness, as demonstrated with our UNESCO programs with traumatized children or those caught in conflict, a subject of my Chap. 17. Indeed, the concept of *social* harmony dates back to ancient China, the Eastern Zhou Dynasty and the time of Confucius, when music, according to Confucian concepts was seen as a means to create balance within individuals, nature and society, along with social order (Wikipedia 2015).

Music fundamentally embodies communication beyond the constraints of the verbal connectedness that otherwise forms the limits of our consciousness. Our appreciation of music is however normally basically formed within the cultural world and expectations within which we have grown up.

Perhaps transcending this cultural envelope, there is, however, 'sacred music'. The music of our wider humanity. To explore our humanity we must move outside our protective domain of local meaning. This is what Stomu Yamash'ta, colleague in this Book and Musician is contributing to our understanding with his

---

[3]See Chap. 17, Stephen Hill. 'Sacred Silence: The Stillness of Listening to Humanity'.

inter-religious "On Zen" performances which have inspired our Kyoto Symposia and discussions, along with his written contributions within the Book.

Extending beyond the immediate pragmatic world, beyond the 'expected' harmonies of experience, reaching towards the human universal, sacred music—for those who *listen*—takes us to the limits of our humanity, to the organizing harmony of the universe to which we all belong. The depth of our humanity is what is 'sacred', entitled to reverence or respect.

6 An Agenda for Transformation: From Individual Action to Global Change

6.1 Listening

Here lies the starting point for transformation, 'listening'—across cultures and across difference, truly hearing others in *their* terms—the basis for all human sharing. As I concluded in my Chap. 17.

> "At the heart of *all* policy and organizational action is this single cultural idea … "sacred silence", suspending the 'noise' and 'listening', then applying this core vision to *everything* from negotiations with the political environment and shareholders to implementing CEO decisions right down to organizational detail"… "Focus on the meanings, the culture and its transformation need to be around a single clear vision."

Listening allows us to understand, to share. Action that follows is then fundamentally about cultural change, and cultural change is about transformation of meaning, a holistic phenomenon based on sharing a common all-encompassing vision.

6.2 Mindfulness

The Dalai Lama brings the qualities of oneself to bear on decision-making that follows by drawing on Buddhist philosophy, introducing '*mindfulness*' to action. He is quite specifically relating this to management within a business organization—effective leadership (Dalai Lama and Muyzenberg 2008).

Based on 'the six perfections—generosity, ethical discipline, patience, enthusiastic effort, concentration and wisdom (Dalai Lama and Muyzenberg 2008, p. 36), he demonstrates the power of wider consciousness, embodied in "Right View":

> 'Right View' consists of two parts: the decision-making process and the three values or concepts that have to be respected in every decision … the goal is not to respond from a self-centered point of view but from the point of view of the company and all the people and organizations affected by the decision. (Dalai Lama and Muyzenberg 2008, p. 18).

The 'three values' join cause and effect, action and consequence within 'Dependent Origination', and comprise,

Intention – at minimum, the action causes minimal harm to others;

State of mind – recognize the origination of any negative effects on the mind, such as defensiveness or anger, and be able to return the mind to a calm, collected, and concentrated state; and,

Effects of the decision – to be beneficial (at the end of the decision-making process). (Dalai Lama and Muyzenberg 2008, p. 19)

Mindfulness requires training and discipline in order to develop the capability to distinguish feelings, perceptions and consciousness, and to be able to consider different perspectives ... to *listen*.

As the Dalai Lama concludes:

With Right View you will examine your intentions and make sure that you consider the consequences of your actions on yourself, your organization, and others, and will do your utmost to avoid harm and increase the wellbeing of others. You will also be able to reduce the negative thoughts and emotions that lead to wrong decisions and unhappiness for yourself and others. (Dalai Lama and Muyzenberg 2008, p. 185)

Immediately 'listening' and 'mindfulness' demonstrate the first line of attack against the 'grammar' of global economics.

As Schumacher demonstrates, the underlying economic thinking, or 'grammar' (my term not his), is that the marketplace equates everything with everything else—through the mechanism of *price* that allows them to be exchangeable ...

"If economic thinking pervades the whole of society, even simple non-economic values like beauty, health, or cleanliness can survive only if they prove to be 'economic'." ... "To the extent that economic thinking is based on the market, it takes the sacredness out of life, because there can be nothing sacred about something that has a price." (Schumacher 1973, p. 20)

Relating listening and mindfulness to the problematique of this Chapter, i.e.: reversing the valence of economy over society as the objective of action, policy is both explicit and implicit.

In the case of economic policy for example, impact on local culture and community empowerment is implied and needs to be taken into account in planning *all* economic strategy. Promotion of economic growth, for example, is *not* an end in itself, but must be examined for consequent *benefits* to community, equity and empowerment.

In the case of social policy, local community engagement and understanding must be included quite explicitly. Policy needs to be based on listening and community engagement that is genuinely open rather than directed to secure an outcome that government has already decided. Bring 'sacred silence' and 'mindfulness' into governance.

Mindfulness extends however to *all* humanity. That *is* our human community, as demonstrated in the earlier comments by President Kennedy and Allan Moorehead.

All of us, but particularly those in positions of power, need to maintain this wider awareness in taking actions or generating policy that may have significantly wider consequences.

6.3 Expansion from the Local to Global Localism

As I presented in my Chap. 18, my position here is based on the power of individual action, and the power of inter-subjective *community*. For *meaning* is constructed within our 'world within reach', in subjective relations to others, in socially producing together, in direct sharing ... in our *local world. Our culture is not produced elsewhere!*[4]

Wider social empowerment starts in the same place, within our local world. For it is here that *humanity*'s strength resides.

"Our quest is then to build what I call 'global localism', capturing the power of the local where meaning is constituted, our immediate and subjective relationships and culture, and exploding our connectedness at this human level across the global human world."[5]

Concentrated attention on helping the local community to transform itself, can then be turned into wider application through using this community as base for networking, training, mentoring and inspiring others. In my Chap. 18, I presented a detailed case study of our UNESCO work with the community of the Indonesian village of Banjarsari to demonstrate action that works.

The *human* focus is at local level. Its application is *global*—hence, global localism. It is the power of community that is then determining economic advantage.

7 Changing the Dynamics of Economic Action: From Growth to Nutritive Stasis

7.1 The 'Other Way Round'

Theodore Roszak observes in his Introduction to E.F. Schumacher's book, 'Small Is Beautiful',

> What sort of science is it that must, for the sake of its predictive success, hope and pray that people will never be their better selves, but always be greedy social idiots with nothing finer to do than getting and spending, getting and spending? It is as Schumacher tells us: 'when

---

[4]See Chap. 18, Footnote 10.
[5]See Chap. 18, and in particular, Footnote 11.

the available "spiritual space" is not filled by some higher motivations, then it will be necessarily be filled by something lower – by the small, mean, calculating attitude to life which is rationalized in the economic calculus. (Roszak 1973)

If instead, we look at the market place from 'the other way around', that is, from the perspective of human needs and aspirations, there are a number of strategies that we can capture.

We then *must* confront the reality that world society has reached its global economic limits to sustainability. All action needs to be focused on translating an economy based on limitless growth to one based on serving the real needs of the society it is supposed to serve, replacing growth with nutritive stasis.

7.2   Introducing Human Values into the Market Place

Exercise the power of 'listening' and 'mindfulness' at the level of individual decision makers and political actors. Promote the concept and teaching of mindfulness in all Business School and Company Training programs. Not only is this going to lead to a wider social base for decisions, but also to a more effective and sustainable organization. Build 'mindfulness' as the new OK approach to good management.

Develop public awareness programs to capture the attention of consumers as individuals within the market system towards consumption according to carefully assessed need rather than image. Again, exercise 'mindfulness'.

Promote economic strategies that follow a mindful objective, i.e.:

Using Public Pressure: Large corporations, including those involved in mining, forest exploitation, use of labor in poor countries, are usually very sensitive to public moral pressure. Their 'bottom line' of shareholder investment is at stake. Already there is an increasingly large number of examples where public pressure has led to transformation of enterprise to less exploitative, more ecologically and labor sensitive production, and support for the *local* community economy, e.g.: with coffee products, community sensitive mining and forestry.

To quote Jared Diamond:

Businesses have changed when the public came to expect and require different behavior, to reward businesses for behavior that the public wanted, and to make things difficult for businesses practicing behaviors that the public didn't want. I predict that in the future, just as in the past, changes in public attitudes will be essential for changes in businesses' environmental practices. (Diamond 2005)

Social Business: Models are now developing of 'social business', i.e.: companies producing products for the poor in return for which costs are paid but not excessive profits—as one component of moral business, i.e.: economics *for* the community.

> Muhammad Yunus, Nobel Prize winning founder of the Grameen Bank, is a champion. The principle is for business enterprise to be "a non-loss, non-dividend company designed to address a social objective". One example is 'Grameen-Adidas. Yunus recognized that shoes are a necessary object for people in poor countries, e.g.: to avoid hook worm and injury. He convinced Adidas to produce the first shoe accessible to the poor, at less than one Euro in cost. (Yunus 2007) He is expanding the same idea to other large corporations.

Cooperative Business Organizations: Already cooperative non-for-profit, but shared advantage organisations have made major inroads into the international market place, for example, in banking and insurance.

> The United Nations estimates from data from 145 countries that there are over 2.6 million Cooperatives, comprising a billion memberships and clients. Holding $(US)20 trillion in assets, together the Cooperatives generated over $(US)2.98 trillion in annual revenue, making the 'Cooperatives Economy' larger than the economy of France and only just behind that of Germany, the fifth largest national economy in the world. (Grace et al. 2014)

Within a cooperative, there is greater scope for mindfulness as the clients are also the decision makers on management, whilst excessive profits and exploitation are not supported.

Ecological Sensitivity: Whilst pressure from the public and shareholders will impact on corporate policies and consciousness, enforcing the necessary action to slow the rate of carbon and methane escape into the atmosphere, to conserve un-renewable resources and energy production, and to care for threatened fauna and flora species, requires action at government policy level. I will come to this shortly.

Social Media: The power of social media can be capitalized on to popularize and force change to happen, such as with 'moral' pressure and development of 'social business'. Social media can be good at getting an idea up for general support—even high impact promotion, such as with 'flash crowds' and for support of the *local* economy and alleviation of inequality through crowd funding. As examples crowd funding is now being used to help the poor (Benevolent Net), to fund disaster relief (Global Giving), and, in particular, to assist entrepreneurs in developing country communities to whom banks will not give start-up loans (African Entrepreneurs).

Transformation of Vision: Cultural change of an organization, a community, or a public value, requires transformation of their organizing *vision*.

There are two key elements: a single clear vision communicated and implemented with strong leadership, and application of this vision to *everything*—from the CEO's or leader's own actions right down to the workers who may clean the toilets. Monica Barone, CEO of the City of Sydney Council in Australia, introduced a values-based leadership,

> "Our values guide us in how we work, interact with each other and make decisions. They help us deliver on the City of Sydney's purpose to 'lead, govern and serve'"

> ... the vision of 'attention always to community service' and it swept through the entire Council with significant consequences.[6]

Two specific applications follow:

> The transformation of vision in the ultimate purposes of *government policy*, i.e.: to put culture and social/local community at the center of *all* policy, including very specifically, economic.

> The transformation of all *design*, in particular of physical, social and organizational space and boundaries that encourages community and its creativity as a whole – for creativity is essential to escape the habit of current practice.

7.3 Capturing the Power of Humanity's Spirituality

The final issue we must address—both at local community level and globally, is capturing the power of humanity's spirituality. As I observed earlier in this Chapter, humanity is what we *can* be as a human race;

> Empowered, fulfilled individuals, whose own identity and meanings are deeply woven into caring and sharing with others across our separate cultural worlds. A people who have learnt from their past and can share across boundaries of apparent difference. A people who can live together, understand each other and accept difference. Who can live in peace through a continuous and collective quest for mutual empowerment and inner fulfillment.

My point now is that we *must* capitalize on this resource, this highest power of human capital, to have the strength to fight for our human survival.

Power lies in collective community vision of spirituality, holding as reference point and 'frame' for human action and commitment, humanity's highest values of connectedness, empathy and vision—expressed in 'community' not economic demand. The lesson is a return to humanity's plan for a future that is ruled by the human-centered principles expressed in Ancient Greek Philosophy and Society ... and spirituality—a fundamental lesson from history (Hill 2010, 1988, pp. 37–39).

Stomu Yamash'ta is showing us the way—both in practice, such as through his *On-Zen* performances, and in his philosophy—expressed elsewhere in this Book.

Our Book, "The Kyoto Manifesto for Global Economics" delivers a challenging program of change—turning the frame of our world community from 'economics'

---

[6]Presented in an interactive lecture to the University of Wollongong Summer School on community empowerment which John Hatton and I developed—in cooperation with Glenn Mitchell in 2009–2010. For Council strategy see City of Sydney (2011). The Lectures are available on the University of Wollongong website.

to 'society, humanity and spirituality'. Ultimately we otherwise confront major threat to our very survival beyond the 21st Century. Re-asserting human 'community' lies at the core of transformation. Setting some starting points for the framework of action is a very daunting task and at every step along the way I can see a whole corridor of further research we need to explore. There is much further to go.

Ultimately the task of our Kyoto Symposium Series and Book is however to take the first steps along the path towards a world guided by spiritual wisdom that *cares* —to build these values into 'community' at all levels, and into global economic activity and demand.

It is unlikely to be the theorists who make this happen. Change will come from the people capturing the power of their humanity.

What is blazing in neon lights of clarity as a guide to this path is my main message,

Humanity needs a new global economics!

And we are most likely to discover this 'new global economics' through,

Listening to and Building the Harmony of Humanity

References

African Entrepreneurs Turning to Crowd funding|Africa|DW.COM. http://www.dw.com/en/african-entrepreneurs-turning-to-crowdfunding/a-17830318.
Arrington, C. E., & Francis, J. (1993). Accounting as a human practice: The appeal of other voices. *Accounting Organization and Society, 18*(2/3), 105–106.
Benevolent Net. http://www.benevolent.net/in.html.
Boulding, K. E. (1973). Attributed in: United States Congress, House (1973), Energy, Reorganization Act of 1973: Hearings. Ninety-third Congress, first session on H.R. 11510, p. 248.
Canada. (2016). Global affairs. Canada's response to the conflict in Syria. October 26th. http://www.international.gc.ca/development-developpement/humanitarian_response-situations_crises/syria-syrie.aspx?lang=eng.
City of Sydney. (2011). Councils, community and you. http://www.cityofsydney.nsw.gov.au/council/about-council/careers/our-vision-and-values.
Dalai Lama, His Holiness, & Van Den Muyzenberg, L. (2008). *The Leader's way—Business, Buddhism and happiness in an interconnected world*. London, Boston: Nicholas Brearley Publishing.
Diamond, J. (2005). *Collapse: How societies choose to fail or succeed* (Chapter 15). New York: Penguin. http://www.jareddiamond.org/Jared_Diamond/Collapse.html.
Gandhi, Mahatma. (1925). *Young India*. January 8th. Notable quotes: Mahatma Gandhi quotes. http://www.notable-quotes.com/g/gandhi_mahatma.html.
Global Giving. http://www.globalgiving.org.
Grace, Dave & Associates. (2014). *Measuring the size and scope of the cooperative economy: Results of the 2014 global census on co-operatives, for the United Nations Secretariat*. Department of Social Affairs, Division of Social Policy and Development, April.
Hill, S. (1988). *The tragedy of technology—Human liberation versus domination in the late twentieth century*. London: Pluto Press.

Hill, S. (2010). Ways of seeing—Science and technology within their cultural setting. In A. Jain (Ed.), P. Chatapadhyaya (Series Ed.), *Civilization, Philosophy, Science and Culture*: Volume in Series. *Science and the public. Section: 'science in society'* (pp. 252–280). New Delhi: Sage.

Hill, S., Murphy, P., et al. (1994). *National Board of Employment, Education and Training. 'Study of quantitative indicators of research'*. Commissioned Report No. 27 prepared by the Centre for Research Policy. AGPS, Canberra. May.

Hill, S., & Turpin, T. (1995). Cultures in collision: The emergence of a new localism in academic research (Chapter 7). In M. Strathern (Ed.), *Shifting Contexts*: Vol. 1. *The uses of knowledge: Global and local relations. The reshaping of anthropology*. London: Routledge.

Kennedy, J. F. (2017). *Transcript. 'Ich bin ein Berliner' Speech* (June 26, 1963). Charlottesville, VA: The Miller Center, University of Virginia. http://millercenter.org/president/speeches/speech-3376.

Lutz, M. A. (1990). Social Economics in a humanistic perspective. In M. A. Lutz (Ed.), *Social economics: Retrospect and prospect* (pp. 235–268). Boston/Dordrecht/London: Kluwer Academic Publishers.

Mackay, H. (2007). *Advance Australia ... Where?* Australia: Hachett (used in radio interviews when promoting the Advance Australia book: personal communication).

Moyal, Ann. (2014). *A woman of influence—Science, men & history* (p. 81). Crawley, Western Australia: University of Western Australia Press.

OECD. (2014). Migrant policy debates. p. 2. www.oecd.org/migration.

Roszak, T. (1973). Introduction. In *Schumacher*. See also http://www/ditext.com/schumacher.

Schumacher, E. F. (1973). *Small is beautiful—Economics as if people mattered*. New York: Harper and Row.

Schumpeter, J. (1942). *Capitalism, socialism and democracy*. New York: George Allen and Unwin.

Schweiker, W. (1993). Accounting for ourselves: Accounting practice and discourse of ethics. *Accounting, Organizations and Society, 18*(2/3), 231–252.

Sen, A. (2007). *Identity and violence: The Illusion of Destiny*. India: Penguin Books.

Shearer, T. (2002). Ethics and accountability: From the for-itself to the for-the-other. *Accounting, Organizations and Society, 27*, 541–573 (p. 541).

Smith, A. (1973). *An inquiry into the nature and causes of the wealth of nations (1776)*. Pilgrim Classics.

Smith, A. (2008). The concise encyclopedia of economics. Library of Economics and Liberty. Para I.2.2. http://www.econlib.org/library/Enc/bios/Smith.html.

Vinsel, L. (2016). Silicon folly: The pitfalls of innovation policy. *The Saturday Paper*. August 27th. https://thesaturdaypaper.com.au/opinion/topic/2016/08/27/silicon-folloy-the-pitfalls-of-innovation-policy.

Wikipedia. (2015). Harmonious society, (October 14th). pp. 1–2. https://en.wikipedia.org/wiki/HarmoniousSociety.

Yunus, M. (2007). *Creating a world without poverty*. Google Books. Also quoted in www.destinationchangemakers.com/discover/definitions/social-business.

Chapter 22
The Future of Capitalism and the Islamic Economy

Shinsuke Nagaoka

1 Introduction

"Abuses of socialism and illusions of capitalism," replied the late Professor Hirofumi Uzawa, a leading economist in Japan, to Pope John Paul II in 1991, when he was asked to describe briefly the problems facing the contemporary world. This dialogue was held when the Pope proposed a new encyclical to celebrate the 100th anniversary of the encyclical of the *Rerum Novarum* issued by Pope Leo XIII just one hundred years before. *Rerum Novarum* is known as the first foundational text on modern Catholic social teaching, and it called for improving the status of workers suffering at the bottom of the capitalist hierarchy. Pope Leo XIII identified the main problems of the world at the time as "the abuses of capitalism and illusions of socialism." Uzawa offered his own version for the new encyclical issued a hundred years later.[1]

This episode clearly implies that people are still maintaining some hope that capitalism can bring about a better life than other economic systems, although modern history proves that capitalism has brought about various adverse effects. Can capitalism respond to such a faint hope? Or is it just an illusion, as Uzawa pointed out? In the past, active discussions were held over the potential and limitations of capitalism. This was because an epic laboratory for socialism called the Soviet Union existed, and the choice of "capitalism or socialism" was a real and

---

[1]This episode is referred to in Uzawa (1993).

S. Nagaoka (✉)
Graduate School of Asian and African Area Studies, Kyoto University, Kyoto, Japan
e-mail: nagaoka@asafas.kyoto-u.ac.jp

imminent issue for the global population. The discussions formed a common arena where both those who supported capitalism and those who opposed it could participate.

The collapse of the Soviet Union at the end of the twentieth century made us realize that socialism is just an illusion, and capitalism succeeded in occupying the position of being a unique hegemonic economic system. However, capitalism continues to produce many adverse effects and evils, and its negative impact merely increases. For example, during the global financial crisis triggered by the bankruptcy of Lehman Brothers in 2008, high-finance capitalism was subjected to intense criticism. To respond to this, various ideas, theories, and movements are being developed in order to overcome the negative impacts and evils of capitalism while aiming for a new alternative economic system. We can observe such kinds of alternative trends in various places and at various levels from ideas linked to the genealogy of Marxism, as represented by Michael Hardt and Antonio Negri's "multitude" (Hardt and Negri 2004), to grassroots movements such as local currency and fair trade.

However, current discussion on the pros and cons of capitalism has not formed a common arena as in the past. Modern economics, which has continued to support capitalism in theory as its greatest advocate, is trying to find a better form of capitalism in its academic framework. However, there is not necessarily a direct connection with the anti-capitalist movement or alternative systems. Modern economics rarely focuses on discussions that do not share its theoretical assumptions, while anti-capitalist or alternative movements deny the usefulness of modern economics by negatively labeling it "market fundamentalism." Despite a shared recognition that current capitalism is at a crossroads, the argument over its future has been highly segmented.

Under such circumstances, there is still a common discussion arena over the future of capitalism where heated discussion has been exchanged among participants from various positions, including modern economics and anti-capitalist or alternative movements. That is the Islamic economy and its leading practice, called Islamic finance. Islamic finance came into the spotlight globally during the latest global financial crisis as an alternative financial system that can overcome the problems of existing capitalist financial systems. Islamic finance is often considered an anti-capitalist movement only for Muslims because of the religious term, Islam. However, the practice of Islamic finance, or more broadly the idea of an Islamic economy, cannot fit in the existing framework of anti-capitalism. There, we can find useful wisdom for conceiving the future of capitalism from a perspective beyond the differences between pro and anti conflicts, or among religious beliefs. This chapter focuses on some practices of the Islamic economy, especially Islamic finance, and clarifies the wisdom of the Islamic economy behind these practices. Then chapter will consider what we can learn from this teaching for a better future.

2 The Revival of the Islamic Economy and the Rise of Islamic Finance

2.1 The Rapid Growth of Islamic Finance

A rapid quantitative growth clearly demonstrates the vibrancy of Islamic finance in the twenty-first century. Figure 1 shows the growth trend for the total global assets of the Islamic banking sector from 1997 to 2012. While no clear trend can be observed before 2002, a clear positive growth trend is observable thereafter. By the end of 2012, the global assets of the Islamic banking sector totaled USD1.2 trillion (IFSB 2014: 14).

Geographic diffusion, one of the characteristics of Islamic finance in the twenty-first century, is contributing to its rapid quantitative growth. There are more than 600 financial institutions providing Islamic financial services in over 50 countries. Figure 2 clearly shows that the commercial practice of Islamic finance is ongoing, not only in Muslim-majority countries from North Africa to Southeast Asia, but also in other regions such as Western countries and sub-Saharan Africa.

Figure 3 shows the distribution of the Islamic banking sector's assets by county in 2012, explicitly demonstrating that Malaysia and the Gulf countries stand together as the global hub of Islamic finance. Malaysia has the largest share, while the Gulf countries (Saudi Arabia, UAE, Kuwait, Bahrain, and Qatar) comprise more than half (56.3%) of the world total. The Islamic financial industry in these countries also has a significant share (over 20%) of the banking sector (see Fig. 4), as it does in other countries such as Bangladesh and Iraq. Although Islamic finance's share of global banking assets is less than 1% (MGI 2008), its share in

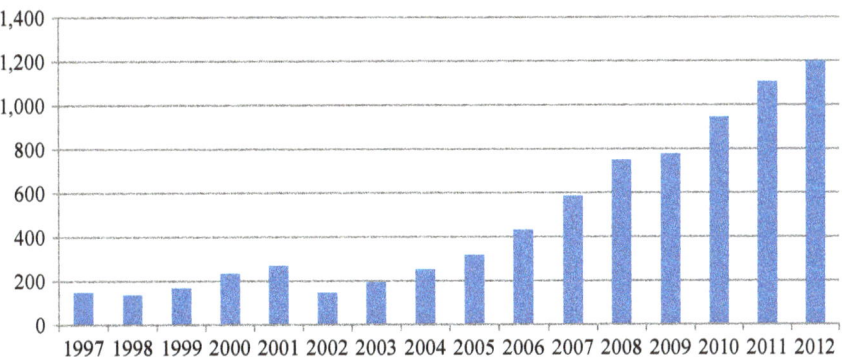

Fig. 1 Growth trend of the total global assets of the Islamic banking sector. *Source* Prepared by the author, data based on CIBAFI (General Council for Islamic Banking and Financial Institutions), ISFB (Islamic Financial Services Board) and TheCityUK

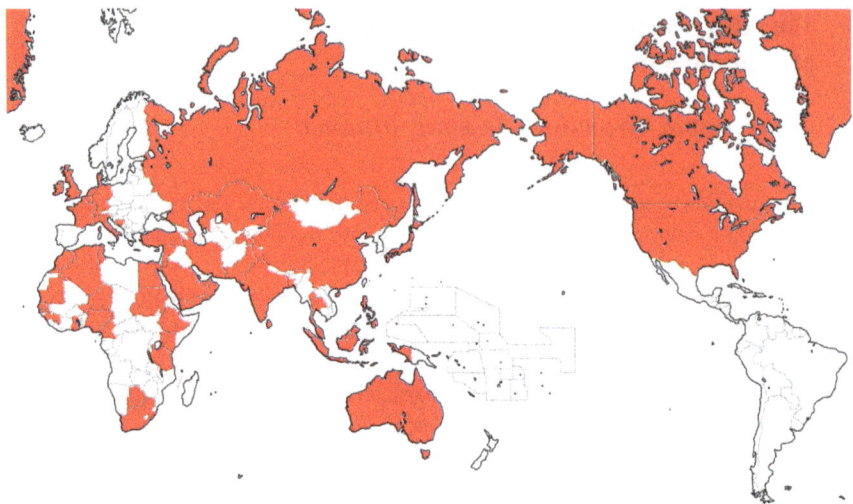

Fig. 2 Geographic diffusion of Islamic finance. *Source* Prepared by the author

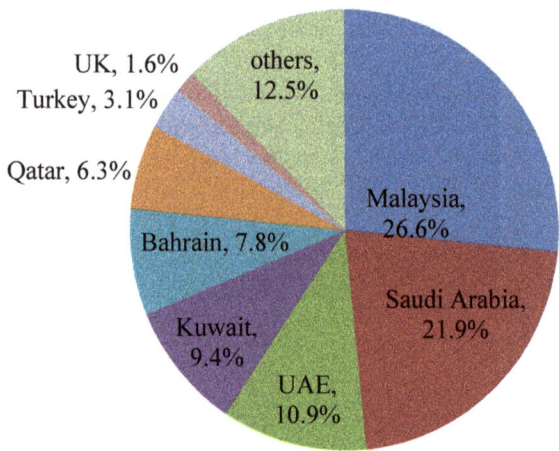

Fig. 3 Asset distribution of the Islamic banking sector by county in 2012. *Source* Prepared by the author, after deducting Iran from TheCityUK (2013: 1)

Asian countries (excluding East Asia) is around 15%, according to the author's own calculation. In the global financial market, some Western banks such as HSBC, Standard Chartered and Citibank have entered the Islamic financial market and provide a wide variety of services (banking, investing, funding, and insurance) to both Muslims and non-Muslims. This current situation implies that Islamic finance is now playing a significant role not only in the development of the financial sector of emerging countries but also in the global financial system.

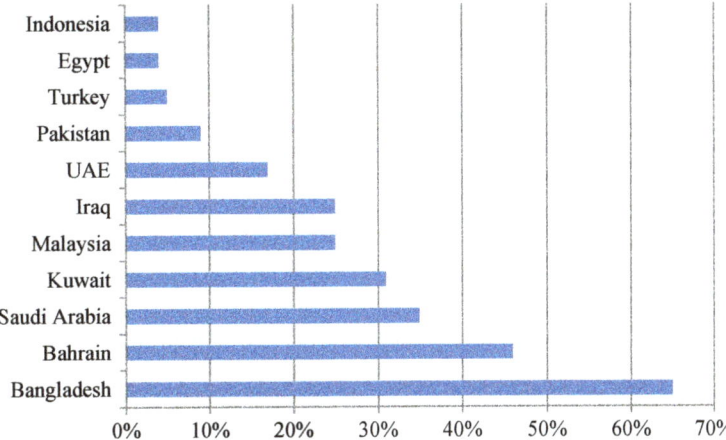

Fig. 4 Market shares of Islamic banks in selected countries. *Source* Prepared by the author, based on TheCityUK (2012: 4)

2.2 The First Steps of Islamic Finance

It was in the middle of the twentieth century that the practice of Islamic finance was initially conceived. Muslim countries, under the strong influence of the post-colonial West, sought not only political independence but also economic independence. As one of these movements, the Islamic revival movement, which aims to struggle against Western hegemony by reconstructing a modern civilization based on the idea of Islam, succeeded in forming a global network beyond existing nation states and national economies.

One lecture held at Aligarh Muslim University in British India in 1941 offered a major opportunity to create Islamic finance. The lecture was given by Abū al-A'lā Maudūdī, who was the founder of the largest Islamic organization in Asia, named Jamā'at-e-Islāmī. In his lecture, entitled "The Economic Problem of Man and Its Islamic Solution," he pointed out various adverse effects created by capitalism and called for a fair economy and society based on the idea of Islam.[2] He also mentioned a desirable Islamic financial system, where lenders and borrowers work together and share profit and loss, in order to defeat the existing financial capitalism where a privileged few monopolize wealth based on unearned income, such as banking interest. This idea is exactly the basic concept of Islamic financial products. Therefore, Maudūdī is called "the father of Islamic finance."

The followers of Maudūdī began making his idea fit for practical use. Not only Islamic scholars but also a wide variety of people such as economists and bankers participated in this magnificent project, and their dream and intellectual task was to

---

[2] An English translation of the lecture was later published (Maudoodi 1947).

establish a distinctive financial system based on the idea of Islam, something totally different from conventional systems. Therefore, they were vividly aware of both capitalism and socialism, which were in the ascendant at that time. For example, Anwar Iqbal Qureshi in Pakistan was one of the earliest economists who worked on the project, and he published a book entitled *Islam and the Theory of Islam* (originally published in English in 1946 [Qureshi 1946], later translated into Urdu). As he mentioned in his book, the book's title is a tribute to John Maynard Keynes's *General Theory of Employment, Interest, and Money* which was published ten years earlier. *Iqtiṣādunā* (originally published in Arabic in 1968 [al-Ṣadr 1968], retitled *Our Economy* in its English translation) written by Muḥammad Bāqir Ṣadr, who was one of the prominent Shi'ite scholars, is conscious of Karl Marx's *Capital*, and argues for the characteristics of an Islamic economic system by comparing capitalism and communism. These examples imply that scholars did not ignore the existing financial system but learned its strengths and advantages, and then utilized this knowledge in forming the Islamic financial system.

2.3 The Rediscovery and Renovation of Islamic Civilization

In addition to the use of knowledge of the existing financial system, the pioneers of Islamic finance rediscovered the legacy of Islamic civilization in the pre-modern era, and renovated it so that it meets the demands of the modern world. *Muḍāraba* (مضاربة), which is a representative financial product in Islamic finance and also mentioned by Maudūdī, was originally used as a funding instrument in distant trade in the medieval Islamic world. In the original form of *muḍāraba*, a local merchant trusts his funds to a trade merchant, and the latter merchant conducts business in various cities. The profit and loss from the business are then shared by both merchants.

Figure 5 shows a modern *muḍāraba* scheme as a financial instrument in Islamic finance after modern renovation. Each customer (depositor) puts his/her money into a bank account. Unlike deposits in conventional banks, his/her money is not deposited in the account but invested in the bank's business (*muḍāraba* A). The bank then lends the funds to borrowers (companies and individuals). Again the money is not lent, but invested in their businesses (*muḍāraba* B). The profit and loss from the businesses are firstly shared by the bank and the borrowers (*muḍāraba* B), and then the bank's quota is shared by the bank and the depositors, which implies that the depositors take a risk of losing their principal (*muḍāraba* A).

We can find two renovated mechanisms in modern *muḍāraba* which did not appear in the original form of *muḍāraba*. One is that two different *muḍāraba*s (*muḍāraba* A and B) are used between customers and a bank, and between the bank and borrowers, and they are linked via the bank. Another is that the bank is entrusted with funds from multiple customers, and also entrusts the collected funds to more than one borrower. These two renovations make it possible to replace some functions of conventional finance by pooling funds at a mediator between the two

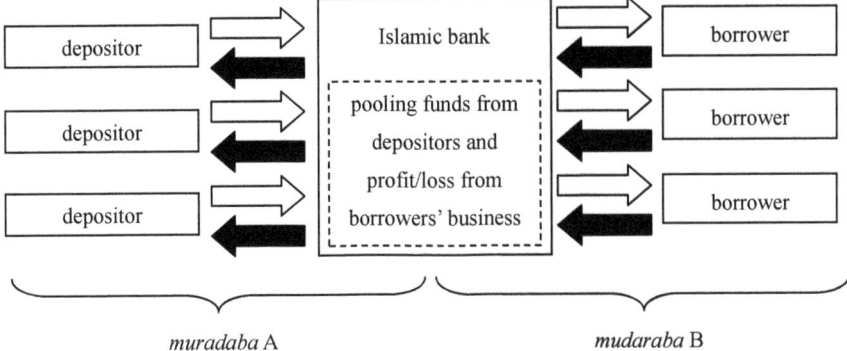

Fig. 5 Bank *mudaraba* renovated in the modern world. *Source* Prepared by the author

muḍārabas, that is, a bank. For example, even if one borrower fails in business and reports a loss, the bank can compensate the loss by the profits generated from other borrowers. Thus the bank can lower the credit risk, which is a very basic function of conventional finance.

2.4 The Development of Islamic Finance

It was in the 1970s that the ideas of Islamic finance such as those mentioned above were put into practical use. In particular, 1975 is called "the year of Islamic finance": this is because two Islamic banks commenced operations. One was the Islamic Development Bank (IDB, the head office is in Jeddah, Saudi Arabia) which was established by the member countries of the Organisation of Islamic Conference (OIC, recently renamed the Organisation of Islamic Cooperation). The IDB contributes to the economic development of Muslim countries by financing infrastructure construction, trade promotion and small and medium enterprises. Another was the world's first commercial Islamic Bank, Dubai Islamic Bank in the United Arab Emirates (see Fig. 6). Both banks provided financial services based on the mechanisms of Islamic finance that had been cultivated so far. Thereafter, the establishment of commercial Islamic banks continued one after another in the Middle East (Kuwait, Sudan, Egypt, Jordan, and Bahrain) in the 1970s.

There are two reasons for the boom of Islamic finance in the 1970s. One is the existence of enormous amounts of petrodollar flowing into the Middle East. During the 1973 Arab–Israeli War, the Arab oil-producing countries took measures to reduce or turn off oil supplies to Israel-friendly countries. As a result, crude oil prices soared, and enormous quantities of petrodollar flowed into the Arab oil-producing countries. With this abundant petrodollar, it was possible for these countries to establish Islamic banks with sufficient capital.

Fig. 6 Head office of Dubai Islamic Bank in the United Arab Emirates. *Source* Prepared by the author

Another reason is the penetration of the Islamic revival movement. After the Second World War, Arab nationalism had great influence among the people in Arab countries. However, Arab nationalism waned due to the Arab countries' losses in the Six-Day War in 1967, and the Islamic revival movement gained popularity as an alternative to Arab nationalism. It involved not only political slogans but also faithful economic activities being upheld among the people. In fact, in the Middle East there were many people who were allergic to the banks originally introduced by the West. In Saudi Arabia, where the king is appointed the title of "the guardian of the two holy cities of Islam (Makka [Mecca], Madīna [Medina])," the institution which plays the role of the country's central bank is called a "monetary agency," and avoids the designation "bank." Those who did not like to use a bank protected their wealth instead by buying gold and its processed items (bracelets and necklaces). However, as Islamic banks appeared, these people rushed to them to deposit their money. Some Islamic banks do not use the designation *"bank* (بنك),*"* which means bank in Arabic, but use another word, *"maṣrif* (مصرف),*"* which also means bank in Arabic, in order to take such disapproval into account (see Fig. 7). The word *maṣrif* derives from money-changers (*ṣarrāf*, صرّاف) who have been popular in the Islamic world since pre-modern times.

Upon their success in the 1970s, two Saudi-based Islamic banking groups (DMI Group, Albaraka Group) actively began overseas expansion in the 1980s. These banks not only extended to Muslim countries but also advanced into Europe, in cities such as London, Geneva, and Luxembourg. This was a direct first contact with Islamic finance for Europe. The main purpose was asset management for wealthy Muslims residing in Europe. However, since Islamic finance was providing services with a different mechanism from conventional systems, it was a puzzle for European financial authorities. In the UK, tighter regulations on deposit reserves in 1991 made it difficult for Islamic banks to provide *muḍāraba*, which resulted in the withdrawal of Albaraka bank from the UK market.

Fig. 7 An example of using the designation of *"maṣrif"* in Arabic at Sharjah Islamic Bank in the United Arab Emirates. *Source* Prepared by the author

In the 1980s, the practice of Islamic finance was launched in Southeast Asia. In 1983 Southeast Asia's first commercial Islamic bank (Bank Islam Malaysia) started operations. After that the Malaysian government strongly promoted Islamic finance. In particular, after Prime Minister Mahathir bin Mohamad announced the long-term development initiative project "Vision 2020 (Wawasan 2020 in Malay)" in 1991, which advocates economic development in an Islamic way, Islamic finance became likely to play a central role as a driving engine (see Fig. 8). Under the support of the government, various infrastructure and epoch-making products were developed in Malaysia, which supported the rapid growth of Islamic finance in the 2000s as mentioned above.

Fig. 8 Combination of mosque and Petronas Twin Towers in Kuala Lumpur as a symbol of Malaysian way of economic development. *Source* Prepared by the author

3 Islam and Capitalism

3.1 *Capitalism Revisited*

What is the distinctive economic idea of Islam behind such practicing of Islamic finance? To consider the characteristics of Islamic economic ideas, we need to review the characteristics of the most familiar economic system to us, that is, capitalism. The term "capitalism" has been understood in a very diverse manner depending on how it is analyzed: whether it is a historical concept or used to overcome the limits of arguments.

Those scholars such as Karatani (2005) and Iwai (1994) who try to grasp the commonality of the dynamism of capital in the various economic systems which have existed define capitalism as the principle of the infinite growth of capital which is achieved by the endless pursuit of profit, which in turn relies on some sort of "difference system." When we understand capitalism in this way, economic activities or systems which can be regarded as capitalist can be found in various places from the earliest times, as Karl Marx implicitly pointed out with his metaphor of the ubiquitous gods in Epicurean theology.

Historically, several types of capitalism have been observed which are distinguished by the characteristics of a difference system. Merchant capitalism can be defined as a profit-making system which utilizes the difference of prices between two geographically distant points; industrial capitalism utilizes the difference of labor wages and raw-material prices between urban and rural areas; financial capitalism earns a profit by making use of the difference in our preferences between the present and future. Although the characteristics of the difference system vary across the ages, the characteristic of the dynamism of capital which seeks profit from some sort of difference remains unchanged.

Meanwhile, the dynamism of capital penetrated into all the economic domains in Europe after the industrial revolution in the second half of the eighteenth century. Penetration of the dynamism of capital refers to the process whereby every item of capital, such as land, labor, and money, is incorporated into difference systems, namely, markets. Thereafter, this penetration was globalized by swallowing up not only Europe but also peripheral areas, and this resulted in the emergence of so-called global capitalism. From the standpoint of emphasizing the penetration of the dynamism of capital, the term capitalism can be understood as a modern phenomenon which is clearly distinguished from economic systems of the previous era.

3.2 *The Islamic Economy as Super Capitalism*

The religion of Islam was born in Makka on the Arabian Peninsula in the seventh century. Believers aim to reach heaven through the judgment of God (*Allāh*, الله) at the end of the world. In order to fulfill this purpose, they must live according to

God's instructions in this world. The guiding principle of their lives is the scripture of the *Qur'ān* (القرآن, Koran). The *Qur'ān* is a book which compiles God's revelations received by the Prophet Muhammad over the 23 years from 610 to 632 AD. All Muslims firstly refer to the *Qur'ān* about everything in their daily lives. This means that everything related to the lives of believers must be posted in the *Qur'ān*. Therefore, the *Qur'ān* includes not only religious acts such as worship, fasting, and pilgrimage, but also social acts such as marriage, divorce, and inheritance.

Economic activity is also included in the *Qur'ān*. The ideal form of economic activity for believers is abundantly mentioned. Therefore, it is necessary first to unravel this in order to know the ideas and specific rules of the Islamic economy. Here are some of the clauses of the *Qur'ān* regarding economic activities[3]:

God has allowed trade... (2: 275)

You who believe, do not wrongfully consume each other's wealth but trade by mutual consent. (4: 29)

...if you keep up the prayer, pay the prescribed alms, believe in My messengers and support them, and lend God a good loan, I will wipe out your sins and admit you into Gardens graced with flowing streams (5: 12)

First of all, before the content review, it is surprising that the *Qur'ān* describes the ideas of the economy directly and clearly. Moreover, these ideas, such as the acceptance of business, the denial of waste, and the promotion of work and charity, are quite understandable in our modern sense. If we boldly try to apply the analytical concept of economics to them, these ideas can be explained as "profit maximization through market exchange," "optimal allocation of resources," "labor theory of value," and "income redistribution."

Generally, we imagine that any economic idea in religion is rather ascetic, and emphasizes a future profit rather than one in the present world, which is contrary to so-called economic rationality. Even in Max Weber's *The Protestant Ethic and the Spirit of Capitalism* (*Die protestantische Ethik und der Geist des Kapitalismus*, 1904–05), Weber argues that the profit motive of the Protestant dissenters is not driven by a direct doctrine on encouraging business but is an incidental product arising as a result of encouraging faith and labor in the present world in order to gain confirmation that God will save them.

In comparison, the profit motive in Islam is quite simple and reasonable in the sense that it directly connects to salvation in the hereafter: the more profit in this world, the greater the possibility of being saved in the afterlife. Such a philosophy of affirming wealth in this world is quite compatible with the universal principle of capitalism which seeks the infinite growth of capital by the endless pursuit of profit. Therefore, it can be concluded that Islam is more familiar with capitalism than Protestantism.

---

[3]English translation of the *Qur'ān* is based on (*The Qur'an* 2004) with some author's revisions.

3.3 Religion as a Constraint?

While having the philosophy of affirming wealth in this world, there are some clauses where the *Qur'ān* imposes certain restrictions on the acquisition of profits:

> Whatever you lend out in *ribā* to gain value through other people's wealth will not increase in God's eyes... (30: 39)
>
> You who believe, do not consume *ribā*, doubled and redoubled. (3: 130)
>
> You who believe, beware of God: give up any outstanding dues from *ribā*, if you are true believers. (2: 278)
>
> But those who take *ribā* will rise up on the Day of Resurrection like someone tormented by Satan's touch. ... God has ... forbidden *ribā*. (2: 275)
>
> for taking *ribā* when they had been forbidden to do so; and for wrongfully devouring other people's property. For those of them that reject the truth we have prepared an agonizing torment. (4: 161)

All of the above clauses forbid what is called "*ribā* (ربا)." *Ribā* has been understood in Islamic jurisprudence as pointing to some inequality of exchange. In the context of Islamic finance, this term is defined as being equivalent to bank interest. This is why Islamic finance is well known as "interest-free finance." Modern *muḍāraba* as mentioned above was invented as a financial product to avoid predetermined bank interest, which is not permitted. Certainly, in *muḍāraba*, the gain received by depositors and bankers is prescribed by the profit which depends on the success or failure of the borrowers' business, and one cannot receive a predetermined bank interest automatically obtained regardless of the success or failure of the banks' investments.

> In addition to the prohibition of *ribā*, there is another kind of clause which imposes certain restrictions on the acquisition of profits:
>
> Keep up the prayer, pay the prescribed *zakāt*, and bow down [to God] with those who bow. (2: 43)

This clause mentions "*zakāt* (زكاة)." *Zakāt* is a kind of charity, and it is counted as one of Muslims' most important obligatory acts. It is the practice of returning a certain percentage of the wealth earned in a year to God. The proportion of payments varies according to the type of wealth, for example, 10% of agricultural products, 1 calf for 30 cows, and 1 sheep for 40 sheep. As for gold, silver, and cash, 2.5% of annual earnings should be returned. Collection and distribution of *zakāt* are managed by professional institutions (*zakāt* institutions) and mosques on behalf of God. They distribute the collected *zakāt* to eight targets (the poor, the needy, *zakāt* administrators, converts to Islam, slaves released, debtors, those who strive for God, and travelers) as prescribed in the *Qur'ān*. Such a mechanism implies that *zakāt* takes on the role of income redistribution through God. This is similar to tax systems in our sense. However, in contrast to tax systems where taxpayers can benefit from public services, *zakāt* payers receive no benefit in this world. In return, they receive full benefit in the afterlife. Therefore, in this world wealth flows unilaterally from payers to beneficiaries through God.

In addition to *zakāt*, there are other charitable systems in Islam such as *ṣadaqa* (صدقة) and *waqf* (وقف). *Ṣadaqa* is an act of returning wealth to God voluntarily; there is no limit on the amount of payment. *Waqf* is a mechanism for donating a private property, where the income from the property is used for a special purpose (charity and family support) specified by the donor. Historically, these systems were prevalent throughout the majority of the Islamic world in the pre-modern era, and they played an important role in the Islamic economy and society. After the advent of the modern era, these practices declined in many regions owing to westernization and secularization. But recently new attempts to revitalize these systems can be found in several Muslim countries. There, governments, companies, and NGOs re-evaluate their roles for the sustainable development of the Muslim community, as well as for tapping new markets for the Islamic economy. Islamic finance is also included in this revival movement of traditional charitable systems in Islam.

The prohibition of *ribā* and obligation of *zakāt* mentioned above seem like constraint conditions for acquiring wealth in the world. In other words, in Islam, Muslims are not allowed to simply pursue infinitely the profits of this world, and wealth acquisition is only justified in Islam by fulfilling these conditions. If we apply this mechanism in Islam to the preceding argument over capitalism, it can be explained that the Islamic economy does tolerate the universal principle of capitalism which seeks the infinite growth of capital by the endless pursuit of profit. On the other hand, a religious belief in Islam imposes certain constraints on this principle, and refuses the penetration of the dynamism of capital. Then, is this explanation really correct? While keeping such reservations in mind, this chapter next looks at cases of Islamic finance and Islamic charitable systems.

4 The Wisdom of the Islamic Economy

4.1 Wealth or Islamic Legitimacy?

A mechanism that imposes certain constraints on the dynamism of capital can be found in the practice of Islamic finance. In other words, the profit in Islamic finance is only justified by properly performing interest-free transactions and paying *zakāt*, although profit seeking through the provision of financial services is highly encouraged, as is conventional finance. However, the application of these constraints is not necessarily uniform. Some Islamic banks apply more relaxed or realistic constraints, focusing on competitiveness with conventional banks. Others apply more rigid or idealistic constraints with an emphasis on Islamic legitimacy. Therefore, there is still a heated debate over how to balance the capitalist motive of acquiring wealth and Islamic legitimacy which imposes constraints. This debate leads to the diversity in the practice of Islamic finance.

Some people have sought to devise financial instruments that emphasize the acquisition of more profit under an interest-free constraint. "*Bay' dayn* (بيع دين)," developed in Malaysia in the 1990s, was one such method, and sparked a debate over its Islamic legitimacy.[4]

Generally, the money lent out by a bank is recorded as a claimable asset until its maturity date. The more the bank lends out, the more the claimable asset will increase. Under such circumstances, there may not be sufficient cash on hand in the bank when the depositor requests a withdrawal. In conventional finance, an interbank market is available in preparation for such a situation. In the interbank market, banks with sufficient cash on hand can lend money at low interest rates to banks with insufficient cash. However, in Islamic finance, such an interbank market has not been developed because of the prohibition of *ribā* (interest). Therefore, Islamic banks need to suppress lending and keep excess cash on hand in preparation for withdrawal by depositors. This situation results in an inefficient management of Islamic banks, and has been a hindrance to the development of Islamic finance for a long time.

Bay' dayn, developed by Malaysia, was a groundbreaking idea to create cash on hand by selling receivables to other banks at a discount price. For example, when bank A, holding a receivable of 100 US dollars due to *muḍāraba* lending, needs immediate cash, bank A can obtain cash by selling the receivable to bank B for 90 US dollars. Bank B can earn a profit (10 US dollars) from this *bay'dayn* transaction by receiving 100 US dollars from the original borrower at the maturity date.

This instrument was welcomed as an alternative for Islamic finance to the interbank market, and thus as enhancing the competitiveness of Islamic finance, that is, generating more wealth. However, some scholars and bankers cast doubt on the legitimacy of *bay' dayn* because the transaction of selling receivables at a discount price may conflict with the prohibition of *ribā*. Certainly, the term "bank interest" is not found anywhere in this transaction. However, critics say the above bank B's profit is the same as the interest in conventional loans, because bank B earns a profit by doing nothing except for two monetary transactions: just buying a receivable at a discount price and collecting a claim at the original price. Scholars and bankers defending *bay' dayn* refute the criticism as follows. Bank B becomes a new partner of the existing *muḍāraba* on behalf of bank A, and the items sold by bank A include not only the mere receivables but also the right to engage in business by *muḍāraba*. This right is an entity like a commodity; therefore, both banks can trade this entity at any price they can agree on, which is compliant with the idea of Islamic jurisprudence.

As cases of Islamic charity, the flow of wealth in *zakāt* is unilateral from payers to beneficiaries through God as mentioned above. In this flow, collected *zakāt* must be immediately distributed to beneficiaries. However, recently some *zakāt* institutions have started to consider investing collected *zakāt* in Islamic finance. If *zakāt* investment is successfully managed, the institutions can provide greater distribution

---

[4]For more details on the debate on *bay' dayn*, see Nagaoka (2007).

Fig. 9 An example of renovated *waqf* properties in Singapore. *Source* Prepared by the author

to the beneficiaries. As another example from *waqf*, some institutions collaborating with Islamic banks have started establishing new *waqf* properties or renovating old *waqf* properties by receiving funds from investors. Here, the original donors of *waqf* are investors. Generally, donors of *waqf* cannot receive any benefits from the property, but investors can receive dividends from this newly introduced scheme. If *waqf* properties are successfully managed, investors can enjoy a greater return while at the same time beneficiaries can receive a greater distribution (see Fig. 9).[5]

These new attempts in *zakāt* and *waqf* are contrary to the principle of the flow of wealth. In *zakāt* investment, there is a risk of reducing the principal of the collected fund in the event of mismanagement. This implies that humans intervene in the wealth redistribution process conducted by God. With the *waqf* fund, there is a reverse flow of wealth from *waqf* to donors by distributing the profit from *waqf* properties to investors, which is contrary to the original flow of wealth in *waqf* from donors to beneficiaries. Some scholars criticize these modifications because they make Islamic religious acts "money games." Others defend these modifications because they can contribute to revitalizing these traditional charitable systems. This implies a compatibility of faith and the pursuit of wealth.

---

[5]For more details on renovation of *waqf* properties in Singapore, see Nagaoka (2016).

4.2 Islamic Finance as an Embedded System

What do these cases imply? From a simple point of view, as explained many times, there is a conflict of two opposing views: whether to emphasize the capitalist character of acquiring wealth or to emphasize Islamic legitimacy by imposing constraints on the dynamism of capital. However, both parties share one common platform. It is that only the profit from a real economy is Islamically justified.

In the case of *bay' dayn*, critics argue that the buyer of receivables earns a profit by doing nothing except for two monetary transactions and they then conclude that such transactions are similar to interest-based loans. This suggests that if the profit could arise from non-monetary transactions, *bay' dayn* could be acceptable for them. It turns out that the logic of this suggestion can be shared with the argument of those who permit *bay' dayn*: that the core of the transactions is a trade of the right to engage in real business by *muḍāraba*. In the case of the *waqf* fund, those who are critical of fundraising using Islamic finance are concerned that it may be a money game, in other words, a transaction that diverges substantially. On the other hand, its proponents emphasize the investments in substantive business of *waqf* properties.

From the above discussion, a logical structure as an inherent characteristic of the Islamic economy emerges, clearly distinguishing between real transactions and monetary transactions. This structure can also be derived from the structure of the prohibition of *ribā*, which indicates the essence of a prohibition that we cannot clarify by merely identifying it as bank interest. Table 1 shows the structure of the prohibition of *ribā*, summarizing a perpetual discussion since the seventh century in its simplest form.

The prohibition of *ribā* becomes an issue in two aspects of transactions. One is the quantity of goods exchanged, and the other is the timing of the exchange. Regarding the quantity of goods, the unequal exchange of monetary goods is prohibited; otherwise, any exchange is permitted if the parties agree. Regarding the timing of the exchange, a deferred exchange of monetary goods is in principle prohibited except for an exchange between difference goods (gold and silver); otherwise, any deferred exchange is permitted.

Under such a structure of the prohibition of *ribā*, what kind of form can be provided if you want to operate money lending? As a matter of first priority, the moneylending must be a credit transaction. A moneylender that you borrow money from and return it to immediately is meaningless. Furthermore, as long as it is a commercial business, some kind of profit is necessary. If we consider these conditions, transactions can be only available on the righthand column of the table. In

Table 1 Structure of the prohibition of *riba*

	Monetary goods	Other goods
Unequal exchange	No	Yes
Deferred exchange	No (partially Yes)	Yes

Source Prepared by the author

other words, it is the essential meaning of this prohibition of *ribā* that, even if you lend money, it is impossible to do business without actually involving real goods in transactions. Therefore, the unique characteristic of the Islamic economy, in which only the profits from substantive transactions are Islamically justified, was concealed in the structure of the prohibition of *ribā* long before this characteristic was revealed in the debate on Islamic finance today. This chapter calls this characteristic of the Islamic economy a "financial system embedded into the real economy," which is a paraphrase of Karl Polanyi's famous term: an "economy embedded into society" (Polanyi 1977: 53).

Furthermore, where is the boundary between real and monetary transactions? In contemporary financial transactions, as mentioned above, it is not easy to distinguish between them. Therefore, opinions and practices change depending on where to draw the line between the two. As mentioned earlier, most debates on Islamic finance are described as conflicts between two opposing views: whether to emphasize the capitalist character or to emphasize Islamic legitimacy. However, a binary confrontation only emerges when we try to understand what each view is familiar to. The essence of the debate is focused on the one issue of what constitutes a real or substantive transaction. It is neither more nor less than this.

The characteristics of the Islamic economy as mentioned above should therefore be revised. The prohibition of *ribā* is not a constraint as a negative assertion but an incentive device which induces people to perform economic activities based on real or substantive transactions. In other words, in Islam it is considered that people can obtain a more desirable future in this world and in the afterlife by concentrating their resources on such economic activities.

4.3 Self-interest as a Core of Islamic Morality

The characteristics of *zakāt* can be also considered from another perspective apart from an economic-constraint view. *Zakāt* has been explained as Muslims' obligatory acts, so that they "must" pay from their annual earnings. This implies the *zakāt* system reduces their material satisfaction from a constraint point of view. However, *zakāt* also implies that no matter how much wealth you earn you should pay *zakāt*. In our society (especially in Japan), we tend to hold a mixed view of jealousy and envy towards those who earn too much wealth but, as mentioned above, in Islam the more profits in this world increase the more the possibility increases of being saved in the afterlife. This implies that earning wealth in Islamic society is directly linked to personal piety.

This logical structure in *zakāt* makes people work hard for the accumulation of wealth in this world in order to maximize the possibility of their own salvation in the afterlife, which inevitably means that the amount of *zakāt* increases as well. The ratio of *zakāt* payment in cash is fixed at 2.5%, so if one earns ten times more, the amount of *zakāt* will also increase by ten times. This leads to the enhancement of welfare by distributing more funds to beneficiaries. In our society, the enhancement of welfare, in particular by charity, depends greatly on the altruistic mindset and morals of people who earn wealth. Originally charitable activities started based on philanthropy and brotherhood. When we see businesspersons who are enthusiastic about charitable or social-welfare activities, we admire them for being altruistic. However, we criticize businesspersons who are not concerned about others, operating with a profit-first principle, saying that they have no morality or altruistic mindset.

In contrast, *zakāt* in Islam is based on thorough self-interest, on one's own desire to be saved in the afterlife. The payment of *ṣadaqa* and the donation of *waqf* are also for the purpose of one's own salvation. That is why people strive at these charitable acts. We cannot find any fundamental elements of altruistic spirit or morality there. However, a so-called moral economy emerges as a result of the enhancement of welfare based on the pursuit of self-interest. When we look at the logical structure of Islamic charitable systems, it is not a constraint on the universal principle of capitalism, which seeks the infinite growth of capital in order to enrich community welfare, but a personal incentive device which induces people to maximize their total benefits in this world and in the afterlife.

From the above analyses of Islamic finance and Islamic charitable systems, we can redefine the Islamic economy as a peculiar type of capitalism employing two incentive devices with religious origins. Generally, there are two opposing views of the characteristics of the Islamic economy: capitalistic or non-(anti-) capitalistic. Such differences in view depend on how the system's peculiarity is evaluated.

5 Conclusion

The word "future" makes us feel bright. This is because we use this word in the expectation that a better future is waiting, compared to our present lives. It is obvious that current capitalism is at a crossroads. Various ideas, theories, and movements are being developed in order to overcome the evils of capitalism. Under such circumstances, what can we learn from the Islamic economy and Islamic finance? A "financial system embedded into the real economy," and the "enrichment of welfare based on thorough self-interest." These are the teachings that the Islamic economy offers us. It is uncertain how these can contribute to a "bright" future. However, as long as we see the latest global financial crisis as something caused by highly leveraged financial products and the inevitability of wealth concentration and disparity in capitalism, as clearly revealed by Piketty (2014), it seems worthwhile seriously considering the significance of the teachings of the Islamic economy, which can provide another way of alleviating such maladies of capitalism. The wisdom in a "financial system embedded into the real economy" helps to curb the running away of financial capitalism. The wisdom in the "enrichment of welfare based on thorough self-interest" helps to achieve the correction of economic disparity without restraining economic development. Moreover, interestingly, the examples of *zakāt* and *waqf* show that corrections to disparity can be achieved by an autonomous route without national intervention.

The teachings of Islam say that a bright future will come if you engage in economic activities according to its ideas. However, both the prohibition of *ribā* and obligation of paying *zakāt* are based on faith in Islam. It is not easy for non-Muslims, who do not share the faith, to understand these ideas and to perform their economic activities based on them. Therefore, it is necessary to verify what kind of effects these teachings offered by Islamic finance have on human society as a whole, using various analytical frameworks including economics. This is an attempt to universalize the teachings of the Islamic economy. Therefore, we need to run concrete simulations for universalizing the teachings: for example, how we can universally induce economic behaviors based on the teachings; how we can design universal institutions based on the teachings, and so on.

Islamic finance does not become feasible merely by inheriting the legacies of Islamic civilization before the modern era, but by renovating them with reference to the teachings of our own capitalism to meet the demands of the modern world. In this way Islamic finance can achieve a remarkable development. Now is our turn to learn and utilize the wisdoms of the Islamic economy. Is this possible? When we trace back through history, we find several experiences of learning from and utilizing the legacies of Islamic civilization. For example, the check was widely used in the pre-modern Islamic world and then imported into Europe (Çizakça 2011: 46–47). Also it is said that the concept of the shareholding company, which constitutes the core of capitalism, originates in *muḍāraba* in the pre-modern Islamic world (Udovitch 1962). These show that the teachings of the Islamic economy are not distant from us. When we understand the essence of the Islamic economy correctly, an economy which does not share the excessive "illusions" of capitalism but does not at all reject capitalism, we may find clues for designing our better future.

References

Çizakça, M. (2011). *Islamic capitalism and finance: Origins, evolution and the future*. Cheltenham and Northampton: Edward Elgar.
Hardt, M., & Negri, A. (2004). *Multitude: War and democracy in the age of empire*. New York: Penguin Press.
Islamic Financial Services Board. (2014). *Islamic financial services industry stability report 2014*. Kuala Lumpur: Islamic Financial Services Board.
Iwai, K. (1994). Sai to Ningen (Difference and human). In *Shihonshugi wo Kataru* (Talking about capitalism). Tokyo: Chikumashobo (in Japanese).
Karatani, K. (2005). *Transcritique: On Kant and Marx*. Revised Edition. Cambridge: MIT Press.
Maudoodi, S. A. (1947). *The economic problem of man and its Islamic solution*. Pathankot: Jama'at-e-Islami Publication.
MGI. (2008). *Mapping Global Capital Markets*, 5th ed. Mckinsey Global Institute.

Nagaoka, S. (2007). Beyond the divergence/convergence theories in Islamic finance: Analytical reflections on *murabahah* and Islamic securities in Malaysia and the Gulf countries. *Kyoto Bulletin of Islamic Area Studies, 1*(2), 72–91.

Nagaoka, S. (2016). Revitalization of *waqf* in Singapore: Regional path dependency of the new horizons. *Kyoto Bulletin of Islamic Area Studies, 8,* 4–18.

Piketty, T. (2014). *Capital in the twenty-first century* (A. Goldhammer, Trans.). Cambridge: Harvard University Press.

Polanyi, K. (1977). *The livelihood of man.* In: H. W. Pearson (Ed.). New York: Academic Press.

Qureshi, A. I. (1946) *Islam and the theory of interest.* Lahore: Muhammad Ashraf. al-Ṣadr, M. B. (1968). *Iqtiṣādunā.* Beirut: Dār al-Fikr.

TheCityUK. (2012). *Islamic finance.* London: TheCityUK.

TheCityUK. (2013). *UK, the leading western centre for Islamic finance.* London: TheCityUK.

The Qur'an. (M. A. S. Abdel Haleem, Trans.). (2004). Oxford and New York: Oxford University Press.

Udovitch, A. L. (1962). At the origins of the Western commenda: Islam, Israel, Byzantium? *Speculum, 37*(2), 198–207.

Uzawa, H. (1993). 'Rerum Novarum' inverted: Abuses of socialism and illusions of capitalism. In M. Baldassarri & R. Mundell (Eds.), *Eastern Europe's transition to a market economy* (pp. 19–31). Basingstoke: Macmillan.

Author Biography

Shinsuke Nagaoka is Associate Professor of Graduate School of Asian and African Area Studies at Kyoto University. He was awarded Ph.D. in Area Studies from Kyoto University in 2009. He is a leading expert in the fields of Global Islamic Economic Studies, Islamic Finance, Comparative Economic Thought & Economic History, and Islamic Area Studies. His research focuses on both the theory and practice of Islamic finance, and launches a new methodology toward criticizing modern capitalism and economics both polyphonically and internally. He has experiences of visiting research positions at Islamic Research and Training Institute (IRTI), Islamic Development Bank and Durham University. Dr. Nagaoka has field research experience around the Islamic world which include Middle East (Egypt, Jordan, Saudi Arabia and the Gulf countries) and Southeast Asia (Malaysia, Indonesia, and Singapore). He has written extensively in published in books, referred academic journals, chapters in edited books, and articles in both Japanese and international journals and magazines. His forthcoming publication is *Islamic Economics and Finance in Action: Inventing a New Universal Paradigm* (Brill 2017).

Chapter 23
Buddhist Economics: A Cultural Alternative

Juewei Shi

1 Introduction

Watching weeds grow in the garden turns out to be a powerful lesson outside the classroom. First, the weeds look innocently beautiful until they start invading the space of the expensive grass that is fighting for survival. Alarmed, the gardener moves into action with industrial-strength weedkiller. Before long, the herbicide poisons both the weeds and grass. Alas, weeks later, it is the weed that manages to survive the new level of toxicity in the soil and springs back to life ahead of the grass. The battle resumes with the weeds ahead.

Buddhist teachings focus on purifying the mind of "weeds" such as greed, anger and delusion. A practitioner does so by "planting" seeds of virtues such as right view, right thought, right speech, right action, right livelihood, right effort, right mindfulness and right concentration (collectively known as the Noble Eightfold Path) and encouraging the training of ethics, meditative concentration and wisdom. The goal of Buddhist practice is to lessen suffering, for the self and others. This objective is accomplished by the cultivation of one inexhaustible natural resource, the mind, in order to produce human virtues. According to Zsolnai, unfortunately, such Buddhist teachings are in opposition to western economics (Zsolnai, Why Buddhist Economics? 2011, p. 3). One system encourages the moderation of desires for the benefit of self, community and nature. The other encourages hedonism and the accumulation of wealth. The battlefield within individual minds also extends to the physical world. The training of the mind to be less dependent on toxic sensations will help to assure balanced co-existence of both systems, assuring mental and physical wellbeing, for the self and others.

J. Shi (✉)
Director of Humanistic Buddhism Center and Lecturer of Applied Buddhist Studies at the Nan Tien Institute, Wollongong, Australia
e-mail: juewei@ibps.org

Without "throwing the baby out with the bathwater," this chapter surveys contemporary economic models and "experiments" that inject Buddhist principles into secular systems as well as economic exchanges in Buddhist sanctuaries. I shall explore the ongoing dialogues between these two apparently incompatible systems and study how Buddhist communities have engaged in a harmonious partnership that combines Buddhist values and wisdom with existing economic paradigms. The critical success factor for this paradigm shift lies in the Buddhist discovery of the truth of karma and *pratītyasamutpāda* (dependent co-origination).

2 Secular Communities

2.1 Buddhist Teachings and Western Economic Models

Buddhists realise that there are causes and conditions behind every phenomenon. In other words, each event is dependent on the co-arising of a complex network of causes and conditions (dependent co-origination). Karma, a kind of power formed as a result of each past deed, speech or thought, determines which sets of conditions arise. Since these causes and conditions are transitory in nature, attachment to any phenomenon will only result in *dukkha* (unsatisfactoriness). This dependent co-origination model explains that attachment to income and wealth or any transitory mental and physical phenomena only provides for temporary satisfaction (Ash, Happiness and Economics: a Buddhist perspective 2007, p. 214) and will inevitably result in further suffering (Ash, Do Our Economic Choices Make Us Happy? 2011, p. 119). Ignorance to the working principles of karma and dependent co-origination can lead to erroneous decisions driven by greed, anger and delusion (the three principal Buddhist poisonous causes) that will not lead to balanced co-existence and optimum results.

One important result of the Buddhist teachings of karma and dependent co-origination is the promotion of cyclical rather than linear thinking, as well as awareness of a spectrum of interdependent factors. Permaculture today has utilised such principles. For example, free-range chickens have a symbiotic relationship with the environment, eating weeds, fallen fruit and insect pests. In return, chickens provide manure and clean the environment of rotten fruit and pests. By caging chickens, farmers broke the cycle and had to busy themselves with feeding, cleaning and pest control activities. Worse, toxins released from the pesticides resulted in a self-degenerating system (Linear vs. Cyclical Paradigms and Permaculture Mind). Mindfulness of such natural interdependence can lead to alternative commercial decisions.

Buddhists do not object to economic progress unless it causes suffering for the self and others. One purpose of Buddhist practice is to seek joy, peace and harmony, not only for oneself but also for all sentient beings. This is no different from the original aim of economics. Smith (1723–1790), recognised as the father of classical economics and a moral philosopher, believed in human perfection and happiness and that each individual lives as a member of a family, state and "society of mankind" (Powers 1956, pp. 223–224). In this model, self-interest can be balanced with greater good. Unfortunately, economic policies of recent times narrowed the goals to full and efficient employment of people and capital, economic growth, and the reduction of income inequality (George 1975, p. 284). With these limited goals, the capitalist system has generated some impressive results. Between 1990 and 2013, the number of people living in extreme poverty dropped by more than half, from 1.85 billion to 770 million, and child mortality has dropped by nearly half, while literacy and vaccinations have all increased (Duflo and Mosenkis 2017). However, the 2016 World Happiness Report indicates that happiness inequality has increased significantly among the world's population and such inequality leads to a reduction of happiness (Helliwell et al. 2016, p. 4). Findings such as this undermine the belief that self-centred financial capital growth can lead to happiness.

Recent attention to the topic of happiness is encouraging. Humanity has often envisioned a better world or looked back towards a Golden Age of peace, harmony, stability and rule by the wise and compassionate. This universal pursuit finds common ground between economics and Buddhism. The highly-competitive and global agenda today represents one extreme of radically autonomous and self-interested societies while the utopian connected, altruistic and cooperative economy another extreme (Nelson 2011, p. 29). Advocating either end of the spectrum leads to dualistic thinking and will only lead to unhealthy opposition. In this world of constant flux, there is a Middle Way.

The application of economic ideas that stem from Buddhist thought is commonly known as Buddhist Economics (Alexandrin 1993, p. 3). The pioneering *Small is Beautiful: economics as if people mattered* by E.F. Schumacher (1911–1977) in 1955 uses the principles of right livelihood, inter-dependence and Middle Way to propose a non-violent way in economic and political life. His ideal model maximises satisfaction rather than consumption, measures harmony rather than annual consumption, and seeks to raise the value of an employee instead of viewing him as a cost item (Guruge 2008, pp. 41–42). Schumacher makes a strong case against the western belief that universal prosperity will bring about peace, but instead argues that the world's population strife for wealth will only widen the poverty gap and over-stretch the planet's fossil fuel reserves (Schumacher 1973). Unfortunately, Schumacher's argument for a human-centred economic model that would enable human and environmental sustainability has been labelled as "romantic idealism" (Bunting 2011).

Although this ideal did not materialise, it inspired subsequent models that became the basis of several successful implementations.

Buddhist economics is determined by an individual's behaviour which in turn is governed by the mind. Hence, Buddhist training emphasises and begins with the acquisition of right view through education. Decision-makers need to be aware of the problems created by the existing economic system(s) and the inescapable laws of dependent co-origination. Stemming from Schumacher's proposal, the training also involves right understanding so that decisions not only optimise human satisfaction (quality of life) but also complement nature and the society-at-large (Prayukvong 2005, p. 1174).

Thailand's Venerable Payutto Dhammapitaka's (b. 1938) published *Buddhist Economics—a middle way for the market place* in 1992. He proposes a spiritual approach to economics based on personal development called "harmonious happiness." In this model, economic transactions are altruistically based (motivated by goodwill and compassion) and directed towards the wellbeing of society (Guruge 2008, p. 57). It predicates upon the practice of meditation and mental training to contemplate the mental conditions (motivation) leading to (un)ethical behaviour, thereby helping one to better resist unwholesome compulsions (Guruge 2008, p. 62). Payutto also advocates meditation (rather than wealth) as a means to inner peace because it enables one to use wealth for social good rather than for personal gratification (Guruge 2008, p. 63).

Magnuson's *Pathways to a Mindful Economy* reminds readers that active social participation is a mindful practice that the Buddha recommended (Magnuson 2011, p. 99). In a mindful economy, smaller-scale local economic systems become the starting point for more comprehensive changes to evolve. An example is a growing socially-responsible community of more than 1600 for-profit companies from 42 countries and over 120 industries certified as "Beneficial Corporations" because they meet rigorous social and environmental performance, accountability, and transparency standards (What are B Corps? 2017). People in mindful economies such as B-Corps are motivated by core values that are not greed nor self-indulgence-based. The issue now is how to steer companies away from growth-oriented, profit-driven capitalist systems into community-based, sustainable systems (Magnuson 2011, pp. 105–107).

Chang believes that the evolution of economic systems today has prepared companies to adopt a Buddhist wisdom-based economic model (Chang 2006, p. 173). In this ideal state, decisions are coordinated to yield harmony for the animate and inanimate realms. With high levels of insight based on Buddhist wisdom, individuals do not rely on consumption for happiness (Chang 2006, p. 175). Contrary to popular paradigm, the self becomes the factor of production that can be sacrificed (Chang 2006, p. 179). In this wisdom-based model, the right view of karma and dependent co-origination enables the self to be sacrificed for greater public good.

The preceding discussion is by no means an exhaustive listing of Buddhist economic models nor an attempt to demonstrate the superiority of Buddhist paradigms. Buddhists are encouraged to avoid the temptations of self-righteousness and instead, be open to engaging with businesses, governments and the larger suffering world (Nelson 2011, p. 32). Below we shall explore how the Buddhist economic theories are put into practice in secular communities.

2.2 Buddhist Economic Practice in Secular Communities

The most visionary model in practice today comes from the Buddhist kingdom of Bhutan with its famous Gross National Happiness (GNH) index defined in terms of the four pillars of economic development, good governance, cultural preservation and nature conservation. The Buddhist Noble Eightfold Path is mapped to each GNH component for the wellbeing of the nation through a mixed economy that does not adopt the extremes of either capitalism or communism. Bhutan is attempting to exercise the Middle Way by "mixing" market forces with some central government leadership, with a more holistic and systemic human life understanding (Tideman 2011, pp. 146–150). GNH, coined in 1972 and institutionalised in 2008, has been Bhutan's contribution to the world. The 2015 GNH index findings show that there was a 1.8% increase in GNH over the previous five years and a 2.5% increase in its population being happier (Centre for Bhutan Studies and GNH Research 2015). Still in its early stages of implementation (compared to capitalism which can be traced to the Middle Ages in Europe), the GNH model will need time to mature and for its long-term effects to be assessed.

The Royal Thai Sufficiency Economy Model, launched by the late King Bhumibol Adulyadej (1946–2016) after the 1997 economic crisis, operates on the principles of moderation, reasonableness, self-immunity, wisdom and integrity (Essen 2011, p. 61). Essen gives an example of a Thai mulberry paper business that refused bank loans and would only expand according to the availability of surplus funds. The owner invested in employee training and environmental wellbeing. As at the writing of the paper, the enterprise had 400 employees (Essen 2011, p. 67). This sufficiency model is compatible with capitalist economy but does not over-extend the businesses into credit.

Thailand has experimented with complementary economic models. Prayukvong examined three rural communities that fared better than major institutions during the financial crisis of 1997. The leaders of the successful Na Muen Sri Weaving Group, Bor Kul Housewives Group and Ta Mod Farmer's Group were committed to the community groups they belonged even though they could have made more money if they had set up their own businesses. By not putting personal interests as their first priority, these compassionate leaders chose "a path whereby they as individuals can coexist with society and nature to achieve a certain quality of life" (Prayukvong 2005, p. 1184). In addition, the Ta Mod group engaged both Buddhist monks and eminent Muslims in its project. Such interfaith collaboration underlines the wish for all humanity to live together peacefully.

Also in Thailand, the Santi Asoke Buddhist Reform Movement of Thailand eschews material comfort in order to attain spiritual freedom. Members practise right livelihood in the Three Professions of natural agriculture, chemical-free fertiliser, and waste management, with work perceived as meditation and a path to enlightenment. However, the general Thai public deemed this Reform as being too austere for ordinary farmers (Essen 2011, pp. 68–70).

In Sri Lanka, another Buddhist country, the Sarvodaya Shramadana movement serviced 15,000 villages in just over half a century (History 2017). On its website, Sarvodaya publishes its mission to create a "no poverty, no affluence, and a conflict-free society" in order to "uplift and empower the most disadvantaged people in Sri Lanka" (Philosophy and Approach 2017). Sarvodaya believes that a country does not have enough resources to provide affluence to all, that the social, environmental, moral and cultural costs incurred in the process of attempting to build an affluent society are too high, and that an affluent society is not necessarily a happy one (Ariyaratne 1999, p. 36). Instead, the goal is awakening at the individual,[1] family,[2] village, urban, national and global levels (Philosophy and Approach 2017). To this goal, Sarvodaya provides simple means to satisfy basic human needs such as water, clothing, food, housing, healthcare, communication, energy, education, culture and spiritual needs (Ariyaratne 1999, p. 37). Underlying the aim to build a full-engagement society is the important concept of right livelihood and not full employment, as western economics will have it. Every individual, including children and elders, must be socially engaged in meaningful ways to meet the basic needs spelled out.

Based on the experiences of implementing variants of models based on Buddhist teachings, it seems that harmonious co-existence of humanistic values and the existing systems of the state is possible. Through moderation in production and consumption, ethical behaviour, mindful consumption and altruistic, compassionate action that are aligned to the Buddha's teachings (and incidentally, not very different from Adam Smith's propositions of moral sentiments), there will be respectful consideration for resources (natural and manmade), dignity accorded to the human being (rather than being relegated to the role as a factor of production), and analysis of impact to environmental, human, social, cultural and other factors before production.

2.3 Practice at a Personal Level

Economic or any action, for that matter, is driven by one's motivation. Amartya Sen (b. 1933), recipient of the 1988 Nobel Prize in Economic Science, vehemently disagrees with the first principle of economics that claims "every agent is actuated only by self-interest" and proposes commitment as an important behaviour determinant (Sen 1977, pp. 317 & 343). His assertion is confirmed by new neuro- and behavioural science findings that discovered that human nature is not driven by greed and egoism only; equally important are principles of justice, cooperation and

---

[1]The four sublime abodes of individual awakening are: loving kindness, compassion, joy and equanimity.

[2]The four Buddhist prescriptions of family awakening are: giving, kind and intelligible words, right livelihood, and equality.

altruism (Tideman 2011, p. 144). Tideman notices that every market player is an active co-creator of a continuous dynamic process, much as in the principle of dependent co-origination. A giant of western American philosophy, Charles Pierce (b. 1953), proposed that the driving force in successful human life is not greed but compassion (Lancaster 2006, p. 47). Judging from the intuitive right choices that enable the survival of the human race, Pierce argues that compassion is a part of human nature while selfish actions are learned attitudes. This position is very much in line with the intrinsic Buddhist Buddha nature theory.

How do these apply to the contemporary economic problem? Buddhists and non-Buddhists admit the same issues; however, their problem-solving methods are different. Buddhists acknowledge that tangible resources (including manpower) are limited in supply. Instead of setting price points to match or curtail demand, they advocate cherishing all direct and indirect, natural and manufactured resources. Waste is frowned upon. For example, orientation of newcomers to Buddhist temples often include an admonition to "cherish the possessions of the temple as though protecting one's eyeball." Buddhist monastics set an example by consuming only just sufficient basic necessities for survival and dedicating themselves to self-study and service to others. Buddhists remain a part of the economic cycle but are taught to become disciplined, ethical and responsible consumers.

While Buddhist monastics take a vow of poverty, householders do not. In the *Anguttara Nikāya*, the Buddha recognises the need for a layperson to spend on food, clothing and shelter; attending to family members, relatives, friends and guests; illness and emergencies; charity; alms and meritorious activities; and payment of taxes (Guruge 2008, p. 45). The householder is not advised to spend his wealth indulging in sense pleasures. The Buddha's definition of prosperity includes both abundance of material good as well as virtue and knowledge (Guruge 2008, p. 44) Right livelihood,[3] interpreted as the foundation of Buddhist economics by Schumacher, excludes trade in weapons, living beings, intoxicants and poisons; slaughtering animals and fishing; military service; deceit and treachery; soothsaying; trickery and usury (Guruge 2008, p. 48). The benefits of such livelihood include longevity, good complexion, health and comfort, as well as energy or power that is, overall wellbeing (Guruge 2008, p. 49).

Shinichi Inoue, former President of the Japanese Miyazaki Bank and reputed economist, demonstrated the possibility of putting Buddhist teachings into practice. In his book, *Putting Buddhism to Work*, Inoue combined the best of capitalist and socialist economic models into an inter-dependent, sustainable and ecologically sound system (Weeraratna 2012). Inoue claims that the one should not engage in businesses that do not serve the world and that the goal of business should be to serve the community with the profit coming as a by-product (Zsolnai, Why Buddhist Economics?, 2011, p. 7).

---

[3]One of the Noble Eightfold Paths: right view, right thought, right speech, right action, right livelihood, right effort, right mindfulness, and right concentration.

In order for people and nature to co-exist on this increasingly fragile planet, Venerable Master Hsing Yun (b. 1927) promotes the Five Harmonies[4] to the world. It starts with inner peace and works its way to world peace. He proposes "harmony" as a precious universal value that allows one to transcend the self towards the greater good, and asserts that "money, wealth and love" are nothing without harmony (Hsing Yun, 365 Days with Traveler, 2015a, p. 320). The claim of this international Buddhist leader has been proven by research on group practice of Transcendental Meditation. Collective meditation practices, which builds inner peace in individuals, have resulted in fewer traffic accidents, reduction in violence, increase in optimism and greater order in Israel and Lebanon in 1983 (Orme-Johnson et al. 1988).

Meditation is not the only way to further the goals of the society. Diligent work can also build a prosperous nation. In a youth conference in 1997, Venerable Master Hsing Yun recommends youths to work hard to acquire wealth morally (right livelihood), value work to be a form of service and cultivation (rather than for material ends only), and to generously contribute towards charitable and religious causes (Chandler 2004, p. 96). Work becomes practice because industry at work focuses the mind in the same way as meditation, and service to liberate others avoids one's tendency towards selfish enlightenment (Chandler 2004, p. 97). Such diligence in turn helps build a nation. Venerable Master Hsing Yun believes that only a prosperous nation is able to strengthen its defence, raise its standards of education, increase the standard of living, and encourage the cultivation of virtues among its people (Hsing Yun, Buddhist View on Economic Issues, 2005, p. 315). A strong advocate of co-existence, Venerable Master Hsing Yun urges nations to co-operate to actualise world peace and the wellbeing of humanity. Hence, Buddhist teachings do not contradict national objectives but can support a country's agendas.

2.4 Summary

Schumacher's human-centred, Payutto's harmonious happiness, Magnuson's mindful and Chang's wisdom-based Buddhist economic models are by no means exhaustive. They represent a range of ideals that build on Buddhist principles but these cannot be put into practice without education and re-training. It is unlikely and impractical that any Buddhist economic model can replace the well-entrenched standards of either free market economies or centrally planned socialist communities (Guruge 2008, p. 103). There is no need to: Buddhists do not frown upon economic success that alleviates suffering. In the *Aṅguttara Nikāya*, the Buddha

---

[4]The Five Harmonies are "Individual harmony achieved through joy; family harmony achieved through deference; interpersonal harmony achieved through respect; social harmony achieved through cooperation; world harmony achieved through peace".

recognises that wealth, when ethically obtained, leads to "four sources of worldly happiness: economic security, having enough to spend generously on oneself and others, the peace of mind that accompanies freedom from debt, and the peace of mind of knowing that one has earned one's wealth blamelessly (A II 62)" (Ash, Do Our Economic Choices Make Us Happy? 2011, p. 118). The problem only arises if one clings to the wealth with greed.

To achieve sustainable harmony or equilibrium (a goal of both Buddhists and economists), practice should start from the personal level. Mosini notes that classical economists defined equilibrium as selfish individuals achieving harmonious outcome with political, social and moral order (Mosini 2007, p. 1). While neo-classical economics referred to the equilibrium of supply and demand of commodities, they also recognised that any disturbance to the system would lead to a tendency back to (harmonious) equilibrium. In the *Mahāyana Awakening of Faith*, bodhisattvas[5] are reminded to remain unchanged within the flow of fluctuating conditions. Treating diligent work as a form of service for the benefit of the society-at-large, one will avoid the dangers of greed-motivated decisions. Mutual thoughtfulness and respect will build strength and prosperity, from the family through the nation to the world. Hence, harmonious co-existence is the common goal of both Buddhist and economic enterprises.

3 Economics in the Buddhist World

3.1 Buddhist Teachings Meet Contemporary Economics in the Sanctuary

This section explores an alternative paradigm that is in part based on abundance economics and the gift economy where the "commodity" is merit or endless human virtues. Progress is now measured in more intangible terms where the harmony of individual self-interests may be achieved in today's market mechanism. Noted economists such as Adam Smith, Karl Marx, Thorstein Veblen, John Keynes, and more recent thinkers such as R. H. Tawney, John A. Hobson and Eric Zimmerman taught "abundance economics" where everyone has abundant healthcare, nutrition, education, transportation, recreation, housing, self-expression, and personal security (Peach and Dugger 2006). Leaving the academic debate that ensues aside, the economy of abundance brings about a paradigm shift that can enable a movement from competition to collaboration, from self-interest to shared-interest, and from

---

[5] A bodhisattva is a "Buddhist practitioner intent on the attainment of enlightenment based on profoundly altruistic motivations" (Muller, Bodhisattva, 2013). Two distinguishing features of bodhisattvas are their realisation of the empty nature of all mundane phenomena (hence, impermanence and interdependence) and their deep compassion for the suffering of all beings. These characteristics drive bodhisattvas to practise the six perfections of endless generosity, discipline, tolerance, perseverance, mindful concentration and *prajñā* wisdom..

greed to generosity. At a mental level, the Buddhist philosophy of formlessness, selflessness and desirelessness assumes an abundant world that is inexhaustible, boundless and infinite (Hsing Yun, Original Intents, 2016, p. 30). *Sūtras*[6] are filled with such awe-inspiring cosmic scenes of mental constructs. Buddhists believe in the power of the mind, that is, the abundance and infinity that can be construed through the mind can be turned into physical possibilities.

The notion of abundance precedes a gift economy. Today, the internet and MOOC (Massive Open Online Course) are well-known examples. In gift economies, goods and services are exchanged without explicit agreement upon a *quid pro quo* (Lillington 2006, p. 7). The assumption of abundance is an important motivator. Another is that in a volatile, uncertain, complex and ambiguous (VUCA) world, friendship is better than money. A piece of Brazilian popular adage says "a friend on the market is better than money in your pocket" (De L'Estoile 2014, p. 62). Of course, we shall also be careful not to simplify the relationship to friends are better than money.

The idea of "gift" naturally brings to mind Mauss' thesis that every gift is part of a system of reciprocity, or that there is not a free (altruistic) gift (Mauss 1990, p. ix). Mauss argues that stability comes from exchanges to create mutual interests and satisfactions in a so-called civilised world (Mauss 1990, p. 106). Unfortunately, this argument creates tensions for the Buddhist sangha (monastic community).

The sustenance of the Buddhist sangha depends on the contribution of laity or householders. In the simplest model, monastics work towards their own salvation but also teach/serve the world. Lay devotees offer to monastics food, medicine, clothing and shelter as well as donation towards building or restoring religious buildings (Coderey 2005, p. 405). Such *dāna* (offering) is meritorious. Hence, the donor can expect better rebirths as well as better karma in this life. While there is not supposed to be any expectation of reciprocity in such religious exchanges, that is practically not so. Based on Mauss' observation, a bond is created between the recipient and donor through the gift. This bond exists through the expectation of some return, possibly intangible such as *puṇya* (merit). Buddhist *puṇya* is the cause of wholesome karma and is often associated with virtue, fortune and goodness (Muller, Merit, 2010), while merit builds religious capital for Buddhist adherents. Having considered the ethical consequences of each action mindfully and wisely, each action becomes the cause for a better future. Hence, gifts (material or otherwise) made in the present serve as investment for the growth of one's meritorious religious capital. It is the growth of such intangible, inexhaustible capital that Buddhism encourages rather than economic growth at the expense of non-renewable resources. Furthermore, meritorious religious capital can co-exist in any economy.

Puṇya has given Buddhist communities economic momentum. While the *Adbhutadharmaparyāya Sūtra* assures monastics that the accumulation of merits can lead to the extermination of all defilements leading to Buddhahood, the

---

[6]*Sūtras* are Buddhist canonical texts.

Drumakinnararājaparipṛcchā Sūtra confirms that lay practitioners can accumulate merits for divine protection. Furthermore, merits can be dedicated to someone else, known as *pariṇāma* (merit transfer). Technically, this means turning around one's "good roots and virtues of one's own religious practices" and directing them to somewhere else (Kawamura and Kawamura 1991, p. 149). In the *Sukhāvatīvyūha Sūtra*, a person transfers the merits of practising wholesome deeds, upholding vegetarian fasts, erecting *stūpas* and images, feeding the sangha, and supporting the monastery to the vow of rebirth in an Amitabha Buddha's pure land. In the Mahāyana spirit, the purpose of such dedication was for the benefit of all suffering beings (Wong 2012, p. 202). The *Avatamsaka Sūtra* tells of great enlightening beings who dedicate roots of goodness by wishing all sentient beings to be purified and filled with inexhaustible and indestructible virtues so that they may "rest securely on innumerable great foundations of goodness, to be forever free of poverty, to be fully equipped with seven kinds of wealth—faith, self-control, shame, conscience, learning, generosity and wisdom" (Cleary 1984, p. 533). There are many reasons to present gifts to the sangha.

The preceding description seems to reinforce Mauss' observation that people give for the sake of reciprocal benefits, which can be larger than the original gift. However, more recent works by Testart (2013) and Florence Weber (Weber 2012) recognise that the obligation to reciprocate, especially with some "thing" of a higher value, is not universal (Sihlé 2015, p. 353). Buddhism teaches a higher order of giving that is based on the non-substantiality of the act of giving, that is, the donor, beneficiary and gift are intrinsically empty. In the *Vajracchedikā Prajñāpāramitā Sūtra* (better known as the *Diamond Sūtra*), "a bodhisattva should practise giving without abiding in form, nor should he give abiding in sound, smell, taste, touch or dharmas" (Hsing Yun, Four Insights for Finding Fulfillment, 2012, p. 91). Practitioners are advised to give without attachment to phenomena, ideas or outward appearances and not to discriminate who to give to and what to give. Only such giving will have limitless merit. The family is an example of such a gift. Parents offer unconditioned love to their children. Buddhists are not the only ones who believe that the care parents provide to their children is immeasurable, and in Buddhist parlance, worthy of limitless merit.

A question naturally arises about giving to the sangha. Although Buddhist texts label the sangha an incomparable merit field, economists may not agree with how much a group of renounced labour can contribute to the mainstream economic engine. Stereotypes picture monastic communities as cloisters of monks and nuns in solitary devotion, being parasitically dependent on laity for their material wellbeing. Such monastics are believed to be socially withdrawn. However, not all sangha members belong in cloistered communities. Ash confirms that a sangha can be "productive" because the Dharma taught makes those actually engaged in the workforce more trustworthy (reducing transaction costs and sustaining trade), and encourages co-operative ventures (reducing the costs of doing business) (Ash, The Monastic Sangha: "an incomparable field of merit".. and wealth creators?, 2006, p. 218). Buddhism can continue to serve humanity by ensuring the progress is not only measured by economic growth. People can transcend their limits of self-centredness. Hence, *dāna* is an effective gift as long as the virtuous monastics practise and teach. If done well, spiritual and material wellbeing will go hand-in-hand.

3.2 Practice in Sacred Communities

The aforementioned system of offering and merit has operated in Buddhist communities for over two thousand years. However, when it encounters modern economics, this system faces some challenges. There is a distinction between those brought up in a culture where Buddhist gift-giving is embedded and those living in urban environments coming into contact with Buddhism. While the ideal Buddhist gift is an act of asymmetrical and unreciprocated generosity, the predisposition to give without being asked is marker of Buddhist virtue and faith that only those growing up in such cultures appreciate (Caple 2015, pp. 467–468). Below are a variety of models that show how sangha communities sustain themselves in the modern world, given these economic dichotomies.

Campergue surveyed over 290 Tibetan dharma centres in France to determine the western perspective of the Buddhist gifting practice. Unfamiliar with the traditional Buddhist practice of merit, adaptations have resulted in commodification of Dharma teachings as seen in the high costs of retreats, conferences and teachings (Campergue 2015, p. 449). These centres collected donations, offerings, and teaching fees. Westerners were willing to make monetary and other donations to their masters for alleviating their personal health or other existential issues, a practice that some centre administrators labelled as *upaya* (skilful means) for the promotion of the Dharma (Campergue 2015, pp. 451–453). The Dharma encounters turned transactional in an environment unfamiliar with the concepts of *dāna* and *puṇya*.

Myanmar, a Buddhist country, presents a case study that represents the other end of the spectrum. The concepts of *dāna* and *puṇya* were so much a part of the nation's culture that they were used in the traditional healing sector whereby donations were offered to healers. Traditional healers (monks, diviners, spirit mediums, exorcists, and traditional specialists of indigenous medicine) in the central Rakhine state present their services freely as tokens of loving kindness and generosity. Their healing is perceived as a form of *dāna* guided by Buddhist texts (Coderey 2005, p. 407). Patients present voluntary donations in return for the service to avoid being in an inferior position of indebtedness and to acquire karmic merit (Coderey 2005, p. 418). The healer is rated according to his loving kindness, while the patient is seen as the one who is fortunate enough to show his or her respect and gratitude through a meritorious donation which contributes to the efficacy of the healing session (Coderey 2005, p. 419).

Although several dynasties in China's long history adopted Buddhism as a state religion, gifting to temples in recent times represents a religion in flux. The Buddhist temple economy has been influenced by the capitalist model (Wang 2006,

p. 251). For example, several temples, such as Jing-an Temple in Shanghai, were dependent on real estate income in the Republic era. Many temple patrons were rich businessmen who helped to promote Buddhism through charitable, cultural and educational undertakings (Wang 2006, p. 252). In a study of Chinese Buddhists frequenting Tibetan centres in China, two levels of financial transaction were seen: (1) gift devoid of any expectations of return; and (2) exchange in which a service is delivered (Caple 2015, p. 476). The more faithful will give to the temple, leaving the natural karmic laws to determine intangible merit received, if any. Of course, the relationship is complex, with moral, economic, political and social interests and implications (Caple 2015, p. 477). Whatever the sponsors' motivation or economic background might be, monastics claimed that they could put the funds to good use (Caple 2015, p. 473), thereby generating wholesome karmic merit for all benefactors.

These examples are by no means exhaustive but serve to illustrate some of the issues encountered when tradition meets modernity. Buddhist economics take on new levels of innovation when applied within the sacred communities.

3.3 A Socially-Engaged Buddhist Economic Model

Buddhism is a practical religion. It was the traders who took Buddhism beyond its birthplace in India through the Silk Roads. Together with Buddhist relics, texts and images, the caravans also carried silk, precious gem and glass (Lancaster 2006, p. 41). The Buddha did not advise his lay disciples to give up worldly activities; instead, he advised them to combine economic and spiritual values for the sake of maximising all round benefit, for the individual and the society (Balachandran 2006). In this form of engaged Buddhism, wealth, both tangible and intangible (such as wisdom and virtues), play an important role. Stability and harmony in society arise from equality and fair distribution of wealth.

One form of socially-engaged Buddhism promoted in China, first by Master Taixu (1890–1947) and now practised by Venerable Master Hsing Yun and others, is seen as the Buddhist response to the changing Chinese economic climate. Humanistic Buddhism reflects the values of self-development and active engagement in society, while restoring the conscience (Buddha nature) lost through commercial competition (Wang 2006, pp. 258–259). Instead of engaging in consumerism or hoarding, these Buddhists are taught that they truly possess wealth when their money is put to good use. In this model, Buddhist congregations spend their wealth and effort on educational, cultural, religious and/or charitable enterprises. The wealth of these temples come from pooled resources (which include talents and time). The positive affinities built from the investment of their resources in turn become part of their merit field, as a matter of course.

This merit field represents religious, social, moral and spiritual capital. Selfless bodhisattvas contribute to this merit field with no expectation of returns. This new paradigm is rather different from goal-oriented capitalists who invest to earn positive dividends and increase asset value for their stakeholders. Instead, Buddhist *sūtras* are filled with teachings that infinite merits can be gained without the intention of reaping rewards.

To illustrate, let us look at Fo Guang Shan, a curious economic miracle. Chandler argues that Fo Guang Shan encourages behavioural patterns conducive to capitalist enterprises (Chandler 2004, p. 5). Its founder, Venerable Master Hsing Yun, has built over two hundred temples and set up art galleries, libraries, publishing houses, bookstores, television, tea houses, mobile clinics, orphanages, senior homes, Buddhist colleges, and universities worldwide (Hsing Yun, Hear Me Out, 2015b, p. xi). Venerable Master Hsing Yun is keen to ensure that his Buddhist sangha contributes positively to economic and social wellbeing. When asked how a monk with no assets in the beginning managed to build a multinational monastic enterprise, Venerable Master Hsing Yun often said that he only knew how to manage his own mind. In 2015, he published his economic wisdom based on Buddhist principles in *Hear Me Out: message from a humble monk*. His tenets of wisdom related to economics include "nothing is mine; everything is public property," "enjoy poverty, a different type of happiness," and "settling with simplicity, a confident manager of money" (Hsing Yun, Hear Me Out, 2015b, pp. 16–18). Venerable Master Hsing Yun declares that it is not in his nature to accumulate wealth or possessions, but rather is always happy to share with others (Hsing Yun, Hear Me Out, 2015b, p. 21). In fact, he constantly invests to expand the scope of his activities without any accumulation, "accepting money with one hand and immediately giving it away with the other" (Chandler 2004, p. 235). For example, donors may offer a fortune for one piece of his calligraphy, but Venerable Master Hsing Yun did not have access to even a dollar because the entire sum of donation would immediately be deposited into one of his educational and cultural foundations.

Since the Venerable Master did not complete primary education, he taught himself on-the-job. Although he did not know the textbook versions of successful business models, he had a clear mission to awaken people from their destructive worldview and habits when he edited a Buddhist magazine *Awaken the World* in the 1950s. His motivation was never financial nor for himself. He was nevertheless a pragmatic and entrepreneurial monk. He supports capitalism because it provides opportunities to those who are industrious (Chandler 2004, p. 92). To Venerable Master Hsing Yun, economic activity can be beneficial to self-cultivation if the service and resources help others (Chandler 2004, p. 92). Fo Guang Shan expands itself continuously in noteworthy causes, believing that financing will come later (Chandler 2004, p. 103). According to Chandler, monastic life has been transformed into a paragon of entrepreneurial spirit (Chandler 2004, pp. 103–104):

> Foguang clerics exemplify the capitalist work spirit at its very best: they are a highly organized, diligent labour force, remaining frugal in personal life, but daring to expand the horizons of the "occupation." Most important, the dualism between secular occupation and religious cultivation collapses: to practise Buddhist teachings is to serve others productively, and any beneficial service is an expression of Dharma.

Fo Guang Shan presents an interesting case whereby religious symbols and resources foster a fruitful interaction between capitalism and the Buddhist Dharma (Chandler 2004, p. 94). Instead of avoiding the seductive power of wealth and worldly possessions, Venerable Master Hsing Yun sees the endless possibilities for improving the human condition through prudent financial management (Chandler 2004, p. 104). Donations are well-utilised (and hence, meritorious) if they serve a larger and longer-term purpose. Education and culture are the most difficult financially but the most meritorious in terms of building moral, social and spiritual capital for the society. Take for example, Fo Guang Shan Nan Tien Temple in Wollongong, Australia. Devotees, volunteers and visitors generously donate time and material goods to support the cultural, educational, charitable and missionary causes of the Temple. As a result, Nan Tien Temple gave Australia its first accredited institution of higher education based on Buddhist values and wisdom. Nan Tien Institute is made possible by the "reinvestment" of donations and alms towards higher education. Both Nan Tien Temple and Nan Tien Institute run programs to encourage mindfulness, ethics and sustainability. Not only did these institutions not shy away from the economic engine of the day, but they participated fully in the process for the benefit of the society-at-large.

Whatever the motivation of the donors, socially-engaged temples put these gifts to use for the greater good. In a recent analysis of 801 wish cards collected from Nan Tien Temple in December 2015, 58% of adults prayed for good health, 21% happiness, 18% peace and 17% career. A similar pattern can be seen among children: 42% health, 24% happiness and 18% peace. These wholesome wishes were dedicated primarily to the self (57% of adults and 79% of children) and to the family (63% of adults and 50% of children). Interestingly, only 38% of children writing in English dedicated their wishes to their family while 75% of Chinese children messages did so. Among the adults, they are rather balanced at 64% English and 62% Chinese. This "reality check" demonstrates that most people seek merit for self-centred purposes. Only a few children wished for "world peace." It was unlikely that these patrons cared very much about how their *dāna* went towards the development of Nan Tien Institute or other noble causes. They were contented with the fact that the Temple would "invest" their *dāna* in meritorious activities so that their prayers could be "answered." Knowingly or unknowingly, the act of giving has created a causal network of partnerships stemming from the individual onto the world.

3.4 Summary

The Buddhist sangha is continually looking for ways to sustain itself in a world that seems less and less dependent on a community of virtuous representatives of Truth.

Ominously (for the sangha), the Oxford English Dictionary named "post-truth[7]" as the word of the year in 2016, which among other things, imply that a selected few who claim to know the "truth" and have access to the mechanisms to promulgate such knowledge own the right to impose this truth on others (Saul 1995, p. 24). This is opposed to Buddhism that believes in ultimate equality: that everyone owns the Buddha Nature (the Truth). In addition, humanity seems to be losing its struggle to the darker side of self-destructive self-interest (Saul 1995, p. 35). Not only are we uninterested in public good, we are also not interested in confronting reality. Grasping the way things really are is the crucial step toward happiness (Greenblatt 2011, p. 199) and that includes understanding that the universe is not all about us and our destiny (Greenblatt 2011, p. 238). Perhaps the cause of disinterest with and competing distractions against supporting the Sangha may also be the very reason to sustain the diminishing guardians and practitioners of Buddhism.

The economics of the Buddhist sangha presents an interesting case study: a community of dedicated monks and/or nuns living on minimum desires but still dependent on others for sustenance. This dependence, in turn, generates a positive application of the Dharma. Buddhist merit is measured by the extent of one's altruism: how far-reaching the benefits are to others and into the future. Merit is also accrued when one does not require "return on investment." Trust the natural laws of karma to return wholesome effects eventually to the entire system (of which the individual is a part). Hence, every kind deed, word or thought is an investment towards a Pure Land on earth for the self and others.

The vision of selfless bodhisattvas building a meritorious Pure Land together for future generations is still an ideal. In reality, many temple patrons wish for personal and family wellbeing. Education is the key to shifting paradigms, worldviews and value systems. Supporting the shift has to be communities of practice to build new habits. Mindful habits at the personal level can extend to peaceful interaction with family and friends; collaborative community-building can lead to social harmony and world peace. The Buddhist sangha, such as Fo Guang Shan, can be an example in generating positive socio-economic impact through spiritual practices in human enterprises.

4 Conclusion: Path to Co-operative Harmony

Buddhist and western economic paradigms are not necessarily conflicting. They propose different measures and paths to help humanity be happier. While Buddhists focus on mental/spiritual attributes, western economics emphasise the tangible. However, neither system denies the existence of other attributes. Increasingly,

---

[7]According to the Oxford Living Dictionaries, "post-truth" is "relating to or denoting circumstances in which objective facts are less influential in shaping public opinion than appeals to emotional and personal belief".

scientific studies are confirming much of the benefits of Buddhist practices of altruism, mindfulness and ethics.

The Buddha did not invent the laws of karma, dependent co-origination, nor the empty, impermanent nature of all things. He discovered these natural laws of being as well as how the human mind trapped itself in a relentless cycle of tension. Attachment to sensory pleasures is a form of (self-centred) greed and will inevitably lead to unwholesome result. Buddhist training involves mindful contemplation of conditions leading to the reality of the present, followed by the practice of contributing to the economy altruistically and compassionately for co-operative harmony. Hence, economic progress is intended to serve the nation, and national progress will serve every individual. Ideally, humanity makes progress spiritually and materially through this positive cycle of virtues.

Living in a complex world, we should be careful to identify the weeds from the grass, and apply the right herbicide. We may draw some lessons from Saul who points out that a "knowing" person advances carefully, recognising that what he or she knows is only a fraction of the larger picture, whereas a specialised, technocratic elite is dangerously "shielded by childlike certainty" (Saul 1995, p. 5). In humanity's zest to overturn blind faith, superstitions and pessimism of tradition, modernity has promoted progress by mastering nature and expanding economic output (Cohen et al. 2011). The perils of modern commerce is that humans are treated as means to an end, and hence, people feel manipulated, exploited or manoeuvred (Klein 2012, p. 28). Science and ego have taken over religion and the tradition of volunteerism. The sense of community has become about rights rather than service. Self-righteousness and hostility inevitably increase.

Eradicating the weed that has grown stronger over time is not going to be effortless nor quick. It will take the injection of much healthy grass and other ingredients to strengthen the soil. Such cultivation on the mind is not a luxury, but a matter of necessity and urgency. The modern consciousness emphasises human concerns; humanistic Buddhism adds to that dialogue a reminder for compassionate activities within this human sphere in response to timeless human needs. Sustainable happiness of a community in harmony requires co-operation rather than competition. The path to co-operative harmony can take place in one's personal, work and community life, with every action taken, speech made and thought generated. Many Buddhist leaders and communities have engaged society to demonstrate possible ways to minimise one's self-centred needs as the origin of economic relationships. It begins with one opening up one's heart to the needs and conditions of others (human beings, as well as all animate and inanimate things), beyond theory into practice.

References

Alexandrin, G. (1993). Elements of buddhist economics. *International Journal of Social Economics, 20*(2), 3.

Ariyaratne, A. (1999). *Buddhist economics in practice: In the Sarvodaya Shramadana movement of Sri Lanka*. Salisbury: Sarvodaya Support Group UK.

Ash, C. (2006). The Monastic Sangha: An incomparable field of merit. and wealth creators? In A. W. Guruge (Ed.), *Hsi Lai Journal of Humanistic Buddhism* (Vol. 7, pp. 214–221).

Ash, C. (2007). Happiness and economics: A Buddhist perspective. *Society and Economy, 29*(2), 201–222.

Ash, C. (2011). Do our economic choices make us happy? In L. Zsolnai (Ed.), *Ethical Principles and Economic Transformation—a Buddhist approach* (pp. 111–131). Dordrecht, Netherlands: Springer.

Balachandran, P. (2006, May 15). Plea to adopt Buddhist economics. *The Hindustan Times*.

Benn, S., & Giurco, D. (2014, February 25). *Explainer: What is the circular economy?* Retrieved May 24, 2016, from The Conversation: Academic rigour, journalistic flair: http://theconversation.com/explainer-what-is-the-circular-economy-23298.

Bunting, M. (2011, November 10). Small is beautiful—an economic idea that has sadly been forgotten. *The Guardian*.

Campergue, C. (2015). Gifts and the selfless work ethic in Tibetan Buddhist centres in France. *Religion Compass, 9*(11), 443–461.

Caple, J. (2015). Faith, generosity, knowledge and the Buddhist gift: Moral discourses on Chinese patronage of Tibetan Buddhist monasteries. *Religion Compass, 9*(11), 462–482.

Centre for Bhutan Studies & GNH Research. (2015, 11). *Bhutan's 2015 Gross National Happiness Index*. Retrieved November 11, 2017, from Gross National Happiness: http://www.grossnationalhappiness.com/SurveyFindings/Summaryof2015GNHIndex.pdf.

Chandler, S. (2004). *Establishing a pure land on earth: The Foguang Buddhist perspective on modernization and globalization*. Honolulu: University of Hawai'i Press.

Chang, O. (2006). The Buddhist approach to economic development: The path to a wisdom-based economy. In A. W. Guruge (Ed.), *Hsi Lai Journal of Humanistic Buddhism* (Vol. 7, pp. 173–181).

Cleary, T. F. (1984). *The flower ornament scripture: A translation of the Avatamsaka sutra*. Boulder: Shambhala Publications.

Coderey, C. (2005). The healing power of the gift healing services and remuneration in Rakhine (Western Myanmar). *Religion Compass, 9*(11), 404–422.

Cohen, M., Gough, I., Tienhaara, K., Peine, J. D., & Sim, S. (2011). The end of modernity: What the financial and environmental crisis is really telling us. *Sustainability: Science, Practice, & Policy, 7*(2).

De L'Estoile, B. (2014). Money is good, but a friend is better: Uncertainty, orientation to the future, and the economy. *Current Anthropology, 55*(S9), 62–73.

Duflo, A., & Mosenkis, J. (2017, January 10). *Greater Good: the science of a meaningful life*. Retrieved January 13, 2017, from Why 2016 Was Actually One of the Best Years on Record: http://greatergood.berkeley.edu/article/item/why_2016_was_actually_one_of_the_best_years_on_record?utm_source=Newsletter+Jan+11%2C+2017&utm_campaign=GG+Newsletter+Jan+11+2017&utm_medium=email.

Essen, J. (2011). Economic Sufficiency and Santi Asoke. In L. Zsolnai (Ed.), *Ethical principles and economic transformation—a Buddhist approach* (pp. 61–77). Dordrecht, Netherlands: Springer.

George, J. S. (1975). The goals of economic policy. *The Journal of Law & Economics, 18*(2), 283–292.

Greenblatt, S. (2011). *The Swerve: How the world became modern*. New York: W.W. Norton.

Groenewegen, P. (2009). Introduction in a. Marshall, *Principles of Economics* (pp. 1–10). Cosimo Classics.

Guruge, A. W. (2008). *Buddhist Economics and Science*. Bloomington, IN: Authorhouse.
Helliwell, J., Layard, R., & Sachs, J. (2016). World happiness report 2016. In J. Helliwell, R. Layard, & J. Sachs (Eds.), *World happiness report 2016 update* (Vol. 1, pp. 2–7). New York: Sustainable Development Solutions Network.
History. (2017). Retrieved January 09, 2017, from Sarvodaya: http://www.sarvodaya.org/history.
Kawamura, G. N., & Kawamura, L. S. (1991). *Mādhyamika and Yogācāra: A Study of Mahāyāna Philosophies: Collected Papers of G.M. Nagao*. Albany: SUNY Press.
Klein, D. (2012). *Travels with epicurus: A journey to a Greek island in search of an authentic old age*. Melbourne: Text Publishing.
Lancaster, L. (2006). Buddhism and the study of philosophical approaches to economics. In A. W. Guruge (Ed.), *Hsi Lai Journal of Humanistic Buddhism* (Vol. 7, pp. 41–63).
Lillington, K. (2006, January 6). Gift economy keeps on giving in virtual utopia. *Irish Times*, p. 7.
Linear Vs Cyclical Paradigms and Permaculture Mind. (n.d.). Retrieved May 25, 2016, from (Perma)Culture and Sanity: http://permaculture-and-sanity.com/index.php.
Magnuson, J. C. (2011). Pathways to a mindful economy. In L. Zsolnai (Ed.), *Ethical principles and economic transformation—a Buddhist approach* (pp. 79–107). Dordrecht, Netherlands: Springer.
Mauss, M. (1990). *The Gift: The form and reason for exchange in archaic societies*. (W. Halls, Trans.) London: Routledge.
Mosini, V. (2007). Three ways of looking at economic equilibrium. In V. Mosini (Ed.), *Equilibrium in economics: Scope and limits*. London: Routledge, Taylor & Francis Group.
Muller, C. (2010, October 26). Merit. *Digital dictionary of Buddhism*.
Muller, C. (2013, March 28). Bodhisattva. *Digital dictionary of Buddhism*.
Nelson, J. A. (2011). The relational economy. In L. Zsolnai (Ed.), *Ethical principles and economic transformation—a Buddhist approach* (pp. 21–33). Dordrecht, Netherlands: Springer.
Orme-Johnson, D. W., Alexander, C. N., Davies, J. L., Chandler, H. M., & Larimore, W. E. (1988). International peace project: The effects of Maharishi technology of the United Field. *Journal of Conflict Resolution, 32*(4), 776–812.
Peach, J., & Dugger, W. M. (2006). An intellectual history of abundance. *Journal of Economic Issues, 40*(3), 693–706.
Philosophy and approach. (2017). Retrieved January 09, 2017, from Sarvodaya: http://www.sarvodaya.org/philosophy-and-approach.
Powers, R. (1956). Adam Smith: Practical realist. *The Southwestern Social Science Quarterly, 37*(3), 222–233.
Prayukvong, W. (2005). A Buddhist economic approach to the development of community enterprises: A case study from Southern Thailand. *Cambridge Journal of Economics, 29*, 1171–1185.
Riedy, C. (2013, November 14). *The sharing economy spooking big business*. Retrieved May 24, 2016, from The Conversation: Academic rigour, journalistic flair: http://theconversation.com/the-sharing-economy-spooking-big-business-19541.
Sandberg, A. (2014, May 9). *The five biggest threats to human existence*. Retrieved May 24, 2016, from The Conversation: Academic rigour, journalistic flair: http://theconversation.com/the-five-biggest-threats-to-human-existence-27053.
Saul, J. R. (1995). *The unconscious civilization*. New York: The Free Press.
Schumacher, E. F. (1973). *Small is beautiful: Economics as if people mattered*. New York: Harper & Row.
Sen, A. K. (1977). Rational fools: A critique of the behavioral foundations of economic theory. *Philosophy & Public Affairs, 6*(4), 317–344.
Sihlé, N. (2015). Towards a comparative anthropology of the Buddhist gift and other transfers. *Religion Compass*, pp. 352–385.
Smith, A. (1790). *The Theory of Moral Sentiments* (6 ed.). London: A. Millar.
Testart, A. (2013). What is a gift? *HAU: Journal of Ethnographic Theory, 3* (1), 249–261.

Tideman, S. G. (2011). Gross National happiness. In L. Zsolnai (Ed.), *Ethical principles and economic transformation—a Buddhist approach* (pp. 133–153). Dordrecht, Netherlands: Springer.

Wang, Z.-y. (2006). Humanistic Buddhism and economic progress: Economic growth in 20th and 21st century in the Yangzi River Delta in China. In A. W. Guruge (Ed.), *Hsi Lai Journal of Humanistic Buddhism* (pp. 246–263).

Weber, F. (2012). The gift: Towards an ethnography of non market services. In M. Mauss (Ed.), *The gift*. New York: Routledge.

Weeraratna, S. (2012). *Review of Putting Buddhism to Work: A New Approach to Management and Business by Shinichi Inoue*. Retrieved January 05, 2017, from BuddhaNet: http://www.buddhanet.net/budwork.htm.

What are B Corps? (2017). Retrieved January 06, 2017, from https://www.bcorporation.net/what-are-b-corps.

Wong, P. (2012). *Acculturation as seen through Buddha's birthday parades in Northern Wei Luoyang: A micro perspective on the making of Buddhism as a world religion*. Los Angeles.

Yun, H. (2005). Buddhist view on economic issues: Speech by venerable master Hsing Yun on 7 August 2003. *Universal Gate Buddhist Journal, 26*, 315–353.

Yun, H. (2012). *Four Insights for Finding Fulfillment: A practical guide to the Buddha's Diamond Sutra*. (R. Smitheram, Trans.) Hacienda Heights, California: Buddha's Light Publishing.

Yun, H. (2015a). *365 days with travelers: Wisdom from Chinese literary and Buddhist classics*. Kaohsiung city, Taiwan: Venerable Master Hsing Yun Public Education Trust Fund.

Yun, H. (2015b). *Hear Me Out: Messages from a humble monk*. (Miao Guang, You Zai, & Zhi Yue, Trans.) Kaohsiung, Taiwan: Fo Guang Shan Monastery.

Yun, H. (2016). *Humanistic Buddhism: Holding true to the original intents of Buddha*. (Miao Guang, Trans.) Kaohsiung, Taiwan: Fo Guang Cultural Enterprise.

Zsolnai, L. (2011). Why Buddhist economics? In L. Zsolnai (Ed.), *Ethical principlese and economic transformation—a Buddhist approach* (pp. 3–17). Dordrecht, Netherlands: Springer.

Author Biography

Juewei Shi is the Director of Humanistic Buddhism Centre and Lecturer of Applied Buddhist Studies at the Nan Tien Institute, Australia. She holds a Ph.D. from University of the West in USA; a Master of Arts in Buddhist Studies from Tsung-Lin University in Taiwan; a Master of Business Administration from Cranfield University in the UK; and a Master of Science in Computer Science and Engineering from the University of Michigan, Ann Arbor in the USA.

Venerable Dr. Juewei's research interests include Buddhist Economics, Humanistic Buddhism, and Buddha's birthday festivals. As part of her belief in the education and practice of humanistic values in today's world, she advocates alternative models inspired by Buddhist values and wisdom that fit with modern-day paradigms and improve the quality of life.

The worldwide tour: 'Buddha's Birthday Education Project—Through These Doors: Connecting Past and Present, East and West' is based on Venerable Dr. Juewei's dissertation and book, *Parading the Buddha*. She heads the tour, and also directs the creation of the website: www.paradeofthebuddhas.org and several mobile apps which makes relevant research, literary and artistic information accessible to a worldwide audience.

Chapter 24
Informal Economy and Diversity: The Role of Micro-producers

Tadashi Yagi

1 Introduction

The concept of market competition has long dominated the field of economics, and many of us believe in the benefits of it. Market competition improves the efficiency of the economy, as predicted by the first basic principle of welfare economics, which proclaims that a competitive economy achieves the most efficient allocation of resources. However, this principle is not valid in situations where economies of scale are evident in the whole economy [see Bator (1958) for discussion of the non-convex economy].

In the real world, there are many reasons that economies of scale are found in the economy. First, production cost per unit decreases as production equipment capacity increases. Second, the negotiating power for purchasing intermediate goods increases as the amount of trade increases. In addition to these properties, the more complex issue still remains as to the relation between a competitive economy and diversity, as discussed by Tisdell (2013).

As the economy becomes globalized, economies of scale increase because of the expanding market size. In this process, the size of global companies and their price competitiveness increase, which results in an oligopolistic market structure. In other words, the diversity of products decreases as the number of producers decreases.

Contrary to the prediction of economic theory, many micro-producers still exist in the economies of developing countries such as India, and they improve the functioning of the whole economy by providing diversity. Trienekens (2012) argues that the competitiveness of value chains depends on business models that link small producers to the global value chain, regardless of the weakness of small producers in various areas such as their financial situation.

T. Yagi (✉)
Faculty of Economics, Doshisha University, Kyoto, Japan
e-mail: tyagi@mail.doshisha.ac.jp

The key characteristics of micro-producers are discussed by Silva et al. (2016), who conclude that financing systems for micro-producers are vital to their success [see Marconatto et al. (2016) for the definition of microfinance]. By providing a system of microfinance, it becomes possible for micro-producers to survive and improve their quality of life by engaging in creative activities. According to Silva et al., it is estimated that 30 million people have accessed microfinance services worldwide over the last 25 years. These microfinance services, however, are hindered from reaching their full value because of the lack of systematic government oversight of their operations (Ahmed et al. 2013).

In this chapter, we theoretically discuss the economic conditions that allow micro-producers to exist in the market, and derive some insights into the diversified market.

2 Conventional Approach to Diversity in the Economy

2.1 Dixit–Stiglitz Type Diversity Model

Concerning diversity in the economy, Dixit and Stiglitz (1977) present an influential mathematical model. In their model, they assume a constant elasticity of substitution (CES) type utility function U, which is specified as

$$U = \left(\sum_{i=1}^{n} x(i)^\rho \right)^{\frac{1}{\rho}}, \quad 0 < \rho < 1, \tag{1}$$

where $x(i)$ is the ith good, and the elasticity of substitution σ is defined by

$$\sigma = \frac{1}{1-\rho}. \tag{2}$$

The budget constraint is given by

$$\sum_{i=1}^{n} p(i)x(i) = Y, \tag{3}$$

where $p(i)$ is a price of good i, and Y is income. Maximizing Eq. (1) subject to Eq. (3), we derive the following demand function:

$$x(i) = \frac{Y}{p(i)^\sigma P^{1-\sigma}}, \tag{4}$$

where

$$P = \left(\sum_{i=1}^{n} p(i)^{1-\sigma}\right)^{\frac{1}{1-\sigma}}. \tag{5}$$

In the case of symmetric equilibrium, Eqs. (4) and (5) are rewritten as follows:

$$\begin{aligned} p(i) &= p \\ x(i) &= x \\ P &= n^{\frac{1}{1-\sigma}} p \\ x &= \frac{Y}{np}. \end{aligned} \tag{6}$$

In their model, it is assumed that the same production technology prevails throughout the region, and the cost function is given by

$$C = cq + F, \tag{7}$$

where c is the marginal cost, F is the fixed cost, and C is the total cost. In this case, the profit function π is given by

$$\pi = (p - c)q - F. \tag{8}$$

The optimality condition for profit maximization gives

$$p = \frac{\eta}{\eta - 1} c, \tag{9}$$

where η is the demand elasticity of price, defined as

$$\eta \equiv \frac{p}{q} \frac{\partial q}{\partial p}. \tag{10}$$

Combining this elasticity equation with the demand function derived above, we get the following.

$$\begin{aligned} p &= \frac{c}{n-1} \frac{\sigma+1}{\sigma-1} \\ q &= \frac{Y(\sigma-1)(n-1)}{c\{\sigma(n-1)+1\}} \end{aligned} \tag{11}$$

Assuming free entry to the market, new entrants continue until the profit level shrinks to zero. Thus, the zero-profit condition assures that

$$(p-c)q = F, \qquad (12)$$

which allows us to derive the following equilibrium:

$$
\begin{aligned}
n^* &= 1 + \frac{1}{\sigma}\left(\frac{Y}{F} - 1\right) \\
p^* &= \frac{\sigma c}{(\sigma - 1)\left(1 - \frac{F}{Y}\right)} \\
q^* &= \frac{(\sigma - 1)F\left(1 - \frac{F}{Y}\right)}{c\{\sigma(n - 1) + 1\}}
\end{aligned}
\qquad (13)
$$

From the equilibrium values given by Eq. (13), Dixit and Stiglitz derive the following properties of the equilibrium.

(i) The degree of diversity is an increasing function of income.
(ii) The degree of diversity is a decreasing function of fixed cost in production.
(iii) The degree of diversity is a decreasing function of the elasticity of substitution σ. This value goes to infinity as the value of ρ converges to 1. This implies that the degree of diversity converges to 1 as goods become completely substitutable. This means that the degree of diversity at the equilibrium increases as consumers differentiate between goods.
(iv) Equilibrium price increases linearly as the marginal cost of production increases.
(v) Since

$$\frac{dp^*}{d\sigma} = \frac{-c\left(1 - \frac{F}{Y}\right)}{\left((\sigma - 1)\left(1 - \frac{F}{Y}\right)\right)^2} < 0,$$

the equilibrium price decreases as the degree of substitutability increases.
(vi) Since

$$\frac{dp^*}{dF} = \frac{\sigma c(\sigma - 1)}{\left((\sigma - 1)\left(1 - \frac{F}{Y}\right)\right)^2} > 0,$$

the equilibrium price increases as the fixed cost increases.
(vii) Since

$$\frac{dp^*}{dY} = \frac{-\sigma c(\sigma - 1)F}{\left((\sigma - 1)\left(1 - \frac{F}{Y}\right)\right)^2 Y^2} < 0$$

the equilibrium price decreases as the income level increases. Intuitively, this seems strange. However, the constant marginal cost assumption implies that the average cost decreases as demand increases, and it is plausible that the lower equilibrium price reflects the decrease in the average cost.

(viii) The equilibrium demand is an inverse function of the equilibrium price. Thus, demand decreases as the marginal cost increases, increases as the degree of substitutability increases, decreases as the fixed cost increases, and increases as the income level increases.

2.2 Extension of the Dixit–Stiglitz Model

In this section, we discuss the extension of the Dixit–Stiglitz model from various points of view. In the previous section, we discussed the implications of diversity in the context of market equilibrium. This provided us with insights on the mechanisms of how diversity affects the market equilibrium under the assumption that individual preferences are same among all consumers, and that all goods affect utility in the same way. Our question now is how market mechanisms are affected by relaxing these assumptions.

2.2.1 Diversity in Preference

The assumption that all consumers have the same preferences has a strong impact when discussing diversity. In the extreme, it is possible to imagine a case in which an infinite number of producers make goods and each consumer's preferences are completely different from other consumers. In this case, each consumer has a unique consumption bundle, and each producer produces products for one consumer. Since fixed costs exist and the production costs exceed the zero-profit level, no producers can survive. Thus, only a finite number of producers who can attract a certain number of consumers survive in the market.

The question is how the selection mechanism works between consumers and producers. The producers that attract many consumers can gain a positive profit because the price of goods and the quantity produced increase. However, since we assume free entry into the market, new entrants continue to enter the market until the profit becomes zero. Since the cost function is same for all the producers, the zero-profit condition predicts a uniform price for all products.

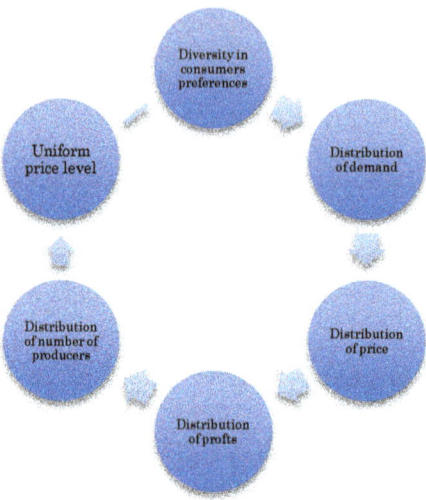

2.2.2 Diversity in Quality and Preference

In the Dixit–Stiglitz model, it is assumed that the same production function prevails over all producers. In reality, the production function differs among producers, and the quality of products differs among them. The consequence of unequal production functions is not complicated unless the quality is equal. The equilibrium price prevails in the market, and the profit level differs depending on producers' cost functions. Thus, profit level is unequally distributed among producers.

In the case where the quality of products and cost functions differ among producers, the market equilibrium becomes complicated. First, it is necessary to clarify the matching mechanism between producers and consumers. The amount of willingness-to-pay for a product depends on the quality of the product. For example, consumers who are sensitive to the safety of foods have a high willingness-to-pay for organic foods. Thus, the price set by the producers of organic foods can be high. In this case, a producer can survive in the market even when the cost of production is relatively high.

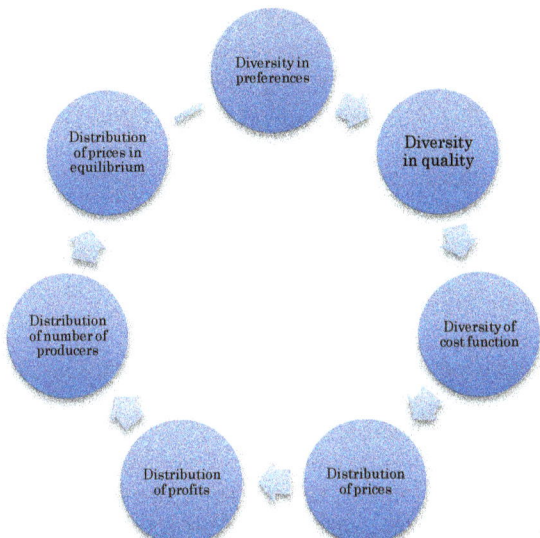

In this matching process, consumers seek various types of information, such as price and quality. In this type of transaction, the cost of collecting information could be quite high because the factors affecting the quality of products can be very large. In the example of organic foods, some consumers will care about the traceability of foods. This kind of information is hard to obtain through the market.

In the Dixit–Stiglitz model, only price is used as the signal for both consumers and producers. Quality information is assumed to be completely perfect, and the cost of collecting information on quality is ignored. In the real world, serious asymmetry exists between producers and consumers concerning information about quality. This problem becomes more serious for consumers as the degree of diversity in the market increases because the number of choices increases as the number of goods increases. For this reason, it is useful to explore the matching process for transacting diversified products.

2.3 Matching Process for Transacting Diversified Products

We assume a positive value for information cost I, which is given by

$$I = \psi(n, \omega), \quad \frac{\partial \psi}{\partial n} > 0,$$

where n is the number of products, and ω is the market system. Suppose that two types of market systems exist. In one type of market, it is assumed that there exists a monopolistic producer that produces n product variations; in the other type of market, it is assumed that there exists n producers and each producer produces one type of differentiated product. The former type of market is referred to as "the monopolistic (M) market," and the latter type of market is referred to as "the network of micro-producers (N) market."

2.3.1 Monopolistic Market (M-Market)

We examine the transaction pattern for each market type. First, in the M-market, there is only one producer, so this producer can control the market price even when the substitutability among products is large.

The cost function in this market type is quite complicated because some products are jointly produced, and economies of scale and scope may potentially exist in the production function. The source of economies of scale is the decreasing average cost, which reflects the strong negotiation power in the procurement of intermediate goods. The advantage of a single producer producing various types of products is the efficient utilization of administration. Because of these economies of scale and scope, the monopolistic producer can enjoy price competitiveness.

The monopolistic producer sets prices so that the marginal revenue equals marginal cost. If the prices exceed the prices set by new entrants to the market, the equilibrium prices will decrease until the profit level of new entrants decreases to zero. Thus, equilibrium price for a good will be determined at a level between the monopoly price and the competitive price. The size of the difference between the monopoly price and competitive price depends on the degree of economies of scale and scope enjoyed by the monopolistic company.

2.3.2 The Network of Micro-producers Market (N-Market)

In this market type, we assume a large number of micro-producers with each producer producing one type of differentiated product. Each product market is assumed to be competitive, and monopolistic competition prevails in the market. Thus, each micro-producer determines the output level at the point where the marginal revenue equals marginal cost, and the equilibrium price given to the producer is determined at the level where the profit of the producer becomes zero.

2.3.3 Comparison Between the M-Market and N-Market

The condition that determines whether a market becomes an M-market or an N-market depends on the difference in cost functions and the differences in the cost structure for consumers collecting information. If cost conditions are beneficial for a monopolistic producer, it is difficult for micro-producers to survive in the market. It is quite evident that the cost condition is quite beneficial to monopoly producers in the apparel industry. The examples of large-sized apparel companies such as Zara, H&M, and Uniqlo show us why economies of scale prevail in the apparel industry. As a result, the market share of large producers has been expanding in the world apparel market. For example, the sales volume of large apparel companies has been expanding, while the total market size of the apparel industry in Japan has been shrinking. According to Gyokai-search.com, the top ten companies in terms of market share occupy around 70% of the total market. In particular, Fast Retailing (Uniqlo) takes around 23% share of the total market.

One possibility for reducing costs would be an association or network of micro-producers. Joint procurement of intermediate goods may possibly reduce costs, and joint promotion or advertisement of products may also work well. These forms of cooperation, however, cannot overwhelm the cost advantages of the large producers because the micro-producers will also incur the coordination costs necessary to manage the association or networks of micro-producers.

2.3.4 Foundation for the Sustainability of Micro-producers

As discussed in the sections above, there exists little foundation for the existence of micro-producers in a competitive market when only price is used as the endogenously determined signal. In the market, however, other endogenously determined signals such as "trust" also exist. Certain asymmetries concerning information between consumers and producers may also exist and benefit micro-producers.

Large companies have numerous procurement channels, and production sites are located around the world. It is difficult for large firms to monitor their production processes carefully, and these global operations are necessary to achieve economies of scale and reduce the cost of production. However, this manner of operating can make it difficult for consumers to find information about the company's products and can result in damaging information being spread to consumers. For example, a consumer may not be able to know whether chemical fertilizers were used in producing foods. In an actual case, a major hamburger chain was accused of improper food processing in one of its factories, which was revealed to the public via online video.

These problems are found not only in the food industry but also in the manufacturing industry. In both cases, trust formation in the market has been the important issue. For example, safety and long-term support of products are major concerns in the automotive industry. Another prominent example of a market where trust formation plays a crucial role is the medical industry. Patients choose a medical clinic to build a trusting relationship with a doctor. Since knowledge of a patient's health history is important for evaluating health troubles, a long-term relationship is valuable both for both the patient and the doctor.

Information cost I is given by the equation

$$I = \psi(n, \omega), \quad \frac{\partial \psi}{\partial n} > 0,$$

where ω includes various factors affecting information cost. Trust is one of the most important factors, and it is formed through a continuous relationship between consumers and producers. For example, trust concerning organic food is formed through the conversation and knowledge shared between producers and consumers, and the experiences of consuming organic foods.

Another important example is handicrafts, which are closely related to the artistic activities of a city or region. The producers of handicrafts have the experience of receiving art training, and skills are formed by practicing within a certain network of producers and art schools. The evaluation of products is continuously conducted. The pricing of diversified products is informed by the history of evaluation of the producer, and trust formation plays an important role in evaluation.

The competitiveness of micro-producers depends on the efficiency and effectiveness of trust formation. In the matching process, the search process continues until the marginal expected return from search and the marginal cost of search become equal. The marginal cost of search includes information collection cost. Trust formation contributes to a decrease in the marginal cost of search because the information collected through repeated evaluation is reliable and detailed.

In this matching process, price is only part of the important information used to make purchase decisions, and other important factors such as trust and reputation are also exchanged in the market. The advantage of micro-producers is the accumulated trust and detailed information in the local market. Large producers, in contrast, are limited in their ability to use face-to-face trust formation. As is discussed in the example of a major hamburger chain, the traceability of its foods material is limited, and trust in the producer easily erodes after even minor incidents because the production process is a black box to the consumer.

When we incorporate the matching process into the consideration of the competitiveness of micro-producers, the probability of survival for a micro-producer increases when the micro-producer has an advantage in trust formation compared with large producers.

2.4 Insights on the Properties of Diversified Markets

This discussion now examines various insights into the properties of diversified markets. Key insights are as follows.

(1) Diversified markets depend on the cost structure and the efficiency and effectiveness of trust formation in the market.
(2) Micro-producers have less advantage in terms of production cost, and large producers with economies of scale and scope dominate the market.

(3) Micro-producers potentially have various advantages in trust formation in the local market because of the face-to-face interaction between producers and consumers. In this case, a micro-producer may be competitive in a diversified market.

3 Essence of Diversity

The purpose this section is to clarify the source of diversity in India, and examine how the economy and society benefit from maintaining diversity. Our hypothesis is that the importance of community in India is a critical factor in various areas, such as the economy and cultural activities. Taking this hypothesis to its extreme, the community, rather than the household, can be viewed as the decision-making unit in India. Thus, the traditions and rituals of a community are highly esteemed and have a dominant meaning in life. This allows communities to sustain their economic activities and life in a diverse manner.

In India, we presume the culture is diversified in a way that reflects the history of the different peoples in the region. These differences are reflected in various cultural goods such as music instruments. One typical example is the stone instrument in India, which captures various aspects of cultural diversity in India. One aspect would be as a spiritual icon used during rituals. These rituals are a vehicle for maintaining the community's culture.

In Western economies, companies that exhibit low-cost structures dominate the high-cost companies. Economies of scale are pursued by companies and diversity is discarded. The question is why small companies in India are not dominated by the large companies to the same degree as in the West. One hypothesis is that the community is the key unit of the economy, and respect for tradition, history, and local culture helps maintain the diversity in the economy.

In the current globalized economy, creativity is the main source of competitiveness. In the creative economy, community plays an important role in knowledge creation. Since the community is the source of diversity and creativity is generated from the mixture of different knowledge, we expect that India excels in creating new culture. The case of the stone instrument is a good example that illustrates this hypothesis.

In addition, we would like to know how the unity of community is kept in India, specifically in regards to the roles of religion and rituals. Our hypothesis stems from the idea that common values shared by members of the community are necessary for keeping unity. Moreover, it would be necessary for a community to cooperate with other communities for various reasons such as economic reason or political reason. In this case, the common values shared by the different communities are important to consider.

4 Concluding Comments

This chapter theoretically discussed the sustainability of micro-producers. Economic mechanisms work to reduce the number of micro-producers, which are relatively inefficient in comparison to large firms. This economic force puts diversity in society at risk, which can then harm the culture of the region. It is necessary to explore the essential importance of diversity before taking policy actions. Differences in geography, climate, history, and environment have brought about the uniqueness of the culture of each region. Each people in a region has continued their creative activities based on their own culture, and this in turn generated a diversity of products. Thus, policies for improving the efficiencies of micro-producers, such as provision of microfinance, coordination of networks and associations, and human capital development in the field of business activities will contribute to the sustainability of diversified culture in the world.

References

Ahmed, F., Brown, B., & Williams, S. P. (2013). Is it time to regulate microfinance? *Progress in Development Studies, 13*(3), 209–220.
Bator, F. M. (1958). The anatomy of market failure. *The Quarterly Journal of Economics, 72*(3), 351–379.
Dixit, A. K., & Stiglitz, J. E. (1977). Monopolistic competition and optimum product diversity. *The American Economic Review, 67*(3), 297–308.
Marconatto, D., Cruz, L. B., & Pedrozo, E. A. (2016). Going beyond microfinance fuzziness. *Journal of Cleaner Production, 115*, 5–22.
Silva, W. A. C., Fonseca, R. D. F., & Santos, A. D. O. (2016). Microbusiness development and quality of life of microentrepreneurs's family. *Revista de Administração Mackenzie, 17*(4), 176–200.
Tisdell, C. A. (2013), *Competition, diversity and economic performance.* Edward Elgar Publishing.
Trienekens, J. H. (2012). *Value chains in developing countries.* Global Value Chains.

Chapter 25
"The Future's Not What It Used to Be"—Ogden Nash

Stephen Hill

1 Trump's Card Play

Currently, the 'Harmony of Humanity', a quest of my previous Chap. 18, is deeply disturbed, most evocatively, by the 2016 Presidential Election in the United States. The whole development of the current book's argument preceded this event.

We now must take the presence of President Donald Trump in the world's political and economic landscape into account for it deeply affects the real-life context within which we are developing a humanistic/social alternative platform for re-examining global economics.

We have therefore included this additional chapter.

On Friday 20th January 2017 at 11.47 am Donald Trump was inaugurated as President of the United States. The implication is concerning many not just within the United States but worldwide.

Having lost all three Public Debates against Democratic Party opponent, Hilary Clinton, plagued by persistent allegations of sexual predation, promoting fake news, links with Russian hacking and espionage support, making then retracting outrageous false accusations even within the same speech, expressing pride as a successful billionaire in paying zero tax for the last 15 years … most of America was simply *stunned*. And, I might add, many did not vote as they did not care until they saw the outcome.

The rest of the world watched in disbelief as a posturing, aggressive, habitually lying, self-centered billionaire businessman with zero international diplomatic or policy experience … became the most powerful man in the world.

Every card in Trump's hand appeared to be a loser, a knave or a joker. Yet he convincingly 'trumped' the opposition.

S. Hill (✉)
University of Wollongong, Wollongong, Australia
e-mail: sthill@uow.edu.au

© The Editor(s) 2018
S. Yamash'ta et al. (eds.), *The Kyoto Manifesto for Global Economics*,
Creative Economy, https://doi.org/10.1007/978-981-10-6478-4_25

How could this happen?
It is clear that there were a number of political forces in favor of Donald Trump.

The first was the relative unpopularity of his opponent, Hilary Clinton – a legacy of her vote on the Iraq War, the Benghazi attack in Libya, controversial decisions she made during her husband's Presidency.

Second, Hilary was 'stained' by Bill Clinton's past and her own inattentive use of emails within her official role as America's most senior diplomat – reinforced by crippling allegations by the Head of the FBI immediately prior to the election that further investigation of Hilary Clinton was to go ahead – even though finally rejected as unproblematic ... but too late. The stain was already indelible.

Third, and most importantly though, was that Hilary was an uninspiring symbol of 'more of the same' whilst Trump represented a refreshingly outrageous proponent of *change*.

Even so, Hilary actually won nearly 2.9 million more popular votes than Trump —with Hilary even surpassing President Barack Obama's 2012 popular vote total by 389,944 votes. (Kreig 2016) Many people, unfortunately, did not vote.

But the final US election process—mediated via State Electoral College Representatives—worked strongly in Trump's favor—particularly as Trump had "swooped down on the Midwestern States—Michigan, Ohio, Pennsylvania and Wisconsin—like a vulture claiming the carcass left behind by Clinton" (Roysam 2016).

As stated on US ABC News:

This means that it doesn't matter if Mrs Clinton won by almost 2.5 million votes in California, or that Mr Trump won by almost a million votes in Texas — the number of electoral college votes awarded would be the same as if they had won by one vote. Mr Trump has won smaller vote margins in the states, but he has won states rich in electoral college votes, such as Florida, Pennsylvania and Ohio, which helped him reach the magic number of 270. (ABC 2017)

Michael Moore, ascerbic commentator and film-maker on American and world issues, accurately predicted the election result well in advance – along with the *real* reason Trump was elected.

From Green Bay to Pittsburgh, this, my friends, is the middle of England – broken, depressed, struggling, the smokestacks strewn across the countryside with the carcass of what we used to call the Middle Class. Angry, embittered working (and nonworking) people who were lied to by the trickle-down of Reagan and abandoned by Democrats who still try to talk a good line but are really just looking forward to rub one out with a lobbyist from Goldman Sachs who'll write them a nice big check before leaving the room. What happened in the UK with Brexit is going to happen here. Elmer Gantry shows up looking like Boris Johnson and just says whatever shit he can make up to convince the masses that this is their chance! To stick it to ALL of them, all who wrecked their American Dream! And now The Outsider, Donald Trump, has arrived to clean house! You don't have to agree with him! You don't even have to like him! He is your personal Molotov cocktail to throw right into the center of the bastards who did this to you! SEND A MESSAGE! TRUMP IS YOUR MESSENGER! (Moore 2016)

As Business Reporter David Taylor observed, "Donald Trump is both unconventional and, in effect, a-political." ... "That means that President Trump has the ability to *surprise*." "He created his own popularity" and with this came his power base" (Taylor 2017).

2 A Contested Game

A deep division has been left however within America.

Even well before the election itself, the protests against Trump started to build up.

One of the most creative was delivered at the time of the July 2016 Republican Convention.

> As a way of lampooning Donald Trump's controversial call for a "great, great wall" on the US-Mexico border to stop illegal immigrants, an artist who calls himself 'Plastic Jesus', installed a tiny 15 cm high concrete wall around the Hollywood 'Walk of Fame' Star awarded to Trump for his work on America's TV show, 'The Apprentice' – the 2327th Star on the Hollywood Walk. Topped with razor wire, miniature US flags and 'Keep Out' signs written in both Spanish and English, the miniature wall attracted world wide attention. (Avis 2016)

Far more significantly, on Saturday 21st January 2017, the day after Donald Trump's Inauguration, hundreds of thousands of women flooded the streets of Washington, and many more marched in cities across the country. As the New York Times reported, participation in the City of Washington likely surpassed a half million, more than 400,000 marched in New York City, 175,000 in Boston, and hundreds of thousands more in Chicago and Los Angeles and other cities where demonstrators took to the streets—a total US protest easily passing the participation of one million people (Chira and Alcidor 2017).

> The women were marching to protest against an incoming President who promised action to oppose abortion rights, cut funding for anti-domestic violence, and a range of other actions that disproportionately affect women and minorities … and, who had been outed by a number of women for arrogant sexual abuse. (Chira and Alcidor 2017)

> Marching against a President who proudly pronounced his elitist, anti-feminist, racist, xenophobic, isolationist agenda and who quite comfortably lied in public view.

The protest numbers far exceeded the number of people who attended the Inauguration Ceremony for Donald Trump the day before, and—from aerial photos of the crowds, Trump attracted a much smaller crowd than did Barack Obama's 2009 Inauguration, and again in 2013—a fact that was reinforced by the number of people riding Washington's mass transit system on the day, even compared against Obama's 2013 Inauguration—782,000 for Obama versus 571,000 for Trump just over four years later, in 2017 (Davis and Rosenberg 2017).

Trump's response revealed his priority to project personal image and lies over presidential leadership.

> As the incoming President of the USA, Trump's *first Press Conference* did not use the occasion to announce policy or reflect on the significance of the day.

> Instead, he personally dispatched his White House Press Secretary, Sean Spicer, to claim to the media, that "this (his Inauguration crowd) was the largest audience to ever witness an inauguration, period." Confronted by clear visual recorded evidence contradicting this assertion, the press were told that *these* were "alternative facts." (Bradner 2017)

Even those within Trump's own Republican Party expressed opposition and fear.

> The Trump business empire spans more then 140 companies, with interests in at least 25 countries, according to filings with United States regulators. This has raised considerable fears within the Republican Party, let alone elsewhere, that the President's commercial interests could taint decision-making on both domestic and foreign policy. (Lang 2017)

> With this in mind, on Tuesday 24th January, just four days after Trump's Inauguration, Richard Painter, a lawyer who advised former President George W. Bush on ethics, and has strong ties with the Republican Party, admitted he had voted for Hilary Clinton rather than Donald Trump. He then zeroed in particularly on the billionaire businessman's connections to international companies and countries, observing that Trump would be breaking with the US Constitution's requirement that, as a person in a position of trust dealing with foreign governments and companies controlled by foreign governments, he must not receive profits or other benefits from these sources. (Grant 2017)

President Trump's own financial business is particularly compromised where Trump must resolve conflict in countries where the results depend on his negotiating or power role as US President, such as between Russia and Turkey (where he has both friendship with President Putin in Russia along with business interests, and in Turkey where Trump owns golf courses and other interests).

Most important is Donald Trump's already biased decisions concerning the Middle East.

By Executive Order, as 'protection for US citizens', President Trump banned citizens from seven Islamic countries from entry to the United States: Iran, Iraq, Libya, Somalia, Sudan, Syria and Yemen.[1]

> No American citizens were killed on American soil from citizens of any of these nations between 1975 and 2015 according to detailed statistics compiled by the CATO Institute in the US. (Nowrasteh 2016)[2]

> In the meantime however, 3000 Americans were killed by citizens from Saudi Arabia, the United Arab Emirates and Egypt in the same time period — with the bulk of those killed being victims of the 9/11 attacks. These three Islamic countries were excluded from President Trump's Executive Order so their nationals are still welcome to apply for US visas and travel permits.

Trump's global business empire—which he has refused to rescind ownership of—holds multi-million dollar licensing and development deals in all of these three countries, raising potential conflict of interest concerns and alarming questions over what actually went into the decision process behind the Executive Order banning *some* Moslem immigration to the United States (New York Daily News 2017).

---

[1] Iraq was subsequently removed from this banned list as the US's defense engagement in Iraq required continuing exchange of personnel across borders.

[2] A side-note of relevance, given that refugees tend often to be targeted for exclusion is that the CATO Institute calculates that the chance of being killed by a refugee is 1/3.64 billion, compared with 1/3.9 million killings by people entering the United States on a Tourist B visa, the normal mode of entry. Many individual crimes by Islamic immigrants were against the murderer's spouse and completely unrelated to terrorism (Nowrasteh 2016).

Indeed, in August 2015, according to the Washington Post, shortly after launching his bid for the US Presidency, Donald Trump registered eight companies in Saudi Arabia tied to his hotel interests.

> "They buy apartments from me," Trump said during an Alabama rally. "They spend $40, $50 million. Am I supposed to dislike them? I like them very much." (Sabransky 2016)

Yet Trump offers little protection against such compromise, having handed over management of his financial affairs to his family whilst still maintaining ownership. He still *knows* what personal financial benefits are accruing according to his Presidential decisions.

> Richard Painter states, "He will conform to the constitution or we will remove him. That is done in the United States." In other words, impeachment is possible, though perhaps unlikely as long as President Trump can "figure it out". (Grant 2017)

In the meantime, Donald Trump remains in position—as the most powerful person in the world.

3 Leader of the 'Free' World!

As a clear example of his influence, President Donald Trump is having serious impact on global economics. He has become the single biggest global market influence.

> When, following his election to Presidency, Trump broadcast a 'tweet' (140 characters) on internet stating that Lockheed Martin's costs were "out of control", stock of a company, worth $(US)75 billion, immediately slumped by three percent, or $(US)2.25 billion. (Taylor 2017)

> On the day Trump won the election, the stock market had one of its biggest swings in recent memory. At the time of his Inauguration, according to Wall Street traders, hundreds of billions of dollars were on the move, which if bond trading is included added up to *a trillion dollars*. (Taylor 2017)

The dark side of the economic influence card is Trump's immediate action to take climate change and environmental concern off the American agenda, and ultimately to impact strongly on the globally mandated commitment to reduce human impact on the environment, given the US's dominant share in contribution to global warming.

Moments after President Donald Trump took the oath of office, all traces of previous President Obama's climate change initiatives were removed from the White House website (Parker 2017).

Disturbingly, Doug Eriksen, Head of Communications in the Trump Administration's Environmental Protection Agency (EPA), announced four days after Trump's Inauguration that scientists who want to publish or present their scientific findings are likely to need their work reviewed on a "case by case basis" before it can be disseminated, i.e.: politically screened: As Erikson said,

> We'll take a look at what's happening so that the voice coming from the EPA is one that is going to reflect the new administration. (Rott 2017)

Such review directly conflicts with the EPA's 2012 "scientific integrity policy" which forbids any form of repression, alteration or impeding of scientific findings and conclusions. Furthermore, political review prior to release of research based information potentially limits the EPA's ability to pursue independent research on environmental concern (EPA 2012) The proposed review is particularly worrisome when the defense already used by the Whitehouse for not accepting clear evidence of crowd size supporting Trump was the invention of "alternative facts", i.e.: not based on evidence.

As at the time of writing, the world awaits the social, political, international and economic impact of this wild-card President who promises a firm leadership agenda though based on a chimera of lies that change literally moment to moment, are strongly influenced by personal interest, and against already strong domains of popular opposition.

Still, 49% of Americans surveyed by a Reuters/IPSOS Poll on 30th to 31st January 2017 supported Trump's Moslem-specific immigration bans at the time he signed the Executive Order—larger than the 41% who opposed it—although the division was largely on political lines, Republicans versus Democrats (Kahn 2017).

4 Trump's Appeal

Michael More expressed it well in the quote I used earlier. Trump is appealing to the re-capture of 'The American Dream' which has been steadily dissipating under the negative influences of globalization on the American workforce and 'invasion' of outsiders who take jobs away and threaten the American way with an alternate ideology.

Trump offers a simple set of solutions and the people in general have accepted his rhetoric—even though there remains deep and heart-felt opposition from those who look more broadly at the future.

> I will make American business come back and give you jobs and the chance to re-engage in the American Dream. Social welfare is an unfortunate casualty. Environment impact is a necessary cost. I offer jobs now!

Donald Trump promises expansion of jobs in industries that are intrinsically in decline, rather than preparation for the future that will shortly be upon us.

With all policy cast within the 140 characters of Tweets!

The subtext of the mantra is coming from the people who supported Trump in the election:

> Please protect us, allow us to rest in the safe shallows of our national boundary rather than make us swim any more in the open ocean of globalism.

The people appear ready to accept that research and innovation to prepare for a future that is different to the past needs to be sidelined and will have to remain in a funding vacuum. And any information that might compete with Trump's take on the world may need to be suppressed in the interest of maintaining his primary agenda.

What Donald Trump offers, as solution, is a return to the past!
A remembered place of security.
Where jobs remain in established industry
that previously powered modern development.

Rather than the title of the 1985 American science fiction adventure comedy film, "Back to the Future", Trump promises *"Forward to the Past"*.[3]

The strength of this popular demand to return to the past is demonstrated by the political absurdity of the man the United States system has elected to lead the world! But the people can see immediate personal advantage, and follow towards a blinkered vision of what the future might hold—in particular, for their children and grandchildren.

Indeed, Trump offers a disturbing vision for the future, uncomfortably reminiscent of Hitler's invention of National Socialism in Germany in the 1920s to 1930s .... The 'Fuhrer Principle—a belief in the iron infallibility of the leader; his assertion of superior ability ("only *I* can fix it")—that the people must *trust*, even without information on how the 'fix' would be achieved, trust even against demonstrable lies; the targeting of clear enemies to welfare, i.e.: in this case, not Jewish people but Mexican immigrants and Moslems (Range 2016)—"an instant leap from despair to utopia" as historian Fritz Stern expressed it (Stern 1974).

Rhetoric, national command over industry, megalomaniac individualism of the *One Leader who can fix things* ... lies and propaganda to support ... declaring boundaries and de-legitimizing whole peoples in favor of America's re-discovered 'Greatness'.

To be clear, I must emphasize that Trump does not represent Hitler's inhumanity and racism, only a much less violent parallel in xenophobia: protectionism against those from outside the US borders and central religion who might disturb the national US system, namely, Mexicans and Moslems, from crossing the borders into the protected territory and beliefs of the American people.

As with Trump's political promises in general, the message that many people in the US want to hear is *simple!* And focused on their *main* life-world problem—*ensuring employment-based income* and *preservation of the consumer-based lifestyle they have got used to*. Fear of Islamic terrorism has focused attention on the

---

[3] After 'inventing' this title, I discovered that Tim Dunlop had also come up with the same epithet. However, whilst I am talking of the 'Trump Phenomenon' and its reflection of an attempt to recreate a previous industrial age, Dunlop is talking about return to community as it existed in pre-industrial times. Dunlop speaks disparagingly of this *social* reversion, whereas I argue for its necessity in the context of building a society-base for our future economy. See, Dunlop (2016, Loc 2121).

need for the United States to protect its borders from the effects of globalization, and to re-assert the 'American Dream'.

This is not just a crazy President appealing to threatened middle American workers with the mantra of 'jobs, jobs, jobs!', and protection from foreigners taking away these jobs or 'our way of life'.

As demonstrated earlier, Trump is having enormous impact on world economic markets—with each tweet or signed-off (and personally presented on TV) Presidential Executive Order.

However, what is more important is that the appeal of Donald Trump in the US is not unique. The same public fear that supports Trump is spreading across the developed world as we move through this second decade of the 21st Century.

> There appears to be a broadly based movement across Western Europe towards the political right, what Jean-Claude Juncker, President of the European Commission, called "galloping populism". Juncker was referring to movements like the Sweden Democrats, the National Front in France, the Party for Freedom in the Netherlands – voices calling for their once open national borders to close up and for the society to turn inward ... away from globalization. Clearly triggered by a political backlash to the Syrian refugee crisis of the Summer of 2015, the underbelly of fear is deeper. It is a return to isolationism. (Shuster 2016)

> In the case of the BREXIT vote by citizens of Great Britain in 2016 to leave the European Union, the British response was more directly also to the threat to disappearing jobs posed by open borders to the rest of the EU as well as threatening 'our' traditional British culture.

> Both far right wing Presidential candidates for election in 2017, Marine Le Pen in France, and Geert Wilders in the Netherlands, have collected strong support for extremist isolationism. Both are talking of following Britain out of the European Union, the consequence of which would almost certainly sink European collaboration into the mire of past history. (Pasha-Robinson 2016; Express 2016)

> Neither did win. However, their strong presence in the political agenda of Europe signals a clear message of isolationism from the negative effects of globalization.

Donald Trump's election is likely to embolden ultra conservatives in both cases. He stands as symbol and focus for a serious 'tipping point' in globalization.

Even Australia's recent national elections show a similar picture, with the rising popularity of Pauline Hanson from Queensland and her 'One Nation Party', again, concerned about protecting Australia's borders.

Donald Trump therefore represents a leading edge symbol and inspiration of an emerging moment in global capitalism generally—where the people are starting to get scared and are drawing in the boundaries to protect themselves.

Certainly, as is demonstrably the case in Europe under the openness of both internal and external EU borders, from migrants from poorer countries seeking a better life, and now, in particular, from the *one million* Syrian refugees who have escaped from the violence of Syria, of which 150,000 have declared asylum in the EU; and, in the US, more related to illegal Mexicans crossing the border, this is protection from 'invasion'.

In both Europe and the US, 'invasion' is by those who have been excluded from the benefits of global development and are desperate for a different future. And threatening access to disappearing jobs in their countries of adoption as globalized companies generally transfer to where labor cost advantage is best.

Or those who are refugees from despotic or corrupt regimes where benefits have been distorted towards the powerful.

Or, where current terrorist movements, in particular, ISIS and the Taliban, ultimately fighting against globalization's capitalist values and religions, kill all who do not support *their extremist version* of Islamic ideology.

All products of 21st Century globalization. And Americans, fear the consequences, as already has been very dramatically demonstrated with the 9/11 terrorist attack at the heart of America.

But, the success of Trump's 'America First' agenda is most strongly influenced by the 'invasion' of globalization on American *employment* - disappearance of manufacturing jobs in Middle America as the US companies transferred overseas to capture cheaper labor advantage.

There is no question that employment in manufacturing, Trump's main target for action, has been declining at an ever increasing pace in the US. And export of US manufacturing capability has been expanding to countries where the factor cost of labor is cheap.

> Although in the US there was a boost to overall manufacturing employment from 2010 to 2016 of 4.8%, it was preceded by a decade of decline and over the longer term, the number of jobs in manufacturing in the US has dropped from a peak of 19,553,000 in 1979 to 12,322,000 in April 2015, that is a decline by 7,231,000 or 37%. In the case of the apparel industry, employment decreased by 85% over this time. This overall loss in manufacturing employment represents a decline since 1979 in the percentage of US non-institutional employment population from 12.5% to today's 4.9%. (US Bureau of Labor Statistics 2015; Jeffrey 2015; TED 2017)

However, the level of job-loss in the United States was steeper than in many peer countries, particularly Germany, where the level of employment in manufacturing remains at 19.8% of the German workforce, and where decline in manufacturing employment was only 10.3% over the same period as the United States.

The reason? Germany saw the trend emerging and implemented serious policy reforms to do something about it, in particular, bolstering the science, technology and innovation ecosystems that underpin the competitiveness and innovation potential of their private sector enterprises. Japan, Korea, Holland, Taiwan and even China followed suit.

Meanwhile, the UK and the United States R&D and innovation support languished and job losses increased. (Innovation Files 2014) Australia followed suit with the promise to honor a commitment made back in 2014 to cut 20% of the budget from support of Australia's university system, i.e.: a projected $(A) 3.2 billion saving to the national budget, a sacrifice of Australia's future that some have described as a "zombie" measure (Knott 2016).

Trump is making no such investment in the future as did Germany—with demonstrated results.

Instead, he is now trying to bring back the jobs of the past rather than reach forward towards the future through a broad ranging technological innovation initiative that *prepares* for the future rather than denies the implications of global warming and IT productivity based loss of employment.

In policy actions which Donald Trump is now initiating he is also sweeping aside any environmental, human rights or cultural constraints on creating this future, as is evidenced in his immediate signature of his Executive Orders on January 24th 2017, four days after Trump's Inauguration, to build the Keystone XL Pipeline from Canada to US refineries located along the Gulf of Mexico and to complete the Dakota Access Pipeline under Lake Oahe in North Dakota—across territory, water supply and sacred sites of the Standing Rock Sioux tribe and against their protest. In the case of the Keystone XL pipeline, Trump is reversing a major and courageous policy decision of previous President Obama. This original decision was designed, even against US economic benefit, to prevent potentially significant impact on climate change from the heavy duty processing required to turn the piped tar sands crude oil into a marketable product. In both pipeline cases there has been entrenched opposition from environmental and human rights groups to the pipelines being constructed. Trump does not care (Wald 2017; Mufson and Eilperin 2017).

Internationally, President Trump is asserting America 'above all' rather than seek international cooperation for shared benefit.

> Most significantly, he is making this assertion via the cancelation of long-negotiated multi-lateral trade agreements such as the Trans Pacific Partnership Agreement (TPP) in favor of bilateral trade where America calls the shots. (Diamond and Bash 2017)

> As a demonstration of diplomatic attention to international relations and one of America's closest traditional allies, Australia, Trump rudely hung up on the Australian Prime Minister, mid call, as he was unhappy with the deal Australia had already negotiated for resettlement of some refugees into the US. (Rucker 2017)

Withdrawal to self-interest and a past that seemed to work. Little concern about global cooperation or welfare.

However as I noted earlier, in line with the other countries drawing back to the security of isolationism, *globalization* has reached a critical *tipping point,* not just for the US but increasingly across the globe. Trump is the most out-there exponent of withdrawal and self interest.

If only this was a withdrawal from globalization's external *economic* command over the strength of local community—a step to recapture 'society' from the stranglehold of globalized neoliberal 'economics'.

But it is not. Instead, what President Trump is doing is the assertion of self-interest and denial of our wider humanism. This message is catching on elsewhere.

An immediate danger exists, i.e.: the collapse of international *multi-lateral* (shared) cooperation within the global economy, the consequence of which is likely to be a terrible contradiction.

On the one hand, the people are rejecting globalization as it negatively affects them across their national borders, so they are building walls – both real and metaphorical, in an attempt to protect their own self-interest.

On the other hand, what will be left is rapacious and unconstrained capitalist enterprise world wide – unmediated by cross-nation agreement – where everyone competes rather than cooperates, and the most powerful will win – including penetrating deeply across national borders.

Seeking to escape globalization by the strategies of Donald Trump is likely to trap the world's people into an even worse form of globalized impact on their lives. And preparation on a global level for a global warming future will go out the window.

Most importantly though, what we see emerging with the Trump Phenomenon is a familiar story of potential *social failure*—from the Fall of Empires to the collapse of business corporations.

When they reach their zenith of greatness, the State or organization is often too conditioned to continue with the practices that got them there in the first place whilst the world around them has changed and these practices are no longer likely to be successful.

As Jim Collins observed in his 'five stages of decline', drawn from 6000 years of combined corporate history surveyed over 25 years,

Great enterprises can become insulated by success; accumulated momentum can carry an enterprise forward for a while, even if its leaders make poor decisions or lose discipline. Stage 1 (of decline, 'Hubris Born of Success') kicks in when people become arrogant regarding success virtually as an entitlement… (Collins 2009)

Check out just about every regime of the past, the Egyptian Old Kingdom, the Chou Dynasty, the Hittite Empire, Athens, Rome. The British Empire was well on its way to failure as it crossed into the 20th Century, still wedded to its earlier success via steam power when electricity was taking off as the base of production in Germany whilst Britain arrogantly believed their command over world production and trade and their Global Empire could not fall. Meanwhile, America and its consumer focused culture was rising in global significance (Hill 1988, p. 15, 148).

Kodak is a case in point if referring to business corporations.

In 1962 Kodak employed 75,000 people, controlled 70% of the US film market and earned more than $(US) 1 billion in US sales alone. But the company was wedded to its enormous success in marketing film photography. Consequently, even though Kodak invented digital cameras, the company stubbornly refused to support the development of this rival product to their core business, film. …In January 2012, this billion dollar corporation filed for Chap. 11 bankruptcy. (Brachman 2014)

Trump is unknowingly embedded in an agenda of failure, even to deliver what he promises to the American people. And the consequences for global cooperation are immense.

5 The Trump Card: Addressing the Decline in Manufacturing Employment

The cards in Trump's hand come from the past not the future. He is *demanding* the return of manufacturing company production to the United States from countries where, according to labor cost advantage, they had previously re-located.

However, as with King Canute (or King Knud) early 11th Century ruler of Britain, Denmark and Norway, who attempted to turn back the ocean tide, the flow of global employment transformation is irrevocably advancing over the shore of time where 'King Trump' sits in his regal arrogance in the United States Presidential Chair facing this advancing ocean. King Canute recognized that no matter what his obsequious courtiers said was his power, he *could not stop the tides*, thus recognizing his limits of power (Rhodes 2015). President Trump has yet to develop such humility.

The problem with the core popular appeal of Trump—protecting jobs in manufacturing industries—is that in the longer term it will inevitably fail—and leave the United States weakened in its capacity and the commitment required to handle the future.

Global capitalism means that production will relocate to wherever costs are cheapest. And no matter what the US might do, the country remains *surrounded* by a global capitalism context and deeply *injected* with its power.

Apparently in Trump's favor, some American companies such as General Electric, Walmart and Zentech, which previously moved their manufacturing plant from the United States to China to capitalize on cheap labor, are now closing down the Chinese factories and moving back to the United States, a process called "Reshoring"—*because it is economically more profitable for them to do so* (Robinson 2013).

However, whilst perhaps 4000 jobs may have been lost in the US when production moved off shore because of cheap labor advantages, 'reshoring' is likely to create maybe 120–200 jobs. The new factor cost advantage that allows return to the US is via technological innovation and the shedding of workers.

Furthermore, take the case of Apple. It may not be possible to bring the full employment envelope of Apple to America even if the company relocates.

> Apple, for example, manufactures iPhones in seven factories, six in China and one in Brazil. Their own global workforce constitutes just 110,000 people. If Apple were to assemble the phones in the US rather than China and Brazil, the cost of the final product would increase by $(US)30 to $(US)40 each – but less than 100,000 employees would move.
>
> Meanwhile, Apple's outsourced *suppliers* employ more than 1.6 million workers in 346 factories in China, 126 in Japan, Taiwan 41, and the US, 69, i.e. 12% of suppliers are already in the US. If these (non-Apple) overseas suppliers could be persuaded to move to the US the cost of the phone in the US would increase by a further $(US)30 to $(US)40 partly because of higher labor costs but also higher cost of shipping parts not the finished product to the US. If all were to move to the US the factories would be very likely

uncompetitive because most of the goods required would run at low volumes, thus raising the cost differential with Asia even higher.

Most importantly however, the Apple phone uses 70 elements from the periodic chemical table. The elements that need to be mined and processed cannot all be sourced from the US. This is particularly the case with the so-called rare earths such as hafnium and neodymium, absolutely essential for the i-Phone, but sourced primarily from China which produces 85% of the world's output.

Apple is deeply embedded in the global economy. Relocating the majority of the workforce that feeds production of i-phones to the United States is virtually impossible (Kakaes 2016).

And IT based global business platforms, perhaps *the* major wave of the future, employ few people.

Facebook, for example, with vast international reach, employed just 7185 people in 2013—whilst its owner, Mark Zuckerberg, is the sixth richest person in the world, worth $(US)44.6 billion. Amazon warehouses are increasingly populated by interacting robot *stackers*, whilst those *packers* who are still left are housed in what the company euphemistically calls "Fulfillment Centers" (Dunlop 2016, Loc 1184–1195). Unfortunately 'fulfillment' basically means keep doing a repetitive boring job whilst the robots gather around you and until you are forcefully 'retired' when a robot takes over your chair.

So, no matter what Donald Trump might wish, he is fighting—without apparently being aware—against the core dynamic of current global capitalism, technological innovation. He may get some factories to 'reshore', but with massively decreased workforces compared with what they used to have prior to moving offshore.

Trump's intervention agenda is unlikely to create any significant change in this rate of decline in the United States or elsewhere—*in the longer term*.

6 March of the Machines

Ultimately, the most efficient 'ideal' production systems will require no human labor, just machines that do the job and even then design and produce increasingly efficient machines of manufacture (through IT intelligence) and fix them whilst the owner and shareholders remain on the sidelines watching their money accumulate. This is already happening.

There is of course a problem here. If there are no consumers with money, there is no market for the capitalists to sell their products to. I will come to this paradox shortly.

Be that as it may, the leaders of global production continue to reach for competitive cost savings—now moving on from labor cost benefits in poor low-salary countries to technology-based productivity. A benefit of 'globalization'.

Technological innovation, and in particular, artificial intelligence based change is increasingly and rapidly extending back up the chain of production towards job replacement for the sake of financial efficiency. Eighty five percent of the job losses in US manufacturing from 2000 to 2010, a period when 5.6 million factory jobs disappeared, were caused by technology sourced productivity gains whilst only 13% were attributable to trade (Griswold 2016).

What is most indicative of this productivity trend however is that the highest productivity growth was in the production of computers and electronic products ... 829% versus just 6.0% for nonmetallic mineral product manufacture—demonstration of the rapidly increasing presence of IT and computer intelligence across economic production and consumption (Hicks and Devaraj 2015).

> To take one example, 'Baxter', the latest humanoid robot from *Rethink Robotics*, released towards the end of 2012, received an overwhelming response from the manufacturing industry in the US. At just $(US)22,000, Baxter is cheap to buy, easy to train, can work side-by-side with workers ... or, replace them! In particular, from warehousing and laboring jobs. (Briody 2013)

> To take a second example, already in place, based on using cloud computing combined with robotics, robots interact successfully with 'unstructured environments' by talking with each other and checking their knowledge against the vast data banks stored in cloud-computer environments. Amazon is using robots developed by a company, Kiva, designed to work in warehouses.

>> The robots move around storage racks filled with boxes of items. There can be hundreds and thousands of them in a warehouse, and they increase efficiency amazingly. What makes it all work is that these robots are all talking to each other. They are constantly communicating. They work together to coordinate traffic patterns, and if conditions change, like one robot finds a bit of grease on the floor, it instantly alerts the others to avoid it. (Dunlop 2016, Loc 967–978)

> Foxcon, tech suppliers to Apple and Samsung, replaced 60,000 workers with robots this year, and that is just one factory. (Gilmore 2016)

Robots and machines are on the March. Donald Trump should be paying particular attention.

The total robotic patent applications by China over the period from 2006 to 2015 end up in 2015 at more than double the applications made by US interests. The US applications grew steadily by a factor of three over this decade to 1500 whilst China's applications rose from below 500 per year to over 3000 per year, a rise by a factor of six, a geometric curve that appears to be continuing. Europe basically flat-lined at less than 500 patent applications per year (Chanseau 2016).

Meanwhile, economies world-wide are increasingly moving from a manufacturing base into service sectors. To take the US and Australia as examples:

> The latest data for the United States (2014) shows Manufacturing employment at 8.1% of the overall workforce, decreasing at the compound rate of 1.6% per year. Meanwhile, the Services Sector employed 80% of the workforce and was increasing at the compound annual rate of 0.9%. (US Bureau of Labor Statistics 2015)

> In Australia, data from February 2016 shows Manufacturing employment also in decline – by 5% over the year since 2015 and employing 11.7% of the workforce. The Service

Sector, meanwhile is growing overall by 2.7% per year. Financial and Insurance Services are growing the fastest – at 9.7% pa, then Administrative and Support Services – 9.3% pa, while the Health and Social Assistance Sector is growing at 5.8% pa. (Vandenbroek 2016)

Machine intelligence and robots are in fast pursuit.

Courtesy of a software platform, Baxter can do a more complex sequencing of tasks, for example, picking up a part, holding it in front of an inspection station and receiving a signal to place it in a 'good' or 'bad' pile. Via a further software kit to allow third parties to play, the CEO of Rethink Robotics, Baxter's creator, envisages Baxter "flipping burgers in Macdonalds, folding t-shirts for Gap, or pouring coffee for Starbucks." Already MIT has developed 'Bakebot' that can read recipes, whip up cookie dough and place it in an oven. Robot waiters are serving tables at restaurants in Japan, South Korea, China and Thailand (Briody 2013).

Truckers, bus drivers and taxi drivers are threatened by self-driving vehicles.

Fastbrick Robotics, an ASX-listed company based in Perth, Australia, has created a robot bricklayer, a form of 3-D printing which can build the shell of a house without being touched by human hands. The 'Hadrian 105' robot hit a bricklaying speed of 225 standard bricks per hour, or about a half days work for a top human bricklayer. The company is now developing its 'Hadrian X' robot which will have the capacity to lay 1000 bricks in an hour, equivalent to over two days work for a top bricklayer—who would cost between $(A)1500 and $(A)2000 for the same job. The brick laying market in Australia, the UK, US and Canada is currently worth around $(A)12 billion (Pash 2016).

An academic friend who recently returned to Australia from Cambridge University in the UK told me that not only are they working with a robotic brick layer there, but developing a robotic system to *produce* the robotic bricklayer.

Meanwhile, in China, WinSun Decoration Design in Shanghai is now using 3D printers to build ten houses on a block of land in 24 h—each 6.6 m high, 10 m wide, and using a mix of cement and construction waste. And, the 'Tiger Stone Paving Robot can lay a road at four times the speed of a team of human workers (Dunlop 2016, Loc 978).

Moving on, high status cognitive jobs are now under threat.

Early in 2016, 'ROSS', a legal practice dedicated version of IBM's supercomputer, 'Watson', famous for beating a (human) champion in the TV show 'Jeopardy', was launched as the first artificial intelligence lawyer.

On the medical side,

An artificial intelligence (AI) machine outperformed human surgeons in stitching up a pig. (Welsh 2016)

A British digital health startup known as 'Babylon' is developing a medical ap that "can decode symptoms and prevent illnesses before they occur, by tracking the patient's daily habits, integrating with this data on heart rate, diet and medical records". (Al-Khatib 2016)

And 'Watson' is now acting as medical diagnostician.

A hospital in California has replaced all their pharmacists with machines which work faster and more accurately than their human counterparts. (Gilmore 2016)

Indeed Deloitte predicts that robots will replace 25% of business service workers in the UK by 2035, less than two decades hence, that is 800,000 to one million jobs from a field of 3.3 million jobs that can be classified as business services in the UK (Spence 2016).

Meanwhile, robots and drones are marching onto or overflying the battlefield.

> One potential combatant developed by South Korean engineers, the Super aEgis II is a robotic gun turret than can identify, track and shoot targets up to four kilometers away with a .50 caliber gun.

> General Robert Cone, Head of Training and Doctrine Command in the US Army confidently predicts that by 2030, a quarter of US combat soldiers will be replaced by robots. (CBS 2014)

7 Pretending to be Human

Forget machine-looking robotic applications that impact on manufacturing, health delivery and business service workers and fight wars for us. Robot companions are already coming into our homes—pretending to be human.

Robots are likely to play a particular role in care for the aged. By 2030 it is estimated that the number of elderly in the world will *double* from 600 million today while a shortage of care givers for the aged will need to be addressed by a dramatic rise in numbers (Gorges 2016).

In 2015 robots with friendly humanoid faces but on wheels were tested in a nursing home in Florence, Italy. With sensors, cameras, wireless access to real-time cloud data and advanced algorithms, they accompany the elderly to the dining room, remind them of daily tasks and when to take their medications. They are able to extrapolate from behavior whether a senior is showing signs of dementia and track their progress or memory over time. They *will* be capable of having conversations with seniors to keep their minds sharp and fend off loneliness and despair.

In France, a home robot, Kompai, is also fitted with a screen that allows videoconferencing with healthcare workers, friends and family. Kompai robots talk, understand speech, remind people of meetings, keep track of shopping lists and play music. Response from the elderly is very positive (Gorges 2016).

Already around for more than a decade, there is also a robot that needs to be cared for. It is Paro, modeled on a harp seal, the robotic toy created by Takanori Shibata in Japan. It serves a key role in occupational therapy, with its ability to "learn", remember its own name, and, in particular, respond to physical touch. For example, a dementia patient can look into the seal's eyes, brush its whiskers and tickle its nose. The seal wriggles, flaps its flippers, gazes back at the person and makes small, seal-like noises—with a musculature in its face that gives a real "living" feeling. Two-way care! It works wonderfully in encouraging social communication amongst the elderly, and calming distressed patients (Griffiths 2014).

Not only that. With careful attention to modeling detail and plastic based face design, cyborgs are now being built to mirror specific human counterparts. *The advent of the robotic doppelganger!*

> David Hanson, CEO of Hanson Robotics and his engineers have developed Sophia, an advanced android inspired by Audrey Hepburn and Hanson's wife, Sophia.
>
> Sophia's (the robot's) lifelike skin is made from patented silicon and she can emulate more than 62 facial expressions. Cameras inside her "eyes", combined with computer algorithms, enable her to "see", follow faces and appear to make eye contact and recognize individuals. A combination of *Alphabet's Google Chrome* voice recognition technology and other tools enable Sophia to process speech, chat and get smarter over time.
>
> As Hanson commented:
>
>> "Our goal is that she will be as conscious creative and capable as any human". "We are designing these robots to serve in health care, therapy, education and service application." (Taylor 2016)

Even further down the cyborg track, leading Japanese robot developer, Professor Hiroshi Ishiguro, of Osaka University, has built a robot modeled, with intricately accurate facial features and expressions, on himself. Named 'Geminoid' a prototype of a doppelganger type android, he operates it remotely via internet to give lectures at conferences around the world instead of appearing in person (Stafford 2016).

Ishiguro observes that at this *early* stage of developing Geminoid, he feels he is looking in a distorted mirror, but other people see *him* reasonably clearly in the android's face. His own tests found that 80% of people greeted his most human-like androids with "hello", initially mistaking them for real people.

He is now creating a line of robots to serve different functions. The most human-looking are best suited to roles such as hotel receptionists, museum tour guides, and language tutors. Ishiguro is now running field tests to demonstrate the 'healing power' of robots—using robots to interact with people with dementia and children with automism—where a *mechanical-looking robot* works better:

> "They (the children) do not like to talk to the human or very human-like, robot". "But as they grow up they accept a more humanlike robot." (Taylor 2016)

Robots may indeed provide seriously beneficial support for humans in the near future—although this future is rather scary.

Meanwhile, there is simply no question that, if we wish and can afford it, we will be able to purchase an extraordinarily life-like, interactive, and personally engaging model of ME within a decade, or at most, two decades. Perhaps like Hiroshi Ishiguro, we can send our doppelganger out to go to work for us … maybe, even stand in for us in job interviews … for whatever employment might still be around!

I will not pursue this now. But, I must leave in the wings of the present discussion the question, "What impact is this going to have on our very humanity, self-identity, and interactions with others?"

8 What Is Left for Us Humans

It is clear that not only repetitive work in structured environments is likely to be replaced easily and soon. IT based production efficiency gains will also be delivered for systems that are far more flexible and informed, combining interrogative interaction between robots with access to cloud computing information.

The McKinsey Global Institute examined over 2000 work activities in every industry sector across the US economy, and classified the automation potential of each sector by adapting *currently demonstrated technology*. As indicator, the percentage of time in present jobs that can be automated, is highest in 'predictable physical work' (78%), 'data processing' (69%) and 'data collection' (64%). Less susceptible to automation are 'unpredictable physical work' (25%), then, 'stakeholder interactions' (20%).

As the authors conclude, the hardest activities to automate with currently available technologies are those that involve managing and developing people (9%), or that apply expertise to decision making, planning, or creative work (18%) (Manyika et al. 2016a, b).

A parallel conclusion is made by the Committee for Economic Development of Australia (CEDA). Almost 40% of current jobs have a moderate or high chance of disappearing in the next ten to fifteen years—as a consequence primarily of five emerging technologies responsible for the increasing automation of work: cloud services, the Internet of Things (IoT), big data, artificial intelligence and robotics and immersive communications. Where humans will continue to have the advantage is in:

> Problem-solving, digital and social skills are a worker's best defense against the impending technological revolution set to disrupt the way we work. (Burgess 2016)

Visionary educationists are now starting to look forward to what will need to be taught in future education. I had the privilege of sharing a dinner conversation in June 2016 with Professor Juichi Yamagiwa, President of Kyoto University and author of Chap. 19 in the present book. He wisely observed that, looking ten to twenty years into the future, universities will particularly need to focus their teaching not so much on specific career program such as for accountants, lawyers, business managers and medical practitioners, but on our humanity—developing creativity, empathy, resilience, problem solving, social awareness and relationship skills; exploring our human context through philosophy and history.[4] Needless to say, up-to-date IT skills and creativity will, in parallel, be of particular importance.

---

[4]Juichi Yamagiwa, Personal Conversation, Yase Rikyu Hotel, Kyoto, June 5th, 2016.

9 Tarot Cards of Our Future

There are massive implications for the present Kyoto Book's argument!

> "The future is not what it used to be" as Ogden Nash observed some decades ago, the opening quote for this Chapter.

A large proportion of the world's population is surplus to the needs of capital—in particular because of the accelerating 'March of the Machines'—and their rapidly expanding role in labor-displacing productivity growth.

Any economic analysis now must look forward to a future dominated by rapidly encroaching machine intelligence, radically transformed demand for human employment *across all spheres of work*, including even of services and human care, and a society that effectively progresses without employment-based income to power consumption.

As Tim Dunlop observes:

> The argument is that we have already entered a period where the prospect of a job – providing an ongoing and adequate source of income derived from employment that can support a person across their lifetime – is increasingly remote and that this situation is only likely to be exacerbated by technology. (Dunlop 2016, Loc 2296)

Meanwhile, we *must* not lose sight of the need to maintain and build the power of our humanity, not subjugate it to 'necessary' requirements of soul-less economic demand. Cyborg replacements for us are, quite frankly irrelevant—a side-trip.

Without this power of human creativity and resilience, humanity faces really serious threats to its very survival in a world already seriously challenged in having adequate resources, even of air and water, to sustain the people or our future world. These are living and potentially beautiful human beings like you and me, your mum and dad, your children … in particular, *your own grandchildren*—given current global population and environment degradation trends.

Lets face it, your own grandchildren are likely to be around until at least the next century … and have to handle the consequences of what you and the rest of us decide NOW and force into action. Even my own University ID card as a (lifelong) Emeritus Professor lasts optimistically until the year 2043, by which time, God willing, I would be 100 years old … and there are likely to be few new employment opportunities around, even if I was capable of applying.

As a conservationist quote that has now been around for forty years, and sourced in slightly different words to Wendell Berry, observes:

> We do not inherit the earth from our ancestors; we borrow it from our children.
>
> (Berry 2013)

The future requires not 'more of the same'—as delivered by present neoliberal economics, the doctrine of globalization. Instead, we need a new human-centered economics, one that even sidelines employed labor as the basis for income.

The central issue is our very survival as a human race!

Our future depends on how we play these cards

10 A Hand that Might Work

There is however a powerful idea emerging!

The idea, first proposed 500 years ago by Thomas More in Utopia' (1516) of "everyone with some livelihood" as his antidote for crime (Guardian 2016), is resurging in different work-clothes, a "Universal Basic Income". As one example, Nick Srnicek and Alex Williams, in their book, 'Inventing the Future' see a Universal Basic Income (or UBI) as the platform for what they call, a society of 'Full *Un*employment' or a 'Post-work Future' (Srnicek and Williams 2015).

And, remember, the issue is not just about having money to allow a consumer base to exist as a requirement for the continuation of capitalist production. Instead, it is about forging a new society for the future—one where UBI offers "financial independence and freedom of choice for individuals between work and leisure, education and caring, while recognizing the huge value of unpaid work" (Reed and Lansley 2016). One direct positive outcome of financial transfers to low income families was observed by Kristin Butcher, that is, the long-run benefit to children of the families—in terms of better diet, health and education that impact on their future life chances (Butcher 2017).

Tim Dunlop observes that a UBI provides empowerment for those at the bottom of the job-search ladder. He refers to the argument of Joel Mokyr, Chris Vickers and Nicolas Ziebarth, that under current 'poverty-alternative' based economic assumptions affecting the very poor who *must* find (now, increasingly casualized) work to survive, the employers are in a position of power to build their work force on minimizing worker rights and benefits.

> For the person to be truly free in making choices in particular about casual work and its conditions, UBI must meet the three conditions – *universal, adequate and unconditional* for "this gives the worker a genuine choice, genuine flexibility in choosing whether to take the job or not. And then whether to leave it." (Mokyr et al. 2015)

Most importantly, we do not only work for income. It also provides meaning and a sense of purpose to our lives—a connection to society as a whole both in terms of purpose and social relationships, a discipline for the day, our personal identity—progressively lost as a person who, previously employed, confronts longer term unemployment (Windshuttle 1981). As a signal of the wider social importance of work, two-thirds of Americans, when asked in a 2013 Gallop Poll, said they would continue working even if they won $(US)10 million in the lottery (Newport 2013).

Introduction of a Universal Basic Income must be accompanied by a developed community empowering strategy as well—apart from anything else, to ensure replacement of the social supports for identity and wider community connectedness.

Paul Mason, in his book, 'Post Capitalism', projects the humanistic change in thinking about technology, ownership and work itself, that will be the most basic revolution of all in forming a UBI based society.

> When we create the elements of the new system we should be able to say to ourselves and others: this is no longer my survival mechanism, my bolt-hole from the neoliberal world, this is a new way of living in the process of formation. (Mason 2015, 2016)

Tim Dunlop projects therefore a 'Distributionist Model' to underlie 'Full Unemployment' or 'Postwork Society' (Dunlop 2016, Loc 2299–2304).

Tadashi Yagi, colleague in producing this book, proposes a number of 'distributionist' mechanisms for income redistribution which provide excellent support measures, e.g.:

> Reduction of the disposable income of the richest income class with consequent tax revenues being utilized for the improvement of social welfare;
>
> Development of parity between the wage rate for non-regular workers and that of regular workers;
>
> Provision of subsidies for education so that learning opportunity is universally available, thus lessening the transmission of inequality over generations;
>
> Offering of public services such as job training at cheap cost; and,
>
> Development of international regulation to control tax haven behavior.[5]

I would propose one further force for 'distribution', that is, the development of company taxation regimes based on the *difference* between the highest and lowest income of employed workers—including the CEOs.

The idea of a guaranteed basic income goes further however. Even with these mechanisms to reduce inequality, the assumption remains whilst a neoliberal economic regime is in place that unemployment *will* exist and *will* continue to expand in its reach, and thus human inequality and exclusion will remain.

Already the movement exploring the idea of a Universal Basic Income has begun.

> Small scale schemes have been introduced in the developing nations of Kenya, Uganda, and India.
>
> Iran became the first country in the world to establish a full nation-wide basic income in 2010, financed from oil revenues. (Tabatabai 2011)

In the developed world, the idea of a universal basic income was tested in the 1960s in the Canadian town of Dauphin, Manitoba, and President Richard Nixon even suggested the idea in the 1970s (Jakzek 2017).

Right now however, a widespread movement is starting to develop.

> Switzerland held a referendum in April 2016 on introducing a Universal Basic Income, but, with its impact potentially doubling welfare spending and with a lack of government backing, only 25% of the population supported the idea.

---

[5]Tadashi Yagi, Personal Note, January 2017.

Trials however are being considered in Scotland by councils in Fife and Glasgow, as well as in the Netherlands cities Utrecht, Tilburg, Nijmegen, Wageningen and Groningen, testing different models of the scheme – with a range of restrictions and sanctions.

Italy is starting to explore. (Whigham 2017) The Italian city of Livorno began providing the city's 100 poorest families a guaranteed basic income of just over Euro500 a month in June 2016, whilst Ragusa and Naples are considering similar trials. (Henley 2017)

The Canadian province of Ontario is developing trials to be implemented later in 2017 where 2500 people will be given a basic income of $(C)1320 ($(US)970) per month with no strings attached. As Hugh Segel, a former senator and basic income advocate who wrote the study on which the trials are based, stated:

> Instead of traditional welfare systems, which assume that the poor are fundamentally lazy and have to be incentivized to work with an intricate system of carrots and sticks, basic income assumes that if you support people, they will go on to greater things. (Jakzek 2017)

'Y-Combinator', a Silicon Valley incubator firm, will sponsor a similar test as that being carried out in Finland in Oakland California. (Guardian 2016)

Even Australia has been toying with the idea.

The formative work of Professor Ronald Henderson from the University of Melbourne, founding father of Australia's poverty studies (and, also my Masters thesis mentor and examiner in 1965), identified a minimum economic line of poverty for Australians. Appointed Chair of the Commission of Enquiry in 1972, he developed a 'Poverty Line', set at a benchmark income of $62.70 pw for the September quarter 1973, which was around the value of the basic wage plus child endowment (an earlier version of family allowance), for a reference family of two-adults with two children. Adjustments were then made for other household types. Henderson promoted the idea of this being the indicator of a universal basic income in Australia. (Henderson 1975; Henderson et al. 1970)

Ross Garnaut, former senior advisor to Prime Minister Hawke, Ambassador to China and now Professorial Fellow in Economics at the University of Melbourne, subsequently proposed a UBI mechanism:

> A simple way of making it work would be to give all Australian citizens or residents (an) automatic payment into their bank account every fortnight subject to a means test, principally an assets test (and) you'd be taxed at a basic rate from the very first dollar of income. (Guardian 2016)

Meanwhile, Tim Dunlop has written an excellent book, published in 2016 promoting the idea for Australia. (Dunlop 2016)

So far, however, the idea has not taken hold.
Finland, on the other hand, has already commenced large-scale trials.

On January 1st 2017, the budget proposal for an experimental first phase of a larger basic income pilot study, came into force, having been approved by Finland's Parliament just over two months earlier (Ministry of Social Affairs and Health 2016). Its goal is to *promote employ*ment in an already existing context of limited employment opportunity for the people involved, not (yet) to develop UBI for all. But, this experiment leads the way.

The Study includes a test group of 2000 randomly sampled unemployed Finns aged 25 to 58 – excluding students and old age pensioners, all of whom will receive a tax free basic income of EUR 560 per month ($(US), equivalent to the level of labor market subsidy and basic daily allowance and replacing existing social benefits. This income will be paid even if they find work. (Ministry of Social Affairs and Health 2016; Henley 2017)

11 Where Next?

One can't be totally pessimistic.

Universal Basic Income offers a realistic and increasingly tested framework for our future global economics and therefore, society. It is just that we *must not forget* the critical importance of the social empowering dimension of whatever system may be introduced—plus, of course, maintain the agenda for reducing impact on our physical environment. Plus, ultimately, to find ways of limiting population growth, and distributing the benefits of globalization to those who are currently the most desperate non-participants in its benefits.

Powerful ideals! Increasingly difficult to implement globally. But, we must never lose sight of them if we are to maintain what our *humanity* is—our connectedness and care for *all!*

Everything I have suggested about our future, including serious socially responsible application of Universal Basic Income, are *political concerns*. To be fought in our Parliaments, on our streets, in fostering cooperation within our local communities. Helping people *understand.*

All else proposed throughout this book, 'The Kyoto Manifesto for Global Economics', remain as projects and strategies. That is, as objectives, to focus on 'community' rather than 'economic demand', to build empowerment and human connectedness.

And, all the strategies proposed through the book remain, such as community-centered action, expansion of the local power to global strategies, development of economic action such as via micro-financing of the local, and alternative Buddhist or 'Hospitality' (gift-based) dimensions of future economic activity, subjects of previous chapters.

Our final Concluding Chapters in 'the Conclusions Suite' will revisit all of these alternative strategies, and, in the context of a Universal Basic Income Strategy, propose a way forward. The prime concern of our book is to put humanity to the fore rather than globalized (neoclassical) economic demands, as the platform for humanity's future.

Our Manifesto for Global Economics!

In the meantime, we must admit Donald Trump to our drama. Even though, as at the time of the original drafting this Chapter he has been in power for just 67 days.

He is a new totally negative and powerful force for going backwards at least in the short term – on desirable social and economic issues as well as environmental protection for the future sustainability of humanity as a whole.

But he captures the fear of the intrusion of global economics into the US peoples' daily lives and opportunities.

Trump represents a tipping point in globalization generally—where the people are scared not just in the United States but across the developed world, and wish to recapture their past and selectively isolate themselves from the impact of globalization and open borders.

He must fail, at least in the longer term, as his strategies are simply WRONG.

However, we must wait for the American peoples' resolution of this drama before the world will go forward to a realistic and sustainable future!

And, clearly we must take this 'tipping point in globalization' into account.

References

ABC. (2017). Donald Trump's inauguration: Who is (and isn't) performing?—US.... *ABC News*. www.abc.net.au/news/2017-01-14/who-is-and-isnt-attending-the-donald-trump-inauguration/8180122.

Al-Khatib, T. (2016, February 4). Robo-lawyers, farmers, docs: Our future on autopilot. *Seeker*. http://www.seeker.com/robo-lawyers-farners-docs-on-autopilot-177083892.

Avis, D. (2016, July 22). BBC's UGC and social news team. *US Election: Artist Builds Wall Around Trump's Hollywood Star*. http://www.bbc.com/news/uk-england-36854572.

Berry, W. (2013, January 22). The unforeseen wilderness: An essay on Kentucky's Red River Gorge. *Quote Investigator*. http://quoteinvestigator.com/2013/01/22/borrow-earth.../.

Brachmann, S. (2014, November 1). The rise and fall of the company that invented digital cameras. *IP Watchdog*. http://www.ipwatchdog.com/2014/11/01/the-rise-and-fall-of-the-company-that-invented-digital-cameras.

Bradner, E. (2017). *Conway: Trump White House offered 'alternative facts' on crowd size*. https://edition.cnn.com/2017/01/22/politics/kellyane-conway-alternative-facts/.

Briody, B. (2013, March 26). The robot reality: Service jobs are next to go. *The Fiscal Times*. http://www.cnbc.id/100592545.

Burgess, M. (2016, April 4). Robots and automation to replace 40% of today's jobs so workers need to re-skill now. *News Corporation, Australia, Career One*. http://www.news.com.au/finance/work/careers/robots-and-automation-to-replace-40-per-cent-of-todays-jobs-so-workers-need-to-reskill-now/.

Butcher, K. F. (2017, January 27). Assessing the long-run benefits of transfers to low-income families. *Hutchins Center Working Paper No. 26*. Brookings. https://www.brookings.edu/wp-content/uploads/2017/01/wp26_butcher_transfers_final.pdf.

CBS. (2014, January 23). News. U.S. Army general says robots could replace one-fourth of combat. *CBS News*. http://www.cbsnews.com/news/robotic-soldiers-by-2030-us-army-general-says-robots-may-replace.

Chanseau, A. (2016, August 10). Robot companions are coming into our homes. How human should they be. *World Economic Forum*. https://www.weforum.org/agenda/2016/08/robot-companions-are-coming-into-our-homes-how-human-should-they-be.html.

Chira, S., & Alcindor, Y. (2017, January 21). Defiant voices flood US cities as women rally for rights. *New York Times*. https://www.nytimes.com/2017/01/21/us/women-march-protest-president-trump.html.

Collins, J. (2009, May). How the mighty fall. *Business Week*. http://www.jimcollins.com/books/how-the-mighty-fall.html.

Davis, J. H., & Rosenberg, M. (2017, January 21). *With False Claims, Trump Attacks Media on Turnout and Intelligence Rift*. https://www.nytimes.com/2017/01/21/us/politics/trump-white-house-briefing-inauguration-cr.

Diamond, J., & Bash, D. (2017, January 24). Trump signs order withdrawing from TPP, reinstate "Mexico City policy" on abortion. *CNN Politics.* http://www.cnn.com/.../trans-pacific-trade-deal-withdrawal-trumps-first-executive-order/.

Dunlop, T. (2016). *Why the future is workless.* Sydney: New South Publishing.

EPA. (2012). Scientific integrity policy. US EPA. https://www.epa.gov/osa/basic-information-about-scientific-integrity.

Express. (2016, September 14). Now for NEXIT? Dutch 'turn to the right' as eurosceptic Geert Wilders soars in polls. *Express.* http://www.express.co.uk/news/world/7717904/Nexit-Dutch-turn-right-euroscepticism-..../.

Gilmore, J. (2016, November 23). The inconceivable truth: Our jobs are not coming back. *News.com.au.* http://www.news/com.au/finance/work/careers/the-inconceivable-truth-our-jobs-are-not-coming-back.

Gorges, M. (2016, May 16). A role for robots in caring for the elderly'. *Newsroom.* http://newsroom.cisco.com/feature-content?type=webcontent&articleId=1763666.

Grant, S. (2017, January 24). Trump must conform with constitution or he will be removed, ex Bush adviser Richard Painter says. *ABC News.* http://www.abc.net.au/news/2017-01-23/trump-will-conform-or-be-removed-former-bush-adviser-richard-painter-says.

Griffiths, A. (2014, July 8). How Paro the robot seal is being used to help UK dementia patients. *The Guardian.* https://www.theguardian.com/society/2014/jul/08/paro-robot-seal-dementia-patients-/.

Griswold, D. (2016, August 1). Globalization isn't killing factory jobs. Trade is actually why manufacturing is up 40%. Center for Business Growth, Ball State University. Op-Ed, *Los Angeles Times.* http://www.latimes.com/opinion/op-ed/la-oe-griswold-globalization-and-trade-help-manufacturing-20160801.

Guardian. (2016, November 10). Basic income for all: a 500-year-old idea whose time has come? *The Guardian.* https://www.theguardian.com/business/2016/nov/11/basic-income-for-all-a-500-year-old-idea-whose-time-has-come.

Henderson, R.F. (1975). (Chairman). Poverty in Australia first main report April 1975. In *Commission of Inquiry into Poverty,* AGPS, Canberra.

Henderson, R. F., Harcourt, A., & Harper, R. J. A. (1970). *People in poverty—A Melbourne Survey.* Melbourne: Chesire.

Henley, J. (2017, January, 4). Finland trials basic income or unemployed. *The Guardian.* http://www.theguardian.com/world/2017/jan/03/finland-trials-basic-income-for-unemployed/.

Hicks, M. J., & Devaraj, S. (2015). *The Myth and the reality of manufacturing in America.* Indiana: Center for Business and Economic Research, Ball State University, June 2015, p. 3. http://conexus.cberdata.org/files/MfgReality.pdf.

Hill, Stephen. (1988). *The tragedy of technology, human liberation versus domination in the late 20th century.* London: Pluto Press.

Innovation Files. (2014). How America's manufacturing job loss outpaces other leading industrialized countries. *Innovation Files.* http://www.innovationfiles.org/how-americas-manufacturing-job-loss-outpaces-other-leading-industrialized-countries.

Jaczek, H. (2017). Minister of Community and Social Services, Canadian Government. Canada's basic income experiment—Will it work?, reported by Mukherjee, A. (2017, February 2). *Reuters* (Anindito Mukherjee). https://weforum.org/agenda/2017/02/canadas-basic-income-experiment-will-it-work/.

Jeffrey, T. P. (2015, May 12). 7,231,000 lost jobs: Manufacturing employment down 37% from 1979 peak. *CNS News.* http://www.cnsnews.com/news/article/terence-p-jeffrey/7231000-lose-jobs-manufacturing-employment-down-37-%-from-1979-peak.html.

Kahn, C. (2017, January 31). Reuters, Poll: 49% of Americans agree with Trump's immigration ban. *Business Insider.* https://article.wn.com/view/2017/01/31/Poll_49_of_Americans_agree_with_Trumps_immigration_ban/.

Kakaes, K. (2016). The All-American iPhone. *MIT Technology Review,* 119(4), 35–37.

Knott, M. (2016, August 3). Universities Australia urges Turnbull government to abandon $3.2 billion 'zombie' cut. *The Sydney Morning Herald*. http://www.smh.cm.au/federal-politics/universities-australia-urges-turnbull-government-to-abandon-$3.2-billion-zombie-cuts.html.

Kreig, G. (2016, December 22). Its official: Clinton swamps Trump in popular vote. *CNN*. http://edition.cnn.com/2016/12/21/politics/donald-trump-hillary-clinton-popular vote.

Lang, S. (2017, January 20). Donald Trump's presidency will be 'hopelessly conflicted', corporate governance expert says. *ABC News*. http://www.abc.net.au/news/2017-01-19/donald-trump-presidency-to-be-hopelessly-conflicted.

Manyika, J., Chui, M., & Miremadi, M. (2016a, July). Where machines could replace humans—And where they can't (yet). *McKinsey Quarterly*. http://www.mckinsey.com/business-functions/digital-mckinsey/our-insights/where-machines-could-replace-humans-and-where-they-cant-yet/.

Manyika, J., Chui, M., & Miremadi, M. (2016b, July 11). These are the jobs least likely to go to robots. *Fortune*. http://fortune.com/2016/07/11/skills-gap-automation/.

Mason, P. (2015, July 17). The end of capitalism has begun. *The Guardian. Economics*. http://www.theguardian.com/books/2015/july/17/the-end-of-capitalism-has-begun/.

Mason, P. (2016). 'PostCapitalism': A guide to our future. *Farrar, Straus and Giroux*. http://www.barnesandnoble.com/w/post-capitalism-paul-mason/1121817838.

Ministry of Social Affairs and Health. (2016, October 20). Legislative proposal on basic income experiment submitted to Parliament, Ministry of Social Affairs and Health (Finland). *Press Release 178/2016* (published in English on October 25th, 2016). http://stm.fi/en/article/-/asset-publisher/lakiehdotus-perustulokokeilusta-eduskunnan-/.

Mokyr, J., Vickers, C., & Ziebarth, N. L. (2015). The history of technological anxiety and the future of economic growth: Is this time different? *Journal of Economic Perspectives, 29*(3). quoted in Tim Dunlop (2016). Loc 1997.

Moore, M. (2016). 5 reasons why Trump will win. http://www.alternet.org/election-2016/michael-moores-5-reasons-why-trump-will-win/.

Mufson, S., & Eilperin, J. (2017, January 24). Trump to give green light to Dakota Access, Keystone XL oil pipelines. *The Washington Post*. https://www.adn.com/nation-world/2017/01.24/trump-to-give-green-light-to-dakota-access-keystone-xl-piplines/.

Newport, F. (2013, August 14). In U.S., most would still work even if they won millions. *Economy*. https://www.gallup.com/poll/163973/work-even-won-millions.aspx/.

New York Daily News. (2017, February). Trump's Muslim ban excludes countries linked to his businesses. *New York Daily News*. http://www.nydailynews.com/news/politics/trump-muslim-ban-excludes-countries-linked-businesses-art/.

Nowrasteh, A. (2016, September 2016). Terrorism and immigration—A risk analysis. *Cato Institute—Policy Analysis*. https://object.cato.org/sites/cato.org/files/pubs/pdf/pa798.2.pdf.

Parker, A. (2017, January 21). Donald Trump inauguration: White House website removes Obama climate change initiatives. *Sydney Morning Herald*. http://www.smh/com.au/world/donald-trump-inauguration-white-house-website-removes-Obama-climate-change-initiatives-20170120-gtvwmm.httml.

Pash, C. (2016, July 27). VIDEO: A one-armed Australian robot can build a house four times quicker than a brickie. *Business Insider*. http://www.businessinsider.com.au/video-a-one-armed-australian-robot-can-build-a-house-four-times-quicker-than-a-brickie.

Pasha-Robinson, L. (2016, November 20). Marine Le Pen takes huge lead over Nicolas Sarkozy in French first round presidential election poll. *The Independent Online*. http://www.independent.co.uk/news/world/europe/marine-le-pen-election-odds-latest-french/.

Range, P. R. (2016, July 27). Hitler expert says comparing Donald Trump to Hitler isn't as far-fetched as it sounds. *Sydney Morning Herald*. http://www.smh.com.au/comment/comparing-donald-trump-to-hitler-isnt-as-farfetched-as-it-sounds.

Reed, H., & Lansley, S. (2016). Universal basic income: A idea whose time has come? In *Compass*. London: Impact Hub Islington. https://www.compassonline.org.uk/wp-content/uploads/2016/05/UniversalBasicIncomeByCompas. Also, quoted in Henley, J. (2017, January 4). Finland trials basic income or unemployed. *The Guardian*. https://www.theguardian.com/world/2017/jan/03/finland-trials-basic-income-for-unemployed/.

Rhodes, B. M. (2015, June 22). Canute (Knud) the great—The King who could not stop the sea but stemmed the Viking tide on England's Shores. *The Viking Network*. http://viking.no/the-viking-kings-and-earls-knud-the-great/.

Robinson, A. (2013, September 25). The reshoring trend is good for U.S. Engineers and America'. *Cerasis*. http://cerasis.com/2013/09/25/reshoring/.

Rott, N. (2017, January, 25). EPA scientists' work may face "case by case" review by Trump Team, Official Says. *The Two-Way Breaking News From NPR*. http://www.nprorg/sections/the%20two-way/2017/01/25/511572169/epa-scientists-work-may-face-case-by-case-review-by-trump-team-official-says.html.

Roysam, V. (2016, November 11). 7 Reasons why Donald Trump won the Presidential campaign. https://www.yourstory.com/2016/11/why-donald-trump-won/.

Rucker, P. (2017, February 2). (White House Correspondent). Breaking news: Trump, Australian PM Turnbull have tense phone call over Muslim refugees. *CBS News*. http://www.cbsnews.com/news/trump-australian-pm-turnbull-have-tense-phone-call-over-muslim-refugee.

Sabransky, R. (2016, November 21). Trump registered eight companies in Saudi Arabia during campaign: Report. *The Hill*. http://thehill.com/blogs/blog-briefing-room/news/306990-trump-appeared-to-register-eight-companies-/.

Shuster, S. (2016). European politics are swinging to the right. *Time*. http://time.com/4504010/europ-politics-swing-right/.

Spence, P. (2016, July 12). Robots will replace a quarter of business service workers by 2035, says Deloitte. *The Telegraph*. http://www.telegraph.co.uk/business/2016/07/11/robots-will-replace-a-quarter-of-business-service-workers-by-2035-says-deloitte.

Srnicek, N., & William, A. (2015). *Inventing the future: Postcapitalism and a world without work*, Verso. https://www.versobooks.com/books/1989-inventing-the-future.

Stafford, A. (2016, November 3). Android clone v human: Will you be able to tell the difference at work?. *The Guardian*. https://theguardian.com/sustainable-business/2016/nov/03/android-clone-v-human-will-you-be-able-to-tell-the-difference-at-work/.

Stern, Fritz. (1974). *The politics of cultural despair: A study in the rise of the germanic ideology*. Berkeley: University of California Press.

Tabatabai, H. (2011). The basic income road to reforming Iran's price subsidies. *Basic Income Studies*, 6(1), 1–24.

Taylor, D. (2017, January 24). Donald Trump becomes the single biggest global market influence. *ABC News*. http://www.abc/net/au/news/2017-01-24/how-trump-has-become-biggest-influencer-on-global-markets.

Taylor, H. (2016, March 16). Could you fall in love with this robot? *CNBC-PRO*. http://cnbc.com/2016/03/16/could-you-fall-in-love-with-this-robot.html.

TED. (2017, February 1). Employment in apparel manufacturing decreased by 85% over last 25 years. *The Economics Daily*. https://www.bls.gov/opub/ted/2017.employment-in-apparel-manufacturing-decreased-by-85-percent-over-last-25-years.html.

US Bureau of Labor Statistics. (2015, December 8). *Employment projections: Employment by major industry sector*. https://www.bls.gov/emp/ep_table_201.htm.

Vandenbroek, P. (2016, April 14). Employment by industry statistics: A quick guide. Australian Parliamentary Library. *Research Papers 2015–2016*. http://www.aph.gov.au/About_Parliament/Parliamentary_Departments/Parliamentary_Library/.

Wald, E. R. (2017, January 24). Here are the jobs the Keystone XL Pipeline Would Create Under Trump's Executive Order. *Forbes.com*. http://www.forbes.com/ellenrwald/here-are-the-jobs-the-keystone-xl-pipeline-would-create-under-trumps-executive-order.

Welsh, S. (2016, September 1). Are we ready for Robotopia, when robots replace the human workforce. *The Conversation*. https://theconversation.comare-we-ready-for-robotopia-when-robots-replace-the-human-workforce.

Whigham, N. (2017, January 4). *Finland begins Universal Basic Income trial as the world watches*. http://www.news.com.au/technology/innovation/finland-begins-universal-basic-income-trial-as-the-world-watches/.

Windshuttle, K. (1981). 'Unemployment', A Social and Political Analysis of the Economic Crisis in Australia' (Revised Edition). Australia: Pelican/Penguin Books.

The Conclusions Suite Finale: 'The Kyoto Manifesto—From Exploration of the Sacred Essence of Humanity to Daily Life and Economics'

Chapter 26
"The Sacred Symphony" (Overture)

Stephen Hill, Stomu Yamash'ta and Tadashi Yagi

1 Beyond the Tipping Point

Globalization has reached its Tipping Point along with the growth-based neo-classical economics that lie at its cold heart.

As Stephen Hill quoted back at the start of this book from Hugh Mackay, Australian social survey leader, "*We used to live in a Society. Now we live in an Economy.*" What this means is observed by E.F. Schumacher over 40 years ago, "*The marketplace equates everything with everything else – through the mechanism of price that allows them to be exchangeable.*" (Schumacher 1973, p. 20) We live, express, and act, within this 'grammar' of daily life.

We therefore now *live* within the frame of our economy's demands rather than by our humanity's values—right down to the very ways we communicate with each other, the values we live by, and under the ultimate command of a highly concentrated group of immensely wealthy, globally powerful, corporate interests.

Please note that citations are only provided through this Conclusions 'Suite' if an author or reference is used which have not been cited in the Chapters these Conclusions refer to. The reader can find citational support for the argument by referring back to the Chapter identified.

S. Hill (✉)
University of Wollongong, Wollongong, Australia
e-mail: sthill@uow.edu.au

S. Yamash'ta
Center for the Study of the Creative Economy, Doshisha University, Kyoto, Japan

Sound Core Co., Ltd., Kyoto, Japan
e-mail: info@sound-core.jp

T. Yagi
Faculty of Economics, Doshisha University, Kyoto, Japan
e-mail: tyagi@mail.doshisha.ac.jp

As but one indicator of the atrophy of our humanity—presented in Hill's Chap. 2, global inequality is steadily getting worse in a world of plenty, whilst eight men, just eight men, bask in fabulous wealth equivalent to the collective income of *half* of the rest of the world's population. All at the expense of the finite environment and food resources on which we all depend.

Something is terribly wrong. The immensely wealthy elite may say 'let them eat cake' as attributed (incorrectly) to the out-of-touch arrogance of Queen Marie Antoinette at the time of the French Revolution. But, *one third* of the world's people today are lucky to find a disposed piece of stale bread, or discarded remnants of a meal of rice, in the rubbish bin. Meanwhile, the ecological world on which even the rich depend, may well not be there in the near future, unless dramatic alternative action is taken now.

Cracks are starting to appear, however, in the golden and calming promise of neo-classical economics—to not only provide a rich consumer-based lifestyle for all, whilst ensuring the sustainability of the world of our future, and stopping the increasing descent into increased inequality world-wide, and so bring the 2.2 *billion* people of our shared humanity above their current two dollars-per-day poverty line. Silent in these promises, is addressing perhaps the most important social dynamic of all, the paralysis that globalization's economics has injected into the resilience of society to respond, to act together … in time. Quite simply, this economic ideology is not working in support of a caring and harmonious society

However, in a note of promise, as Leonard Cohen, the recently departed Canadian singer and song-writer, wrote,

Everything has a crack in it. That's how the light gets in.

2 The Kyoto Manifesto: From Exploration of the Sacred Essence of Humanity to Daily Life and Economics

This Manifesto seeks to focus and strengthen this light.

Tadashi Yagi, in his Chap. 4, looks towards the East and Eastern philosophy as do others through this book—whilst lessons to be learnt from economics within other belief systems, Buddhist and Islamic, as well as from other economic entities such as micro-producers, presented in Chaps. 22–24, by Shinsuka Nagaoka, Juewei Shi, and Tadashi Yagi respectively, are also important in the Manifesto this book constructs. Ed Arrington, in his Chap. 20 demonstrates from detailed analysis of Western philosophic argument that a similar concern to that of Buddhist economics for a 'sharing' and 'hospitality-based' society also has been developing in the West.

Most fundamentally though, our argument for economic transformation now is based in seeking to understand the essential character of humanity and social community. This quest has taken us to the deepest of explorations of the character of humanity's spirituality, even back to the cosmos and evolutionary forces which have produced our current human society, presented in particular in Kazuyoshi

Yoshimura's Chap. 9 and Stomu Yamash'ta's Supplement Chap. 10. It takes us, as with Juichi Yamagiwa's Chap. 19 to human evolution from our primate roots and to the unique development of 'community' amongst hominoids.

We have moved on to develop the social platform from which a new economics must be developed—starting with the qualities of humanity, including the creativity necessary for paradigm change as presented, for example, in Tadashi Yagi's and Stomu Yamash'ta's Chaps. 7, 8, 10 and 13, and moving from the individual and communication, including across cultures, then progressing through an understanding of 'community', followed by an analysis of requirements to achieve global harmony as progressively developed through Stephen Hill's Chaps. 17, 18 and 21.

Ours is a reasoned call for major change—not, however, by minor adjustments to economic theory and action, but by going back to the essence of what our humanity is and can be. For it is in this resource that we will find the "light" we need for the very survival of humanity beyond the dawning of the next Century.

Connecting this quest with the relatively recent exploration of extrinsic factors to established fundamental principles of neo-classical economics, our book explores the deeper dimensions of the concept of economic "Sunspot Equilibria"—extrinsic random variables that are outside the normal economic fundamentals, such as preferences, resources, and economic systems, which are normally employed in predicting movement of the economy. The idea of sunspot equilibria is that *extrinsic* uncertainties such as changes in beliefs or trust in a society can drastically change the behavior of economic agents, and as a result, change the economic fundamentals.[1] An unexpected 'economic bubble' and its transmission across national economic borders could result, to take but one case.

As behavior is predicated on emotion, and humans are essentially emotional animals, factors that affect emotion therefore can play a crucial part in changing economic behavior. Thus, while emotions lie way outside normal economic scrutiny, the effectiveness of economic and social policy will be dependent on positive emotion-supportive incentive structures. For mainstream neo-classical economics however, such influences on policy lie, in general, in the domain of extrinsic uncertainties, territory which is excluded from calculation.

This concept of sunspot equilibrium activity lies, it would appear, at the front edge of factors that are yet to be included into mainstream economic theory and equations … but, which have the potential, if understood, explained and linked, to offer even possible revolutionary reformations of basic economics. i.e.: they potentially lie at the front end of paradigm change.

Most of what we are exploring in our Manifesto is 'sunspot activity'- dimensions not normally included into theoretical economics fundamentals, like 'trust',

---

[1] The metaphor of 'sunspots' was developed somewhat whimsically by David Cass and Karl Shell in 1983, from the earlier econometric work of William Stanley Jevons who explored correlation between sunspot activity and the price of corn, publishing his results in *Nature* in 1878. Cass and Shell used the metaphor as shorthand for the technical term, "extrinsic random variable" (Cass and Shell 1983). For an example of application of the concept in econometrics, see Kamihigashi (1996).

emotions, inter-subjective communication, sympathy, empathy, community, business organization decision and participation structures … and ultimately, referring to the basic platform then guide from which all of these 'sunspots' can be derived, "human spirituality".

Contrasting this book with current neo-classical economic texts, and as metaphor,

> We are turning 'sunspots' into 'sustaining daylight'.

Our approach moves outside the mainstream, and explores the consequence for neo-classical economics of the quote presented earlier from Leonard Cohen,

> Everything has a crack in it. That's how the light gets in.

The 'Kyoto Manifesto for Global Economics' explores the light coming through the 'crack', the source of the economic 'sunspots'. We are seeking to develop the platform for change from the 'light' that we can see if we look beyond the immediate 'sunspots'.

Our analysis is informed deeply from the practice of searching for what is 'sacred', the ultimate essence of our humanity, what we *can* be as a human race—empowered, fulfilled individuals, deeply sharing and caring for each other across our separate cultural and life worlds—understanding the fundamental *depth* of our shared lives. It is our spirituality which opens our inter-subjective door of sympathy and empathy, qualities which are denied under the emotional clothing of self-interest.

To explore our humanity-base for a new Economics, we have brought together a quite extraordinary range of broad-thinking contributors in three International Symposia, all held in Kyoto, Japan, in 2014, 2015 and 2016. The contributors to the book have been informed by many others in our presentations and debates. They spread in expertise across many disciplines, and certainly not just economics, although, with our base in Doshisha University's "Center for the Creative Economy", we have had an excellent economics base and guiding force for the economic implications of our conclusions.

As the reader will have seen in getting to this point in the book, the breadth and depth of contributions range from sacred music to quantum physics; primatology, comparative anthropology, and sociology; history, philosophy and ecology; Buddhist economics, Islamic economics … and mainstream political economics. Deep within our debates has been exploration of the lessons to be drawn from the variety of philosophies, generally classified together as from the East, as well as from explorations of new ways within the West.

All of these inputs are necessary as our quest has been to reach right back to seek the essence of what our humanity is, and the strengths we can draw from this.

In developing the book, we have organized the Sections of separate readings as in a Symphony, and with the 'voices' of Shinto, as outlined in our Introduction. The expression of Shinto within the book is as in a "Polyphony", both within and across Symphonic Movements—the welding of two simultaneous themes—nature and humanity—into a coherent harmony. However, in developing the synthesis required in our Conclusions, we have reverted to the Symphonic form in which the book was written, so present Conclusions in a 'Suite', as in a musical composition which progressively follows the arguments within each Movement. This overall Symphony then forms the Performance on the basis of which we present our Encore, "The Kyoto Manifesto for Global Economics".

We find however, that elements or harmonies from across all Movements need to be inserted into our progressive development of argument at places in the Score where a new 'improvisation' drawn from elsewhere in the Symphony, strengthens the passage we are performing at that time. The result, however, is overall evocative harmonic progression from the creative synthesis of all the inputs along the way—to a dramatic and definitive final crescendo of the Suite and its Encore.

We trust, of course, that the audience will applaud.

References

Cass, D., & Shell, K. (1983). Do Sunspots Matter? *Journal of Political Economy, 91*(21), 193–228.

Kamihigashi, T. (1996). Real business cycles and sunspot fluctuations are observationally equivalent. *Journal of Monetary Economics, 37*(1), 105–117.

Chapter 27
Recognizing the Need for Change (First Movement)

Stephen Hill, Stomu Yamash'ta and Tadashi Yagi

The vision of the light emanating from the 'crack' in global economics, remains, however, obscured. People are starting to recognize a problem with globalization, but many are moving in the wrong direction to address it.

Newly elected President Trump of the United States is seeking to paper over the cracks—to create, as is demonstrated in Chap. 25, a world of *denial*.

The fact that he was voted in as US President demonstrates, however, that he is not alone. The exit of Britain from the European Union through 'Brexit', the broad-ranging rise of 'populist' right wing political candidates across the developed world seeking to limit globalization's impact for their own constituents, attest to a wider international movement.

As demonstrated in Stephen Hill's Chap. 25, Donald Trump's success is built on the fears of people who find the doors to their protected interests have been opened too wide, so wish to close down national boundaries, and return to a nation-focused industrial past from which the world has moved on. They are seeking isolation from others crossing their own international borders, bringing with them the religious and ideological diversity that characterizes a *world* of open borders rather than one of a

---

Please note that citations are only provided through this Conclusions 'Suite' if an author or reference is used which have not been cited in the Chapters these Conclusions refer to. The reader can find citational support for the argument by referring back to the Chapter identified.

S. Hill (✉)
University of Wollongong, Wollongong, Australia
e-mail: sthill@uow.edu.au

S. Yamash'ta
Center for the Study of the Creative Economy, Doshisha University, Kyoto, Japan

Sound Core Co., Ltd., Kyoto, Japan
e-mail: info@sound-core.jp

T. Yagi
Faculty of Economics, Doshisha University, Kyoto, Japan
e-mail: tyagi@mail.doshisha.ac.jp

© The Editor(s) 2018
S. Yamash'ta et al. (eds.), *The Kyoto Manifesto for Global Economics*,
Creative Economy, https://doi.org/10.1007/978-981-10-6478-4_27

'protected' local community. This global movement threatens the locals' entrenched and comfortable beliefs. Indeed, it would appear Donald Trump has appealed to those fearful of losing 'The American Dream" that his people cherish, raise flags in their front yards for, and send their children off to war to protect. *"America"*, he preaches, *"will be great again!"*

Trump, however, is moving "Forward to the Past". He *denies* what by far the majority of scientists in the world assert, that is, 'Global Warming is very real; carbon dioxide emissions are a major contributor; and, this force will inevitably cause major disruption to our world unless it is stopped.

But, staring him down is the future, for it is here NOW!

Global warming is already upon us. As reported in Stephen Hill's Chap. 2, 744 scientists, the best from around the world, producing the 2015 United Nations Intergovernmental Report on Climate Change, reviewed 12,000 of the latest relevant scientific studies to conclude,

> Warming of the atmosphere and ocean system is unequivocal.

Indeed, the World Meteorological Organization (WMO) concluded three years ago that we were about to breach the level of carbon dioxide in the atmosphere that could cause enough sea level rise, drought, and severe weather to significantly harm human populations. By their 2014 data and projections, we may now, in 2017, have already crossed this threshold.

Check out the "Earth System Trends" Fig. 3 in Ryuichi Fukuhara's Chap. 3 if you need any more convincing. Amongst other indicators, *exponential growth* is demonstrated just since *1950*—in carbon dioxide, nitrous oxide and methane gas emissions; in surface temperature; ocean acidification; terrestrial biosphere degradation; tropical forest loss; and, marine fish capture.

Behind these frightening indicators is the core dynamic of neo-classical economics and the associated philosophy of neo-liberalism, *"let the market rule"*. Fukuhara demonstrates, through the case-study of cotton farming and use, how powerful major agricultural industry expansion decisions have been on causing massive environmental damage. In complete harmony with the neo-classical/neo-liberal creed, care for the ecosystem that supports cotton production is, 'necessarily' sacrificed for the sake of maximum short-term profit. Most importantly, this dynamic of greed and growth, required expanding cotton cultivation to unsuitable regions at too large a scale. Amongst other things, cotton production has all but dried up the Aral Sea, the world's fourth largest lake until the 1960s, shared between Kazakhstan and Uzbekistan. Globally, cotton production now consumes 2.5% of the total water withdrawal from the earth … whilst millions of children around the developing world cannot access clean water to drink.

The neo-classical economic dynamic reaches even further into creating enormous danger, in this case, to our food supplies. Biodiversity of humanity's main staple food crops now lies firmly in the hands of a very limited number of executives of major transnational corporations. Hill provides a number of examples in Chap. 2. Most alarmingly, *three* agrichemical firms, Monsanto, DuPont and

Syngenta, control over *half* of the global commercial seed market. Increasingly, genetic engineered seeds are replacing natural seeds—so natural diversity is severely impacted. A key reason why genetically altered seeds are needed is to resist the anti-weed 'Roundup' chemical spray that Monsanto sold to the world earlier, creating the need, as it turned out, for their next product. Consequently, Monsanto's biotech-sourced seeds accounted for 87% of the total world area devoted in 2007 to farming from genetically engineered seeds, whilst this genetic seed market is rapidly expanding, as is the land area devoted to genetically manipulated seeds. In the United States, to take a leading example, between 86% and 93% of the three major commodity crops, soybean, cotton and corn, are genetically engineered, whilst canola checks in at 64%. Monsanto alone controls the patents for 90% of soybean production and 80% of corn grown in the US. The seeds are intentionally sterile. Farmers, even in the poorest countries, must purchase seeds for their next crop *every* year. Again, this is entirely in keeping with good neoclassical economic practice. It is just that the dimensions of power and centralized control have been added.

The average citizen however has turned his or her eyes away from these dangers. For they have enjoyed luxuries from the massive post-Industrial Revolution growth in industry and consumerism that could never have been available before. Thus, they have become hooked on the growth-based economic dynamic that feeds this lifestyle. Trump's support in the United States is not about limiting consumerism or handling the future. It is about recovering a lost past.

However, along with continuing economic growth and its expansion of exploitable resources, our world population exploded, as Ryuichi Fukuhara demonstrates in Chap. 3, from 800 million in 1750, to four billion in 1980, and then, in just over the last 35 years, to seven billion—many of whom are seeking to participate in this apparently limitless consumer culture. As example, 70% of Indians possess mobile telephones while 40% have toilets. The exponential curves of environmental impact follow, as globalization extended its profit-centered interests out to serve this rapidly expanding market—chasing the potential consumer down, even to the poorest of villages and farms. Indeed, as Fukuhara reports, the impact of humans on the very basic dynamics of our planet is now so great that an official expert group reporting to the 2016 35th International Geological Congress in South Africa, recommended declaration of a new geological epoch, the "Anthropocene", beginning in 1950—a depiction of the new period of the earth's history when humans are actually *changing* the earth's environmental dynamics at a global planetary level.

Donald Trump denies all this. And, his views represent those of many Americans. As Grace Gonzalez and Ed Arrington observe in Chap. 5, 50% of American adults do not believe climate change is a product of human activity. So Trump's leadership in denial is disturbing. To justify his assertions, President Trump produced "alternative facts" (that is, unsubstantiated lies)—usually, in messages within the 'tweet' limit of 140 characters.

Employing social media is a great strategy for propagating 'alternative facts', and creating a highly dangerous "post-truth future". As these assertions get picked up and passed on to a geometrically expanding number of others – that is, "going viral", they assume the legitimacy of public acceptance over expert knowledge – a serious problem of knowledge validity in our present age. 'Tweets', in particular, are a further threat as, within just 140 characters, they can be nothing but a summary assertion with no evidence-based support whatsoever. Indeed, as Juewei Shi points out in Chap. 23, the Oxford English Dictionary named "post-truth" as their 2016 "word of the year".

As observed in Hill's Chap. 25, Trump's 'tweets', and consequent policy actions, excused his reversal of ecologically and culturally conscious decisions that previously prevented the building of major pipelines to carry piped tar sands crude oil from America's North to West Coast refineries where this crude oil requires particularly polluting heavy-duty processing to turn it into a marketable product. Additionally, it is basic to Trump's 'jobs' strategy to give his permission for continuing and uncontrolled pollution by American industries—based on the power generated by politically-washed "clean coal" for immediate short-range (political and commercial) advantage… and JOBS! Even, as Hill observes in Chap. 2, the officially independent Environmental Protection Agency of the United States can not provide a voice of reason any more for they must now have all scientific reports approved or censored by White House staff before publication to ensure they align with President Trump's "vision".

Meanwhile, the damage being done to the social fabric of care for the dispossessed globally is being torn apart—primarily to ensure tax breaks for the rich and unconstrained expansion of greed.

Both Stephen Hill's Chap. 2, and Tadashi Yagi's Chap. 4 demonstrate the level of inequality that follows. Just 0.01% of the world's population control 30% of the world's wealth while 99.1% control just over *half* of this level of wealth, that is, 19%; and 34% of the world's population live in abject poverty, surviving on an income of less than two dollars per day. One-third of our humanity is unlikely to have access to safe water, decent food, any welfare or health support, or education —living in a pit of desperation to survive, and for their children to grow up to maturity.

Meanwhile, as noted earlier, *eight men* face the poorest half of humanity, 3.6 billion people, with the same level of wealth as all of them put together.

Actually, they don't 'face' the poorest. Instead, they fly over them in their personal, polluting, jet planes, to enormously expensive resorts, often carved out of previous ecologically pristine natural environments, where they can relax amongst the glitterati, even … the Kardashians.

Meanwhile, the neo-classical economics of globalization is not improving inequality. It is making it worse. As Thomas Piketty comprehensively demonstrates, our economics regime has done so through the entire history of capitalist-based industrialization—largely because inherited wealth is passed on and builds the platform for subsequent wealth expansion of an increasingly smaller elite! Even more basically, the underlying power dynamics behind the exercise of neo-classical economics—in its practice globally, have an enormously distorting influence to keep the rich wealthy, and to impoverish the poor. At heart is the value of self-interest.

Tadashi Yagi, in Chaps. 4 and 14 (with Yamash'ta), demonstrates ways in which this happens under a monetary economy. People who are poor in monetary terms are likely to remain poor and disadvantaged as they cannot get to first base in the wealth-generating economy. High volatility in employment opportunities and inflation impact the lives of workers in urban areas because the owners of capital generally see labor as a cost to be minimized rather than an organization community to be nurtured. So, income inequality expands and emotional happiness is lost.

As Stomu Yamash'ta and Tadashi Yagi show in Chap. 14, in a society where efforts to build *trust* are neglected—not even a measured factor in neo-classical economics, the economy becomes inefficient. When people are monitored by employers and transactions are based on contract, mutual assistance cannot be expected, and psychological resistance to committing crime is lowered when people are not emotionally connected. Without an environment of trust, individuals will look for advantage by whatever means, and must develop countermeasures against attacks from other members of the society. Alternatively, where there is trust, individuals feel sympathy for their employer, feel others are thankful for their contribution, and will therefore be more creative and productive. Besides, the potential cost of monitoring does not exist.

As Yagi demonstrates, emotions are therefore central in economic activity, but generally neglected within neo-classical economics models of what people are expected to be. Mainstream neo-classical economics is increasingly finding it difficult to deal with the person and the essence of our humanity.

Meanwhile, neo-classical economics has put control of the economy into the hands of a very small number of corporate heads as demonstrated by Stephen Hill in Chap. 2. Just 147 companies, therefore, 147 CEOs, control nearly 40% of the monetary value of all transnational corporations—and the majority are 'super-entity' *financial* institutions, not producing anything, but pursuing the singular objective, *profit*. How their subordinate and networked companies produce this profit for them is irrelevant. To a large extent, the ultimate controlling corporations are outside public visibility, so remain unaccountable.

But, these global corporations call the shots—right down to the lives of peasants in remote societies, as is demonstrated in the opening depiction of the Ladakh community on the Tibetan Plain of Northern India in Stephen Hill's Chap. 18. Consequently, as for this remote community, the powers that control the global economy into which the Ladakhs became embedded since the 1970s, is way outside their sphere of influence. It cannot be interrogated or confronted—a context to which they must be obedient but cannot change, or, even understand.

Here lies the problem for the world as a whole. Control of the global economy is so far away from peoples' life world that it seems there is no way of attacking or changing it. Even behind the corporations that stand in front of daily experience, there is a powerful backroom command interested in nothing else but profit!

We therefore confront a paralysis. Whilst protests and committed movements for change are emerging, and indeed make incremental progress, they are fundamentally likely to be sidelined or beaten down by both direct action and advertising 'spin' under command from the corporate interests that stand way behind the immediate experience of the public—but continue to maintain the economic 'frame' for global society, that is, the hidden 'grammar' for daily life expression.

> As example, in the last week in Sydney, Australia (this is late April 2017), one of the commercial TV channels has been broadcasting so-called 'documentaries' of one-sided support for a commercial corporation's programs, funded by the corporation, but with reference to corporate 'interest' buried in nothing but a rapidly-disappearing logo in the final credits – that is, with no declaration of interest. It is but a long, one-sided commercial attempt to fool the public into support for the corporation in a situation of continuing public contest. The 'public' community, needless to say, cannot afford an equivalent TV documentary response.

Consequently, the global economy today not only invades, but *disempowers* alternative action at the same time. As Ed Arrington and Grace Gonzalez observe in Chap. 5, capitalism at its core not only misrecognizes others who remain at a distance, but under cover of social contract and the doctrine that actions are right if they are useful to the majority, remains morally indifferent to them just as it exploits them.

The philosophy behind neo-classical economics is that of 'neo-liberalism' … 'let the market rule', as we noted earlier. As Arrington and Gonzalez demonstrate, neo-liberalism has colonized the political with the economic, or, more accurately, with the capitalistic. When politics are colonized, so too are ethics. Therefore, disempowerment, or the conviction that one cannot change the current economic regime, is deep, for the values that underlie the neo-liberalism frame around our lives have become our own.

As Arrington and Gonzalez observe,

> Ethics – the question of how we ought to live – is, in its economic context, reduced to questions of property rights, of individual identity understood as autonomous action in markets, and of the good society as that which protects those rights and those markets.

Consequently, life goals come to be understood in economic terms—responsibility to manage one's own human capital to maximal effect, and therefore achieve stable employment, housing and even health services. Neoliberalism sees competition as the defining characteristic of human relations. Citizens are re-defined as *consumers*, democratic choices are best exercised by *buying and selling* against which one's merit by the criterion of efficiency is measured. Our world is a competitive stage. Attempts to limit competition are inimical to liberty.

Tadashi Yagi's Chap. 4 further demonstrates the limitation of neo-classical economics to solve key issues in globalized society. 'Efficiency' cannot stand for 'fairness and justice', values of far greater importance for people in a globalized world. Indeed, Yagi takes us back to the birth of modern-day economics and Adam Smith's "the invisible hand"—the concept that resources are allocated efficiently in markets through transactions of goods and services where consumers seek to maximize their own utility and producers seek to maximize profits whilst the market mechanism thence operates without any human controls. Selfish behavior, by this theory, leads to social harmony. The economic theory assumes humans act as "homo economicus"—with no ethical requirements and only economic concerns, and the mistaken belief that no harm will come to society from a collection of selfish individuals. Laissez-faire economic liberalism follows—privatization, fiscal austerity, deregulation, free trade, reducing government spending to enhance the role of the private sector in the economy. Profit for the few.

However, as Tadashi Yagi also demonstrates, most modern economists did not explore the other side of Adam Smith's argument, for he also recognized "greedy capitalism", the *immoral* behavior of economic agents versus the importance of 'sympathy' in building *trust*. Yagi takes this argument further, pointing to what is left out of our humanity, the emotional factors that real human beings must confront —sympathy, joy, anger, and the relation of these emotions to social structures—that reinforce culture, community and religious beliefs. All left out of the neoclassical economic equation.

Demonstrably, global capitalism has *not* led to harmony, for inequality is getting progressively worse, with consequence for not only those forced to live in desperate poverty, but also, as a breeding ground for conflict, and terrorism against the wealthy 'West'. Meanwhile, control of wealth transactions is becoming enormously centralized … and further away, wealth safe in Swiss Banks and tax-free havens, and corporations safe behind official State security protection.

Where, therefore, in this economic 'progress' is our shared "humanity"? Our ability to determine our collective future according to humanity's values, rather than have it determined for us by an elite interested in nothing else but private profit and personal advantage?

Trump, discussed in Stephen Hill's Chap. 25, and representing the worst of denial, is, however, the President of the United States, arguably the most powerful person in the world. He cannot be dismissed as an ignorant self-centered clown—because, enough of the people of America voted for Trump and precisely these policies. They voted because of unexamined *fear* of what globalization is doing.

More importantly, the movement in world opinion and power Trump represents is increasingly being reflected in popular right-wing movements across Europe and other developed countries, as we observed earlier.

These are the dangerous times to which our book refers, the platform for us developing "The Kyoto Manifesto for Global Economics".

Donald Trump is likely to be left soon in the ideological shadows from which he emerged, hopefully having not caused significant damage before he leaves office. However, although, he has sought to paper them over, Trump has focused world attention on the 'cracks' in the fabric of globalization, and, for this, we should be grateful.

Others can see the cracks. But the light getting in remains dim.

Chapter 28
"Foundation Stones of Spirituality" (Second Movement)

Stephen Hill, Stomu Yamash'ta and Tadashi Yagi

1 The Significance of 'Place'

Kyoto, the 'place' is an excellent foundation for building a platform for change.

Twelve hundred years old, Kyoto was established as Japan's capital in A.D.794, under the name, "Heian-kyo", and remains the spiritual 'heart' of Japan, a crucible for the development and practice of Buddhism. Even now, there are over 3085 active temples in Kyoto, whilst Shinto and Buddhist ritual are deeply embedded in daily life. Consequently, as Manami Oka demonstrates in Chap. 6, Kyoto is a spiritual center for those following a more introspective and reflective journey, a center from which the wisdom of this journey diffuses throughout Japan.

Traditionally, the home of the most advanced crafts, Kyoto epitomizes the interaction between culture and nature, a fundamental tenet of Japan's indigenous Shinto beliefs which Tadashi Yagi speaks about in Chap. 4, and follows the dynamics of 'aesthetics' in design of everything, and 'harmonization with nature'.

Please note that citations are only provided through this Conclusions 'Suite' if an author or reference is used which have not been cited in the Chapters these Conclusions refer to. The reader can find citational support for the argument by referring back to the Chapter identified.

S. Hill (✉)
University of Wollongong, Wollongong, Australia
e-mail: sthill@uow.edu.au

S. Yamash'ta
Center for the Study of the Creative Economy, Doshisha University, Kyoto, Japan

Sound Core Co., Ltd., Kyoto, Japan
e-mail: info@sound-core.jp

T. Yagi
Faculty of Economics, Doshisha University, Kyoto, Japan
e-mail: tyagi@mail.doshisha.ac.jp

Kyoto's age and history represents the longevity of what is most sacred in our collective humanity. Oka also points to the power of the women of Kyoto, to their particular role as artesans at the same time as household managers, and, represented in the satirical comedy drama form of "Kyogen" by the archain phrase, "wawashi" which meant they were skilled at outwitting men.

Kyoto as *place* therefore sets the discussions from which the Kyoto Manifesto for Global Economics originated, within the deepest and widest context of our humanity. The combined Shinto and Zen ritual of Stomu Yamash'ta's *On Zen* performances at Daitokuji Temple, have preceded each International Symposium through which the Kyoto Manifesto has been formed, thus celebrating and communicating the essential spirituality that lies at the core of Kyoto *as place* and the very essence of our humanity which provided the platform for our discussions.

Additionally, the signature of Kyoto's conservation culture was written on the world's first serious deliberations to produce the United Nations "Kyoto Protocol"—mandatory targets to reduce overall greenhouse gas emissions by at least 5.2% compared with the world's 1990 level, over the commitment period, 2008 to 2012 (UNFCCC 1997).

Symbolically and physically, Kyoto therefore provided the ideal platform for developing The Manifesto for Global Economics which this book presents.

So, whilst we end up with specific recommendations for social and economic action, the reservoir for strength to act is our humanity. Our immediate goals are ecological and social sustainability. However, beyond this, our goal is to re-assert our humanity in the modern age—light the way for the *people* to know and act.

Kyoto has been the light-house.

2 Essential Roots of Humanity: Finding Harmony Between Spirit and the Cosmos

As we noted above, each International Symposium was preceded by Stomu Yamash'ta's "On Zen" Performance and the cross-religious Zen/Shinto Ritual at Diatokuji Temple in Kyoto. Entré to both our discussions and the societal platform we are constructing here was therefore deeply woven into and from the spirituality which forms the essence of humanity and its highest goals, and in particular, Stomu's mission to find and express global harmony and peace based on spirituality and its expression in sacred music.

This is therefore where we start our analysis of the transformation required to base future global economics on humanity and society rather than constrain these essential human qualities within the abstract and soul-less demands of our current global economic frame. For as Hill reports in Chap. 17, E.F. Schumacher reminded us nearly 50 years ago,

> "To the extent that economic thinking is based on the market, it takes the sacredness out of life, because there can be nothing sacred about something that has a price". (Schumacher 1973, p. 20)

Stomu Yamash'ta, is a major internationally-famous professional classical *and* rock musician who created furor in London and Paris with his revolutionary rock-style performance, as Tadeo Takemoto observes in Chap. 11. However, in a search for inner and global peace, Yamash'ta then left the international rock scene and its benefits behind, to return to Japan to study Buddhism and Buddhist music as a novitiate for three years at the To-ji Temple in Kyoto, the head temple of the Esoteric Shingun Sect. At the end of this period, when Stomu had finally completed his allocated task of cleaning out a long-disused temple, and came to the Head Monk for further guidance, the Head Monk of the Temple instructed Yamash'ta to follow a mission in the secular world rather within the cloisters, to *"bloom the flowers of the sounds in the real world"*.

Stomu Yamash'ta took this advice and immediately discovered the power of Sanukite Stone. This particular stone has had a special place in Japan's historic culture since the Paleolithic Period, employed not only for adornment of important tombs, but, because of its metallic-sounding high notes when drummed, used for alarm or ceremonial purposes for at least 2200 years until being superseded in the middle of the Zhou period (BC 900–800) by the Bronze Age and the ability to make metal instruments. Stomu has now spent 30 years, as he describes it, in *dialogue* with the Sanukite stone musical instrument he has collaboratively developed and uniquely plays.[1]

Yamash'ta listens to the voice of the stone and at the same time communicates with it as it has a mystical power, able to activate the human brain with its more than two-minute resonance including inaudible high frequency waves more than 500,000 Hz, which some believe have a healing effect. Hearing the *"grandeur of the memorial vibrancy"*, Yamash'ta observes,

> In all the energy of nature, the universe generated from the Void coexists here and now in the actual world of earth in which stone and human beings live together as the result of the miraculous phenomenon woven through eternal time.

Stomu Yamash'ta has returned to this historic place before the Bronze Age. From his dialogue with the beautiful tones produced from naturally occurring material, Stomu has learnt to 'hear' in tune with the vast timelessness of the world which surrounds him, and thus to live in relation to it—to live slowly and gently ... a dialogue where he can feel that *"we live together"*.

He contrasts this with the increasing dependence today on digital (sampled) music, pointing to the difference in wave motions and wave lengths to those of natural sound—to the consequent decline in multidimensional thinking and originality, the ongoing loss of cultural diversity in a globalized world. Exploration of the artistry of music—one of the greatest and most valuable objectives of humanity, Stomu Yamash'ta argues, requires us to be our *'natural selves'*, to connect with the fullness of our natural environment. Natural music communicates through wave patterns that harmonize with nature and our interaction with it. Stephen Hill

---

[1]For a more complete description of the age, character and qualities of Sanukite Stone, see Tadao Takemoto's Chapter 11 in this Book.

demonstrates in Chap. 17, that music rather than words has the power to *heal* in situations where children are seeking to adjust to conflict or trauma.

It is here that Stomu Yamash'ta's Chap. 8 reminds us of the essence in Buddhist philosophy of our humanity, that is, we exist as humans in an intrinsically mysterious world, consisting of both "non-existence"—intangible, immaterial phenomena, and "existence"—of physical substance. In his Chap. 10 Supplement to Kazuyoshi Yoshimura's Chap. 9, Yamash'ta also points to the contribution of the great Chinese monk, Xuanzang, and the "Heart Sutra" which Xuanzang brought from India and translated into Chinese characters from Indian Sanskrit texts, in particular, the longer Prajna Paramita Sutra.

Buddhism had come to Japan from China via Korea through ruling class interactions a century earlier, when Xuanzang translated the Sutra in the mid-seventh century AD. The Sutra was quickly picked up and became influential in Japan. The Heart Sutra teaches the transcendence of all dualities, and starts from the assumption that the body is material and the spirit is the non-real existence. The Heart Sutra asserts that the 'Void' or 'emptiness' is the state of impermanence, but also the heart of the energy which generates everything in the 'real' world. For example, in line 9, the Sutra on 'the heart of the perfection of wisdom', states according to the teaching of 'Sariputra', one of the direct disciples of Gautama Buddha, 'there is 'no materiality; there is no physical feeling, no active process of understanding, no establishing or maintaining the thought stream, no consciousness'. At the heart is emptiness.

But this is where one's spirit exists. Stomu Yamash'ta explores this space in the spiritual music he unveils in his On-Zen performances.

At an individual level this reflection on 'emptiness' is directly parallel to the state of the non-materiality or emptiness of the center of the cosmos as determined by the latest of scientific research—in the mathematics and observations of contemporary quantum and cosmic physics—presented by Kazuyoshi Yoshimura's Chap. 9 and Stomu Yamash'ta's Chap. 10 Supplement. As an apparent paradox, in both cases—Buddhist and Scientific, emptiness is the source of infinite energy… or, wisdom.

Yoshimura demonstrates that the miraculous energy of this world and the universe emerges from the "Void"—from the 'singularity', the infinitely small point of space-time focus. This is the *point* of the massive concentration of energy from which the universe was created through the "Big Bang", and also the non-material *point* of the entire energy of every star that collapses … into a singularity.[2] Continuous interaction between matter and non-matter. As Albert Einstein further demonstrated, there is no separation between space and time. The singularity of the universe's ultimate energy therefore is both 'here and now', and timeless.

---

[2]For many, the mathematical base of Kazuyoshi Yoshimura's Chapter will be unfamiliar and difficult to unpack. For these readers what matters is the authority of his conclusions. The mathematical development remains in our text however for those who are more expert in understanding the mathematics and underlying physics. This way, the strength of Yoshimura's 'proof' is verifiable.

Tadeo Takemoto concludes in Chap. 11,

> Irrationality of Zen Buddhism and uncertainty of quantum theory face each other in concord.

Perhaps for those not familiar with this concept of the Void as the base of all creation and energy and the idea of 'zero' (Void) versus 'one' (Substance), these explanations may sound fanciful. However, be reminded that they have been tested by *both* millennia of Buddhist practice and experience, *and* the very latest research in physics and chemistry.

Indeed, as further clarification, Yoshimura demonstrates in Chap. 9, that 'space', according to the latest scientific research, is a 'Void', but paradoxically, *not empty*. It is full of nets of gravity waves—an energy fabric woven out of space and time, but, in keeping with the zero/one principle, warped by the *mass* of all suns and planets—as gravity energy is the force of attraction between two masses, so is affected by mass. Gravity waves are distorted in space-time—like the indentation in a safety net into which a basket-ball has been dropped.

Therefore, to take the classic observation which proved this effect of mass on light energy, predicted by Einstein, light from a solar *mass* behind, *bends* around an observed planet. Further, as Einstein demonstrated 100 years ago in his famous equation, $E = mc^2$, where c = the speed of light (a constant representing ultimate speed in the universe), energy and mass are interchangeable. But if you reflect for a moment on this equation, the amount of energy released from mass is enormous: c = approximately 300,000 km per second, so squared, the multiplier in converting one kilogram of mass to energy 'joules' is 90 million x one million, i.e.: 90 billion, to bring it back to meters, the unit of calculation. Thus, one kilogram of mass could power a 100 W light globe (using 100 joules of energy per second) for 31.5 million years. Now, that beats the hell out of what can be delivered to your house from a kilogram of coal bunt in your local power plant.

This conversion is going on all the time in space, so the 'Void' is incredibly busy —continuously full of participles (electrons or matter) and anti-particles (positrons or anti-matter), which collide, disappearing at once in what physicists call "pair annihilation," but leaving behind a vacuum 'point' of enormous energy whilst producing gamma ray emission that either, through radioactive decay or collision with an atom, produces more positrons, and so the process continues ceaselessly. As Stomu Yamash'ta observes in his Chap. 10 Supplement to Yoshimura's Chap. 9 , this process is directly what we experience as the eternal theme of humankind—in life versus death, or disappearance into the Void—and generation of our 'material' progeny who themselves will die and disappear, but produce the next generation.

All matter, all humanity, is therefore ultimately connected to the vast energy sink of the cosmic Void. We are both one and zero, matter and non-matter. Stomu Yamash'ta observes this, and Tadeo Takemoto later develops the concept in Chap. 11, towards his conclusion of "Being Now" as the essential quest of future society. For it is here that the most fundamental character of humanity, the essence of our ultimate spirituality, lies—outside linear time.

Some may represent this ultimate spirituality in the form of a personalized God with infinite power (energy) to create, and connected to us through belief and prayer. Buddhist philosophy accepts this connection through meditative experience. Others in our modern age explain our connection to the cosmos and its essence in the total energy of the Void, as scientific reality—proven by both observation and mathematics. By whichever path we arrive, the power and connection cannot be denied.

Takemoto however, observes that human *experience* must not pay ultimate obedience to scientific explanation—for this is born out of a logic that excludes the irrational, non-recurrent, non-constant phenomena that make up this human experience, and can connect us out of the material and into the immaterial world of the Absolute, the Zero, and the soul. For some of these phenomena could 'relativize even life and death' the primary concerns of people dealing with their material world and existence. As Indian guru, novelist and scientist, Raja Rao, observed,

> Why are the Western people likely to dramatize the door between life and death? Death is the path to the light.

Stomu Yamash'ta, in his Chap. 10, further points to the parallel search of music, his vehicle of understanding, in contrast with contemporary scientific exploration. Both are struggling to uncover the truth behind the (apparent) real world, in keeping with the ideal of harmonizing nature and humankind. Indeed, Yamash'ta, in his Chap. 8, declares his own musical search now is to unite religion, art and science through dialogue—and that this ultimately must be the united quest of humankind for the future and sustainability of our society and world.

Consequently, by letting go of the demand on consciousness by our material existence and world, by non-attachment, we are able to appreciate the ultimate essence of what our humanity is—infinite connectedness with the vacuum world of the cosmos—*"without being imprisoned by self-interest, the value of which is negligible in the universe"*.

3 Implication of 'the Void' for Social Arrangements

Akio Tanabe takes us in his Chap. 12 from this demonstrated scientific and philosophic position, i.e.: the existence of the Void, or Absolute, into its implication for social organization and political democracy, as already practiced in India.

India is, as Tanabe demonstrates, one of the most diverse and disadvantaged populations in the world—with 22% living below the poverty line; 18% of urban populations living in slums; 25% "Scheduled Castes and Scheduled Tribes"; 40–50% "Other Backward Castes"; 20% belonging to various "religious minorities." All "exceptions" to the norm of a democratic society, with the number of "individual citizens", able to act with 'agency' and fully participate in democracy, being a minority. In this context, the workings of governance remain, at best, fragmentary, too complex and heterogeneous to be governed in a uniform way—leading to a vast space beyond the rule of law.

From extensive field research in India, Tanabe recognized, however, that beyond the more common dimensions of social analysis of Indian society, employing caste-division, status, and the dominance of power, a deeper *social* dynamic operates. His term for this is "ontological equality"—based on spiritual exploration and ideation—across the Vedas and Brahmanism, Bhakti, and Buddhist movements.

"Ontological Equality" is the idea that the Absolute, while transcending all beings, is at the same time, immanent, permeating through each being in the world. As Tanabe then continues,

> This means that all beings – whether human or non-human, alive or non-alive – are equal at the ontological level, as their spiritual essence is one and the same.

The consequence is not just limited to the religious domain in the narrow sense, but has the potential of becoming a common cultural resource which makes possible the flourishing of social and cultural *diversity*—which, instead of delivering division and exclusion, offers mutual dependency and value.

Tanabe carries this idea forward to demonstrate that, as in India, "Vernacular Democracy" has developed, the vibrancy of the clamor of diverse voices mingling and interacting with each other to form an inseparable whole—operating however, in the "subaltern" realm, recipients rather than active agents. *This* is where "vernacular democracy" fits in and allows the vast diversity of India to be not only governable, but engaged in "deepening its overall democracy—based on assertion and tolerance of diversity, itself based on ontological equality derived from the Absolute Reality of the Void.

> "Vernacular Democracy", is, as Tanabe concludes, "a creative way and process of imagining a world where both diversity and equality can stand together" - where "a sustainable relationship between humanity and nature, are important agendas not only for India, but also for the entire world."

The basic platform is, however, the essence of human spirituality and its ability to connect with the ultimate Void of the cosmos. Tadeo Takemoto draws us towards the essential conclusion from the Kyoto Symposia which have been developing the societal platform for a new Global Economics. His advice, based on extensive philosophic analysis, is that the future societal platform has to be based on the depth of humanity's spiritual culture, our intrinsic connectedness with the ultimate timelessness of the cosmos, a society where "Being Now" is its values priority.

References

Schumacher, R. F. (1973). *Small is beautiful—Economics as if people mattered*. New York: Harper and Row.

UNFCCC, Kyoto Protocol—Toward Climate Stability ... http://kyotoprotocol.com/; United Nations framework convention on climate change: 'A summary of the Kyoto protocol', UNFCCC, 1997: http://unfccc.int/kyoto_protocol/background/items/2879.php.

Chapter 29
"The Dynamic of Creativity" (Third Movement)

Stephen Hill, Stomu Yamash'ta and Tadashi Yagi

Central to the very concept of the Void is creativity. The core dynamic of the universe is creation of the new, destruction of the old, to be replaced by new creation.

Indeed, referring back to the previous discussion of 'Place' and Kyoto, Yagi observes in his Chap. 7, that, in parallel, the culture of Kyoto has, for 1200 years, been characterized by a repetition of creation and revival. Many traditions and heritages remaining in Kyoto today are the living evidence of a past which has transcended time—a traditional culture with memories of fusing Eastern and Western Cultures. The 'Festivals', commonly practiced in Kyoto, are central in revivification of this traditional spirit. However, *"people, objects or matters, keep on evolving with the times."*

There is thus a close connection between spirituality and creativity …. and *place* … as argued by Stomu Yamash'ta in Chap. 10, and by Tadashi Yagi in his Chap. 7. Yagi points to the redevelopment of the concept of "space" to the idea of "resonance field" in Chap. 15 to explain the mechanism of innovation creation. Paradigm shifting innovations are nurtured in a resonance field that is defined by the *place* of the emergence, and stimulated by the *interaction* among people with different knowledge and experiences. Most importantly however, *emotion* is central to creation.

This observation immediately takes us in our quest for change from spirituality and the cosmos into the inner world of the person. Yamash'ta and Yagi further

---

S. Hill
University of Wollongong, Wollongong, Australia
e-mail: sthill@uow.edu.au

S. Yamash'ta (✉)
Center for the Study of the Creative Economy, Doshisha University, Kyoto, Japan

Sound Core Co., Ltd., Kyoto, Japan
e-mail: info@sound-core.jp

T. Yagi
Faculty of Economics, Doshisha University, Kyoto, Japan
e-mail: tyagi@mail.doshisha.ac.jp

develop this argument in Chap. 13. Six "senses", they argue, play crucial roles in improving the value of creativity—design, story, symphony, empathy, play, and meaning. All derive from "right brain" activity which controls emotion and holistic understanding, thus the genesis in emotion, as opposed, to linear logical brain activity. Creativity is directly associated with well-being, and being able to see how to *change* things—moving beyond established explanation. As Albert Einstein observed of the importance of creative enterprise,

> We cannot solve problems with the same thinking we used when we created them.

The *act* of creation involves 'connecting the dots'—identifying order out of chaos, discovering connection between seemingly unrelated things. This too is the most significant base for humor ... and, of 'letting go' so we can enjoy a new vision of the 'same-old' world. It is within this laterally explored new world that we can let go of the material things and fixed beliefs which constrain our exploration, and search the non-material Void. Meanwhile, as Yamash'ta and Yagi observe in Chap. 13, creativity is cultivated by the accumulation of high-quality emotional experiences and knowledge—such as feeling the beauty of nature and enjoying art performances.

Most importantly, as demonstrated throughout this book, and specifically, in the introduction to this present Conclusions Suite, we *have to* change things, in particular to break out of the cement cast that neo-classical economics has hardened over our society and future. We cannot leave this task for a 'creative elite', but need to build a society and organizations where this is the 'norm' of daily activity and purpose.

A healthy society is a participative society, not one ruled from elsewhere by either a political or expert elite—particularly from the distance of globalized economic control. As demonstrated, in particular, by Stephen Hill's Chaps. 2 and 17, the result is dependency, inability to feel in control and therefore valuable, and paralysis of taking the action required to escape the situation. *"Necessity is therefore the mother of invention"* as Yamash'ta and Yagi observe in Chap. 13, but, as dependents on the 'system' the people are incapable of finding and holding on to the reins of transformation to deal with what must be done.

As Yagi and Yamash'ta further argue, a central quest of this Book is to identify the optimal economic and social system for producing the *fabric* of a creative economy.

At the level of international action, the 2004 UNESCO initiative to promote a "Creative Cities Network" promotes multiplication of art, music and other domains of creative expression as the desired creative norm of the overall society, or city, or community. This community creativity design does fundamentally enrich the life and satisfaction of the people as a whole.

BUT, this is not enough. Whilst an emphasis on creative industries, art, music, culture and so on, attaches emblems of activity to the fabric, what matters is weaving the overall fabric as a whole—producing a creative and responsive *society*.

This objective therefore does not just imply fostering creative *activities*, conducted and presented in separate organizational domains and to separate audiences. Instead, it implies building creativity rather than rote learning into the education of children, fostering creativity across physical science and humanity domains in subsequent education—in particular at the postgraduate research level, building physical spaces that encourage connection and creative engagement into the architectural design of everything from city design to offices to local communities, and fostering government policy that rewards creativity and new enterprise—in particular, for the general social good rather than just commercial profit.

Yamash'ta and Yagi point to the economic benefit, even as measured by correlation of the World Competitiveness Yearbook (WCY) Index and the Global Competiveness Index (GCI), which, combined, produced the 'National Quality Competitive Index (NQCI) all developed by the World Economics Forum from a wide range of indicators. The main factors that determine national competitiveness were innovation capability and infrastructure capability for innovation—building a creative economy and society, not just promoting separate creative and arts activities. In the context of demonstrated economic advantage however, Yamash'ta and Yagi argue that innovation needs to be directed towards improving society rather than profit making as such. They refer to the Aga Khan Foundation as example. The Foundation has implemented innovative developments by organizing communities since the 1970s—a model of participatory rural development which combines development principles with a community's specific context and needs in a flexible manner. The authors therefore reinforce the importance of paying attention to underlying societal factors in sustaining creativity.

Again, though, let us remember, as Yamash'ta and Yagi remind us in Chap. 13, the source of creativity lies with the individual, their emotions and lateral exploration. They point particularly to the role of art, always seeking to capture—and generate—the emotions of individual human beings, joy, anger, pain, and connectedness.

Our creative capacity is severely constrained however, when we get caught up in the world of the material, the quest for immediate selfish advantage and material rewards ………the very platform for neo-classical economics.

But, bringing this quality forward and nurturing creativity is a social organizational task. Yamash'ta and Yagi particularly, demonstrate the importance of the personal *inter-subjective* relationship within these organizational arrangements in their Chap. 14—not one of 'contract' but one of *trust*. Yet again, a neglected dimension of Western-inspired business and its neo-classical economic base. Counter to most Western business practice, *trust* rather than contract is most commonly the relationship for doing business in many Eastern countries, where previous traditional ways of relations have resisted the international onslaught of the cold litigational heart of neo-classical economics. Instead, Eastern business or commitments often rely on a handshake. To carry this further, trust is a basic dimension of the *social capital*[1] that provides serious *social wealth* to a group or society. As defined by one quoted author,

---

[1] We use the term 'social capital' here with some degree of caution as it implies looking at people as a production cost factor and our entire approach is to avoid this minimization of their full worth

Social capital consists of the features of social organization, such as networks, norms, and social trust that facilitate coordination and cooperation for mutual benefit.

Indeed, it is important to note that even at the front-end of institutionalized creative activity globally now, i.e.: scientific research, *openness*, and therefore trust, now seems to rule the international research community, not closed institutional boundaries to protect self-interest, and to prevent new good ideas to escape whilst protecting possible self-interested patent rights (Hill 1993; Hill and Turpin 1994, 1995). Indeed, it is inter-subjectivity and *mobility* of scientists, carrying with them their 'tacit' knowledge gained from experience (observed by Yagi in Chap. 15), that most matters in developing new major initiatives and networks within the scientific community—not internet, nor citation allegiance, and not immediate selfish protection of one's own or corporate-endorsed ideas. Hill and colleagues' own research to demonstrate this included a survey with results from 10,132 scientists, 8008 of whom were from the Asia-Pacific area (Hill and Turpin 1995; Turpin et al. 2008; Woolley et al. 2008).

Yagi, in his Chap. 15, observes that these same principles apply to creative organization in general. 'Open Systems', network organization and autonomous actors are central principles. Decentralized organization allows rapid response to organizational change.

Careful balance is also necessary however against poor decision location and control. Decentralized organization can lead to lack of discipline in following the overall organization's objectives, so hierarchical monitoring and assertion of a central vision, can also be important. What matters is full participation, not centralized command.

Yamash'ta and Yagi demonstrate in their Chap. 13, the importance of code, icon and symbol as means of *transferring* tacit knowledge, and this applies well in the realm of wider and more anonymous society. However, contemporary scientific relations are not just passing on tacit knowledge, but at the same time, building creative new explorations and resolutions. … it is the *inter-subjective quality of communication* that appears to matter more in the case of building scientific relations and creativity.

Back to the power of the individual and intuitive knowledge—at the forefront of global change.

Back to the individual and their emotional life.

Back to the non-material Zero and Void of the creative cosmos.

Again, creativity and its organization require *open boundaries* of the organization, *sharing* within, *trust,* not self-interest ………….back to the personal bases of creativity, but now cast into organization and cross-organization domains. Critical, and oft-neglected managerial lessons follow—lead with vision rather then hierarchical control, build autonomous teams, nurture rather than demand!

---

as people. However, 'social capital' is a familiar phrase in economics, so we live with the expression for now and trust the reader will appreciate our caution.

Creativity and its organization also imply quite different regimes for training in general, and in particular, post-graduate experience. Still, most universities teach science and engineering in isolation from the humanity and humani*ties* courses that lie alongside, but way across the other side of the disciplinary quadrangle, unknown and unexamined.

Yamash'ta and Yagi, in their Chap. 13, therefore promote the idea of bringing engineers into direct contact with art during the course of their training. They present the recently-founded University of Aalto in Finland as a best-practice example—particularly, in promoting design and design processes into the strategic development of Finish companies.

Resistance to this widening of education experience for inclusion into the 'left-hemisphere' disciplines, goes further. Rarely are the science and engineering graduates adequately prepared for the organization world into which they are about to transfer as they have little or no training or disciplined experience of the social/emotional dimensions of working with others creatively across knowledge boundaries, or crossing the cultural divide between academia and industrial or commercial life. The lesson of C.P. Snow and his depiction of the separation between the "Two Cultures"—humanities versus the sciences (Snow 1959),[2] remains unaddressed even though Snow's illuminative observation was originally made 60 years ago.

Herbert Marcuse warned us 47 years ago of the immediate danger,

> The industrial society which makes technology and science its own is organized for the ever more effective domination of man and nature, for the ever more effective utilization of its resources. (Marcuse 1970, p46).

To which Rachel Carson's observation six years earlier circles us back to the importance of the person, and the 'human' side to natural science.

> Man's attitude to nature is today critically important simply because we have now acquired a fateful power to alter and destroy nature. But man is part of nature, and his war against nature is inevitably a war against himself. (Carson 1964).

However, since the time when Carson and Marcuse wrote, subsequent progressive expansion of disciplinary specialization and concentration on (left-brain) logic on the 'one' side of the cosmic 'one-zero' equation, has dominated, as has the

---

[2]Snow's 1950s observation of the uncrossable dividing line between Humanities and Natural Science in British Universities applies today with even greater force. Snow, however, identified the problem for the UK at that time, as too heavy a focus on the classics, Greek and Latin, at expense of Natural Science—which, he observed, had been the engine for winning World War II. He wrote originally, as it turned out, at the 'tipping point'. From there on, the balance reversed as the world of the 1960s became enchanted with science and its power … to even land a man on the moon during a decade where commentators preached the infinite benefits of scientific progress and the *only* critique of the impact of science on society or our environment was Rachel Carson's 'The Silent Spring' which exposed the impact of pesticide DDT on the environment—even into remote previously pristine animal habitats (Carson 1962, 1964). However, the disciplinary separation remained.

eviction of the *'holistic experiential person'* out of the knowledge apparently required by neo-capitalist economics where the anonymous objective of profit rules.

Indeed, under the current world-wide trend of university management, Presidential or Vice-Chancellorial CEOs generally rule, not knowledge leaders; profit outdistances knowledge as criterion of excellence; and universities are judged by an honor list contrived from KPIs or key performance-indicators—abstracted and partial criteria that can be quantitatively presented. As attractors to fee-paying students, this abstract quantification abides by the rule of neo-classical economic competition. Courses have increasingly been targeted to specific job-related skills rather than wider knowledge, reflection and creativity development. … and 'knowledge' gained or transmitted, appears secondary.

Some University Presidents have the vision to escape this neo-classical economic trap, but not many. In their hands, however, lies the future.

Consequently, knowledge creation and training to produce it for the world's future is largely entrapped within the demands of neo-classical economic advantage… and, therefore, prestige and salaries of the CEO's, now measured against leading corporate executives and in their million dollar territory, rather than the Professorial and other senior knowledge-focused academics over whom their 'executive system' rules.

Knowledge for our future 'escape' is therefore deeply trapped within the limiting grasp of neo-classical economics. Whilst the Void is glimpsed at the end of quantum and cosmic physics mathematics, its significance for humanity and 'living now' is entirely neglected … or, rejected, as far as economic analysis is concerned.

This has to change if we are to survive!

References

Carson, R. (1962). *The silent spring*. Houghton-Mifflin: Boston & New York.
Carson, R. (1964). CBS documentary: Quoted in NRDC (2015).
Hill, S. (1993). Visions of the 1990s: New perspectives on global science and technology policy. In S. Okamura, F. Sakauchi and I. Nonaka (Eds), *Science and technology policy research, new perspectives on global science and technology policy* (pp. 413–433). Tokyo: MITI Press.
Hill, S., & Turpin, T. (1994). Academic research cultures in collision. *Science as Culture, 4*(20), 327–362.
Hill, S., & Turpin, T. (1995). Cultures in collision: The emergence of a new localism in academic research. In S. Marilyn (Ed.), *The uses of knowledge: Global and local relations. The reshaping of anthropology*, Vol. 1 (Shifting Contexts, Routledge, London, 1995).
Marcuse, H. (1970). *One dimensional man*. London: Sphere Books.
NRDC (National Resource Defense Council). (2015). *The story of silent spring*. 13 Aug 2015, https://www.nrdc.org/stories/story-silent-spring.
Snow, C. P. (1959) (2001). *The two cultures*. London: Cambridge University Press.

Turpin, T., Woolley, R., Marceau, J., & Hill, S. (2008). Conduits of knowledge in the Asia Pacific. *Journal Asian Population Studies, 4*(3), 247–265.

Woolley, R., Turpin, T., Marceau, J., & Hill, S. (2008). Mobility matters: Research training and network building in science. *Comparative Technology Transfer and Society, 6*(3), 159–184; 259–260.

Chapter 30
"Building the Kyoto Platform for Change" (Fourth Movement)

Stephen Hill, Stomu Yamash'ta and Tadashi Yagi

1 From the Individual to the Social

We have now established the fundamental piers on which we can build a new Global Economics platform.

As demonstrated so far, our central reference point lies at the depth of our spirituality, and this, in turn, is anchored at its deepest level in the cosmic Void and our 'non-material' genesis within a material world. We can see the connectedness of human spirituality with creativity, the basic human power we need to make change happen. The world of creativity is an *open* world, not closed into self-interested separation. Creativity is fed by 'tacit knowledge', intuition, sharing … trust—the *experience-base* of humanity.

Tadao Takemoto then demonstrates in his Chap. 11 observation noted earlier, that human *experience* must not be limited in validity to what is legitimated by scientific explanation—for this is born out of a logic that excludes the irrational,

---

Please note that citations are only provided through this Conclusions 'Suite' if an author or reference is used which have not been cited in the Chapters these Conclusions refer to. The reader can find citational support for the argument by referring back to the Chapter identified.

S. Hill (✉)
University of Wollongong, Wollongong, Australia
e-mail: sthill@uow.edu.au

S. Yamash'ta
Center for the Study of the Creative Economy, Doshisha University, Kyoto, Japan

Sound Core Co., Ltd., Kyoto, Japan
e-mail: info@sound-core.jp

T. Yagi
Faculty of Economics, Doshisha University, Kyoto, Japan
e-mail: tyagi@mail.doshisha.ac.jp

© The Editor(s) 2018
S. Yamash'ta et al. (eds.), *The Kyoto Manifesto for Global Economics*, Creative Economy, https://doi.org/10.1007/978-981-10-6478-4_30

non-recurrent, non-constant phenomena that make up this human experience, and can connect us out of the material and into the immaterial world of the Absolute, the Zero, and the soul. Indeed, to drop this observation into an economics context, limitation to just what can be explained through mathematized basic economic processes, leaves out the 'Sunspots' that might well offer wider, more humanistic character to economic explanation.

Additionally, with a primary focus on the genesis of life and progression to ageing, Masatoshi Murase in Chap. 16, observes that in the context of complexity, unexpected, even small, but *systemic*, forces, such as 'sunspot' influences may represent, can lead to system-wide impact. He draws a lesson from fractals, or self-similar static structures—where characteristic patterns of structures appear successively at descending or ascending scales so that at any scale they are similar in shape to the whole. Murase then develops the concept of *self-similar dynamic processes* in order to explore simple principles that explain complexity. In keeping with the idea of fractals, underlying principles—across all orders of magnitude—should be self-consistent. 'As above, so below!' Ultimately, in constructing the Kyoto Manifesto, we are building complexity from universal principles of humanity and spirituality—and these apply at all levels of aggregation and application. At the core of 'everything', is a central *vision!*

Our task now is to build the social platform for a new Global Economics. To do this, we start from the individual within society and reach forward to the essence of sociality—building and sustaining community. From here we then explore social harmony at a global level.

Our starting point lies in Stephen Hill's observation at the opening of his Chap. 17,

> To truly engage with our shared humanity requires bringing others—even from across different cultural worlds—into our very self. We must truly listen—suspend the noise of our own inner dialogue of consciousness that otherwise gets in the way. It is here and in our immediate social world that our meanings and culture are formed, not elsewhere.

This aligns closely with Tadeo Takemoto's admonition that 'Being Now' must be a fundamental principle of consciousness for a future sustainable and fulfilling society.

Hill goes on to demonstrate from work with children caught in major conflict or trauma that, healing occurred when the vehicle of communication was music, not words—moving behind the fears and hostilities that were embedded in their verbal screen of consciousness. Further, he demonstrates from a case study of a hostage crisis involving his own United Nations staff, that negotiation only started to work when the mediators learnt to 'listen' to the needs of the tribal West Papuan freedom fighters *in their very different cultural terms* rather than through the assumptions the negotiators imported with them from their international cultural world. Once we 'listen' across cultures, we have much to learn—as in this case of West Papuan tribes, from the integrity of values, strength of acceptance once trusted and admitted to the group (even to fight to the death to protect the person), even in handling inter-group conflict—where the fight is largely symbolic: as soon as one person is killed or seriously injured, victory is declared and the fighting finishes.

Equally, we have much to learn from history. The richness of humanity has been formed over thousands of years. We stand today at the intersection between the cultural history that formed the meanings within which we now participate, and the contemporary diversity of today that both challenges and enriches our connection to humanity as a whole. Again though, we must silence our own language of consciousness, our formed expectations, in order to learn openly from a past where humanity lived within *different* times, opportunities and constraints

As Hill later goes on to observe in his subsequent Chap. 21, the practical application of 'sacred silence' is in the practice of "mindfulness", a Buddhist-based concept, but of direct use in the organization and values of business enterprise today. Mindfulness means suspending immediate self-interest, and making decisions in full consciousness of the people, organization and wider community impact of the decision—all informed by the past and previous experience. The goal is minimal harm, maximum benefit to all. Apart from anything else, this makes for good business organization. Most importantly though, mindfulness represents the first line of attack against the *'grammar'*, or, underlying assumptions, of global economics. We therefore return to this as an early action point in the Kyoto Manifesto.

Stephen Hill then demonstrates the power of inter-subjective *community*: "meaning is constructed within our 'world within reach', in subjective relations with others, in socially producing together …. In our local world." It is here that our *humanity's* strength resides. *Place*, as discussed earlier in relation to Manami Oka's Chap. 6 on Kyoto and Tadashi Yagi's Chap. 7 Supplement, is therefore important.

Hill refers to the instructive case study of the people of Ladakh, "Little Tibet", within northern India but on the Tibetetan Plateau. Here, within 20 years, a people living in full harmony with their environment and others, in a reciprocity-based society, were virtually destroyed by an Indian Government initiative to 'develop' the society—bring them into the globalized world. In the example of Ladakh, one can see what has happened to our whole global society over 250 years, condensed into one-eighth of this time.

What lies at the heart of the human drive to community is the need, as social animals to 'belong', to have an anchor of meaning that allows people to act, to share, to feel appreciated or loved—included—to have a personal identity that others reinforce. At the core of working and living together in true community is the *social capital* of mutual *trust*, the importance of which was revealed earlier in Yagi and Yamash'ta's Chap. 14.

Juichi Yamigawa in Chap. 19 observes from primatology research that whilst humans share sociality with the great apes, 'community'—in which two or more different social units support each other via frequent interactions, was a novel characteristic of human societies.

There is a biological basis. Food sharing, he argues, was the first driving force for the evolution of human sociality. Food sharing emerged in species due to the slow maturation of offspring. Whilst food sharing is practiced in some primate groups, only one species, *Homo Sapiens*, share food with non-kin individuals and outside groups. Partly through the benefit of bipedal movement, and thus the ability to forage and transport the food, hominoid individuals collected more food than they could use, so brought it back to camp to share and eat with their fellows. We use food as a social tool for communication, and according to rituals and practices that vary across cultures. But all human groups have developed a practice of sharing.

The second 'foraging revolution' during the period from 2.5 to 1.8 million years ago, was associated with the first sign of an increase in hominoid brain size following the emergence of stone tools and increased meat consumption. The dietary innovation of collecting high quality foods, including meat, preceded encephalization and promoted division of labor between the sexes for foraging. Increased brain size led to allocation of energy during early growth to rapid brain growth and a delay in somatic growth. Again, there was a social/community consequence, unique to humans. Childhood and adolescence periods developed, thus further fostering pair bonding of male and female parents as they needed to care longer for their offspring, and fostering the wider development of 'community'. Maintenance of community relations required inter-subjective connection, and thus enhanced empathy and sympathy among group members, producing a strong identity of the individual hominoid with his or her wider community.

Yamigawa then explores where violence came from in relation to this emerging sociality. War, even hunting, are not human nature, he argues. For most of human evolutionary history, it was the other way around, being hunted as *prey,* a basis for collective action to survive.

Aggression *between* species is normal for the purpose of eating. Aggression *within* a species is derived from competition over food, resting places or mates. Where the competition is reduced, so too is the need to fight, and the aggression can result in stronger bonds for coexistence via reconciliation and consolation. However, strong empathy and identity with the community enabled our human ancestors to benefit from the power of the collective, and to expand their habitats to include risky environments.

However, development of language and subsequent managed food production (agriculture and animal domestication) led to the emotional traits associated with protecting commodities and land, thus coalitions amongst people within a community along with increased hostility between communities, leading to violent interactions. What is interesting to add here though is, as reported in Stephen Hill's Chap. 17, traditional indigenous communities such as those in West Papua, have over time, developed inter-tribal traditions and rituals over the last 10,000 years, to *contain* this inter-community violence.

Yamigawa emphasizes however as noted before that violence is *not* an intrinsic human character. He observes that in 7 million years of human evolutionary history, distinct hunting tools, such as spears, first appeared just 0.4 million years ago, whilst evidence for violence with weapons among humans appeared only very recently, and seems to be associated with the emergence of agriculture—that is, possessions, territory, and self-interest.

Violence, apart for food capture, is therefore, not an intrinsic quality of being human but a consequence of 'attachment' to material goods and territory.

Yamigawa is thence particularly concerned about the conditions to produce violence in contemporary globalized society. The social cement provided by community is breaking down with the massive growth of cities where anonymity rules both in city design and in life choices. Communication by electronic means rather than direct inter-subjective relations marginalizes empathy and mutual understanding. Action to acquire individual benefits dominates … the rule of neo-classical economic values, the cage within which contemporary society is imprisoned. Globalization separates inter-subjectively at the same time as it pretends to connect us through other means. As a consequence, lethal violence amongst human is now six times higher than the average in all other mammals.

Yamigawa concludes we therefore must pay attention to these lessons learnt from primatology and early human development in constructing our future society. It is not an intrinsic character of being human to be violent, but a product of self-interest and atrophy of community—and 'community' *is* a unique human feature. At the center therefore of a positive future for humankind is empathy, sympathy, community empowerment, sharing even across community boundaries.

Again, back to "trust".

'Trust is basic for relationships of sharing and giving, reciprocity over self-interested exchange. This is precisely the moral philosophy developed by Ed Arrington in his Chap. 20, *"the presumption of hospitality"*—He quotes from Dostoevsky's "The Brothers Karamazov", *"To welcome a friend is splendid. To welcome a stranger sublime."*

Humanity's strength therefore resides here and now in this reciprocal, hospitable local world. As Hill argues in his Chaps. 17 and 18, *social empowerment* starts in the same place.

Stephen Hill moves on to discuss *non-place-based communities* within present-day globalization.

Most significant are 'elective communities', spread potentially across enormous territory and not determined by place, formed through networks of common interest, such as religious belief, ethnic origin, hobbies. These offer the individual support for various facets of their personal identity and sense of belonging. But elective communities can only offer a range of identities from which the individual selects to locate themselves within a globalized world, whilst depth of belonging is intrinsically fragmented.

Increasingly, in our internet-communicating world, 'cyber-communities' are developing, linking people via networks such as Facebook and Twitter. But others are only known via electronically mediated information (e.g.: 350 "friends" on Facebook), cannot provide full inter-subjective communication and understanding, indeed, may well be used, as with pedophilic 'grooming' of young people, as disguise. Certainly, as noted earlier in the Overture to this Conclusions Suite, the new world of internet is a world where "alternative facts", of 'un-truths' can explode across a global population and be accepted without evidence.

These non-place communities can be useful supports in developing and communicating a reciprocal, hospitable personal world, and a sense of belonging.

However, social empowerment comes not from here, but from the inter-subjectivity of direct relationships, place and the local.

There are then many examples of newly developed local communities that form and exercise internal cohesion, reciprocity and care. Helena Norberg-Hodge's "Local Futures" initiative, discussed in Hill's Chap. 18, is one such movement—to popularize and implement a focus on building and sustaining *local* economies against the destructive winds of globalization.

What particularly matters though is not stopping at a local level, but instead, to capture an effective dynamic to *expand* from this cultural and community platform —to capture the power of the local, and explode our connectedness at this human level across the global human world. The problem then is that in the world of the 21st Century, the 'local' is embedded in and deeply penetrated by globalism's economic values and control. Effective change *must* take these forces into account.

The phrase Hill uses for this dynamic is "global localism". He presents a detailed case study of UNESCO's intervention to assist the local community of Banjarsari in Indonesia not only to transform itself into a resilient, environmentally focused community within an poor urban setting, but also to influence many other communities—like a pebble dropped into a pool, to send out ripples of influence both locally and globally.

A powerful further example is that of the Basque Cooperative Movement, based in Mondragon, Spain. Conceived on a local basis in 1959 between a handful of workers in a disused factory, the Movement is based on workers being co-owners, inclusive democracy on a proportionate basis—whilst allocating adequate proportions to cover education, health and support. Mondragon production employs the latest technologies but members enjoy job security, though *all* wage rates can go up or down according to overall productivity. The 'idea' has expanded rapidly. There are now 266 Mondragon-inspired and linked Cooperatives across the world—all committed to developing employee ownership on a case-by-case basis—consistent with local laws, customs and other cultural and economic considerations. The Mondragon Movement now offers jobs for 83,800 workers and benefit from annual sales of $(US)20 billion. (Mathews 2012).[1]

Indeed, the Cooperative Movement in general is already a major player in the world economy. As Stephen Hill observes in Chapter 21, from United Nations data, there are now 2.6 million Cooperatives across 145 countries, comprising a billion memberships and clients with a collective 'economy' larger than the economy of France.

The power of community, and the wider influence of community based on place and social values rather than those of neo-classical economics, is therefore emerging within global society. The task however is to strengthen this movement and to escape the stranglehold of globalized neo-economics control.

---

[1] We will come back to the Mondragon Model and a number of its principles in our final Manifesto, our 'Encore'.

Stephen Hill's Chap. 21 then goes on to draw these dynamics together into an overall synthesis at the global level. He looks at the market place from 'the other way around', that is from the perspective of human needs and aspirations. From this he develops a number of strategies we can capture to 'listen to the harmony of humanity' in order to explore the dimensions of a new paradigm for economic-oriented action. These include exercising the power of listening and mindfulness, developing public awareness programs, promoting economic strategies that follow a mindful objective, developing social business into 'normal' economic business, stimulating and supporting cooperative ecologically-sensitive business organizations—and, fundamentally, transforming a shared economic vision towards one based on our humanity and its ultimate source of power in spirituality, social resilience and reciprocity. These strategies are carried forward directly into the Kyoto Manifesto which follows.

Additionally, the strategies carried forward must reflect a realistic view of the accelerating impact of technological transformation on current economic productivity and its organization, as discussed in Hill's Chap. 25. Serious consideration has to be given to the very real possibility of a future 'economy of *unemployment*' as one quoted author describes it, where alternate means of acquiring and distributing wealth will need to be conceived and 'universal basic income' considered —along with serious action to reduce the massive and destructive gap between the very rich and the very poor.

2 Some Lessons from Economic Action Based on Alternate Systems of Belief or Action

Taking these foundations and construction lessons into account we now move on towards final resolution in a human-centered economics.

Here, we reflected against alternative economic systems based on alternative belief systems and social/economic dynamics as platform—in this Movement—for the Conclusions Suite which follows.

The book therefore includes two Chapters which specifically explore practicing economic activity under the umbrella of alternate religious values—Islamic and Buddhist, as well as from economic philosophies such as is practiced in a village-level Indian economy which supports rather than marginalizes the micro-producer and the value of 'small is beautiful'.

We can learn from these accounts, so include their lessons into our subsequent Conclusions Suite.

In the case of the Chap. 22 exploration of the future of capitalism and the Islamic Economy, Shinsuke Nagaoka points to the failure of both capitalism and Soviet-style socialism. He further observes that the Islamic Economy and its leading practice, Islamic Finance, do not, as many may assume, represent an anti-capitalist movement, but is an alternative practice *within* global capitalism.

Consequently, from a conceptual base in a 1941 lecture at Aligarh Muslim University in pre-independence India by Abul A'la Maududi on the economic problem of man and its Islamic Solution, the movement grew, particularly from 2002 onwards. Over the period from 2002 to 2012, the Islamic Banking Sector expanded at a growth rate of 73% per year, to the control of global assets of $(US) 1.2 trillion. With 600 financial institutions providing Islamic financial services to over 50 countries, Islamic Banking has a market share of banking up to 65% in Bangladesh and 45% in Bahrain. Islamic finance is therefore a rapidly emerging new force within the global financial market place.

Nagaoka argues that whilst Islamic finance still requires renovation to fit into the 'wisdoms' of capitalism to meet the demands of the modern world, lessons may be adopted into the current global economic system, thus representing a change in global economic values.

Specifically he points to two key principles of Islamic finance—forbidding of 'riba' or unequal exchange—hence, 'interest-free finance'; and the demand for 'zakat'—return of a percentage of income to God—in general within the modern world, 2.5%.

Thus, 'riba' is avoided through both investors and the bank sharing proportionately in the final profits. Interest on the loan may or may not be adjusted continuously according to demand and market conditions, but the investor gains only at the end from the success or failure of the borrower's business. Meanwhile, 'zakat' contributors receive their full benefit, not now, but in the afterlife. Additionally, investment, according to Islamic values is 'Haram', forbidden, in areas regarded as unethical or immoral, such as casinos, alcohol, nuclear energy and the military, though what is included as Haram rather than 'Halal', permitted, is debated.

The main implication is that the Islamic economy tolerates the universal principle of capitalism which seeks infinite growth of capital by the endless pursuit of profit, and *encourages* self-centered profit-oriented business activity as this provides greater 'zakat' for God and the cause of Islam. Exercise of these values in practice varies and mechanisms developed such as for Islamic banks to legitimately sell receivables at a discount price to be fully compensated on maturity (developed originally within Malaysia), remain contested.

The main difficulties of absorbing Islamic financial practices into a reform agenda of global capitalism is that the system *supports* strong growth-oriented capitalist development through a values focus on self-interest, and, whilst the return of a percentage of income to charitable pursuits is an excellent principle, the reward within Islam is in a later life. In an ecumenical world, belief in later life is very divided, so the principle of zakat cannot be applied universally. Perhaps, reference to the mechanism developed within the Mondragon Movement for allocation of a percentage of shared incomes to be to social support is more workable—but this fundamentally depends on a core principle of economic activity being the sharing benefit from mutual labor rather than self-interested benefit from others' labor.

The Mondragon model focuses on organization values. Juewei Shi takes us, in her Chap. 23 discussion of Buddhist Economics back to the personal level, to the power of integrity and inner-peace to influence society as a whole.

Shi points out that there is no necessary conflict between Buddhist values and economic activity. What matters is the objective, and personal values in action. Basic is the *consciousness* of the "Noble Eightfold Path": right view, right thought, right speech, right action, right livelihood, right effort, right mindfulness and right concentration. The objective is to relieve suffering not just for oneself, but for all. At a personal level, relief of suffering requires recognizing the reality identified in the earlier discussion of spirituality in this Chapter Suite, i.e.: everything is impermanent, including, in particular, matter. To be 'attached', for example, to income or wealth therefore can *only* provide very temporary satisfaction, and certainly will distract personal values from the principles expounded in the Noble Eightfold Path, and from inner peace.

Wealth, instead, is to be used for social good rather than personal gratification …… and greater happiness is the product, not just for oneself but for all others. Shi refers to the teaching of Venerable Master Hsing Yun that people and nature co-exist—thus, the principle of 'dependent co-origination' or all events arising out of a complex set of relationships and factors. The healthy and sustainable society starts from the individual recognizing this, so acting as a kind of 'beam of light' within this complexity—starting with one's own inner peace and radiating out ultimately to create social harmony, even to a global level. Happiness and inner peace catches on. In generating this power, one's own karma is formed, or one's unintended impact on the positive or negative character of the complex surrounding conditions for oneself in the future.

Indeed, the idea of 'happiness' rather than 'economic wealth' being the measure of a society's welfare is now gaining ground internationally, led from the tiny Buddhist kingdom of Bhutan. As Shi points out, Bhutan developed its Gross National Happiness (GNH) index to replace the traditional Gross National Product (GNP) economic index generally used to measure national welfare. Bhutan has a mixed economy and seeks to chart a 'Middle Way'—between the extremes of capitalism and communism, mixing market forces with some central government leadership, whilst maintaining a more holistic and human life understanding. Similar values are successfully carried into the economic mainstream, as Shi observes. Shinichi Inoue, former President of the Japanese Miyazaki Bank, claims that one should not engage in businesses that do not serve the world; instead, the goal of business should be to serve the community with profit coming as a by-product.

In alignment with the idea of a 'gift' giving or 'hospitality' based social order developed in Ed Arrington's Chap. 20, Buddhist practice teaches that compassion, giving unconditionally, are basic to social harmony—as well as for acquiring 'merit'. The benefit of Arrington's analysis is that he constructs it from deep interrogation of Western philosophic literature. The 'idea' of a 'hospitality'-based social order is therefore not just an Eastern phenomenon, but a global concern.

Indeed, the idea is represented in totally practical terms in the Spanish Basque community's Mondragon Movement discussed earlier.

Juewei Shi points to practical models of Buddhism applied to national economic activity to demonstrate, as with the Royal Thai Sufficiency Economy Model, that avoidance of greed leads to more sustainable and happy business enterprise, that is, activity based on principles of moderation, reasonableness, self-immunity, wisdom and integrity. Material benefits are to be cherished. Waste is to be avoided.

Centrally, as also demonstrated in Stomu Yamash'ta's and Tadashi Yagi's Chap. 14, *trust* becomes the core dynamic of relationships, yielding both a happy and productive work environment as well as personal satisfaction. Workers have to trust that by not being self-centered, they will benefit more. Shi demonstrates further that trust is basic to all Buddhist economic activity, for harmony, happiness and merit are achieved by giving without expectation of immediate return and 'trusting' that rewards will accrue anyway.

Reward comes from "karma". In keeping with the way minor interventions can alter a total complex physical or organizational system, karma represents the 'rippling' influence of even a tiny small act on the entire cosmic (non-material) (timeless) environment of which the person is part and from which he or she will, depending on actions, be rewarded with wholesome benefits—either in this life or the next. Consequently, greater 'merit', the currency, as it were, of karma, is measured by the extent of one's altruism and how far-reaching the benefits are to others and into the future.

Juewei also seeks to clarify the often-mistaken assumption that Buddhism in daily life requires commitment to poverty, though this is the principle of non-attachment required of nuns and monks within the monastic sanctuaries. The Buddha did not advise his disciples to give up everything, but admonished them to not get 'attached' to material things for self-reward. Instead, economic activity can be beneficial to the self-cultivation *if* the service and economic rewards received are used to help others. Shi also notes, that there has to be some level of abundance before a gift economy is going to work anyway. Reflecting back to Juichi Yamagiwa's Chap. 19 observations on early humans, 'community' was specifically a product of some level of abundance beyond immediate individual needs.

Juewei Shi observes the difficulties which some Buddhist Temples and movements have had with being embedded within a wider neo-classical economic environment, principally, in marketing objects, prayers or teaching for wealth. However, she concludes from examination of a number of implemented economic models based on Buddhism but in the wider community, harmonious co-existence and the existing system of the State is possible—but at the center there has to be an altruistic view of possessions and wealth and their purpose, and … trust. As she concludes:

> Through moderation in production and consumption, ethical behavior, mindful consumption and altruistic compassionate action that are aligned to the Buddha's teachings (and incidentally, not very different from Adam Smith's propositions of moral sentiments), there will be respectful consideration for resources (natural and manmade),

dignity accorded to the human being (rather than being relegated to the role as a factor of production), and analysis of impact to environmental, human, social, cultural and other factors before production.

Shi also refers to the work of E.F. Schumacher and his classic, 'Small Is Beautiful', the original Western work that introduced Buddhist practice into economics.

This takes us directly to the Tadashi Yagi's Chap. 24 and his argument concerning "micro-producers" and the "informal economy". As in the case of India, even against the onslaught of the economies of scale from very large and international corporations, micro-producers exist and improve the functioning of the whole economy by providing diversity that is largely written out of very large companies' business practice. Yagi observes indeed that the competitiveness of value chains depends on business models which link small producers into the global value chain, even if the small units are financially weak. However, to sustain and develop the micro-producer enterprise, systems of micro-financing are vital for their survival and improvement of quality of life through engagement in creative activities.

Yagi then explores the conditions needed to maintain micro-producer diversity through extending and applying the Dixit-Stiglitz mathematical diversity model. If price alone is the arbiter of business survival, then micro-producers are likely to fail in a competitive economy. However, other endogenous signals, such as *trust* come into play. Large international companies are remote, often making it difficult to find information about the processing quality or exploitation that stand behind the product on the shelf. Not only price, but trust and reputation are also exchanged in the market—thus providing an advantage for the local small-scale producer who is likely to have direct and repeated face-to-face contact with the purchaser.

Additionally, as is the case in India, micro-producers are embedded in a highly diverse cultural context. Community, generally however, is highly valued. Respect for tradition, history and local culture helps to maintain local diversity even against cost efficiencies of large producers seeking to penetrate the market. The local culture will call forth specifically local products—from clothing to musical instruments. In this case, the market vitality is a direct result of common shared values of the community—both product of and sustenance for social unity and harmony.

Trust, valuing diversity, sharing and care. Basic principles for market success by people-centered standards.

From here, we move on to the wrap-up of the main messages of this book in Chap. 31, 'The Way Forward' from our Conclusions Suite, the next 'composition'.

Chapter 31
The Way Forward

Stephen Hill, Stomu Yamash'ta and Tadashi Yagi

We return in a full circle to where we started in this Conclusions Suite, to the essential character of humanity and social community—and their ultimate base in spirituality. This is our strength to deal with a very troubled future.

The current neo-classical global economics framework, which largely commands current political action and business enterprise, does not provide the solution. It is, as we have demonstrated, the problem.

Fundamentally, the current neo-classical economics principle, 'let the market rule' is of itself limiting, but has been further distorted in delivering equity and value for all, by power and centralized ownership, themselves properties of neo-liberal economic opportunity.

Our global economic system is predicated on and fosters self-interest, separation, and *dis*-harmony as, ultimately they are good for business. The system fosters the fundamental problems today in our globalized world—inequity, conflict and violence, rapacious exploitation of limited physical resources, and exploitation or marginalization of people as but cost-factors in a profit-centered equation where saving by casualization or eviction from the labour force is a beneficial strategy.

Certainly, consumer wealth and comfort is a product for the fortunate. But, as with the Myth of the Faustian Bargain, the 'devil' is already claiming back his

---

S. Hill (✉)
University of Wollongong, Wollongong, Australia
e-mail: sthill@uow.edu.au

S. Yamash'ta
Center for the Study of the Creative Economy, Doshisha University, Kyoto, Japan

Sound Core Co., Ltd., Kyoto, Japan
e-mail: info@sound-core.jp

T. Yagi
Faculty of Economics, Doshisha University, Kyoto, Japan
e-mail: tyagi@mail.doshisha.ac.jp

bargain's reward for the gifts of short-term benefits given. Meanwhile, the value, the power, the dignity of our humanity has been evicted out of the economic equations—ultimately for the self-centered benefit of the few.

Most importantly, growth-based intrinsically exploitative, neo-classical economic ways MUST fail as it is logically and environmentally impossible for infinite growth to continue within a finite system. This is dramatically demonstrated in Fukahara's Chap. 3 where he demonstrates that the *first* main crop supporting industrial development, cotton, now absorbs 2% of the world's water and has massive continuing impact on the world's environment. Further conflict is inevitable as overall resources deplete. The only question is when. Already, as demonstrated earlier 'The Future is Now!'. We are already close to or at the 'tipping point'.

As this book has demonstrated, the current economic system has therefore failed us. We *have* to change it, even if just to survive into the next Century, and for our grandchildren to have a future.

Our argument therefore explores and asserts the power of our humanity to make the difference—promoting the 'other way around' in society's relationship to its economic frame for action and meaning.

Our basic principles are derived from our spirituality, itself sourced in humanity's inescapable connectedness with the infinite and timeless cosmos, the energy and wisdom of which we can experience, with discipline and non-attachment to material distractions.

Even by the principles of modern physics and chemistry, there is a universal, continuous, destructive, but creative interaction between matter and non-matter, so attachment to physical things or consumer products, can provide no more than a very temporary satisfaction, and hold us back in our immediate physical world. Physical things are intrinsically impermanent.

'Connecting', as we have demonstrated, means suspending the prejudices, thoughts and material interests that hold us back on one side of a material-non material cosmos, and being prepared to look over the edge of the precipice, to throw ourselves into and then experience the 'Void' of emptiness but infinite energy in a timeless universe—of which we are all a part. Letting go of self-interest, unconditional sharing with all others in our humanity, allows us to be part of the harmony of all that there is. Buddhists would describe this as 'enlightenment', the source of ultimate wisdom. As Tadeo Takemoto concludes, our resilience and community of future society depends on us "Being Here Now".

There are various routes to access this power and connectedness—whether it be via religion or science, or reflective altruistic care. Harmony is at the heart.

As a note to the reader however, don't get lost here. We are not preaching religion, just drawing together *evidence* from both empirical science and from long-term human experience, to establish the *human* and *societal* foundation for future *economics*.

Action for change, for establishing wider global harmony and peace, starts and ends with the individual, you and me. Remember the power of Mahatma Gandhi, Martin Luther King, and Nelson Mandela, none of them wealthy or powerful in the wider economic world, indeed, all marginalized by the establishment but followed by the people. Each of them changed the world based on the strength of their individual integrity, courage, and commitment to care and equity for all.

As demonstrated throughout this book, what then matters in our participation in the immediate world is sharing and 'hospitality' not self-interest; cherishing and conserving our limited material resources, not unnecessarily exploiting or wasting them.

The core dynamic in social relations is *trust*—letting go of attachment to our material possessions for they can provide no more than transitory satisfaction anyway; letting go of our prejudices so we can truly listen and be mindful, including across cultures and across the gap of difference. *Giving* with no expectation of immediate reciprocal return, but trusting all will be all right or balanced in the end. Trust, participating without demand or personal discord with the other, is the basis of harmony.

We are, as in this book's structure of development, playing individually within the polyphonic platform of a Symphonic Orchestra of many players, indeed, the rest of the world's community—including those yet to be born. If we pay attention to harmonize with what everyone else is playing, across different sections (or cultures) of the orchestra, strings, brass, woodwind, percussion, and so on—as well as others within our own orchestral group; if we seek to contribute in ways which not only complement but *strengthen* their harmonic welfare ... then we will all, individually, benefit from the power, the compassion, the harmony of the overall orchestra's performance. We will share in our harmonic cooperation. In the meantime, we will have created quite extraordinary music together—from our orchestral community.

We therefore contribute to and benefit from the group, the 'community'. Our need for community, as demonstrated in this book, is unique to humans—the security of belonging and to feel valued, to act together for both meaning and protection.

Empowering community universally is therefore critical for our future and for being able to deal with the very significant problems we now confront—specifically with increasing inequality and environmental destruction.

Violence is not a *natural* human characteristic, but a product of protecting our attachment to material possessions and *our* territory and *our* way of life, asserting *our* way is the only way—or, not being satisfied, heading off to take it away from others who are 'different'.

On the other hand, as shown through this book, *diversity* can be a strength, even in economic activity and benefit. Creativity, and its organization, derive from our subjectivity and emotion, require openness not self-centeredness, but provide empowerment of the community at large and the dynamic of transformation.

Direct implications for economic and urban policy follow. Amongst others,

1. Economic growth should be regarded as a means, not an end: the goal instead is viable stasis.
2. Emphasis in national investment strategies should be to promote 'mindful' industries and corporations, e.g.: where people and community are valued rather than treated as cost-factors; where wider social benefit is featured; where environmental impact is minimized; and, where core business feeds substantive needs rather than fashion.

3. Community-level initiatives and small scale entrepreneurial practice should be supported both through targeted small-scale financing and linkage into wider economic activity.
4. Taxation regimes should distinguish between profits made through physical capital and those made through financial capital, and favor physical capital support; provide tax incentives to corporations with minimal difference between highest and lowest salaries; encourage cooperative based organizations.
5. Design of urban open and living space should encourage community interaction and creative activity—promote "Musubi" or sharing a sense of consciousness of and with others.

We now have the tools in hand to start to rebuild economics in such a way that our humanity is at the core rather an excluded or marginalized element in the dominating demands of our current global economic system. Matoshi Murase provides heart for our quest in his Chap. 16 in pointing to the observation that in the context of a complex system—as with the current global economic frame, a minor event can precipitate a sudden 'emerging new order', ending up in either 'abrupt disruptions' or major new advances, for example, in different ways of doing things, or, knowledge. It follows that the 'minor' event of the Kyoto Series of Symposia *can* have a major ripple-effect across the global economy.

Furthermore, Murase's idea of 'fractals' offers a core principle of our Manifesto, that is, the same configuration of values and vision at every progressively aggregating level of economic impact. The source of all is our spirituality—our central *vision*.

We now call forth the resulting Kyoto Manifesto for Global Economics, our *Encore!*

Encore

Chapter 32
"The Kyoto Manifesto for Global Economics". "The Platform of Community, Humanity and Spirituality"

Stephen Hill, Stomu Yamash'ta and Tadashi Yagi

Preamble

Together, the arguments and evidence presented in the 2014 to 2017 Kyoto Series of International Symposia and which are captured in this Book, lead us to the *Kyoto Manifesto for Global Economics* based on its *Platform of Community, Humanity and Spirituality*. This Manifesto offers an alternative, rewarding and sustainable future, based on society being the determinant of our economic regime, not the other way around as is the case at present.

1 Basic Principles

1. *People matter*:

The Economics Domain must serve peoples' needs and *value their humanity*, not treat people as mere cost factors, demand and reward life-goals based on separative self-centered values, and require obedience to power which is all encompassing and elsewhere. Human dignity and equality need to be central qualities in economics, whilst diversity is encouraged rather than global conformity.

S. Hill (✉)
University of Wollongong, Wollongong, Australia
e-mail: sthill@uow.edu.au

S. Yamash'ta
Center for the Study of the Creative Economy, Doshisha University, Kyoto, Japan

Sound Core Co., Ltd., Kyoto, Japan
e-mail: info@sound-core.jp

T. Yagi
Faculty of Economics, Doshisha University, Kyoto, Japan
e-mail: tyagi@mail.doshisha.ac.jp

© The Editor(s) 2018
S. Yamash'ta et al. (eds.), *The Kyoto Manifesto for Global Economics*,
Creative Economy, https://doi.org/10.1007/978-981-10-6478-4_32

2. *The Essence of our Humanity is our Spirituality*:

What is sacred or of imperishable supreme value for humanity is what we *can* be as a human race—empowered, fulfilled individuals, in harmony, deeply sharing and caring for each other across our separate cultural and life worlds—understanding the fundamental *depth* and *equality* of our shared lives. Economic activity must be built with human spirituality as its center, not as an accidental and marginalized byproduct.

3. *Our Spirituality is Fundamentally Connected with the Cosmos*:

We are therefore connected with the creative matter-non-matter dynamic of the cosmos, where discovering and enriching our soul lies in dialogue with the 'void', the "emptiness" of both non-attachment and the center of creation and energy in the cosmos as a whole, source of infinite energy and wisdom—where self and self-interest can be nothing but a tiny blip on the distant horizon. Non-attachment in daily life to physical things and to (transitory) social status is essential for us to discover and enrich our spiritual experience. Recognizing the timelessness of the cosmos, the basic philosophy of self and society needs to be guided by 'Being Now'!

4. *The Ultimate Goal of Humanity is Harmony*:

Humanity's welfare and ultimate survival is based on harmony and living in peace in a sustainable physical environment which we cherish rather than exploit and waste.

5. *Achievement of Wider Social Harmony Starts with the Individual and Positive Emotion*:

To share, have sympathy and empathy, we must suspend our inner voice of prejudice and self-interest to 'listen' across cultures and across difference, recognizing we are all joined in 'ontological equality', equal as participants in the cosmic drama.

We must act mindfully, seeking maximum benefit for others and minimum harm.

In Business, mindfulness, moderation, avoidance of greed and waste, along with integrity, are values to be applied.

6. *Interaction with Others Must Be Based on Trust*:

According to principles of sharing and empathy, all interactions, including in particular, in economic exchange, must be based on *trust* rather than on immediate litigation-supported self-gain—offering without expectation of immediate reward in a gift-centered, or hospitality-based relationship.

7. *The Power of People to Act Together lies in their Community*:

It is here that values and mutual care are formed within inter-subjective relations, and empowerment is possible. A 'community' dynamic is possible world wide, according to the principle of 'global localism'.

8. *The Goal of Economic Policy must be to achieve 'Viable Stasis'*:

Economic growth is therefore a means of supporting humanity and their community not an end. Infinite growth within a finite system is impossible in the longer term.

2 Applications

The above basic principles may well sound a philosophic ideal, not applicable to economic action in practice. But, this is not so.

1. There are six basic *Principles of Action for change* that follow from the argument of this book: "dialectic confrontation", "fractals", "small intervention swarming", "the creativity imperative", "global localism", and "sunspot equilibria".

    (1) By the principle of *dialectic confrontation*, the 'antithesis' derives from the 'thesis', so we focus on weaknesses within the 'thesis' as platform for change.

    (2) By *the principle of 'fractals'* the same configuration (of new values) can nest within ever wider levels of aggregation. The culture of an entire organization can be transformed through leadership around a single coherent vision—applied to *everything* and to every employee from the CEO to the cleaner.

    > For example, this principle worked in reformation of a local Council in Sydney, Australia, where responsiveness to constituents was important; and in a United Nations body which needed to develop a vision of universal support for service in the field rather than bureaucratic demand at headquarters. Both of these examples represent actual successful cases of change management.
    >
    > Similarly, as but one of a number of major social innovations, such as those developed under the Aga Khan Foundation, the Spanish Basque Cooperative Mondragon Movement now includes over 83,800 people, all committed to a different way of doing business, one that is inclusive and democratic, values the person and their labor, shares economic rewards as a result of what all produce rather than according to wide differentiation in roles and incomes, values creativity … and works! It is of particular relevance to note that in the Basque region where the Mondragon Movement came from, there is no need for a police force. Instead, there is harmony and mutual respect.

    (3) Furthermore, there is clear evidence that *a small disturbing intervention into a complex system* can fundamentally transform the system as a whole. In the strategy presented in this Kyoto Manifesto, the plan is for there to be a *swarm* of small interventions—across all levels of aggregation within the economic system. So, impact on the current economic system and its governance can ultimately lead to wide-spread transformation. As Len Fisher observes:

    > "The swarming order arises from rules of interaction between individuals which produce dynamic patterns of interaction. The resulting set of emergent patterns characterizes the society as a whole rather than its individual members." (Fisher 2009, p. 3)

    (4) The human strength of empowered action resides within *local* inter-subjective meaning and culture. Change needs to start and refer to the local level. However, according to the principle of '*Global Localism*' the power

of local community can and should, as a matter of design, be expanded and multiplied into the wider global community.

(5) At the core of any positive transformation is building widespread ability and interest in "creativity", *"The Creativity Imperative."*

(6) Finally, whilst all the core values basic to the Kyoto Manifesto, trust, emotion, altruism and so on, remain excluded from the fundamentals of current neo-classical economic calculation, they are starting to appear as '*Sunspot Equilibria*'—outside fundamental principles by which economic activity is calculated. As such, they may, if understood, and included into mainstream economic thinking, be revolutionary, a prequel to paradigm change.

Therefore, we are proposing that the values within the Kyoto Manifesto are ideals to be applied in *every* situation, and at *every* level of governance and business enterprise.

As with 'fractals', the design of input and impact is identical at all levels of scale but organized around a central coherent vision.

As with the sensitivity of complex systems to small irritant inputs, the impact of a swarm of humanity-centered interventions can cause fundamental change overall.

New solutions and designs will be required, so encouraging creativity in every aspect of learning and community participation matters.

As with admission of Kyoto Manifesto values into economic activity as yet-to-be-explained 'sunspots', the power of the people can finally be admitted into theory and economic principles as a revolutionary force to be included, leading to paradigm change.

2. Specific actions follow. To take some examples:

(1) *Capture the Power of Humanity-focused Vision*:

Put *mindfulness* at the center of all decision-making from the top of government to business managers to daily action of each individual. In all cases this will lead to stronger, more positive performance which contributes to the *general* good.

There is good evidence also that the use of brief meditation prior to learning or daily business will produce better attention and mindfulness. Meanwhile, no matter what belief system the individual may follow, by suspending attention to the material world, takes each of us closer to dialogue with the non-material center of our spirituality and provides greater strength to live and influence creatively and for the common good. To 'let go' and *trust!* There can be no stronger or resilient society than one that is based on mutual trust and care.

(2) *Capture the Power of Community*:

At government policy level, in architectural design, in local community organization, maintain the priority of *building* and *empowering* local community. Maintain a 'village' design with open spaces design to 'connect' the people who live nearby, promote small scale locally (diversity) focused enterprise, such as, for example, farmers' markets, networked local shops, restaurants and street markets, local industries and crafts such as ceramic kitchen ware, woodworking, herbal products and so; encourage people to do produce together, such as in community gardens or development of shared community business—in particular, following principles such as those of the Mondragon Cooperative.

Then, expand and connect—promote the principle of 'global localism' as outlined in this Book. Where a community has been successful, develop links with other areas and communities where the people might learn from the successful example. There are numerous ways in which this can be achieved, for example, the pairing of two urban areas in 'sister-city' ways, with exchanges and involvement in each other's activities, mentoring, training and experience programs. Children are great ambassadors. Target wider groups such as the scouting movement to learn from the demonstration village and take the message across the country via the wider movement (as demonstrated did work in Indonesia).

However, the core principle must be maintained, that is, to *focus* on the inter-subjective 'local' as the core principle to be diffused, whilst the value that must remain at the center of all action is *trust* and sharing, not suspicion and self-interest. Finding a committed informal leader and assisting them to take initiatives, including through training, can be very important.

(3) *Capture the Power of Creativity*:

Creativity lies at the center of the cosmos, its dynamic, and our human relationship to all that is—therefore, of our spirituality. We live in uncertain times so finding creative solutions—through exploring the source of our spirituality, will be necessary, even for our very survival.

Openness, access to not only technical knowledge but also tacit 'experience'-based knowledge of others, are important. In an organizational context this requires following democratic principles which honor all team members and their capabilities, and maintains a 'flat' non-hierarchical relationship between the people.

All education needs to put the development of creative potential at the core. This applies from per-school to school entry level where children should be encouraged to experiment, to play, to be creative and proud of their creative achievements, rather than dominated by curricula knowledge requirements. Equally, 'creativity' should be at the center of all further education, in particular, university and post-graduate education. The current separation between arts and natural science streams needs to be re-examined to encourage all students to have a wider understanding and to see, for example, the social and cultural context (including art, design and social organization) to which their scientific learning is developing and into which it can be applied. In the case of business education specifically, management to promote the values of mindfulness and creativity need to be central to the curricula.

Additionally, promotion at all levels of music, art, and other forms of creative expression is of general benefit to the society at large. The core principle however is not to just establish creative *activities*, but to establish the fabric of a creative *society* as a whole.

(4) *Promote Economic Strategies which follow a Mindful Objective*:

(i) *Social Business*: Non-loss, non-dividend companies designed to address a social objective.

(ii) *Cooperative Business*: Not-for-profit, shared advantage organizations—where clients are also the decision-makers on management, whilst excessive profits and exploitation are not supported.

(iii) *Environmentally-Sensitive, Morally-Conscious Business*: Wider value and status can be accorded to morally sensitive business, for example, in awards from business chambers, media and government. Meanwhile, public pressure has already proven itself to be a powerful influence on exploitative business internationally, or example, with respect to child labour, pollution, forest exploitation, etc.

(iv) *A Sharing Investment Strategy*: Mainstream the core investment strategy objective as practiced in Islamic Financing, that is, to reward the investor as a result of the shared support and thus success of the business enterprise funded, rather than through benefit from immediate and continuous interest rate fluctuations. In this way, the investor and the business engage in a shared enterprise rather which is supportive of physical capital development and therefore longer-term human value, rather than the investor benefitting from financial capital development which, of itself, leaves nothing behind for the future of others.

(5) *Change the Criterion of National Welfare*:

Governments should explore the applicability of a Gross National Happiness (GNH) Index as employed in Bhutan, to complement specifically economic indices, and start to influence national policy away from singular attention to economic wealth alone. For governments to take this action will almost certainly require individuals and social movements to demand attention to the wider person and their humanity within measurement of the success of government strategy.

(6) *Prepare for a Humanity-Centered Society of Non-Work*:

The role of labor as basis for income and consumption in the global economy will go through major transformation in the near future as a result of technological change and robotics. Economists, government leaders and the community must start preparing now, in particular, in testing universal basic income initiatives. The core of transformation objectives must capture the benefit of this change to foster humanity-centered objectives rather than rely on inequality and marginalization when people as cost-factors in production are no longer there.

3 The Future

As this book has consistently argued, the principles of the Kyoto Manifesto are basic not only to a humanity and spirituality-centered society of benefit to all, to redressing the widening gap in inequality, but also are *essential* if we are to have the capacity to act in time to maintain the viability of our physical environment to support humanity beyond the next Century and to handle the massive social change which is likely to happen in the meantime—largely driven by demands of the current economic machine.

References

Fisher, L. (2009). *The perfect swarm-the science of complexity in everyday life*. Basic books.

Index

A
Abducted, 287
Absolute belief, 30
Abundance, 518
Acausality, 174
A cause-and-effect, 267
Accessibility, 74
Accidental culture, 300
Accountability, 93, 102
Actors, 277
Administrative and civil control, 26
Adolescence, 340
Adolescent growth spurt, 338
Aesthetics, 78, 296
African apes, 334
Aga Khan Foundation, 205, 503
Agamben, G., 187, 189
Age at first parturition, 335
Aggression, 349
Aging, 258, 280
Agriculture, 338
A healthy society is a participative society, 502
A holistic view, 259
Air markets, 73
Aissez-faire economic liberalism, 64
Aleppo, 56
Algorithms, 381
Alien, 299
Alliances among males, 342
All modulations of the voice, 133
al-Qaeda, 25
Alterity, 366
Alternative facts, 451
Altruism, 225, 518
Altruistic behavior, 233
Ambassadors, 324
America first, 457
Amida, 115
Amino acids, 267

Amoeba management, 83
Amu Darya, 35
Amyloid Precursor Protein (APP) of beta-amyloid, 272
Analytical ability, 199
An arrow-like view, 267
Anatta, 79
Ancient pentatonic, 134
Annihilation, 143–147, 149, 151, 152
Annihilation operator, 145, 147, 149, 150
Anomalies, 219
Anonymity, 513
Anonymize, 381
Anonymized, 317
Anthropocene, 44, 487
Anthropocentric, 367
Anti-feminist, 451
Antimatter, 143
Antiparticle, 143, 152
Antithesi, 321
Ape-men, 348
Aporia, 372
Apple, 460
Arab nationalism, 402
Aral sea, 35
Arashiyama, 115
Aratama, 159
Aristotle, 90, 97
Art, 198
Artificial intelligence, 462
A Sharing Investment Strategy, 532
Asian cultural influence, 82
Aspiration, 77, 320
A spiritual center, 493
Astronomy, 157
Astrophysics, 157
Attached, 517
Attachment, 523
Australia, 456

Authenticity, 78
Authority, 300
Autonomy, 240
Axiology, 366, 369, 372

B
Backroom command, 489
Bacteria, 265
Bamayan Buddhas, 312, 367
Bamiyan Statues, 292
Banjarsari, 304, 323, 514
Bank Islam Malaysia, 404
Banned, 452
Bāqir Ṣadr, Muḥammad, 400
Bardeen-Cooper-Schrieffer (BCS), 149
Bashō, Matsuo, 170
Basic infrastructure capability, 201
Battlefield, 464
Baxter, 462
Bay Dayn', 409
BCS Hamiltonian, 150
BCS theory, 149–151
Bednorz and Müller, 151, 153
Behavioral economics, 67
Beheading of innocents, 31
Being now, 6, 166, 510
"Being Now" as the essential quest of future society, 497
Belonging, 314
Bentham, Jeremy, 96
Bhakti, 180
Bhutan, 421
Big Bang, 144, 145, 152
Bipedalism, 335
Bogoliubov, 150
Bogoliubov pseudo-particle, 151
Bogoliubov transformation, 150
Bohm, David, 169
Bohr magneton, 143
Bohr, Niels, 142, 262
Bon festival, 113
Bonus structure, 234
Bose-Einstein Condensation (BEC), 145, 147, 149, 152
Bose-Einstein distribution, 145
Boson, 145, 147
Bougainville, 299
Boundaries, 305, 315
Boundary membranes, 268
Bracket vectors, 144
Brain activities, 134
Brand New Britain, 200
Bread, 300
Breathing, 360, 362, 364, 368

Bregman, Rutger, 373
BREXIT, 23, 91, 456
Bridges, 304
Brillouin zone, 146
Broad-thinking contributors, 482
Buddha, 163
Buddhahood, 54
Buddhism, 54, 164, 180
Buddhist, 210
Buddhist economic models, 420
Buddhist economic practice, 421
Buddhist economics, 75, 517
Budding, 264
Built on the fears, 485

C
Cage, John, 170
Caliphate, 26
Capital, 524
Capital accumulation, 298
Capitalism, 395, 405
Capitalist ethics, 94
Capital, Marx's, 400
Caputo, John, 98, 99, 361, 363
Care, 392, 523
Caring, 311
Cartesian thought, 164
Cash economy, 300
Catastrophe, 271
Causality, 173
Celebrations, 217
Censorship, 293
Cercopithecus monkeys, 330
Ceremonies, 295
CES, 438
Champions, 324
Change, 315, 321, 509
Character of humanity's spirituality, 480
Chest-beating, 348
Chew, Geffrey, 168
Childbirth, 368, 370
Child labor, 80, 232
Choice, 290
Christianity, 39, 167
Christianity and Islam, 76
Cities, 513
Civilization, 340
Civil society, 191
Civil wars, 348
Classical economics, 51
Classics, 297
CLCC, 293
Climate change, 453
Clinton, Hilary, 450

Clones, 262
Closed innovation, 242
Code, 217
Code, icon and symbol, 504
Co-evolve, 271
Coexistence, 130
Cognitive approach, 215
Cognitive diversity, 244
Cognitive systems, 277
Cold war, The, 41
Collective, 322
Collective electrons, 149
Collective hysteria, 220
Collective intelligence, 220
Collusion, 74
Combination, 240
Combinatorial control, 266
Command, 4
Commoditization of education, 75
Commonality, 285, 318
Common knowledge, 244
Common purpose, 320
Communal breeding, 338
Communism, 39
Communities of Innovation (CoI), 205
Community, 20, 293, 310, 330, 375, 511, 513, 517, 523, 528, 531
Community in India, 447
Compassion, 138, 339, 517
Compete, 310
Competition, 245
Complementarity perspective, 262
Complexity, 280
Compost, 324
Compromised, 452
Concentration points, 325
Concept creation, 240
Concept justification, 240
Concept of capability, 68
Concept of minimalism, 81
Concept of void, 81
Conflict, 5, 298
Confluence Approach, 216
Confront, 383
Confront the assumptions, 379
Confucius, B.C., 133
Conjugate operators, 144
Connectedness, 384
Connections, 323
Conscientiousness, 229
Conscious Business, 532
Consciousness, 286
Consolation, 349
Consortship, 342

Constituent molecules, 267
Consumer, 316
Consumer credit, 381
Consumerism, 310
Consumption, 300
Continental influence, 129
Continuous complexation, 262, 264
Contractarian ethics, 94
Contradictions, 273
Control, 20, 489
Control of fire, 339
Cooking, 339
Cooperation, 223, 245
Cooperative based organizations, 524
Cooperative breeding, 338
Cooperative business, 532
Co-operative harmony, 432
Cooperative movement, 514
Cooper pair, 149, 151
Co-opting, 30
Coordination costs, 445
Co-owners, 514
Copernican revolution, 257
Core dynamic of neo-classical economics, 486
Corporate Social Responsibility (CSR), 239
Correlation effect, 146
Cosmic inflation, 145, 152
Cosmopolitan, 363
Cosmopolitanism, 363
Cosmos, 522
Cost and benefits of cheating, 68
Cotton, 36
Coulomb interaction, 146
Coulomb repulsion, 146
Council of Kyoto's Traditional Culture and Forestry, The, 110
Court music, 134
Crafts, 493
Creation, 144, 146, 147, 149, 151, 497
Creation operator, 144, 145, 147, 149, 150
Creative cities network, 199
Creative city, 198
Creative director, 243
Creative economy, 198
Creative workers, 199
Creativity, 9, 197, 209, 501, 523
Creativity imperative, The, 530
Crime, 292
Crisis, 277
Critical theory, 89, 90, 93
Critique, 377
Cross cultural, 291
Cross cultural understanding, 287
Crusader campaign, 27

CSR training, 239
Cult, Cargo, 316
Cultural diversity, 82
Cultural divide, 505
Cultural environment, 380
Cultural history, 511
Cultural innovations, 341
Cultural noise, 296
Cultural politics, 363
Cultural surplus, 99, 100
Culture, 316, 329, 388, 510
Curie temperature, 148
Cyber-communities, 318, 513

D
Dāna, 426
Dakota Access Pipeline, 458
Danger, 458, 486
Dead hand, 27
de Broglie, L., 142
de Broglie particle wave, 145
Decentralized management, 293
Decline, 457
Defect, 143
Dehydration, 270
Deleuze, 182
Demand for change, 10
Democracy, 179
Demonstration communities, 324
Denial, 491
Dentity, 512
Dependency, 502
Dependent co-origination, 418
Derrida, Jacques, 101, 102, 363, 365
Descartes, René, 363
Design, 81, 198
Design for living, 301
Dialectic, 320
Dialogue, 318, 495, 498
Dichotomy, 261, 262
Digested, 296
Digital (sampled) music, 495
Dirac equation, 142, 143
Dirac formalism, 144
Dirac, Paul, 142
Disabilities, 69
Disagreeableness, 229
Disassembly, 266
Disconnect, 322
Discovery, 95, 96, 98, 99
Disempowerment, 383
Disempowers alternative action, 490
Dis-harmony, 521
Dislocation, 143

Dismal theorem, 17
Distributed, 15
Distributionist Model, 469
Distributive justice, 89, 90
Diversity, 181, 188, 190–192, 205, 244, 285, 348, 437, 499, 523, 527
Diversity in preference, 441
Dividing cells, 262
Division, 451
Division of labor, 237, 330
Divisiveness, 24
Dixit- Stiglitz mathematical diversity model, 519
Dixit–Stiglitz type diversity model, 438
DNA, 264, 267
Doctor, 325
Dōgen, 165
Domestication, 338, 349
Dominance ranks, 334
Domination, 505
Dongria Kondh, 185
Douglass North, 40
Downsizing, 235
Dualism, 164
Dubai Islamic Bank, 401
Dynamical magnetic susceptibility, 148
Dynamic mechanism of knowledge creation, 245
Dynamics of knowledge creation, 245

E
Early hominids, 334
Early weaning, 337
Earth's environmental dynamics, 487
Earth system, 42
Eastern and western cultures, 210
Eastern cultures, 29
Eastern intellectual trends, 129
Eastern paradigm, 78
Eastern philosophy, 259
Ecological perspective, 40
Ecological sensitivity, 390
Econometrics, 377
Economic, 381
Economic ethics, 89, 94, 95, 97–100
Economic growth, 15, 39
Economic imaginary, 89, 365, 366
Economic justice, 361
Economic policies, 419
Economic progress, 418
Economic responsibility, 359
Economic take-off, 57
Economies of scale, 437
Economies of scale and scope, 444

Economism, 372
Economy, 4, 311
Economy of unemployment, 515
Economy's demands, 479
Ecotourism site, 325
Ecumenical, 30
Education, 293, 323, 419, 502, 531
Edward said, 53
'Efficiency' cannot stand for 'fairness and justice', 490
Efficient resource allocation, 63
Efficient utilization of administration, 444
Eigenvalue, 142
Einstein, Albert, 141, 142, 165, 497
Einstein's theory of relativity, 142
Elayed maturation, 338
Elective communities, 513
Electron, 142, 143
Electron-pair, 146, 149
Electron-phonon, 150
Elemental, 365, 366, 368, 370, 372
Elementary particle, 142
Elementary particle physics, 145
Emergent, 259, 277
Emergent diseases, 258
Emerging new order, 524
Emotion, 84, 198, 220, 503
Emotional ability, 199
Emotional experiences, 209, 502
Emotional factors, 63
Emotional intelligence, 221
Emotion-driven behavior, 84
Emotion innovation, 243
Emotions are therefore central in economic activity, 489
Empathy, 81, 86, 198, 225, 338, 512
Employment opportunities, 77
Employment systems, 86
Empowered, 293, 528
Empowerment, 468
Emptiness, 496
en, 130
Encapsulate, 270
Encephalization, 337, 512
Endocytic-exocytic cycle, 263
Endocytosis, 263
Endo-system, 269
Enframement, 377
Engage, 293
Enjoyment, 365, 366
Enlightenment, 39
Enma, 112
Enmity, 310
Entitlements, 95, 99

Entity, 73
Entry competition, 71
Environmental conditions, 332
Environmental costs, 40
Environmental degradation, 47
Environmentally, 532
Environmental threat, 18
EPA's 2012 "scientific integrity policy", 454
Equality, 331, 348, 429
Equality principle, 331
Equalization of factor prices, 197
Equity, 5, 20
Equity, Reciprocal, and Competitive (ERC) theory, 233
Erosion of trust, 233
Essences of the universe, 157
Essential, 157
Estate tax, 233
Estrus sign, 342
Ethics, 431, 490
Ethnic culture, 135
EU, 456
European culture, 82
European Technology Platform (ETP), 203
Evacuated, 292
Evolution, 271
Evolutionary history, 333
Evolutionary psychology, 84
Exclusion, 315
Executive Order, 452
Existence, 136, 496
Existence and non-existence, 158
Exocytosis, 263
Exogamy, 330
Exo-world, 269
Expand consciousness, 5
Expansion of jobs, 454
Exploitation, 521
External bridging, 223
Externality, 316
Externalization, 240
Extinction, 311
Extrinsic uncertainties, 481

F
Face-to-face, 318
Factor cost advantage, 460
Fair distribution of wealth, 429
Fairness, 234
Fair trade, 75, 396
Fair treatment of members, 234
Fare subsidies, 70
Fashion, 381
Fecundity, 337

Feelings of anxiety, 224
Feelings of attainment, 224
Female-bonded, 330
Female-dispersal, 330
Fermi-Dirac distribution, 145
Fermi energy, 146, 150
Fermi liquid, 146
Fermion, 147
Ferromagnet, 147
Fertile crescent, The, 56
Financial capital, 99, 101
Financial capitalism, 405
Financial Conduct Authority (FCA), 204
Financial institutions, 5
Finite system, 522
First artificial intelligence lawyer, 463
First basic principle of welfare economics, The, 437
Flame, 294
Flat hierarchy, 224
Flatter hierarchical control, 84
Flower Garland Sutra (Avatamsaka Sutra), 167
Food distribution, 332
Food sharing, 511
Food supplies, 486
Food transport, 335
Foraging revolution, 512
Forward to the past, 455, 486
Foucault, Michel, 90, 94, 369
Four voices, The, 8
Fractals, 257, 510, 524, 529
Fragmented, 317
Frame, 4
France, 456
Fraser, Nancy, 90, 92, 100
Fraud, 233
Freedom, 16, 288, 348
Freedom in life, 74
Freezing, 376
Friendly competition, 86
Frozen, 312
Fuhrer principle, 455
Fulfillment, 298
Full spectrum of human and academic knowledge, 6
Fushimi Inari Taisha, 107
Fusion process, 82
Future, 24

G
Gaia system, 276
Galloping populism, 456
Geertz, Clifford, 301
Geiko, 127

Geminoid, 465
Gene-centric, 265
Genetic, 296
Genetically engineered, 22
Genetically engineered seeds, 487
Genoplore model, 215
Giant Water Basin of Kyoto, The, 109
Gibson-Graham, J.K., 102
Gift, 289
Gift economy, 426
Glebe, 319
Global capitalism, 89, 93, 94, 100, 373, 405
Global competitiveness index, 200
Global corporations, 310
Global economics, 499
Global economics paradigm, 13
Global economy, 197
Global financial crisis, 65, 91, 396
Global hub for innovation, 203
Globalism, 296, 348
Globalization, 91, 93, 96, 320
Global localism, 304, 383, 388, 529
Global market influence, 453
Global value chain, 437
Global warming, 486
Global winter, 27
Glocalism, 321
Gor'kov Hamiltonian, 150
Grameen Bank, 206
Grammar, 302, 316, 376, 511
Gravity waves, 497
Great acceleration, 42
Great divergence, 47
Great transformation, 44
Greedy capitalism, 64, 76
Green Ban, 319
Greening, 323
Gross National Happiness (GNH) index, 73, 421, 517
Growth, 311
Guano, 49
Gusmao, Xanana, 295

H
Haber-Bosch process, 49
Habermas, Jürgen, 91, 100
Habitats, 512
Habituation, 330
Halal, 516
Hamiltonian, 142
Hand, Seàn, 371
Happiness, 223, 227, 419, 517
Happiness research, 313
Happiness studies, 72

Haram, 516
Harmony, 4, 67, 89, 101, 102, 375, 425, 491, 518, 523, 528
Harmony with nature, 78
Hata, 107
Hata no kawakatsu, 120
Hawking, Steven, 145
He_3, 151
Heal, 286
Heart Sutra, 158
Heian capital, 109
Heidegger, Martin, 366
Heisenberg's uncertainty principle, 261
Heisenberg, Werner, 142, 168
Helium-4, 145
Heller, Agnes, 100, 370
Hermeneutical circle, 366
Highest power of human capital, 391
High fecundity, 334
Highly centralized control, 382
High-$T_c$cuprate, 149, 151
Historic legacies, 312
Hobbes, Thomas, 96, 362
Holistic, 378
Holistic approach, 78
Holistic experiential person, 506
Holistic recognition, 219
Holistic understanding, 198
Holocene, 44
Holstein-Primakoff model, 146
Homo economics, 51, 65, 361
Homo faber, 365
Homo sapiens, 45
Hōnen, 165
Honneth, Alex, 94
Honorable poverty, 80
Hormone, 341
Hospitality, 359, 361, 362, 364, 366–372
Houris, 30
Hsing Yun, Venerable Master, 424
Hubbard Hamiltonian, 146
Hubbard model, 146
Hugo, Victor, 170
Human bab, 337
Human-centered economics, 467
Human clade, 333
Human community, 383
Human creativity and resilience, 467
Human experience, 498
Human family, 330
Humanistic Buddhism, 429
Humanitarian, 290
Humanity, 3, 285, 297, 481, 527
Human nature, 362, 364, 369

Human-nature dualism, 52
Human spirituality, 482, 528
Hunting, 333
Hunting hypothesis, 348
Hydration, 270
Hypercycle, 271

I
Icon, 217
ICRC, 288
Ideal platform, 494
Ideal type, 302
Identity, 315, 340
Ideological extremism, 25
Ideology, 291
Imanishi, Kinji, 53
Imminent collapse, 17
Immoral behavior of economic agents, 64
Impact, 26
Impermanent, 517
Implicate and explicate order, 169
Incentive structure, 79, 239
Incest avoidance, 345
Incest taboo, 330
Inclusion, 384
Inclusive, 29
Income-generating activities, 324
Income inequality, 197
Independence, 295
India, 179, 499
Indigenous societies, 315
Individual, 522
Industrial capitalism, 405
Industrialism, 297
Industrialization, 14, 379
Industrial revolution, The, 38, 348
Inequality, 19, 47, 223, 233, 331, 480, 488
Inequality principles, 331
Inequity aversion, 234
Infanticide, 332
Inflation, 77
Informal economy, 519
Information, 240
Information cost, 443, 445
Information revolution, 348
Inherited wealth, 488
Initiative, 324
Inner fulfillment, 385
Inner peace, 420, 517
Innovation, 198, 503
Innovation capability, 201
Innovation community, 204
Innovation hub, 204
Inspiration, 138, 456

Inspiring, 326
Institutionalized religion, 29
Insulated by success, 459
Integrationist approach, 259, 278
Integrity, 311, 385
Interactions, 314
Inter-birth interval, 335
Interdependence, 418
Interest, 30
Internal bonding, 223
Internalization, 240
International attention, 290
International Biosphere and Geosphere Program, The, 41
International Council of Science, The, 41
International development assistance agencies, 310
International Geological Congress, 44
International Labour Office, 91, 92
International Monetary Fund, 91
International multi-lateral (shared) cooperation, 458
Internet, 318, 348, 380
Interpersonal altruism, 234
Interpretation, 90, 93, 95, 99, 101
Inter-subjection meaning, 529
Inter-subjective, 291, 511
Inter-subjective collective, 317
Intersubjectivity, 361, 364, 366, 369, 371
Intracellular Society, 262
Intrinsic instability, 261
Invasion, 457
Invention, 95–99
Investment theory, 216
Invisible hand, 63
Invisible world, 132
Irrational, 171
ISDS, 23
Ise Shrine, 115
ISIS, 25, 56
Islamic Banking, 516
Islamic Development Bank, 401
Islamic economy, 396, 515
Islamic finance, 396
Islamic ideology, 457
Islamic revival movement, 402
Island communities, 323
Itinerant-electron, 148
Itinerant-electron magnetism, 149
Itinerant ferromagnet, 146
Itinerant system, 146
Itoh Jakuchū, 54

J
Japanese knowledge creation, 240
Japanese macaques, 329
Jaspers, Karl, 165
Jeremiah, 165
Jevons, William Stanley, 46
Job opportunity, 74
Joint liability, 207
Jung, Carl, 165
Jungle, 288
Justice, 361, 363

K
Kant, Immanuel, 359, 362, 372
Karma, 418, 517
Katsurame, 123
Keyes, R., 91
Keynes, John Maynard, 361, 373, 400
Key performance indicators, 378
Keystone XL pipeline, 458
Kibune Shrine, 112
Kimono, 127, 138
King Kong, 348
Kinship, 295
Kiyomizudera, 112
Knowledge, 14, 237, 240, 296
Knowledge creation, 205, 237, 506
Knowledge creation mechanism, 244
Knowledge-enabling conditions, 240
Knowledge resonance, 240, 242
Knowledge transfer, 240
Kobayashi, Hideo, 165
Kojève, A., 181
Kushimitama, 159
Kyogen, 123
Kyomachiya, 126
Kyoto, 7, 8, 131
Kyoto culture, 129
Kyoto Manifesto, 3
Kyoto Manifesto for Global Economics, 527
Kyoto, the place, 493

L
Ladakh, 309, 511
Lā Maudūdī, Abūal-A, 399
Landes, David, 47
Land tenure, 349
Language, 329, 349
Last common ancestor, 333
Lateral inhibition, 274
Leadership, 244
Learn, 311

Learned Helplessness, 24
Levinas, Emmanuel, 359, 361, 363–368, 371
Lévi-Strausse, Claud, 169
Leung, G., 363
Liberation theology, 101
"Life and death", 158
Life goals come to be understood in economic terms, 490
Life history, 335
Life history strategies, 338
Lifestyle, 487
Lifeworld, 91, 93
L'il y a (there is), 366
Limited, 322
Linguistic silence, 286
Listen, 510
Listened, 325
Listening, 10, 285, 386
Listen to the Future, 137
Living now, 506
Local, 513, 529
Local activation, 274
Local culture, 83
Local currency, 396
Local diversity, 519
Logical thinking, 221
Long-run evaluation system, 234
Long-runself-interest, 234
Lt Colonal Stanislov Petrov, 28

M
Machine age, 379
Machines, 461
Macromolecules, 266
MAD, 299
Magnon, 146, 147
Magnon theory, 146
Malabou, C., 101, 102
Malleability of beliefs, 225
Malraux, André, 165
Malthus, Thomas, 50
Management innovation, 243
Mandala, 137
Manifesto, 471
Manufacturing employment, 457
Many-body problem, 150
Man'yoshu, The, 79
Marginal cost pricing rule, 69
Marginalization, 297
Marginal tax rate, 233
Market, 461, 494
Market competition, 437
Market mechanism, 63
Market value of innovation, 243

Martyr, 30
Marxism, 39, 396
Marx, Karl, 366, 405
Maslow's hierarchy of needs, 204
Mass, 497
Matching mechanism, 442
Matching of researchers, 243
Matching process, 443
Material spirit voice, 8
Maternity, 368
Matrilineal societies, 345
Matrix mechanics, 142
Matsuno Taisha, 112
Matter, 143
Matter wave, 142
McCloskey, Dierdre, 89
McNeill, John, 42
Mean field theory, 146, 150
Meaning, 81, 85, 198, 300, 314, 468, 511
Meat, 334
Meditation, 420
Mentoring, 326
Merchant capitalism, 405
Merit, 426, 518
Metaphysics of presence, 361
Michael Hardt and Antonio Negri's "multitude", 396
Microfinance, 438
Micro-financing, 519
Micro-producers, 437
Middle American workers, 456
Middle way, 419
Military opposition, 26
Milky Way, 157
Millennials, 92, 93
Mindful economy, 420
Mindful industries and corporations, 523
Mindfulness, 80, 386, 431, 515, 530
Minimal harm, 511
Minimum living condition, 80
Miraculous energy, 496
Miroku (Maitreya), 117
Mirror samadhi, 175
Mobs, 319
Mode-mode coupling, 148
Moderation, 518
Modern, 310
Modern economics, 396
Modernity, 360
Modernized beliefs, 29
Mohamad, Mahathir bin, 404
Molecular chaperones, 266
Mondragon, 514
Mondragon cooperative, 531

Monetary economy, 77
Money, 310
Mongolia, 294
Monitoring costs, 77
Monogamous, 330
Monogamous families, 339
Monopolistic (M) market, 444
Monotheistic religions, 76
Moral behavior, 224
Moral economy, 413
Moral education, 226
Moral formation, 84
Morality, 84
Moral ontology, 95, 371
Moral sentiments, 232
Moriya-Takahashi, 147
Mott transition, 146
Mozambique, 57
Muḍāraba, 400
Muhammad, Prophet, 406
Multidimensional, 136
Multi-lateral trade agreements, 458
Multi-level community, 344
Multi-level society, 333
Multiple universes, 158
Muromachi period, 123
Music, 385, 496
Music theory, 133
Mutation, 272
Mutual trusts, 86
Mystical approach, 213
Myths, 217

N
Nagarjuna, 181
Nambu, Yoichiro, 176
Narrative unity, 301
National branding, 199
National Quality Competitive Index (NQCI), 200, 503
National Science Foundation (NSF), 201
Natural mutation, 22
Natural selection, 260
Natural selves, 136, 495
Negative effects of globalization, 66
Negative happiness, 224, 230
Neg-emergence, 260
Negotiation power, 444
Negotiations, 288
Neo-classical economics, 50, 95, 480
Neo-classical global economics, 521
Neoliberal, 89, 90, 95, 99
Neo-liberalism, 89, 90, 94–96, 99
Netherlands, 456

Networking, 326
Network of micro-producers (N) market, 444
Networks, 295, 317
Networks of common interest, 317
Neurodegenerative disorders, 272
Neuroticism, 229
New global economics, 392
New paradigm, 375
New solutions, 28
Niels Bohr, 142
Niels Bohr's complementarity principle, 262
Nigimitama, 159
Nishijin, 120
Nitrogen fixation, 49
Niyamgiri, 185, 186
Noble eightfold path, 517
Nogaku, 120
Noh, 79, 168, 241
Noh performance, 219
Non-attachment, 74, 528
Nondividing cells, 262
Non-existence, 496
Nonlinear effects of collaboration, 245
Norberg-Hodge, 309
No-self, 73, 224, 231, 234
Nothing, 81
Nothingness, 81, 364
Not improving inequality, 488
Notion of en, The, 127
Nuclear war, 27
Number operator, 145, 148

O
Objective property, 379
Offering, 426
Oharame, 109
Oligopolistic market, 437
Olivier clément, 167
Onnes, 149
Ono no Takamura, 112
On-the-job training, 240
Ontological equality, 180, 181, 188, 190
On Zen, 10, 314
On Zen ceremony, 138
On Zen performances, 494
Open innovation, 242
Openness, 504
Open systems, 504
Operator, 142
Opportunistic behavior, 226
Opposition, 273
Option value, 68
Organic waste, 323
Organizational change, 305

Organizational intent, 240
Organizational theory, 237
Organizational trust, 224
Organization for Economic Co-operation and Development (OECD), 92
Origin of life, 260
Origin of sin, 349
Orissa, 183
Orphanages, 286
Other-regarding behavior, 339
Ovulation, 341
Oxford Happiness Index, 73

P

Pair annihilation, 143, 497
Pair bonding, 338
Pair creation, 144
Pair creation operator, 146
Paradigm, 4
Paradigm change, 481, 530
Paradigm of the west, 78
Paradigm shift, 243, 280
Paradigm-shifting innovations, 243
Paralysis, 480, 489
Pareto, Wilfredo, 361
Participatory parity, 90, 93
Particle, 143, 152
Past, 295
Patent applications, 462
Paternal care, 342
Patrilineal societies, 345
Pauli paramagnetic, 145, 146
Pauli's exclusion principle, 146, 149
Paul II, Pope John, 395
Peace, 286, 385, 528
Peer group effect, 71
Penrose, Roger, 273
Perceptions of fairness and equality, 75
Perceptive illusions, 278
Percussion instruments, 134
Performativity, 102
Permeable, 320
Personal identity, 317
Personal image, 451
Personality trait, 229
Phallocentric, 364
Phenomenologists, 302
Philopatry, 339
Philosophy, 297
Philosophy of descartes, 78
Phonon, 150
Phronesis, 98
Phronimos, 97, 98
Phylogenetic model, 329, 330

Piketty, Thomas, 361, 372, 413
PISA, 72
Place, 8
Place-centered cultures, 311
Planck, Max, 142
Plastic changes, 261
Plato, 165
Plato stated, 133
Play, 81, 198
Polanyi, Karl, 44, 412
Policy, 305, 503
Political, 471
Political democracy, 498
Political economy, 360, 361
Political forces, 450
Pollution, 323
Polygynous, 344
Polymerization, 269
Polymers, 268
Polytheism, 137
Poor, 309
Pope, 290
Popper, Karl, 361
Population, 18
Populist right wing political candidates, 485
Positive and negative happiness, 69
Positive emotion-supportive incentive structures, 481
Positive happiness, 224
Positron, 143
Positron annihilation, 143
Post-graduate, 505
Post-rational economics, 372
Post-reproductive period, 338
Post-truth, 91
Posturing, 449
Post-work future, 468
Poverty, 518
Poverty line, 19
Power, 14, 312
Power house, 304
Power structure, 82
Pragmatic approach, 213
Praxis, 360
Precipice, 31
Predation pressure, 332
Pribram, Karl, 169
Price, 494, 519
Price competitiveness, 437
Price mechanism, 232
Primary activity capability, 201
Primary reinforcers, 220
Principles of action for change, 529
Problematique, 387

Problem-solving, digital and social skills, 466
Procurement channels, 445
Productivity gains, 462
Profit, 5, 313
Progress, 491
Promiscuous mating system, 342
Properties of diversified markets, 446
Properties of the universe, 157
Prosocial consciousness, 84
Pro-social ethics, 232
Prosociality, 339
Protection, 319
Protect us, 454
Protein–protein interactions, 266
Proteins, 267
Protestantism, 406
Protest movement, 319
Protests, 451
Protocols, 305
Prototype creation, 240
Protoviruses, 271
Prudence, 360
Pseudo-particle, 149, 151
Psychodynamic approach, 214
Psychometric approach, 214
Puṇya, 426
Public, 389
Public arena, 191
Public pressure, 389

Q
Qualia, 220
Quality information, 443
Quality of innovation, 245
Quality of life, 74, 198
Quantum and cosmic physics, 496
Quantum Electro-Dynamics (QED), 144
Quantum field theory, 144, 149, 151
Quantum mechanics, 146, 149
Quantum physical science, 151
Quantum physics, 152
Quantum theory, 174
Quaternary, 45
Qurān, 406, 407
Qureshi, Anwar Iqbal, 400

R
Radical change, 375
Radicalization, 27
Random Phase Approximation (RPA) theory, 147
R&D, 198
Reassembly, 266
Re-assert our humanity, 494

Rebuild, 295
Reciprocity, 234, 340
Reconciliation, 349, 512
Recycling, 324
Redistribution of income, 76
Redler, L., 371
Reductionism, 78
Reductionist approach, 259
Redundancy, 240
Refugee, 348, 369, 457
Regenerate, 296
Regime, 291
Relative universalism, 53
Relaxed education policy, 75
Release, 288
Renaissance, 296
Rentiers, 96, 99
Repression, 312
Reproducibility principle, 261
Reproductive success, 332
Reputation, 519
Rerum Novarum, 395
Reshoring, 460
Resilience of local culture, 83
Resilience, The, 83, 340, 347
Resonance field, 243
Restoration, 314
Retributive justice, 363
Reverse innovation, 235
Reward system, 245
Ribā, 407, 516
Ricardo, David, 51
Ricoeur, Paul, 364
Right brain, 198
Right livelihood, 64
Right of movement, 74
Right of starting up new business, 74
Rimbaud, Arthur, 170
Robot bricklayer, 463
Robot companions, 464
Robotic doppelganger, 465
Robots, 462
Rosato, Jennifer, 368
ROSS, 463
Rote learning, 293
Royal Thai Sufficiency Economy Model, 421, 518
Roy, Arundhati, 100

S
Sabotage, 77
Sacred, 6, 482
Sacred Houses, 294, 318
Sacred music, 385

Sacred symphony, 10
Sadaqa, 408
Sallis, John, 366
Salvation, 30
Sangha, 427
Santi Asoke Buddhist Reform Movement of Thailand, 421
Sanukite, 173
Sanukite stone, 495
Sanukitoid, 173
Sarvodaya Shramadana, 422
Saudi Arabia, 453
Save, 324
Scavengers, 325
School district system, 72
Schools, 293
Schrödinger, Erwin, 142
Schrödinger wave-equation, 142
Schumacher, E.F., 46, 364, 382, 419, 519
Schweiker, William, 93, 94, 100
Scientific explanation, 498
Scientific knowledge, 6
Scientism, 97
Scientistic, 378
SCR theory, 148
SCR theory of spin fluctuations, 147
SECI, 240
Secondary reinforcers, 220
Second quantization, 144, 145, 149, 151
Security, 348
Seed ownership, 21
Self, 291, 510
Self-actualization, 204
Self-assembly, 265
Self-Consistent Renormalization (SCR) of spin fluctuations, 147
Self-cultivation, 518
Self-folding, 265
Self-interest, 73, 79, 224, 231, 320, 513
Selfishness, 382
Self-learning ability, 75
Self-nested hierarchical structures, 278
Self-nested hierarchies, 258
Self-nonself circulation process, 266
Self-Nonself (or Endo–Exo) Circulation Theory, 264
Self-organization, 273
Self-perpetuating cycle, 227
Self-preservation, 299
Self-replicating units, 268
Self-similar dynamic processes view, 258
Self-similar dynamic systems view, 259
Self-templating structure, 264
Sense of achievement, 73

Sense of insecurity, 73
Sense of security, 227
Sensitive, Morally, 532
Separation, 299
Sergey Eisenstein, 168
Sexual coercion, 332
Sexuality, 341
Share, 305
Sharing, 318
Sharing and hospitality-based society, 480
Sharing benefit, 516
Sharing of tacit knowledge, 240
Shinto, 6–8, 78, 86, 160, 164, 210, 482
Shirakawame, 123
Shōbōgenzō, 165
Shotoku, Prince, 119
Signs of estrus, 340
Single-minded nature worship, 129
Singularity, 160
Simple, 455
Site, 241
Six-Day War, 402
Six factors, 81
Six "senses", 198, 502
Skilful means, 428
Slavery trade, 39
Small Business Innovation Research (SBIR), 201
Small intervention swarming, 529
Small is beautiful, 73
Small-scale, 322
Small scale entrepreneurial practice, 524
Smith, Adam, 50, 380
Social brain hypothesis, 338
Social business, 206, 390, 515, 532
Social capital, The, 223, 314, 503
Social complexity, 338
Social empowerment, 513
Social fabric of care, 488
Social failure, 459
Social fairness, 76
Social good, 503
Social harmony, 517
Social infrastructure, 69
Social innovation, 211
Social interactions, 329
Socialism, 395
Sociality, 329, 361, 365, 370, 371
Socialization, 240
Social media, 390, 487
Social Networking Services (SNS), 205
Social networks, 224
Social objectives, 206
Social order, 296

Social organization, 498
Social organizational task, 503
Social pathologies, 371
Social-personality approach, 215, 216
Social perspectives, 239
Social preference theory, 234
Social psychology, 234
Social relationships, 84, 332
Social security system, 69
Social structure, 335
Social supports, 224
Societal conflicts, 83
Societal interest, 232
Societal platform, 499
Society, 329
Society of 'Full Unemployment', 468
Socio-ecological model, 332
Sociological imagination, 291
Solar system, 157
Solidarity, 90, 94–96, 101, 102, 384
Solid-state physics, 145, 147
Solid-state quantum physics and chemistry, 141
Solid-state science, 152
Solitary, 344
Solution, 521
Song of the precious, 175
Sound spirit, 135
Sound Spirit Voice, 8
Sovereignty, 24
Soviet Union, The, 35
Space, 497
Spaceman Economy, 17
Spears, 289
Specialization, 313
Spectators, 277
Spin excitation, 146, 149
Spin fluctuation, 149
Spin-lowering operator, 147
Spin of electron, 146
Spin operator, 146
Spin-wave, 147
Spirit, 89, 98, 101, 102, 496
Spiritual, 29
Spirituality, 3, 89, 102, 167, 314, 391, 494, 509, 522
Spivak, G. C., 182, 183
Spontaneous symmetry breaking, 144
Standardization of culture, 83
Standard of living, 74
Stationary state, 51
Stone, M., 363
Stoner theory, 146, 147
Stone (sanukite), The, 131

Story, 81, 198
Strategy, 305, 322
Strongly correlated electron superconductor, 151
Structural barrier, 74
Stuart Mill, John, 51
Subaltern, 183, 184, 188
Sub-group trust, 227
Subjective experience, 315
Sufficiency, 322
Sunspot Equilibria, 481, 530
Super analogue, The, 139
Superconducting, 151
Superconducting gap, 150
Superconductivity, 149, 151
Superconductor, 151
Superfluidity, 151
Superpower, 27
Supplemental education costs, 71
Suppressed, 455
Survivability, 20
Survival, 312
Sustainability, 304, 389, 431, 480
Sustainability of the nature, 80
Sustainability of the resonance field, 244, 250
Sustainable capability, 201
Suu Kyi, Aung San, 298
Suzuki, Daisetzu, 165
Sweeping assumptions about people, 377
Swelling of sexual skins, 341
Symbol, 217, 299, 316
Sympathy, 232, 338, 4912
Symphonic Orchestra, 523
Symphony, 8, 81, 198, 482
Symposia, 3
Synchronous failure, 58
Synthesizer, 135
Syr Darya, 35
Syrian civil war, The, 56
Syrian refugee crisis, 456
System, 5, 313, 378
Systemic, forces, 510
Systemic problems, 257

T

Tacit experience-based knowledge, 531
Tacit knowledge, 219, 240, 509
Tacit-knowledge formation at the site, 241
Tagore, Rabindranath, 165
Talented individuals, 198
Tales of Genji, The, 79
Tanabata, 217
Tanabata festival, 129
Taxation, 524

Index
549

Taxation of income, 233
Taxation of wealth, 233
Taxes on inheritance, 233
Tax evasion, 68
Tax havens, 67, 232
Taylor, Charles, 360
Team creativity, 244
Team diversity, 244
Team logic, 241
Technical knowledge, 531
Technological systems, 380
Technological transformation, 515
Technologies of the self, 369
Technology innovation, 243
Temples, 295
Territoriality, 344
Testis weight, 342
Tetralemma, 181, 189–191
Theory of moral sentiment, The, 64
Theory of relativity, 141
The outward "diffusion" of the four spirits, 160
Thermal spin fluctuation, 148
"This universe and that universes", 158
"This world and that world", 158
Threat, 319
3D printers, 463
Three mountains of Kyoto, The, 109
Timor Leste, 294
Tipping point, 13, 18, 456, 479
Tonga, 300
Topos Conference, 204
Torrance tests of creative thinking, 214
Total Factor Production (TFP), 48
Totalitarian, 292
Toulmin, Stephen, 360, 362, 364
Toynbee, Arnold, 46, 167
TPP, 23
Traditional, 309
Traditional societies, 28
Traditions, 295
Training, 324
Transfer integral, 146
Transformation, 285
Transformation of vision, 390
Transients, 261
Transnational corporations, 66
Tribesmen, 288
Trump business empire, 452
Trump, Donald, 220, 449
Trust, 76, 223, 227, 245, 314, 382, 445, 489, 503, 513, 518, 519, 523, 528
Trust-consistentself-interest, 231
Trust formation, 224, 445
Truth, 381

TTIP, 23
Tuition fees, 74
Turner, S., 91
Twelve-tone, 134
Two-fold problem, 277
2.8 million children, 27
2001: A Space Odyssey, 348
Tzu, Lao, 165

U
Umbilical cords, 100, 370
Unconsciousness, 138
Unequal pay by gender, 75
Unequal societies, 76
UNESCO, 199, 294
Unethical, 516
Unfair contracts, 232
Unfair markets, 73
Uninspiring, 450
Unique development of community, 481
United Nations, 288
Unity in diversity, 385
Unity of community, 447
Universal, adequate and unconditional, 468
Universal basic income, 468, 515
Universalism, 363
Universal mundane, 132
Universal pragmatics, 90
Universe, 144, 145, 152
Unlike in humans, sharing foods, 334
Urban, 317
Urbanization, 340
Urban open and living space, 524
US President, 485
Utilitarianism, 94, 96
Utility, 94, 96, 361, 367, 369
Utility maximization, 361

V
Vacuum, 141, 143–145, 151, 157, 160
Vacuum breaking, 144
Vacuum state, 141, 142, 144, 146, 147
Vacuum void, 158
Vacuum world, 136
Valence, 31
Value chains, 437
Values, 313
Van den Akker, R., 93
Van Rym, Rembrandt, 172
Vermeulen, T., 93
Vernacular democracy, 179, 182, 188, 192, 499
Verter, Mitchell, 367
Vesicles, 264

Viable stasis, 523
Village life, 300
Violence, 348, 512
Vision, 504, 515, 524
Visual illusion, The, 274
Voice, 293
Voice of Mathematical Spirit, 9
Voice of spirit, 9
Void, The, 131, 141, 143, 495, 522, 528
Von Uexküll, Jacob, 53
Voucher system, 71

W
Walzer, Michael, 95–100
Waqf, 408, 410
Waste, 518
Water footprint, 38
Watsuji, Tetsuro, 53
Wave function, 142, 145
Wave mechanics, 142
Wave number, 146
Wave vector, 150
Way of seeing, The, 379
Weakened, 383
Weakening cooperation, 233
Weaknesses of the economic, 5
Weaknesses within the system, 376
Weak selection, 268
Weapons, 349
Weber, Max, 406
Welfare economics, 361
Well-being, 69, 198, 224
Western science, 260
Western scientific thinking, 259
West Papua, 288
What is Life?, 259
Who I am, 315
Widespread movement, 469
Wike, R., 92

Willingness-to-pay, 442
Wisdom, 493
Wisdom of the ages, 312
With female kin, 330
Wolfe, C., 102
Women of Kyoto, The, 108, 494
Work incentive, 233
World Competitiveness Yearbook (WCY), 200
World Economic Forum, 200
World heritage, 288
World population exploded, 487
World within reach, 302
Worship of ancestors, 87
Worshipping nature, 87
Worthiness of immigration, 384
Wrigley, Tony, 47

X
Xenophobic, 451
Xuanzang, 158

Y
Yang, 160
Yasurai festival, 129
Yin, 160
Youth, 325

Z
Zakāt, 407, 409, 412, 516
Zambrana, Rocio, 90, 94
Zeami, 120, 170
Zen, 129, 160
Zen Buddhism, 164, 211
Zenith, 459
Zen philosophy, 81, 213
Zero, 158
Zero-point spin fluctuation, 148
Zoroaster, 165